THE HIDDEN VICTIMS

The Princeton Economic History of the Western World

Joel Mokyr, Series Editor

A list of titles in this series appears in the back of the book.

The Hidden Victims

Civilian Casualties of the Two World Wars

Cormac Ó Gráda

PRINCETON UNIVERSITY PRESS

PRINCETON AND OXFORD

Published by Princeton University Press
41 William Street, Princeton, New Jersey 08540
99 Banbury Road, Oxford OX2 6JX

press.princeton.edu

All Rights Reserved

Library of Congress Cataloging-in-Publication Data

Names: Ó Gráda, Cormac, author.
Title: The hidden victims : civilian casualties of the two World Wars / Cormac Ó Gráda.
Other titles: Civilian casualties of the two World Wars
Description: Princeton : Princeton University Press, [2024] | Series: The Princeton economic history of the Western world | Includes bibliographical references and index.
Identifiers: LCCN 2023057832 | ISBN 9780691258751 (hardback) | ISBN 9780691258744 (ebook)
Subjects: LCSH: Civilian war casualties. | World War, 1914–1918—Casualties. | World War, 1939–1945—Casualties. | BISAC: HISTORY / Wars & Conflicts / World War I | POLITICAL SCIENCE / History & Theory
Classification: LCC U21.2 .O37 2024 | DDC 940.3—dc23/eng/20240222
LC record available at https://lccn.loc.gov/2023057832

British Library Cataloging-in-Publication Data is available

Editorial: Joe Jackson, Emma Wagh
Jacket: Karl Spurzem
Production: Danielle Amatucci
Publicity: William Pagdatoon
Copyeditor: Wendy Lawrence

Jacket Image: Courtesy of the State Library of South Australia / Wikimedia Commons

Printed in the United States of America

10 9 8 7 6 5 4 3 2 1

CONTENTS

Introduction

War is a violent teacher. It brings people down to the level of their circumstances.
—THUCYDIDES, *HISTORY OF THE PELOPONNESIAN WAR*, C. 400 B.C.

By some queer change in international outlook, things that were condemned as crimes against humanity twenty-five years ago seem today to be accepted as part and parcel of the inevitable consequence of "total" war. . . . Then, an air raid on a peaceful city was stigmatised as an act of barbarism; now the rival belligerents openly boast of the extent of the destruction that they have caused to each other's centres of population.
—*IRISH TIMES*, APRIL 19, 1941

All major wars are and always have been against the civil population.
—SIR ARTHUR TRAVERS "BOMBER" HARRIS, 1977

Many histories of war are military histories—but not this one. It focuses instead on the millions of civilians killed and injured during the twentieth century's two world wars (World War I and World War II). By "civilians" we mean all those men, women, and children who did not bear arms or set out to kill—that is, noncombatants. The numbers who perished are staggering. The estimates of civilian deaths that Walter Clemens and David Singer (2000) propose—9.7 million during World War I and 25.5 million during World War II, respectively—are, as we shall see, too low; war-induced famines alone may have cost 30 million lives or more during the two wars.[1] Estimates of 25 million for all war deaths in the Soviet Union during World War II and 14 million in China, on which more will come later, imply a global aggregate of well over 50 million lives, or well over the entire populations of France or the United Kingdom at the time.[2] Much more speculative estimates of the cost in lives of earlier wars imply that only gigantic, long-lasting conflicts involving the likes of Genghis Khan in the early thirteenth century, Timur (or Tamerlane) in the fourteenth, the Shunzhi Emperor in the mid-seventeenth, or the Taiping Heavenly Kingdom under Hong Xiuquan and his followers in the mid-nineteenth are likely to have come anywhere close to the twentieth-century's world wars in terms of total deaths, and those estimates do not distinguish between military and civilian deaths.[3]

During World War II, more so than during World War I, most if not all the warring parties countenanced civilian deaths on a mass scale. Lofty prewar commitments to sparing civilians evaporated once the dogs of war were let slip. Given the lack of an enforcement mechanism, laws agreed upon in peacetime were nearly always broken whenever they got in the way of military goals. Meanwhile, both sides accused the other of atrocities against civilians and reaped the propagandistic rewards to be had from such claims. Eventually civilians, too, called for retaliation and revenge against enemy civilians. War transformed how people felt about civilians; at the height of World War II, novelist and journalist George Orwell denounced "all talk of 'limiting' or 'humanizing' war [as] sheer humbug."[4] That is far from saying that all sides were equally guilty. But the history of the two world wars is a reminder that the only sure way to prevent the huge cost of war in innocent civilian lives is to prevent war itself.

The bloody events that produce the outcomes described in what follows have qualitative and quantitative dimensions, which are strongly complementary. This is not a book about numbers for the sake of numbers. Yet without getting the numbers right when possible and pointing out when that is impossible, we cannot argue with those who, innocently or otherwise, deny or exaggerate wartime savagery. Getting the numbers right also helps us to show not only how human savagery and brutality survived the Enlightenment but how the technological progress that the Enlightenment helped engender made it more effective. Against the belief in human progress due to better technology and the rise of "state capacity," often deemed to have been a good thing, the numbers speak louder than words.

Death came to civilians in many gruesome guises, some familiar since antiquity and some novel. Both world wars caused several famines. Both spawned genocides, above all the Jewish Holocaust. Both targeted civilians as a means of winning: during World War I through blockades and forced labor, during World War II through expropriation and far more forced labor, and through aerial bombing on a massive scale, culminating in the atomic bombs dropped on Hiroshima and Nagasaki in early August 1945. Both wars led to huge enforced displacements of civilian populations, both planned and unplanned. Long-range artillery and aerial bombardment killed relatively few civilians during World War I, but they caused hundreds of thousands of deaths during World War II.[5] World War I did not cause but exacerbated the influenza pandemic of 1918–19, which cost tens of millions of lives. And for every civilian who died there were more who were injured, who endured physical and sexual assault, who were displaced and impoverished and bereaved, or who suffered trauma. These various causes of civilian death and injury are among the subjects of this book.

Why do noncombatants die during wars? It may be helpful to distinguish between two broad categories of victim, even if the dividing line between them is blurry. The first includes those civilians who die as the unintended collateral damage of war, people who are just in the wrong place at the wrong time or who are victims of actions meant to accomplish something else but end up killing instead or who succumb to the crises created by mass conflict (e.g., famines, infectious diseases, a lack of shelter and exposure to the elements). The second is the *deliberate* killing of civilians, either because of a belief that such will help to win a war (e.g., through aerial bombings or the starvation of besieged cities) or out of pure malice and hatred for a perceived enemy during the fog of war, as in the cases of the Holocaust or the Armenian genocide.

Civilians in Earlier Wars

"War is hell." When General William Tecumseh Sherman spoke these words to a class of graduating cadets at the Michigan Military Academy in 1879, he was not referring to his infamous march through Georgia in the later stages of the American Civil War but to the carnage that had resulted from the Union and Confederate armies engaging each other in battle.[6] In fact, although Sherman's march destroyed much of Georgia's industrial infrastructure and deprived its people of foodstuffs, his troops, like General Philip Sheridan's in the Shenandoah Valley, were disciplined, and civilian casualties were few. The same holds for the American Civil War more generally: civilians made up only a small fraction of all deaths. The war cost as many as 750,000 military lives, but its most eminent historian has estimated the number of civilian deaths at about 50,000, or 7 percent of all deaths. While no precise numbers are forthcoming, the lack of serious epidemics and the relatively small number of violent incidents involving civilians point to a low number. In 1863 the war produced the Lieber Code to govern the conduct of soldiers on the Union side, but the code was concerned with issues such as the treatment of guerrilla fighters and Black escapees rather than civilian welfare.[7]

Historical context matters. Did the American Civil War reflect an earlier stage in the history of war, when civilians were much less likely to suffer? Were World War I and World War II defining moments for civilian vulnerability in wartime? Did they bring the killing of civilians to a new level? How different were the causes of such deaths? Is it true that before the twentieth century, "war [was] an ugly thing, but we had rules in which we made sure that soldiers fought soldiers but did not victimize civilians"?[8] One can think of some wars that support such a claim—it has been argued that, in Europe at least, for some decades during the nineteenth century "people's wars" gave way to "wars between armies of the states." But that was merely an interlude before World War I and World War II "civilianized" war again.[9] Nowadays, there is a growing consensus that throughout the ages civilians have suffered much in wartime. Even in nineteenth-century Europe, wars in the Balkans and in the East exacted a high cost in civilian lives. One analysis based on nearly five hundred wars since AD 1700 suggests that on average civilians made up half of all deaths, with little change in that proportion over time. Colonial and civil wars result in higher civilian shares than interstate wars, and ethnoreligious conflicts produce the highest proportion of civilian casualties.[10] Again, such statistics render the American Civil War exceptional in terms of civilian deaths.

Julius Caesar has been dubbed "the first *génocidaire* in European history," but thanks to the Athenian historian Thucydides, war-linked genocides in Europe can be documented back to 416–415 BCE, when an Athenian army destroyed the island of Melos (today's Milos), slaying its entire adult male population and selling its women and children into slavery.[11] The Hebrew Bible, too, contains many references to wars that would strike the modern reader as genocidal, such as those against the Amalekites and Midianites, but historians and archaeologists question the historicity of those accounts. In later times, others more than matched the barbarism of ancient Greece and Rome. Nongenocidal wars repeatedly targeted civilians too, with some, such as the Napoleonic Wars in Iberia and the Thirty Years' War (1618–48), standing out.[12] In the history of the latter, incidents such as the Sack of Magdeburg in 1631 are notorious, but in the course of that war, it is reckoned that more than a quarter of the inhabitants of the area comprising modern Germany died. The overwhelming majority of those were civilians, with more succumbing to hunger and infectious disease than to bloody atrocities. The same holds for the "Spanish Fury" of Antwerp in November 1576, when Spanish forces massacred thousands of civilians sheltering in the city. Similarly, Cromwellian outrages in mid-seventeenth-century Ireland have a prominent place in popular history, but famine and plague were mostly responsible for the accompanying demographic catastrophe that may well have exceeded, in relative terms, the Great Irish Famine of the 1840s. According to economist and colonizer Sir William Petty, in Ireland between 1641 and 1652 "about 504 [thousand] of the Irish perished, or were wasted by the Sword, Plague, Famine, Hardship, and Banishment." Petty's calculations were often cavalier, but this figure tallies with recent assessments that war-related losses, mainly in 1649–52, reached 20 to 25 percent of the population.[13] Today some historians would categorize the Irish colonial wars of the late sixteenth and mid-seventeenth centuries as genocidal, following a pattern whereby genocidal wars happen "after extreme social and political crisis, where normal rules of behavior are suspended and violence is honored."[14]

Again, most war-related civilian deaths in the past were not due to systematic killings but to the hunger and diseases attendant on warfare. What was new about the twentieth century was not civilian casualties but the widespread humanitarian concern for civilians, as reflected in international law and in the rise of nongovernmental organizations directed at aiding and protecting civilians.[15] The International Committee of the Red Cross (ICRC) was founded in 1863 after the carnage at the Battle of Solferino (1859) moved its founder, the Swiss-born philanthropist and Nobel Peace Prize winner Henri Dunant, to form a society to relieve soldiers wounded in future wars. But its remit related solely to military victims. On the eve of World War I, in 1912, the Red Cross extended its mission to include prisoners of war, and during World War II, it sought to help victims of all kinds. The Commission for Relief in Belgium (1914), Save the Children (1918), Oxfam (1942), Catholic Relief Services (1943), and Médecins sans frontières (1971), among others, targeted civilian victims of war from the outset.

Today it is common to contrast "old wars," which were "grand clashes between two or more sides in which battle . . . was the decisive encounter," and "new wars," in which "battles between armed groups are rather rare and most violence is directed against civilians." The chronological dimension of this contrast is reflected in the assertions from the Carnegie Commission on Preventing Deadly Conflict in 1997 that "in some wars today, 90 percent of those killed in conflict are noncombatants, compared with less than 15 percent when the century began" and from the United Nations (UN) Development Programme in 1998 that "civilian fatalities have climbed from 5% of war-related deaths at the turn of the century to more than 90% in the wars of the 1990s." In *New and Old Wars*, Mary Kaldor, an influential theorist of modern warfare, invoked such numbers to argue for her characterization of wars in the modern era, albeit without the caveat "in some wars" at the beginning of the first quotation.[16] Many plausible reasons for the reversal have been proposed: greater access to lethal weapons, the intensification of racial and religious hatred, new military technologies, a greater acceptance of terrorism, and widespread contempt for international humanitarian law. As Robert Gerwarth notes, during World War I there were no significant differences in terms of brutality between Allied and Central Powers troops, and the brutality of World War II was subject to significant regional variation. Much more important, according to Gerwarth, was the violence linked to population transfers and to militias of both the Left and Right in the immediate post–World War I era.[17]

Evidence for the reversal proposed by Kaldor and others is mixed, however. On the one hand, as already noted, the civilian share of war deaths before the twentieth century was much higher than assumed and comes close to or matches the World War I and World War II shares mentioned above. On the other hand, during the major wars of recent decades, military deaths have tended, if anything, to exceed civilian casualties, as during the Vietnam War (1965–75), the Arab-Israeli War (1967), the Indo-Pakistani War (1971), the Yom Kippur War (1983), the Iran-Iraq War (1980–88), and the U.S. War in Afghanistan (2001–21). That also holds for the ongoing war in Ukraine, with the Israel-Hamas war being a glaring exception.[18] Civil and quasi-civil conflicts come closest to being "new" wars; for example, military casualties outnumbered civilian during the Gulf War of 1990–91, but civilian casualties dominated in the uprising against the Iraqi government that followed that war. Civilian deaths also outnumbered military in the Bosnia-Herzegovina war of 1992–95 by 54 to 46 percent.[19] In several civil conflicts in Africa since the 1960s, the civilian share was higher, often exceeding a ratio of eight to one or ten to one.[20] But it is difficult to see the world wars as marking some kind of dividing line between "old" and "new" wars in this sense.

Innocent Bystanders?

World War I, known as the Great War before an even greater war began in 1939, was not the first war to be fought on a global scale. The Seven Years' War (1757–63) involved most of the European great powers and military action in Asia, Europe, and North America. The reach of the French Revolution and the Napoleonic Wars (1792–1815) was even wider, touching places as far apart as Ireland and Haiti, Cairo and Hyderabad, Moscow and Louisiana. However, in terms of scale, World War I and World War II represented a new era of "total war." The emergence of the term "total war" is often associated with the publication of German general Erich Ludendorff's *Der totale Krieg* in 1935, with an English translation, *The Nation at War*, following in 1936. Indeed, the *Oxford English Dictionary* attributes the term to him. But it was already in circulation during World War I, as evidenced in a letter from Captain Peter Strasser, commander of the German navy's Airship Division, to his mother:[21]

> We who strike the enemy where his heart beats have been slandered as baby killers and murderers of women. What we do is repugnant to us too, but necessary, very necessary. A soldier cannot function without the factory worker, the farmer and all the other providers behind them. Nowadays there is no such animal as a noncombatant. Modern warfare is total warfare.

Strasser, who would die in the last Zeppelin attack over Britain in early August 1918, was claiming that killing civilians reduced the enemy's resources in a war that was total. Around the same time in France, the right-wing journalist Léon Daudet (son of the well-known writer Alphonse Daudet) also used the term—"a total war: us or them"—and in April 1918 he published *La guerre totale*, a fierce polemic against a negotiated settlement with Germany.[22] The term resonated more widely during World War II. It appeared in the *Irish Times* for the first time on December 23, 1939, citing a pamphlet produced by the United Kingdom's Ministry of Information: "To keep their air force going in a 'total' war against Britain and France, the Nazis would need to make up for losses amounting to at least fifty per cent a month." On February 13, 1940, the same newspaper cited Reich Minister for Labour Franz Seldte as saying "Remember we are waging total war, and we have to demand a great deal, not only of the soldiers, but also of the home front." Total war, in other words, entailed bigger and longer wars and therefore unprecedented material sacrifices from the civilian population. On the eve of the German Blitzkrieg, the prime minister of France, Édouard Daladier, also repeatedly referred to "total war." But the term achieved a new, more sinister resonance in the wake of Joseph Goebbels's chilling *totaler Krieg* speech in Berlin's *Sportpalast* on February 18, 1943, a fortnight after the rout of the Wehrmacht at Stalingrad.[23]

In Britain, World War I seems also to have spawned several other terms that put civilians on central stage, such as "war effort" (1914), "rationing" (1915), "propaganda film" (1916), and "home front" (1917).[24] The first use of "home front" identified in the *Oxford English Dictionary Online* dates from April 11, 1917, in the *Times*; the expression appeared in the *Irish Times* for the first time on June 12, 1918. This new rhetoric of mobilization seemed to be redefining the role of noncombatants, even if the concept of total war was anticipated in France in 1793 in a decree declaring a *levée en masse* (mass conscription), which began:

> From this moment, until when its enemies have been swept from the territory of the Republic, the whole of France is permanently at the service of its armies. The young people will do the fighting; married men will forge arms and transport provisions; the women will make tents, clothes and serve in hospitals; the children will convert old linen to lint, and the old men will be driven to public places to cheer on the fighting men, to preach hatred for kings and the unity of the Republic. Public accommodation will be converted into barracks, public places into workshops for armaments, cellar floors will be washed to extract saltpetre. Firearms will be exclusively reserved for those who face enemy, civil society will make do with hunting rifles and knives. Saddle horses will be needed for the cavalry corps; draft horses other than those used in agriculture will drive artillery and supplies.

The American and French Revolutions of the late eighteenth century introduced an era when armies, wars, and mentalities were "democratized"; indeed, such democratization was probably a precondition for the French *levée en masse* of 1793. Yet in relative terms, recruitment in France during the Revolution and the Napoleonic Wars (2.6 million men aged over twenty, or more than a third of a total male population aged twenty to fifty-nine of 7.5 million) fell far short of that achieved in 1914–18 (8 million, or almost four-fifths of a male population aged twenty to fifty-nine of 10.5 million over four years).[25] In the wars against Napoleon, the British army peaked at 250,000 (out of a male population aged twenty to fifty-nine of about 7 million in Great Britain and Ireland) in 1813, whereas Britain mobilized over

6 million by the end of World War I (out of a male population aged twenty to fifty-nine of over 11.3 million), and 2.9 million served in World War II (out of a male population aged twenty to fifty-nine of about 12 million). Total German and French deployments during the Franco-Prussian War of 1870–71 were 1.5 million and 2 million, respectively. During World War I, they were 11 million and 8 million; during World War II, they were 13.6 million and 5 million. The two world wars cost much more in aggregate budgetary terms than the American Civil War; its $80 billion was dwarfed by their $2 trillion and $10 trillion, respectively, using 2011 purchasing power parities. In terms of military spending as a percentage of gross domestic product, the cost of fighting the American Civil War (84 percent) shaded that of World War I (78 percent) but was dwarfed by that of World War II (246 percent).[26] All these numbers are, of course, approximations, but they are indicative nonetheless. Their flip side is the cost in foregone consumption.[27] Nor do they factor in the devastation caused by war.

Insofar as the *levée en masse* and *Volkskrieg* both privileged mass conscription, the potential remained to keep the distinction between civilian and military. But the unprecedented mobilization of resources also increased the incentive of those at war to target civilians, both as contributors to the "war effort" and as citizens. And the mobilization for total war as represented in contemporary propaganda blurred the distinction between soldier and civilian that international law sought to establish in Geneva in 1949. In the wake of World War II, a U.S. legal scholar used the terms "noncombatant" and "civilian" interchangeably "to include all peaceful inhabitants of a country, not attached to or accompanying its armed force." But he then claimed, ignoring the young, the elderly, and those who looked after them, as well as the ill and the inactive, that the distinction between combatant and noncombatant had been "so whittled down by the demands of military necessity that it has become more apparent than real."[28]

The rhetoric of wartime leaders also placed their civilians at risk. On August 7, 1914, a few days after the outbreak of hostilities, Prime Minister René Viviani appealed to Frenchwomen to take to the fields that their menfolk had been forced to leave behind: "Prepare to show them tomorrow the land cultivated, the crops harvested, the field sown! No work is menial in these grave times."[29] British prime minister Winston Churchill went further in 1940, declaring that "the front line runs through the factories. The workmen are soldiers with different weapons but the same courage."[30] Such morale-boosting rhetoric has its darker corollary. Just a fortnight before the bombing of Hiroshima, a last-ditch Japanese effort at a *levée en masse* prompted the declaration in a U.S. intelligence report that "the entire population of Japan is a proper target. . . . There are no civilians in Japan." General Curtis LeMay, commander of the bombing campaign in Japan at its climax, felt the same: "There are no innocent civilians," he would later say. "It is their government and you are fighting a people, you are not trying to fight an armed force anymore."[31] By the same token, in the wake of World War II some observers defended the mistreatment of German civilians on the grounds that they had brought it upon themselves by voting for Hitler. And, indeed, a week after Hamas's barbaric outrages against Israeli civilians on October 7, 2023, Israeli president Isaac Herzog said of civilians in Gaza, "It's not true, this rhetoric about civilians being not aware, not involved. It's absolutely not true. They could have risen up, they could have fought against the evil regime which took over Gaza in a coup d'état."[32]

One particular group, mainly women, highlights this issue. During World War I, the number of women working as *munitionettes*, or "canary girls" (because filling shells with TNT turned their skin yellow), in the United Kingdom reached 0.6 million, distributed across over two hundred plants controlled by the Ministry of Munitions (figure 0.1). During World War II, the munitions workers, now more likely to be known as "bomb girls," peaked at nearly a million in the United Kingdom. In France during World War I, the number of munitionettes reached over 0.4 million. They mattered, even if General Joseph Joffre, commander in chief of the French forces at the time, greatly exaggerated in 1915 by claiming "If the women employed in the factories stopped work for twenty minutes, the Allies would lose the war."[33] Without them, it is true, there would have been fewer fighting soldiers. In Germany, where munitions workers numbered a million in 1917–18, the greater reliance on men meant the diversion of hundreds of thousands of soldiers from the front.

Still, in international humanitarian law a civilian is simply someone who is not a member of the armed forces and does not take part in hostilities. The ICRC's interpretation is that taking part in war involves actions causing, or intending to cause, harm to military or civilian adversaries—of being what sociologist Anthony Giddens has dubbed the "specialist purveyor of the means of violence."[34] That interpretation does not embrace munitions workers, though it probably should include those who shielded or provided useful information to the armed forces. Most of the millions of civilian victims described in the following chapters were innocent victims. A majority were women and children. They endured and perished from famine, from indiscriminate bombing from above, from infectious diseases, from forced and

FIGURE 0.1. Munitionettes at work in Nottinghamshire, England, 1917

often violent displacements, and—most horrific of all—from genocide. The data analyzed in what follows, however imprecise, reflect the ICRC's view.

Killing Civilians and Moral Equivalence

Protagonists sometimes argue that counting and publishing estimates of civilian casualties while a war is still in progress can only help the enemy; as the chief of the U.S.-led International Security Assistance Force lamented in 2009, "The perception caused by civilian casualties is one of the most dangerous enemies we face."[35] Meanwhile, propagandists on both sides of conflicts tend to exaggerate or conceal civilian casualties, as the case may be. Other observers believe that full knowledge of the cost in lives may prevent future wars. "If the evils of war are in reality larger and the benefits smaller than in the common view they appear to be," wrote economist John Bates Clark in 1916, this should "afford a basis for an enlightened policy whenever there is danger of international conflicts."[36] Either way, therefore, adding up civilian casualties in order to get a better sense of the costs of war is not a morally unambiguous exercise.

Some civilian deaths during World War I and World War II were deliberate or intentional, but more were not; some might seem justifiable in the circumstances, but more were emphatically not. Summing up deaths from a vast range of contexts in order to produce an aggregate toll is therefore controversial. It can be seen to imply that all civilian deaths were equally reprehensible, thereby obscuring the contexts in which they occurred and implying "a sort of moral bookkeeping that offsets one series of atrocities against what might be considered another."[37] That statement recalls a letter to the *Times* at the start of the Nuremberg trials in October 1945 from the campaigning philosopher Bertrand Russell, in which he expressed outrage at the mass expulsions of ethnic Germans from Eastern Europe by asking, "Are mass deportations crimes when committed by our enemies during war and justifiable measures of social adjustment when carried out by our allies in time of peace? Is it more humane to turn out old women and children to die at a distance than to asphyxiate Jews in gas chambers?"[38]

Even today, granting that Russell's protest was well meant, the moral equivalence underlying it is troubling. Historian Atina Grossmann's bitter critique of Helke Sander's *Befreier und Befreite* (*Liberators Take Liberties*), a feminist film about the mass rape of German women by Soviet troops at the end of World War II, offers an opposing perspective on this issue. Grossmann bristled at whether what "may be a horrifically accurate estimate (of rapes committed) . . . has something to do with precisely a competitiveness about the status of victim . . . so sensitive in the context of World War II." For Grossmann this story of rape is not "universal": it is one of German women, often racists and enthusiastic Nazi supporters, being raped by Soviet soldiers who defeated Nazi Germany and who had "liberated death camps." Grossmann worried that the mass rape would become part of a narrative "that might support postwar Germans' self-perception as victims insofar as it might participate in a dangerous revival of German nationalism, whitewash the Nazi past, and normalize a genocidal war." She, in turn, has been accused of insensitivity toward the suffering of war rape victims.[39]

Similarly, passionate critics of the Allied bombing campaign against civilians, such as author and historian Jörg Friedrich and novelist W. G. Sebald, have been accused of ignoring both the context of the bombing and the much greater suffering endured by the victims of Nazism elsewhere. For example, in a hostile review of Richard Overy's *The Bombing War* (2013) the U.S. military strategist Edward Luttwak juxtaposed the fatalities resulting from the firebombing of Hamburg in late July 1943 and the "achievements" of that city's notorious Reserve Police Battalion 101 during the slaughter of tens of thousands of Jews in the Lublin district of eastern Poland four months later.[40] But surely historians can explain different sets of atrocities without slipping into moral equivalence? This work attempts to do so, but it will probably not please everybody.

The "Dark Figures" of War

Sociologists and criminologists refer to the "dark figure" of crime as a means of highlighting the limitations of recorded data. The expression has broader resonance for estimates of death tolls in past wars. First, it recalls the definitional and contextual issues just discussed, which must be kept in view. Second, the sheer elusiveness of accurate estimates of civilian casualties makes them "dark figures." The fog of war makes it inherently difficult to count people, dead or alive; as we shall see, the lack of accurate data creates a vacuum for wild guesstimates that tend to be recycled and eventually treated as fact. A glance at Wikipedia's "List of Wars by Death Toll" highlights the problem. Where a range is given, the average gap between Wikipedia's low and high estimates of death tolls prior to World War I is nearly double, with a coefficient of variation of 0.83. Sometimes the width of the range, as with the 20–70 million given for the Taiping Rebellion (1850–64), makes numbers meaningless, other than as a rhetorical device. And sometimes—as with the 36–40 million given for the Three Kingdoms war in China (184–280 CE)— the estimate is both too big and too narrow to be credible.[41] The trouble is that there is a ready market for data, no matter how questionable. Spurious numbers have a habit of taking on a life of their own. As economic historian Greg Clark remarks, "Among modern economists there is a hunger by the credulous for numbers, any numbers however dubious their provenance, to lend support to the model of the moment."[42] Nevertheless, there is a role as well for cautious estimates, presented with suitable caveats, if only to rule out more farfetched numbers. Sometimes, too, it is appropriate to point out that no numbers are better than bad numbers. And Albert Einstein's familiar bon mot, "Everything that can be counted does not necessarily count; everything that counts cannot necessarily be counted," is also apposite here.

Although the numbers are better for World War I and World War II than for most earlier wars, gaps and uncertainties remain. In an age of industrialized slaughter, states went to great lengths to record military casualties, but civilian fatalities frequently went uncounted; indeed, figures were often deliberately obscured. That is why some historians avoid estimates of civilian casualties.[43] Still, establishing a figure for civilian fatalities can reveal much about the nature of modern war. Our concern in the following chapters is not only to build on earlier estimates of casualties from a range of causes, some reliable, some approximate at best, but also to warn against spurious precision when even approximations are impossible. Thus, for example, while the human toll of the Jewish Holocaust is generally agreed to have been about 6 million,[44] the tolls of two other war genocides, those of the Armenian community in Turkey during World War I and of the European Roma community during World War II, cannot be determined with any precision. Scholarly estimates of the former range from 0.6 to 1.2 million and of the latter from "at least 130,000" to "between 250,000 and 500,000," and higher numbers have been cited in both cases.[45] During World War II, Chinese civilians faced both a civil war and Japanese occupation. No estimate of the resultant civilian deaths, which range from an implausibly low 2.5 million to 20 million, is reliable.[46] One of the fruits of this book is a negative one: offering some sense of what war casualties are beyond estimation.

The numbers of victims of aerial bombing during World War II are less contested, but they have provoked controversy in the past. Today the generally accepted estimate for all deaths (though mostly civilians) from U.S. bombing in Japan during World War II is about 0.4 million, but initially the U.S. Strategic Bombing Survey placed the number at 0.9 million plus 1.3 million injured. A UN estimate of 140,000 for the death toll in Hiroshima is now preferred to an earlier tally of 260,000 by Japan's Pacific War National Air-Raid Victim Consoling Association.[47] It is now also widely accepted that initial estimates of the number of civilian deaths caused by the notorious bombings of the German cities of Hamburg and Dresden during World War II were far too high. The same holds for an estimate of 0.8 million hunger-related deaths in Germany during and in the wake of World War I, where the true figure may have reached 0.4–0.5 million.[48]

And so some estimates are set deliberately low in a spirit of denial; some are exaggerated for effect; some were never intended to be taken literally.[49] Estimates of famine deaths in Vietnam in 1944–45 range from 0.4 to 2 million and in Java from 1.3 to 2.4 million. Similarly, estimates of the German refugees murdered in Czechoslovakia in the wake of World War II range from the 15,000 to 40,000 claimed by Czech historians to the 2.23 million claimed by the German historian Heinz Nawratil.[50] The Nazis' chief propagandist, Joseph Goebbels, put the death toll in Dresden in February 1945 at 250,000, and a near-contemporary account claimed that "no survivor could report on the events in the center of Dresden, where 300,000 persons were reported killed in 24 hours." In one of her last essays, Susan Sontag would recycle an estimate of "more than a hundred thousand German civilians, three-fourths of them women," but the expert consensus on the true death toll is now about 25,000.[51] People will sometimes pick the number that suits them: in an interview in 1977 Marshal Sir Arthur Travers "Bomber" Harris, head of the Royal Air Force's Bomber Command at the height of World War II, recycled an implausibly high figure for the Allied blockade of Germany during World War I as a way of making the numbers killed by the Bomber Command during World War II seem "small."[52]

In addition to those who perished were those who survived but were physically or mentally scarred by war. They include the injured and the bereaved, those traumatized by what they witnessed and experienced, and those suffering the long-term consequences of being in utero or being born during or in the wake of war. They must also find a place in what follows. And here, too, one encounters great discrepancies in estimates: for instance, the estimated number of women raped by Soviet and Western forces at the end of World War II ranges from less than hundreds of thousands to over two million.[53]

Finally, fallibility aside, figures are a cold way of capturing the enormity of civilian losses during World War I and World War II. Soviet journalist Vassili Grossman's verbal depiction of what he witnessed in Treblinka in mid-August 1944 captures its horrors much more effectively than his feeble attempt at estimating (or exaggerating) the number who perished there.[54] In the end there remains Sherman's aphorism: "War is cruelty and you cannot refine it."[55] Aren't any estimates of the aggregate civilian fatalities—which are by definition, refinements—inadequate and unavailing for explaining the experience of war? How does one measure cruelty? How does one measure grief? History demands a figure, but the figure somehow occludes the darkness that underlies it. Big anonymous numbers may have shock value, but they compromise compassion and empathy. And counting deaths risks equating them in morally troubling ways.

In contemplating the horrors of the world wars, genocides, bombings, and atrocities spring to mind more readily than famine, and much has been written about them. Yet if war-related deaths in the new Soviet Union in 1918–22 are included, hunger, famine, and associated diseases were the single biggest cause of civilian mortality during World War I and World War II. And whether those post-1918 deaths are included or not, famine deaths during World War II exceeded those during World War I by a big margin. The role of famine is paramount, and that is why the first part of our account describes famine in both wars in some detail. Some of those famines will be familiar and well documented, while others have attracted research only recently, and a few await systematic analysis. Some of these war famines broadly replicated earlier famines in terms of proximate causes and symptoms, but others differed in a number of ways. And whereas a few were deliberate, more were the by-products of strategic decision-making that placed military goals before civilian needs. As we shall see, relatively affluent economies were not immune from hunger and starvation; famines in the heavily urban western Netherlands and in Leningrad (today's Saint Petersburg) during World War II have yielded precious data that shed light on aspects of other lesser-known famines.

The Guns of August, V-E Day, "the eleventh hour of the eleventh day of the eleventh month": dates linked to World War I and World War II are engraved in our memories. Yet it has been argued that World War II began in 1931,[56] and certainly events in Ethiopia and in Spain and in China may be seen as dress rehearsals for what was to follow. And there is a good case for arguing that World War I did not end until the Russian Civil War and the Greco-Turkish War were over. Indeed, one of the foremost historians of World War I, Jay Winter, has described July 24, 1923, the day on which representatives of Turkey and Greece signed a peace treaty in Lausanne, as *The Day the Great War Ended.*[57] Similarly, the embers of World War II were not extinguished until 1946 or 1947. Our discussion reflects these broader chronologies. The approach is thematic rather than chronological. The order in which settings and victims are discussed, whether by chapter or within chapters, is not intended to relativize them. Chapters 1 to 3 are devoted to hunger and famines during World War I and World War II. They pay particular attention to aspects such as the demographic impact and characteristics of war famines, the constraints on relief efforts in wartime settings, the use of blockades as a military tactic, food rationing and the operation of black markets, and the long-term health impacts of hunger. The enormous cost of famine in terms of lives lost during the two wars will be highlighted, even if questions remain about the accuracy of some of the data invoked. Chapters 4 and 5 shift the focus from famine to the more familiar territory of war-related genocides, particularly the Jewish Holocaust. Chapter 6 describes the impact of a new and controversial form of war tactic that disproportionately targeted civilians, aerial bombing. There is broad consensus now on the death tolls from bombing in Europe and Japan. The figures for elsewhere in Asia are of poor quality, but the global total killed from the above during World War II was well over a million and possibly 1.5 million. Chapter 7 is devoted to war-related migration, involving displaced persons fleeing for their lives, refugees, and forced laborers. Both wars produced unprecedented numbers of human migrants, both during the fighting and in its wake. Not easily quantified but possibly numbering 100 million or more in total, these, too, were nearly all innocent victims. Reliable numbers on another category of victim, those targeted by sexual violence and other atrocities, are even more elusive. They are the focus of chapters 8 and 9. Chapter 10 examines the impact of World War I and World War II on civilian morale and trauma, both in the short run and the long run. A century ago the term "trauma" (from τραῦμα, Greek for "a wound") referred to physical injury; only in the post–World War II period has it been in widespread use in its modern sense of psychic injury. Nowadays the UN is ubiquitous, and it features prominently and controversially in the literature on both world wars. Chapter 11 summarizes and concludes with some broader speculations.

1

Mobilization, Relief, and Famine

Those in the country will die by the sword;
Those in the city will be devoured by famine and plague.
—EZEKIEL 7:15

In what follows, famines are understood as shortages of food or purchasing power that lead directly to excess mortality from starvation or hunger-induced diseases.[1] Not all wars cause famines in this sense, but wars invariably put pressure on the living standards of civilians. They divert labor and capital from agriculture and consumption in general and they destroy crops. They disrupt economic activity and reallocate resources toward war-connected industries by restricting the flow of goods, people, and information, and they entail occupation and exploitation. In all these ways, wars make famines more likely. And when they do cause famines, they make it more difficult to relieve and to end them.

Such factors have applied throughout history. But they mattered much more after industrialization, mass politics, military technological change, and conscription made *totale Kriege* possible. During both world wars, total war massively diverted prime males away from agriculture on a scale previously unmatched. More than ever before, wars reallocated food to high-priority consumers (soldiers and armament workers) and away from everybody else, and horses and fertilizer went from farming to military use. The attendant physical destruction, trade disruption, blockades, plunder, mayhem, and mismanagement added immeasurably to the vulnerability of the civilian population. Such was the pressure of total war on civilian living standards that it reintroduced serious malnutrition and famine to some relatively well-off economies that had not experienced them for generations.

Both world wars led to hunger and starvation on a massive scale. Somewhat paradoxically, perhaps, given that global living standards had risen in the interim, World War II was much more murderous than World War I in this respect. The size of the difference depends on whether the Russian Civil War in the wake of World War I (1918–22) is included. Technically, Russian involvement in World War I ceased on March 3, 1918, at the signing of the Treaty of Brest-Litovsk between the new Bolshevik government and the Central Powers. However, it was the arrival by sealed train in Petrograd on April 3, 1917, of Vladimir Lenin and thirty or so other revolutionary exiles that spawned both the October Revolution and the civil war that lasted until 1922.[2] Though distinct events, the continuity between World War I and the Russian Civil War of 1918–21 is indisputable. At stake in the calculations are about five million famine deaths in 1921–22.

I begin this account of civilian casualties of war with a discussion of famines because famine was the greatest single killer of civilians during both world wars. Between them, World War I and World War II spawned famines in over two dozen countries and led to the deaths of between thirty million and thirty-five million civilians from starvation and associated diseases. In a timely caveat, as will become clear all figures are necessarily approximate. During World War I, if war-related deaths in the Soviet Union after 1918 are included, famine deaths clearly exceeded all battlefield deaths, and during World War II the ratio was about two-thirds. This arithmetic is not reflected in the literature on the two wars. There is no general account of the role of famine during either World War I or World War II, although many studies of individual famines exist. Yet while famines such as the Great Bengal Famine of 1943–44, the Leningrad Blockade famine of 1941–43, and the much smaller Dutch Hunger Winter famine of 1944–45 are familiar, several others are poorly documented, and most are known only to specialists. Nor were the "forgotten" famines the smallest: perhaps three times as many perished in the Dutch East Indies in 1944–45 as in Leningrad in 1941–43, and three times as many died of starvation and related diseases in Vietnam in 1944–45 as in Greece in 1942–43. Twice as many succumbed to starvation in French mental hospitals during World War II as in the whole of the western Netherlands in late 1944 and early 1945, and twice as many again starved in German mental hospitals.

War and mobilization for war increased the likelihood of famines, and the authorities sought to mitigate their impact in various ways, as the present chapter will show. The following two chapters are devoted to describing the main famines of World War I and World War II and their demographic aspects.

Mobilization and Food Availability

Both wars involved levels of mobilization of economic resources on a scale almost certainly unprecedented in human history (figure 1.1). France and Germany devoted over half of their gross domestic product (GDP) to military expenditure during World War I; in the United Kingdom the proportion was two-fifths in 1916–18. Mobilization during World War II far surpassed that during World War I except in France, which was forced to bow out early, and the United Kingdom. By 1943 Germany was committing 70 percent of its national output to the war, compared to the Soviet Union's 60 percent and the United Kingdom's 40 percent. Data implying that on the eve of surrender both Germany and Japan were spending the equivalent of their entire GDP on the war (as Russia had done in 1917 and, even more so, in 1919) indicate total war, very literally. Such data should be taken with a grain of salt, but they are probably not too far off the truth and are indicative of the degree of mobilization involved.[3] In the case of Germany, the plundering of occupied countries and minorities is part of the story; figure 1.1 (on which more will be discussed below) speaks volumes in this context. By the end of World War II, the United Kingdom, Germany, the Union of Soviet Socialist Republics (USSR), and Japan had spent three times or more of their GDP on their war effort.[4] By comparison, military spending in the United States during the American Civil War had peaked at 11.7 percent of GDP in 1865 while toward the end of the Napoleonic Wars the United Kingdom had been spending about one-fifth of national income on defense.[5]

The levels of mobilization reached during the world wars led to severe labor shortages everywhere. The wars militarized much of the civilian population and greatly increased women's participation in the labor force. In France the increase in the female labor force was most dramatic in department's with the heaviest military losses.[6] During World War I, the proportion of women in the UK labor force rose from less than a quarter to nearly two-fifths. Their share rose fastest from 1916 on in the wake of what was known in Britain as the "shell scandal" of May 1915, when the failure of an offensive at Aubers Ridge on the Western Front was blamed on a lack of munitions. Female employment rose most dramatically in the munitions sector, and

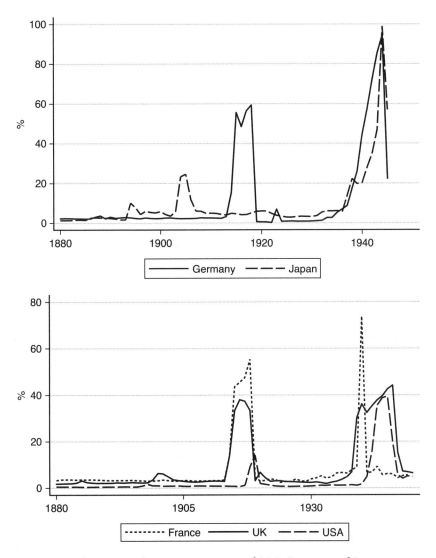

FIGURE 1.1. Military expenditure as a percentage of GDP, Germany and Japan
Source: Our World in Data
Note: Q = consumption; M = imports; C = consumption

by mid-1918 nearly one million women were employed in UK munitions industries.[7] In Germany and in France, too, women substituted for men on the home front, but they were more likely to be employed in agriculture than were British women. Still, by the end of the war French *munitionnettes*, who by then numbered 0.4 million, had produced three hundred million shells and over six billion cartridges, and in the massive Renault works in

Paris, the female share of the labor force had quintupled, rising from 3.8 to 31.6 percent.[8] In the UK between 1939 and 1945, against the significant fall in the number of insured male employees (from 11.4 million to 8.6 million) and the increase in their average age, the number of females in the labor force rose from 4.4 to 7.4 million. Germany dragooned Belgian and Polish workers into its factories during World War I and relied on such labor to a much greater extent after 1939. It is reckoned that imported, and in many cases forced, labor produced about one-fifth of its food during World War II.[9]

Agriculture and light industry, not heavy industry, bore the brunt of conscription. Women, prisoners of war, and in some case, forced laborers were used as substitutes, but they could not make up for the missing skilled male labor. In Great Britain during World War I, about fifty thousand women were put to work in agriculture, with preference given to those with some experience of working on the land. During World War II, the number of "land girls" from the Women's Land Army engaged in farm work peaked at eighty thousand in 1944, but farmers were skeptical of their added value. In Germany mobilization removed two-fifths of its laborers from agriculture, and the number of seasonal laborers also dropped. Most of the workers sent to replace them lacked experience and motivation.[10] The mobilization of labor for war constrained the productivity of agriculture everywhere.

None of the belligerents in 1914 foresaw a war that would last four years and cost so many lives. Yet although Kaiser Wilhelm II famously promised departing German troops that they would be back "before the leaves fall from the trees," historians have been tilting away from the view that the military top brass on both sides suffered from "short war illusion." The prevailing military consensus, it is now believed, was that the war would be very bloody but last no more than two years.[11] Therefore, guaranteeing food supplies was not a preoccupation at the outset. From 1916 on, however, the threat of famine would become very real.

Because Britain's area under cereals and potatoes had diminished so much over the previous half century—by over a quarter since 1870—it was in a good position to expand tillage as required after 1914. All the authorities needed to do at the outset was to ensure that farmers were adequately compensated. Not until January 1917 did they introduce more interventionist measures, such as compulsory tillage orders and subsidized tractors. By contrast, the United Kingdom introduced tillage orders almost immediately after the start of World War II, on September 15, 1939. The huge increase in the arable acreage (from 8.9 million in 1939 to 14.6 million in 1944) varied by region, with the smallest increases in the already heavily arable eastern part of the country.[12] On the eve of World War I in Germany, by comparison, the tilled area was almost one-fifth higher than in 1870, leaving little scope for further expansion; in France it was only 5 percent lower, and in addition German occupation entailed the loss of 5 percent of France's best arable land.

The contrasting evolutions of agricultural output during both wars, as reflected in cereal and potato production in Great Britain, Germany, France, Italy, and the Soviet Union, are striking and were important for food security. They are compared in figure 1.2. Great Britain stands out as exceptional in both wars, but its achievement in almost doubling the number of domestically produced calories by 1943–44 during World War II was particularly outstanding. By contrast, German output in 1918 was about half its 1914 level, and this, combined with very limited access to outside food supplies, led to serious hardship and, ultimately, famine conditions in 1918 and 1919. German agriculture fared much better during World War II, however, at least until 1944.

While Italian agriculture proved resilient enough during World War I, its performance during World War II was disastrous. The difference is mainly a reflection of World War I being fought on Italy's mountainous northeastern border, while World War II involved invasions, air strikes, and lengthy occupations across the peninsula. The decline in French agricultural output during World War I may be attributed to the reduction in manpower, horses, and fertilizers and the loss of land in the North and East. Output at the end of World War II was only two-thirds that before the war, but most of that decline occurred in 1939–40. Thereafter, under pressure from the Germans to deliver, French output held its own, or even increased slightly, although hampered by shortages of manpower and other inputs. At the end of 1940, France's agricultural labor force was 13 percent less than before the war, and those missing were "often the fittest and the strongest." Horse numbers fell from 2.7 million in 1938 to 2.1 million in 1944, and nitrogenous fertilizer inputs fell by half.[13] About 15 percent of all bread grains and meat produced and one-fifth of fodder grains were delivered to Germany.[14] The impact of the reduction in entitlements on health and nutritional status during World War II was severe. In the Soviet Union, the trends in both wars were remarkably similar, with potatoes holding their own and cereal production collapsing. The collapse in cereal production during World War II was in large part due to the loss of much of the Soviet Union's most productive acreage, particularly in Ukraine, during most of the war. Chapter 2 discusses the importance of potatoes for survival in some detail.

The data in figure 1.2 refer to tillage, which was the priority everywhere. In addition, as competitors with humans for calories, pig numbers fell

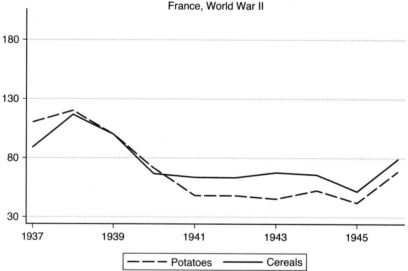

FIGURE 1.2. Trends in cereal and potato production during World War I and World War II

Source: Russian data from Andrei Markevich, "Russia in the Great War: Mobilisation, Grain, and Revolution," *VoxEU*, March 9, 2019; Suhara 2017: table 3.3. Data for other countries are taken from Mitchell 1975

Note: Production measured in tonnes, 1914 and 1939 set at 100 (except in Soviet Union where 1941 = 100)

FIGURE 1.2. (*continued*)

heavily in Germany (by 60 percent) and in France (by 38 percent) during World War I, but the decline was much smaller (18 percent) in Britain, where there was less pressure on food availability and a much larger share of meat supplies imported. During World War II, the decline in pig numbers was most dramatic in Britain (from 3.8 million in 1939 to 1.6 million in 1943) and in the Soviet Union (from 12.2 million in 1940 to 4.2 million

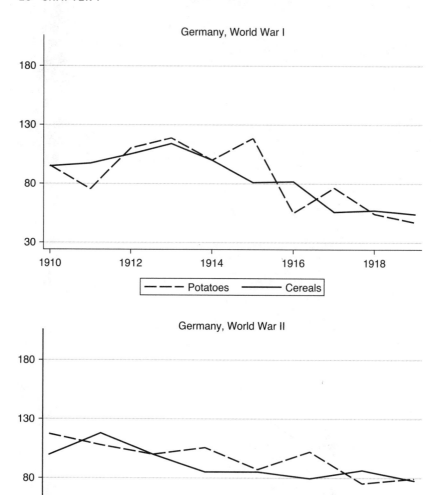

FIGURE 1.2. (*continued*)

in 1944).[15] Pig numbers in Germany also fell during World War II, but more gradually, from 25.2 million in 1939 to 15.3 million in 1944 (data for 1945 are lacking).

In one respect Germany might have been luckier with its agriculture during World War I. The output of nitrogenous fertilizers using a process

FIGURE 1.2. (*continued*)

discovered by one of its own foremost scientists, Fritz Haber, which had just recently become commercially viable, rose from sixty-three hundred metric tons of fixed nitrogen in 1913 to almost two hundred thousand metric tons in 1918, while output using the less energy-efficient Frank-Caro process rose from forty-three hundred metric tons to fifty-five thousand metric tons

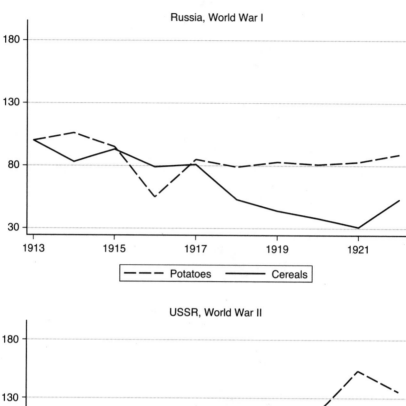

FIGURE 1.2. (*continued*)

over the same period. By war's end, Germany's output of fixed nitrogen was about three times that of prewar nitrate imports from Chile.[16] But in the choice between guns and butter, guns won out, and in any case, potash was an imperfect substitute for nitrates, the input of which per cultivated acre fell by half during the war.[17] In Germany a serious outbreak of *Phytophthera infestans*, or potato blight, led to a disastrous potato harvest in 1916, and

TABLE 1.1. Agricultural produce delivered to Germany by France and by the occupied USSR, 1940–44

Item	France to Germany, 1940–44 (tons, unless otherwise indicated)			Item	USSR to Germany, 1941–44 (tons, rounded)		
	Quantity	Kcals/ton	M. kcals		Quantity	M. kcals
Bread grain	2,950,000	3,284,000	9,687,800	Bread grain	5,016,000	16,472,544
Meat	891,000	2,500,000	2,227,500	Meat	563,700	1,409,250
Eggs (1,000)	311,000	60,000	18,660	Eggs (1,000)	1,078,000	64,680
Fats	51,200	3,000,000	153,600	Oils	20,500	61,500
Butter	88,000	7,000,000	616,000	Butter	206,800	1,447,600
Potatoes	752,000	702,127	527,996	Potatoes	3,281,700	2,304,156
Sugar	99,000	4,000,000	396,000	Sugar	401,000	1,604,000
Wine (hl)	10,400,000	70,000	728,000			
Milk (hl)	1,445,000	60,000	86,700			
Cheese	45,000	4,000,000	180,000			
Total (m. kcals)			14,622,256			23,363,730

Source: derived from Lyautey and Elie 2019: table 1a and 1b, applying above kcal conversion rates.

output failed to recover thereafter, while cereal yields fell by one-third during the war. The lack of food had a major impact on German civilian morale from 1916 onward.

German agriculture proved much more resilient during World War II than during World War I. But Germany extracted a lot of food from its occupied territories, most notably from France and the Soviet Union. Table 1.1, based on data collated by Margot Lyautey and Marc Elie, indicates that, very roughly, France and the occupied regions of the Soviet Union (and particularly Ukraine) supplied about forty trillion kilocalories to Nazi Germany during the war. A daily intake of two thousand calories per adult equivalent would mean enough to feed about 50 million people for a year, or 12.5 million annually between mid-1941 and the end of the war. Between 1939 and 1944, aggregate deliveries from abroad accounted for 12 percent of German civilian and military consumption.[18]

As noted in the introduction, the two wars produced several examples of blockades aimed at restricting the food supply, with fatal consequences. The blockade of Germany in the wake of World War I in particular contributed to the deaths of perhaps 0.4 million civilians. Although intended as a "weapon of starvation" from the outset, the blockade did not begin to bite until 1916. Thereafter, the *Burgfrieden*, or social partnership, agreed upon between competing economic and political groups in Germany at the outset of the war was severely threatened as the hungry sought out scapegoats, both urban and rural. A prewar assessment by the Royal Society that a full blockade on Germany would reduce proteins and fats below the threshold for health and efficiency was more than borne out.[19] According to Matthias Blum, toward the end of the war civilian deaths almost matched military deaths, with urban dwellers, the poor, Catholics, and those living in "the highly integrated, food importing regions along the Rhine river and the North- and Baltic Seas" most at risk.[20] On the insistence of the French of the need "to remind the Germans that the blockade shall cease at the same moment as the state of war" and despite British protests, the blockade was not lifted until after the ratification of the Treaty of Versailles on July 12, 1919. Inevitably, "the ignorance and stupidity of man" and the cutting off of previous sources of food in the East played a part in the tragedy. But given the disastrous impact of the blockade on food availability in Germany from 1917, blaming "general exhaustion brought on by all the operations of war, of mismanagement, and of placing military demands before civilian needs" seems beside the point.[21]

In March 1919, Winston Churchill, then the British secretary of state for war, made no bones about the blockade against Germany being a "weapon of starvation,"[22] and the code name given to the highly successful aerial mining campaign conducted by the U.S. XXI Bomber Command against Japan in the spring of 1945, Operation Starvation, tells its own story, although it did not lead to outright famine. Indeed, the author of a 1974 RAND Corporation study of Operation Starvation tried "to avoid this unfortunate code name by resorting to various circumlocutions" or by calling it the "mining campaign" despite concluding (approvingly) that it had virtually destroyed Japanese maritime trade and that by its end "food supplies had fallen below subsistence level."[23] It was the aerial campaign of mining Japanese waters that "finally strangled Japan." Between April 1945 and the war's end, submarines sank only 17–18 percent of the total vessels and tonnage lost by the Japanese.[24]

The Wehrmacht's decision to let the civilian population of the besieged city then called Leningrad (today's Saint Petersburg) starve was in the spirit of the genocidal Backe Plan to ensure relief was not allowed to get in the way of providing food for Germany.[25] The blockade began on September 8, 1941. By the time it was completely lifted on January 27, 1944, from 0.7 to 1.0 million Leningraders had perished of starvation. Blockades also resulted in, or accentuated, famines in Lebanon in 1916 and in Greece in 1941–43.

Although, like Leningrad, India was never occupied by the enemy during World War II, the Great Bengal Famine of 1943–44 was indisputably a war famine. It was due in large part to the refusal of the authorities, for war-related reasons, to acknowledge that Bengal was suffering from a food availability decline (FAD) until it was too late. The insistence that Bengal contained enough food throughout to feed the entire population suited the military priorities of the Allies, but it made involuntary war casualties of over two million Bengalis. In Vietnam in 1944–45, the impact of typhoons and flooding in the Gulf of Tonkin was there for all to see, but neither the Japanese nor French occupiers took worthwhile remedial action, and U.S. bombing of the communications infrastructure made shipping food supplies from surplus to deficit areas virtually impossible. Elsewhere the exploitation that accompanied occupation was enough to create famine conditions, as in Java, China, and Ukraine during World War II. All these famines are discussed in more detail in chapter 2.

Markets, Rationing, and Famines

During threatened or impending subsistence crises in wartime, the authorities are typically and understandably reluctant to sacrifice guns for butter, but the pressure to "do something" is strong. In a context in which most adult males have enlisted or are already employed, public works are no longer expedient, although other classic remedies such as soup kitchens or canteens may be in some settings. Assisted migration may also provide a limited way out. In wartime, too, philanthropy can play a particularly powerful role. In Britain, World War I saw an unprecedented degree of volunteering, while the Commission for Relief in Belgium, a citizens' initiative orchestrated by future U.S. president Herbert C. Hoover, helped to sustain millions of civilians in German-occupied Belgium and northern France and inspired the American Relief Administration's massive efforts in the Soviet Union in 1921.[26]

During World War I and World War II, the authorities relied heavily on a new or at least unfamiliar form of relief, food rationing. Although *cartes de rationnement* were issued in Paris during the Commune (1870–71), the word "rationing" was new in English in 1914, at least in the sense understood today; prior to that one might have referred to "the daily rationing of children attending schools" during the Great Irish Famine or to "the soldier's ration." The earliest use reported in the *Oxford English Dictionary* of the term "rationing" in the modern sense was in 1914.[27] In 1916 economist

A. C. Pigou used the term "rationing" with inverted commas in *The Economy and Finance of the War* while economist Moritz Bonn referred to the "so-called process of 'rationing'" in the *Quarterly Journal of Economics*, and F. Y. Edgeworth used "rationing" in inverted commas in a review of Pigou's essay in the *Economic Journal*.[28]

Rationing marked the suspension of market forces as the main means of distributing staple foodstuffs. It entailed both price controls and shifting entitlements since ration coupons entitled consumers who might have been unable to pay free market prices to a stipulated amount of the rationed good per day, week, or month. In a classic paper, economist Martin Weitzman described the conditions under which the rationing of a deficit commodity works best.[29] He showed that the more uniform the need for the commodity and the more unequal the distribution of income, the more rationing proved effective "in matching up the limited supply of a deficit commodity with those users who need it most." Such conditions always loom large whenever famine threatens during wartime. But Weitzman does not dwell on the institutional context, which is crucial. For rationing to be effective, the authorities need to exercise control over both the supply of and demand for the rationed commodities. Bread is the classic rationed food. When the rationed goods are not necessities, proposed Yale economist James Tobin in a famous 1952 paper, it would make sense to permit people to sell their rations, thereby increasing the economic well-being of both those who sell and those who buy. But when such sales threaten the life of card holders or their dependents, that welfare-improving framework does not apply. Nor does it apply to secondary trading in markets that specialize in stolen goods.

The system the authorities impose must, by definition, involve sacrifices on the part of most people, but in order to work, it must also be seen to be "fair," or equitable. That does not necessarily mean that everyone is treated equally; due allowance must be made for physical needs and the nature of the work performed. For example, in France during World War I there were separate entitlements for infants, adults, young people, workers, agriculturalists, and older adults. Under the system introduced in the Soviet Union in July 1941, manual workers in war industries were entitled to twenty-eight ounces of bread, whereas white-collar workers got only eighteen ounces and children under twelve years of age, fourteen ounces.[30] Such distinctions made sense, but they risked undermining people's belief that the system was "fair."[31]

Given that markets for staple foods usually involve vast numbers of producers, distributors, and consumers, making rationing work is never going to be easy. To be effective it requires a strong state and, in essence, central planning, with the power to control both supply and demand. The state must become both monopolist and monopsonist simultaneously.[32] That is not easily achieved when thousands or millions of agents are involved. It helps if the rationed commodity is homogeneous; the rationing of meat, for example, can give rise to accusations of favoritism and sharp practice.

For centuries it was common for governing elites to alleviate food shortages through holding stocks in reserve, imposing restrictions on the movement of cereals, seeking supplies from abroad, prohibiting the nonfood uses of grains, and controlling prices. The authorities in cities under siege sometimes resorted to rationing, as in Bologna in 1590, Lucknow in 1857, Paris in late 1870 and early 1871,[33] and Mafeking in 1899–1900. At the start of the siege of the Indian city of Lucknow in 1857, for example, "women got three-quarter rations, children half"; later on, those shares were reduced to half a ration for women and one-sixth for children.[34] During the 1870–71 Siege of Paris, meat rationing was introduced on October 6, 1870, and in mid-December horses were requisitioned for food. By then fuel and meat were virtually unavailable. On January 18, 1871, bread rationing was introduced at three hundred grams daily for ten centimes for adults, but three weeks later the mayor brought the rationing of bread to an end. Rationing was also part of the *loi du maximum général* in force during the French Revolution in 1793–94. But protracted nationwide rationing in wartime as practiced during the twentieth century was something new.

Rationing during World War I

In Germany during World War I, converting dwindling aggregate supplies of food to basic entitlements for the mass population was an enormous challenge. The authorities intervened early, setting a maximum price for potatoes in late 1914 and, in the following months, rationing bread, banning the foddering of grain, commanding farmers to kill off livestock, and confiscating the potatoes used to feed cattle. From the beginning bakers were allowed to supplement the standard inputs of rye and wheat with potato flour in their bread; other additives were allowed later. The resulting ersatz product, known as *K-Brot*,[35] was widely reviled (figure 1.3). Food rationing on the scale forced on Germany during World War I was unprecedented and posed enormous administrative challenges. In late January 1915, the authorities banned private transactions in grain and began to centralize all grain stocks. Bread rationing was introduced, with a daily allocation of about

FIGURE 1.3. German Interior Ministry propaganda postcards

250 grams or its equivalent in flour; the precise figure varied from city to city. That would have amounted to 600 to 700 kilocalories, or about half the amount required to keep an inactive male adult alive. It reflected what grain the authorities were able to collect after the lack of manpower and nitrates had begun to bite. Potatoes were rationed in 1916 and meat in 1917 (250 grams weekly, equivalent to about 600 kilocalories). In Berlin the disastrous harvest of 1916 led to the bread ration being reduced to 1,600 grams weekly. In January 1917 ration cards were issued for turnips for the first time, and the potato ration was reduced to 750 grams (or 750 kilocalories) daily. Hopes that Russia's withdrawal from the war in March 1918 would lead to ample imports of grain from Ukraine were not realized.[36]

Rationing in Germany probably saved lives, even though the rations were very meager, equivalent to about a thousand calories daily in mid-1917.[37] Anything was better than nothing. Table 1.2 describes how the value of the food ration dropped as the blockade began to bite. As supplies dwindled, the authorities sought to enhance entitlements through vast soup kitchens (figure 1.4), but they were ineffective in the face of a rampant black market: according to Avner Offer approximately "one-fifth to one-third of food could only be obtained through illegal channels."[38] The gap between official and black market prices widened over time but differed considerably across products and, presumably, between places. The price of the bread ration did not rise, but its quality fell, as inferior grains were substituted for wheat. Rationing often entailed queueing in vain for long hours—"dancing the polonaise," as it was described in Berlin—an added cost that brought its own tensions. Long queues, mainly of women, would form at night. Figure 1.5 shows queues in Germany and in Britain during World War I. The image from Luton accompanied the following in a local newspaper:

TABLE 1.2. Wartime rations relative to peacetime consumption in Germany (%)

Item	July 1916–July 1917	July 1917–July 1918	July 1918–Dec. 1918
Potatoes	71	94	94
Flour	53	47	48
Vegetable fats	39	41	17
Pulses	14	1	7
Butter	22	21	28
Cheese	3	4	15
Meat	31	20	12
Fish	51	..	5
Eggs	18	13	13
Sugar	49	56–67	80

Source: Hardach 1977: 119.

Throughout the week there had been queues in the principal streets, and whole families have been hunting from breakfast time to shop closing time. . . . So general has this become and such a tax on some of the shopkeepers, that in some instances shops have been closed throughout the morning in order that the assistants might prepare for the afternoon rush. . . . This morning before 10 o'clock a crowd approaching 500 assembled on the market hill waiting for the shops to open. . . . At one shop in High town this morning over a thousand customers were served out with small packets of goods before ten o'clock. . . . Police have been on duty regulating crowds every day, and matters have now got to such a pass that in Luton at any rate there would be general satisfaction if Lord Rhondda (the Government's Food Controller) carried out the suggestion of the Luton Food Committee and instituted compulsory rationing.[39]

In Berlin some people would join the queue equipped with stools or mats:

The others stand there apathetically, some asleep while standing, and the moonlight makes the colourless faces look even more wan. Constables appear and walk up and down morosely. Dawn breaks. New droves draw near. . . . At last selling begins. And the result: a miserable half, or if one is very lucky, whole pound each of meat, lard or butter for half the purchasers, while the other half have to go away empty-handed.[40]

Adding to the hardship was that the ration card did not guarantee food: it was merely a statement of the maximum entitlement when available. Ration

FIGURE 1.4. Canteens and soup kitchens in Germany, World War I

FIGURE 1.5. Queuing for food in England and Germany during World War I

FIGURE 1.6. Ration cards/books from World War I and World War II (including from Leningrad and the Rzeszov/Reichshof ghetto)
Source: Judenrat of Rzeszow by the Nazi Generalgouvernement, USHMM, https://collections.ushmm.org/search/catalog/pa1095750

cards came in many sizes and shapes; those in figure 1.6 include cards for turnips and potatoes in the German cities of Erfurt and Trier during World War 1 and cards from Leningrad and the Jewish ghetto in Rzeszov/Reichshof during World War II.

In Germany during World War I, most bread and potatoes were traded through legitimate channels, but one-quarter to one-third of dairy products and one-third to one-half of meat products, fruit, and eggs made their way to the black market.[41] The pain was spread unevenly; a recent study of the heights of male survivors suggests that the gap between rich and poor, using the father's occupation as a proxy for income, increased during the war, which has been attributed to the greater reliance of the poor on the inadequate rationing system.[42] In Germany hunger spawned political disaffection and heightened resentment against middlemen and farmers and led to industrial unrest, food riots, and increases in petty crime from the autumn of 1915 onward.[43] The increasing gap between official prices and (black) market prices diverted other foodstuffs and other resources away from the poor. The lack of food helped to bring Germany to its knees and resulted in hundreds of thousands of deaths from hunger and starvation. During the war, of course, the end of imports from Russia; the removal of men, horses, and nitrates from German agriculture; and the role of price controls in further diminishing agricultural output (see figure 1.2) magnified the impact of the Allied blockade. The continuation of the blockade until the Versailles Treaty was signed in June 1919 exacerbated the hardship.

French civilians felt the pinch too. France switched to summer time on June 15, 1916, as an energy-saving measure;[44] petrol rationing and *cartes d'alimentation* for sugar, bread, and coal followed in 1917, and rationing became general in 1918, first in Paris in February and nationwide in June. Peasant hostility to controls and the availability of imports, in particular of frozen meat, help explain why the rationing of bread (coupled with a prohibition on pastries) was introduced so late, in August 1917. The rationing of other items followed. Still, the sense that farmers got richer while urban dwellers went hungry inflamed urban-rural tensions.[45] Rations were meager: workers were entitled to 700 grams of bread daily, other adults to 600 grams, and children under seven years to 300 grams. These entitlements were reduced to 500, 400, and 100 grams, respectively, on October 10, 1918.[46] The sugar entitlement was 750 grams a month, and meat was available initially twice a week but in 1918 hardly at all, whereas the milk ration varied regionally.

In Russia at the outset the main concern of the authorities was provisioning a massive army. Their woefully inadequate response to growing shortages in the cities—including an attempt at food rationing—led to the collapse of the czarist regime. In late March 1917, the Provisional Government that succeeded it sought to establish a state grain monopoly based on the procurement of surpluses above the necessary rural consumption at a fixed price. But the peasants resisted, a strategy justified in retrospect by the doubling of the official price in August. In Petrograd rationing failed and led to the downfall of the Provisional Government; the daily bread ration was only 205 grams on the eve of the Bolshevik takeover.

The Bolsheviks' initial "struggle for bread" fared no better; in May 1918 Lenin lamented that the state grain monopoly system still existed only on paper, thwarted by recalcitrant peasants, a dilapidated transport network, and the prevalence of urban "baggers" who scoured the countryside for food.[47] But to judge from the pioneering food consumption surveys carried out by Soviet statisticians at the time, conditions in urban areas improved from mid-1919 on. In Petrograd (renamed Leningrad in 1924), consumption by average daily workers' families rose from 1,598 kilocalories per adult equivalent in March–April 1919 to 2,242 kilocalories in December 1919 and 3,375 kilocalories in October–November 1920. The levels in Moscow were 2,066, 2,791, and 2,744 kilocalories, respectively. But these numbers were achieved at the cost of a mass exodus of people from city to countryside. In 1921–22, as harvest failures resulted in severe malnutrition and famine in rural areas, consumption levels in the cities remained adequate.[48]

In Britain the situation was very different, and despite the German submarine campaign against merchant navies bringing food to Britain, rationing was limited to sugar and meat toward the end of the war. There was a leveling down in nutritional levels; during the war the calories available to working-class families did not fall but those available to skilled workers' families did. Comparing estimates of food consumption by working families in 1904 and 1918, Ian Gazeley and Andrew Newell find that the lack of price controls on fruit and vegetables diverted consumption away from them and toward foods like bread, bacon, and condensed milk, which lacked the same nutrients. Table 1.3 describes the shift from butcher's meat to bacon and ham and from butter to margarine and the sharp rise in potato consumption.[49]

Rationing during World War II

Rationing was quasi-universal during World War II, although its effectiveness varied greatly. So were its constant companions, the gray and black markets. Gray markets entailing the sale of legally obtained goods were widely tolerated, black markets involving clandestine transactions less so. The authorities made a show of clamping down on the latter, with varying success and propaganda posters against black marketeers were ubiquitous

TABLE 1.3. Weekly consumption per capita of basic foodstuffs in the United Kingdom during World War I

	Kg	1909–13 = 100	
Item	1909	1917	1918
Flour	1.94	110	112
Butcher's meat	0.92	82	62
Bacon and ham	0.15	106	135
Butter	0.14	65	55
Margarine	0.05	218	200
Lard	0.05	73	136
Potatoes	1.66	105	143
Sugar	0.66	68	64

Source: W. Beveridge, British Food Control (Oxford: Oxford University Press, 1928), p. 311, as cited in Hardach 1977: 131.

(figures 1.7 and 1.8). Everywhere, the system was based on each individual receiving a given number of coupons for a stipulated period, often a month, to be redeemed in an appointed shop or restaurant. Rations generally reflected some definition of "need," whereby the military and those engaged in heavy labor were granted extra calories, and women and children were generally entitled to less; in Britain invalids were allowed extra food in exchange for sugar entitlements, and in besieged Leningrad a scientific and artistic elite received favored treatment. The perception that rationing was a shared privation probably boosted morale.[50] D. V. Pavlov, the city's food supremo during the blockade, later reminisced about the reaction on the street when a bread-van driver was killed by a shell:

> The loaves of bread were scattered all over the pavement. Conditions were favourable for looting. Yet the people who gathered around the wrecked vehicle, raised the alarm, and guarded the bread till the arrival of another truck. All these people were hungry, and the temptation to grab a fresh loaf of bread well-nigh irresistible. And yet not a single loaf was stolen.[51]

Pavlov was being more than a little naive, however, for there was widespread criminality in Leningrad too.[52]

During World War II in Britain, Germany,[53] and Japan, rationing was effective; even though food availability declined almost everywhere, few died of literal hunger (table 1.4). In Nazi Germany the calories available from

FIGURE 1.7. World War II anti–black-market posters (occupied France and the Netherlands)

the domestic production of cereals and potatoes in 1944 were still 80 percent of those available in 1939. A striking feature is the share of potatoes in the total: well over one-third throughout, except in 1943 when the potato harvest was poor and the wheat harvest particularly good. Tables 1.4 and 1.5 and figure 1.9 imply that food availability held up well until 1945; note that

FIGURE 1.8. Policing the black market in Brussels during World War II
Source: Cegesoma/State Archives

TABLE 1.4. Average daily calories per civilian

	Japan	UK	Germany	US
Prewar	2,265	2,987	2,907	3,080
1944	1,900	2,923	2,941	3,215
1945	1,680	..	1,721	..

Source: Garon 2017: 48, citing Cohen 1949: 386n53; USSBS 1945a: 132.

while the first of these refers to calories from all sources, others refer to ration allowances only.

GERMANY

The bureaucratic arrangements for rationing in Germany were already in place and the hoarding of goods banned when the war began. Initially, most foodstuffs were rationed together with clothing, shoes, leather, and soap. The list did not include bread, but within some months it would be rationed too.

TABLE 1.5. Ration allowances (in kcals)

Place	1939	1940	1941	1942	1943	1944	1945
Germany		2,125	2,020	1,845	1,990	1,930	1,671
Belgium		.	1,360	1,365	1,320	1,555	
France		.	1,300	1,115	1,080	1,115	
Netherlands		.	1,925	1,805	1,765	1,580	
Norway		.	1,620	1,385	1,430	1,480	
Poland			845	1,070	853	1,200	
General Government		.	1,250	1,235	1,135	1,160	
Baltic lands		.	.	1,305	1,305	1,420	
Protectorate		2,045	1,820	1,785	1,860	1,740	
Croatia		.	.	815	905	915	
Serbia (Belgrade)		.	.	580	1,035	960	
Greece	2,300		930	1,700			
Japan					2,270	1,816	
Leningrad			900	460			
Italy						763 (South)/ 906 (urban)	

Source: Klemann et al. 2012: table 17.1; Stanford website, https://web.stanford.edu/~ichriss /GR-WWII/GR-WWII-44.JPG (Greece, Italy); Wright 2010: 61 (Japan).

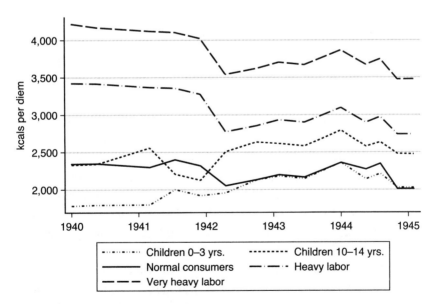

FIGURE 1.9. Estimated calorie consumption in Germany during World War II
Source: Goldman and Filtzer 2015: 29

Until April 1942 the bread allowance consisted of half white and half dark bread. Thereafter, the proportion of white bread decreased to one-fifth. In April 1942 cuts in the rations for meat and fat were also introduced. The meat ration was initially generous (500 grams weekly), but after December 1941 the weight of attached bone matter was included, and by war's end the meat entitlement had dropped to 250 grams. While German civilians did not starve—and that was in part due to their ruthless exploitation of the countries they conquered[54]—the quality and variety of their food suffered considerably. Moreover, controls over the sale of clothes were strict and severe.

At the outset the black market was restricted to informal barter between people who knew each other, but as rations were cut in 1941 and 1942, its scope broadened. The authorities permitted trades between consumers but outlawed those between producers and consumers, and restricted products could not be sold without authorization. The penalties for flouting the rules were severe—"Every day announcements of executions for this offence appeared in the German papers"[55]—but the black market endured and grew. For a clandestine market to function, its location had to be well-known but at the same time not too obvious, and it should have a means of quick escape. In Berlin it usually took place in bars and restaurants, although the destruction of much of the city in 1944 forced more black market activity outdoors. Food and clothing accounted for nearly half of the items traded; tobacco was important too. Most of the trade happened in the city center.[56]

A major scandal in early 1943 involved the upmarket delicatessen owner August Nöthling and members of the Nazi elite who had been buying from him at bargain prices without the required ration coupons. Clients included household names such as Joachim von Ribbentrop (foreign minister), Karl Doenitz (navy admiral), Wilhelm Keitel (field marshal), and Berlin's police chief, Wolf-Heinrich Graf von Helldorff (later executed for his part in the July 20, 1944, plot to execute Hitler). Goebbels, Gauleiter of Berlin, fumed that such behavior amounted to war sabotage, particularly in his own bailiwick "because any misbehaviour on the part of the elite affects morale in the imperial capital." But Hitler washed his hands of the affair. Nöthling's customers escaped with reprimands, while Nöthling, on remand in prison, gallantly brought an embarrassing situation to a resolution by taking his own life on May 9, 1943.[57]

As Soviet advances deprived Germany of food supplies from the East, the situation looked increasingly ominous. Still, in April 1945 an American official described the newly conquered German countryside as "fat and prosperous. The people are fat, well dressed, and smug with good living.

Even the dogs are fat."[58] Even if that was somewhat of an exaggeration, the situation contrasted starkly with that at the end of World War I. Toward war's end the plundering of Wehrmacht supplies and dehoarding staved off a crisis until the second half of 1945. Hendrik Jüerges's analysis of the calorific value of the average adult male daily ration in Wuppertal in western Germany confirms the adequacy of the intake during the war but with a downturn in early 1945: between February and April 1945, the average daily caloric intake plummeted from 1,603 to 678. These are allowances: as noted, they were most likely supplemented by dehoarding and plunder. From then on food shortages were serious.[59] Thereafter, the average intake varied between 1,000 and 1,500 until mid-1948. Calories, of course, are only part of the story; in terms of fat, the situation was worse in 1946 and 1947.[60] Although the seriousness of the malnutrition was hotly contested at first, soon skepticism regarding German hunger turned into concern and action, and "occupied Germany had become the recipient of the largest food-aid program in history."[61]

THE UNITED KINGDOM

Britain's rationing system during World War II was probably the most elaborate and embraced all main food items except bread and vegetables, as well as clothing. The absence of bread rationing implies that calorie consumption was unconstrained and explains why it remained basically flat throughout the war. Rationing was effective in the sense that it was widely considered to be fair, and there was widespread compliance. In a survey in January 1941, 63 percent expressed satisfaction with the system, another 19 percent satisfaction with qualifications, and only 12 percent dissatisfaction; a year later 82 percent approved of "all persons convicted of black-market dealings in food [being] sent to prison without the option of a fine."[62] The perception that the system was fair was borne out by data published later. Before the war the calorie and protein intakes of working-class households lagged behind those of middle-class households by margins of 15 to 20 percent, but they were virtually identical in 1944 and 1955.[63]

Key features included resorting to bulk buying by government agency, which was easier in an island economy where government-controlled shipping imported much of the food.[64] This helped control supplies, as did concentration orders, which reduced the number of producers. The government also reduced consumer choice by limiting the number of products. Regulation was enforced by an army of civil servants, consisting of 0.2 percent of the civilian labor force by the end of the war. The scope and the need for black-market activity were thus limited.[65]

GREECE

In Greece, where rations were minimal, control of supplies ineffective, and the normal functioning of markets lacking, black markets were ubiquitous. As early as January 1941, the nutritional value of rationed food in Athens-Piraeus was down to 458 calories; it troughed at 183 calories in November and was only 353 in March 1942. Communal canteens added a further 140 calories or so. It was reckoned that even after taking black-market consumption into account, per capita consumption in the city was no more than 600–800 calories, or far below the minimum needed to sustain life. Clothes, household goods, medicinal drugs, and sex were exchanged for food, but at prices beyond the reach of the poor, and in the end even black-market supplies of foodstuffs periodically dried up. Both the occupiers and the Greek resistance sought to curb the black market; the former by severely punishing speculators, the latter by requisitioning hoarded food for redistribution in famine-stricken neighborhoods. But in a report on the food situation in May 1942, a group of Greek economists dismissed the role of the official market and insisted that "it is only the 'Black Market' which has been supplying the population of Athens and Piraeus," even if "at exorbitant prices."[66] According to Violetta Honiton, foremost historian of the Greek famine, overregulation, extreme price volatility, and the sheer lack of food were too much for any market, black or otherwise, to overcome.[67]

POLAND

According to Robert Ley, who was head of the German Labour Front (Deutsche Arbeitsfront, DAF) and close to Hitler, soon after the German occupation of Poland, "A lower race needs less room, less clothing, less food, and less culture than a higher race. The Germans cannot live in the same fashion as the Poles and the Jews. . . . More bread, more clothes, more living space, more culture, more beauty—these our race must have, or it will perish." Rationing in Poland reflected Ley's views. In Poland in December 1941, the allocation for those of German nationality was 2,310 calories per diem. Foreigners were entitled to 1,790 and Ukrainians to 930 calories, whereas the rations allocated by the occupiers to ethnic Poles and to Jews were 654 and 184 calories per diem, respectively. Not surprisingly, there was widespread resort to black markets, especially in the General Government (the part of Poland controlled by the Germans but not formally annexed by them or the Soviet Union in 1939) and in Warsaw. Laws against involvement in black markets were draconian but the means to make them effective lacking; according to historian Jerzy Kochanowski, "Polish society owes its survival" to the illegal market. Such was its size that various towns within reach of Warsaw by rail specialized in different forms of contraband. Those who gained the most were the most daring and resourceful among rural producers, particularly wealthier peasants who were in a good position to bribe officialdom, but officials who facilitated the illegal traffic also stood to gain.[68]

THE SOVIET UNION

In the Soviet Union, rationing (introduced in July 1941) was highly centralized. Rations were allocated according to perceived nutritional needs, with bread the main item in the diet. In 1942 manual workers in war industries were allocated twenty-eight ounces of bread; other manual workers, twenty-one ounces; white-collar workers, eighteen ounces; dependents aged twelve and up and children, fourteen ounces. Workers exceeding their quotas were granted extra rations, and in March 1943 miners and some other workers were allowed thirty-five ounces daily. The system relied on the private sector, as represented by allotments and collective farm markets, to supplement rations, with the latter's contribution "carefully planned and implemented by a powerful organizational network of party, soviet, and union organizations."[69] In addition, citizens had recourse to the "free" market supplied by collective farms, but it is important to point out that most of the available food was rationed and sold at controlled prices. Free-market prices were high everywhere but higher in the East than in Moscow. The government also established centrally run clothing and food stores in the main cities to moderate free-market prices, a strategy that seems to have worked well. Certain categories of workers, such as factory workers and war heroes, were allowed discounts at such stores.[70] Black markets flourished too; there were markets even in ration cards. Indeed, the People's Commissariat of Food came to see merit in trade as long as the goods traded were not stolen and resold. But theft perpetrated by both the poor and the rich was pervasive, and favoritism and corruption were rife. Still, as Wendy Goldman and Donald Filtzer point out, by incentivizing producers and increasing the entitlements of ordinary people, albeit at a cost, the black market had its benefits. The lack of food was a more fundamental problem than its misappropriation; given the constraints it faced, it is the effectiveness of Soviet rationing during World War II that is rather remarkable. Perhaps that is what has prompted one historian of Soviet Russia to muse "whether this perceived effectiveness suggests a partial *post facto* justification of the brutal imposition of collectivization in the 1930s."[71]

The situation in Leningrad was particularly grim. It had its black markets too: according to one of the city's many war diarists, in the spring of 1942 the city was "one big black market." Trade usually took the form of barter, but there were cash transactions too. While the official price of a loaf of bread was two rubles, prices such as sixty rubles for a loaf of bread, three hundred rubles for a sack of potatoes, or twelve hundred rubles for a kilogram of meat were mentioned. Again, although markets were in theory illegal, the authorities turned a blind eye to the bartering of personal items such as watches, books, and pieces of furniture for heating fuel, food, and even vodka and, indeed, realized the usefulness of such petty trading.[72] But those trading in ration cards or stealing or diverting food from the state system could face summary execution. It was said that for a time, Leningrad Communist Party boss Andrei Zhdanov personally "was the only man allowed to replace a lost ration card."[73] To judge from diaries kept during the blockade, black marketeers were universally despised, yet many diarists used them, supporting "Soviet moral codes about private trade at unregulated prices with their words, but not their deeds."[74] Despite increasingly brutal repression, crime rates rose in Leningrad during the siege.[75]

The Food Commission's remit was to ensure that the available food kept as many people alive as possible, and it also decided on the added entitlements of those social and professional groups on whom the survival of the city depended, such as industrial workers and plant managers. A small group of scientists and artists were given preferential treatment.[76] But while Leningrad's system provided a "fairer" allocation of food supplies, those supplies were simply inadequate to sustain life. On November 20, 1941, workers' calorie allocation was reduced to 707 daily and that of office staff to 473.

FRANCE

As always, the political context mattered. Whereas in besieged Leningrad "the authorities and the public shared the same goal: survival," in Vichy France the resistance might plausibly protest that "Pétain urges French peasants to deliver all their wheat, but it is not for the French, it is for the *boches*."[77] In the months before the German occupation, France did not

FIGURE 1.10. The pro-Nazi Milice française distributing black-market contraband in a school in suburban Paris, April 28, 1944

impose any restrictions on food markets. As elsewhere, the occupation led to significant requisitioning by the occupiers, but the administrative structure the Vichy regime created to identify, collect, and distribute supplies was never fit for a purpose. Both producers and distributors cooperated in diverting supplies to a burgeoning and ubiquitous black market. This made it impossible for the state to meet even basic needs. It is reckoned that nearly half of all chickens and one-third of all eggs were sold on the black market by 1943; the proportions were almost certainly higher later.[78] Not surprisingly, individuals who had traded legitimately before the war tended to dominate the black market during it: they had the right connections. Ration cards were pilfered and trafficked, and the forging of ration cards seems to have been widespread as well.

The failure of controls is reflected in the huge number of prosecutions—about two million—brought between 1940 and 1944 for abuses of the system. Most prosecutions were either for profiteering or the illegal trade in foodstuffs and livestock. They resulted in a fine rather than a court case, and even though the penalty for trafficking was execution, no trafficker received the death sentence during the occupation.[79] While the fines imposed on major traders could be heavy, the authorities were inclined to go easy on small-scale purchasers of food. The relatively short terms of imprisonment imposed on farmers reflected the authorities' concerns that imprisonment would negatively affect farm production. A frequent feature in northern France was town dwellers having their bags inspected at railway stations for contraband in the form of potatoes, vegetables, and meat. On occasion, confiscations resulted in rioting, so often the police turned a blind eye to small-scale purchases of necessities.[80] But they also used their interference as a propaganda tool (figure 1.10).

Research conducted in the wake of the occupation implied that by the time the Germans departed, 30–40 percent of food was passing through gray or black markets. Gray-market prices were twice the official prices and black-market prices, five times.[81] Those numbers, even if only approximately true, highlight how the Vichy regime's ambitions for *ravitaillement général* remained a pipe dream, as does the cameo of black-market restaurants serving a lavish "prewar menu" of food diverted from official markets or the following account of a "fashionable restaurant" in Paris in 1941:

> Full house . . . No restrictions whatsoever. Forbidden beefsteaks are concealed under fried eggs. Nouveau riche clientele. The finest wines are flowing. The well to do triumph in the New Order. With cash, lots of cash, one can still fill oneself to the gills whilst housewives queue for hours in the snow to get hold of a bit of swede. It sickens me, but I stuff my face all the same, for the days "without."[82]

In sum, France's ineffective rationing under German occupation yielded inadequate calories—an average of 1,180 in 1941–44—with resultant increases in mortality in some areas and widespread resort to black markets.[83] As a *préfet* in Haute-Savoie lamented in late 1941: "Peasants are visited at home by town-dwellers, who pay a high price for easy-to-hide stuff such as eggs, poultry, butter, cheese, etc. We would need a gendarme in each farm."[84]

ITALY

Rationing (*razionamento*) was introduced in Italy at the outbreak of war. Civilians were not fooled by early propagandistic efforts to reduce demand on the grounds that overeating was unhealthy or unpatriotic ("*Se mangi troppo derubi la patria*"). But the authorities had little control over farm output, with the result that rations were meager and of poor quality. The black market operated almost from the start and dominated transactions involving food toward the end of the war. According to the estimates provided by the Allied Labor Subcommission, 39 percent of a stipulated food budget in September 1942 could be obtained by ration card and the remaining 61 percent via the black market, but two years later rationing provided only 26.2 percent of the total and by March 1945 only one-twelfth of a theoretical food budget adequate for a household of five. Most people had to rely on the black market to provide the rest. As in Greece, a highly inadequate

TABLE 1.6. Daily rations in Italy in 1944–45

	Bread (grams)	Spaghetti (grams)
Anglo-American diplomats	500	200
Policemen, merchant seamen	435	85
Hospital patients	350	100
Refugees in camps	300	100
Civilian prisoners, army recruits	250	80
Italian civilians	200	80

Source: Anonymous 1945: 890.

rationing system spawned a thriving black market that became "a way of life involving the entire population."[85] As elsewhere, many urbanites headed to the countryside to buy food. In one tragic event near Balvano in the region of Basilicata on the night of March 2–3, 1944, about five hundred Neapolitan unfortunates, many of them stowaways in search of food, died of smoke inhalation when the train they were traveling in got stuck in a tunnel. This was the worst train disaster in Italy's history.[86]

Toward the end of the war, daily rations of the two staples in the Italian diet were as described in table 1.6. The impact on health was reflected in significant increases in the death rate toward the end of the war, as noted further in chapter 2.[87]

JAPAN

During World War II, pressures on Japanese crop yields and production owed less to a lack of labor than to shortages of equipment and of fertilizer. Adult per capita food consumption fell from a norm of about 2,100 calories per capita before Pearl Harbor to 1,900 calories in mid-1944, falling further to 1,680 calories by the war's end. The share of rationed goods in the total fell by more, particularly in the last year of the war. Moreover, the range and quality of foods available worsened. As imports from Korea and Taiwan plummeted, rice available for domestic use dropped from 153 kilograms to 119 kilograms per capita and fish from an average of 63.6 grams per diem in 1939/41 to 31 grams in 1945.

Figure 1.11 charts the trends in production and supply of rice between 1937 and 1945, highlighting the food supply problem from early on but especially in 1945. Wheat, barley, soybeans, potatoes, and yams were substituted for

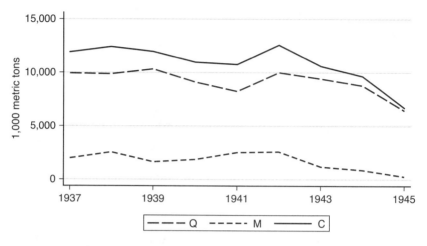

FIGURE 1.11. Production and consumption of rice in Japan
Source: Cohen 1949: 368–69
Note: Q = consumption; M = imports; C = consumption

rice. The lack of fish and fresh fruit and vegetables led to protein and vitamin C and B_1 deficiencies; there were significant increases in the incidence of beriberi (vitamin B_1 deficiency) and tuberculosis, and the physical growth of children was severely constrained.[88] For much of the war, supplementary rations were available for certain categories of workers, but the deterioration of supplies led to increased reliance on the black market. Still, although malnutrition led to widespread incidence of beriberi and tuberculosis and reduced worker productivity and morale, classic famine symptoms and excess mortality were absent in wartime Japan.[89]

The Food Control Law enacted on February 21, 1942, less than two months after the attack on Pearl Harbor, introduced a strict and far-reaching rationing system, which covered food, clothing, cooking oil, and much more. The distribution of food passed from designated merchants to quasi-governmental bodies. The system worked smoothly and equitably in 1943 and 1944, relying on neighborhood associations to distribute rations and operating on the assumption that "people could not face cheating the people they had to live next door to."[90] The authorities managed to maintain a daily ration of 2.3 *go* (1,158 kilocalories) for normal consumers, though with an ever-diminishing rice share.[91] After the U.S. capture of the island of Saipan in July 1944, followed by the increasingly intensive bombing of Japanese cities, rations became more erratic, and citizens increasing resorted to the black market. The gaps between official and black-market prices began to widen. The official price of rice remained constant during the war, but the estimated quarterly rise in black-market rice prices rose from 38.2 percent in 1943Q2–44Q2 to 49.4 percent in 1944Q2–45Q2.[92]

In Japan, rationing predated World War II and would also outlast it. The rice ration accounted for the bulk of consumption at the outset, but by mid-1942 it provided only two-thirds. By the autumn of 1944, it was reckoned that the black market provided nearly two-fifths of the fish and over two-thirds of the vegetables consumed. Still, it was after this time that black-market prices began to diverge markedly from official prices. The authorities fought against the black market with propaganda and mass arrests. By August 15, when the emperor made his speech conceding defeat, the black market had become "the de facto civilian economy itself."[93] Per capita consumption fell from a norm of 2,000 calories per capita before Pearl Harbor to 1,900 calories in 1944, falling further to an average of 1,680 calories by the war's end.[94]

A Few Broader Patterns

Table 1.7, based on research by Matthias Blum, shows that in Germany before World War I a consumer could obtain 288 kilocalories of beef, 5,300 kilocalories of rye flour, or 4,475 kilocalories of wheat flour for one mark. Toward the end of the war, they could obtain only 61 kilocalories of beef, 167 kilocalories of rye flour, or 179 kilocalories of wheat flour for a considerably depreciated one Papiermark.[95] Note the ensuing sharp shift in relative prices: whereas before the war a mark would pay for 16 times as many calories in cereals as in meat, four years later that ratio was only 3.3. As food became scarcer, consumers focused on nutrition. Even though the prices of basics rose more than those of discretionary items, the former still tended to offer more calories at the end of rationing.

Table 1.8, which reproduces data from the Netherlands during World War II, tells a similar story to that told by table 1.7. Whereas one gulden would purchase 10.7 (i.e., 2040.8/191.7) times as many kilocalories in the form of bread as in beef on the black market in 1942, in the famine conditions of 1944–45 the ratio fell to 2.6 (i.e., 50/19.2). Again, in Austria in 1945–46 (tables 1.9 and 1.10) the same pattern may be detected in the gap between relative values in kilocalories of flour/bread versus beef/pork in official and black market prices. Finally, table 1.11 describes the increases in the black market prices in Japan relative to the official price between late 1943 and the end of the war. Note that relative price movements once again broadly mirror those already described in tables 1.7–1.10.

TABLE 1.7. Prices and kilocalories in 1914 and 1917–18 in Germany

Product	1914 official	1917–18 official	1917–18 black market	1917–18 ratio	1914 kcals/ RM	1917–18 kcals/ RM on black market
Beef	1.0	2.8	4.75	1.7	288	61
Veal	1.0	2.8	5	1.8	235	47
Pork	0.8	..	6	..	328	44
Smoked ham	1.2	..	13	..		..
Olive oil	3.0	..	50	..	775	47
Beef tallow	0.4	2	14.5	7.3		..
Schmaltz	0.8	5	18	3.6		..
Condensed milk	0.5	1.7	4.5	2.6		..
Salad oil	1.4	..	24	..		..
Quark	0.2	2.3	3.5	1.5		..
Eggs	0.06	.4	.65	1.6		..
Rapeseed oil	0.60	5.0	21.5	4.3	3,750	105
Bacon	0.7	2.75	15.5	5.6	2,686	121
Butter	1.3	3.4	14	4.1	1,492	139
Rye flour	0.15	1.85	4	2.2	5,300	167
Wheat flour	0.2	..	4	..	4,475	179
Rice	0.25	..	8	..	3,440	143

Source: Blum 2013a: 279 (citing Anne Roerkohl, *Hungerblokade und Heimatfront* [Stuttgart, 1991]).

TABLE 1.8. Prices and calories in the Netherlands, 1942–45

			Kcals/gulden			
			Official	Black market prices		
Item	Unit	cal/100 gr	1944	1942	1943	1944/45
Bread	kg	200	8,421	2,040.8	2,040.8	50.0
Butter	kg	776	2,985	310.4	172.4	51.7
Cheese	kg	400	2,286	727.3	266.7	66.7
Milk	liter	600*	3,529	750.0	600.0	60.0
Beef	kg	115	1,917	191.7	76.7	19.2
Sugar	kg	310	5,636	775.0	221.4	38.8
Beans	kg	170	3,400	618.2	566.7	42.5
Wheat flour	kg	354	13,615	1,011.4	708.0	59.0
Oatmeal	kg	364	10,706	485.3	455.0	66.2

Source: derived from de Zwarte 2020: 173; cal/kg from www.calorie-charts.net.
Note: *kcals per liter

TABLE 1.9. Official prices in Austria, 1945–47 (in schillings)

Commodity	Official price		Kcals/schilling on official market		
	Dec. 1945	July 1946	Kcal/100 g	Dec. 1945	July 1946
Flour, white	0.56	0.48	354	6,321	7,375
Bread, dark	0.34	0.34	220	6,471	6,471
Milk (liter)	..	0.50	330		6,600
Bacon	2.16	2.16	548	2,537	2,537
Lard	2.16	2.16	900	4,167	4,167
Sugar	0.76	0.78	310	4,079	3,974
Beef	1.80	1.80	115	639	639
Pork	2.60	2.50	105	404	420
Wine (liter)	4.00	4.00	85	213	213

Source: Kravis 1948. Price per kg unless otherwise noted.

TABLE 1.10. Black market prices in Austria, 1945–47 (in schillings)

Commodity	Black market price		Kcals/schilling on black market		
	Dec. 1945	July 1946	Kcal/100 gr	Dec. 1945	July 1946
Flour, white	45	55	354	78.7	64.4
Bread, dark	25	30	220	88	73.3
Beef	50	85	115	23	13.5
Pork	200	175	105	5.3	6.0
Bacon	800	250	548	6.9	21.9
Lard	..	325	900	..	27.7
Sugar	80	160	310	38.8	19.4
Milk (liter)	..	..	330	..	..
Wine (liter)	40	70	85	21.3	12.1

Source: Kravis 1948. Price per kg unless otherwise noted.

Naturally, the black market was disproportionately the preserve of the better off. Household expenditure data gathered by statistician and demographer Pierpaolo Luzzatto-Fegiz illustrate this clearly for northeastern Italy in 1942–43. Table 1.12 shows that the poor (Class A) relied on their ration cards for 52 percent of their oil, 72 percent of their potatoes, and 89 percent of their sugar, whereas for well-off and rich households those percentages ranged from 5 percent for maize flour to 30 percent for oil. This pointed to

TABLE 1.11. Black market food prices as percentages of official prices: Japan, 1943–45

Item	Dec. 1943	June 1944	Nov. 1944	July 1945
Rice	600	2,800	4,400	7,000
Edible oil	517	1,379	4,138	7,586
Soy	375	625	1,625	4,750
Sugar	2,273	9,091	13,636	24,091
Dried bonito	479	1,027	1,507	3,562
Pork	300	1,400	1,700	2,700
Wheat flour	533	1,467	2,000	2,667
Potatoes	500	700	1,600	2,600
Soybeans	750	1,375	1,750	3,000
Beef	219	844	1,250	1,875
Butter	171	789	1,579	1,579
Salt	600	900	800	800
Salted salmon	341	750	795	568

Source: Davis and Engerman 2006: 380.

TABLE 1.12. Percentage shares of four food items acquired by ration card and black market: Northeast Italy, 1943

Item	Class	Per 100 kg or liters		Per 100 lire expenditure	
		Ration card	Black market	Ration card	Black market
Oil	A	51.9	48.1	14.5	85.5
	B	38.2	61.8	8.7	91.3
	C	30.0	70.0	6.1	93.9
Maize flour	A	29.7	70.3	7.7	92.3
	B	14.1	85.9	3.2	96.8
	C	5.0	95.0	0.8	99.2
Potatoes	A	71.8	28.2	57.5	42.5
	B	74.1	25.9	58.2	41.8
	C	56.7	43.3	37.7	62.3
Sugar	A	89.4	10.6	65.2	34.8
	B	70.5	29.5	34.9	65.1
	C	49.0	51.0	17.2	82.8

Source: Luzzatto-Fegiz 1946b: 328.

Notes: A: poor (0–550 lire monthly per consumption unit); B: middle income (551 https://web.stanford.edu/~ichriss/GR-WWII/GR-WWII-44.JPG 1,000 lire); C: comfortable or rich (>1,000 lire) the redistributive effect of rationing and also to the inability of the poor to capitalize much on the black market.

Another likely feature of black markets everywhere is that prices varied significantly from place to place. Hard evidence is scarce, but in Tuscany in mid-1944, for example, the kilogram of cherries that sold for twenty-five lire in Lucca might cost fifty lire in Pietrasanta forty kilometers away; in Florence "the fruit and vegetables brought into the city [were] sold to consumers at very different prices from district to district, from square to square, from shop to shop." A study of black markets in Bavaria in 1947–48 reveals coefficients of variation ranging from 14 percent for cigarettes in 1947 to 70 percent for flour and 78 percent for meat in 1948.[96]

Moral Economy and Food Riots

In a well-known 2001 paper, Daron Acemoglu and James Robinson described how in nondemocratic societies the threat of violence by the disenfranchised poor can sometimes, and perhaps only temporarily, extract concessions from the ruling elite. Such a threat is more likely when the costs of resistance are lower, as in times of high unemployment.[97] Acemoglu and Robinson were influenced by events in twentieth-century western Europe and Latin America, but their approach also has resonance for contexts where there is a risk of famine. Riots as reactions against food shortages were commonplace in the past in urban areas. From Roman times to the twentieth century, the less well-off have insisted on an equitable distribution of what is available in times of food scarcity. As such, food riots have generated an important literature around the English social historian E. P. Thompson's concept of *moral economy*, by which Thompson meant a system of exchange perceived as "fair" by the common people. Thompson's focus was on food riots in early modern England, but the remit of his moral economy is now much wider. Food riots were commonplace during World War I and much less so during World War II.

Food riots were contests with uncertain outcomes between the rioters and the authorities. There was implicit bargaining going on. The rioters weighed the hope of relief against the risk of repression; the authorities balanced avoiding bloodshed against upholding the strict letter of the law. Riots kept recurring because even though they might attract repression, *on average* they brought some respite, and there was no obvious alternative. Their actions, be they blocking exports, seizing food directly, or forcing prices down, succeeded in extracting concessions from the elite. Predicated on the moral economy conviction that necessity knows no law, the transfers of resources they extracted saved some lives. Rioting worked. Although their protests sometimes turned violent, the rioters were on the whole disciplined. Moreover, food riots, unlike agrarian protest, did not threaten the status quo. The distinction was not lost on the elite at the time, but they also had reason to fear that what began as a food riot might, given the right circumstances, morph into something much more serious. John Bohstedt surmises that food riots were partly responsible for the elimination of famine in England after the 1620s, citing with evident glee E. P. Thompson's panacea for famine: send cadres of food-riot instructors to countries at risk.[98] But the above is all subject to an important caveat: while riots may offer respite in situations of mild FADs, they are unequal to the kind of FAD typically associated with famines.

Food riots were common, if not ubiquitous, when food shortages or famine threatened during World War I. There were riots in Belgium, Austria, Russia, Germany, Italy, the Netherlands, France, the United States, the United Kingdom, Australia, and Japan. The targets were mostly profiteers, real or alleged, and the demands were for "fair play," but citizens also protested against occupying forces plundering and exporting food. In October 1915 in the town of Bogorodsk, not far from Moscow, riots initiated by a small group of women protesting the price of sugar led to thousands of workers going on strike, which resulted in a 20 percent pay rise for the workers. In late February 1917, rioting that began with thousands of women in Petrograd shouting "Down with hunger!" escalated into tens of thousands of striking workers making more political demands in the following days and, on March 2, the abdication of Czar Nicholas II. In Amsterdam a week of rioting known as *het aardappeloproer* (the potato riot) culminated on July 5, 1917, in soldiers and police shooting 9 demonstrators dead and injuring 114 more. In Germany, as early as November 1914 a ceiling was placed on the price of potatoes in response to popular discontent. When rumors of the authorities' plan to remove the ceiling caused the potato supply to evaporate, rioting ensued. In mid-October 1915, rioting by women protesting the price of butter straddled several working-class areas of Berlin. According to Belinda Davis, military and civilian officials at this point "rapidly responded to each of the episodes . . . by attempting to meet popular desires in some form." As the supply situation worsened, there were further, increasingly subversive, riots in August 1916, mid-1917, and early 1918.[99]

Did any of this rioting fill bellies or save lives? Clearly, rioting could not reproduce the biblical miracle of loaves and fishes: food availability set a limit to what riots, or the fear of riots, might achieve. Perhaps they provided respites in Germany up to 1916 and in Bogorodsk in 1915, but they were powerless to prevent hunger and, indeed, famine thereafter. Anton Vrints's assessment of the situation in Belgium during World War I has a broader resonance: while protests could sometimes be counterproductive insofar as they led to black markets and producer boycotts, they also pressurized Belgian elites into pursuing interventionist policies, such as food rationing, that increased the entitlements of the most destitute.[100]

Protests about food were much rarer during World War II. That was partly because harsh repression by the authorities, particularly the Nazis and the Soviets, was much more likely. In Paris in June 1942, for example, six people were sentenced to death and six others to hard labor for life for participating in a food riot in which two policemen were killed.[101] Yet in her account of popular protest in the northern départements of Nord and Pas-de-Calais, Lynn Taylor discovered a "startling amount of room" for protest in France. There were food protests in the South too. In January 1942 riots prompted the Ministry of the Interior to rush "hundreds of tons of food to the Departments of Hérault and Gard following hunger disorders that lasted for days." At the same time, house-to-house searches for instigators were conducted as the riots took on "a political aspect." In all cases a majority of the food rioters were women and children. The French Communist Party, which played a leading role in orchestrating protests both in Paris and generally, considered such action as "women's spaces and food scarcity as a specifically women's issue."[102] There were scattered, spontaneous protests in Italy too, as in Parma in mid-October 1941 and in Sardinia and Milan in May 1942. The widespread food rioting in Rome on December 7–8, 1944, was directed mainly at traders accused of profiteering. On the first day of the riots, the frightened fruit and vegetable stall owners at Campo dei Fiori "made the best of a bad situation by distributing their products free to avoid having their stalls smashed or being beaten up." On the following day, the rioting continued, "an interesting example of popular justice, whose effectiveness will depend on the ability to keep it within bounds." Those incidents ended without bloodshed, but in Rome on April 7, 1944, ten women were shot by the SS (*Schutzstaffel*; protection squadron) when caught raiding a bakery.[103] In Vienna in early October 1944, a public announcement that food rations would be reduced by 10 percent led to widespread rioting and the deaths of dozens of protestors.[104]

2

Hunger and Famine

If the assailant does not venture to pass by a position, he can invest it and reduce it by famine.

—CARL VON CLAUSEWITZ, 1832

Starvation is a heinous, medieval method of warfare which must be outlawed once and for all. By taking action the UN Security Council sends a powerful signal to all states and individuals that are guilty of this crime.

—SIGRID KAAG, DUTCH FOREIGN MINISTER, 2018

The famines of World War I and World War II varied greatly in nature, duration, and cost in lives. Many generated the behaviors and reactions generally associated with famines throughout history, ranging from rising intrafamilial tensions and child desertion to theft and violence. A few led to incidents of cannibalism. Most were the by-products rather than the intentional outcomes of warfare, but some were deliberate. Blockades, an age-old tactic of warfare, were employed in both wars. During World War I an Allied blockade targeted civilians in Germany and resulted in the death of about 0.5 million and a blockade affecting a mountainous part of present-day Lebanon perhaps 0.2 million more. During World War II, a German blockade targeted the civilian population of Leningrad and starved between 0.7 million and 1.0 million while a shorter German blockade of the Warsaw ghetto led to the death of perhaps 0.1 million more.

Famines occurred at various stages during the two wars, but in most cases, perhaps not surprisingly, they were more likely to strike towards their end, or even in their wake, when resources and resilience were exhausted. During World War 1, the earliest famine struck in 1915, when starvation was used as a genocidal weapon against Armenians in their forced expulsion from Asia Minor.[1] The Third Horseman struck again in the Middle East in 1916. In Germany, hunger-related excess civilian mortality mounted from 1916 on but did not peak until after the fighting had stopped. After October 1917 the Bolshevik Revolution turned the food crisis that led to it into a major famine, and the ensuing starvation lasted until 1922. During World War II, mortality in Leningrad and in Athens peaked in the winter of 1941–42, in Bengal in mid-1943, in the Netherlands and in Vietnam in 1945, and in some places after peace had been declared. Most famines occurred in relatively poor countries, but blockade and disruption also caused death in places that had been spared serious famines for decades and even centuries.

World War I and its aftermath were linked to famines in Russia, Germany, Austria, Italy, the Balkans, and parts of the Ottoman Empire, Persia (Iran), and Africa. In most cases reliable data on excess mortality are lacking. Most of the deaths occurred in Russia, which was at war until 1923, though the worst of the fighting ended in 1921. Famines were more widespread during World War II. In this chapter we describe the famines of World War I and World War II country by country. In chapters 3 and 4, we discuss these famines more thematically.

World War I

THE SOVIET UNION

A recent careful estimate of the civilian death toll in the Soviet Union between 1914 and 1923 puts total deaths at 11.4 million. Most of those deaths were due to famine-induced pandemics; Wheatcroft's famine death toll of 8 million from famine (5 million in 1915–20 and 3 million in 1921–22) would leave room for 3.4 million by other means. This figure exceeds the most plausible estimates of famine deaths in Stalin's Soviet Union in 1931–33 and matches or exceeds those during World War II. Indeed, relative to population the years of famine between 1914 and 1922 were the worst in Russia since the Time of Troubles that preceded the accession of the Romanov dynasty in the early seventeenth century.[2]

The Russian Revolutions of 1917, by-products of World War I, were both fueled and threatened by food shortages. The Provisional Government that assumed power in March 1917 almost immediately introduced measures to control and centralize the supply of grain, which the peasant masses strenuously resisted. The Provisional Government's efforts at both peaceful and armed procurement failed, with urban consumers increasingly reliant on self-procurement by so-called bagmen in the countryside. By autumn the situation was out of control, with dwindling supplies in the cities, food rioting, and galloping inflation. Petrograd's plight, intensified by immigration, facilitated the Bolshevik takeover under Lenin in early November. Aside from continuing with the procurement policies of their predecessors, the Bolsheviks sought to ease the food supply problem by ceding Poland, Finland, and the Baltic countries to local administrations, moving the capital from Petrograd to Moscow and, on March 3, 1918, signing a separate peace treaty with the Central Powers. Still the crisis escalated, and the authorities substituted formal requisition with simply commandeering what they could find by force of arms. This improvised policy, which alienated the peasantry further, came to be known as *war communism*.

As economic historian Stephen Wheatcroft has explained, the famines that devastated the new Bolshevik state can be divided into two phases. Famine struck first in urban areas in the north of Russia (1918–20), where they reduced the population of Petrograd (today's Saint Petersburg) by over two-thirds and of Moscow by half through a combination of death and outmigration. In Petrograd the bread ration was reduced from an already miserable 500 grams per day (or about 1,300 calories) in February 1917 and 300 grams in October 1917 to 150 grams on January 27, 1918; 100 grams on February 14, 1918; and 50 grams (equivalent to about two slices of bread) on February 28, 1918. The exodus from the city was prompted by the closure of munitions and armament factories and by famished workers' hopes of acquiring land in the countryside. For the Bolsheviks, who had achieved control of Petrograd on November 7, 1917, this represented an erosion of their proletarian base, prompting Lenin's lament that "people have run away from hunger; workers have simply abandoned their factories, they set up housekeeping in the countryside and have stopped being workers."[3] In 1919 over 7 percent of Petrograd's population succumbed to famine-related epidemics and starvation. That famine was caused by the civil war and by the inability of the state to procure grain from areas occupied by anti-Bolshevik forces.[4]

Famine then struck further southeast in the Volga and Ural regions during the civil war and its aftermath (1921–22), compounded by atrocious weather in 1920 and 1921. A contemporary League of Nations report described "the Russian Famine of 1921–22" as "the worst, both as regards the numbers affected and as regards mortality from starvation and disease, that has occurred in modern times."[5] Agricultural output fell from 88 percent of its prewar level in 1917 to 60 percent in 1921. The food consumption per capita of adult workers in the southern Volga region was half or less its normal level; in parts of the North Caucasus, Ukraine, and Kazakhstan at the height of the crisis, it was about fifteen hundred kilocalories per day.[6] Wheatcroft distinguishes between these two phases by comparing trends in food and nonfood prices and in household food consumption in Moscow/Leningrad and the Volga region. He notes that in Moscow the ratio of food to nonfood prices fell up to September 1917, but by January 1918 it was double its 1913 level and quadruple its prewar level by May 1918. The ratio declined slowly until late 1920 and fell rapidly thereafter, until it was only two-thirds of its prewar level by January 1923. Official household food consumption survey data indicate that the worst was over in Moscow and Leningrad by 1920, whereas both price and consumption data imply little pressure in southern cities such as Saratov and Samara in 1918–19 but famine conditions in late 1921 and early 1922 (figure 2.1).[7]

The authorities resorted to the food seizures and rationing associated with what their leader Vladimir Lenin rather disingenuously described in April 1921 as "that peculiar war communism forced upon us by extreme want, ruin, and war." Recognizing that "requisitions in the villages and the direct application of communist principles" were getting them nowhere, in March 1921 the authorities sought to replace force by a tax in kind and market incentives. And in October 1921, Lenin would openly acknowledge the cost of the mistakes made:[8]

> The defeat we have suffered on the economic front at the beginning of 1921, in our attempt to make the transition to communism, has been much more serious than any we have suffered at the hands of Kolchak, Denikin, or Pilsudski. The defeat means to us that the economic policy of our leaders has got entirely out of touch with its base and has utterly failed to effect a revival of production.

From mid-1921 the Bolsheviks also resorted to seeking help from abroad, and Maxim Gorky's famous appeal for bread and medicine was widely publicized in the West in July. There followed a "treaty," signed on August 20, 1921, between the Soviets and Herbert Hoover, U.S. secretary of commerce, governing aid in the form of food, medicine, clothing, and personnel through the American Relief Association (ARA). Over a period of a year, some three

FIGURE 2.1. Famine in Russia, 1921–23
Source: International Committee of the Red Cross Audiovisual Archive

FIGURE 2.1 (*continued*)

hundred ARA employees hired 120,000 Russians to distribute relief, and it was claimed that 768,000 metric tons of relief reached as many as 20 million Russians. The ARA's efforts led neither to any permanent improvement in United States-Soviet relations nor to the eventual resistance from within that the staunchly anti-Communist Hoover had envisaged. But they did help relieve the crisis, as the Soviets recognized.[9]

GERMANY

Both World War I and World War II involved industrial powers, the United Kingdom and Germany, heavily reliant on food imports. On the eve of World War I, imports provided about two-fifths of the United Kingdom's calories. Germany imported 20 percent of its calories and 27 percent of its proteins,[10] as well as much of the sodium nitrate it used as fertilizer. Although never formally declared as such, the Central Powers were subjected to an Allied naval blockade almost from the outset. Germany was the worst affected. It was not only at the mercy of a Royal Navy capable of blocking its access to the sea by mining neutral waters; its important prewar links to Russian and Danubian wheat were also sundered.[11] The Allies' blockade of Germany lasted five years (August 6, 1914–July 12, 1919). Germany had anticipated a blockade but had seriously underestimated the damage it could cause and was unprepared when it happened.[12] It was relatively lax before mid-1916, when trade with neutrals effectively ended. Although at the outset it managed to import some food from neutrals, little was imported starting in 1916. German imports of grain fell from 240,000 metric tons in 1916 to 36,000 in 1917 and 6,000 in the first half of 1918. The real value of total imports had dropped to one-fifth of their 1913 level by 1918.[13] For the Habsburg Empire, which had been self-sufficient in cereals in 1914, the problems differed: it lost Transylvania, its main breadbasket, for the entire duration of the war, while within the dual monarchy of Austro-Hungary, resentment in Austria grew as imports of foodstuffs from Hungary plummeted (figure 2.2). Hungary simply kept more of its own declining production for itself, as Austria's output faltered (figure 2.3).

At the start of World War I, both Germany and the United Kingdom envisioned starving each other into submission. The German U-boat campaign initially consisted of sinking enemy and neutral ships carrying contraband after their crews had vacated them, but in February 1917 it switched to a policy of unrestricted shoot on sight. Still, although the U-boat campaign ultimately led to the sinking of over six thousand merchant ships weighing an aggregate 12 million tons, besides presumably deterring others from sailing

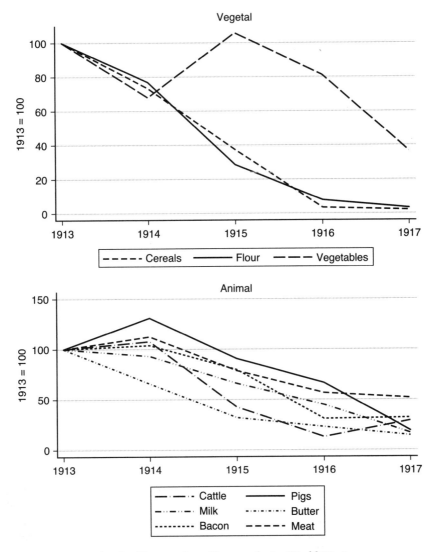

FIGURE 2.2. Austrian food imports from Hungary during World War I
Source: Citing H. Löwenfeld-Russ, *Die Regelung der Volksernährung im Kriege*
(Vienna: Hölder-Pichler Tempsky, 1926), p. 61

it failed to stop British food supplies from abroad. The expected impact on British morale did not materialize. Moreover, the campaign prompted the United States to break off diplomatic relations with Germany on February 3, 1917, and, three months later, to join the war. That was a gamble that did not deter Ludendorff or von Hindenburg—"I do not give a damn about America," proclaimed the former to the latter—but it proved disastrous in the end.[14]

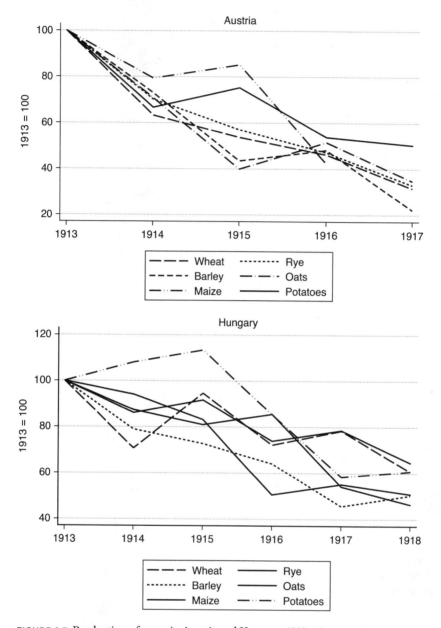

FIGURE 2.3. Production of crops in Austria and Hungary, 1913–18

The "largely unseen" pressure that the Royal Navy placed on Germany has been described, albeit controversially—see below—as Britain's "greatest contribution to the allied cause" during World War I.[15] Winston Churchill, first lord of the Admiralty between 1911 and 1915, is frequently cited as later claiming (and the statement is not out of character) that the blockade "treated the whole of Germany as if it were a beleaguered fortress, and avowedly sought to starve the whole population—men, women and children, old and young, wounded and sound—into submission." That was also the view of the first official historian of the war.[16]

Hunger, exacerbated by cold in wintertime, was a constant problem in Germany from 1916. As an oft-quoted Australian musician trapped in Leipzig during the war described to her sister in February 1917:

> Coal has run out. The electric light is cut off in most houses (I have gas, thank Heaven!), the trams are not running, or only in the very early morning, all theatres, schools, the opera, Gewandhaus and concerts and cinematographs are closed—neither potatoes nor turnips are to be had—they were our last resource—there is no fish—and Germany has at last ceased to trumpet the fact that it can't be starved out. Added to that the thermometer outside my kitchen window says 24 deg. Fahr. *below zero*. I have never seen that before.[17]

A combination of three factors led to significant excess civilian mortality in Germany starting in late 1916. The first was military mobilization, which reduced domestic agricultural output; on the eve of World War I, agriculture required one-third of Germany's male labor force, but the war deprived it of two-fifths of those. Soldiers came before civilians: "Feed me at once, [Big Bertha, World War I siege howitzer] screams, or I will kill myself. Stay me with lard, comfort me with pork, or I will bring the roof down." After 1916, when the military became responsible for food distribution, the guns-versus-butter trade-off tilted even more against the civilian population. Alan Kramer, indeed, has argued that "if the 'excess mortality' of civilians during the war was a war crime, then German war policy bore the heaviest responsibility," but that fails to account for the fact that much of the excess mortality occurred after the armistice of November 11, 1918.[18] Second, the war deprived Germany of its main prewar foreign sources of nutrition when an increasingly effective Allied blockade really began to bite in 1916. It lasted for eight months after the armistice. The potato harvest of 1916 was poor, and during the bitterly cold Steckrübenwinter (turnip winter) that followed malnutrition became widespread. Official data imply that total calories generated domestically by cereals and potatoes in 1918 were only about 55–56 percent of those produced in 1914,[19] and since imports could not be counted on in 1918, the decline in calorie availability would have been even greater. The role of the potato was crucial, yielding about one-third of the calories available from grain and potatoes except in 1916 when, as noted, the potato harvest was very poor. Since at the outset pigs were consuming perhaps one-fifth of the available potatoes, the huge reduction in the pig population—from twenty-five million in 1914 to eleven million in 1917—led to a considerable increase in the potato's share of human calorie consumption. Indeed, given how potatoes economized on land compared to cereal crops, it is hard to imagine how Germany could have survived to 1918 without them.

The privations of war had a disproportionate effect on the lives of older adults; "that part of the population most innocent of the war suffered most from it."[20] Civilian cases of famine edema were first noticed in Berlin, Hamburg, the Rhineland, and Vienna in early 1917,[21] but German civilians experienced no respite until the peace treaty was signed in July 1919. The supplies of Ukrainian wheat envisaged by Germans after the Treaty of Brest-Litovsk, which stipulated the arrival of the equivalent of a million tons of bread per annum, proved a mirage.[22] In mid-February 1919, an inquiry conducted by the UK War Department recommended against removing "the menace of starvation by a too sudden and abundant supply of foodstuffs. This menace is a powerful lever for negotiation at an important moment."[23] The worsening food crisis adversely affected the morale of civilian and soldier alike. Toward the end, all one heard from better-off train travelers was talk "of Sparticide terror, of greed and brutality by workmen, of the hopelessness of the industrial future." In third or fourth class, all the talk was "of famine, of impossible prices, and of profiteers."[24]

The resulting death toll is still contested. In his classic study of the impact of the blockade, Avner Offer ruled out a famine in the sense that "people did not, as a rule, drop dead in the streets" and dubbed the cost as "hardly crippling" in historical perspective. Others, however, have painted a bleaker picture and argued for an excess mortality figure of 0.4 to 0.5 million (compared to 1.8 million German deaths on the battlefield). The excess death estimate in table 2.1 assumes that 1913, when deaths numbered 945,835, was a normal year, which seems reasonable, but it makes no allowance for deaths from the flu pandemic of 1918–19, which took about 225,000 lives. Allowing for the likelihood that malnutrition inflated the latter suggests a blockade-induced death toll somewhat short of 0.5 million.[25] In Berlin the blockade led to a sharp rise in illegitimate infant mortality that lasted until 1922, and stillbirths and maternal mortality greatly increased. The blockade led to the loss of British lives too, though not from hunger: Germany's U-boat campaign killed nearly fifteen thousand noncombatant British merchant seamen and fishermen.[26]

Hitler's understanding of the impact of the Allied blockade on Germany during World War I—"What we failed to do, the enemy did, with amazing skill and really brilliant calculation"[27]—convinced him of the urgency

TABLE 2.1. Deaths in Germany, 1914–19

Year	Military deaths	Civilian deaths	Excess deaths
1914	241,343	988,204	42,369
1915	434,034	954,706	8,871
1916	320,468	957,586	11,571
1917	281,905	1,000,433	68,598
1918	379,777	1,216,882	271,047
1919	14,314	1,017,284	71,449
Totals	1,671,841	6,135,095	473,905

Source: Howard 1993: 166.

of guarding against a repetition during World War II. Part of the Nazi response was an unmerciful focus on plundering the resources of captured lands during World War II. How this applied has been in highlighted in Götz Aly's influential bestseller, *Hitler's Beneficiaries: Plunder, Racial War, and the Nazi Welfare State* (2007) and in the more technical analysis of how Filippo Occhino, Kim Oosterlinck, and Eugene White exploited France.[28] Another part was the Nazis' so-called Hunger Plan, which entailed the conquest of Ukraine as Germany's eastern breadbasket "in order that no one is able to starve us again, as in the last war." The plan would, if implemented, have entailed the death through starvation of many millions of civilians in wheat-deficit areas. Poor Nazi planning and Soviet resistance effectively constrained its implementation, but probably five million to six million perished of famine in the occupied Soviet Union in any case.[29] The main point here is that Germans, excluding those targeted by the regime, were adequately fed during World War II.

AUSTRIA-HUNGARY

Austrians also endured severe food shortages during World War I and immediately afterward due to the combined effects of the loss of their breadbasket (Galicia) for the entire duration of the war, declining domestic production, and a lopsided distribution of Austro-Hungarian supplies. In calorie equivalents, the basic food ration in Vienna dropped from 1,300 kilocalories at the outset of the war to 830 kilocalories by 1917.[30] By 1918 both troops and civilians were severely undernourished. Morale plummeted, as reflected in the repeated references to food shortages in letters intercepted by the security forces. Hunger bred resentment against the authorities and against the greed of farmers and middlemen, stoking ethnic tensions and anti-Semitism. Rudeness and demoralization replaced trust and civility. In May 1918 a Vienna newspaper described the prevailing attitudes thus: "I'm afraid of my landlady. I could just as well have said the cleaning lady, the coffeehouse waiter, the greengrocer, any bureaucrat, tram conductor or barber. I see this cold, compassionless hatred between people all around."[31] As common in food crises, the poor believed there was enough food to go around and blamed producers, middlemen, immigrants, and the authorities. As the Habsburg Empire collapsed, particular fury was reserved for Hungarian producers, on whom Austria had heavily depended before the war.

Again, the data are incomplete, but Anatol Schmied-Kowarcik's careful calculations put the civilian death toll in the whole of Austro-Hungary during and in the wake of World War I at 465,000 civilians.[32] That would include deaths from typhus, which was rife on the Eastern Front toward the end of the war, and those due to wartime atrocities but not those from the flu pandemic: most of the deaths would have resulted from hunger and related diseases. The situation in Vienna, where a man-made *Hungerkatastrophe* accounted for one death in ten during the war, was particularly acute and spawned serious urban-rural and intercommunal tensions. Jewish refugees from Galicia were accused of smuggling and profiteering, and their properties were sometimes attacked and plundered. Soup kitchens served twenty million free meals in 1916 and forty-one million in 1918.[33] The crisis is reflected in the decline in birthweights in Vienna from a pre–World War I mean of thirty-one hundred to thirty-two hundred grams to below three thousand grams in 1921.[34] The Hungarian part of the empire, with an estimated eighty thousand deaths, escaped much more lightly.[35] Viennese doctors attributed nearly one-tenth of deaths in the city during the war to "inanition." In the end the lack of food undermined the Habsburg regime's legitimacy.[36] As figure 2.4 indicates, famine exacted a heavier toll in Austria toward the end of World War I than in the wake of World War II, with Allied food aid crucial to keeping deaths down in 1945 and after.

THE LOW COUNTRIES

The contrasting impact of World War I on occupied Belgium and neutral Holland is captured rather well in the trends in birth and death rates (figure 2.5). Most dramatic was the plunge in the birth rate in Belgium, while that in the Netherlands was only marginally affected. Some indications of excess mortality are evident in Belgium too; while much of the spike in deaths in both countries in 1918 was due to the flu pandemic described in more detail in chapter 9, the rise in mortality in Belgium preceded the flu and

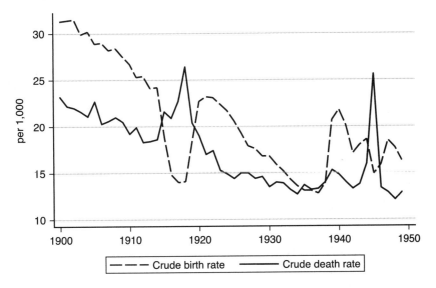

FIGURE 2.4. Birth and death rates in Austria, 1910–49
Source: Statistik Austria (as cited in https://en.wikipedia.org/wiki/Demographics_of
_Austria)

was somewhat greater in 1918. Hunger-induced increases of 3 per 1,000 in
the death rate in Belgium in 1917 and 1918 would have entailed excess mortality of about 45,000, and the aggregate shortfall in births between 1915
and 1919 approached 250,000. But the true death toll was probably higher:
soon after the war, a Belgian sociologist put the number of excess civilian
deaths at 82,000 (nearly 1 percent of the population).[37] Occupation and war
seriously compromised Belgium's food production. Under international law
Germany, as the occupying force, was responsible for the nutritional status
of Belgians but refused to honor its obligations until the Allies allowed in
food via the neutral Netherlands. A combination of Belgian initiatives and
Herbert Hoover's Commission for Relief in Belgium helped mobilize food
aid from afar, almost certainly avoiding a serious famine surely worse than
the Dutch Hunger Winter of 1944–45. Nonetheless, the hardships Belgium
endured amounted to what two Belgian scholars have described as "a small-
scale replica of the great crisis of the mid-19th century."[38]

THE BALKANS

The Balkans experienced significant hunger-related excess mortality during
World War I. Precise data are lacking; one accessible source claims that food
shortages caused 100,000 deaths in Bulgaria while a combination of food

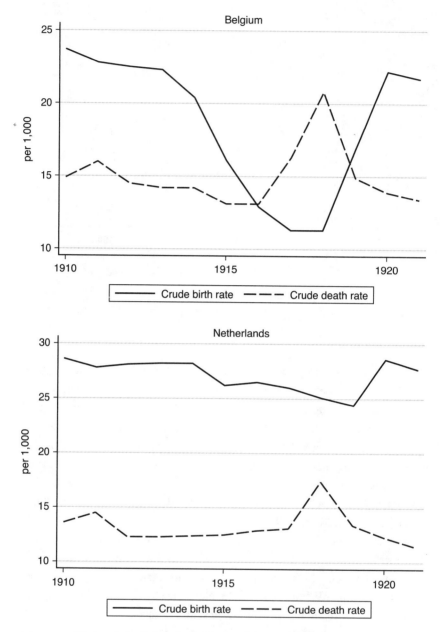

FIGURE 2.5. Birth and death rates in Belgium and the Netherlands, 1910–21
Source: Mitchell 1975: 114, 117

shortages, epidemics, and the Spanish flu caused 430,000 deaths in Romania and 450,000 deaths in Serbia.[39] The latter figure is obliquely reflected in pre- and postwar population estimates for Serbia (4,576,508 in 1914, 4,041,427 in 1921). In November 1915 the Serb army, almost encircled by enemy forces, sought to escape to the Adriatic coast via Albania and Montenegro instead of surrendering. About 220,000 civilians, including an older King Peter and most parliamentary deputies, joined this "Great Retreat" into exile, which entailed crossing difficult mountainous terrain in the depth of winter. Food was extremely scarce and, naturally, troops took precedence over civilians. An estimated 160,000 civilians perished en route, mostly from exposure, disease, and starvation. Another 11,000 would die later. Austro-Hungarian and Bulgarian forces' capture of the multiethnic town of Prizren, now in Kosovo, where a large Serb population had taken refuge, led to forced Bulgarization, the internment of the Serb population, and the deaths of several hundred from starvation and disease. The Serb delegation to the Paris Peace Conference produced an estimate of 845,000 deaths for its Reparations Commission, whereas, as noted, Hersch's more plausible estimate of 450,000 refers to southern Serbia and Montenegro only but includes deaths from atrocities and influenza.[40] An aggregate toll for Serbia of 0.5–0.6 million civilian deaths from all causes, and of 0.3 million from famine and typhus, is not implausible. Thanks mainly to excessive requisitioning by occupying forces—*Raubwirtschaft*—Romania was reduced to famine toward the end of the war. It is reckoned that as many as 0.4 million died of hunger and disease, with pellagra and typhus rampant, but perhaps the flu epidemic was responsible for some of those. For Greece, Hersch opted for a "purely hypothetical figure of 150,000."[41] A round figure of 1 million for the entire Balkan region is suggested here.

POLAND

The territories that would combine to form Poland in 1918–19 suffered severely during World War I and in its wake. Food and fuel were in short supply, especially in the cities, and the constant movement of refugees and the military facilitated the spread of typhus. Mortality rates from tuberculosis soared, at least in the cities. However, the nutritional status of the population is poorly documented, and hard data on famine mortality are lacking. The population of post-1918 Poland is reckoned to have fallen by over 4 million between January 1914 and January 1919. Most of that decline was due to emigration and displacement; hundreds of thousands of civilians were either deported to the Russian interior or moved to Germany as forced laborers, and hundreds of thousands more, including many Jewish refugees, escaped to the West. Much of the migration was motivated by a wish to escape conscription by either Russian or German armies. On the basis of necessarily fallible data, in 1939 an official at the Central Statistical Office of Poland put the total number of emigrants in 1914–1918, forced or otherwise, at 3.7 million and the number of excess deaths at 0.4 million; the latter figure, in particular, is probably on the low side. The losses in population were greatest in eastern Poland. The immediate postwar years brought significant repatriation, especially from the east. An excess mortality of 0.3 million due to famine and hunger-related diseases seems a conservative guesstimate.[42]

ITALY

Famine also caused excess mortality in Italy during World War I but on a much smaller scale. After the disaster of Caporetto in October 1917 and the retreat of Italian forces to the river Piave, the provinces of Udine and Belluno and parts of Treviso and Veneto fell to the Austrians. About 0.3 million of the occupied region's population of 1.2 million, disproportionately the healthier and better-off, followed the retreating army. Mortality among the 0.9 million left behind, who competed for food and accommodation with about 1 million Habsburg, mainly Hungarian, troops, was high. The statistician Giorgio Mortara estimated excess deaths during *l'an de la fàm* (October 1917–October 1918) in the northeast of Italy at 27,000,[43] with the occupied part of Treviso Province, where the excess death rate reached 61 per 1,000, the worst affected. If Mortara's calculations are correct, the town of Valdobbiadene and its hinterland in Treviso suffered an excess death rate of 123 per 1,000 during the occupation.[44] In Valdobbiadene itself a plaque reads: "Cittadini uccisi da proiettili n. 51—Cittadini morti per fame n. 484." Violence, starvation, and disease all contributed to mortality. Mayors, priests, and hospital administrators complained of people being reduced to gathering edible herbs and grasses fit for animals and of famine diseases being widespread, particularly among older adults and children. An account from Calalzo in the Venetian Dolomites recorded: "We went looking for edible herbs: radishes, wild spinach, nettles, sorrel, '*pèti da pra*' (carlina) and roots to boil. Around eleven o'clock you could hear only the blows of the '*pestarola*,' a large knife that crushed the grass to be seasoned with sour milk."[45]

Mortara deemed the estimated 9,797 deaths from starvation reported to the authorities as unsafe, given the difficulty of defining starvation; he concluded that malnutrition was the main or contributory cause of at least

FIGURE 2.6. Rats and mice being dried for food, northeast Italy, 1918
Source: Biblioteca civica di Belluno - Collezione Massenz-Badlini

half the excess deaths.[46] Outside the region occupied in 1917–18, and setting aside deaths from influenza, war-related excess mortality in Italy was relatively light. However, the increased deaths from malaria in 1918 in Sardinia, Basilicata, and Puglia could be linked to the war. Quite apart from the issue of wartime privation, troops infected in the war zone carried the disease to their places of birth and recuperation.[47] Scolè reckoned the aggregate excess civilian deaths in 1918,[48] compared to the 1911–13 average at 532,457, most of which would have been due to influenza. If we accept Fornasin et al.'s estimate of 411,000 flu deaths in 1918,[49] that leaves about 0.1 million for other causes, mainly famine. In our summation below, we put the Italian toll at 50,000–0.1 million. Figure 2.6 shows *pantegane* rats and mice being hung out to dry during the *an de la fan* in Belluno.[50]

FINLAND

Although on a lesser scale, the twelve thousand or so leftist prisoners who died from starvation and related diseases in concentration camps during the Finnish civil war of 1918 were mainly male civilians. Conditions in the camps were atrocious; in the most notorious of them, Tammisaari in southwest Finland, three in every ten prisoners perished. Two-thirds of these deaths may be considered famine deaths; the remainder would have been flu victims. For survivors the suffering did not end there. Recent research suggests that the longer they spent in prison, the greater the adverse impact on their survival prospects in old age.[51]

THE OTTOMAN EMPIRE

Data on famine mortality in parts of the collapsing Ottoman Empire are less precise. In Mount Lebanon, then a *mutasarrifiyya*, or semiautonomous province of Ottoman Syria composing the mountainous part of present-day Lebanon, a combination of wartime requisitioning, poor harvests, and a British-imposed blockade on food imports lasting from mid-1915 to late 1918 contributed to famine. Other factors—a locust infestation that virtually destroyed the 1915 cereal harvest, inadequate relief from the Ottomans and their suspicion of the Arab population's loyalties, rampant corruption, and poor communications—also played a role in the lead-up to extreme famine conditions in 1916. The archival evidence is sparse and of dubious quality, but it is reckoned that 80,000 had died in Mount Lebanon by the end of 1916; during the following two years, further crop failures, an Arab revolt, and the blockade, "unmercifully constant throughout the war . . . and therefore . . . the primary cause of famine in the coastal regions," increased the death toll to beyond 0.1 million in Mount Lebanon and 0.5 million across Bilad al-Sham, as the area comprising Lebanon, Palestine, Jordan, and Syria was known.[52] The French, who sought to relieve the area's mainly Maronite Christian inhabitants by easing the blockade, believed that the British "consider the famine as an agent that will lead the Arabs to revolt."[53] Not far from Lebanon, perhaps a million Armenians perished from famine-related causes during their Aghet (catastrophe), which is discussed separately in chapter 4.

The Muslim population of eastern Anatolia, at the epicenter of the empire, also suffered. It is supposed that up to 1.5 million perished from the combined effects of intercommunal strife, famine, and disease during World War I and its sequel.[54]

AFRICA

Reliable estimates of civilian mortality in Africa during World War I are lacking. A figure of 0.7 million from a combination of massacre, disease, and famine has been proposed by Joe Harris Lunn merely as "a frame of reference for further inquiry." One detailed study of hunger in the Dodoma region of central Tanzania, then under German control, puts excess mortality at 30,000 out of a population of 150,000. The troubles began when the Germans started to requisition grain and livestock and, later, to conscript men as soldiers and porters. Porters, or carriers, were crucial for all sides on terrain without a road network. A British estimate put the number conscripted by the Germans at 35,000, but after the British took over the region, "The only change in the situation . . . was the language in which the demands were made." The civilian population sought to survive by flight and by hiding what food they could in the bush.[55] More generally, war meant the disruption of farming and the plunder and requisitioning of foodstuffs across extensive parts of eastern, southern, and southwestern Africa. In addition, all sides conscripted African labor as carriers, who played an indispensable role in a mobile war. It is estimated that 95,000 African men supporting British troops died, over 40,000 from German East Africa (encompassing present-day Tanzania, Burundi, and Rwanda), parts of which had been captured by the British. The deaths of porters supporting the Belgian army in the Congo have been estimated at 24,000. Perhaps, in all, 0.2 million carriers employed by the various armed forces perished, mostly succumbing to a combination of overwork, inadequate rations, and disease. About 1 million Black Africans worked as porters for Allied forces and an unknown but much smaller number for the Germans. Here we attribute half of Lunn's figure, or 0.4 million, to famine and famine-linked diseases, but this can be no more than a guess.[56]

PERSIA/IRAN

Persia's neutrality during World War I did not spare it from military invasion, infiltration, and occupation; the requisitioning of food, livestock, and oil; sabotage and disrupted communications; and severe droughts. This combination of factors culminated in famine in 1917–19. The leader of a British force described the scene on arrival in Hamadan in western Iran in early 1917:

The evidences of famine were terrible, and in a walk through the town one was confronted with the most awful sights. Nobody could endure such scenes if he were not endowed with the wonderful apathy of the Oriental: "It is the will of God!" So the people die and no one makes any effort to help, and a dead body in the road lies unnoticed until an effort to secure some sort of burial becomes unavoidable. I passed in a main thoroughfare the body of a boy of about nine years of age who had evidently died during the day; he lay with his face buried in the mud, and the people passed by on either side as if he were merely any ordinary obstruction in the roadway.

The same source reported that "corpses strewed the road between Kasvin (close to Tehran) and Hamadan at intervals throughout its length" and that there were cases of cannibalism in Hamadan.[57] He offered no indication of the death toll, for which there is no robust evidence. Iran's first census dates from as recently as 1956, and its demographic trajectory before then is but poorly understood. At one extreme, one "best estimate" of population trends between 1900 and 1966 leaves little room for major excess mortality and does not even mention famine during World War I, whereas at the other extreme is the claim that the famine reduced Iran's population by two-fifths (from a counterfactual nonfamine estimate of 18–20 million to 10–12 million). Some *engagé* accounts recycle the latter estimate, but few specialist scholars take it seriously. Others opt for a figure of 2 million, but on flimsy evidence.[58] Given a likely prefamine population of about 10 million, 2 million deaths may seem on the high side, even though the famine seems to have extended over a wide area. Moreover, given a succession of devastating droughts in 1916 and 1917, it is probably unfair to blame war for all the resultant mortality. Our guesstimate of 0.5 million is necessarily arbitrary; it may err on the side of caution.

World War I: The Reckoning

Table 2.2 summarizes our estimates of the aggregate death tolls from famine during World War I. Bear in mind that all figures are approximate, that some are contested, and that they err, perhaps, on the conservative side; this aspect is clear from the final columns in the table. During World War I, if war-related deaths in the Soviet Union after 1918 are included—as they should be—famine deaths clearly exceeded battlefield deaths. These deaths accounted for two-thirds of World War I famine deaths and 8–9 percent of the population of prewar Russia. During World War I, famine deaths were mostly confined to Europe, and apart from in the Ottoman Empire, the

TABLE 2.2. Deaths from hunger and famine during the First World War (1914–22)

Place	Number (millions)	Observations, provenance
Soviet Union	8	"May well have been about 8 million" (Wheatcroft 2017: 229); data on rural areas lacking. Compare Adamets 2002: 163–44; Harrison and Markevich 2011: 679.
Germany	0.5	"Most recent estimate . . . extrapolated from mortality estimates from Berlin" (Cox 2019: 242). Includes up to seventy thousand inmates of mental institutions (Engwall 2005). See also Kramer 2014a.
Austro-Hungary	0.3	Schmied-Kowarcik 2016
Belgium	0.05	Olbrechts 1926: 40, as cited in Majerus and Roekens 2017: 26
Italy	0.03	Mortara 1925
Poland	0.3	No hard data[a]
Finland	0.008	Register of war victims (accurate)
Ottoman Empire	1.5 to 2	Schatkowski Schilcher 1992; Brand 2014
Balkans	1.0	Mougel 2011; Radivojević and Goran Penev 2014 (Serbia only); Hamlin 2009 (Romania)
Persia/Iran	0.5	See text
Africa	0.4	Lunn 2015
Total	12.5 to 13	

[a] Anonymous 1939: 233.

numbers were mostly small relative to population size. The share of what might be called colonial famines was much higher during World War II than World War I, and China, which suffered badly during World War II, was spared during World War I.

World War II

The incidence and spread of death from hunger and disease during World War II were different. Remarkably, all the main actors with the exception of the Soviet Union largely escaped famine, at least until near the end—though this claim does not extend to their colonial possessions. Why this was so is further discussed below. Death tolls from famines elsewhere, however, were massive in both absolute and relative terms. In South Asia, Vietnam,

Java, and Bengal suffered greatly as colonies of the French, Dutch, and British, respectively. Even in Europe, "in Poland, Greece, parts of Yugoslavia, and Albania distribution was irregular and consumption fell for shorter or longer periods to levels of semi-starvation or outright famine."[59] Jozo Tomasevich refers to near or outright starvation as "widespread" in Croatia but offers no numbers.[60]

POLAND

Almost immediately after invading Poland, the Germans annexed territory ceded to Poland under the Treaty of Versailles, renaming it the Warthegau. They sought to Germanize the region by expelling about 0.5 million Poles and replacing them with a smaller number of ethnic Germans. More Poles were expelled elsewhere; perhaps 1 million in all were sent to what was left of Poland after outright annexations, the occupied area known as the General Government (*Generalgouvernement* was the term used by the Germans). Throughout World War II, food was scarce in the General Government, and the authorities made a policy of distributing what there was very unequally. Rationing was introduced in December 1939. In 1941, ethnic Germans were entitled to 2,613 calories daily and other foreigners to about 2,000 calories, compared to 699 for Poles and 184 for Jews in the ghetto. In order to survive, Poles and Jews struggled to supplement those meager allocations via charity or clandestine means. In the Warsaw ghetto in December 1941, beggars were reckoned to have consumed only 784 calories daily and the general population, 1,125 calories a day.[61]

Table 2.3 is taken from an official report produced in Poland after the war. It refers to all war victims; given the Holocaust's toll of 3 million Polish Jews, it supports the claim that more than half of all the reported Polish lives lost were Jewish victims of the Holocaust. The numbers do not identify famine deaths separately, though to assume that half of the 1.3 million who reportedly perished in prisons, concentration camps, and forced labor camps and half of the 0.5 million who perished outside the camps were civilians who succumbed to hunger-related causes is hardly far-fetched. From this comes the guesstimate of 0.9 million in table 2.10 below.

GREECE

The death rate from famine in Greece was probably higher than in any other European country with the exceptions of the Soviet Union and Poland. Following its occupation by Axis troops in April–June 1941, the British navy,

TABLE 2.3. War-related deaths in Poland, 1939–45

Cause of death	Number (1,000s)	Percentage of population
Direct military action	644	2.4
Murdered in extermination camps, executions, ghetto liquidation	3,577	13.3
Death in prisons, concentration camps, from epidemics, forced labor	1,286	4.7
From wounds, beatings, overwork	521	1.8
Total	6,023	22.2

Source: *Report Relating to Casualties and War Damages of Poland between the Years 1939–1945* (produced by the Polish government in January 1947), http://amularczyk.pl/wp-content/uploads/2017/09/raport-straty-wojenne-ang.pdf.

which controlled the Mediterranean, blocked sea access to Greece. Greece was one of the few Nazi-occupied economies that depended on imports for much of its food. The theft of meat and dairy cattle in the area around Athens for army use quickly followed occupation.[62] Very soon, essential foodstuffs became scarce, particularly in Athens, which led to a famine at its most intense in 1941–42. The capital and its port city of Piraeus and some of the islands were hit particularly hard. The context was one of hyperinflation, an Allied blockade, and state-sponsored theft by the occupation forces.

Accurate estimates of the death toll in Greece in 1941–43 are lacking since the registration of deaths during the war was incomplete, but deaths in Athens and Piraeus are believed to have exceeded 2,000 daily at the end of January 1942, and about 40,000 died of famine in Athens and Piraeus in 1941–42. In addition, famine struck various parts of Greece at different points between 1941 and 1945; an aggregate estimate of about 0.3 million out of a population of 7.3 million is widely accepted.[63] Local data for Athens/Piraeus and some of the Greek islands shed light on several aspects of the famine's demography, including the extent of excess mortality; its main causes; and its gender, age composition, and occupational profile.[64] A Red Cross report described the scene in Athens:

> The first to succumb were the old, the infirm, and stunted children. They died quietly; the rest did not give in so easily. A famished mob roamed the streets, dressed in foul-smelling rags and faces contorted by hunger and vermin, devouring no matter what refuse they found. Robbing and pillaging at will, they might even kill for a few morsels of food. But they too succumbed in due course. In working-class neighbourhoods, pale

children scratched themselves to relieve the itch caused by fleas. Indoors, in semi-darkness, one might discern the dying, their bodies swollen by oedema and covered with septic wounds.[65]

Agricultural statistics imply a huge reduction in output in 1941 and 1942 (see table 2.4). This is partly because Bulgaria had taken away parts of northern Greece—Thrace and Eastern Macedonia—that normally supplied 25–30 percent of farm output while containing only 13 percent of the population. The Ionian Islands, which specialized in olive production, had been declared Italian territories. Other factors, such as the reduced supply of farm machinery and horses, wartime disruption, low regulated prices, and excessive taxation and procurements, also tended to depress food availability. Still, the fall in output was probably less than the data imply because some produce was hoarded and concealed from the authorities and made its way to the black market. Indeed, Violetta Hionidou goes so far as to argue that the output estimates "reflected the collected tax in kind" rather than true output.[66]

There was rationing but the rations were meager because the authorities managed to centralize only a fraction of output. Of the 1941 harvest, only 22,400 tons of corn and 10,200 tons of other cereals were available to distribute. The bread ration in the main towns and cities began in April 1941 at one hundred *dramia* (320 grams) per head, but that was reduced in steps to sixty, forty, and thirty dramia, and supply became increasingly irregular. In April 1942 the average daily ration in the capital, even after supplementation by the Red Cross, was still only sixty dramia per capita. Sometimes polenta was substituted for wheat bread. During the first year of occupation, the Germans imported about 80,000 tons of grain to feed the Greek workers they employed.[67] Too late, they and the Italians imported 17,000 tons of grain in late March 1943 to relieve the cities.

By the time food relief from abroad began to arrive in Greece, the worst of the famine was over, but relief undoubtedly played a part in preventing a recurrence. Between October 1941 and March 1942, food deliveries from abroad amounted to only 7,500 tons, at a time when the local relief organizers reported to Geneva that they would require 90,000 tons of corn and an equivalent amount of other food items for the first four months of 1942.[68] Most relief was channeled through the International Committee of the Red Cross, with ships carrying the flags of neutral Sweden and Turkey playing a key role. Turkey was first off the mark, and its SS *Kurtulus* made its first delivery on October 6, 1941. Between September 1942 and March 1945,

TABLE 2.4. Greek agriculture: "Production" and foreign trade, 1938–42 (1,000 metric tons)

Item	1938			1939			1940			1941		1942
	Q	M	X	Q	M	X	Q	M	X	Q	M	Q
Wheat	983	475	.	1,042	366	.	905	275	.	566	198	343
Other cereals	722	105	.	757	69	.	697	20	.	458	21	369
Dry vegetables	90	20	.	129	9	.	119	4	.	35	6	32
Potatoes	143	3	.	163	3	.	190	3	.	143	.	99
Olive oil	94	.	21	125	.	29	102	.	30	84	.	90
Olives	23	.	14	79	.	12	19	.	10	20	.	22
Dry raisins	189	.	104	170	.	177	166	.	40	110	.	63
Dry figs	.	.	19	.	.	11	22	.	18	22	.	22
Sugar	.	81	.	.	68	.	.	44	.	.	10	.

Source: Helder 1949: 25, 28. Q = output; M = imports; X = exports.

the Greek Red Cross distributed 463,000 tons of imported corn, 99,000 tons of dried vegetables and soups, and 18,000 tons of meat and fish.[69] This ensured that in Athens between September 1942 and October 1944 over 1 million people received a daily bread ration of sixty-eight dramia, equivalent to 4.5 kilograms of flour monthly, and in addition, through groceries, 2.9 kilograms of various other foods. In rural areas the commission fed an average of 0.8 million people, who received an average of 3.2 kilograms of flour per month. In Athens this translated into a daily equivalent of 840 calories; certain categories with special needs and children fed in canteens received over 1,100 calories (figure 2.7).[70]

In Athens and its port city, Piraeus, the cold weather also played a role during the winter of 1941–42. The Greek demographer Vasilios G. Valaoras studied the correlation between mortality, on the one hand, and the daily bread ration and the mean daily temperature, on the other, in the city between October 1941 and April 1942.[71] While he found no apparent link between daily deaths and the bread ration, there was a clear correlation between deaths and temperature. That is not to say that nutrition did not matter; the problem was that being able to survive the cold required an expenditure of calories in addition to the inadequate allowance that had already seriously weakened the constitution.

The Joint Relief Commission managing Greek relief conducted a series of inquiries into the nutrition of working-class households in Athens and Piraeus during the occupation, following the method used in inquiries in 1938–39 and 1941–42. The surveys were carefully carried out but involved small samples. They targeted the most disadvantaged, and many of the household heads were casual laborers or unemployed. The outcome in table 2.5 underlines the parlous nutritional status of these urban households and implies that they were on the verge of starvation in late 1941 and early 1942.

Famines have a history of spawning nongovernmental organizations (NGOs). Just as one of the world's best-known NGOs, Save the Children, was born as a response to the threat of famine in Germany and Austro-Hungary in the wake of World War I, another, Oxfam, was a by-product of famine during World War II.[72] In 1942–43 the Greek famine was being widely reported in the British press. The publicity led to the formation of the Oxford Committee for Famine Relief, which began in October 1942 as the local branch of a national Famine Relief Committee (FRC). The FRC had been founded in London on May 29, 1942, by a group of pacifists. In the spirit of "humanitarian neutrality," they opposed the British policy of blockading enemy-occupied countries such as Greece and Belgium and thereby making

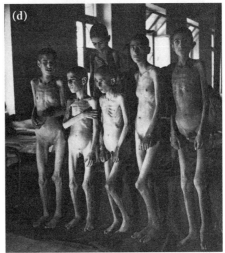

FIGURE 2.7. Greece, 1941–42
Source: International Committee of the Red Cross Audiovisual Archive
a. Island of Chios, June 2, 1942
b. Children in a Greek Red Cross convalescent home in Athens, winter 1941–42
c. Dead victims, 1941–42
d. Children in a convalescent home

it impossible to supply food relief. The FRC's initial request that milk and vitamins by allowed through was rejected initially on the basis that any such help would be diverted to the enemy war effort and that it was the responsibility of the occupying power to feed civilians. Some relief reached Greece from Turkey and Sweden. In 1942 British policy was relaxed, enabling aid to reach Greece through the Red Cross, which had managed to establish a passage for food relief into Greece. But it was not until March 1943 that the

TABLE 2.5. Mean consumption in hectograms per week of households consisting of two adults and two infants in Athens, 1938–44

Item	Nov. 38–Jan. 39	Dec. 41–Mar. 42	Feb. 43–Mar. 43	Apr. 43–Jul. 43	Nov. 43–Dec. 43	Feb. 44–Jun. 44
Milk	27.3	5.7	12.1	15.9	14.9	13.6
Cheese and eggs	4.7	.	0.0	0.5	.	0.3
Olive oil	10.8	6.0	10.1	7.3	2.8	3.0
Meat	10.8	1.9	1.1	1.9	0.6	1.1
Fish	8.1	1.5	0.3	1.3	1.0	2.8
Flour, oatmeal, pasta	8.3	3.8	32.1	10.8	8.0	5.1
Bread	94.4	28.3	61.8	63.5	82.8	78.7
Fresh fruit and vegetables	91.5	91.7	80.3	83.5	73.4	61.1
Dried fruit and vegetables	12.1	20.4	32.9	27.1	29.7	35.0
Sugar, honey, etc.	10.4	4.2	2.8	2.0	1.1	0.1
Other	2.2	0.1	.	.	.	.
Calories per adult male equivalent per diem	2,429	1,176	2,062	1,703	1,671	1,690

Source: Helder 1949: 604–6. The calories are derived from the totals given on page 606 and assume that a household of four equals three adult equivalents.

committee was registered as a charity under the War Charities Act. Then it could appeal for funds, and during the summer of 1943, the Oxford committee first raised £3,000 from members of the university while a gift shop in a prominent location raised another £3,000. Before too long, £12,700 had been raised, all of which was sent to the Greek Red Cross representative in London.[73]

AUSTRIA

Austria, too, experienced famine conditions toward the end of World War II and in its immediate wake. The output of cereals and potatoes had been falling since the beginning of the war, but the fall had been cushioned at the outset by grain imports. In 1945 production was down to half its prewar level, and imports were no longer available. That potatoes accounted for one-third of the calories provided by cereals and potatoes combined was a reflection of Austrian poverty at the time. The consequences for food availability were disastrous in 1945, and may be inferred from the peaks in the crude death

FIGURE 2.8. Births and deaths in Austria, 1935–50

rate and the infant mortality rate (which reached 350 per 1,000 in Vienna in July 1945); births also dropped sharply in 1945 (figure 2.8). The situation in parts of Austria, especially in the capital, bordered on famine. In 1946 and 1947, it would have been cataclysmic but for the departure of hundreds of thousands of refugees and the availability of relief aid from the United Nations Relief and Rehabilitation Administration (UNRRA).

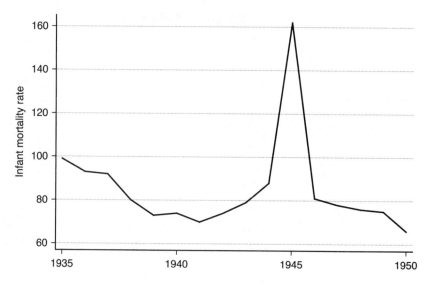

FIGURE 2.8. (*continued*)

THE NETHERLANDS

Far more died in Greece in 1941–44 and in Austria in 1945–46 than during the Dutch famine of 1944–45, but the so-called Hunger Winter is more familiar for being the locus classicus for fetal origins hypothesis–related research on famines.[74] This was more a reflection of the quality of Dutch recordkeeping than the severity of the famine in question. The famine, which was responsible for about 20,000,[75] struck toward the end of World War II, when the Dutch government-in-exile in London ordered a railway strike in support of the airborne Allied troops who had landed in the southern Netherlands on and after September 17, 1944 (figure 2.9). In return, the Germans halted all shipping traffic for three weeks, cutting off access to outside food supplies in the German-occupied, heavily urbanized western Netherlands. Transport constraints and winter weather continued to severely restrict food imports for several months. Food availability gradually shrank; the gravity of the situation by late January 1945 is reflected in the issue of instruction by the Rijksbureau vor Voedselvoorziening (National Office for Food Supply) on how to store, prepare, and cook tulip bulbs.[76] The last remaining food supplies were distributed at the end of April; fortunately, the famished area received relief a few days later. Stein et al. tracked birth weights by month in different parts of the country, and those data offer quite a precise guide to the famine's duration and intensity.[77] Rations in the affected area were reduced to 600–800 calories per diem, forcing an increasing reliance on

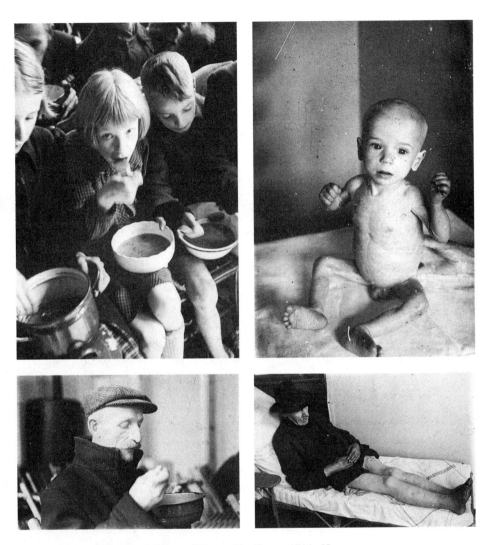

FIGURE 2.9. The Dutch Hunger Winter, The Hague, 1944–45
Source: The Menno Huizinga Collection, NIOD, Amsterdam

the black market for survival. Farmers profiteered and urban consumers turned to sugar beets and tulip bulbs as supplementary foods. Although mortality was already rising before the famine, which makes estimating excess mortality tricky, the famine likely resulted in about 20,000 excess deaths in a population of 4.5 million (the population of the affected area, not the Netherlands as a whole). Age and gender mattered. For example, nearly four-fifths of all deaths from malnutrition in The Hague during the first half of 1945 were of people aged fifty-five years and above, while those aged twenty to thirty-nine years accounted for less than 4 percent of the total. Those who suffered most, relatively speaking, were adult males from working-class households. Deaths in working-class households were also more likely to be from malnutrition, although the number of deaths in The Hague due to malnutrition was also significant in middle-class households, reaching two-fifths at the peak in April.[78]

Here is a piece of oral history from the town of De Bilt on the outskirts of Utrecht:

> My father went on his bicycle with massive tires on his way to Gelderland and I believe also to Friesland, to buy food. Many people made such "hunger journeys." It's hard to imagine; such trips when he himself was so hungry. In the beginning, he brought some coffee and tea from home, as he worked at an office that traded in those goods. The farmers gladly exchanged them for potatoes. When that source ran out, he took my mother's gold watch to barter. It was her wedding present. My mother and father also bought flower bulbs and sugar beets somewhere. Those flower bulbs were fried in a little rapeseed oil or boiled, but that made us sick. The sugar beets were also cooked and we made syrup and a kind of pulp from it. We even went to beg people for pulp. In the evenings at an oil pit we sometimes sat around the table singing.[79]

ITALY

In two of the countries at war, Italy and France, the classic symptoms of biblical famine may have been missing during World War II, but the lack of food is reflected in reductions in births and increases in infant and child mortality.[80] In Italy food consumption per capita fell from a pre–World War II daily mean of about 2,600 calories to 2,000 by 1943 and 1,733 in 1945, with the share of calories derived from protein falling in tandem. Official efforts at providing basic food requirements at regulated prices failed miserably. Both infant mortality and deaths from infectious and respiratory diseases rose, first in the Southern Italy, then in the North.[81] Soon after arriving in Naples in October 1944, British army intelligence officer Norman Lewis observed a "remarkable spectacle" of "hundreds, possibly thousands" of Neapolitans searching for edible plants in roadside fields some ten to twelve kilometers from the city. Among the fifteen or so plants being collected, Lewis recognized only dandelions. Meanwhile, "innumerable children" were reduced to gathering limpets along the seashore at Santa Lucia and butchers to selling chickens' heads and gizzards. The near-starvation was reflected in increases in infant mortality, in decreases in the heights of children, and in widespread prostitution and petty crime.[82]

In late 1945 the *Monthly Labor Review*, published by the U.S. Bureau of Labor Statistics, offered an insight into the impact of food shortages on mortality in Rome. In 1944 the death rate in the Eternal City was 50 percent above its prewar rate, and births exceeded deaths for the first time since the flu pandemic of 1918: "The infant mortality rate is reported to be approximately 50 percent; and the press states that in one foundling home 40 percent of the children are dying of malnutrition."[83] An indication of the increasing privation in northeastern Italy is the rising share of household income spent on food. An invaluable survey of household budgets carried out in Trieste and its hinterland in 1942–43 shows that for the poorest households the share rose from 55.9 to 61 percent between 1942 and 1943; for the very richest, increasingly reliant on the black market, the share rose from 32.7 to 54.8 percent.[84]

FRANCE

In France the situation throughout most of the war was described by the minister responsible for food supplies during the second collaborationist government led by Pierre Laval, Max Bonnefous, as "slow famine." In a speech to the municipal council of Paris in June 1943, he referred to ten million French citizens with "only their ration tickets to subsist on."[85] Rationing under German occupation was quite ineffective,[86] however, and yielded inadequate calories—an average of 1,180 in 1941–44—with resultant increases in mortality in some areas. Aggregate data on births and deaths before and during the war reveal the emergence of a classic pattern consistent with famine conditions (figure 2.10), with the death rate peaking and conceptions at their lowest point in 1940. The trends in infant mortality were different, with the infant mortality rate of births within marriage peaking in 1940 and 1945 and those of more vulnerable single mothers worsening as the war wore on.

Although about half of the civilian demographic deficit was due to the Holocaust and the bombing of civilians after D-Day, that still leaves about 150,000, attributable to a combination of excess deaths and lower fertility. That figure includes one category of deaths that is easier to measure: about 45,000 resulting from the literal starvation of inmates in France's mental hospitals, leaving room for a similar or somewhat higher number of hunger-related deaths elsewhere. The deaths in psychiatric institutions are discussed separately below.

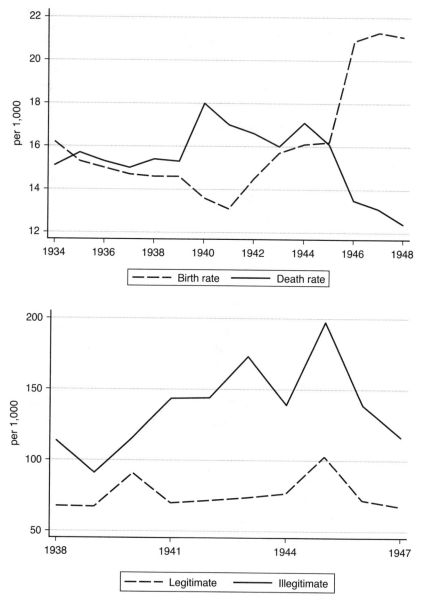

FIGURE 2.10. Birth and death rates in France 1934–47
Source: Derived from Mitchell 1975: 115 (military losses excluded); Rollet et de Luca 2005: 264, 276

THE SOVIET UNION

As during World War I and in its wake, Soviet civilians suffered most during World War II. Most of the deaths there were in German-occupied areas, with Ukraine particularly badly affected. In the besieged Soviet Union, the suffering in Leningrad in 1941–43 is best known, but hunger and starvation were widespread until very near the end of the war, particularly in the cities. A lower-bound estimate of deaths in Leningrad is 0.7 million, but many more Leningraders perished during or in the wake of evacuation. And hundreds of thousands of Soviet civilians perished elsewhere of starvation and tuberculosis. Particularly at risk were prisoners in the gulags and displaced minorities such as ethnic Germans and Chechens. Rewarding white-collar officials and healthy and productive *Stakhanovite* workers with food may have been good for overall labor productivity—although this is debatable—but it further compromised the vulnerability of the weak. We put the total in the unoccupied Soviet Union at 2 million. The impact of the famine blockade in Leningrad reached its height in 1941 and 1942, as reflected in the fall in the number of registered births from 4,229 in January 1942 to 109 in December 1942, but deaths elsewhere in the Soviet Union peaked in 1943. Deaths would undoubtedly have been higher but for strenuous and broadly successful efforts to keep infectious diseases at bay. There was no cure for typhus at the time apart from symptomatic treatments,[87] so great efforts were put into tracing sources of the disease.[88] More generally, benign weather and a massive increase in reliance on the potato also helped to keep famine mortality down.[89]

That the civilian death toll in the Soviet Union dwarfed civilian casualties anywhere else during World War II is not in doubt, but estimates vary widely, from 7 to 20 million. Since the 1990s Soviet sources have reckoned their number at 11.5–12 million (with an added 2 million deaths in German labor camps),[90] while a recent estimate by Donald Filtzer and Wendy Goldman suggests that 14 million died from starvation or violence. Mark Harrison opts for a round 25 million "plus or minus a million" excess deaths in total, including military casualties. These figures include the deaths of victims of the Leningrad blockade and of the Holocaust, of shootings and bombings and of malnutrition in German labor camps; they also include men enlisted in anti-Soviet forces and nonconscripted partisans.[91] Deaths from hunger and related diseases may have reached 6 to 8 million, mostly in areas occupied by the German army. Between mid-1941 and the end of 1942, excess mortality was mainly confined to the very young and very old and to those with predisposing illnesses. Food supplies reached their nadir in 1943, when the group to suffer most was adult males, and the main causes of their deaths were starvation and tuberculosis.[92]

Were it not for the role played by the potato, the situation in the Soviet Union would have been much worse (table 2.6). Acreage and output were hit by the Nazi occupation of the Soviet Union's most fertile land in 1941–42, but output in the Soviet zone rose considerably thereafter to 1945. Urbanites, predominantly female, were instructed in how to grow potatoes. Wherever there were vacant spaces, households were assigned plots to grow vegetables, especially potatoes. The word came from on high that "if you want to participate in the victory over the Fascists, you must plant as many potatoes as possible," and the proportion of households with a garden plot reached almost two-fifths in 1943.[93] The area under potatoes in 'victory gardens' rose from 150,000 hectares in 1942 to 243,000 hectares in 1943.[94] Those totals represented 18 and 24 percent of all land in garden plots in 1942 and 1943, although only a small fraction of the total acreage was under potatoes. By 1943 potato consumption per inhabitant from garden plots was 52 kilograms, but with a very wide variation across republics and districts. In Siberia, the annual consumption per capita exceeded 100 kilograms, whereas it was zero or minimal in the Turkic republics and in Georgia.[95] Assuming conversion rates of 329 and 87 kilocalories per 100 grams of grain and potatoes, respectively, implies that potatoes provided 14.8 percent of the kilocalories provided by both cereals and potatoes combined in 1940. That share plummeted to 9.7 percent in 1942 but recovered again to 14.2 percent by 1945.

Table 2.7 reproduces Jacques Vallin et al.'s estimate of excess deaths in Ukraine between 1941 and 1948. Presumably, a significant proportion of these were due to famine. Three-quarters of the wartime casualties were male. A very rough estimate of the number of civilian casualties may be obtained by doubling the female totals. That would imply a toll of well over three million for 1941–45, or nearly 10 percent of Ukraine's population on the eve of the war.

We must not forget that nearly all Ukraine was occupied by the Nazis from late August 1941 and that they were not driven out entirely until the beginning of 1945. In 1941 the retreating Soviets blew up what they could not dismantle and carry with them to Russia. There was also large-scale civilian migration from Ukraine to Russia. The Nazi control of Ukrainian agriculture left the cities in a grim situation. Occupation and requisitioning not only limited food availability but destroyed farm capital, seriously hindering production. The number of tractors in collective farms fell from

TABLE 2.6. Potato production in the Soviet Union, 1940–45

Year	Area sown (1,000 ha)	Million ton	Yield [tons/ha]
1940	4,077.6	36.4	8.9
1941	4,046.0	24.7	6.1
1942	3,628.5	22.5	6.2
1943	4,419.2	30.4	6.9
1944	4,815.1	35.2	7.3
1945	5,114.3	34.7	6.8

Source: Suhara 2017.

TABLE 2.7. Excess mortality by gender in Ukraine, 1941–48 (1,000s)

Year	Males	Females
1941	1,591	242
1942	1,596	491
1943	1,057	622
1944	755	191
1945	341	135
1946	33	16
1947	174	122
1948	20	12
1941–45	5,339	1,682
Total	5,567	1,831

Source: Vallin et al. 2012: 70.

ninety thousand to thirty-four thousand between 1940 and 1945 and that of combine harvesters from thirty-one thousand to seven thousand.[96] The cities were particularly at risk; the death toll from famine in Kharkiv in the East was seventy to eighty thousand, and many also perished in Kiev. Vallin et al.'s numbers just about support Timothy Snyder's claim that "in absolute numbers more inhabitants of Soviet Ukraine died in the Second World War than of Soviet Russia."[97]

The famines that followed in the Soviet Union in the wake of World War II are also part of the reckoning. In February 1946, U.S. president Harry Truman warned of a global famine that "may prove to be the worst in modern times." Truman's worst fears were not realized; thanks in part to the Marshall Plan, malnutrition was widespread but famine was averted in most places.[98] Still, Tokyo suffered a severe food crisis bordering on famine in the second half of 1945, and a real famine cost up to a million lives in the Soviet Union in 1946–47. The situation in Germany, where the average ration allowance fell to eight hundred calories between April and July 1945 and was also very low (one thousand to twelve hundred calories) in the spring of 1946 and 1947, was a cause for serious concern.[99] There were widespread reports of hunger edema in Hamburg and the Ruhr, and Herbert Hoover reported in autumn 1946 that hunger had increased the death rate of those aged over seventy by two-fifths in the occupied English and American zones. There was severe hunger, certainly, but no mass starvation—and nothing to match 1918–19.[100] Soviet-occupied eastern Germany experienced hunger, too, though excess mortality is impossible to gauge. In Chemnitz in August 1946, the Soviet authorities reckoned that 600 of its population of 0.2 million were dying monthly due to malnutrition, whereas infectious diseases such as typhus, typhoid, and diphtheria were on the rise in Mecklenburg in late 1945 and early 1946, thanks probably to the immigration of refugees from Poland.[101] Much more serious was the situation in the East Prussian city of Königsberg (Kaliningrad from 1946), conquered by the Soviet army after a very bloody battle in April 1945. Civilian casualties during the fighting were very high, and deaths from hunger and starvation after the region became part of the Soviet Union, lasting into 1947, added to the death toll. A recent estimate puts the number of German dead at about 60,000. Corruption, incompetence, and a lack of resources all played a part, but it would seem, too, that the Soviets were largely indifferent to the fate of their ex-German subjects. Thus, food rations were much more generous in the Soviet occupation zone in east Germany than in Königsberg/Kaliningrad.[102] The number of German deaths from malnutrition in 1939–47 is put at 0.2 million in table 2.10 below, but this is highly speculative. These included tens of thousands who died of malnutrition in German psychiatric institutions during the war.

The Soviet famine of 1946–47 was proportionately most severe in Moldova, where 120,000, or 5 percent, of the population perished, but costliest in numbers of lives in Ukraine (360,000, or 1 percent, of the population) and elsewhere in the Soviet Union (630,000, or 0.6 percent, of the population). Excess mortality in Moldova is inferred from official data in table 2.8; this assumes that the death rate was back to normal in the fall of 1947. Donald Filtzer has likened this famine to a nuclear explosion, with its epicenter in Moldova and Ukraine but reaching out in ripples to "the very end of the USSR."[103] In a report prepared for the United Nations in early 1947, UNRRA's chief medical officer in Ukraine reported that the ration scale for workers in

TABLE 2.8. Mortality in the Moldovan Soviet Socialist Republic in 1946 and 1947

Month	1946	1947	Difference
January	4,466	19,133	14,667
February	4,347	23,791	19,444
March	5,633	25,953	20,320
April	4,588	15,034	10,446
May	3,782	14,938	10,616
June	3,676	24,701	21,085
July	5,235	16,418	11,183
August	5,313	8,346	3,033
September	4,544	5,248	704
October	5,799	[4,000]	−1,799
November	5,753	3,264	−2 489
December	9,650	[4,000]	−5,650
Total			119,637

Source: Council of Europe Parliamentary Assembly, Document 12173, March 2010, https://assembly.coe.int/nw/xml/XRef/Xref-XML2HTML-en.asp?fileid=12386&lang=en. The bracketed totals of October and December 1947 are my interpolations.

heavy industry had been reduced from the equivalent of 3,888 calories up to the end of September 1946 to 3,040 calories in February 1947; that for workers in light industry from 1,916 to 1,512 calories; and that for employees (office workers, caretakers, and the like) from 1,294 to 1,1010 calories. Open markets provided little respite. The price of bread doubled between June 1946 and February 1947, while the price of other foods hardly rose, and by the latter date cereals and sugar were unobtainable.[104]

As with all Soviet famines, the underlying causes of this famine have been bitterly disputed. Severe drought in the spring of 1946 in the wake of an occupation that left an economy flattened and twenty million dead is one possibility; official culpability for prioritizing grain exports at the expense of the starving masses is another. In 1946, for the fifth year in a row, grain output in the Soviet Union was less than half its prewar average.[105] William P. Forrest believed that in Ukraine it had taken a herculean effort to plant "over 80 percent" of the 1940 harvested area but that the crop yield per acre could not, "at the most optimistic estimate," have been much more than 40 percent that of 1940.[106] Michael Ellman does not question the severity of the harvest failure but still pronounces the famine a food availability decline (FAD) 2 famine (i.e., a famine in which alternative policies could have prevented or significantly alleviated mortality),[107] on the argument that more forceful relief could have avoided much of the mortality. The Soviets did provide some relief but not enough; Moldova's original grain procurement target was set at 265,000 tons but was reduced to 161,000 tons on June 26, 1946, and 72,000 tons on August 19, 1946. At the height of the famine, Moscow sent Alexei Kosygin, vice president of the Council of Ministers, to Moldova, where he criticized local leadership for their silence and failure to organize relief. A loan of 24,000 tons of grain was provided, and over a thousand canteens were opened all over Moldova in January–March 1947. According to local historian Igor Casu,[108] however, these measures "were not very effective in combating the famine because of a combination of bad management and theft." Stephen Wheatcroft describes the 1946–47 famine as following a Soviet pattern whereby pressures on urban food supplies led to increasing pressure on the peasantry, resulting in disaster when drought and harvest failure struck.[109] But an additional factor in 1918–22 and 1946–47 not present in 1932–33 was the impact of war and the associated reductions in production, transportation, and stocks. There was also a brutal realpolitik at work in 1946–47. The famine struck at the dawn of the Cold War, when it suited both Truman and Stalin, for different reasons, to conceal its true scope, and during what Wheatcroft dubbed "the most serious global food shortage of modern history."[110] What is not in dispute is the catastrophic outcome of Europe's last brush with biblical famine.

LENINGRAD

More has been written about the siege famine of Leningrad than perhaps any other famine discussed in this book. It is also distinctive for the sources it has generated, reflections of the city's cultural sophistication and relatively advanced economy. One of these sources is the scores of diaries kept and left behind by *blokadniki* (survivors of the blockade). These have been published separately or in anthologies, have recently been analyzed by the American historian Alexis Peri, and also inform the work of Saint Petersburg historian Sergey Yarov. Physicians living in the city during the blockade produced another unique document, a thirty-minute educational film of people suffering from nutritional dystrophy. *Distrofiia* (1943), graphic and disturbing, was intended for medical students so they would recognize the onset of dysentery and learn how to treat it before it was too late (figure 2.11).

The crisis that would soon lead to famine began when the Nazis cut off all land routes to the city on September 8, 1941. By early December, deaths

FIGURE 2.11. Leningrad, 1941–42
a. Civilians on a street, December 10, 1942 (*Source:* RIA Novosti archive, image
#2153 / Boris Kudoyarov / CC-BY-SA 3.0)
b. Bodies being gathered for mass burial (*Source:* RIA Novosti archive, image #216 /
Boris Kudoyarov / CC-BY-SA 3.0)

FIGURE 2.11. (*continued*)

c. Civilians of Leningrad fetching water from a broken water pipe, December 1941–January 1942 (*Source:* RIA Novosti archive, image #35 / Vsevolod Tarasevich / CC-BY-SA 3.0)

d. Russian civilians transporting the remains of a dead relative along Nevsky Prospect, Leningrad, April 1942 (*Source:* RIA Novosti archive, image #324 / Boris Kudoyarov / CC-BY-SA 3.0)

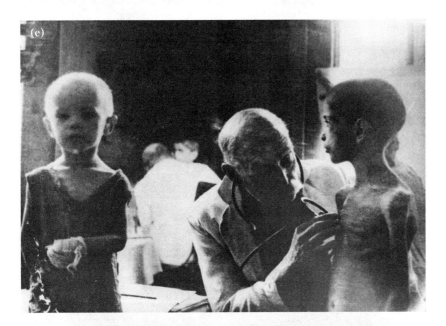

FIGURE 2.11. (*continued*)
e. Children undergoing medical examination (*Source:* Boris Utkin, "Children of Blockade. Leningrad, 1942." Collection of the Multimedia Art Museum, Moscow [MAMM])
f. The Opakhov family on a walk along a street in Leningrad, April 1942 (*Source:* A. Adamovich, D. Granin "The Blockade Book." May 1942)

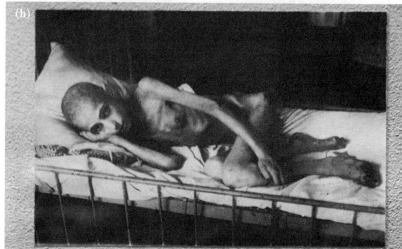

ДИСТРОФИЯ АЛИМЕНТАРНАЯ (ГОЛОДНАЯ БОЛЕЗНЬ) – НАРУШЕНИЕ ОБЩЕГО ПИТАНИЯ ОРГАНИЗМА ВСЛЕДСТВИЕ ДЛИТЕЛЬНОГО НЕДОЕДАНИЯ, КОГДА ПИЩА СОДЕРЖИТ НЕДОСТАТОЧНОЕ КОЛИЧЕСТВО КАЛОРИЙ, СРАВНИТЕЛЬНО С ЗАТРАЧИВАЕМОЙ ЭНЕРГИЕЙ. ПОСЛЕ ВОЙНЫ У ДИСТРОФИИ ПОЯВИЛОСЬ ЕЩЕ ОДНО – НЕОФИЦИАЛЬНОЕ НАЗВАНИЕ – "ЛЕНИНГРАДСКАЯ БОЛЕЗНЬ"

FIGURE 2.11. (*continued*)

g. Female workers in a factory in Leningrad, Russia, January 1, 1942 (*Source:* RIA Novosti archive, image #348 / Vsevolod Tarasevich / CC-BY-SA 3.0)

h. Patient with dystrophy (*Source:* I, George Shuklin, CC BY 2.5, via Wikimedia Commons) were averaging 954 a day and by the end of the month were 2,340 a day. Three-quarters of the deaths were from dystrophy, with deaths from inflammation of the lungs or the consumption of substitute and poor-quality foods next in line. The crisis intensified in January and February, exacerbated by a bitterly cold winter. Over 28,000 people died in the first ten days of January 1942, and during January as a whole the daily death toll averaged about 3,000, the monthly average in a normal year. The number of deaths in February matched January's, but in the spring the death rate slackened. In April monthly deaths totaled 56,000 and in May, 50,000.[111]

The authorities, by forcefully enlisting virtually the entire able-bodied population in mass cleanup campaigns organized by the local sanitary inspectorate, succeeded in keeping epidemics at bay. The clean-ups were brutally enforced by the police, with no excuses accepted for nonparticipation.[112] In April 1942 open platforms attached to the city's trams were diverted to removing garbage, ice, and snow; by mid-April about one million tons of waste material had been carried away from courtyards, bomb craters, and streets. Well might a local poet claim: "It was a stupendous feat, performed by people worn down by months of starvation. The Augean Stables were child's play in comparison."[113] The trams carried passengers once more from April 15 onward.[114]

But the city's battered and broken sanitary infrastructure would pose a serious threat in the wake of the blockade, as displaced Leningraders began to return in numbers. In the postwar city, sewerage and sanitation systems were in a state of virtual collapse, soap was scarce, and access to bathhouses and to indoor water was limited. The authorities focused on disease prevention rather than on restoring the public health infrastructure.[115]

While epidemics were prevented, scurvy was very common and so was dysentery. In a context where running water was scarce and many pipelines carrying water and sewage destroyed by bombing, outbreaks of dysentery were inevitable, although they did not reach epidemic proportions. The dysentery prevalent at the height of the famine in November 1941–March 1942 was very unusual in the clinical sense and seen as a complication arising out of nutritional dystrophy; clinicians referred to it as "starvation diarrhoea" or "colitis of the starving."[116] Scurvy was eliminated with the help of more than 16 million doses of a concoction made with pine needles, saccharine, and berry juice distributed in 1942.[117] A new nosological category, nutritional dystrophy (*alimentarnaia distrofiia*), was born in Leningrad, and the first deaths from this cause were recorded in mid-November 1941. Official data put the average weight loss across the city's population during the winter of 1941 at 22.7 percent—surely unique in the history of mankind.[118]

Appearances could sometimes be misleading. A visitor to a *banya* (public bath) in Leningrad in May 1942 "was completely astounded by the large number of well-fed Rubenesque young women with radiant bodies and glowing physiognomies." But these women were almost certainly not Leningraders but militia women sent in from outside to defend the city. Very different were the bathers described by another diarist who visited the banya on Il'ichevskii Sidestreet on March 1, 1942: "All the bathers, men and women, were so identical . . . that you wished to stand out from them immediately. Everyone is shriveled, their breasts sunken in, stomachs enormous, and instead of arms and legs [there are] just bones poking out through wrinkles, like an elephant's skin." From this *distrofik* perspective in the banya, the blockade was "a horrible equalizer."[119]

Famines always entail a hierarchy of suffering. The poorest perish, most somehow muddle through, and a small minority may even gain. In 1941–42, however, famine in Leningrad pushed virtually an entire population to the limits of human endurance. The authorities, ruthlessly and brutally, sought to stretch the miniscule supplies of food as far and as fairly as possible. Party Secretary Andrei Zhdanov would not allow "even a suspicion" of dishonesty in the state's handling of food, using local Young Communists to set traps and carry out raids. The penalty for breaches was usually death by shooting, carried out with little attention to legal niceties. Ration coupons, which were virtually the only way of obtaining food, could be redeemed in food stores or in canteens/cafeterias. Not all canteens were equally good, and some food stores might be better supplied than others. Inevitably, such differences bred favoritism and resentment. And, on the whole, rations reflected the calorific requirements imposed by work, age, and gender. Zhdanov and his popular deputy, Alexei Kuznetsov, working day and night, lived on the military ration of "a pound of bread a day plus a bowl of meat or fish soup and some *kasha*." Inevitably, there was corruption and the resentments it bred—diary accounts are full of them. But, ultimately, the problem in Leningrad was not corruption but the sheer unavailability of food: at the beginning of the war, rations were set at 1,000 grams, but when rations hit rock-bottom in November–December 1941, workers were entitled to 150–250 grams per day and public servants, children, and dependents to 125 grams per day. Workers were entitled to 1.5 kilograms of meat, 2 kilograms of noodles, 0.8 kilograms of fat, and 1.5 kilograms of sugar monthly, while civil servants were allowed 800 grams of meat, 1.5 kilograms of noodles, 400 grams of fat, and about 1.2 kilograms of sugar. Subsequent increases in the bread ration—by March 22 most workers were entitled to 600 grams of bread daily, dependents to 400 grams—increased morale, even though the death toll continued to rise.[120]

The famine was at its most intense between November 1941 and May 1942, and most of the excess mortality occurred during those months. The ice road across Lake Lagoda (discussed in chapter 6), which began to evacuate huge numbers of Leningraders from January 1942 on, provided a partial respite, though many emaciated refugees died in transit or in reception points in Vologda, Yaroslavl, and elsewhere.[121]

SPAIN

A combination of vicious civil war, misguided agricultural policies, and Allied blockade in response to the Franco regime's pro-Nazi stance produced food shortages that resulted in considerable excess mortality between 1939 and 1942.[122] Disentangling civilian from military deaths between 1936 and 1942 is not straightforward, but the number of civilian victims of malnutrition and associated diseases may well have reached 0.2 million. This famine is discussed in more detail in chapter 7.

COLONIAL FAMINES

During World War II, famines in India, Vietnam, and Java cost five to six million lives. Famine in northern China, much of which in this period was occupied by the Japanese, cost another one to two million lives. All these famines were the consequences of significant war-related FADs in ecologically fragile countries where the majority scraped a living on tiny holdings. Tawney's metaphor describing the condition of northern China's rural population in the early 1930s as resembling "that of a man standing permanently up to the neck in water, so that even a ripple is sufficient to drown him" has deservedly achieved the status of a cliché. Equally apt was the depiction of a French civil servant of the situation in Tonkin, northern Vietnam: "*Ce n'est plus de l'agriculture, c'est du jardinage* (It's no longer agriculture, it's gardening)." Nevertheless, these were FAD2 famines: in other words, policy options could have prevented or at least alleviated mass mortality, as distinct from classic FAD1 famines where feasible human actions to avoid famine are lacking.[123]

BENGAL

The Great Bengal Famine of 1943 has generated a considerable specialist literature, thanks mainly to Nobel laureate Amartya Sen, who introduced it to a global audience. Sen famously acknowledged a moderate shortfall in rice production in 1942 but largely agreed with contemporary policymakers in London, Calcutta, and Delhi in placing the main emphasis on an "exceptional shortfall in *market release*" as the cause of the famine.[124] In other words, producers either held on to more rice than normal, and/or millers and traders hoarded rice, anticipating further increases in the retail price of the grain. In Sen's account such excessive hoarding and the ensuing "administrative chaos," as the authorities sought control of the rice needed to feed Calcutta and, in particular, workers involved in war-related production, fostered the speculative purchasing and withholding of stock.

However, well-informed observers at the time reckoned that the harvest deficit was between one and two million tons, and several features of the famine suggest that hoarding was of minor importance relative to the shortfall in the main crop aman harvest.[125] First was the failure of the "food drives" launched by H. S. Suhrawardy of the Muslim League, the minister responsible for civilian food supplies in Bengal, in rural areas in June 1943 and then in Calcutta and Howrah in August 1943. Instead of unearthing vast supplies of hidden rice as Suhrawardy had predicted, the food drives laid bare the real situation.[126] Second, the huge increase in forced land sales and the rise in peasant indebtedness also suggest a poor harvest rather than hoarding. Third, the strikingly small number of traders prosecuted for profiteering in rice at the height of the crisis compared to other essential items such as kerosene, flour, and coal suggests that the authorities exaggerated the extent of rice hoarding. Finally, the movements in prices in Bengal during and after the famine are not easily squared with hoarding and speculation. Had the speculative hoarding of rice been widespread in 1943, then the market release of hoarded supplies in early 1944 (when there was a bumper crop) should have caused a much bigger than normal price drop. Although the market price of rice converged with the official controlled price at the end of 1943, prices remained higher than before 1943. As always during famines, delaying relief—in this case by denying there was a problem—cost lives. Even the well-known, graphic images of destitution published in the press came late in the day: the *Statesman*'s first were published on August 22 and *Amrita Bazar Patrika*'s (*ABP*), on August 26. Ironically, the *ABP* had published a photograph of two women taking bark off a tree for food a week previously, but that image came from China. Figure 2.12 has been copied from anthropologist Tarakchandra Das's study of destitute migrants who had come to Calcutta "for a morsel of food".[127]

The dead in Bengal were casualties of British wartime priorities. Food and ships could have been found to relieve them, at the cost of diverting

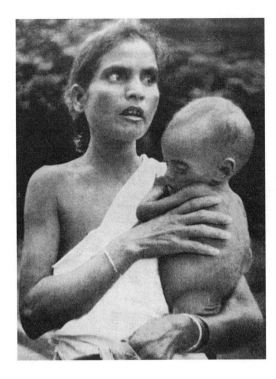

FIGURE 2.12. Bengal, 1943
Source: Das (1949: frontispiece)

resources from campaigns in North Africa and in the Mediterranean. The doctrine of "sufficiency, sufficiency, sufficiency" articulated by the colonial authorities and by Suhrawardy—that is, the assertion that there was enough food in Bengal to feed everybody if only speculation and profiteering would end—served as a rationale for inaction.[128]

British rule in Bengal before and during World War II was benign when set against the exploitative ruthlessness of the Japanese in Java and Vietnam. But the British were very concerned with Calcutta's industrial contribution to the war effort, which entailed that its workforce be well fed. Moreover, foremost in the viceroy's mind in early 1943 was that Bengal's local leaders "simply must produce more rice out of Bengal for Ceylon even if Bengal itself went short!"[129] Ceylon was strategically important due to its rubber plantations and its location as a military base.[130] It suited the authorities in London, Delhi, and Calcutta to blame the crisis that led to famine on war-induced hoarding, and public policy during the famine was based on that premise. Until the crisis degenerated into out-and-out famine, the mantra was that the problem was "grave maldistribution." And although Suhrawardy warned Delhi in early July that the province was "in the grip of a very great famine," representatives of other Indian provinces ignored him and applauded instead the claim that "the only reason why people are starving in Bengal is that there is hoarding." In late July the viceroy, Lord Linlithgow, changed his tune and demanded food imports as a matter of extreme urgency, no matter "how unpalatable this demand must be to HMG."

Too late, the secretary for state for India, Leo Amery, began to listen and to argue the case at the war cabinet. The head of British forces in India, echoing Amery's request, pleaded with London that "so far as shipping is concerned, the import of food is to my mind just as if not more important than the import of munitions." But to no avail. Another rebuff by the war cabinet prompted Amery to muse in his diary that "Winston [Churchill] may be right in saying that the starvation of anyhow under-fed Bengalis is less serious than sturdy Greeks, at any rate from the war point of view, but he makes no sufficient allowance for the sense of Empire responsibility in this country." Although in mid-October Amery was still referring in public only to "scarcity verging on famine," in private he knew that the game was up. Churchill's lack of empathy for India did not help; his immediate reaction to Amery's last-ditch plea for more shipping was "a preliminary flourish on Indians breeding like rabbits and being paid a million a day by us for doing nothing about the war." The problem in Bengal in 1943 was the imperial power's failure to make good a harvest shortfall that would have been manageable in peacetime. The situation was not helped by political divisions and communal tensions.[131]

As with many other famines, there is uncertainty and controversy about the death toll in Bengal, but Arup Maharatna's authoritative estimate is 2.1 million.[132] Famine deaths in India were not restricted to Bengal; officials reckoned there were 176,827 and 52,146 excess deaths in the states of Madras and Orissa (present-day Odisha), respectively, from May 1943 to April 1944. Like Bengal, both states had been food deficit areas in 1942–43, with Orissa, just south of Bengal, suffering from the same disastrous cyclones that had hit its neighbor. Maharatna notes that these mortality estimates for Madras and Odisha/Orissa make no allowance for underenumeration; an aggregate toll of 0.3 million or more is certainly conceivable. In addition, famine and famine-related diseases caused over 0.1 million deaths in food import–dependent Travancore, part of the present-day state of Kerala, and along India's southwestern coast generally.[133]

JAVA

Even at the best of times, most inhabitants of the densely populated Dutch East Indies island of Java (area, 138,794 kilometers squared; population, 42 million) were malnourished. Per capita calories available in 1941 averaged 2,068 across the island but with considerable interregional variation in supplies (1,341 calories in Bogor in West Java, 3,245 calories in Besuki on the northern coast of East Java, with a coefficient of variation of 0.24 across all twenty-one residencies).[134] Before the Japanese takeover in early 1942, thanks mainly to a well-organized Dutch colonial storage and redistribution system, 29 percent of Javanese rice output moved across the island in 1941.[135] However, the Japanese banned all unregulated trade during the war on pain of the death penalty, which reduced the incentive to cultivate in surplus areas, resulting in a drop of 36 percent in aggregate daily calorie supplies from the five main food crops (from 2,068 to 1,316 calories) between 1941 and 1944, and 1945 saw no respite. Moreover, the falls were regionally very uneven; calories per day in 1944 ranged from 835 in Madiun in the interior of East Java to 2,386 in Besuki, with a coefficient of variation of 0.28). Japanese policies outlawing interregional trade in rice have been blamed for exacerbating the crisis by reducing the incentive to cultivate. The revealing statistic here is that Java's cropped area fell by almost a quarter between 1941 and 1944. Severe drought in 1944 almost certainly also played a role, although it would not have affected other food crops as much as rice: data from Java's "rainfall stations" suggest that annual precipitation in 1944 was one-third below normal.[136] So great was the fall in food availability that even without Japanese requisitioning, a famine in 1944–45 would have been hard to avoid. As in Bengal, the famine prompted mass migration to the cities, notably Djakarta. But that did not prevent famine in Java from leading to nearly 2 million deaths and 1.5 million lost births.[137]

VIETNAM

The proximate cause of famine in the coastal Tonkin and northern Annam area of Vietnam was poor weather culminating in a disastrous typhoon season in 1944, which brought much flooding, major losses of cultivated land, and ensuing damage to rural infrastructure. But if adverse weather reduced food availability, it was the war that converted an undoubted crisis into a disastrous famine. Until then the aggregate reduction in output in the affected area had been modest: a decline of 12.5 percent between 1942 and 1944. But the vulnerability of the region's impoverished population to any reduction bears emphasis, as does the exacerbating factor of unusually cold weather and the collapse of imports of rice from southern Vietnam in 1942–44. That vulnerability is well captured by David Marr's calculation that dividing Tonkin's output of 1.68 million tons of paddy across the whole population of nearly ten million would have meant 171 kilograms per head until the next harvest in June 1945. Assuming that every kilogram of rice yielded 1,500 calories, even such a division of available supplies would imply a FAD of famine proportions. But given the rapacity and corruption of government officials, black marketeers, plantation owners, and rice merchants, anything approaching an equitable distribution was a utopia.[138] At the time there was uncertainty about the famine's death toll; in Vietnam itself denying a figure of two million deaths was considered tantamount to ignoring the crimes of French colonialism and Japanese fascism. Nowadays, however, it is accepted that in 1944–45 about one million or 8.3 percent of the total population of Tonkin and the two worst-affected provinces of North Annam perished. Most died next to the paddy fields, but huge numbers sought relief in Hanoi, where they also died in the thousands.[139]

Could the Tonkin famine have been prevented? In theory, emergency shipments of rice from the Mekong delta in southern Vietnam, where there was a surplus, could have been used to alleviate the FAD in the North. In practice, wartime priorities dictated otherwise. The relentless Allied bombing and mining of Vietnam's railway and coastal arteries had reduced the line from south to north into segments linked by ferries and gangs of local laborers, making north–south trade virtually impossible. Coastal shipping was constrained by mines and submarines, and traffic on the main highway linking north and south faced blown-up bridges and a scarcity of fuel. Moreover, the French colonial authorities prohibited interprovincial trade in food, and permission to trade even small quantities of rice intraprovincially was constrained by bureaucracy. Between 1941 and 1944, rice imports from the South dwindled from 186,000 tons, or enough to feed nearly a million people for a year,[140] to only 7,000 tons.[141] In March 1945 the Free French pleaded in vain for a temporary halt to U.S. bombing of northern ports, while Vichy French bureaucratic controls on the movement of rice exacerbated food shortages. By May 1945, when the Vichy French had gotten the Japanese to agree to free trade in small quantities of rice, it was too late. Marr makes a strong case for a feasible counterfactual scenario whereby French and Japanese officials could have mitigated the crisis, outlining a combination of coastal and rail facilities that could have been used and insisting on the Vietnamese civil society's eagerness to help. The problem was that neither the French nor, what mattered most, the Japanese "put a high transport priority on rice to feed starving Vietnamese civilians"; their focus throughout was on "their own military logistics."[142]

In a very interesting analysis of household-level "memory data" collected in nine high-mortality provinces during the 1990s, Gregg Huff estimated the impact of land endowments on famine deaths. The data refer to provinces with a combined population of over five million that cover two-fifths of the Tonkin and North Annam area affected by the famine. Statistical analysis suggests that possessing land led to a drop of almost one-third in death rates and, indeed, that the possession of a tiny parcel of land reduced the household death rate significantly.

Figure 2.13 describes the relationship between the decline in calorie supplies (Java) and rice output (Vietnam), on the one hand, and mortality, on the other, across administrative regions. The contrasting slopes are explained by how the impact on mortality is measured. In Vietnam it is measured by an estimate of the death rate; in Java, by the estimated percentage change in population.[143] The outcome underlines the role of food availability in both cases, although, as explained above, the reasons for the declines differ. The failure of a similar exercise for Bengal to produce a similar result may be due to the quality of the data but may also reflect the likelihood that while in non-crisis years grain flowed to deficit provinces in the East, this did not happen as usual in 1943—as implied by the huge gaps between black market prices in the west and east of the province. That the damage to the main-crop aman harvest in 1942 in those eastern provinces was proportionately lower was of little consolation to their starving inhabitants.[144]

CHINA

There is some controversy about when World War II began in China. In China itself this is often linked to the so-called Mukden Incident of September 18, 1931, which the Japanese Kwantung Army used as a pretext for occupying cities and towns along the South Manchurian Railway north of Mukden.[145] But the Japanese invasion began in earnest in July 1937, after a dispute between Chinese and Japanese troops known as the Marco Polo Bridge incident. In a desperate attempt to halt Japanese advances, the Chinese Guómíndǎng (GMD) government took the drastic step of "using water instead of soldiers" by breaching a major dike on the Yellow River at Huayuankou (Flower Garden Mouth) in Henan Province in June 1938, hoping to slow the advance of the Japanese. The ensuing catastrophic flood removed two million acres from production for nearly a decade. The flood engulfed parts of Hebei and Henan Provinces, while drought ruined crops in the neighboring province of Shandong. The combined effect resulted in nearly a million (mostly civilian) deaths in 1938–40.[146] A few years later, a combination of the effect of the Yellow River breach, a yearlong drought, and violent wartime requisitioning

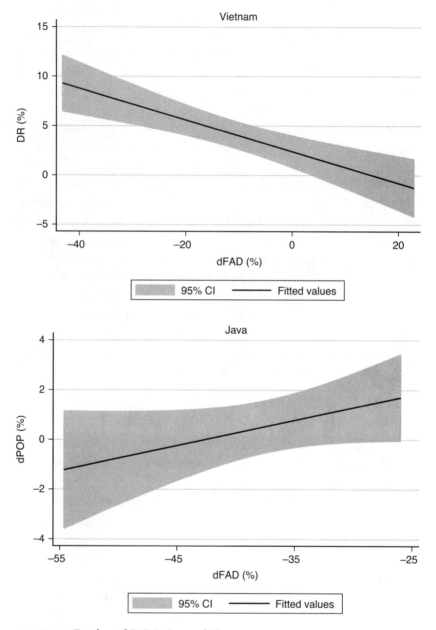

FIGURE 2.13. Deaths and FAD in Java and Vietnam
Note: DR = death rate; DFAD = change in food availability; dPOP = change in population; CI = confidence level

led to the widely reported Henan famine of 1942–43, in which another one to two million died.[147] Adverse weather, winds, and locusts cut grain yields by more than half, but the fall in output relative to before the flood was even greater: banking intelligence suggests that the autumn 1942 harvest was only 33.7 percent of the 1938–41 average.[148] Mark Baker highlights the added burden imposed by state procurements. The initial target for Henan in 1942 was 0.3 million tons or, it turned out, one-quarter of the 1942 harvest. But that was not all: local levies were added on, which "anecdotal evidence from the frontline suggests . . . could be almost as serious to cultivators' food access as the tax and purchase system."[149] As the extent of the harvest failure became clear, the requisitioning continued. Only in late September did GMD leader Chiang Kai-shek reduce the wheat requisitioning target from 0.3 million to 0.17 million tons. Baker estimates that despite this concession, "between one-fifth and one-seventh of 1942 provincial food production was requisitioned by the state, bringing average per-civilian calorie availability down from a very low 1,000–1,100 calories per day to the level of dangerous malnutrition at 800–940 daily calories per capita."[150]

The American journalist Theodore White, who was in Henan during the famine, furnished graphic accounts of parents tying children to a tree "so that they would not follow them as they went in search of food," of children being sold into slavery, and of one Mrs. Ma who was charged with eating her little girl and "merely protesting that she had not killed her." White also described a banquet in Zhengzhou to which he and a colleague had been invited by GMD officials: "We had two soups. We had spiced lotus, peppered chicken, beef and water chestnut. We had spring rolls, hot wheat buns, rice, bean-curd, chicken and fish. We had three cakes with sugar frosting."[151]

The death toll in Henan remains controversial. In March 1943, White predicted that "five million will have died by the time the new harvest is gathered," and this is the number Stephen Devereux uses in his list of major twentieth-century famines.[152] Elsewhere, White guessed that "probably two or three million had fled the province, and another two or three million had died of hunger and disease."[153] Three million is a more common estimate but, as Anthony Garnaut has noted, that figure does not derive from any demographic data. Garnaut makes the case for a much lower toll, on the basis of analysis of a contemporary Guomindang survey and birth cohorts by region in the 1980 China census. The survey proposed a figure of 1.5 million deaths, higher than the "well under one million" he suggests. Garnaut's revision is surely in the right direction; note, however, that his maps imply that the famine was not confined to Henan Province and that mortality was probably not confined to

1942. Li quotes a figure of 200 to 300,000 for famine deaths in southern Hebei province, just north of Henan province. In 1943–44 it was the turn of the southern province of Guangdong; reports of the situation there were widespread in the Western press, but no reliable estimate of the death toll is available.[154] U.S. photographer and journalist Harrison Forman wrote the following in his diary in October 1943:[155] "Toishan hills [in Guangdong Province] full of unburied bodies. Picked bones. Smell. Skulls. All poor people died off. Those starving now are middle class dying in their own homes. Too proud to beg. Sold everything. Just sit. 40% of people already died off." We propose a round figure of 5 million for famine in a land where hunger, violence, and forced migration were pervasive between 1937 and 1945. That includes about 0.5 million for the aftermath of the 1938 flood and 2 million for Henan and Hebei.

Deaths from Starvation in Psychiatric Institutions

Back in 1977 historian Jay Winter argued that World War I had a beneficial impact on the health of Britain's laboring population; only the very old, for some reason, did not share in the general improvement.[156] Mental institutions provide one small but shocking (and largely forgotten) exception to the present consensus that World War I did not increase civilian mortality in Britain. The number of inmates in such institutions did not change much during the war, but the death rate per hundred patients rose from 9.9 in 1913–14 to 12.4 in 1916 and 17.4 in 1917 and reached 20.3 percent in 1918. The last figure is somewhat inflated by deaths from influenza, but deaths from dysentery and typhoid fever were also double their 1913–14 rates in both 1917 and 1918, and the death rates from tuberculosis rose from 12.5 per thousand in 1914 to 37 per thousand in 1917 and 51.8 per thousand in 1918. Clinical psychiatrist John Crammer invoked data on the weekly food allowances for male staff and patients in Buckingham Mental Asylum to argue that the latter were effectively starved. Whereas staff were allowed the equivalent of 4,327 calories per diem, the former received only 1,580 calories. Crammer accused medical superintendents of never mentioning the word "calorie" nor of checking whether the rise in the death rate—which they were aware of—might have been diet related. Tellingly, in Scotland, where asylum diets during the war were much better, mortality hardly rose. While Crammer links the deaths directly to malnutrition, a recent monograph by Claire Hilton posits that the increases in asylum deaths stemmed from factors such as overcrowding, inexperienced staff, and "inadequate food, fuel, clothing, bathing routines and other basic amenities."[157] Assuming that the war increased mortality in mental institutions by 5 percent in 1915–18 is consistent with the former's estimate of 17,000 excess deaths.

During World War I, death rates were also high in mental hospitals and institutions in Belgium, Germany, Sweden, and, most likely, elsewhere. In Belgium, admittedly on the basis of extrapolations from partial data, over four thousand inmates of mental and psychiatric institutions are believed to have died. While mortality in Belgium generally is estimated to have risen by over 1 percent, that in mental institutions rose by 23 percent.[158] The dead in Germany included up to seventy thousand inmates of psychiatric hospitals, a key factor being that inmates of mental hospitals were provided with smaller rations than patients in general hospitals. Two features that distinguish between asylums for the "feebleminded" and hospitals for the mentally ill are noteworthy. Death rates in the asylums were lower because they were often located in rural areas and included vegetable gardens. Moreover, their smaller size may also have led to patients receiving better care.[159] Note the implication that a significant share of all hunger-related deaths in World War I Germany were of asylum inmates.

During World War II, about forty-five thousand inmates of French psychiatric institutions died of hunger-related causes.[160] The rise in deaths in mental hospitals was greatest in state-run institutions. Religious and privately run institutions fared better, but that was also the case before the war. Demographic analysis suggests that deaths peaked in 1941 but remained high while the occupation lasted, and as is common during famines, men fared worse than women. Inmates regularly visited by family members were much more likely to survive.[161] The deaths in French mental hospitals were revealed to a broader public for the first time in a dissertation by Max Lafont, an intern at the giant Vinatier mental institution near Lyon. Lafont's thesis, first published in book form as *L'extermination douce* in 1987, ascribed the deaths of inmates to cowardice and a lack of concern on the part of hospital personnel, rather than to eugenicist ideology or a deliberate Nazi-inspired policy of extermination. In the ensuing debate, however, others wrote of the *"la génocide des fous"* (the genocide of the insane) or stressed dismal conditions in mental hospitals even before the occupation and the savage budgetary constraints under which they operated during it. The issue of who was responsible is one that still rankles in France.[162]

The situation in psychiatric institutions in the Netherlands is contested. A detailed study of the Willem Arntsz Hoeve in Den Dolder (a village halfway between Amersfoort and Utrecht) by Marco Gietema and Cecile aan de Stegge paints a very bleak picture of conditions during the war by contrasting the relatively benign atmosphere of the pre-1941 period with the harsh regime imposed beginning in 1941. They found that not only did the diet and the care of inmates worsen in both quality and quantity but the transfer of workers and patients from other institutions led to extreme overcrowding. An indication of the gravity of the situation during the months of the Hunger Winter is that family visits were virtually impossible. Of the 1,163 inmates who died in the Willem Arntsz Hoeve in 1940–1945, two-fifths died during those months of famine. And while malnutrition and tuberculosis (for which malnutrition was a major risk factor) accounted for 0 and 8.9 percent of deaths, respectively, in the Hoeve in 1934–39, they accounted for 15.4 and 18.3 percent in 1940–45. However, Gietema and aan de Stegge insist that the high mortality in the Hoeve and elsewhere was not the product of the Hunger Winter per se: it was the culmination of "a long agony." They note that excess deaths from malnutrition had been on the rise in the Hoeve since 1942 and that deaths there peaked in January 1945, two months before the peak elsewhere.[163]

However, the study by Eveline Buchheim and Ralf Futselaar of Denne-noord, a psychiatric institution in the village of Zuidlaren in Drenthe Province, describes a very different outcome. Buchheim and Futselaar find that patients in Dennenoord were well looked after in very difficult conditions and that the eugenics ideas popular with the Nazis and their Dutch supporters and prevalent in German psychiatry at the time, which might have compromised the treatment of patients, held no sway there. This impression of a regime that coped well in very trying times is underlined by the fairly stable death rate among inmates: "Just like before and after the war, patients died in Zuidlaren, but not many more."[164]

Perhaps the contrasting outcomes of these two case studies highlight the risks of overgeneralization. One suspects that the two institutions in question faced different challenges. Note that while Den Dolder was located not far from the epicenter of the Hunger Winter—indeed, its railway station contains a monument commemorating the strike that sparked off the famine—Zuidlaren was located in the far north of the Netherlands, far from the suffering endured by places like Den Dolder. The Hoeve's problem (and this also applied to another institution in nearby Amersfoort) was that it was close enough to the famine zone to become a haven for refugees but not far enough to be spared hunger.

In their new survey of Dutch psychiatric institutions, Buchheim and Fut-selaar broaden the canvas, focusing particularly on four carefully selected case studies but paying attention to others as well. For instance, they describe the appalling situation in the Meer en Bosch home for victims of epilepsy in Heemstede, which was controlled by the NSB (Nationaal-Socialistische Beweging, the Dutch Nazi Party) from 1942 on. While the NSB failed to turn Meer en Bosch into an institution run on Nazi eugenics lines, the death rate under its mismanagement was high, consisting of at least 127 (relatively young) patients.[165] But Buchheim and Futselaar conclude that on the whole inmates were well cared for, that their diet was on par with other civilians, and that the high mortality rates in the institutions stemmed largely from the admission of large numbers of older adults. Combining archival evidence and statistical analysis, they estimate a proportional hazards model to test the hypothesis of whether the duration of stay in an institution increased or reduced the risk of dying. The outcome is striking. Whereas in the early years of the war there was hardly any connection between length of stay and mortality, in the final years of the war short stays were a strong predictor of mortality in all four institutions studied. This corroborates with the contemporary opinion that "many patients were already seriously ill upon arrival and therefore died quickly. In all likelihood, they died not because of conditions in the institution, but despite those conditions."[166]

Official data on the admission, presence, and deaths of patients in all Dutch psychiatric institutions show that the death rate rose from 6.6 percent in 1938–39 to 8.1 percent in 1940–41, 9.2 percent in 1942–43, and 13.2 percent in 1940–45.[167] The number of inmates rose somewhat during the war—peaking at 28,398 in 1943, compared to 26,955 in 1939—but this modest increase conceals the compositional shift toward very ill patients suffering from both dementia and malnutrition. Such inmates were more likely to die, but that does not necessarily imply adverse conditions in the institutions, though they were also bad. Thus, the wartime rise in mortality can be attributed to a combination of overcrowding in some institutions, the poor health of inmates, and the precarious situation in the country at large due to the ongoing war and occupation. Assuming a counterfactual death rate of 7 percent for 1940–45 from the data cited above implies fifty-three hundred excess deaths during World War II, with thirty-four hundred occurring in 1944 and 1945.[168] These may be classified as Hunger Winter–related deaths, due at least in part to the admission of patients who were already ill and malnourished before they arrived.

Mental institutions elsewhere in Europe during World War II were not immune either. In occupied Norway the standardized death rates of males in psychiatric hospitals rose significantly between 1936 and 1940 and 1941 and 1945 but not those of females: "Beriberi was very widespread and star-vation oedema commonplace." In Finnish mental institutions, the situation was analogous, with males again at higher risk than females. While inmates received the same inadequate rations as the civilian population, they lacked the agency to supplement them by stealth or ingenuity. In neutral Sweden, mental institutions did not experience a rise in mortality with one excep-tion, Lund's Vipeholms sjukhus.[169] Its severely handicapped patients, many of whom required special assistance in eating, were twice as likely to die in 1941 and 1942 as before the war. In Greece, where conditions in mental institutions were deplorable in normal times, half of all inmates perished during the famine winter of 1941–42, an outcome stemming from a com-bination of hunger and neglect.[170] In Italy, twenty-four thousand to thirty thousand more inmates died than would be expected on the basis of prewar data, with mortality particularly high in southern Italy.[171] The deaths in these countries were all, or nearly all, due to neglect, not eugenicist intent. The case of Germany during World War II, where starvation was used as a means of ridding institutions of ninety thousand patients with mental disabilities and illnesses, is discussed in chapter 8.

Human Behavior in Extremis

Famines produce their own heroes and villains. They transform how people behave and their view of what is moral and legitimate. Each famine produces both its tales of loyalty and decency and its tales of cruelty, callousness, infanti-cide, exploitation, prostitution, theft, and desertion. Each is specific, but most have a universal resonance. For individuals, bad behavior might increase the likelihood of survival; for society at large, it makes things worse. Describing what she witnessed in County Mayo at the height of the Great Irish Famine of the 1840s, the American evangelist and philanthropist Asenath Nicholson wrote that it had turned many of the local people into "maniacs, some des-perate, and some idiots. Human nature is coming forth in every deformity that she can put on, while in the flesh."[172] A century later and eight thousand kilometers away, the following cameo from Calcutta during the Great Bengal Famine in 1943 illustrates both the descent into tragedy and the reactions to it. It describes a woman who lived in relative comfort in a village at 24-Parganas with her husband, a peasant, and their four children:[173]

> Here is the story. . . . They had two big rooms, a kitchen, a cowshed with a pair of bullocks and a number of agricultural implements. With the

failure of [the] crop last year they had the first taste of difficulty. In the course of June, July and August 1943 they incurred a debt of 100 rupees, and they were forced to sell the pair of bullocks, tins from the roof, windows and doors of one of the rooms. In this way with some earnings of her husband as day laborer they managed with difficulty to live up to the month of August. But then it was difficult to secure any loan. Not getting a full meal every day for over a month, the husband was also unable to do any hard work. Starvation faced the family. They began to sell their household utensils, ornaments and other household furniture. But as most of the cultivators were willing to part with these articles to save them from death by starvation, there was hardly any market for them. And all these articles were sold for a paltry sum of 20 rupees only. In this way they spent another 20 days taking one meal with boiled vegetables and pulses, sometimes with half a seer [about one pound or one-half kilogram] of rice. Now the only thing left was their room in which they lived. They mortgaged it for 20 rupees at an interest of . . . 12.5 percent per month with the intention to release it with the harvesting of the next crop. But by this time rice had disappeared from the market. . . . They had no choice but to live on boiled vegetables. . . . This type of food told on the health of the whole family, and the oldest child of ten years was suddenly attacked with cholera. . . . The child died leaving them in a state of helplessness. . . . The local people . . . help[ed] them cremate the dead child. But this was not the end. In the next three days two more children died of the same disease. . . . The father, unable to bear these calamities, left the house and was not heard from ever after. Hearing this news her mother came and took her to her father's village.

Two recent studies of life in Leningrad during the blockade paint bleak pictures of human behavior under the stress caused by hunger.[174] In a fine study of Leningrad through the lens of diaries kept by *blokadniki*, Alex Peri has described the dissonance between how her diarists wanted to remember the Leningrad siege as a "heroic, triumphant battle, human resistance, collective solidarity" and the bleak and sordid realities expressed in what they wrote. Such dissonance is a common feature of living through famine. Sergey Yarov's *Leningrad, 1941–42: Morality in a City under Siege*, which also draws in part on diaries, consists "primarily [of] tales of how people changed."[175] The evidence is new and unique, but the finding is familiar to all those who have studied famines. In his unduly neglected 2006 oral-historical analysis of the blockade, James Clapperton had already highlighted the tensions—but not necessarily contradictions—between experiencing and remembering in personal accounts, between "myths of heroism," on the one hand, and "stories covering acts of cannibalism and war profiteering," on the other.[176]

One of Leningrad's many blockade diarists, Elena Kochina, gave up her career to be with her husband and child yet at the same time bickered constantly with her husband about his stealing their food. In the end she carried what little she had with her when she left the house, reckoning that strangers were less likely to steal from her than her husband. The case of Iura Riabinkin, a sixteen-year-old lad who lived with his mother and sister and kept a diary until he died in early 1942, highlights the moral dilemmas involved and the choices often made. Rabinkin wrote two months before he starved to death:[177]

> I have slid down into that abyss called depravity, where the voice of conscience is totally silent, where there is dishonesty and disgrace. I am an unworthy son to my mother and an unworthy brother to my sister. I am an egoist, a person who, in a moment of adversity, forgets all about his nearest and dearest. And, while I am behaving like this, Mother is straining herself to the breaking point . . . trying to wrench us out of here. I have lost my belief in evacuation. It has ceased to exist for me. As far as I am concerned, the entire world has turned into food. Everything that is left has food as its purpose, getting it, receiving it. . . . I am a ruined person. Life is over for me. The prospect that lies ahead of me is not life.
>
> I would like two things to happen immediately: for myself to die here and now, and for mother to read through this diary. May she curse me as a filthy, unfeeling, and hypocritical creature, let her renounce me. . . . I have sunk too low, too low. . . . What will happen next?

Blokadnik Lidiia Ginsburg noted after the city was liberated that people had committed "the strangest cruel and dishonest acts" in the struggle to survive, although they preferred to believe that they "had remained in the city, suffered, patiently endured, that they had not feared death, that they had continued to work and to participate in the course of life."[178]

In the western Netherlands during the Hunger Winter of 1944–45, it was a different story. There is plentiful evidence for communal solidarity and a highly functional civil society, and in particular great concern for children.[179] There can be no question but that the social capital of Dutch society kept mortality down for the duration of the famine. This made the Dutch famine rather exceptional, as will become even more plain below. But it is important to remember, too, that the Hunger Winter was a short famine with the prospect of liberation always in sight. As teenage diarist Iura Riabinkin confided in Leningrad, "I feel that, to turn myself back into what I used to be, there would have to be hope, the conviction that tomorrow or the day after my family and I will be evacuated."[180]

Famines make customs and taboos give way to necessity. A valuable anthropological survey carried out at the University of Calcutta of destitute immigrants living on the streets of Calcutta at the height of the Great Bengal Famine of 1943–44 revealed how the rules imposed by culture and taboo yielded to hunger during the crisis:

> Hindus and Muhammadans, Caste Hindus and Scheduled Castes—all received and consumed cooked-food sitting side by side. . . . Hindus received cooked food from Muhammadan houses and Muhammadans reciprocated it. . . . Many . . . said that when the famine would pass away they would again observe the usual caste-rules. It may be said without any fear of contradiction that the destitutes of Calcutta belonged to one caste and that was the caste of the "have-nots."[181]

The impact of the famine on feeding restrictions among the immigrants is summarized in table 2.9. Only 80 of the 565 units sampled followed the customary dietary restrictions. Caste Hindus were the most observant, but only a minority of even those followed the rules. Just over half (304/565) felt some guilt about nonobservance; Muslims were more likely to be in this category than Hindus. The many ways in which famine degraded human behavior and lowered the bar on what was deemed acceptable is also one of the costs of famine.

World War II: The Reckoning

Table 2.10 summarizes our estimates of famine deaths during World War II. Again, note that the figures are best-guess approximations. The numbers imply that famine deaths during World War II, while higher than those for World War I, are lower than the most widely quoted estimates of military deaths (twenty-one million to twenty-six million). As in World War I, the Soviet Union was hit the worst, accounting for over two-fifths of all famine deaths during World War II. During World War I, famine deaths were mostly confined to Europe. The share of what we have called colonial famines was much higher during World War II than World War I.

TABLE 2.9. Observing dietary restrictions during the Great Bengal Famine

Community	Observed	Not observed, now under pressure	No scruple	Total
Scheduled castes	35	159	101	295
Caste Hindus	29	53	42	124
Muslims	16	92	37	145
Christians			1	1
Grand total	80	304	181	565

Source: Das 1949: 88–89.

TABLE 2.10. Deaths from hunger and famine during the Second World War (1939–47)

Place	Number (m.)	Provenance, observations
Soviet Union, occupied	5 to 6	Harrison 2003: 943: "[Total] Soviet war deaths were . . . 25 million plus or minus a million."
Soviet Union, other	2	
Java	1.9	De Vries 1946; van der Eng 2024.
India, Bengal	2.1	For Bengal, "2.1 million (with an associated range of 1.8–2.4 million)" (Dyson 2018: 186).
India, elsewhere	0.4	Estimates of 176,827 in Madras and 52,146 in Orissa without accounting for underregistration (Maharatna 1996: 227); 90,000 in Travancore (Balasubramanian 2023).
China, Yellow River area, Henan, Guandong	5	Estimates for Henan range between 1 and 5 million; Garnaut (2013) reckons "well under one million" in Henan on the basis of cohort depletion analysis but stresses severity of famine in other provinces. Four million allows for other likely deaths from hunger and famine between 1937 and 1945.
Vietnam	1	Estimates range from 0.7 to 2 million; "Probably a million dead over a five-month period" (Huff 2019a).
Soviet Union, 1946–47	1	"Depending upon what is assumed to be normal mortality" (Wheatcroft 2017: 239).
Poland	0.9	Informed guesswork; see text
Greece	0.3	"No accurate figure for the whole of Greece" (Hionidou 2006: 25).
Spain	0.2	Inferred from Ortega and Silvestre 2006; see chapter 7.
Austria	0.1	Inferred
France	0.1	Includes >40,000 inmates of mental institutions
Germany	0.2	0.1 inferred plus 90,000 deaths from malnutrition in psychiatric institutions
The Netherlands	0.015 to 0.025	The Centraal Bureau voor de Statistiek reported only 8,300 deaths from hunger between December 1944 and July 1945, but "the attribution of excess deaths to famine alone is likely to remain arbitrary to some extent" (Ekamper et al. 2017).
Total	20 to 21 million	

3

The Demography of
World War Famines

The demographic aspects of the famines described in chapter 1 and chapter 2 will be further discussed here. First, the proximate causes of famine deaths will be reviewed: Did victims die of literal starvation, or as so often in the past, did they succumb to famine-related diseases? Second, age and gender patterns of mortality and the impact of famines on fertility and on the survival prospects of children, particularly on birth weights and heights, will be reviewed. The chapter will end with an account of how fetal exposure to famine during the wars compromised the adult health of some survivors.

What Did Famine Victims Die Of?

In the past, famine deaths have resulted from a variety of causes, ranging from typhus, relapsing fever, and dysentery to malaria and literal starvation. Famines have also tended to increase the number of deaths from tuberculosis (TB) where housing and sanitation are poor and from epidemic cholera, if present. Broadly speaking, the poorer the region affected, the higher the share of deaths from infectious diseases. That explains why, throughout most of history, the proximate cause of most famine deaths has been hunger-related disease rather than literal starvation.[1]

The famines of World War I were traditional in the sense that, as in the past, infectious diseases rather than strict starvation were responsible for most deaths. For example, in the city of Saratov in Russia's Volga region in 1922, 13 percent of excess deaths were linked to airborne diseases; 26 percent to water and foodborne diseases; 35 percent to other vector-borne diseases; and 16 percent to starvation and scurvy. Among the diseases, the most important were dysentery/gastroenteritis (23 percent of excess deaths), typhus (19 percent), and relapsing fever (10 percent); cholera had also played a significant role the previous year.[2]

Confusingly, the generic term "fever" or "famine fever" embraces two separate diseases, relapsing fever (known as trench fever during World War I) and typhus, which, although transmitted in the same way by body lice, were very different. Typhus was spread by biting lice carrying the bacteria *Rickettsia prowazekii*. Scratching the bites allowed their excrement to enter and infect a host's body cells. Its symptoms, which could last two weeks, were flu-like: high temperature, headaches, muscle pains, and coughing, accompanied by lethargy, brain fog, and a body rash. The bacteria (*Borrelia recurrentis*) that caused relapsing fever were transmitted by the same body lice; its symptoms included high temperature, headache, joint pain, and, in some cases, purple spots on the skin. The incubation period varied from five to ten days, and the symptoms lasted about five days. The immune system often failed to destroy all the bacteria, however, with the result that the victims "relapsed." In the era before antibiotics, both typhus (which was not subject to relapse) and relapsing fever could be lethal, but the former was far more dangerous. Being spread by the same vector, the two diseases often occurred together and were confused. But according to a distinguished epidemiologist, it was possible to distinguish between "sharp crises, relapses, and jaundice, on the one hand [and] rashes, or outstanding brain symptoms, on the other."[3]

In several countries during World War II, however, due largely to the impact of the epidemiological transition, literal starvation rather than disease was the main cause of death. A combination of medical science and public health measures helped to keep killer diseases at bay, even if it could not entirely prevent them. The European famines of World War II were all "modern" famines in this sense; literal starvation did most of the killing. The condition that killed so many of the *distrofiki* of the Leningrad/Saint Petersburg blockade gave rise to a new clinical expression, *nutritional dystrophy*.[4]

During World War I, typhus was an abiding concern. Broadly speaking, insofar as civilian populations were concerned, the saying "no famine, no fever," popularized by the prominent physician Dominic Corrigan during the Great Irish Famine, applied. Hunger weakened the immune system, and the lack of hygiene, clean clothing and bedding, and hot water led to conditions in which lice thrived. Although the role of poor hygiene and poor sanitation in the spread of typhus was well understood, there was no ready-made medical defense against it. Too late, in 1909, French microbiologist Charles-Jules-Henri Nicolle (1866–1936) discovered how typhus was transmitted, which would earn him the 1928 Nobel Prize in Medicine. The discovery in the late 1930s that dichlorodiphenyltrichloroethane (DDT) was an effective way of killing lice also came too late for World War I, and effective antibiotics against typhus were unavailable before the late 1940s.[5] Delousing helped, however, and was standard on the Western Front during World War I. The French army operated sanitary zones behind the lines, complete with mobile bathing facilities, where troops were deloused and their clothes disinfected by heating. The process was cumbersome, requiring segregation and ample facilities for heating water. Still, few if any cases of typhus occurred in either France in 1914–18 or Italy in 1918. British troops were also largely immune, and there were fewer than a thousand cases elsewhere on the Western Front, of which 221 were fatal.[6] In the East, however, despite the fact that the efficacy of delousing was understood, prevention was constrained by poverty, overcrowding, and sanitation, and it was probably civilians who suffered most. Typhus was rampant in famine-stricken Mont Lebanon in 1915–16, in Serbia in 1915–16, in contested territory elsewhere on the Eastern Front, and, in particular, in the Soviet Union in 1917–22, where it is reckoned it infected twenty to twenty-five million people and killed between two and three million.[7]

At a critical stage of the Russian Civil War in late 1919, V. I. Lenin confessed that "the *typhus* is mowing down our troops. . . . *Either the lice will defeat socialism, or socialism will defeat the lice!*"[8] Soldiers and civilians alike were at risk from the situation described by a British military officer in Rostov in December 1919: "There was no fuel to thaw water or heat it for a bath, or to wash clothes in; water pipes had frozen and burst; few people possessed spare shirts or underclothes; and as for avoiding crowds, you could not move a step without running the risk of infection. The railway stations and the trains were the worst typhus traps. Crowds of passengers and soldiers camped in the waiting rooms and public halls. The bitter weather made them keep the windows shut, and the filth, the overcrowding, and the stinking atmosphere bred lice to perfection."[9] In Ukraine, typhus accounted for over four deaths in five from infectious diseases in 1921–23; interestingly, the role played by infectious diseases in the carnage of a decade later was much smaller.[10]

In the East, transient Jewish refugees were particularly susceptible; in Warsaw in 1917, where Jews made up 35–40 percent of the population, they accounted for 11,612 of the 15,871 recorded cases of typhus. In Russia and in eastern Europe generally, anti-Semitism during the epidemic sustained "the stereotype of the dirty, louse-carrying Jew."[11] The situation in the Balkans early in the war was probably just as bad. A major typhus epidemic in Serbia killed "at least 150,000," about one-third of them captured Habsburg soldiers, and fear of infection delayed a counterattack by the Central Powers for several months. Why the Western Front was largely spared is not entirely clear, given the lousy sanitary conditions (literally) in the trenches, but the virtual eradication of typhus in the prewar period almost certainly played a part.[12]

The dysentery bacillus had been discovered by Japanese scientists in the 1890s, and the importance of sanitation, disinfection, and hospitalization was rapidly understood and acted upon. As a result, deaths from dysentery in Prussia plummeted from 1,206 in 1895 to 98 in 1912.[13] During World War I, however, tens of thousands of German troops were hospitalized for *war dysentery*, mainly on the Eastern Front and in the Balkans. The number of cases and deaths reached a peak in 1917, exacerbated by food shortages and woeful conditions on the battlefield. Civilians were not spared. Returning soldiers spread the disease in Germany itself, and there were many civilian casualties: in 1917 reported deaths from dysentery totaled 17,582. The lack of an effective vaccine was a major problem; the *Dysbakta* vaccine developed through a public-private partnership in 1917 came too late to make a difference.[14]

Infectious diseases were less deadly during World War II. However, one-third of a large sample of street destitutes—mostly migrants in search of relief—examined in Calcutta in 1943–44 tested positive for malaria, for which there was no cure at the time.[15] Malaria and "fever" were responsible for most of the excess mortality in Bengal, Vietnam, and Java during World War II.[16] But World War II also introduced a new form of "modern" famine in which most deaths were due to literal starvation, not disease. That was the case in Leningrad as described in chapter 2, in Greece in 1941–42, in the Netherlands in the spring of 1945, and in the ghettos of Warsaw, Łódź, and Vilna before their final destruction. The variation stemmed mainly from higher living standards and better sanitary conditions. In all those cases, shortages of soap and hot water made it more difficult for people to wash themselves and their clothes, previous levels of personal hygiene were difficult to maintain, and there was an infestation of fleas and lice. The main

FIGURE 3.1. Mass cleanup in Leningrad, March–April 1942
Source: RIA Novosti archive, image #36 / Vsevolod Tarasevich / CC-BY-SA 3.0

defense was "an environment virtually free from serious infectious diseases and the existing public health structures."

Still, typhus was a serious problem in the Warsaw ghetto. It is reckoned that 30–40 percent of physicians who stayed on contracted the disease and that many succumbed to it. In the autumn of 1941, a serious outbreak caused thousands of deaths. Yet the toll would likely have been much higher but for the actions taken by the *Judenrat* to reduce the transmission rate below the critical threshold.[17] In the Vilna ghetto in Lithuania, the strict public health regime enforced by the Judenrat helped contain the spread of infectious disease—so much so that "the children in fact suffered less from infestation with lice and nits than Vilna school children before the war."[18] In Leningrad, massive street cleanups in the spring of 1942 and subsequently were used to keep infections at bay (figure 3.1). This helped control the spread of typhus, but inevitably, dysentery was still common.[19]

It could have been very different in 1943 in "overcrowded, under-nourished, louse-infested" Naples, which offered an ideal environment for typhus, and indeed, a serious outbreak of typhus in the city and vicinity caused over four hundred deaths toward the end of the year. The U.S. occupiers took the threat very seriously and began a mass delousing campaign when the epidemic was at its peak (figure 3.2). By the end of May, an astounding

КРАСНАЯ АРМИЯ РАЗДАВИЛА
БЕЛОГВАРДЕЙСКИХ ПАРАЗИТОВ -
ЮДЕНИЧА, ДЕНИКИНА, КОЛЧАКА.

НОВАЯ БЕДА
НАДВИНУЛАСЬ
НА НЕЕ -
ТИФОЗНАЯ
ВОШЬ

ТОВАРИЩИ! БОРИТЕСЬ С ЗАРАЗОЙ!
УНИЧТОЖАЙТЕ ВОШЬ!

FIGURE 3.2. Typhus
a. Delousing soldiers on the Serbian front, 1916
b. Russian antilice poster, 1918–22
c. Gear being deloused (*Source:* National Museum of Health and Medicine;
Reeve 17613)

FIGURE 3.3. Soldiers dusting survivors in Bergen-Belsen with DDT
Source: United States Holocaust Memorial Museum, courtesy of National Archives and Records Administration, College Park

3,265,786 people (including many repeaters) had been dusted with antilouse powders (i.e., either DDT or the somewhat less effective MYL) at one of Naples's forty dusting stations, first with hand dust guns and later with power dusters. In 1945 the director of the public health section of the Royal Army Medical Corps, Brigadier General S. Parkinson, wrote:

> The typhus epidemic at Naples will doubtless stand out as a milestone in the field of public health and disease control. Here it was for the first time that a major epidemic of this vicious disease, which characteristically strikes men when they are down, was not merely curbed but actually brought under control by the vigorous application of delousing measures.[20]

In Germany and Austria in 1945, forced-labor and concentration camps were perfect breeding grounds for typhus. The liberation of these camps in April–May 1945 led to widespread outbreaks in surrounding areas, but the liberal use of DDT quickly brought the disease under control (figure 3.3).[21]

TABLE 3.1. Main causes of death in Athens, 1940–43

Disease	1940 and 1943	1941 and 1942	Difference	% Total
Infectious/parasitic	1,679	2,734	1,055	9.7
Typhoid	*37*	*51*	*15*	*0.1*
Typhus	*0*	*13*	*13*	*0.1*
Malaria	*13*	*61*	*49*	*0.4*
Tuberculosis	*1,276*	*2,083*	*807*	*7.4*
Other	*354*	*526*	*172*	*1.6*
Respiratory system	576	1,170	594	5.4
Digestive system	586	1,597	1,011	9.3
Circulatory system	602	1,198	596	5.5
Nervous system	460	769	308	2.8
Genito-urinary	327	719	392	3.6
Cancer	395	421	25	0.2
Senility	316	1,343	1,027	9.4
Violent deaths	357	5,801	5,444	49.9
Rheumatism et al.	336	424	89	0.8
Ill-defined	197	576	379	3.5
Total deaths	5,832	16,749	10,918	100

Source: Valaoras 1946: 221. Numbers rounded.

Table 3.1 compares the main causes of death in Athens in nonfamine (1940 and 1943) and famine (1941 and 1942) years. Note the increases in deaths from *all* causes; this was not unusual during famines in the past.[22] However, half of all the excess mortality was "violent"—that is, mainly from starvation. Hionidou's account of the situation on the islands of Syros, Mykonos, and Hios also highlights the role of starvation in excess mortality.[23] Strikingly, given the poverty of the setting, infectious diseases associated with famines in the past—typhoid, typhus, malaria[24]—barely registered, although the rise in deaths due to TB is noteworthy. The significant roles of deaths from diseases of the digestive system and senility come as no surprise, either. The contrast with the situation in Bengal in 1943 is stark (table 3.2). The classifications for Bengal are cruder, but the importance of infection in the form of malaria and cholera (in 1943) stand out.

One often lethal disease on which there are data and which reflected conditions during World War I in various countries was TB, an illness closely

TABLE 3.2. Death rates by main causes in Bengal in 1937–41, 1943, and 1944 (per 1,000 population)

Cause of death	1937–41	1943	1944	Excess in 1943	Excess in 1944
Cholera	0.73	3.60	0.82	2.87	0.09
Smallpox	0.21	0.37	2.34	0.16	2.13
Fever	6.14	7.56	6.22	1.42	0.08
Malaria	6.29	11.46	12.71	5.17	6.42
Dysentery/diarrhea	0.88	1.58	1.08	0.70	0.20
All other	5.21	7.20	5.57	1.99	0.36
All causes	19.46	31.77	28.75	12.31	9.28

Source: Derived from Maharatna 1996: 154.

linked to poor housing conditions and malnutrition. The death rate from TB had been declining before the war across all of western Europe, but the war brought that decline to a temporary halt. Mortality rates were higher in eastern than in western Europe before the war, as they would be during it. Figure 3.4*a* compares trends during the war in Belgium, Germany, and Austria, where deaths from TB rose significantly; in Ireland, England, Wales, and the United States, where they did not; and in Hungary, which lay in between. Death rates in 1918 were inflated by the influenza pandemic since some flu deaths were recorded as deaths from TB. Focusing on the change between 1913 and 1917, therefore, in proportionate terms the rise in deaths was greatest in Belgium and in Austria. In contrast, there was little change in the United States, where the impact of the war was modest in 1917, and in Ireland. National-level data are lacking for eastern Europe, where the situation was certainly worse. Figure 3.4*b* accordingly describes the trend in mortality rates in cities in Entente and Central Powers countries and in Poland. Rates rose most in Polish cities, where they were already high, doubling in Krakow and tripling in Warsaw, whereas 1 percent of the population of Łódź succumbed to the disease in 1917. Data on Poland as a whole are lacking, but in Warsaw the rise occurred in a wartime context of a doubled overall crude death rate (CDR) and a halved crude birth rate (CBR).[25] The rises in German and Habsburg cities and their timing (highest in 1917 and 1918) are also striking. Those increases were linked to a context of war, blockade, and malnutrition, if not outright biblical famine conditions. The data imply that TB mortality rates rose in Moscow and Petrograd after 1917, during the civil war.[26]

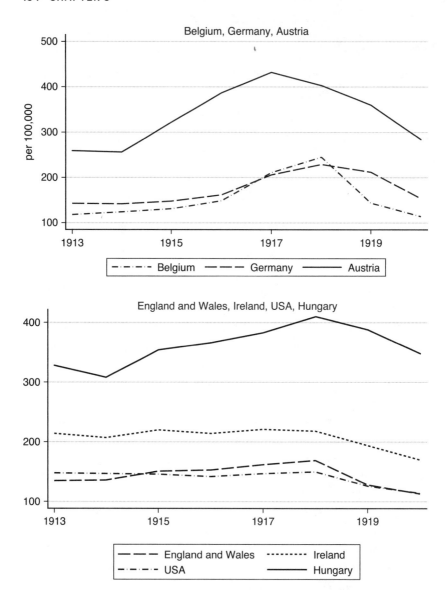

FIGURE 3.4A. The death rate from tuberculosis in selected countries during World War I
Source: Drolet 1945: 691

During World War II, death rates from TB also rose but from lower bases. The biggest recorded increase again occurred in Warsaw, rising from 150 to 500 per 100,000 between 1939 and 1944 compared to from 312 to 974 per 100,000 between 1914 and 1917. In Berlin the death rate peaked at 250 per 100,000 in 1945, up from about 80 per 100,000 before the war. Vienna and

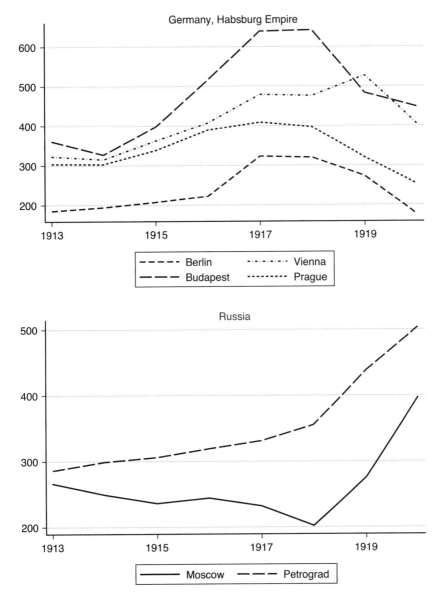

FIGURE 3.4B. Mortality from tuberculosis, 1913–20, in some major cities
Source: Drolet 1945: 692

Budapest suffered similar increases, but that in Hamburg was very modest by comparison. TB was also endemic in concentration camps; two-fifths of the autopsies carried out in Dachau after liberation found evidence of advanced TB, and many of the hundreds of TB patients in other concentration camps died soon after being liberated.[27]

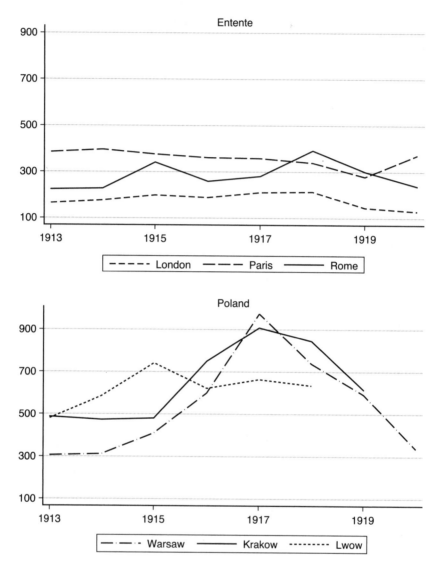

FIGURE 3.4B. (*continued*)

Patterns of Mortality: Age and Gender

Famines nearly always kill more males than females. Culture may play a part in this, but physiology is the main reason.[28] The famines of World War I and World War II display this common pattern of a female mortality advantage (figure 3.5). However, the advantage varied across countries, being much more marked in, for example, Greece than in Bengal, perhaps because starvation

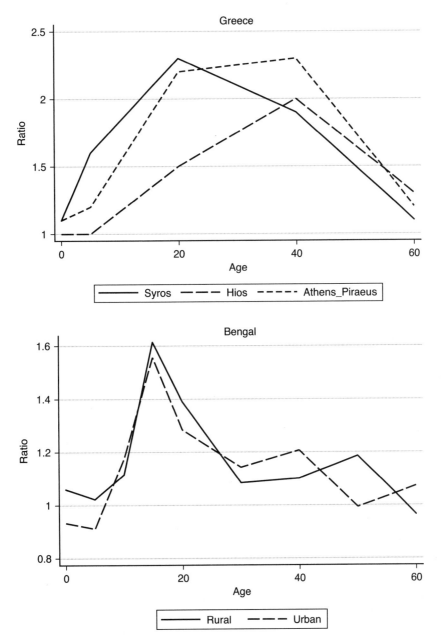

FIGURE 3.5. Age, gender, and death in Greece, Bengal, and Leningrad

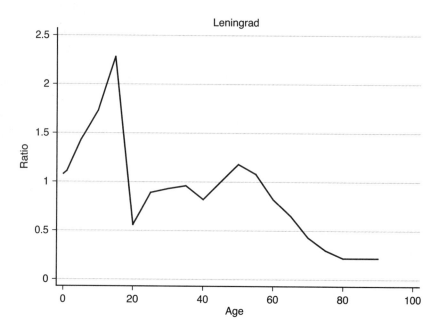

FIGURE 3.5. (*continued*)

rather than infectious disease was responsible for most deaths in the former (panels *a* and *b*).[29] In the affected provinces of the Netherlands, twice as many males as females died during the Hunger Winter; the gender gap in mortality was much more glaring than is typical during famines. In The Hague, the capital city of the Netherlands, nearly two-thirds of those who died at the famine's peak during the first three months of 1945 were male. The wartime context must partly account for this marked male disadvantage, but there was a class aspect to this too. In The Hague, the female share of deaths was 31.5 percent in working-class households, 40.2 percent in middle-class households, and 46.8 percent in the relatively small number of upper-class households. In the very different context of Bengal in 1943–44, men were more likely to perish but by a much narrower margin. In Leningrad (panel C), males in their teens were much more likely to succumb than females, but thereafter the outcome is clouded by conscription, differential migration by gender, and perhaps the higher death rates of males in the past.[30]

The war disrupted the age profile of this new form of death. In relative terms in the Netherlands, male infants, males aged 45–54 years, and males over 70 were the most vulnerable, while children of both sexes escaped lightly. This pattern may reflect, at least in part, the absence of a significant

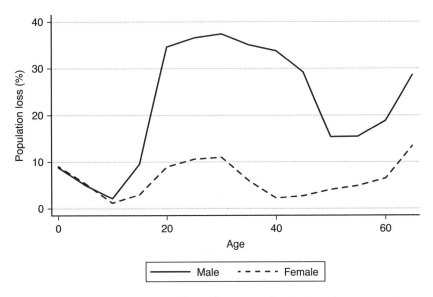

FIGURE 3.6. Demographic impact of World War II on the Soviet Union, 1940–46
Source: Andreev et al. 1992: 115,

number of younger Dutch males in forced-labor camps in Germany. By the same token, as further discussed in chapter 6, the civilian victims of aerial bombing in Europe tended to be older and female. Young children and adolescents were also at severe risk in Leningrad and on the Greek islands of Syros and Mykonos, though on the island of Chios the provision of school meals has been credited with keeping deaths in that age group down. In Greece more generally, the pattern was mixed.[31] Figure 3.6 highlights the impact of age and gender in the Soviet Union during World War II. It compares actual and counterfactual populations in 1946 by imposing 1940 mortality levels on the latter. Note that the calculation does not distinguish between civilians and combatants. The impact on males was catastrophic, with over one-third of those in their twenties and thirties lost during the war. Females were also at greatest risk in their twenties, but this was more likely due to malnutrition and famine.[32]

Infant Mortality and Fertility

Rising infant mortality rates (IMRs; figure 3.7) provide another useful demographic proxy for increasing economic hardship. Here again, trends were quite different in the two wars. By this yardstick Italy and France fared worst during World War I, being particularly badly hit in 1918, while

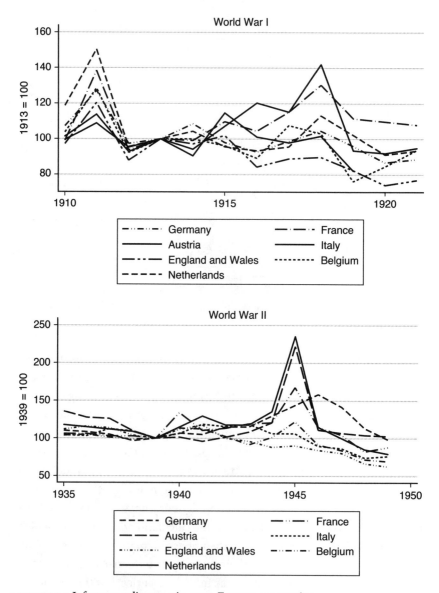

FIGURE 3.7. Infant mortality rates in seven European countries

Germany seemed to have gotten off lightly. In their study of infant mortality in Berlin during World War I, Winter and Cole infer from the data that in the capital, as elsewhere in Germany, "legitimate babies remained remarkably safe from the crisis of the war and the ensuing disturbed period." But they draw particular attention to the plight of illegitimate infants, whose life chances were severely compromised in the immediate postwar period.[33] In western Europe during World War II, IMRs did not rise appreciably, but Austrian and Dutch IMRs rose dramatically in 1945, and German rates peaked in 1946.

The contrasting impact of war in Europe on CBRs, another sensitive indicator of nutrition and economic well-being, during World War I and World War II is striking. This is described in figure 3.8 for six countries, with the requisite data. During World War I, the Netherlands, which was neutral, escaped lightly, as did England and Wales; the worst affected were Germany and Belgium, where birth rates were less than half their prewar levels in 1917 and 1918. The impact on birth rates during World War II was much lighter in the same countries. In England and Wales and in the Netherlands, a dip in 1945 was followed by a sharp rebound in 1946 and 1947. In Leningrad births plummeted in 1942, while in the three worst-affected provinces of the Netherlands they fell by 12–15 percent in the wake of the Hunger Winter of 1944–45. In both instances there was selection. Soviet physician A. N. Antonov's classic study of seventy-nine women who gave birth in a clinic in Leningrad during the second half of 1942, at the height of the German blockade of the city, is a telling if extreme case in point. Of the seventy-nine mothers, fourteen were employed in food industries (as cooks, waitresses, and so on), six were receiving military rations, seventeen were physicians, nurses, teachers, and members of other professions, fourteen were manual workers, and twenty-two were housewives. And had information been available on the occupations of the housewives' husbands, it "would doubtless have strengthened further the assumption that the food of the women who bore children . . . was considerably better than that of the other women in the city."[34] The situation that Antonov was describing was exceptional, however. Elsewhere, men being away and couples choosing not to have children in a period of uncertainty reduced the CBR, as in the United Kingdom during World War II. And in Germany during World War I, the decline in birth rates occurred early in the war, before serious food shortages set in.

Birth rates held their own or rose across the Netherlands during the early years of the war, but the Hunger Winter reversed this in the west of the country. Figure 3.9 highlights birth rates in the affected and unaffected areas. Not only was the decline in births in 1945 more marked in Nord-Holland, Zuid-Holland, and Utrecht; the rebound in the latter places in 1946 was also much more dramatic than in the other provinces.[35] That suggests that

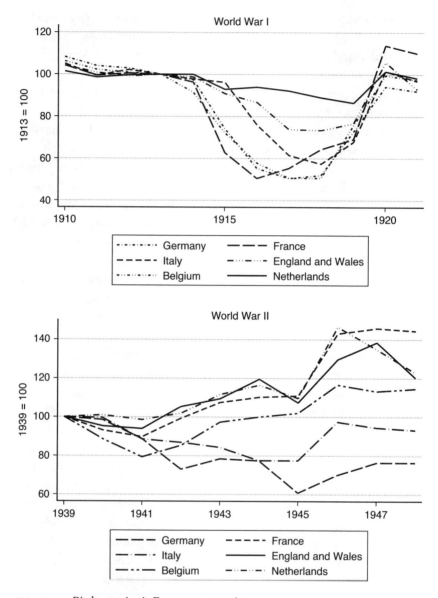

FIGURE 3.8. Birth rates in six European countries

to some extent at least, births may have been postponed rather than lost during the Hunger Winter.

Famine reduced birth rates in Greece, where it was claimed that "a psychological sterility which may have affected both sexes but was evident among women" played a role. The Greek demographer Vassilis G. Valaoras

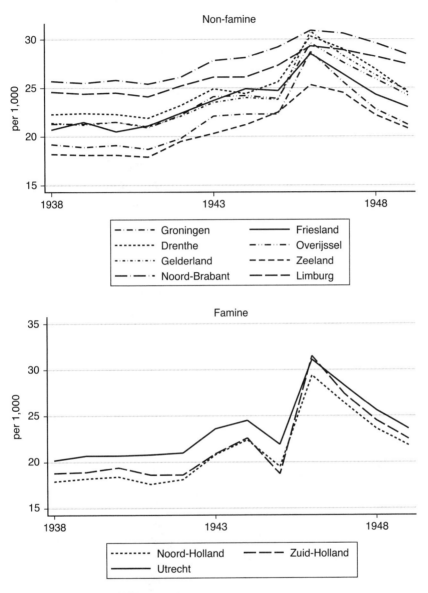

FIGURE 3.9. Birth rates in Dutch provinces, 1937–51

reported that 70 percent of women of childbearing age failed to menstruate. The birth rate recovered as relief became available: "Natality rose in two stages, firstly nine months after the introduction of regular bread rations, and secondly nine months after the introduction of regular distributions through food stores."[36]

BIRTH WEIGHTS AND HEIGHTS

The mean birth weight of a population is a sensitive indicator of the health and nutrition of its mothers and, by extension, of the broader community. Figure 3.10 describes a range of outcomes during World War II. The biggest declines in mean birth weights—about six hundred grams in each case— occurred in Leningrad in 1941–42 and in Vienna in 1944–45. The decline in mean birth weight in the western Netherlands during the Hunger Winter, represented by "Famine Area" and Rotterdam in figure 3.10a, was half to two-thirds that in Leningrad and did not last as long. These numbers mean that approximately 25 percent of Leningrad-siege infants weighed less than twenty-five hundred grams, compared to between 5 and 10 percent of Dutch infants. Declines in birth weights in Germany during and after World War II were modest by comparison (figures 3.10d and 3.10e).[37]

Famines also affected children's growth.[38] In *The Economic Consequences of the Peace*, economist John Maynard Keynes quoted this account from the *Vossische Zeitung* (June 5, 1919) about a visit to a school in Saxony:

> You think it is a kindergarten for the little ones. No, these are children of seven and eight years. Tiny faces, with large dull eyes, overshadowed by huge puffed, ricketty foreheads, their small arms just skin and bone, and above the crooked legs with their dislocated joints the swollen, pointed stomachs of the hunger œdema. . . . "You see this child here," the physician in charge explained; "it consumed an incredible amount of bread, and yet did not get any stronger. I found out that it hid all the bread it received underneath its straw mattress. The fear of hunger was so deeply rooted in the child that it collected stores instead of eating the food: a misguided animal instinct made the dread of hunger worse than the actual pangs."

Stunting was a widespread phenomenon in the wake of malnutrition during both world wars. In most Soviet cities for which data are available, children born in 1942–43 were shorter than those born in preceding or succeeding years, with occupied cities particularly badly hit. The worst affected was Leningrad: enduring and surviving the siege cut 7 centimeters off the average height of a seven-year old boy (figure 3.11a). The data refer to Leningraders born in 1936–37, 1945, and 1958. The impact on children's heights in Japan was also marked but less than in Leningrad (figure 3.11b). In the case of Italy (figure 3.11c), conscripts born in 1945 were about 1 centimeter shorter than those born before and after the war. A study of nearly five hundred women, former students of a university in Poznan born before, during, and after World War II, found that those born during the war were a significant 2 centimeters

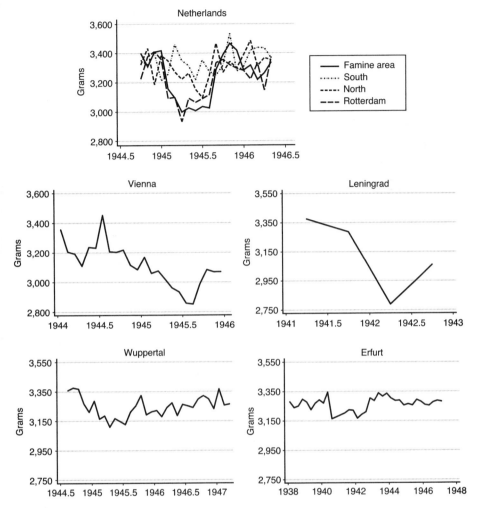

FIGURE 3.10. Birth weights during World War II
Source: Stein et al. 1975; Antonov 1947; Jürges, personal communication; Jürges 2013; Hußlein 1947 (*clockwise from top*)

shorter than the others. The outcome, the authors claim, reflects the stresses and shortages of wartime.[39] Finally, in France, too, malnutrition had its costs in terms of stunting. According to Sarah Fishman,[40] a 1942 study conducted in five industrial towns in nonoccupied Vichy France found that the average weight of boys and girls, controlling for age, was one to seven kilograms less than in 1938, and that boys were 1 to 5 centimeters and girls 1.5 to 2 centimeters shorter than in 1938. The situation in the capital was much worse. There a study of schoolboys aged fourteen to sixteen years in May 1941 found that one-fifth were growing normally and gaining weight, three-fifths were not

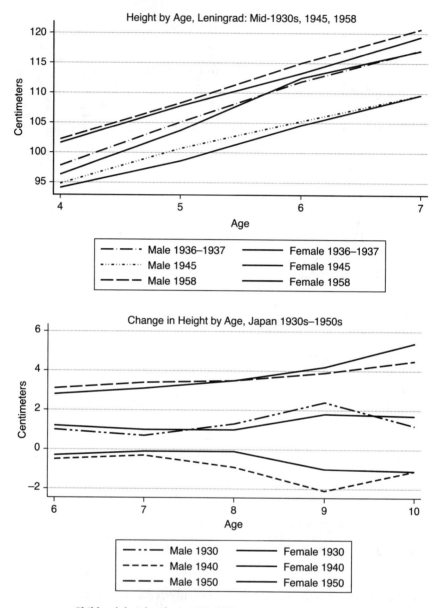

FIGURE 3.11. Children's heights during World War II
Source: Brainerd 2010: 103 (*Leningrad*); Kagawa et al. 2011 (*Japan*); Daniele and Ghezzi 2019 (*Italy*)

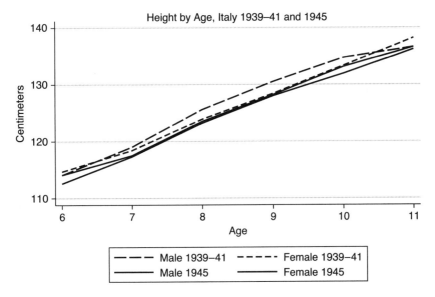

FIGURE 3.11. (*continued*)

gaining weight, and one-fifth were losing weight. Another study of children, this time in the southern city of Montpellier, found that half were suffering from vitamin A deficiency. And in the wake of the war, a study carried out on behalf of the Red Cross found that adolescents aged between thirteen and twenty-one were the group showing the strongest signs of malnutrition.

Schneider et al.'s study of the impact of World War II on the heights of Japanese children finds that the size of the penalty depends on the age at which it was incurred. For those in their late childhood or adolescence, the impact was significant—a loss of 1.7 to 3 centimeters. However, younger exposed children suffered no such penalty, suggesting that a healthy environment after the war allowed them to recoup any losses.[41] Perhaps this explains why the heights of children in Moscow, somewhat puzzlingly, were largely unaffected despite a big drop in daily calorie consumption. Fairer allocation through rationing or catchup in the wake of war could have been responsible, or alternatively, selection could have excluded some of the weaker children from the reckoning.

Fetal Exposure during Famines

The costs imposed by famines outlast them.[42] They have an afterlife in the form of the physical and mental damages inflicted on the health of those born in their wake: "Chronic, degenerative conditions of adult health . . . may be triggered by circumstance decades earlier, in utero nutrition in particular."[43] It has been widely recognized that such research on famines based especially on survivors of the Dutch Hunger Winter of 1944–45 has played an important role in providing human laboratories to study biomedical mechanisms.[44] Research based on data from the Hunger Winter and in Ukraine in 1932–33, Leningrad during World War II, and China in 1959–61 suggests that fetal exposure during a famine doubles the risk of contracting schizophrenia in adulthood and increases the risk of diabetes by 30–50 percent.[45] These findings seem robust; other findings are "still diffuse and conflicting" and have not survived careful critical scrutiny.[46]

Such research outcomes have a broad appeal. In famine historiography they have made the Dutch famine of 1944–45 much better known than, for example, the much more lethal Greek famine of 1941–43. They have prompted advice to women not to try to lose weight during pregnancy and the claim that the famine "may have accelerated brain ageing." Historian and anthropologist Jared Diamond has warned that we ignore the lessons of the Hunger Winter "only at our children's, and our grandchildren's, expense."[47] In a similar vein, a recent paper by a team of epidemiologists claims that China's current type 2 diabetes mellitus epidemic stems in part from fetal exposure to poor nutrition during the Great Leap Famine of 1959–61 and warns that famines have long-term and intergenerational consequences that pose serious risks to public health. More journalistic assertions such as "World War II Dutch Famine Babies' Brains 'Aging Faster,'" "Brief Famine May Boost Cancer Risk," and "Famine Make Future Generations Fat" have become commonplace.[48]

What are the implications of this research for the long-run cost of the famines of these two world wars? That cost may be approximated by multiplying the number of births at risk (B) by the product of the disease prevalence rate (p) and the increase in case numbers caused by a famine (d).[49]

Here we hazard very rough guesses at the impact of antenatal exposure on added cases of schizophrenia during the famines of World War I and World War II. We are not aiming for precision, but if we are willing to invoke the odds ratios generated by the epidemiological research just described (so $d = 100\%$) and $p = 0.5$, combined with estimates of the duration of the famines and the birth rate during them, we can generate rough estimates of the cost of antenatal exposure for schizophrenia.[50] Since reliable hard data on birth rates are generally lacking, here we assume an average birth rate of 20 per 1,000 across all famines, compared to a nonfamine norm of 30 per 1,000, which generates estimates of 16 and 23 million people prenatally exposed to the famines of World War I and World War II. Using $B.d.p$, this

TABLE 3.3A. Schizophrenia and Famine during World War I

Country	Mortality (millions)	Population (millions)	Famine duration (years)	Births at risk (thousands)	Schizophrenia cases (thousands)
Soviet Union	8	138	4	11,040	55
Germany	0.4	63	1	1,260	7
Austro-Hungary	0.3	15	1	300	2
Italy	0.03	37	.5	370	2
Ottoman Empire	1.5	20	2	800	4
Balkans	1.5/2	25	3	1,500	8
Africa	1	20	2	800	4
Totals	11.9/12.4			16,070	82

TABLE 3.3B. Schizophrenia and Famine during World War II

Country	Mortality (millions)	Population (millions)	Famine duration (years)	Births at risk (thousands)	Schizophrenia cases (thousands)
USSR	8	170	5	17,000	85
India, Bengal	2.1	60	1	1,200	6
India, elsewhere	0.3	40	1	800	4
China	2	35	1	700	3.5
Java	2.4	48	2	1,920	9.5
Vietnam	1	25	1	500	2.5
Greece	0.3	7	2	280	1.4
Other	1.4–2.4	40	2	80	4
Total	17.5–18.5			23,200	116

Source: Mortality estimates as in text. "Other" includes estimates of deaths in Poland and several European countries.

yields 82,000 and 116,000 extra cases of schizophrenia in adulthood in World War I and World War II, respectively (table 3.3). In itself, these are "big" numbers, but they are "small" relative to the contemporaneous aggregate death tolls from famine. And they are upper-bound measures of the likely cost because they ignore the losses of those who died before reaching an age at which they might contract schizophrenia.

A related and growing literature focuses on exposure in childhood rather than in utero. A 2013 study of the long-term effects of the Greek occupation is constrained by the data used and focuses on educational attainment as measured in the 2000 Greek census. It finds a negative effect on those in early infancy during the famine, and it was greater for urban populations, as expected. Foreign-born residents born in the same period were not affected. However, the education of those in utero during the height of the famine was not compromised. A related study using European survey data on twenty thousand adults across thirteen European countries in 2009 investigated the impact of war exposure during childhood on adult outcomes.[51] Both studies identified significant costs in terms of other economic and health outcomes. The second found that being exposed to war in childhood was linked to a higher incidence of diabetes (2.6 percentage points relative to a no-war mean of 10 percent), depression (5.8 percentage points), and self-appraisal of health (9.4 percentage points). The impact on economic outcomes was negative too, insofar as schooling (three months less) and life satisfaction (0.3 points lower relative to a mean of 7.6) were concerned, although not net worth. Note again that the focus of this research is the impact of exposure to war in childhood rather than on fetal origins and famine.

Again, a 2021 study of the Vietnam famine of 1944–45 is also concerned with early childhood rather than fetal origins. Using sample data taken from the 1989 census and two rounds (1993 and 1998) of a national survey of living standards, it links province-level paddy production data to a range of outcomes and claims to have found that the famine as proxied by food shortfalls significantly reduced body mass index, weight, height, and arm length of the affected age cohort. Exposure was also linked to lower literacy rates and lower incomes. Nor did the impact end there: the school participation of the offspring of those at risk was also lower.[52] The study by Schneider et al. of the impact of the health shock of World War II on Japanese children's growth patterns finds that those exposed in late childhood and adolescence were worst affected; they not only grew more slowly but were significantly shorter as adults. Children exposed at younger ages did not suffer the same penalty, however: improved living standards after the war enabled them to make up for any losses.[53] Again, evidence from the Leningrad blockade suggests that exposure in childhood or adolescence predicted cardiovascular disease (for men), breast cancer (for women), and higher adult blood pressure (for both), while evidence from France indicates an adverse impact of exposure under age five on a wide range of health conditions in adulthood.[54] All of these studies point to a significant health penalty following exposure to World War II during early childhood.

Finally, Jürges and Kopetsch use a huge data set comprising sixteen measures of morbidity for virtually the entire population to study the link between wartime fetal origins and adult health outcomes in Germany.[55] Their interest is in the hunger years straddling 1945–47. Changes in nutritional status are inferred from data on daily ration allowances, which plummeted to fewer than eight hundred calories between April and July 1945 and were also low (eleven hundred to twelve hundred calories) in the spring of 1946 and 1947. A drawback of this database is that literally nothing is known about the individuals other than their birth dates and a measure of their health status. Although Jürges and Kopetsch interpret their results as highlighting how extreme malnutrition increased the risk of suffering from "a range of chronic conditions," a more cautious reading of their findings yields an intriguing result: the relative morbidity risks later in life associated with an estimated five-hundred-calorie decline in daily food rations—which is considerable—tend to be positive but also modest, and in a majority of cases the change is insignificantly different from zero. In only three cases (out of forty-eight) do the odds exceed 5 percent, and in these cases the confidence intervals are particularly wide.

A concluding caution: all the studies just mentioned focus on odds ratios, not on the number of victims. And, as in cases of schizophrenia and diabetes during the Hunger Winter, the number of victims would have been small relative to the number of deaths during the crises in question.

Appendix: A Note on Neutral Ireland during World War II

Although the Irish Free State remained neutral during World War II, it did not escape the war. It was not immune from the pressures placed by the war on living standards and consumption. Incomes were squeezed, with real earnings falling significantly. In the distribution, manufacturing, and construction sectors, incomes plunged by a mighty 26–39 percent between 1938 and 1944; in agriculture they fell 9 percent; in public service they fell 24 percent; and in the higher professions, incomes decreased by one-third between 1938 and 1943. Those on middling incomes took the biggest hits, but the poor felt the hardships most. Spending on food and alcohol held up during what the Irish called the Emergency, but that on clothing fell by over a quarter and that on fuel, light, and "other goods" by two-fifths.[56] The contrast with World War I, when high food prices in Britain had boosted incomes in a largely agricultural economy, was striking. Of the European neutrals during World War II, Ireland alone suffered a reduction in both

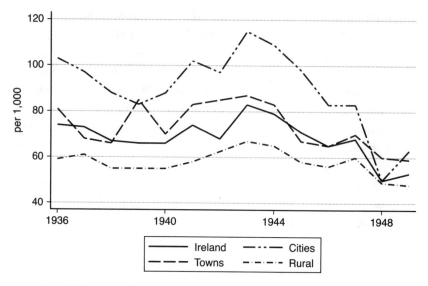

FIGURE 3.12. Infant mortality rates in Ireland, urban and rural, 1936–49

gross domestic product (GDP) and GDP per capita. The ratio of Irish to UK GDP per capita fell from about half before the war to 43 percent by 1943. The fall in personal consumption probably entailed some intrahousehold redistribution: spending on fuel and light and on clothing fell dramatically, while that on alcohol and tobacco held its own. The lack of domestic heating hurt the poor the most. Campaigning pediatrician Robert Collis described how in the wake of a cold spell in early March 1941 he used a subnormal thermometer to take the temperature of a dying infant in a Dublin maternity hospital. It registered 85°F (29.5°C). The infant's young mother revealed that "for the last ten days they had no fire in the room."[57]

The impact of the Emergency on living standards is reflected in demographic data. The IMR increased a great deal in 1943 and 1944 (figure 3.12), while the decline in the death rate from TB stalled (figure 3.13). The rise in infant mortality, mainly due to gastroenteritis, was especially severe in Dublin, where fuel and food were particularly scarce. Note also the contrasting trends in the overall mortality rate in the two Irelands (figure 3.14). While the CDR in the South did not rise during the war, its failure to fall as it did in Northern Ireland and Britain is significant. A rough comparison based on figure 3.14 suggests that the higher death rate in the South from 1942 onward cost some thousands of lives.

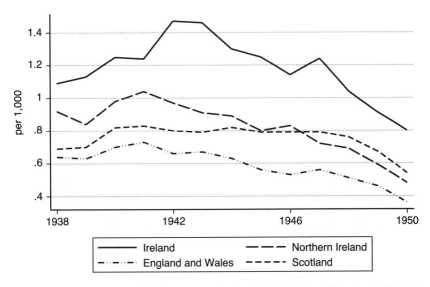

FIGURE 3.13. Tuberculosis death rates in Ireland and in the United Kingdom, 1938–50

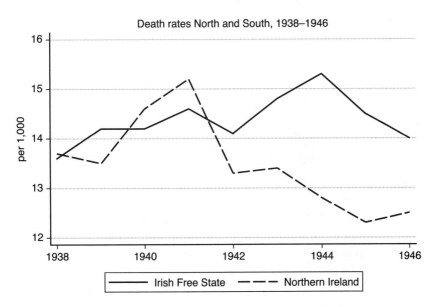

FIGURE 3.14. Death rates in the Irish Free State and Northern Ireland, 1936–46

4

The Genocides of World War I

When the Turkish authorities gave the orders for these deportations, they were merely giving the death warrant to a whole race; they understood this well, and, in their conversations with me, they made no particular attempt to conceal the fact.

—HENRY MORGENTHAU, 1918

In 1944 the Polish-Jewish jurist Raphael Lemkin (1900–1959) coined the term that would become synonymous with the Jewish Holocaust. Lemkin had been moved in childhood by the tales of Christians being fed to lions in ancient Rome, the massacre of Huguenots in sixteenth-century France, and the atrocities inflicted on Armenians and Assyrians during World War I. While studying law in Lwów (then in Poland, nowadays Lviv in Ukraine) in June 1921, he was captivated by news from Germany of the trial of Soghomon Tehlirian for the murder of the Turkish politician Talaat Pasha, the leading perpetrator behind what would later become known as the Armenian genocide. Talaat had escaped from Turkey on a German submarine just before the war ended, but a court martial set up in Istanbul at the insistence of the Allies found him guilty in absentia of the "massacre and destruction of the Armenians." Three men, including the former interim governor of Diyarbakır Province, were hanged in Istanbul in 1919 after conviction by court martial for their role in the deportation and massacre of Armenians. A British observer caustically noted "the manner in which the sentences have been apportioned among the absent and the present so as to effect a minimum of bloodshed."[1]

Tehlirian, many of whose family had perished in the genocide, was one of a group of Armenian nationalists who plotted and carried out the assassination of Talaat in Berlin on March 15, 1921. After the assassination, Tehlirian was heard saying "This is for my mother." A German court found him not guilty on the grounds of temporary insanity due to "psychological compulsion." The verdict unsettled Lemkin, who supported Tehlirian for upholding "the moral order of mankind" yet regretted his having to take the law into his own hands. "At that moment," he wrote in his unfinished autobiography, "my worries about the murder of the innocent became more meaningful to me."[2] Lemkin would not have known then that just two months after the Turks started the deportations, the Allies had announced their determination to prosecute those responsible for "those new crimes against humanity."[3]

In a presentation to a League of Nations conference in 1933, Lemkin referred to such actions as a form of "barbarity" that should be punishable by international law. His focus was on atrocities directed "against the life, the bodily integrity, liberty, dignity or the economic existence of a person belonging to . . . a human group." In 1944 Lemkin coined the term "genocide," with the Jewish Holocaust in mind, defining it in his *Axis Rule in Occupied Europe* as "a conspiracy aimed at the total destruction of a group and thus requir[ing] a concerted plan of action. It is a coordinated plan of different actions aimed at the destruction of essential foundations of the life of national groups, with the aim of annihilating the groups themselves."[4] Elsewhere, however, according to Michael Ignatieff, Lemkin argued for a broader definition: he "always believed that genocide could take non-exterminatory forms, as in the determined attempt he had seen in his native Poland to crush Polish language, culture and faith and turn a people into slaves."[5] Lemkin's campaigning culminated in the United Nations (UN) approval of the Convention on the Prevention and Punishment of Genocide on December 9, 1948. The convention defined genocides as acts "committed with intent to destroy, in whole or in part, a national, ethnical, racial or religious group."[6] Such acts included the following:

   a. Killing members of the group
   b. Causing serious bodily or mental harm to members of the group
   c. Deliberately inflicting on the group conditions of life calculated to bring about its physical destruction in whole or in part

d. Imposing measures intended to prevent births within the group
e. Forcibly transferring children of the group to another group

The UN definition was and remains controversial. It is designedly narrow and does not encompass cultural destruction or ethnic cleansing (what the British politician Lord Curzon dubbed the "unmixing of peoples") through the forcible but nonlethal transfer or expulsion of minorities (which Lemkin would have deemed genocidal acts). By design it does not cover actions against social and political groups or atrocities targeting civilians, such as aerial bombardment. Deaths that are an unplanned but inevitable by-product of a policy, such as those of millions from famine, would not qualify either. Nor would unintended deaths in the wake of the expulsion or dispersal of a minority community—though expulsion accompanied by killing members of the same community certainly would. Some hold that the UN definition is too narrow, while others claim that it must be narrow in order to be meaningful.

The UN definition was narrower than what Lemkin wanted, yet he spent the rest of his life badgering member states into ratifying the convention. With progress stalled by the Cold War, the number of signatories grew slowly; only fifty-six members had acceded or ratified it a decade later. Lemkin died suddenly in 1959, leaving unfinished a multivolume *History of Genocide*. The United Kingdom ratified the convention only in 1970 and the United States in 1988,[7] and it would not be until 1998 that an international court prosecuted anyone for genocide. In that year the International Criminal Tribunal for Rwanda found Jean-Paul Akayesu guilty of genocide and crimes against humanity in the Rwandan town of Taba, of which he was mayor.

Inevitably, the term "genocide" and its usage became highly politicized. According to Ignatieff, Lemkin would have bristled at how, on the one hand, it has been invoked and trivialized by "victim groups of all kinds [who] have pressed it into service to validate their victimization" and, on the other hand, been given a wide berth by powerful states for geopolitical reasons or because of the obligation it might impose on them to take action.[8]

As noted, Lemkin's interest in what he would come to call "genocide" preceded the Holocaust. Being a lawyer and not a historian, he was not best qualified to embark in the late 1940s on a three-volume history of genocides that remained largely unfinished when he died in 1959. The notes that he and his research assistants left behind were largely anecdotal and based mainly on uncritical readings of popular secondary sources, but they are useful for highlighting Lemkin's sense of what constituted genocide. An abiding concern was the plight of colonized indigenous groups in North and South America, in the Belgian Congo, in German Southwest Africa, and in Australasia in the nineteenth and twentieth centuries.[9]

The genocides discussed in this chapter would have qualified as such under both Lemkin's and the UN's definitions. The first, the Armenian genocide of 1915–17, was the last in the Ottoman Empire's series of bloody campaigns against Armenians. Tensions between Armenians and Ottoman Turks were of long standing, fueled by ethnoreligious hostility and economic rivalry; indeed, the atrocities of 1915–7 are at the heart of a "thirty-year genocide" described in a recent account of Ottoman campaigns against Christian minorities that ended only in 1924 and resulted in the murder of hundreds of thousands of Turkish Greeks and the expulsion of well over a million more.[10] In 1894–96 Armenians were subjected to massacres carried out under Sultan Abdul Hamid II, and thousands more perished in the pogrom of 1909 in Adana *vilayet* (province) in southeastern Anatolia. The cost in lives of these atrocities is contested. Estimates for the Hamidian massacres range widely, from 80,000 to 300,000. A German clergyman who championed the Armenian cause, Johannes Lepsius, counted 88,243 deaths and added a round 100,000 more from famine and disease, while another missionary's contemporary estimate of the carnage in Harput Province in eastern Turkey reported 29,544 Armenians killed, plus perhaps another ten thousand who died subsequently of burns, exposure, and famine.[11] On the basis of consular reports, Britain's ambassador put the toll at 100,000. A total of 100,000–140,000 seems acceptable as a cautious compromise.

The Hamidian and Adana massacres, which occurred in peacetime, would also probably qualify as genocides. Such massacres are more likely in wartime, and they were dwarfed by what lay ahead during World War I. Wars always threaten the civil rights of politicized minorities who are suspected of disloyalty or worse and allow long-standing resentments and animosities, dormant in peacetime, to become violent. Wars also generate the proverbial "fog" caused by misinformation and state censorship, in which the truth is easier to hide or distort. The fault lines in the Balkans and Anatolia during the war were ethnonational, and several parties—Ottomans, Russians, Armenians, Germans, Kurds—sought to capitalize on and exacerbate them. The Ottomans had gotten away with murder, literally, in 1894–96 and, on a lesser and more local scale, in 1909, but whether the genocide of 1915–16 would have happened on such a scale in the absence of World War I is unlikely.[12]

In 1915, on the eve of actions that would result in the expulsion and death of hundreds of thousands of non-Turkish residents, an Armenian American geographer aptly described the inhabitants of Turkey, his birthplace, as having "been welded by the run of history into a shadowy political unity which has failed to conciliate their incompatibilities of origin and ideals."[13] Decades before the war, the rise of a "Turkey for the Turks" ethnonationalism had led to outrages against minority populations.[14]

The Ottoman Empire's Armenian minority of about 2 million was concentrated in eastern Anatolia, "many of them merchants and industrialists, . . . appeared markedly better off in many ways than their Turkish neighbors, largely small peasants or ill-paid government functionaries and soldiers." The Armenians were an Eastern Christian minority. There was a legacy of mutual mistrust. For the Turks, the sense that the Armenians represented a potential fifth column was intensified by the Armenian Reform Package of February 8, 1914, whereby the European powers forced the Ottomans to grant Armenian Anatolia a degree of autonomy. The project initially envisaged the creation of a single new province headed by a non-Ottoman governor-general and incorporating the six vilayets with significant Armenian populations (in 1912 Armenians constituted two-fifths of their combined populations of 2.6 million and Kurds, one-fifth). German opposition diluted this idea by dividing the proposed region into two, with capitals in Van and Erzurum. The hard-line nationalists of the Committee on Union and Progress (CUP), also known as the Young Turks, who ruled Turkey during World War I considered the agreement a betrayal by the Armenians, and their reneging on it soon after the outbreak of war only increased Armenian alienation.

Early in the war, gains by czarist forces exacerbated Ottoman fears of Armenian betrayal. In the wake of the virtual destruction of their army at the battle of Sarikamis in eastern Anatolia in January 1915, the Ottoman leadership scapegoated the entire Armenian community for sympathizing and siding with the enemy. Some Armenians, indeed, had joined the czarist army, including Soghomon Tehlirian (see above), who served as a volunteer on the Caucasus front, and there is no denying that many Armenians in Istanbul gleefully celebrated the arrival of French and British fleets in the Dardanelles in early 1915. Such actions at a time when Ottoman armies were vulnerable on three fronts would never justify what was to unfold, but they would prove to be recipes for disaster.

The war, in effect, gave the Young Turks free rein to do as they liked. They began by removing Armenians living around the Gulf of Alexandretta (today's Iskenderun) in the Southeast, which was vulnerable to Allied attacks, and increasingly restricting the movements of the Armenian population. A series of events, including an Armenian insurrection in and around the Anatolian city of Van, the massacre of thousands of Armenians in the cities of Van, Bitlis, and Trebizond, and the arrest and subsequent execution of hundreds of Armenian intellectuals and communal leaders in Istanbul in April–May 1915, were followed by the redeployment of Armenian soldiers in the Ottoman army to labor battalions. This escalation culminated in a campaign to eradicate through forced deportation virtually the entire Armenian community of Anatolia.[15]

The deportations to what is now northern Syria and Iraq and the systematic atrocities that accompanied them, particularly the murder of adolescent and adult males, were well documented at the time. In Britain the young Arnold Toynbee's pamphlet, *Armenian Atrocities: The Murder of a Nation*, appeared before the end of 1915, and Toynbee was also a key contributor to Viscount Bryce's 684-page *The Treatment of Armenians in the Ottoman Empire, 1915–1916*, which was published as a parliamentary document in 1916. In the previous year, Bryce had been the driving force behind the 61-page *Report of the Committee on Alleged German Outrages*, an account of German atrocities in Belgium in the early months of the war. Although still dismissed purely as propaganda by those who deny the Armenian genocide, most specialists on the period would support human rights historian Michelle Tusan's claim that "as a collection of verifiable documents" Bryce's Armenian report "provided clear evidence of the first large-scale genocide of the twentieth century."[16]

According to *The Treatment of Armenians*, the expellees were distributed thinly—or marooned—across far-flung districts inhabited by people alien to them in religion, language, and culture, "the worst districts" at the government's disposal. In April 1915, Mehmet Talaat Pasha, a member of the CUP troika that ruled Turkey who was later assassinated by Tehlirian, explained the thinking behind the plan in the following extract from a coded telegram:[17]

> The objective that the government expects to achieve by the expelling of the Armenians from the areas in which they live and their transportation to other appointed areas is to ensure that this community will no longer be able to undertake initiatives and actions against the government, and that they will be brought to a state in which they will be unable to pursue their national aspirations related to advocating a government of Armenia.

Had this meant that the Young Turks' objective was just ethnic cleansing and not the eradication of Armenians as a race, their action would still have qualified as genocide by Lemkin's early definition, if not that of the UN. But the deportation, accompanied by large-scale killings both beforehand and en route, was a form of ethnic cleansing that placed no value on Armenian lives. Given the terrain they were forced through and their lack of food, sending the Armenians to Syria amounted to condemning them to death.[18] Moreover, the determination to disperse the Armenian population in a manner that would keep their share below 10 percent of the local populations in Iraq and Syria was a mathematical recipe for genocidal massacre. Whereas the Muslim population of the resettlement districts was about 2.2 million, the number of Armenians to be displaced was about 1.2 million.[19]

During World War I, about 1 million Armenian civilians perished,[20] mainly from famine-related causes, during what the *New York Times* at the time dubbed a "policy of extermination directed against the Christians of Asia Minor."[21] As a U.S. consul official explained to Henry Morgenthau Sr., U.S. ambassador to the Ottoman Empire until 1916:[22]

> The alleged destination of those sent from here is Urfa, but I know very well this does not mean the city of Urfa. . . . Whatever the destination may be, the journey from here in that direction at this season of the year is very difficult for one who has made careful preparations and travels by wagon. It is for the most part over an extremely hot plain in which there is very little water or vegetation. There are places where there is no water at all during an entire day's journey by wagon. A crowd of women and children will, of course, require several days to traverse the same distance. They cannot go from here to Urfa in less than fifteen or twenty days. There are only two towns and two or three small villages on this route. It would be impossible to find in these villages food for more than twenty or thirty people and there will be days when neither food nor water can be obtained. People on foot cannot carry enough food and water on their backs to last them between towns. . . . For people traveling as these Armenians who are going into exile will be obliged to travel it is certain death for by far the greater portion of them.

Typhus and dysentery, diseases related to forced migration and famine, were the main killers, but there were massacres too, in which members of Turkey's large Kurdish population were also complicit. In an influential account published just after the war, Morgenthau accused the Turks, by ordering the deportations, of "merely giving the death warrant to a whole race."[23] Of the 1.2 million or more who were deported, only 0.5 million were left in Syria by early 1916. That meant that "by February 1916 there was an excess of approximately 275,000 Armenians whose annihilation was deemed necessary," and that was achieved during the following six months or so by emptying the camps erected in Syria. Talet Akçam surmises that apart from the genocidal logic of the 10 percent rule, the capture of Erzurum by Russian forces in February 1916 "triggered fears" that a large Armenian population in Syria might constitute a future security risk. By 1922 there were only 0.4 million Armenians left in Turkey, and about 1 million had perished.[24] As noted earlier, the postwar Ottoman government, under Allied pressure, set up a court martial to try those responsible for the massacres. But the lack of an appropriate institutional framework to prosecute "crimes against humanity," coupled with Ottoman mishandling of the evidence and the escape of the Young Turk leadership, brought this effort at legal redress to an inglorious end (figure 4.1).[25]

Less well-known are the contemporaneous Turkish campaigns against Anatolia's Assyrian and Greek populations. Informed, dispassionate accounts of the persecution of Assyrians—a group of Syriac-speaking Christian communities scattered across Iran, Iraq, eastern Anatolia, and Syria—are few. Instead of expelling them en masse, in October 1914 the authorities embarked on a policy of plunder, terror, and the forcible resettlement of Assyrians in dispersed Muslim villages in western Anatolia. U.S. ambassador Morgenthau put the number of Greeks forced into the interior at 0.2 million to 1 million, of whom an unknown number died. Although reliable data are lacking, reports that up to 0.2 million of a population of 0.5 million died of violence, disease, and hunger during World War I are credible.[26]

And it did not end there. According to Toynbee, on the eve of World War I in western Turkey "a Greek and a Turkish population which had lived . . . side by side, on the whole peaceably, for at least five centuries—even during the wars between Greece and Turkey in 1821–9 and in 1897—[were] both seized by fits of homicidal national hatred."[27] For both sides, World War I was one phase of a long struggle stretching from the Balkan Wars of 1912–1913 to the Greco-Turkish War of 1919–1922 and the Lausanne Treaty signed on July 24, 1923, which officially sanctioned massive population transfers between both countries. Indeed, refugee movements preceded the Balkan Wars, which displaced 156,000 Greeks within Greece and a further 104,000 in Bulgaria, while more than 200,000 Balkan Turks were forced to flee to Anatolia. At a meeting in Paris in May 1919, the Allies granted Greece jurisdiction over Eastern Thrace (excluding Istanbul) and Smyrna and its hinterland, with the aim of protecting Christian minorities in those areas. Greece's quest to impose its rule over the area began triumphantly but was accompanied by massacres of Muslim civilians both as they advanced and

FIGURE 4.1 Armenia and Constantinople
a. Armenians being escorted under armed guard in Kharpert (Harput), April 1915
b. Armenian dead on a deportation route

as they retreated. Arnold Toynbee, a witness during the early summer of 1921, referred to seeing "something inhuman in the blood instincts of the hunter and in the terror of the hunted."[28]

The Greek invasion ended in what Greeks call the "Asia Minor Disaster" in Smyrna (today's Izmir) in 1922. As the victorious Turks captured the city, the Allies sought to remove citizens trapped within. At first the Allies refused to help the mainly Greek Christian population, but when a conflagration lasting several days (September 13–22, 1922) destroyed much of the city, resulting in the death by fire of perhaps 25,000 ethnic Greeks and Armenians and driving tens of thousands of would-be refugees to the harbor area, the Allies began to evacuate the Greeks and other Christian refugees from Smyrna, and 177,000 refugees of all nationalities were rescued. They did not include the thousands of adult males whom the Turks marched into the interior, where most perished. The evacuation or deportation of the remaining Greeks and Armenians brought the Hellenic presence in western Anatolia to a chaotic end, leading the Greek author Dmitri Penzopoulos to describe 1922 as "the most calamitous [year] in the whole of Hellenic history." Henry Morgenthau witnessed the arrival of some of the refugees in Athens:[29]

> The condition of these people upon their arrival in Greece was pitiable beyond description. They had been herded upon every kind of craft that could float, crowded so densely on board that in many cases they had only room to stand on deck. They were exposed alternately to the blistering sun and cold rain of variable September and October. In one case, which I myself beheld, seven thousand people were packed into a vessel that would have been crowded with a load of two thousand. In this and many other cases there was neither food to eat nor water to drink, and in numerous instances the ships were buffeted about for several days at sea before their wretched human cargo could be brought to land. Typhoid and smallpox swept through the ships. Lice infested everyone. Babes were born on board. Men and women went insane. Some leaped overboard to end their miseries in the sea. Those who survived were landed without shelter upon the open beach, loaded with filth, racked by fever, without blankets or even warm clothing, without food and without money.

The numbers, as happens so often, are in dispute, and estimates vary widely. Rummel puts the number of the Armenian and Greek civilian dead in 1919–22 at 0.4 million and 0.3 million, respectively. In their 640-page *The Thirty-Year Genocide: Turkey's Destruction of Its Christian Minorities,*

1894–1924, Morris and Ze'evi merely venture that between the Hamidian massacres of 1894 and the Lausanne Treaty, from 1.5 to 2.5 million Christians died.[30] As for forced migrations, the Greek census of 1928 put the number of refugees from all affected areas—Asia Minor, Pontus, and Eastern Thrace—at about 1.2 million, of whom 82,000 had arrived before 1922. A comparison with even conservative estimates of the number of Greeks resident in the Ottoman Empire on the eve of World War I—say, 1.3 million in Anatolia and 0.25 million in Eastern Thrace—hints at the high price of the population transfer in terms of human lives lost. The dramatic transfers of 1.2 million Greeks from Asia Minor to Greece and 0.5 million Muslims from Greece to Turkey, respectively, under the Lausanne Treaty brought these refugee movements to a definitive end. In Greece (with a population of 5.5 million) the absorption of such a massive inflow was not made any easier by the hurried departure of the refugees, who were forced to leave most of their wealth behind.[31] Toynbee, who had played a major part in exposing the Armenian genocide in 1915–16, now rounded on the Greeks, whom he deemed just as unfit as their enemies for "governing a mixed population." In defeat "the blood of their slain and the smoke of their burning cry out to Heaven," but he also added that history would not be kind to Lloyd George and his French and Italian colleagues, whose brainchild the Greek invasion had been.[32]

The internal "resettlement" and dispersal of 0.7 million Kurds, another minority suspected of disloyalty by the Young Turks (although Kurds had been heavily involved in attacks against Christians both before and during World War I), from eastern Anatolia in late 1916 to, first, the Urfa region of southeastern Turkey and later, in 1917, to the Konya plain in central Anatolia also led to significant mortality from disease and famine.[33] In all, the ethnic cleansings, expulsions, massacres, and genocides described above, straddling a decade, led to the deaths of perhaps 1.5 million people and the displacement of millions more.

Apart from mass killings in the Ottoman Empire, about 0.1 million Jews perished in pogroms during the Soviet civil war of 1918–21, mostly in Ukraine. From early on many in the majority population considered Jews to be disloyal and pro-Communist, and earlier czarist-era anti-Semitic tropes of Jews as "leeches, who sucked the blood of the peasant and robbed him of the fruits of his economic activity" soon morphed into new anti–Judeo-Bolshevik conspiracy theories. What began as isolated attacks on Jews and their property in late 1918 grew into concerted terror against them across Ukraine in 1919, resulting not only in tens of thousands of deaths but in

TABLE 4.1. Genocides linked to World War I

Years	Victims	Location	Deaths (1,000s)
1894–96, 1909	Armenians	Ottoman Empire	100–140
1915–16	Armenians	Ottoman Empire	1,000
1914–18	Assyrians, Greeks	Ottoman Empire	200
1917–18	Kurds	Ottoman Empire	?
1919–20	Jews	Ukraine	100
1919–23	Armenians, Greeks	Ottoman Empire	500–700
			2,000

Sources: Mayersen 2018: 161–62; Bloxham 2003, 2005: 51; Bloxham and Kieser 2014; Morris and Ze'evi 2019; Heifetz 1921: 180. For more detail, see text.

large-scale displacement and expulsion. The genocidal terror of this period, for which Ukrainian nationalist forces under Symon Petliura were widely blamed, prefigured the even more murderous events of 1941–42. Petliura was shot and killed in Paris in 1926 by Samuel "Sholem" Schwartzbard, who had lost family in the pogroms. Like Soghomon Tehlirian, Schwartzbard was acquitted by the court. Petliura's legacy and his role in the genocidal attacks on Jews in Ukraine are still contested.[34]

All the estimated death tolls discussed above are rough approximations; in reading them in combination with table 4.1, this should not be forgotten. Still, an aggregate figure of 2 million is credible.

5

The Jewish Holocaust

What Winston Churchill described to a close confidant in July 1944 as "probably the greatest and most horrible single crime in the whole history of the world" is the main focus of this chapter.[1] The literature on the Jewish Holocaust is enormous,[2] befitting what Primo Levi, an illustrious survivor, has similarly described as "the greatest crime in the history of humanity."[3] That literature has spawned its share of controversies, some very bitter and some of which impinge on what follows. Many details will already be familiar to readers. Our discussion will center mainly on the death toll and on some of its demographics and its determinants in the countries concerned.[4]

Although virulent anti-Semitism was widespread in Germany and elsewhere in Europe during the decades leading up to World War II, it seems highly unlikely that the Nazis would or could have implemented their genocidal policies without World War II. The war allowed them to marshal their organizational capabilities, to mendaciously blame the Jews for the war, and, for a while, to hide news of the Holocaust from the world. Hitler may have fantasized even before writing *Mein Kampf* of his "first and foremost task . . . once I am really in power . . . [being] the annihilation of the Jews,"[5] but on assuming power in 1933, he and his followers seemed content to pursue their aim of making Germany *judenrein* by forcing German Jewry to emigrate and, in doing so, plundering them of their physical property and other assets.[6]

Escape, Flight

In *The Drowned and the Saved* (1986), Holocaust survivor Primo Levi described "Why didn't you run away . . . before the borders were closed?" as one of the questions most often put to "the saved." Prefacing his answer by noting that many of those threatened by Nazism and Fascism did leave, mainly political exiles and intellectuals, he puzzled over why most of those at risk stayed:[7]

> To ask oneself and us why is once again the sign of a stereotyped and anachronistic conception of history; more simply put, of a widespread ignorance and forgetfulness, which tends to increase as the events recede further into the past. The Europe of 1930–1940 was not today's Europe. To emigrate was always painful; at that time it was also more difficult and more costly than it is now. To emigrate one needed a lot of money, but also a "bridgehead" in the country of destination: relatives or friends willing to offer sponsorship and/or hospitality. . . . Confronted by Hitler, the majority of indigenous Jews in Italy, France, Poland, and Germany itself chose to remain in what they felt was their *patria* for reasons that to a great extent were held in common.

Levi added that German Jews were "organically incapable of conceiving of a terrorism directed by the state even when it was already all round them."[8]

Levi's evocative account oversimplifies. It underestimates both the extent of Jewish emigration from Germany from 1933 on and the desperation of German Jewry to leave after the *Novemberpogrome* or *Kristallnacht* (The Night of [Broken] Glass) of November 9–10, 1938. It also underestimates the difficulties of escaping from France, the Low Countries, Czechoslovakia, Greece, Poland, and elsewhere when "confronted by Hitler," and it forgets both that Italian Jews were relatively safe until the Nazis took over much of northern Italy after the Fascists capitulated in September 1943 and that some thousands emigrated in the wake of the anti-Semitic legislation passed in Italy in 1938–39. Indeed, one of the ironies of the fate of German and Austrian Jews is that, thanks to emigration, a higher proportion of them survived than of Jews in most of the places the Nazis occupied during World War II. The main reason for this is that three-fifths of German Jewry, or over 0.3 million, managed to flee before September 1939. Of the fewer than 0.2 million remaining in Germany when escape was no longer possible, 165,000 perished. And because those who escaped were more likely to be young and male, the unfortunates who perished during the Holocaust were disproportionately older and female. As Walter Laqueur put it, "Of those who remained, many were old and sick or they were so poor that they could not afford the price of a visa and a ticket to their destination."[9]

Levi's account might seem to fit the earliest years of Nazi rule in Germany best. A common view in the Jewish community at that stage was that only a minority would have to leave Germany, and the rest would adjust to the more restricted economic opportunities available in the private sector. Still, 37,000 left in 1933, 23,000 in 1934, and 21,000 in 1935. Those numbers were by no means small; they represented 8, 5, and 4 percent of all German Jewry at the time. In relative terms they dwarf even the emigration rates reached in Ireland or Italy during the mass trans-Atlantic migrations of the pre-1914 era. And there were good reasons for them: from the beginning, intimidation, boycotts, and violence from below and discriminatory legislation from the authorities above made life more difficult for most Jews. The numbers of those leaving rose slightly in the wake of the promulgation on September 15, 1935, of the Nuremberg Laws, which banned marriages and sexual contacts between Jews and non-Jews, prohibited Jews from hiring German women of childbearing age, and deprived Jews of German citizenship. The laws, which acted as a template thereafter for anti-Jewish legislation wherever the Nazis ruled, caused 25,000 to leave in 1936 and 23,000 in 1937, or 6 percent of the remaining population in both years.

It bears noting here that before the outbreak of World War II and indeed until autumn 1941, the Nazis sought to use forced emigration accompanied by the expropriation of Jewish property as the main way of achieving a *judenrein* Germany (and from 1938, Austria); the Final Solution was not yet on their radar.[10] Emigration reached new heights after the murderous state-sanctioned brutality of the *Kristallnacht*, following the assassination of a German embassy official in Paris on November 7, 1938, and legislation proclaiming "The Elimination of Jews from German Economic Life," which passed on November 23, 1938. The exodus reached 40,000 in 1938 and 78,000 in 1939. But even then the Nazis were still bent on expelling the Jews and confiscating their property. Even in his infamous Reichstag speech of January 30, 1939, later interpreted by his followers as prophesizing the Final Solution, Hitler bitterly berated Western countries for their unwillingness to offer a haven to German Jews. At the outbreak of war in September 1939, Germany's Jewish population had shrunk from 0.5 million to under 0.2 million.[11]

Most of the 60,000 or so German Jews who left between Hitler's accession in 1933 and the passing of the Nuremberg Laws headed to Palestine or neighboring European countries such as France, the Netherlands, and Czechoslovakia. Most of those who found a home in Palestine did so through the controversial Haavara Transfer Agreement, negotiated between a section of the Zionist movement in Palestine and the Reich Economics Ministry in 1933, which enabled over 50,000 German Jews to emigrate there before the outbreak of war. Others sought help from the Jewish welfare agency, the Hilfsverein der deutschen Juden, which had been founded in 1901 to help *Ostjuden* and transit migrants. In the 1930s the Hilfsverein helped about 8,500 Jews to escape elsewhere in Europe and 3,600 to emigrate overseas. In addition, about 10,000 children, mainly from Germany and Austria but also from Poland and Czechoslovakia, were rescued by the scheme known as the *Kindertransport*. Funded by the Central British Fund for German Jewry and administered by the Refugee Children's Movement, the scheme originated with a group of concerned Jews and Quakers pleading with the British government to provide a temporary refuge to unaccompanied Jewish children under threat from the Nazis in the wake of *Kristallnacht*. Similar schemes enabled 1,500 Jewish children to escape to the Netherlands and 500 to Sweden. The Refugee Children's Movement's funds dried up just before the war began in September 1939 (figure 5.1).[12]

As part of a Weimar policy to deter capital flight, from 1931 onward all migrants, Jewish and non-Jewish, paid a 25 percent Reich Flight Tax (*Reichsfluchtsteuer*) on assets above 200,000 reichsmarks ($47,600) transferred out of Germany. The Nazis reduced the threshold to 50,000 reichsmarks in 1934 and amended how assets were valued to the detriment of migrants, in effect converting the tax into one targeting Jews tempted to leave out of fear. The new more confiscatory tax regime possibly deterred some from leaving in the period before the Nuremberg Laws. But the revenue raised by the tax rose from 17 million reichsmarks in 1933 to 342 million reichsmarks in 1938, most of which was extracted from Jews fleeing persecution. Nor was that all. Much of the remaining wealth of migrants was credited to blocked accounts in a bank affiliated with the German central bank. These assets could be transferred abroad on payment of an added penalty that rose from 20 percent in 1934 to 81 percent in 1936 and 96 percent in 1939.[13]

It was a far-from-ideal time for would-be escapees. The United States, for example, was a country of net *emigration* in 1931–35, and the unemployment rate in manufacturing there was still over 30 percent in 1935. The situation in

FIGURE 5.1. Getting out

a. Applicants for emigration at Hilfsverein office, Berlin, 1935 (*Source:* United States Holocaust Memorial Museum, courtesy of YIVO Institute for Jewish Research, New York)

b. *Kindertransport* refugees in Swaffham, Norfolk, September 1939 (*Source:* United States Holocaust Memorial Museum, courtesy of Ruth Wassermann Segal)

c. German immigrants having their documents checked in the port of Jaffa (*Source:* National Photo Collection Israel)

FIGURE 5.1. (*continued*)

some of the countries most likely to provide opportunities for immigrants is described in figure 5.2. While in general the worst of the Great Depression was over by the mid-1930s, unemployment was still higher almost everywhere when World War II began than it had been a decade earlier. Immigrants in general were not welcome, and several countries, notably South Africa and in much of Latin America, severely restricted immigration. In the late 1930s, Bolivia, where about ten thousand mainly Viennese Jews found refuge during World War II, was virtually the only country anywhere pursuing an open-door policy toward Jewish refugees.[14]

In 1938, U.S. president Franklin D. Roosevelt convened a meeting of delegates from over thirty countries to discuss the crisis facing would-be Jewish refugees. Alas, most delegates at the resultant conference at the French spa town of Évian on July 6–15 offered sympathy but little else. Roosevelt's promise to allow Jewish refugees to fill the annual combined

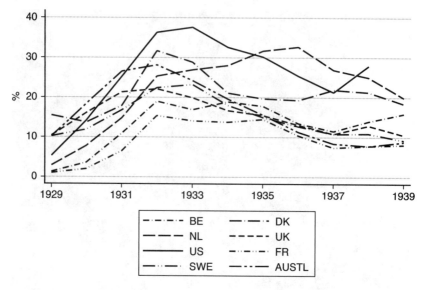

FIGURE 5.2. Unemployment rates in industry, selected countries, 1929–39
Source: Eichengreen and Hatton 1988

German and Austrian immigration quota of 30,000 for three years prompted Australia to commit to 15,000 over the same period, but Canada and France refused to make any commitments, and South Africa would allow in only relatives of those who had already immigrated there. Only the Dominican Republic displayed any enthusiasm for refugees, but few went there and fewer stayed. While some Jewish observers at Évian bewailed the reluctance of Western countries to admit refugees, Zionist observers focused only on emigration to Palestine, which Arab unrest made the British unwilling to allow. One tangible outcome of Évian was the London-based Intergovernmental Committee on Political Refugees Coming from Germany (IGCR), which sought to negotiate an emigration scheme with the Nazis that would allow Jews to leave. In response the Nazis offered a scheme that would be funded by a trust holding all Jewish wealth in Germany and whereby a state-run Office for Emigration would allow 150,000 economically active Jews to leave over a period of five years, followed by the gradual emigration of the rest. This was unacceptable to the IGCR.[15]

Table 5.1 describes the destination countries of Jewish refugees during the 1930s. In terms of absolute numbers, the United States, Palestine, and Argentina received most; relative to population, the most important were Palestine, Shanghai, the Netherlands, Argentina, Belgium, and Bolivia. The wide range of destinations is striking. Those places that took the most refugees

TABLE 5.1. Jewish refugee destinations, 1933–40

Country	Number	Per million population
Soviet Union	200,000 to 300,000	1,200 to 1,800
US	102,000	825
UK	70,000	1,525
Palestine	55,000	37,000
Argentina	45,000	3,782
Belgium	30,000	3,704
Netherlands	30,000	3,797
France	30,000	721
South Africa	26,100	2,373
Poland	25,000	887
China	20,000	6,700
Portugal	12,000	1,765
Bolivia	9,000	3,750
Australia	8,600	1,323
Brazil	8,000	238
Yugoslavia	7,000	486
Switzerland	7,000	1,707
Canada	6,000	571
Czechoslovakia	5,000	357
Italy	5,000	123
The Caribbean	3,500	1,750
Sweden	3,200	525
Syria	3,200	1,600
Hungary	3,000	349
Spain	3,000	128
Norway	2,000	714
Denmark	2,000	571
Venezuela	600	182
Philippines	700	53
Japan	"A few hundred"	.
Uruguay	20	12

Sources: Anne Frankhttps://www.annefrank.org/en/anne-frank/go-in-depth/impossibilities
-escaping-1933-1942/; Pinchuk 1978: 143–44 (on Polish Jewish refugees in the Soviet Union);
Levi 1988: 63; Ellis and Rawicki 2012. For the UK, see fn48. The population of Shanghai in the
1930s was about 3 million; that of Palestine in the mid-1930s was about 1.5 million.

relative to population were by no means the richest nor were they the nearest. A further surprise: among the most "welcoming," in terms of overall numbers though not relative to population, was the Soviet Union, which received between 157,000 and 375,000 mainly Polish refugees. The Jewish flight from Operation Barbarossa, the invasion of the Soviet Union by Nazi Germany and its allies on June 22, 1941, is described below.

The post-1932 exodus, which affected all regions of Germany, had a striking impact on the demographic profile of German Jewry on the eve of the Holocaust. In 1933 the female proportion of Germany's Jewish population was 52.2 percent; only 10.5 percent were aged over sixty-five years, and 15.9 percent were under fourteen. The census of May 17, 1939, reported 217,488 Jews living in Germany, of whom 57.5 percent were female; 21.3 percent of them were aged over sixty-five and 7.5 percent under fifteen.

In 1933–34 Germany and Austria combined contained about 0.7 million Jews. By the end of 1938, 222,500 Jews had left Germany and Austria, nearly half in 1938 alone. Of those, 61,000 headed for other European destinations; 45,000 for Palestine, 52,500 for North America, and 44,000 for Latin America.[16] Of the 0.4 million Jews who had left Germany and Austria between the Nazi takeover and September 1939, some 95,000 emigrated to the United States, 60,000 to Palestine, 50,000 to the Low Countries, 70,000 to the United Kingdom,[17] and about 75,000 to Central and South America. About another 20,000 emigrated to Shanghai, which, exceptionally, required no visas on entry.[18] By the end of 1939, the number remaining in Germany and Austria combined had fallen to fewer than 0.25 million. In 1942, when escape was no longer possible, 139,000 German Jews were left in the Reich, including about 25,000 young people. Since 1933, 278,500 had left, most of them before 1940.

Flight also saved the lives of many of Austria's 0.2 million Jews; in all over two-thirds of Austrian Jewry escaped.[19] Before the Anschluss (March 12, 1938), few left; Austrian Jews, the vast majority of whom lived in Vienna, felt relatively safe under the "middle-of-the road" anti-Semitism of Chancellors Dolfuss and von Schuschnigg. The Anschluss brought panic, arrests, the arbitrary confiscation of property, and despair. The latter was reflected in a significant rise in the number of Jewish suicides.[20] The series of spontaneous cruel and sadistic attacks on Jews in public places during the following weeks, perpetrated both by uniformed Nazis and a subset of Viennese civilians, ended on April 23 when the local Reich Commissioner Josef Bürckel was told to quell the violence and focus on expropriating and expelling Jews.[21] The majority of Austrian Jewry came to see emigration as their only future, and 136,000, including most of the intelligentsia, had left by October 23, 1941, when Himmler issued a decree halting emigration.[22] Two-thirds of the Jews remaining in Austria were women, and only 3,000 were children under eighteen.[23] Family separations had loomed large. About 60,000 would perish in death camps.[24]

As in Germany, at the outset the Nazis in Austria also actively encouraged emigration. Adolf Eichmann's *Zentralstelle für jüdische Auswanderung* (Central Office for Jewish Emigration) used a combination of bullying and terror to expedite the deportation of Jews and the seizure of their assets. Eichmann "demanded an emigration figure of 20,000 Jews without means for the period from April 1, 1938, to May 1, 1939, of the Jewish Community and the Zionist Organization for Austria, and they promised me that they would keep to this."[25] As noted above, between the Anschluss and November 30, 1939, nearly 120,000, or two-thirds, of all Austrian Jews would emigrate under duress. However, the only legal way of doing so was through Eichmann's SS-run agency in Vienna, established in August 1938, which became the model for similar agencies used to implement the deportation of Jews. The agency organized the paperwork and exacted the *Reichsfluchtsteuer* described above and the Jewish Assets Levy (*Judenvermögensabgabe*), both directed at expropriating Jewish assets. The "levy" of 1 billion Reichsmarks ($400 million) was imposed by Hermann Göring on German Jewry on November 12, 1938, two days after the *Reichskristallnacht*, in alleged "atonement" for "the hostile attitude of Judaism towards the German people." The Nazis may have thought that expropriation would yield them a huge fiscal dividend, but this would not prove to be the case because the Jewish share of the aggregate private capital stock was modest and not much more than their share of the population.[26]

The effectiveness of German policy depended in part on Jews being able to find a home elsewhere. For as long as the outflow was relatively modest, as it was before 1938, most of those who wanted to leave managed to do so. The common accusation that "liberal democracies blatantly denied the Jewish refugees arriving at their borders and even on their territory the most fundamental human rights"[27] refers mainly to the crisis period after *Kristallnacht*. Directed especially at the United States and the United Kingdom, it remains a controversial accusation and rings truer for some countries more than others. In 1939 the Netherlands' Jewish population of 136,000 had swollen with about 25,000 refugees from Germany (including Anne Frank and her family); in Belgium refugees accounted for about 22,000 of a total Jewish population of 66,000. Although in the interwar period its immigration policy was vague and admissions were at the whim of the Home Office, Britain took in about 70,000 Jewish refugees in the 1930s, and a further 10,000 arrived during the war.[28] Viktor Ephrussi, a Viennese banking magnate who had been detained and had lost nearly everything after the *Anschluss*, arrived with a single suitcase in London on March 4, 1939. By then one of his daughters was in Switzerland and the other, in Mexico, while his two sons were in America. His wife had taken her own life in October 1938.[29]

Between 1941, when the mass deportations to the death camps began, and 1943, when practically no Jews were left in Germany, three thousand to four thousand German Jews took their own lives. The number of suicides between 1933 and 1941 was probably fewer, but it was widely known that persecution drove many to kill themselves, particularly in the wake of *Kristallnacht*, when "hundreds of Jews died . . . if not one or two thousand." Hundreds more met the same fate in Austria in the wake of the *Anschluss*, prompting Reich Propaganda Minister Joseph Goebbels to gloat in his diary on March 23, 1938: "Many suicides of German Jews in Vienna. Previously, Germans committed suicide. Now it is the other way round."[30]

The Jewish population of Czechoslovakia, of whom about one-third lived in the Czech lands, was about 360,000 in 1933. Between March 15, 1939, when Germany occupied the Czech lands and converted them into its new Protectorate of Bohemia and Moravia, and June 15, 1942, 26,110 Jews emigrated by means of the *Zentralstelle für jüdische Auswanderung*. The *Zentralstelle*, a Nazi creation, was established to rid the protectorate of as many of its Jews as possible. Most of those (19,000) left in 1939; a further 5,000 fled unofficially in that same year. This implies that about 1 in 4 Czech Jews managed to escape. Of the 88,000 or so who remained, 78,150 perished in the Holocaust (figure 5.3).[31]

Before the war the main continental ports of departure for overseas Jewish refugees were Hamburg, Bremerhaven, and Antwerp. Once the war started, Marseille served as an alternative escape route—but only as far as Martinique. Anthropologist Claude Lévi-Strauss, the Russian revolutionary Victor Serge, novelist Anna Seghers, and surrealist painter André Breton were among over 200 refugees who left in one of several ships bound for Martinique in early 1941. The first three were Jewish; Breton was not. Lisbon was the main option from 1940 onward. Portugal, the poorest economy in western Europe, did not welcome permanent residents from abroad, but those with evidence of visas to overseas destinations, paid passages, and enough to pay for their subsistence in Portugal could obtain thirty-day visas. After the fall of France, neutral Portugal offered the main escape route to

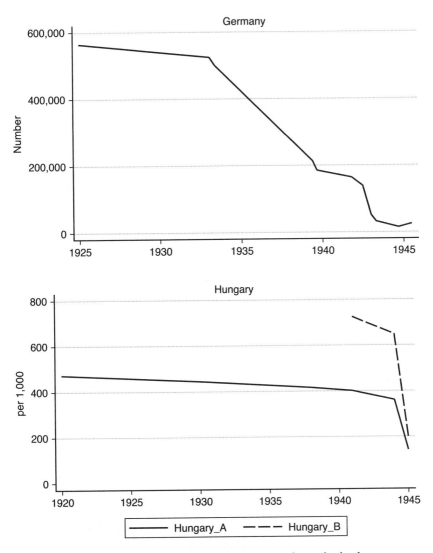

FIGURE 5.3. The Jewish populations of Germany, Vienna, the Netherlands, and Hungary, c. 1900–45
Source: Strauss: 1980: 317 (*Germany*); Dom and Magos 1983 (*Hungary*); Botz 1987; Bukey 2020; Wikipedia (*Vienna*); Wikipedia (*Netherlands*)
Note: Hungary A refers to 1919 borders; Hungary B to 1941 borders

the New World. Almost immediately, the Portuguese allowed the transfer of the main office of the Hebrew Immigrant Aid Society in Paris to move to Lisbon. During World War II, it is reckoned that 50,000 to 80,000 refugees found a safe passage abroad through Lisbon. Notables such as Hannah Arendt and her husband, Heinrich Blucher; Marc Chagall; Max Ernst; Bela Bartok;

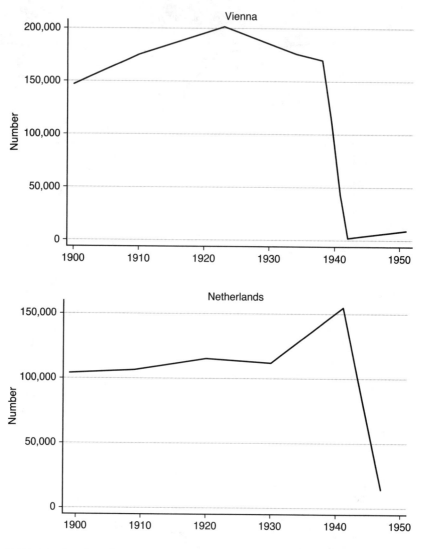

FIGURE 5.3. (*continued*)

André Maurois; Peggy Guggenheim; Lion Feuchtwanger; and Arthur Koestler were among them; Koestler described Lisbon as the "last open gate of a concentration camp." Portuguese policy toward refugees was relaxed by the standards of the time; many had "got into the country with useless visas" (figure 5.4).[32]

The refugees were not a random cross-section of western European Jewry. Matthias Blum and Claudia Rei analyze a data set of these European migrants from Lisbon, who traveled on to New York in 1940–42.[33] Detailed

FIGURE 5.4. Jewish refugees board the SS *Mouzinho* in Lisbon, June 10, 1941
Source: United States Holocaust Memorial Museum, courtesy of Milton Koch

information on personal and socioeconomic characteristics, in addition to anthropometric indicators, allows for a comparative study of the patterns of selection of these wartime migrants. Using adult heights as a proxy for health and human capital, they find that refugees, especially women refugees, were positively selected from their countries of origin. They attribute the strong selection in the data to "the immense difficulty of traveling from European source regions to the south-western tip of the continent in the early 1940s; those who succeeded were not only fortunate, but also well-off."[34]

Johannes Buggle and his coauthors have analyzed some characteristics of a much larger sample (285,000) of German Jewish refugees.[35] A weakness of their data set is the lack of information on education and socioeconomic status, which rules out measurement of the impact of income on migration decisions. Buggle et al. have focused instead on the role of social networks, which they inferred from information included in the database and is highly relevant when migration is driven by the perceived threat of violence. They confirm that migrants were younger than the Jewish population at large and much more likely to be male, while those born outside Germany and those with a traditionally Jewish first name—who were on average poorer— were less likely to emigrate. Similarly, individuals who had been detained at some point were also significantly more likely to go compared to individuals not taken into custody. And, as might be expected, they find that persecution at the city level increased the likelihood of leaving. They also find that one's social network played a significant role only in the pre-1938 period. After the November pogroms, in which everyone across Germany realized that staying posed a significant danger to their lives, additional information on persecution coming from the network ceased to be important. Finally, Buggle et al. find evidence for what they call the "threat effect" through networks offering information on the extent of persecution, as well as the "exodus effect" whereby evidence of others fleeing encourages more to leave. These results lay bare the constraints under which prospective escapees labored. In a similar study, Sascha Becker and his coauthors find that German Jewish university academics—among the first to be affected by Nazi persecution—who had links with others who fled abroad in 1933 and 1934 were more likely to follow.[36]

The age and gender distributions of Jewish refugees differed according to the circumstances. Figure 5.5 compares the age distributions of samples of Polish refugees in Vilna in Lithuania in 1940 with those in the city of Kobe in Japan in 1941 and with German Jewish refugees on board the MS *St. Louis*, which set sail from Hamburg on May 13, 1939. Thousands of Polish refugees fled to Lithuania at the start of World War II; they were a select minority with the means to escape and mostly "from the educated Jewish elite of prewar Poland and represent[ing] a variety of cultural, religious, and political beliefs."[37] A 1941 listing of the Polish Jewish refugees in Vilna who traveled on to Kobe in Japan by means of the Trans-Siberian Express suggests they were a select minority within a minority. The most common occupations for men were "clerk," "merchant," "lawyer," and "journalist," in that order. Among the younger males were many yeshiva students, while hardly any of the women were recorded with an occupation.[38] The saga of the MS *St. Louis*, a passenger ship belonging to the Hamburg-American Line, has often been retold.[39] The ship traveled first to Havana, where only 28 of nearly 1,000 passengers were allowed to land. It then sailed for the United States, where the refugees were refused permission to disembark. Canada also refused them entry. On the ship's return to Europe, the authorities in Great Britain, Belgium, France, and the Netherlands agreed to grant asylum to the remaining 906 passengers. The 288 who landed in London were safe (except for 1 killed during an air raid), and a minority of the remainder managed to escape before Hitler occupied western Europe. But 84 of the 214 who found asylum in Belgium perished in the Holocaust, as did 86 of the 224 in France and 84 of the 181 in the Netherlands.

Of the three groups, the Jewish Poles who fled to Vilna were the youngest, with a modal age of twenty to twenty-four years; refugees aged between

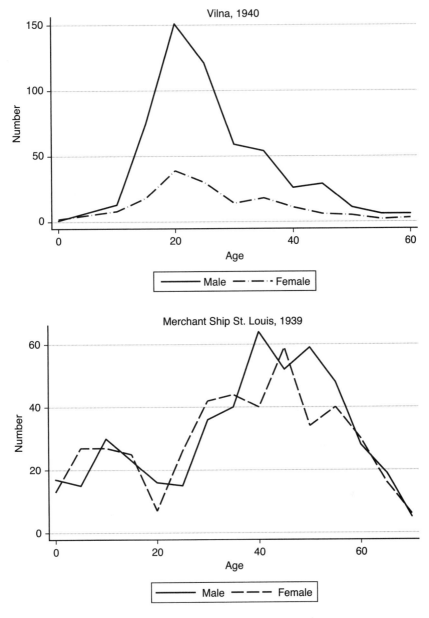

FIGURE 5.5. Age composition of three Jewish refugee flows: Vilna, St. Louis, and Kobe

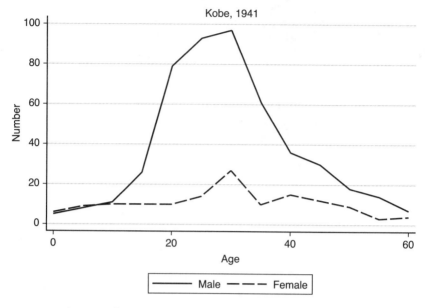

FIGURE 5.5. (*continued*)

fifteen and thirty-nine accounted for 82 percent of males and 74 percent of females. The modal age for those on board the *St. Louis* was double that (forty to forty-nine years), with refugees in the fifteen to thirty-nine age bracket composing 28 percent of males and 33 percent of females. The differences could reflect the more privileged socioeconomic status of the latter and the lower cost of travel from Poland to Vilna, but they could also reflect the fear that Vilna in 1940 was no place for women or older men. The modal age of those who reached Kobe, relatively well-off Orthodox Polish Jews, was thirty to thirty-four years. The refugees also differed by gender breakdown. Whereas females accounted for nearly half of those on the MS *St. Louis*, they made up only 20–25 percent of those in the other groups (figure 5.6).[40]

The Odds of Survival

The age and gender profiles of those Germans and Austrians who managed to escape had an impact on the demographic profile of those who stayed and perished. A profile by age and gender of German victims of the Holocaust may be inferred from the Memorial Book compiled by the Bundesarchiv.[41]

FIGURE 5.6. Jewish refugees

Source: United States Holocaust Memorial Museum

a. Family portrait aboard the MS *St. Louis* (Courtesy of Peter S. Heiman)

b. Passengers on the refugee ship the MS *St. Louis* as it arrives in the port of Antwerp (Courtesy of Fred [Fritz] Vendig)

c. Group portrait, Kobe, May 1941 (Courtesy of Eric Saul)

d. Polish Jewish refugees Henryk and Hanka Starski pose in front of Tamerlane's tomb in Samarkand, Uzbekistan, c. 1942–46 (Courtesy of Peter S. Heiman)

FIGURE 5.6. (*continued*)

Figure 5.7a–c, based on those with surnames beginning with A, summarizes the data for 1942, 1943, and 1944. The preponderance of older people and females in 1942, when the killings were at their height, is remarkable. Over three out of four of the named victims were born before 1900, and of those 64 percent were women. In 1943 the victims were younger—58 percent were born before 1900—with women also forming the majority (56 percent). In 1944, when the number of victims was much lower, the gender difference is less marked, but the victims were still older, with 64 percent born before 1900.

Figure 5.7d describes the age and gender profile of victims of the Holocaust in Czechoslovakia as reflected in the database of people deported, mostly in 1942, to the concentration camp of Theresienstadt/Terezín, located about seventy kilometers north of Prague. For many this camp operated as a waystation to the extermination camps, such as Treblinka and Auschwitz.[42] Only the details of those who were murdered are given. Based again on surnames beginning with A, the picture that emerges is very similar to that for Germany in 1942, with older adults and women overrepresented and young males and females underrepresented. These patterns reflect in part the longer life expectancy of women in normal times and the higher proportion of males among those who fled. They also reflect, if to a lesser extent, male losses during World War I and the higher likelihood of men being chosen for slave labor and therefore surviving.[43]

An extensive literature, most of it based on narratives and case studies, describes how some Jews managed to evade the Nazis. Some accounts highlight the role of luck. In a study of those who died and the tiny minority who survived in the coastal Latvian town of Liepaja, Edward Anders and Juris Dubrovskis write:[44]

In the summer of 1941 . . . men were killed regardless of personal qualities and skills. By fall it was equally dangerous to be old. By winter, it was fatal to be a Jew of either sex and any age, unless one had certain occupational skills. In Riga in 1943/44 it was fatal to be old, or a mother with a young child. But with the increasingly harsh treatment, youth and physical endurance—factors in classical natural selection—began to dominate, especially in Stutthof (a concentration camp located east of Danzig/Gdańsk). Two other Darwinian factors—resourcefulness and intelligence—had been important all along, while other formerly positive factors turned into liabilities: beautiful women attracted the attention of Nazi rapist-murderers, and strong, proud men provoked murderous sadists. Yet the Nazis were determined to prevent survival of the fittest.

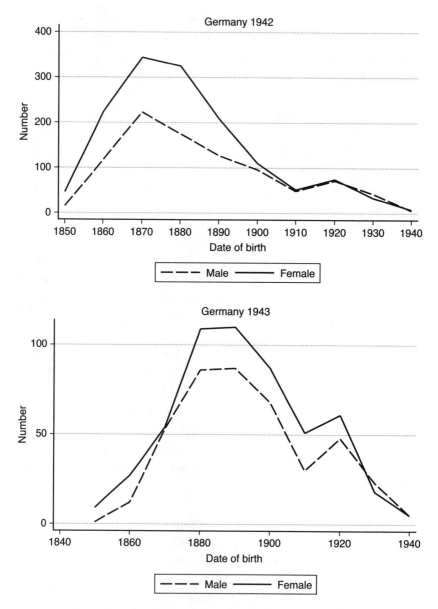

FIGURE 5.7. Age and gender of Holocaust victims in Germany (including Austria) and Czechoslovakia

Source: Bundesarchiv Memorial Book (//www.bundesarchiv.de/gedenkbuch/) (*Germany 1942*); holocaust.cz (*Czechoslovakia*)

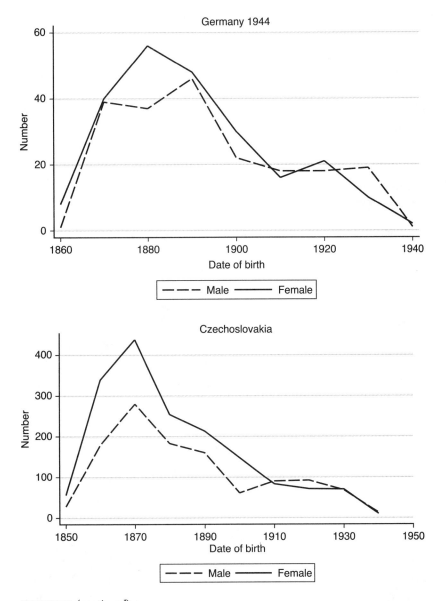

FIGURE 5.7. (*continued*)

A 1942 German document, recommending that Jews be worked to death, warned of the hardy remnant that would remain and might serve as the nucleus of a resurgent Jewish race. All in all, one's survival required not one but several miracles.

The question of who survived the death camps troubled Primo Levi, who entered Auschwitz in February 1944 at the age of twenty-five. He was accompanied by 650 other Italians, of whom 20 survived. Levi had two advantages when he entered the death camp; he spoke German and he was reasonably fit. In the camp, fortune played a part: he grew friendly with an Italian who obtained him some extra food, and the Nazis left him behind as they fled from the camp in January 1945. But it did not end there. Survival meant compromising with evil in what Levi dubbed the "grey zone." And so "the worst survived, the selfish, the violent, the insensitive, the collaborators of the 'grey zone,' the spies. It was not a certain rule . . . but it was, nevertheless, a rule. . . . The worst survived, that is, the fittest; the best all died."[45] However, Levi offers a somewhat different impression in one of his other depictions of Auschwitz:[46]

> In less than ten minutes all the fit men had been collected together in a group. What happened to the others, to the women, to the children, to the old men, we could establish neither then nor later: the night swallowed them up, purely and simply. Today, however, we know that in the rapid and summary choice each one of us had been judged capable or not of working usefully for the Reich; we know that of our convoy no more than ninety-six men and twenty-nine women entered the respective camps of Monowitz-Buna and Birkenau, and that of all the others, more than five hundred in number, not one was living two days later.

A good deal of research has been carried out on the question that concerned Levi: what factors influenced the odds of survival. For example, about 87 percent of Italian Jews escaped deportation, mainly through living in the part of Italy not occupied by the Nazis or by hiding themselves or their identities in the occupied area. Susan Welch has analyzed the fate of the 6,775 who were deported, mostly to Auschwitz, by age and gender. She found that foreign-born Jews, lacking networks and often not knowing Italian, were the most vulnerable and accounted for one-third of those deported. The very old, the very young, women, and those with disabilities were also more likely to be sent straight to the gas chambers on arrival. Nine in ten of those aged fifteen to thirty-four years survived first selection on arrival but only 8 percent of those aged under five or sixty and above. Seventeen percent of young Italian adults aged fifteen to twenty-nine sent to Auschwitz survived but none aged sixty and above. The former included twenty-five-year-old Primo Levi.[47] Another study in the same vein by three Czech economists focuses on the role of networks and social status in influencing the (low) likelihood of surviving the death camps of Theresienstadt, established by the SS in 1941, and Auschwitz-Birkenau. The names of nearly all those sent to Theresienstadt, mostly Czech, German, or Austrian, have been preserved, as has information about their social capital (the presence of other family members or, in the case of Prague, people from the same street) and status (such as education or profession and involvement in predeportation Jewish administrative institutions). The authors show that such factors played a role in protecting victims against death and the likelihood of being sent from Theresienstadt to Auschwitz.[48]

A recent individual-level analysis of Amsterdam Jews by Peter Tammes finds that immigrants were more likely to survive, as were secular, converted, and intermarried Jews.[49] Being married rather than single, divorced, or widowed reduced the likelihood of survival. Class mattered too, with those at the top, such as professionals and white-collar workers, having a marked advantage; unskilled workers were twice as likely to perish as professionals. Males were at marginally greater risk than females. In a related study,[50] Tammes analyzed the influence of the localities in which Jews lived on the likelihood of being deported during the Holocaust. The likelihood was an increasing function of compliant police, "strongest segregation mentality," and "less employment in agriculture." The risk of being deported was highest where the Catholic share of the population was lowest, possibly a reflection of Catholics having less enthusiastically supported Nazism than Protestants, as revealed by voting patterns before 1933. Tammes found that although young males were less likely to die if deported before July 1943, they were more so thereafter, a finding consistent with younger men being made to work at the outset.

A similar study by Marnix Croes focuses on the survival chances of Jews in the eastern Dutch province of Overijssel.[51] It shows that children stood the best chance of not being deported, perhaps because non-Jews were more likely to welcome them and because their parents and aid agencies prioritized their survival. It also confirms anecdotal evidence that belonging to a higher socioeconomic background meant closer integration with non-Jewish society and more influence with the Jewish Council, which could delay transfer to Westerbork transit camp in the province of Drenthe, a staging post for the deportation of nearly one hundred thousand Jews. And it shows that while German Jews could also delay their departure, their overall survival chances remained unaffected.

Péter Tibor Nagy addressed the issue of the likelihood of survival in Budapest using a sample of households in 1941 and 1951.[52] He found that having links to the Christian population increased the probability of survival; being married to a Christian increased survival chances by "a factor of 1.9." He also found that survival chances increased with educational levels and with occupational skills (associated with links to organized labor and ties to the middle classes) and senior public-sector employment in 1941. Wealth helped too: whereas 42 percent of major industrialists classed as Jewish in 1941 survived, only 24 percent of "small" industrialists and wholesalers did. Nagy interprets these and related findings as evidence that the Holocaust was "an event embedded in Hungarian social history."

A microstudy of the thousand or so Jews in the northern French town of Lens also highlights the roles of kinship, wealth, and birthplace in determining whether they stayed put during the war, thereby increasing their risk of deportation.[53] The Jews of Lens, living in a zone ceded to Belgium by the Nazis in 1940, were more exposed than French Jewry generally, and a much higher proportion of them were deported and killed.

Fleeing from Operation Barbarossa

In the East, escape from the Nazis was almost impossible, although not entirely so. In particular, flight and displacement provided a lifeline to perhaps 200,000 of Poland's 3 million Jews. A near-contemporary estimate put the number who fled from German- to Russian-occupied Poland at 1 million, but one careful recent estimate puts the number fleeing east, including to the Soviet Union, at somewhere between 0.2 and 0.3 million. Another estimate suggests that two-thirds to more than four-fifths of the 300,000 to 350,000 Polish Jews who survived the Holocaust did so in Soviet-controlled territory.[54] Some were initially deported as "class aliens" in 1940 before being amnestied in 1941; some were drafted into the Soviet army; some volunteered to work in the Soviet Union; and many more fled east before Operation Barbarossa. Mark Edele and Wanda Warlik include these refugees in the ranks of "Holocaust survivors" as victims who endured a great deal but who, for the most part, survived. Their stories were largely forgotten in the fog of the Cold War. Their memories of exile in the East varied. One wrote in an unpublished memoir: "Looking back, I have no bad feelings about the Soviets. They provided a place for us to go. They let us into their country, unlike what happened in some other countries. It was no picnic, but I survived." "Regardless of the Soviet regime, I had a debt to that land," wrote another.[55]

A smaller number—perhaps 35,000 or so out of a total of 0.25 million— fled from the Baltic states to the Soviet Union. By the time the Latvian border was sealed in July 1941, 15,000 of the country's 85,000 remaining Jews had fled to Russia. About 12,000 of those who fled survived, but only 1,500 of the 70,000 who remained lived. Those who left were more likely to be young and to be Soviet sympathizers; the latter included members of the 10,000-strong Workers' Guard. But family ties kept many behind, and others were reluctant to part with their possessions, while those who had their wealth taken from them by the Soviets were also less likely to leave.[56] About 20,000 Jews fled from Lithuania (as distinct from being deported). They included about 4,000 Communists. Less well-known is the flight of about 4,000 Polish Jewish refugees to Japan and China via Lithuania and the Soviet Union. About 1,000 ended up in Shanghai, mainly destitute and culturally very different from the more Westernized German Jews who had preceded them.[57]

The Jews who fled east to Soviet-occupied Poland in 1939–41 and further east after Barbarossa endured much hardship during the war, as indeed did most inhabitants of the Soviet Union. An unknown number of the refugees did not survive, but those who did constituted the majority of the Jews from Poland who survived the Holocaust. Again, escape to the East saved the lives of hundreds of thousands of Soviet Jews from the claws of the SS and their collaborators.

Vernichtung (Annihilation)

The Nazis and their collaborators' mass killing of Jews began in the ghettos of Poland, the first of which was established in Piotrków Trybunalski in south-central Poland in October 1939, a month after the town had been occupied by the Wehrmacht. The last was established in Dzyatlava (Zdzięcioł) in what was then eastern Poland but is nowadays Belarus, on February 22, 1942. In all, nearly three hundred ghettos were established in Poland, the biggest in Warsaw, which contained over 0.4 million Jews when it was sealed off on November 15, 1940. That is when the Holocaust began in earnest for those trapped inside; between then and the destruction of the ghetto, the Nazis made life in the 3.4-square-kilometer area so unbearable that up to 100,000 inhabitants succumbed to starvation and famine-induced diseases.[58] Although data are lacking, it is not unlikely that the death rates in Warsaw were matched in some other places. For example, in the Łódź ghetto, the second largest, which contained 160,000 people when its gates closed on April 30, 1940, there were 6,851 deaths in 1940; 11,437 in 1941; 18,020 in 1942; and 4,561 in 1943, the year in which most of those still alive were sent to their deaths in Chelmo. The low birth rates in the Łódź ghetto are also telling: in February 1942, 1,875 people died there (three-fifths of them male), while only 45 were born; in the following month, the numbers were 2,244 and 54, respectively. The death rates in Warsaw and Łódź have been reckoned

FIGURE 5.8. Images from the Warsaw ghetto
Source: United States Holocaust Memorial Museum
a. Jews purchase produce from street vendors in the Warsaw ghetto (Courtesy of Rafael Scharf)
b. A beggar on the street in the Warsaw ghetto (Courtesy of Guenther Schwarberg)
c. Two destitute Jews stand among a crowd of people on a street in the Warsaw ghetto (Courtesy of Rafael Scharf)

FIGURE 5.8. (*continued*)

at 17 and 21 percent, respectively, but mortality was much lower in the ghettos of Krakow, Bialystock, Grodno, Kovno, and Shavli. In Kovno between November 1, 1941, and May 1, 1942, 1.1 percent (104/9,898) of females and 1.8 percent (134/7,469) of males died (figure 5.8).[59]

The famine in the Warsaw ghetto generated a unique study of "the physiology and pathology of starvation" conducted by a team of medical practitioners in the ghetto between February and mid-July 1942.[60] With the permission of the *Judenrat*, the team persuaded over a hundred subjects to participate in what they saw as a unique opportunity for studying a famine in real time. During the *Grossaktion*—the deportation of the remaining Jews

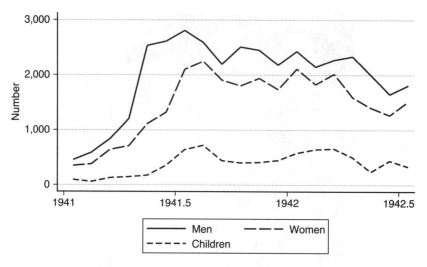

FIGURE 5.9. Monthly deaths in the Warsaw ghetto, January 1941–July 1942
Source: Ferenc Piotrowska 2018: 143–44

from the ghetto in August 1942—they hid their findings in the Jewish cemetery. They were smuggled out later by a Polish colleague and after the war were passed on to the Joint Distribution Committee located in Paris. The physicians' study documented the progressive loss of fat reserves, aging of body tissues, shrinkage of internal organs, and decline in muscle; it proposed how rehabilitation must be very gradual; and it analyzed the psychological impact of hunger. As common during famines, men were more inclined to succumb than women. Even though women outnumbered men in the ghetto at the outset, male deaths outnumbered female by over a third (figure 5.9). Another universal feature of famine demography, a decline in the birth rate, is graphically reflected in the numbers for Jewish Warsaw: 306 births per month in 1940, 229 in 1941, and 85 from January to May 1942.[61]

Although tens of thousands of Polish Jews had already been killed or starved to death in the ghettos before June 1941, it was the invasion of the Soviet Union, code-named Operation Barbarossa, in that month that sealed the fate of European Jewry. The mass murder of Jews in the occupied Soviet Union and in the Baltic countries began as soon as they were conquered. In the end, Germany's Jews accounted for only 3 to 4 percent of the 6 million or so who lost their lives during the Holocaust. Most of the killing was done in the East, and very few of those deported from western Europe to the east by the Nazis survived. The U.S. Holocaust Memorial Museum (USHMM) reckons that nearly half of all victims died in the death camps in the East (Auschwitz, Treblinka 2, Belzec, Sobibór, Chelmno, and Majdanek) or in other concentration camps; another 1.3 million in shooting operations (*Aktionen*) and mobile gas wagons in the occupied Union of Soviet Socialist Republics (USSR); 0.8 million in various ghettos; and close to a million elsewhere. The Nazi murder machine operated efficiently and quickly. Peter Hayes has aptly described it as a "low-cost, low-overhead, and self-financing process of killing with great speed."[62]

Only a minuscule fraction of those sent to Treblinka, Bełżec, and Sobibór survived. The odds of surviving Auschwitz, which was both a forced-labor camp and an extermination camp, were better; about 1.1 million out of 1.3 million were murdered there. Escape from the death camps was virtually impossible. Of the 1.3 million sent to Auschwitz, 928,878 men and 50 women attempted to escape. They included 439 Poles and 213 from the Soviet Union (158 prisoners and 55 prisoners of war, or POWs). Of those, 150 were Jewish, 4 of them women. Other nationalities included Germans and Austrians (49), Roma (41), Czechs (26), and 12 others. Only 196 were successful; another 25 were free for a time but were recaptured.[63] Did inmates have any agency in their survival? Levi says yes, and certainly, the chances of survival increased if one were put into a labor squad. Levi also noted that whether one survived as a laborer was not just a question of luck but also of one's own behavior.

Most of the killing took place in dedicated death camps. A striking feature of the Holocaust in the Baltic states, Belarus, and Ukraine, however, is the relatively small proportion of victims who perished in death camps; most died in a "Holocaust by bullets." *Einsatzgruppen*, special mobile deployment units consisting of members of the SS; the *Sicherheitdienst* (SD, security service); the *Sicherheitspolizei* (*Sipo*; security police); and the *Gestapo* (secret police) who followed the Wehrmacht on its advance east did most of the killing. Four *Einsatzgruppen* were formed in the spring of 1941 in anticipation of Operation Barbarossa; others were established later as the Nazi-occupied territory expanded. In all, *Einsatzgruppen* and their local helpers were responsible for two million deaths, a majority of them Jews. Although other means, such as mobile gas chambers, were also used, mass shootings were the main method employed. A German civilian in charge of a construction firm in Ukraine provided a telling depiction to the International Military Tribunal at Nuremberg:[64]

> I walked around the mound, and found myself confronted by a tremendous grave. People were closely wedged together and lying on top of each other so that their heads were visible. Nearly all had blood running over their shoulders from their heads. . . . The pit was already two-thirds full. I estimated that it contained about 1,000 people. I looked for the man who did the shooting. He was an SS man, who sat at the edge of

the narrow end of the pit, his feet dangling into the pit. He had a tommy gun on his knees and was smoking a cigarette. The people, completely naked, went down some steps which were cut in the clay wall of the pit and clambered over the heads of the people lying there, to the place to which the SS man direct them. They lay down in front of the dead or injured people; some caressed those who were still alive and spoke to them in a low voice. Then I heard a series of shots.

The Last Jew in Vinnitsa an iconic, much-reproduced image most likely dating from the summer of 1941 (figure 5.10), describes another grotesque scene in west central Ukraine. The extermination of the Jewish population of Mizoch (formerly in Poland, now in western Ukraine) was also photographed. The gruesome images show women and children being herded into a ravine outside the town on October 14 or 15, 1942, and being forced to undress before being murdered (figure 5.11).

In Mizoch the Jews were murdered by "German Sipo and SD with the assistance of Ukrainian auxiliaries."[65] According to the Lithuanian American historian Saulius Sužiedėlis, mass shooting worked for the Nazis because they "discovered sufficient man-power for mass murder"[66] locally, and indeed, a key controversy in the Holocaust literature on the Baltic states is the role of local collaborators. In his review of killings in Lithuania, Colonel Karl Jäger, brutal commander of *Einsatzkommando* 3a, notes the crucial part played by local collaborators: "Kovno itself, where trained Lithuanian partisans are available in sufficient numbers, was comparatively speaking a shooting paradise."[67] Thus, the killing of 9,200 people in the notorious *Grossaktion* at Kovno's Ninth Fort over a twelve-hour period on October 29, 1941, could not have been carried out without the presence for every German of "several eager, well-trained, and highly motivated Lithuanians." In the same league, and with inebriated Lithuanian collaborators also playing a leading role, was the *Aktion* in Panevėžys on August 23, which resulted in 7,523 murders, mostly of women and children. In the Vilna suburb of Ponary/ Paneriai, where about 30,000 Jews and several thousand others were shot in the second half of 1941, most of the killings were carried out by Lithuanian volunteers.[68] The depravity of the Lithuanian militiamen is widely attested. In the Panevezys *Aktion*, Lithuanian guards shot the Jews:

The infants were taken by force from their mothers and thrown into the pits. The murderers amused themselves shooting at the infants in the air, before they fell into the pit. The murderers were drunk most of the time, thus missing the infants and many of them fell alive into the pits.[69]

FIGURE 5.10. *The Last Jew in Vinnitsa*
Source: Library of Congress Prints and Photographs Division Washington, D.C.
20540 USA

FIGURE 5.11. Mass murder of Jewish women from Mizocz (now Mizoch in western Ukraine), October 14, 1942
Source: United States Holocaust Memorial Museum, courtesy of Instytut Pamieci Narodowej. Copyright: Agency Agreement. Published Source: *The World Must Know: The History of the Holocaust* . . . by Berenbaum, Michael - Little, Brown and Company

In Utena on the morning of August 7, 1941:

> There were trenches on a hillock which was surrounded by forest on three sides. A Lithuanian was positioned close to the trench. He had a whip in his hand, and was flogging those passing him. The people, frightened by the whip, ran toward the trench, where a German shot them with a machine gun. Next to a car parked close to the trench stood the mayor of the city Z'ukas, the district physician Iasinas, and some other Lithuanian leaders from Utena. They were watching the show.[70]

One of the biggest shootings of all, in which 25,000 Jews (all Latvian except for about a thousand Germans) were murdered, took place in Rumbula forest near Riga on November 30 and December 8, 1941. The *Aktion* was planned by SS *Obergruppenführer* Friedrich Jeckeln, commander of several *Einsatzgruppen* teams. Twelve German SD (*Sicherheitsdienst*) men,[71] using Soviet submachine guns adjusted to shoot bullets individually, shot the victims at close range in the back of the head as they lay face down in pits.

The Germans were assisted by a unit of several hundred men known as the Latvian Auxiliary Security Police led by Viktors Arajs, a group of pro-Nazi and virulently anti-Semitic Latvian volunteers who had helped to clear the ghetto and to finish the off Jews shot en route. The Arajs Commando was involved in all the main massacres in Latvia and in the destruction of Riga's biggest synagogue on July 4, 1941.

Why did Lithuanians and Latvians do so much of the dirty work? Opportunism and greed were presumably part of it, and the interaction between ethnic nationalism and hatred of the Soviets, which the wartime context allowed free rein, was also a factor. Aya Ben-Neftali describes the murders in the Ninth Fort in Kovno as evidence of "the extreme cruelty, high motivation, and passionate enthusiasm that many Lithuanians brought to the task of murdering Jews" and a "fervor . . . deeply embedded in the Lithuanian cultural and religious tradition, in economic, social, and political developments in Lithuanian in the 1920s and 1930s." However, John Klier has downplayed the role of ideology and "traditional anti-Semitism," noting that many of those involved were POWs keen to leave German POW camps.[72]

In western Ukraine, too, the shooting and gassing of Jews were preceded or accompanied by pogroms. Collaboration by elements in the local population in the destruction of Ukrainian Jewry is undeniable. The Germans regarded the Ukrainians as superior to Russians and Poles, and most Ukrainians harbored a hatred of the Stalinist regime. It is believed that 80,000 Ukrainian men assisted the Nazis as *politsaï* (auxiliary policemen). These were mostly ethnic Ukrainians recruited in the regions in which they worked. Ethnic Germans living in Ukraine also helped in the killings and played an added role in translating and in communicating to the German authorities, and some graduated to membership in *Einsatzgruppen*.[73] That said, the intensity of anti-Semitism varied from place to place; it was much milder in Odessa, for example, than in Kiev.[74] The well-known images reproduced as Figures 5.12–5.16 cannot fully convey the unspeakable horrors and cruelty of what Holocaust victims endured, but perhaps they speak louder than most words can.

Surviving documentary evidence on the death toll from the Holocaust is plentiful but fragmentary. Some of it comes from surviving Nazi sources; more is based on demographic inference from pre- and post-Holocaust census data. In an affidavit from an ex-SS prosecution witness read out at the Nuremberg trials, Adolf Eichmann, one of the main organizers of the Holocaust, was reported as declaring in 1944 that about 4 million Jews had been killed in concentration camps and 2 million elsewhere, mainly in the

FIGURE 5.12. Jews from Carpathian Ruthenia (part of Ukraine since 1945) walking toward the gas chambers
Source: United States Holocaust Memorial Museum, courtesy of Yad Vashem (Public Domain)

FIGURE 5.13. Arrival of Hungarian Jews at Auschwitz concentration camp
Source: Bundesarchiv, Bild 183-N0827-318 / CC-BY-SA 3.0

FIGURE 5.14. The "Lietūkis garage" massacre of Jews in Kovno on June 27, 1941
Source: Vilna Gaon State Museum

FIGURE 5.15. Bodies of prisoners at Gusen (Mauthausen) before cremation. Most of these victims were probably not Jewish, but they shared the same fate as the Jewish victims of the death camps
Source: United States Holocaust Memorial Museum, courtesy of National Archives and Records Administration, College Park

FIGURE 5.16. Soviet troops liberate Auschwitz, January 27, 1945

East. Those numbers tally with the broad scholarly consensus today on a figure between 5.5 and 6 million. In 1961 Raul Hilberg arrived at a figure of 5.1 million in a classic study; although carefully calculated, that figure is now generally considered too low. The lower-bound total proposed by the USHMM is 5.8 million. So far, Vad Yashem, Jerusalem's World Holocaust Memorial Center, has compiled the names of over 4.7 million victims and

FIGURE 5.16. (*continued*)

gives lower- and upper-bound estimates of the losses of 5.6 and 5.86 million, respectively. The main reason for the gap between Hilberg's and later
estimates is Hilberg's lower figure for the Soviet Union.[75]

The estimated death rates across Nazi-occupied countries are described
in table 5.2. The greatest uncertainty surrounds the deaths of Soviet Jews:
the USHMM suggests 1.34 million, while Vad Yashem has 1.0–1.1 million.
In table 5.2 I use the compromise range of from 1 million to 1.2 million. The
data for individual countries are contextualized and described in more detail
in an appendix to this chapter.

The variation in death rates across countries is striking and still attracts
comment. The data on potential explanatory variables are too imprecise or
lacking to warrant formal statistical analysis, but the monolithic character
of the Nazi military-industrial complex leaves some room for explanations
that focus on local factors and human agency. As noted above, escape abroad
before borders were finally closed in 1941 helps to explain the surprisingly
high survival rates of German and Austrian Jews as a proportion of both
those who stayed and those who fled, while the might of the Nazi state apparatus explains the near-complete destruction of those whose remained. An
important caveat: it should be noted that not all those sent to the death
camps from the Netherlands, Belgium, or France were Dutch, Belgian, or

TABLE 5.2. Estimated Jewish Holocaust deaths by country

Country	Population	Vad Yashem	USHMM	% (VY)	% (HMM)	% (Avg.)
Lithuania	153,000	141,500	130,000	92.5	85.0	88.7
Poland	3,350,000	2,950,000	2,885,000	88.1	86.1	87.1
Greece	74,500	63,500	61,900	85.2	83.1	84.2
Yugoslavia	82,242	60,300	67,228	73.3	81.7	77.5
Latvia	93,479	70,750	70,000	75.7	74.9	75.3
Czechoslovakia (USHMM)	354,000		260,000	.	73.4	73.4
Netherlands	140,245	100,000	102,000	71.3	72.7	72.0
Hungary (USHMM)	490,621		297,621		60.7	60.7
Norway	1,750	762	758	43.5	43.3	43.4
Belgium	66,000	28,900	24,387	43.8	37.0	40.4
Soviet Union	3,028,538	1,050,000	1,340,000	34.7	44.2	39.5
Luxembourg	4,250	1,950	1,200	45.9	28.2	37.1
Austria	185,026	50,000	65,459	27.0	35.4	31.2
Romania (USHMM)	756,930		236,000	.	31.2	31.2
Estonia	4,500	1,750	963	38.9	21.4	30.1
Germany (pop. 1933)	524,000	138,000	165,200	26.3	31.5	28.9
France	330,000	77,320	73,450	23.4	22.3	22.8
Bulgaria	50,000	11,343	11,343	22.7	22.7	22.7
Italy	58,412	7,680	7,858	13.1	13.5	13.3
Denmark	7,800	60	84	0.8	1.1	0.9
Czechoslovakia (YV)	207,260	146,150		70.5	.	.
Hungary (YV)	825,000	560,000		67.9	.	.
Romania (YV)	609,000	279,000		45.8	.	.
Total	11,400,553	5,738,965	5,800,451	50.3	50.9	50.6

Sources: USHMM, "Jewish Losses during the Holocaust: By Country," accessed December 30, 2023, https://www
.yadvashem.org/holocaust/faqs.html; Yad Vashem, "How Many Jews Were Murdered in the Holocaust?," accessed
December 30, 2023, https://www.yadvashem.org/holocaust/faqs.html. The last column refers to the average of
the two, except for Romania, Czechoslovakia, and Hungary, where the USHMM percentages are used.

French. For example, the Dutch total includes about 25,000 refugees who
arrived from Germany between 1933 and 1940, the likes of Anne Frank and
her family. More generally, the numbers in table 5.2 refer to country of
departure, not country of birth. Although hard data are lacking, it is quite
conceivable that up to 50,000 German-born Jewish refugees were sent to
death camps in the Netherlands, Belgium, France, and elsewhere during

the Holocaust.[76] Including those in the German total would increase the proportion of German Jews lost from less than one-third to one-half.

The role of anti-Semitism is fundamental, but measures of anti-Semitism before the war are lacking and its incidence and character controversial. The Netherlands, where it is generally accepted that anti-Semitism was not widespread, lost most of its Jews, while in Romania, where anti-Semitism was endemic in the prewar era, the prospects of survival were much higher. One might add that whereas an efficient Dutch bureaucracy facilitated the task of locating its Jewish population, the failings of Romania's very corrupt state apparatus made detection more difficult. Again, virulent anti-Semitism has been widely invoked to account for the fate of French Jewry, but in comparative perspective, French Jews were more likely to survive than those in any other occupied country in western Europe outside Scandinavia.

The Nordic countries were *suorum generis*. At the conference at Wannsee on January 20, 1942, at which Hitler's proposed Final Solution was sanctioned by the state bureaucracy,[77] a German foreign office official's suggestion that its imposition in the Nordic countries would lead to "difficulties" and should be delayed was accepted and minuted. According to Paul Levine, Germany's strong interest in maintaining good relations with neutral Sweden conditioned its response to that country, even where the treatment of Jews was concerned. The same held true for Finland, where the Germans knew that "bringing up the Jewish Question in a crass manner would damage Finnish-German relations," and in Denmark, where the occupiers' actions were constrained and delayed by public opinion. The Danes also benefited from the Nazi perception of the Nordic nations as "Aryan."[78]

Of the 107,000 out of a total of 140,000 Jews in the Netherlands who were deported to Nazi camps abroad, only about 5,200 returned.[79] Perhaps 10 percent of captured Poles survived. About 7,000 Jews were living in the death camps in Poland when they were liberated.[80] Polish and Soviet Jews accounted for two-thirds of the total who perished; the worst affected in relative terms were the Baltic states, Greece, Hungary, and the Netherlands. Dutch Jews were lulled into a false sense of complacency by the authorities in the early stages of the war, with the result that fewer of them went into hiding than Jews in France or Belgium.[81] Italian and Danish Jews were the most likely to survive.

Although studies of anti-Semitism in the pre-Nazi era abound, there is no accurate way of measuring trends over time and differences across nations. Table 5.3, based on the work of William Brustein and Ryan King,[82] uses annual data on anti-Jewish events or actions in six countries in the *American*

TABLE 5.3. Anti-Semitic actions in five European countries, 1899–1939 (% of total)

	GB	France	Germany	Italy	Bulgaria	Romania	Total
Legal, statutory	32	26	64	46	35	40	52
Discrimination	*11*	*1*	*28*	*28*	*9*	*17*	*22*
Employment	*11*	*3*	*23*	*15*	*4*	*10*	*17*
Immigration	*3*	*14*	*8*	*0*	*15*	*8*	*8*
Practices	*7*	*8*	*5*	*3*	*7*	*5*	*5*
Violence, threats	29	28	16	0	50	47	27
Assault, murder	*0*	*2*	*3*	*0*	*13*	*10*	*5*
Riots, violent	*6*	*2*	*3*	*0*	*17*	*21*	*9*
Riots, nonviolent	*10*	*20*	*4*	*0*	*13*	*11*	*7*
Vandalism, etc.	*10*	*2*	*3*	*0*	*3*	*3*	*3*
Boycotts, strikes	*3*	*2*	*3*	*0*	*4*	*2*	*3*
Group action	10	8	8	8	7	4	8
Media attacks	26	22	6	31	0	1	7
Raids, confiscations	3	4	4	5	0	2	3
False accusation, imprisonment	3	6	3	10	7	1	3
N	73	49	703	39	46	431	1,341
Population 1930 [m.]	44.8	41.2	65.0	41.2	5.7	18.1	201.3
Per million	1.63	1.19	10.82	0.95	8.1	23.8	6.2

Source: Brustein and King 2004a: 42, 2004b: 700; Mitchell 1975: 20–24.

Jewish Year Book in an attempt to measure differences in anti-Semitism across countries and over time. The reliability of the data depends on two unknowns: editorial discretion and the quality and consistency of local reportage. The latter is probably more of a problem than the former—the *American Jewish Year Book* relied on careful monthly analyses by a multilingual group of researchers of accounts in the most-read newspaper in each country in thirteen categories of actions. The stark contrast between Great Britain, France, and Italy, on the one hand, where antisemitic actions were relatively few, and Germany and Romania, on the other, is perhaps the most striking takeaway. The implied lack of violence against Jews in Italy and the high incidence of legal sanctions in Germany are also noteworthy.[83] By this reckoning, before World War II Jews were most at risk from violent attack in Romania and Bulgaria, but far higher proportions of their Jewish communities survived the Holocaust than those of, say, Greece or the Netherlands, where anti-Semitism was far less prevalent. And here is a further irony: The Wehrmacht murdered Jewish Soviet POWs but not Jewish POWs from Western countries. It is only a mild exaggeration to say that the safest places for a male Jew in German-controlled Europe were the Wehrmacht's POW camps.[84]

The Roma/Romani Genocide

Like the Jews, the Roma (a diverse ethnic group descending from medieval immigrants from northern India) and Sinti (a subgroup found mainly in Germany and neighboring areas) people were a target of Nazi ideology, although unlike the Jews they were never considered an existential threat to the Aryan race. Along with beggars, alcoholics, and nomads, the Roma were considered antisocial and *arbeitsscheu* (work-shy), and in Nazi concentration camps they wore the black triangle badge denoting that category. Although most anti-Roma prejudice, which was endemic in Europe, was directed against nomadic gypsies, in Nazi Germany the most suspect were *Mischlinge* (mixed-race gypsies) who had semi-integrated with the non-Romani population. Indeed, some Nazi ideologues (notably Heinrich Himmler) considered those of pure Romani stock to be Aryan, being originally from India.

Whereas there is broad agreement on the Jewish death toll, estimates of the Roma death toll vary widely, from 0.2 million to 0.5 million and even higher.[85] The *Columbia Guide to the Holocaust* warns that "statistics on Gypsy losses are especially unreliable and controversial." The USHMM's excellent website on the Romani states that while "the total number of Roma killed in Serbia will never be known . . . estimates range between 1,000 and 2,000" and believes that over 1 in 4 of Europe's Roma population was murdered. That same source reckons that the genocide against the gypsies took between 250,000 and 500,000 victims.[86] Guenter Lewy refers to estimates of the number of German and Austrian Sinti gassed in Auschwitz: 15,000–22,000 out of a total population of about 29,000 in 1942. For the rest he cites estimates of about 0.2 million out of a Roma population of 0.8 million and "at least 90,000" in Nazi-controlled territories in the East.[87] The very uncertainty about the death toll points to the marginality of the community before the crisis and its lack of a political voice since then. The reliability of the data varies greatly by country. The gaps between the "high" and "low" estimates provided in the *Columbia Guide* are small or zero in the case of Italy, Germany, France, Greece, and the USSR, but for Hungary the reported range is 1,000 to 28,000; for Slovakia, 400 to 10,000; for Poland, 8,000 to

35,000; and for Yugoslavia, 26,000 to 90,000. The numbers are given in table 5.4. The upper-bound estimates for Slovakia, Yugoslavia, and Romania are probably on the high side. In Slovakia, although many Roma were mistreated and interned, very few were sent to Nazi death camps. As for Yugoslavia, Kenrick and Puxon estimated the number of Roma in Serbia and Croatia in 1939 at 60,000 and 28,500, respectively, and the number of World War II deaths at 12,000 and 28,000.[88] Those latter numbers would tally with the 52,181 Roma in Serbia and 405 in Croatia according to the 1948 census and indicate that the death toll is unlikely to have exceeded 50,000. In 2004 the International Commission on the Holocaust in Romania put the number of Romani victims at 11,000, and that should be regarded as the most reliable estimate available. The *Columbia Guide* suggests the still rather arbitrary toll of 0.2 million.

The violence against the Roma varied considerably across Europe. Because a far lower proportion of Sinti (i.e., a Roma long resident in German-speaking lands) could flee from the Nazis, the death rate of Austrian and German Roma exceeded that of Austrian and German Jews. In western Europe, generally, the Roma were more likely to perish than Jews but not so, apparently, in Romania, Poland, and the former Soviet Union, where they were far more numerous.[89] Germany contained about 30,000 Romani before World War II. Perhaps half of them died at Auschwitz-Birkenau. Before the Anschluss most of Austria's small Roma population lived seminomadic lives in Burgenland next to the Hungarian border. Fewer than a third of them survived. Some died in mobile gas chambers in Kulmhof (today's Chełmno in central Poland); more died in Auschwitz-Birkenau. Most Croatian Roma were murdered by the pro-Nazi Ustaša, which controlled Croatia during World War II. The list compiled at the memorial site of the notorious Jasenovac concentration camp, located one hundred kilometers southeast of Zagreb, contains the names of 16,173 Roma killed there.[90]

Romania, which contained more Roma than any other country in Europe, is of particular interest. The Romanian census of 1930 recorded 262,501 self-declared Roma, most of whom made a living as craftsmen and small farmers; only 15 percent lived in towns. In the 1930s, although eugenicist and racist rhetoric was in the air, the Roma were not considered a problem, and "overall, the relations between the Roma and Romanian peasants were good." Initially, the state leader/dictator Antonescu linked the Roma community in Bucharest to criminality and sought to remove them to new settlements that held 5,000–6,000 households in Bărăgan in southeastern Romania. Although Antonescu wanted ethnic homogeneity

TABLE 5.4. Estimated Romani Holocaust deaths, 1939–45

Country	[1] Roma 1939 population	[2] Low estimate	[3] High estimate	0.5 * [2 + 3]/[1] %
Estonia	1,000	500	1,000	75
Luxembourg	200	100	200	75
Netherlands	500	215	500	72
Yugoslavia	100,000	26,000	90,000	58
Belgium	600	350	500	71
Germany	30,000	15,000	15,000	50
Austria	11,200	6,800	8,250	67
Poland[a]	25,000	8,000	13,500	43
Lithuania	1,500	500	1,000	50
Latvia	4,000	1,500	2,500	50
Bohemia-Moravia	13,000	5,000	6,500	44
France	40,000	15,150	15,150	38
Hungary	100,000	1,000	28,000	15
USSR	200,000	30,000	35,000	16
Romania	300,000	19,000	36,000	9
Slovakia	80,000	400	10,000	7
Italy	25,000	1,000	1,000	4
Greece[b]	.	50	50	.
Bulgaria[c]	130,000	0?	0?	.
Albania	20,000	0	0	0
Total	1,098,000	130,565	285,650	19

Source: Niewyk and Nicosia 2003: 422; Bulgaria and Albania added.

[a] Numbers from Wawrzeniuk 2018.

[b] The Council of Europe's *Factsheet on the Roma Genocide* in Greece states, "There is no existing evidence for Roma victims in Greece during the Holocaust. Consequently, there is no remembrance place for Roma." See https://www.coe.int/en/web/roma-genocide/greece.

[c] The last pre–World War II census in 1926 put the number of Roma in Bulgaria at 134,844 (32,101 in towns and 102,743 in villages). The 1946 census registered 170,011 Roma, 49,671 of them in towns (Marushiakova and Popov 2001: 456).

for Romania, the Roma (unlike the Jews) were not singled out on racial grounds. Most gypsies were not at risk. They served in the army like the rest of the population, and the families of conscripts were exempt from deportation.[91] But in official eyes, there were gypsies and gypsies. The acquisition of Transnistria, a region wedged between Moldova and Ukraine, following

Operation Barbarossa opened the possibility of deporting Roma to outside Romania's boundaries.

The deportation of a section of the Roma population to Transnistria began in the wake of a census conducted on May 25, 1942, on Antonescu's orders that registered 40,909 Roma deemed problematic or "dangerous and undesirable." Those registered included 9,471 nomads; the rest were considered sedentary, recidivist criminals or households unable or allegedly unwilling to support themselves. It bears noting that Antonescu never targeted the Roma population in general. But while race was not used as a pretext for deportation, non-Roma "dangerous" people were not touched.

Antonescu made the decision to deport the Roma across the Dniester in May 1942. Even before the census, Antonescu had decided to deport certain categories of Roma, but the subsequent deportations consisted of the citizens registered in this census. With only a few exceptions, the roughly 25,000 Romanian Roma "evacuated" to Transnistria (about one-eighth of all Romanian Roma) were included on the lists set up by the gendarmerie and police at the end of May. The Roma nomads were the first to be deported. The 13,000 sedentary Roma chosen for deportation were considered "dangerous and undesirable." The remaining 18,941 were to be deported later. The deportees faced harsh living conditions, particularly in 1942–43, and nearly half died of cold, hunger, and disease. The situation improved thereafter, with more work as agricultural labor, in road and railroad repair, and in forestry. By mid-March 1944, when all Romanian citizens were to be repatriated, 12,083 Roma were left in Transnistria. Subtracting that total plus another 2,000 or so who had escaped implies that about 11,000 died and 14,000 survived.[92]

Appendix: Holocaust Deaths, Country by Country

The death rate of Jews relative to their numbers on the eve of Hitler's takeover ranged from Denmark's less than 1 percent to over five-sixths in Greece and in Poland. Some of the factors behind this huge range have just been discussed. This appendix offers brief country-by-country outlines according to the estimated proportion of the Jewish population murdered.

GREECE

Nazi ideologue Alfred Rosenberg complained in 1941 that "for the average Greek, there is no Jewish question. He doesn't see the political danger of world Jewry." Yet Greece probably lost a higher proportion of its Jews than anywhere else during World War II. How much of it was due to anti-Semitism is still contested.[93] But as elsewhere, greed, opportunism, and collaboration on the part of both citizens and the authorities were also at play. Lives might have been saved in Macedonia, which the Nazis occupied between April 1941 and October 1944, in the absence of such tensions and collaboration and the lack of interest in offering protection to Jews at risk, but how many remains moot. The Nazis' grip on Thessaloniki, "the Jerusalem of the Balkans," was tight, and only the very affluent could afford the 150,000 drachmas (worth about $20,000 in 2023) that it cost to escape to Athens.[94]

On the eve of World War II, Greece's mainly Sephardic Jewish community numbered about 80,000. Until September 1943, while the Italians were in control of most of the southern part of Greece (excluding most of Crete), local Jews were relatively safe. Indeed, Jews who fled south to the Italian zone were helped by Italian soldiers and diplomats.[95] But a majority of Greek Jews lived in the North and, in particular, in Thessaloniki, which was under German control from the outset. After subjection to Nuremberg-style laws and the confiscation of much of their property, Thessaloniki's Jews were corralled into ghettos in late February 1943, and finally, the vast majority (45,000) were sent to Auschwitz, where nearly 9 in 10 perished.[96]

Then in 1944 the Nazis rounded up as many of the Jews in the former Italian zone as they could—and in this they were far less successful than in the North—and sent them to their deaths in Auschwitz-Birkenau. Of the half or so who were caught, very few returned alive.[97] On June 8, 1944, Crete's small but ancient Jewish population was forced onto a ship that would take them to Piraeus and on to Auschwitz, but the ship was torpedoed and sunk by a British submarine sixty kilometers north of Heraklion, drowning nearly all the Jews and others on board. The last to be deported were 1,767 Jews from Rhodes and Kos on July 24, 1944; 163 survived.[98]

In all, nearly 9 out of every 10 Greek Jews were murdered. This was mainly due to the ruthless efficiency of the SS in rounding up victims. An added contributory factor was the high death rate in Auschwitz due to the long, exhausting journey from Greece.[99]

POLAND

In 1939 Poland contained more than one-fifth of global Jewry, and they made up one-tenth of Poland's own population. With significant immigration into Poland from the Soviet Union after World War I and outlets for emigration largely closed off, the Jewish population of Poland rose from about 2.8 million in 1921 to nearly 3.5 million in 1939. Very few of those Jews still in Poland after the German invasions of September 1939 and Barbarossa (June 22, 1941) survived. Most of the half million or so who fled east after the first invasion were trapped by Barbarossa. Operation Reinhart, the code name for the plan to exterminate Polish Jewry, was devised in 1941 but gathered speed in 1942. Central to it were the three massive death camps—Belzec, Treblinka, and Sobibór, where much of the mass killing was carried out in gas chambers. The first use of gassing to kill Jews occurred at Chelmo in the Nazi *Reichsgau* (province) of Wartheland on December 8, 1941. Five of the six Nazi extermination camps built by the Nazis were located in that part of Poland known as the General Government, the exception being Chelmo. Nearly half of the 6 million or so who perished during the Holocaust were Polish Jews, and more than half of those perished in Belzec, Treblinka, or Sobibór.

The killings incorporated the whole panoply of "industrial" methods employed by the Nazis: ghettoization, mass shootings, forced labor camps, starvation, mobile gas vans, and gas chambers. Experimentation with gassing had begun in Auschwitz during the summer of 1941; its first victims were not Jews but Soviet POWs and sick Polish prisoners. The camp at Auschwitz (present-day Oświęcim, sixty-five kilometers west of Kraków), formerly a Polish army barracks, was greatly expanded in 1942 to contain not only barracks for prisoners, gas chambers, and crematoria but several industrial plants. The first all-Jewish transports to Auschwitz arrived from Upper Silesia in early 1942. Between then and 1945, about 1.1 million died in Auschwitz, mostly Jews from all over Europe.

Some 265,000 survivors of the Warsaw ghetto perished in the extermination camp of Treblinka II, located eighty kilometers northeast of Warsaw, between July and September 1942; in all about 0.9 million Polish Jews perished there. Another 0.3 million Polish Jews or so died in Auschwitz, 0.7 million in Bełżec and neighboring Sobibór, and 0.3 million in Chelmo. Using data compiled by the Israeli historian Yitzhak Arad from railway records, Lewi Stone reckons that nearly 1.5 million Jews—about 1 in every 4 killed—were murdered in the gas chambers of Belzec, Sobibór, and Treblinka in a period of just over three months.[100]

Fifty to eighty thousand died in Majdanek camp near Lublin in the far east of present-day Poland. Over 40,000 of those perished during what the Nazis called the *Erntefest* (Harvest Festival) *Aktion*, the single biggest massacre carried out by the Germans during World War II. They included 18,000 killed by gunfire on November 3, 1943. The SS carried out the killing with help from the security police (*Ordnungspolizei*) and Ukrainian volunteers. A further 14,500 were murdered in Poniatowa concentration camp, also in the Lublin area, on the following day.[101]

YUGOSLAVIA

The death rate among Jews living in the former Yugoslavia was also very high. Local SS leader Harald Turner claimed in 1942 that Serbia was "the only country in which the Jewish question and the Gypsy question has been solved," and it is likely that 5 out of 8 of the 82,000 Jews living in Yugoslavia when invaded in 1941 lost their lives during the Holocaust.[102] In Serbia, Jewish males were murdered first, many in revenge killings as "hostages," then the women and children were killed, mainly by gassing. In the puppet Independent State of Croatia, most of the killing was done by the Ustaša, which controlled Croatia with Nazi approval from April 10, 1941. They introduced Nuremberg Laws against Jews and Roma and carried out genocidal acts against Serbs living in Croatia and Bosnia. In their concentration camps in Jasenovac, it is reckoned that 80,000–100,000 died between May and August 1941, of whom 20,000 were Jews. Most of the killing of Serb and Croat Jews was conducted within Serbia and Croatia, but about 6,000 Croatian Jews perished in Nazi death camps in eastern Europe.[103]

SOVIET UNION

It has been claimed that "the scholarly consensus is that around 1 million Jewish victims of the Holocaust were residents of the former Soviet Union." "Consensus" is hardly the appropriate word: Snyder puts the number killed in the Soviet Union and the three Baltic states at 1.7 million, while Klier states that "approximately one million Soviet Jewish citizens were killed by the Germans and local collaborators in the period 1941–44," but his estimate includes up to 0.2 million Jewish soldiers. According to the USHMM, about 1.34 million Jews were murdered in the occupied part of the Soviet Union. A precise number is beyond reach, but it is extremely unlikely that the total was as low as 1 million. In table 5.2 we accordingly proposed a range of 1 million to 1.2 million deaths in the Soviet Union and a further 0.2 million in the three Baltic states.[104] Although many Jews, not knowing whom or what to believe, were reluctant to abandon their homes, and while the Soviet authorities doubtless could have done more by prioritizing the evacuation of Jews, nonetheless a million or more Soviet Jews—the Israeli historian Yitzhak Arad has put the number at about 0.8 million Jews from the pre-1939 USSR and another 0.4–0.5 million from territory newly annexed after Barbarossa—survived by finding a safe haven in the East.[105]

BALTIC STATES

On the eve of World War II, the combined Jewish population of the three Baltic states was about 0.25 million (160,000 in Lithuania, 93,000 in Latvia, and 4,000 in Estonia). The Holocaust in the Baltic states was exceptional for the scale of the complicity of the local population. After 1918 the new democracies were ruled by their majority populations for the first time, and this presented challenges to all minority communities. Independence spawned an increasingly assertive majority population, campaigning for a "Lithuania for the Lithuanians" and eager for a bigger share of the national pie. The rhetorical tone of anti-Semitism became coarser. But the conservative dictatorship that ruled Lithuania before the Soviets took over "shielded Jews from the worst of popular anti-Semitism."[106] On the eve of World War II, Jews in Lithuania did not feel threatened: "The common feeling . . . was that . . . Lithuania is one of the best places for a Jew to live in contemporary Europe."[107]

As envisaged under the Molotov-Ribbentrop pact, in mid-June 1940 Soviet troops invaded and quickly occupied the Baltic states. Rigged elections and annexation by the Soviet Union followed. On the night of June 14–15, 1941, just a week before being forced out by the Nazis, the Soviets arrested and deported over fifteen thousand people, or over 1 percent of the total population, from Latvia, making enemies of themselves and friends of the Germans.[108] They expelled a slightly higher number from Lithuania. Those expelled included the cream of society.

The Holocaust brought carnage all over Latvia and Lithuania. It is reckoned that about seventy-five thousand Latvian Jews were captured by the Germans, and nearly half of them were murdered by the end of 1941. About ten thousand survived the war. The outcome in Lithuania, which the Germans invaded on June 22, 1941, was similar, with the extermination of its Jewish population gaining significant support, active and tacit, from the local population. Most of Lithuanian Jewry were murdered by *Einsatzgruppen* of the Nazi paramilitary SS and numerous local collaborators before the end of 1941. Most of those who survived that first phase—about forty thousand—perished in death camps toward the end of the war. About twelve thousand survived the war (including two thousand or so who had fled to the Soviet Union). A striking feature of the Holocaust in the Baltic states is the relatively small proportion of victims who perished in death camps; as in Ukraine and Belarus, most died in a "Holocaust by bullets."

Estonia's tiny Jewish population was more fortunate than those of its Baltic neighbors to the south. While one in ten had been deported as belonging to "socially dangerous elements" by the Soviets, a majority (three thousand) of the remainder, forewarned and broadly sympathetic to the Soviet Union, fled there before the Nazis arrived. Nearly all the thousand or so who remained were killed by *Einsatzgruppen* and a small number of collaborators in the local "self-defense force" before the end of 1941. The Nazis declared Estonia to be *judenfrei* at the Wannsee Conference on January 20, 1942.[109]

The collaboration of significant numbers of civilians in the destruction of Jewish communities has warped the historiography and public memory of the Holocaust in the Baltic states. In 2009 all three embarked on a project to produce an agreed history of "two equal genocides" by the Nazis and the Soviets. This project posited an equivalence between the Holocaust and Soviet oppression during and in the wake of World War II—"The Communists did their murders first," "1940 comes before 1941"—obfuscating or occluding an involvement that went far beyond collaboration by local civilians in the mass murder of their Jewish neighbors.[110]

UKRAINE

Estimates of the number of Jews murdered in Ukraine are contested. The USHMM puts the number in the Soviet Union as a whole at 1,340,000. Assuming 0.4 million for eastern Belarus (see below) would allow for 0.7–0.8 million victims in Ukraine, somewhat fewer than the estimates of 0.9–1.6 million mentioned in Wikipedia; Berkoff puts the toll in *Reichskommissariat Ukraine* at 350,000 in 1942 and 1943. Most of Ukraine's Jews perished in mass shootings, the biggest of which were carried out in Mikolaiv/Nikolaev (35,782, mostly Jews, September 16–30, 1941), Babyn Yar outside Kiev (33,771 Jews, September 29–30, 1941), and Odessa (30,000, mostly Jews, by a combination of shootings and fires, October 22–23, 1941).[111] The carnage in Odessa would have been even greater had half of the city's Jewish population of 200,000 not fled by mid-October 1941 before Romanian troops occupied the city.

In western Ukraine, in particular, pogroms in which locals massacred Jews preceded or accompanied the shooting and gassing of Jews by the Nazis and their helpers.[112] The Germans regarded the Ukrainians as superior to Russians and Poles, and most Ukrainians harbored a hatred of the Stalinist regime. Moreover, much of Ukraine had a history of anti-Semitic pogroms in the 1900s and again during the civil war. It is reckoned that eighty thousand Ukrainian men assisted the Nazis as *politsaï* (auxiliary policemen), most of them ethnic Ukrainians recruited in the regions in which they worked. Ethnic Germans living in Ukraine also helped in the killings and played an added role in translating and in communicating to the German authorities, and some graduated to membership in *Einsatzgruppen*.[113] That said, the intensity of anti-Semitism varied from place to place; it was much milder in Odessa, for example, than in Kiev.[114]

BELARUS

On the eve of Barbarossa, eastern Belarus—that is, the part that remained in the Soviet Union after World War I—contained a Jewish population of 0.4 million, whereas another 0.6 million Jews lived in that part of Belarus that had been made part of Poland. Estimates of the number of Holocaust victims in Belarusian accounts range from 0.2 to 0.9 million.[115] A small number of those from eastern Belarus, perhaps 30,000, escaped from the Minsk ghetto, half of whom survived the war.[116] In Belarus, as elsewhere in the occupied Soviet Union, most Holocaust victims were shot by *Einsatzgruppen* in killing sites, but thousands also perished in the extermination camps of Sobibor in eastern Poland and Maly Trotsdenets, a short distance from Minsk. While the Belarus authorities did not go out of their way to aid Jews, the population at large was less likely to collaborate with the occupiers than in the Baltic states or Ukraine, and thanks to collaboration between Communist and Jewish partisans, several thousand Jews managed to escape from the Minsk ghetto into nearby forests and on to relative safety. In 1941–42, when most of the killings occurred, Germans found that reliable locals were difficult to enlist in Belarus and relied instead on auxiliary police consisting of Lithuanians, Ukrainians, and Latvians.[117]

CZECHOSLOVAKIA

Czechoslovakia contained over 357,000 Jews in 1930, or 2.4 percent of the total population. About one-third lived in what became the German-occupied Protectorate of Bohemia and Moravia in 1939. About 30,000 of those managed to emigrate before 1941; by the end of 1942, most of those left behind had been murdered, and only 15,530 remained in the protectorate.

Of the 89,000 Jews left in Slovakia in 1940—perhaps 5,000–6,000 had fled before the Nazis arrived—69,000 were murdered. Some 10,000 survived the war in Slovakia, and a similar number had survived elsewhere. Nearly 160,000 Jews lived in Carpathian Ruthenia, which Slovakia ceded to Hungary in 1939. About 100,000 of them were murdered. In all about a quarter of a million Czechoslovak Jews perished.[118]

LOW COUNTRIES

When the Germans occupied Belgium in May 1940, it contained about 66,000 Jews, mostly foreign and stateless and mostly living in either Antwerp or Brussels. The Germans immediately imposed laws limiting the rights of Jews. They created the Association des Juifs en Belgique, a *Judenrat* with which all Jews were supposed to register. But only 43,000 did, reflecting a mistrust of authority in the community. German plans were also thwarted by the Belgian civil authorities. The Germans deported 25,000, mainly to Auschwitz, between 1942 and 1944; only 1,207 survived. When the deportations began, Jews began to hide, and by the end of the war, about 25,000 were in hiding, with Catholic clergy playing a prominent helping role. In Belgium efforts by the non-Jewish majority succeeded in saving a significant proportion of the Jewish community. According to Israeli historian Shlomo Kless, "The behavior of the Belgian people may be regarded as the expression of what perhaps should be the normal human behavior of a civilized nation sustained in the face of Nazi occupation." Still, two-fifths of Belgian Jews were lost.[119]

The Netherlands contained about 140,000 Jews when it was occupied in May 1940. Unlike Belgian Jewry, most belonged to a community that could trace its origins back several centuries, but they included about 30,000 refugees from Germany, including Anne Frank and her family. Anti-Semitism was not widespread. Indeed, the protests against the first expulsions of Jews in February 1941 by non-Jewish civilians were unique in western Europe. Those protests, engineered by the outlawed Dutch Communist Party, were short-lived and largely confined to Amsterdam and its hinterland, but they involved significant numbers of people. Over three-quarters of the Netherlands' 140,000 Jews were deported to Nazi death camps, where 96 percent of them perished. Whereas in Belgium the clumsy repression of the authorities prompted Jews to evade captivity, in the Netherlands they subtly lulled Jews into a sense of false security, making it relatively easy to round them up and deport them.[120] In the Netherlands, the religion of the local non-Jewish population is said to have played a role in survival hazards. That Catholics had been less likely to support the local Nazi Party before the war and also less likely to join the auxiliary police that helped to arrest Jews may also have meant they were more likely to help conceal Jews. But protests in August 1942 by the Dutch Catholic hierarchy led to the deportation to Auschwitz and almost certain death of Jews who had converted to Catholicism, whereas those who had converted to Protestantism were sent to Theresienstadt/Terezín, where most survived.[121]

HUNGARY

Thanks to its alliance with Nazi Germany in the interwar period, Hungary had annexed territory containing ethnic Hungarians from Czechoslovakia, Romania, and Yugoslavia. In the enlarged Hungary of 1941, Jews represented 5 percent of the population. Roughly speaking, three-fifths of them lived in Hungary as defined by the Treaty of Trianon (1920), and another fifth resided in northern Transylvania. Hungary took the Axis side in 1939, but heavy losses on the Eastern Front led it to consider surrendering to the Allies. Although Hungary had a history of anti-Semitism, most of its 0.8 million Jews felt secure despite increasingly restrictive anti-Jewish measures including, in August 1941, prohibiting Jews from marrying non-Jews. Not even the deportation to western Ukraine in August 1941 of 20,000 noncitizens, most of them from a region ceded to Hungary in 1939, where they were nearly all slaughtered by the SS, seemed to threaten them. The Nazis occupied Hungary on March 19, 1944, when its alliance with Germany showed signs of wavering. That was when the ghettoization and deportation en masse of Jews began, first from the annexed areas and then from Hungary proper. The plan was orchestrated by Eichmann, with help from Hungarian anti-Semites such as László Endre.[122] By July 6, when the Hungarian leader Miklós Horthy, under heavy pressure from the Allies, ordered a halt to deportations, 437,000 had been deported, and most of the community outside Budapest had already been murdered in Auschwitz. In October 1944, Horthy, keen to make peace with the Allies, was replaced by the pro-Nazi Arrow Cross Party, which was responsible for the deaths of up to 100,000 of Budapest's Jews.[123] The thousands of protective passports issued by Sweden's Raul Wallenberg and other diplomatic representatives of neutral countries gave thousands of Budapest Jews at least a temporary reprieve, but how many lives they succeeded in saving remains controversial.[124]

NORWAY

The Jewish population of Norway increased from 1,500 in 1920 to 2,100 in 1940. Most of the increase was due to immigration, including that of refugees from Germany and Austria in the 1930s. About a thousand escaped to neutral Sweden, and another 100 joined Norwegian forces in Britain before the collaborationist Quisling government started rounding up Jews in October–November 1942. Of the 771 handed over to the Nazis, only 34 survived the Holocaust. An additional 23 deaths were Holocaust related.[125]

ROMANIA

Anti-Semitism had a long history in Romania, where most Jews made their living as middlemen—leasers of land, traders, tax collectors, lawyers, medics, journalists, white-collar workers, and moneylenders—and were resented by both a nascent Romanian commercial class and victims of economic development. Economic resentment was compounded by racial anti-Semitism. There was political anti-Semitism too. As elsewhere in Romania, Jews were overrepresented in left-wing parties, which bred its own conspiracy theories against them. And immigration played a role: the Jewish share of Romania's population rose from about 1 percent in the mid-nineteenth century to 3.3 percent on the eve of World War I and 4 percent on the eve of World War II.[126] When the Soviets occupied the regions of Bessarabia and Northern Bukovina in July–August 1940, some Romanians accused the local Jewish population of collaborating with and welcoming the enemy. This not only fueled violence against Jews in Romania but also led to the murder of thousands of Jews in Bessarabia and Northern Bukovina in the wake of Operation Barbarossa. Paranoia about the pro-Soviet sympathies of the Jewish population, some of whom lived close to the Soviet border, led to a policy of evacuating Jews from the countryside and expelling the Jews of Bessarabia and Bukovina to Transnistria. In July 1941, nearly 15,000 Jews were killed in a pogrom in Iaşi, a small city close to the Soviet border, and perhaps 50,000 more were murdered in Bessarabia and Bukovina after German and Romanian troops occupied those areas.

Romania contained over 0.7 million Jews before World War II. According to the international commission set up by Romanian president Ion Iliescu in 2004, "between 280,000 and 380,000 Romanian and Ukrainian Jews were murdered or died during the Holocaust in Romania and the territories under its control." Half of the 0.3 million living in Bessarabia and Bukovina perished, and over 0.1 million died after expulsion to Transnistria. A further 135,000 Jews living in northern Transylvania, under Hungarian control during the war, were deported and perished in death camps.[127] In the totals given in chapter 4, the killings in Northern Transylvania, Bessarabia, and Transnistria are included in the totals for Hungary and the Soviet Union, respectively.

Marshall Ion Antonescu, *conducator* of Romania from 1941, shifted his stance toward Jews after Stalingrad. In March–April 1943 he halted all deportations despite pressure from the Germans and turned a blind eye to limited Jewish emigration to Palestine. The partial repatriation of Jews from Transnistria began in December 1943, and there were no more deportations. That fewer than one-third of Romanian Jews perished in the Holocaust owed nothing to waning anti-Semitism and everything to the fortunes of war.

BULGARIA

On the eve of the war, Bulgaria contained about 45,000 Sephardic Jews, about half of whom lived in the capital, Sofia. They made up less than 1 percent of the population. Most made their living as street traders or artisans and were not well-off; a more prosperous minority were engaged in the retail trade and in the liberal professions. Bulgaria took the Axis side during the war but did not participate in the fighting on the Eastern Front. Although relations between Jews and the majority population were much better than, say, in Romania, the authorities soon introduced Bulgaria's own version of the Nuremberg Laws and began to confiscate Jewish property. Jews in the main cities were confined to ghettos, and Jewish males of military age served in forced-labor battalions until September 1944. But plans to deport its Jewish population were, for the most part, stymied by resistance from the Bulgarian king, the Orthodox Church, many politicians and intellectuals, and civil society. As a result, at the end of the war the size of Bulgaria's Jewish population was more or less the same as it had been in 1939.

Jews living in the "new lands" of Thrace, ceded to Bulgaria by the Nazis in exchange for participation in the campaigns against Greece and Yugoslavia, did not escape, however. Almost all—numbering 11,343—perished in Treblinka. Responsibility for their fate is controversial. The official Bulgarian position is that the authorities were powerless to prevent the deportations since those territories were under German jurisdiction. This claim is contradicted, however, by extensive evidence of complicity in the Bulgarian state archives.[128]

FRANCE

In 1940 France had a Jewish population of about 330,000, which included 135,000 immigrants, mostly refugees from Nazism. About half of the foreign-born lived in the Paris region. France initially welcomed the refugees, but attitudes and policies hardened over the decade. Still, immigration persisted, much of it necessarily illegal. The Vichy regime, which replaced the Third Republic after France's defeat in 1940, sought to seal the border entirely against refugees and to arrest and intern those who crossed it. It was particularly hostile to refugees who arrived in the wake of the Nazi conquest of France. Yet while much of the historiography of the Holocaust highlights the role of Vichy and its police force in rounding up and deporting Jews, in 2013 the French historian Jacques Sémelin caused a stir by asking why so relatively few French Jews perished, relative to 80 percent in the Netherlands and nearly half in Belgium.

At first the northern half of France was occupied by the Nazis and the southern half by a nationalist-collaborationist regime, but the Nazis took over the entire country in November 1942, apart from a small Italian zone in the Southeast. Still, over three-quarters of Jews living in France in 1940 survived. A benign explanation for this relatively high survival rate is that the French were less anti-Semitic and more willing to help than commonly depicted. Browning highlights the role from 1942 of what historians have dubbed "NGOs for humanitarian relief" and a "supportive web of social relationships" in unoccupied France. These links formed networks and planned escape routes and safe havens in the wake of the deportation crisis of August 1942.[129] It also mattered that whereas in the Netherlands and in Belgium policy toward the Jewish population was exclusively determined by the Germans, in France the Vichy government constrained German actions and in particular allowed its own police to arrest only Jews who were not French citizens.

Vichy blended anti-Semitism and xenophobia. One of its first anti-Semitic laws gave the police discretion to intern *foreign* Jews, and in the following months, it interned ten thousand of them, who were later handed over to the Germans. It was no accident, then, that of the eighty thousand French Jews who perished, fifty-five thousand were foreign-born. Moreover, of the twenty-five thousand French Jews killed, a third were the children of foreigners, and another third were naturalized French citizens. So while over half of Jewish immigrants or the children of Jewish immigrants did not survive the Holocaust, 96 percent of French Jews did.[130]

ITALY

Italy's Fascist government did not introduce its own anti-Semitic legislation until 1938, beginning in July with a law against the public sale of translations of books by foreign Jews. Before then the regime had significant backing from Jews, who had joined the party in roughly the same proportion as non-Jews. The racial laws (*Leggi Razziali*) enacted in November 1938 prompted the emigration of about 6,000 of Italy's 50,000 Jews. However, no Jews were murdered or deported before the downfall of Mussolini's administration on July 25, 1943; indeed, several thousand Jews found refuge in Italy from Austria and the Balkans. The Germans began to round up and deport Jews, mostly Italian but including refugees too, in September 1943. By the end of the war, 8,600 Jews had been sent to Auschwitz, of whom only a thousand survived. In all, 7,680 Italian Jews perished.

DENMARK

With the help of non-Jews and the Danish resistance, 7,220 of Denmark's tiny Jewish population of 7,800 (including about 1,500 stateless refugees), accompanied by 686 non-Jewish spouses, were evacuated across the sound to Sweden on October 1–2, 1943, in order to avoid arrest and deportation. This was done with the knowledge of German naval attaché Georg F. Duckwitz, who sought to have the Jews rescued, and the connivance of local Nazi plenipotentiary Werner Best and the Wehrmacht, who turned a blind eye to the escape to Sweden. Moreover, intercession on behalf of the 464 who were rounded up, most of them refugees, meant they were deported to Theresienstadt—not Auschwitz—where most of them survived. Fifty-two Danish Jews perished there and 1 in Auschwitz. In that way 99.3 percent of Danish Jewry escaped the Holocaust.[131]

FINLAND

In the wake of the Anschluss, the Finnish consulate in Vienna granted visas to a few hundred Austrian Jews. Their arrival provoked an appeal from trade unions fearful of the consequences for employment to deport those admitted and allow no more into the country. In late August 1938, despite loud protests in the press and by left-leaning politicians, a group of 53 Austrians were refused entry and forced back to Germany. Finland contained about 2,300 Jews when war broke out. That included a small number of noncitizens liable to deportation. After the initial successes of the Finnish army (in which several hundred Jews fought) in Karelia, the Jewish population of Finland also included 405 Soviet prisoners who identified as Jewish and presumably several more who did not. News that eight Jewish civilians had been extradited in November caused widespread outrage; 49 of the 521 "troublesome" POWs handed over to the Germans were Jewish, but they were not surrendered because they were Jewish. No anti-Semitic legislation was passed in Finland during the war, and its few synagogues remained open. The Nazis saw Finland as a valuable ally. Public opinion in Finland against handing over its Jews dictated Nazi inaction.[132]

6

Civilian Deaths by Aerial Bombing

What a degrading war this is besides being a bloodthirsty and terrible
one. The poisonous gasses, the Zeppelins, the torpedoes, and the
hidden treacherous mines, all strike a note of mean unfairness; in
modern slang it's simply "not cricket." . . . But as someone said the
other day, "There are no civilians now, we are all soldiers."
—DIARY OF ETHEL BILBROUGH, CHISLEHURST, KENT, 1916

Such wars will be short-lived because their main targets will be the
most vulnerable elements in the countries involved. Perhaps, for all
their attendant atrocities, they will prove more humane than past wars
because, ultimately, they will cause less bloodshed.
—GIULIO DOUHET, ITALIAN AIR WAR THEORETICIAN, 1921

The civilian population must be prepared to suffer harm today from
which a hundred years ago they would have been immune. As Samuel
Johnson remarked in Rasselas: "Against an Army sailing through
the clouds, neither walls, nor mountains, nor seas could afford any
security."
—AN AMERICAN JURIST, 1925

World War I began eleven years after Orville and Wilbur Wright's first thirty-
seven-meter flight at Kitty Hawk, North Carolina, and only five years after
Louis Blériot was the first to cross the English Channel by airplane. Just two

years after Blériot's heroics, on November 1, 1911, an Italian war pilot flew his monoplane over a Libyan oasis and threw four hand grenades out of his cockpit at unsuspecting Ottoman troops six hundred feet below. Whether he succeeded in hitting his target is unknown, but his action is noteworthy for having been the first time aircraft was used in warfare.[1] Although aircraft engineering was still in its infancy in 1914, it was making rapid strides and would make more during World War I. But the war erupted a few decades too soon to replicate the apocalyptic predictions of the science fiction of Pierre Giffard's *La Guerre Infernale* or H. G. Wells's *The War in the Air*, both published in 1908.

In 1910 the Russian and German navies set about creating air arms. The French Navy followed with its Service Aéronautique and the British army with its Royal Flying Corps in 1912. The naval wing of the latter would become the Royal Naval Air Service (RNAS) in 1914. Austro-Hungary and Serbia also realized the lethal potential of airpower and had started building air forces before the start of hostilities. Table 6.1 highlights how future belligerents increased their airpower between 1910 and 1914; the United States, which did not take up arms until 1917, had 73 aircraft in service and 302 more on order by January 1917.[2]

All countries involved in World War I envisaged the aerial bombing of cities as a tactic, and all engaged in it to some extent. In this the Germans would prove the most threatening, if not the most successful. They bombed Liège and Antwerp in August 1914 using the engine-driven, nitrogen-filled airships already commonly known as Zeppelins (a version was patented by Count Ferdinand von Zeppelin in 1895 and first flown in 1900[3]). The nine civilians who died in the former and the ten in the latter would be the first-known victims of aerial bombing.

At first the kaiser refused to sanction aerial bombing—out of concern, it was said, for the safety of his royal cousins in London. The zeppelins began their campaign against Britain on January 19, 1915, days after he relaxed his opposition.[4] Headed for Humberside but driven off course by strong winds, their bombs fell instead on civilians in the Norfolk seaside towns of King's Lynn and Great Yarmouth, killing two civilians in each, "a shoemaker, an old lady over 70 years old, a widow of 26 and a boy of 14."[5] Other raids on Humberside were more successful. The first on June 6, 1915, scored hits on Hull's docks and killed 25 people, and another 51 died in later raids by zeppelins or aircraft. London, which was excluded on the kaiser's orders until May 1915, when he allowed bombing east of the Tower of London, was bombed for the first time at the end of that month. The Germans mounted

TABLE 6.1. Aircraft by country in 1910 and 1914

Country	Airships		Airplanes		Combat aircraft
	1910	August 1914	1910	August 1914	1918
Belgium	2	2	2	16	
Britain	2	0	4	263	3,300
France	3	10	36	165	4,500
Italy	3	—	2	"a few dozen"	1,200
Germany	9	8	5	232	2,390
Austria-Hungary	—	1	—	39*	
Russia	3	4	3	263	
UnitedStates	2	0	2	23	740

Sources: For the United States in 1914: Bergs 2017; for Italy: Caffarena 2014; for Austria: Connor 1986: 258; otherwise Knell 2003. For 1918, Angelucci 2001: plate 7.

Note: (—) indicates "not given"; (*) indicates "operable."

fifty Zeppelin raids in all on England, killing 557, almost all civilians. The airships, quickly dubbed "baby killers" in the British press, were wildly inaccurate in their targeting,[6] and their raids became increasingly hazardous as more effective defenses were deployed, including searchlights, defense aircraft, and incendiary bullets laced with phosphorus (figure 6.1). Thirty of the eighty-four *dirigible* airships involved between early 1915 and late 1916, when raids were temporarily halted, were lost, including Zeppelin L31, captained by Kapitänleutnant Heinrich Mathy and shot down north of London on the night of October 1, 1916, by a B.E.2c biplane. The Germans thereafter switched to employing mainly airplanes, which were more difficult to defend against; but a new Zeppelin model, the S-class, whose cruising altitude of five thousand meters came at a cost in terms of altitude sickness and extreme cold, was also used. In May and June 1917, the first Gulfstream IV biplanes, better known as *Gothas*, were employed in daytime raids on the London area, causing over one hundred civilian deaths. As British antiaircraft and civil defenses improved, the Germans switched to indiscriminate nighttime bombing but suffered heavy losses and limited success. The R.VI, a four-engine strategic bomber developed by Zeppelin-Staaken, was deployed against British targets for the first time on September 28, 1917. By May 1918 R.VI bombers had carried out eleven raids, dropping twenty-seven tons of bombs in thirty sorties.

THE FLIGHT THAT FAILED.

THE EMPEROR. "WHAT! NO BABES, SIRRAH?"
THE MURDERER. "ALAS! SIRE, NONE."
THE EMPEROR. "WELL, THEN, NO BABES, NO IRON CROSSES."

[Exit murderer, discouraged.

FIGURE 6.1. Zeppelin raids
a. In the wake of the first Zeppelin raids in January 1915
b. The super-Zeppelin L31, captained by Heinrich Mathy

Bombs intended for factories, railway stations, dockyards, administrative headquarters, and the like made civilian casualties unavoidable. Even identifying targets was difficult; Zeppelins typically sought out city lights or a river, dropped their bombs, and hoped for the best. Hardly surprisingly, even when intent was lacking the raids were described as acts of terrorism in the British media. Mathy's attack on targets in London on the night of September 8, 1915, with his Zeppelin L13 is a case in point. In a widely recycled account first published in the United States, Mathy explained how "we headed straight for the glow, and soon the city was outlined, still silent below. There were dark spots that stood out from the blue lights in the well-lit portions. The residential sections were not much darkened; it was the dark spots we were after."[7] Mathy may well have been sincere in his wish to spare civilians,[8] but dropping missiles from two miles high in a moving plane was no way to avoid them, as the path over London followed by Zeppelin L13 illustrates. Its first bomb landed on an area surrounded by hospitals in Queen's Square in Bloomsbury, causing no casualties. That was followed by others on a public house at the corner of Lambs Conduit Passage and Red Lion Street, killing two; on Farringdon Road, leveling a warehouse; on a tenement block on Portpool Lane, where four children were killed; on Bartholomew's Close just south of Smithfield Market, where the biggest bomb used so far in the war, weighing three hundred kilograms, killed two men as they emerged from a pub and caused extensive damage to buildings; then over the City of London, causing several major fires but no deaths; and finally around Liverpool Street Station, where two buses were hit, killing twelve people. As L13 headed for home, Mathy also tried, unsuccessfully, to hit Tower Bridge. Less than a month later, he was back with four other airships, one of which (not his) dropped bombs on the West End in what came to be dubbed the *Theatreland Raid*. This raid was far more murderous, costing seventy-one lives (including fourteen soldiers) but causing only £80,000 worth of damage to property.

The Germans attacked Paris too, using both zeppelins and aircraft, leaving 275 dead and 636 injured. The bombing intensified in 1918; the 267 bombs dropped on January 30, 1918, killed 61 and injured 198, and on the night of March 11–12, a panic in a metro station being used as a shelter killed another 76 in northeastern Paris. Calais, Nancy, and Lunéville were among the other French cities where civilians died. The Germans also attacked Polish and Baltic cities, but in those cases civilian casualties were fewer.[9]

Among the combatants, Austro-Hungary's aircraft probably killed the most enemy civilians. In addition to an unknown number killed in the war against Serbia, in Italy they were responsible for 965 deaths and 1,158 wounded, most of them in Veneto (802 and 696, respectively) and Puglia (67 and 103). The city of Venice was a favorite target. It was hit by over a thousand bombs, but fewer (52) died there than in Bassano (274) and Padova (129). Most of Padova's victims were killed in a raid on the city's fortifications, where they were sheltering.[10] However, the dubious credit for the deadliest single action against civilians during World War I goes to the French bomber that killed 117 people, mostly children, attending a circus in the south German city of Karlsruhe on June 22, 1916.[11]

At the outset Russia had the most advanced bomber, the four-engine Sikorsky Ilya Muramets (designed by aviation pioneer Igor Sikorsky and named after one of the heroes of Russian folklore), of which eighty-three were built for the Imperial Air Service between 1913 and 1917. Weighing nearly five tons when loaded and flying a maximum speed of 110 kilometers per hour, they were used mainly to attack frontline positions and railway yards, but they were also used in a bombing attack on Constantinople in August 1915 that cost forty-one civilian lives. During World War I, they performed four hundred sorties and dropped sixty-five tons of bombs.

Although Britain's RNAS aircraft were quick off the mark, bombing Zeppelin bases (with limited success) in September and October 1914 and using shipborne aircraft in a raid on Cuxhaven in Lower Saxony on Christmas Day 1914, plans to carry out long-distance raids on German industrial targets came too late to have much effect. The "really big fire" that would bring Germany to its knees by destroying civilian morale never materialized.[12] Still, by November 1918 the British had dropped 660 tons on German targets, compared to the 300 tons dropped by German airships and aircraft on British targets. But the highest number of civilian casualties caused by a British raid was not in Germany: an air raid on Constantinople on October 18, 1917, killed fifty-four civilians and wounded two hundred. In a report written just after the war, Sir Hugh Trenchard, commander of the bombing campaign that dropped 550 tons on German cities in June–November 1918, admitted that "at present the moral effect of bombing stands undoubtedly to the material effect in a proportion of 20 to 1, and therefore it was necessary to create the greatest moral effect possible." The campaign had resulted in the loss of 109 "machines," with little tangible to show for it.[13]

Serbia's minuscule air force of three airplanes had already seen action during the Balkan Wars. It would begin World War I with nine planes, only seven of which were airworthy. In 1914–15, along with French aircraft, these engaged in both reconnaissance and bombing missions, but soon their main role would turn to the evacuation and rescue of wounded troops. The Serbian air force proved powerless against Austrian attacks on retreating soldiers and civilians in late 1915 and lost all its planes. Those attacks compete for the dubious honor of being the first to expressly target civilians.[14] The Serbian air force reformed on the Thessaloniki front, and by the end of the war, its sixty aircraft had made three thousand combat flights.

Aircraft technology made rapid strides during the war (figure 6.2). According to one authoritative account, "the airplane and its uses in war evolved more in the 52 months of World War 1 than in the 52 years that followed it."[15] In Britain the two-seater Sopwith Tabloids used in 1914 could carry five 9-kilogram (20 pound) bombs at 140 kilometers per hour and had a range of 820 kilometers. The Bristol Braemar Mk. II, first flown near the war's end, had a crew of six, could carry up to 680 kilograms of bombs at speeds of up to 170 kilometers per hour, and had a range 1,600 kilometers. Germany switched from airships to airplanes in 1917; its Gotha G.V (1917) could carry fourteen 25-kilogram bombs at a maximum speed of 140 kilometers per hour and had a range of 840 kilometers, whereas the only slightly slower Zeppelin-Staaken R.VI (1916) could carry up to 2,000 kilograms of bombs for roughly the same distance. At the outset France's Bréguet 4 (1914) could travel at a speed of 138 kilometers per hour and carry 300 kilograms of bombs, but its range was only 400 kilometers. Three years later the Bréguet 14 had a maximum speed of 195 kilometers per hour and could carry up to 355 kilograms of bombs. Rivals copied the Ilya Muramets design, which did not change much after 1914—the Germans apparently learned from the wreckage of the only one shot down—and by 1917 the Russian bomber was no longer supreme (figure 6.2).

As the war intensified, both sides worried less about civilian casualties from aerial bombing, rather like the way in which they shed their scruples about the use of chemical weapons against enemy troops. A French attack on Freiburg-im-Breisgau in December 1914 relaxed the kaiser's angst about using Zeppelins to attack England. The French attack on Karlsruhe, a retaliatory action, raised the stakes further.[16] By 1918 the German War Ministry was condoning reprisals "on the largest possible scale against the populations of capital cities in our enemies' territory," while the chief of the UK Air Staff argued that "the wholesale bombing of densely populated industrial centres would go far in destroying the morale of the operatives."[17] Still, the British position on bombing civilians remained ambiguous.

In all, according to official statistics published in January 1919, German air raids over Britain in 1917–18 killed 1,414 people and injured another

FIGURE 6.2. Rapid technological progress in aircraft engineering:
Sopwith Tabloid (1914) and Bristol Braemar (1918)
Source: Imperial War Museums (*bottom*)

3,416. The physical damage as a result was modest. Its cost has been put
at £3 million, equivalent to 0.03 percent of the gross capital stock of the
United Kingdom in 1914.[18] That was about twice the cost in lives and capital
inflicted by British and French aircraft on Germany. They killed 764 and
injured 1,842 Germans, military and civilian, in 675 raids and destroyed
property worth 24 million marks, equivalent to $6 million or £1.2 million.[19]

During World War I, casualties caused by attacks from above were dwarfed by those from below; in all German U-boats were responsible for the loss of 15,000 lives (as well as of 5,000 ships). In the worst of these incidents, 1,200 passengers aboard the RMS *Lusitania* were drowned when it was torpedoed and sunk off the southwest coast of Ireland on May 7, 1915. Unknown to its passengers, because the *Lusitania* was carrying armaments and munitions for enemy use the Germans considered it a legitimate target.[20]

Between the Wars

Relative to what lay in store for civilians after 1939, these World War I bombing raids did not count for much. They were not very lethal; total civilian casualties on all sides in World War I probably did not exceed five or six thousand. Yet the revolutionary potential of what a future American general called "war in the third dimension,"[21] and of aerial bombing in particular, was much discussed in the wake of World War I. Studies with titles like "The Limitations of Aerial Bombing," "Aerial Warfare and the Laws of War," "Bombing a U-Boat," "The Bombing Tests and Our Naval Policy," "Is It to be Bomb or Battleship?," and "Report of Chief of Air Service, A.E.F.," all of which appeared in 1921, became commonplace. That year also saw the publication by the Italian defense department of *Il Dominio dell'Aria* (*The Command of the Air*) by the Italian general Giulio Douhet (1869–1930), which would prove hugely influential in the interwar period. Douhet's pleas for more airpower during World War I had been rejected by the Italian military establishment. In *The Command of the Air*, he argued for a central role for aircraft as bombers, not merely as ground support for conventional military forces or as spy planes. He envisaged bombing as a primary means of waging future wars on the grounds that it was difficult to defend against and that it reduced enemy civilian morale. Douhet was half right, of course: aerial power would play a crucial role in World War II, but it did not make for a shorter war, and it did not decide the outcome.

The bombing raids of World War I also influenced British and American military thinking in the interwar period. In 1924, in an early recognition of the fear that "the bomber will always get through," Sir Maurice Hankey, secretary of the Committee of Imperial Defence, argued that victory in any future war "will rest with that country whose people will endure bombardment the longer with greater stoicism."[22] Later, the primary aim of Britain's Air-Raid Precautions services, as defined in June 1937, would be "the maintenance of the morale of the people." Toward the end of World War I, the British secretary of state for war counseled the first head of the Royal Air Force (RAF), Air Chief Marshal Sir Hugh Trenchard: "If I were you, I would not be too exacting as regards accuracy in bombing railway stations in the middle of towns. The German is susceptible to bloodiness, and I would not mind a few accidents due to inaccuracy." A decade later, echoing Douhet, Trenchard asserted that airpower should be directed not at the enemy's armed forces but on its industrial hubs and civilian centers of population. Destroying them would lead to victory at a far lower cost in military lives.[23]

The RAF's arsenal grew from 800 aircraft in 1934 to 3,700 on the eve of World War II. The potential of airpower was not lost on the Nazis either. The Treaty of Versailles had banned Germany from having an air force, but the Nazis under Hermann Göring, World War I ace fighter pilot and future war criminal, built one from scratch, first furtively and then openly from 1935 onward. The Luftwaffe's number of serviceable aircraft grew from 75 in October 1933 to 2,893 in September 1939.[24]

The launching of projectiles from balloons "against towns, villages, habitations, or buildings which are not defended" had been prohibited by the 1899 Hague Convention on the Laws and Customs of War on Land. Such acts qualified as terrorism as defined by the *Oxford English Dictionary*: "The unlawful use of violence and intimidation, especially against civilians, in the pursuit of political aims." But who would define what was unlawful? The Hague agreement, which expired in 1904, was renewed in 1907 by Declaration No. XIV of a second Hague conference "for a period extending to the close of the Third Peace Conference." In 1911 the Ottoman authorities formally complained that the Italian aerial attack on their troops in Libya in 1911 was in breach of The Hague rules, against which the Italians countered in rather Jesuitical style that the rules did not apply to heavier-than-air craft. But in any case, neither side had ratified the 1907 treaty. Since the third conference never took place, the 1907 agreement was still in place during World War I, but only the United Kingdom, the United States, and China among the major powers had ratified it. At the outbreak of World War I, combatants initially fretted about the legal implications of bombing, but soon international law was a dead letter.[25]

In February 1923, another international commission of legal experts met in The Hague and drafted new rules on the conduct of aerial warfare. Draft Article XXII distinguished between civilian and military targets, stipulating that "aerial bombardment for the purpose of terrorizing the civilian population, of destroying or damaging private property not of military character, or of injuring non-combatants is prohibited" while Article XXIV declared that "aerial bombardment is legitimate only when directed at a military objective, that is to say, an object of which the destruction or injury would constitute a distinct military advantage to the belligerent." But those rules were never formally enacted in international law, although supported by the United States.

In the interwar period, the imperial powers often employed airpower in colonial wars, as the British did in Afghanistan in 1919, in Somaliland and Iraq in 1920, and in Sudan in 1919–20 and 1930;[26] the South Africans did in Southwest Africa in the 1920s and 1930s; and the French in Syria did in 1926. In 1927 the U.S. Marine Corps, in one of several interventions in the Caribbean in this period, used biplanes to dive-bomb Sandinista positions in Nicaragua, killing at least thirty rebels.[27] Most of the victims of these attacks were not civilians, but in Iraq in 1932 the head of the British colonial administration argued against restraining the RAF on the grounds that "the term 'civilian population' has a very different meaning in Iraq from what it has in Europe. . . . The whole of its male population are potential fighters as the tribes are heavily armed."[28]

In the mid-1930s, a trio of aerial actions on three continents caused widespread outrage. First, during the Second Italo-Abyssinian War (October 1935–May 1936) Italian forces bombed hospitals and dropped chemical weapons on Ethiopian troops. An Ethiopian memorandum submitted to the Paris conference in 1946 claimed that 17,800 women and children had been killed by bombing, but that number is disputed. Second, on April 26, 1937, at the request of Spanish Nationalist forces, the Luftwaffe bombed the Basque city of Guernica (today's Gernika), a strategic location near Bilbao, killing 200-300 civilians in the process. Whether the bombing of Gernika, where the targets were arguably strategic, constituted an act of terrorism is debatable; much clearer cases in point are the Luftwaffe's bombardment of Madrid beginning in November 1936 and the Nationalist and Italian bombing of Barcelona in the spring of 1938. By the end of March 1937 1,500 had been killed and 3,500 injured by aerial bombing in Madrid,[29] and the likely numbers in Barcelona by the end of March 1938 were higher. The Italian air force's attacks on Barcelona on March 16–18, 1938, of which Franco's other ally, the Germans, were highly critical, resulted in about a thousand dead and another two thousand wounded.[30] In all, aerial bombardment during the civil war is unlikely to have cost more than five thousand lives, a small fraction of the total number of civilian victims of the war.[31]

Third, Japan's invasion of Manchuria in 1931 spawned a series of aerial attacks unprecedented in their ferocity and lethality. Its first attack on

Jinzhou, "an unarmed and unwarned city," seems to have targeted railway yards and government offices, but its second, on the Zhabei (formerly westernized as Chapei) district of Shanghai on January 29, 1932, killed "several thousand" civilians.[32] Thereafter until an armistice in May, Japanese planes resorted repeatedly to aerial bombing in and around Shanghai. Claims that their targets were purely military cut no ice with an outraged international community. The next Japanese actions were part of a campaign that became part of World War II. Between July 1937 and the end of March 1940, according to an openly partisan Chinese source, over fifty thousand Chinese civilians died in air raids.[33]

These actions caused international outcries. Lord Cranborne, deputy foreign secretary of the UK, protested at the Japanese bombings:

> Words cannot express the feelings of profound horror with which the news of these raids had been received by the whole civilized world. They are often directed against places far from the actual area of hostilities. The military objective, where it exists, seems to take a completely second place. The main object seems to be to inspire terror by the indiscriminate slaughter of civilians . . . [34]

On September 30, 1937, the General Assembly of the League of Nations unanimously passed an aspirational resolution stating that any subsequent regulations must make the intentional bombing of civilian populations illegal, adding that "Any attack on legitimate military objectives must be carried out in such a way that civilian populations in the neighborhood are not bombed through negligence." U.S. secretary of state Cordell Hull declared that "any general bombing of an extensive area wherein there resides a large populace engaged in peaceful pursuits is unwarranted and contrary to the principles of law and of humanity."[35]

The Japanese, who had withdrawn from the League in 1933 in the wake of its condemnation of their invasion of Manchuria, continued to use incendiary bombing in built-up areas as a tactic against the Chinese. Between 1939 and 1942 they dropped about three thousand tons of bombs, mainly incendiaries, in 268 raids on the temporary Nationalist capital of Chongqing, formerly "a sleepy town perched on a cliff that rises through the mists above the Yangtze river to the sky."[36] The first raid did little damage but the second on May 4, 1939, made world headlines:[37]

> Terror hit Chungking with all the impact of the bombs. . . . Japanese incendiaries started a dozen small fires, which within an hour or two had

met in several distinct patches of creeping destruction that were eating out the ancient slums forever. Within the back alleys, the lanes, and the twisting byways of the city thousands of men and women were being roasted to death; nothing could save them . . . All the compound noises of a great fire were intensified by the setting of the old walled city-there were the whistling and crackling of timbers, the screaming of people, and the intermittent popping of bamboo joints as the lath-and-bamboo slums dissolved in the heat.

Shortly afterwards, just two days before World War II began, President Roosevelt made the following appeal to the governments of Germany, France, Italy, and Poland:[38]

The ruthless bombing from the air of civilians in unfortified centers of population during the course of the hostilities which have raged in various quarters of the earth during the past few years, which has resulted in the maiming and in the death of thousands of defenseless men, women, and children, has sickened the hearts of every civilized man and woman, and has profoundly shocked the conscience of humanity.

If resort is had to this form of inhuman barbarism during the period of the tragic conflagration with which the world is now confronted, hundreds of thousands of innocent human beings who have no responsibility for, and who are not even remotely participating in, the hostilities which have now broken out, will lose their lives. I am therefore addressing this urgent appeal to every government which may be engaged in hostilities publicly to affirm its determination that its armed forces shall in no event, and under no circumstances, undertake the bombardment from the air of civilian populations or of unfortified cities, upon the understanding that these same rules of warfare will be scrupulously observed by all of their opponents. I request an immediate reply.[39]

Roosevelt's statement reflected a revulsion widely shared before September 1939, and both Chamberlain and Hitler reassured Roosevelt that civilian targets would not be attacked. But that was then and this was now. In the war that followed, hundreds of thousands of civilians perished in precisely the circumstances so eloquently decried by Roosevelt. At the beginning of the war Churchill too was horrified at the notion of bombing civilians. As he remarked to a colleague in the House of Commons in 1940, "My dear sir this is a military and not a civilian war. You and others may desire to kill women and children. We desire (and have succeeded in our desire) to destroy German military objectives."[40] Soon all combatants would engage in the "inhuman barbarism" that Roosevelt had condemned so eloquently on the eve of the war. By mid-1943, in wake of the RAF-United States Army Air Forces (USAAF) firebombing of Hamburg, he was already envisaging the use of "Siberian air fields . . . to attack the heart of Japan in a manner she will find it hard to endure." Roosevelt's musings underline what economic historians Lance Davis and Stanley Engerman, in a slightly different context, have called "the adaptability of 'morality' in the face of national self-interest."[41]

Even toward the end of the war, in public U.S. military spokesmen were reluctant to admit that bombing civilians was acceptable. In the wake of Dresden, Secretary of War Henry Stimson promised to "continue to bomb military targets and . . . there has been no change in the policy against conducting 'terror bombings' against civilian populations," and just after the firebombing of Tokyo a month later, a USAAF spokesman denied that there had been a policy shift away from precision targeting. On the day after Hiroshima President Harry Truman described the city as "a military base," adding mendaciously that "we wished in this first attack to avoid, insofar as possible, the killing of civilians."[42]

The prediction of the RAF in 1924 that in a future war "450 tons of bombs would be dropped on London in the first three days and that this would result in 3,800 dead and 7,500 wounded" reflected both recent experience and the limited technological possibilities of the day. The role played by bombing in Iraq, Abyssinia, Spain, and China in the 1930s convinced the British that a future war with Germany would begin with massive air attacks on civilian targets. In the wake of the Nazi bombing of Barcelona, the Committee of Imperial Defence forecast 0.6 million deaths in the first two months and double that number injured. In the wake of the Chamberlain-Hitler meeting in Munich, former prime minister Stanley Baldwin complimented his successor in the House of Lords with the remark that "had there been war there would have been tens of thousands of mangled women and children civilians before a single soldier gave his life for his country. That is a very awful thought." The sense that the Luftwaffe would strike first was widespread: in 1938 a cabinet committee predicted that thirty-five hundred tons of bombs would be dropped on London on the first day and seven hundred tons per day thereafter.[43]

World War II

One of the first actions of invading German forces on September 1, 1939, was the bombing of the Polish border town of Wieluń, which was defenseless and lacked military targets. The cost in civilian lives is unclear; estimates range from the 127 civilians reported in the wake of the outrage to "32 patients of the Hospital in Wieluń and several hundred Poles and Jews who died in other places during the bombing of the city" to "1,290 townspeople killed in their beds."[44] The bombing of other Polish cities, including Warsaw, would follow. The raids on Warsaw on "Black Monday" (September 25, 1939) were the heaviest thus far anywhere. The six hundred tons of bombs dropped were responsible for several thousand civilian deaths; more died from strafing by machine guns. Throughout World War II, however, most of the war in the air occurred on the Western Front. In the East, the Luftwaffe stuck mainly to tactical support for ground forces and aerial combat with Soviet fighter pilots. In this, distance and German fuel shortages played a role; when in the wake of Stalingrad the Wehrmacht asked for aerial attacks on Soviet tank production, only the tank plant at Gorki was within range of Luftwaffe bombers. Soviet civilians were also, for the most part, out of range of German bombers.[45]

The German aerial bombing of British cities—the Blitz—began in 1940. Deaths per month exceeded six thousand in September–November 1940 and in March–May 1941 and petered out thereafter. The Luftwaffe's targets were port towns and cities like London, Liverpool, Hull, Bristol, Cardiff, Plymouth, Glasgow, and Belfast and industrial centers such as Birmingham, Coventry, Manchester, and Sheffield. London, which was hit for fifty-seven consecutive nights, bore the brunt of the attacks. On paper the Luftwaffe forswore attacks aimed at civilians, but all raids were bound to result in casualties. Whatever occurred in the raids on ports and heavily industrial hubs, those on London bore the hallmarks of carpet-bombing, or what would become known euphemistically as area bombing. Figure 6.3 describes the monthly toll in deaths and the seriously injured. As Arthur Harris, commander in chief of the RAF Bomber Command at the height of the bombing campaign against Germany, predicted, the numbers killed in the Blitz were much smaller than in the most lethal raids on Germany in late 1944 and early 1945.

London suffered disproportionately. Liverpool (pop. 800,000), the second most-targeted area after London, lost about 4,000 civilians to the Luftwaffe between August 1940 and May 1941. Liverpool and its satellites of Birkenhead, Wallasey, and Bootle were strategically located and major centers of war-related production. The heaviest bombardment was in May 1941. Birmingham (pop. 1.1 million) was bombed several times between August 1940 and April 1943, destroying or badly damaging the General Electric Company, Birmingham Small Arms Company, and Lucas plants, but the civilian toll was only about one-fifth of Liverpool's. Hull (pop. 300,000), the locus of

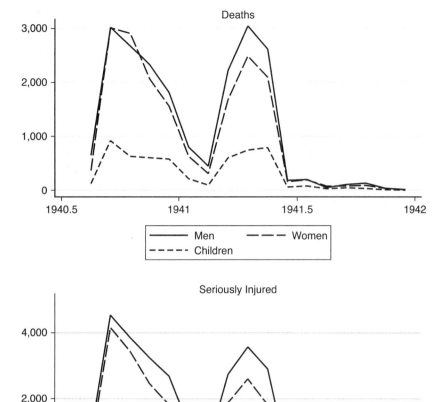

FIGURE 6.3. Bombing casualties during the Blitz, August 1940–December 1941
Source: Overy 2014: 187
Note: Deaths totaled 38,415; injuries totaled 47,616

important docks, railway yards, mills, and barracks, suffered more in terms of "dehousing" than Birmingham—about half its population was homeless at some point or other during the war—and about 1,200 civilians lost their lives. In November 1941 a pioneering secret survey was carried out in Hull to ascertain the impact of sustained bombing on civilian morale.[46] Over five hundred bombers (of which only one was shot down) attacked Coventry (pop.

FIGURE 6.4. Fore Street, Devonport, April 23, 1941

210,000) over several hours on November 14–15, 1940, and in the process inflicted massive damage on its industries—motor construction, machine tools, aircraft, naval ordnance—while also killing nearly 600 civilians.

Plymouth (pop. 220,000) in the Southwest lost 1,172 civilians in fifty-nine raids, most of them in March–April 1941 (figure 6.4). Belfast (pop. 440,000), an industrial city renowned for shipbuilding and aircraft manufacturing and a center for tank, airplane linen, and munitions during the war, was heavily hit on several nights during April and May 1941. The city was poorly prepared in terms of shelters, fire services, and antiaircraft guns. The raid of April 15 killed 900 people, the greatest loss of life in a single raid outside London. The bombing resulted in large-scale evacuations from the city. Another 150 died in a raid three weeks later.

Manchester and Sheffield were also important strategic targets. The former (pop. 700,000), a major center of aero engine and bomber production, was attacked repeatedly, but the worst raids were on the nights of December 22 and 23, 1940. Over 1,000 died in the city and neighboring Salford and Stretford on those nights. The latter (pop. 560,000), a center of steel and munitions production, was severely hit on the nights of December 12 and 15, 1940, in an operation dubbed Schmeltztiegel (Crucible) by the Luftwaffe. In all 660 died. Attacks on the smaller cities of Barrow-in-Furness and Southampton were less lethal. Eighty-three civilians died in Barrow, famous for its Vickers shipyard, in April and May 1941, while over 200 civilians died in the most lethal attacks in November–December 1942, half of them in air raid shelters.

On March 13 and 14, 1941, raids on Clydebank, a town downriver from Glasgow (pop. 1.1 million) and a major producer of ships and munitions, severely damaged a major naval oil storage depot, munitions works, and dockyards. In the process they flattened the town, killing 1,200 people. Before the attack, Clydebank contained about 50,000 people; just after the Blitz only 2,000 remained in the town, and there were still fewer than 7,000 on May 10, 1941. The remainder had trekked their way into the city, "their faces . . . caked with plaster-dust and soot and many were still in their nightclothes."[47] Clydebank's productive capacity returned but not its population.

Finally, Bristol (pop. 415,000), home to the Bristol Aeroplane Company, manufacturer of the multipurpose Bristol Beaufighter and an important port, was a highly visible target. In six major air raids between November 24, 1940, and April 11, 1941, the Luftwaffe dropped over nine hundred tons of bombs and thousands of incendiary cluster bombs on Bristol, destroying over eighty thousand houses and killing 1,300 people. In the wake of the first raid, which killed 207 people, the city's lord mayor lamented that "the City of Churches had in one night become the city of ruins." The bombing took its toll on civilian resolve. In the wake of the November 1940 raids, a doctor revealed a rise in cases of nervous indigestion and of absenteeism to an official of the Ministry of Home Security.[48] In all, the forty thousand tons of bombs dropped during the Blitz of 1940–41 caused an estimated 43,500 civilian deaths and injured as many more. About half of those deaths were in London. The entire German campaign rained over seventy thousand tons on Britain, at the cost of about 60,000 lives (see table 6.2). Industrial and port cities in the midlands and the North suffered badly, but most raids caused hundreds rather than thousands of casualties. Civilian casualties were much higher in German cities, to which we now turn.

In due course, the RAF would more than repay the Luftwaffe in kind. Yet at the outset, fears of retaliation by a much more powerful Luftwaffe had led the British at first to forswear, insofar as possible, any aerial bombing against Germany that would involve the loss of civilian lives. This was less out of respect for international law than the conviction that to provoke German retaliation would be foolhardy. Winston Churchill, who became

TABLE 6.2. Bombs dropped and civilian lives lost, 1939–45

Bombed country	Bombs (tons)	Deaths	Deaths/ton	Deaths per 1,000
Germany	1,360,000	350,000–400,000	0.3	4.7
France	518,000	69,000	0.1	1.7
Italy	370,000	80,000	0.2	1.8
Japan	656,000	400,000	0.6	5.5
UK	74,172	60,600	0.8	1.3

Sources: USSBS 1945c: 84; Overy 2014: 476–77; Overy 1995: 125; John Laurenson, "D-Day Anniversary: France's Forgotten Blitz," BBC News, June 5, 2014, accessed December 6, 2021, https://www.bbc.com/news/world-europe-27703724; half (1,356,829 tons) of all bombs dropped by the RAF and USAAF were dropped on Germany and 13.7 percent (369,554 tons) on Italy.

prime minister in May 1940, had fewer scruples than his predecessor about bombing civilians, but for another year and more the RAF increased its precision bombing of industrial and military targets in low-flying aircraft, with limited success and considerable losses in aircraft and personnel. The combined nighttime raids of Berlin, Mannheim, and Cologne on November 7–8, 1941, marked a low point. Of the 169 bombers sent to Berlin, fewer than half arrived there, and their bombing produced meager results, with minimal damage to property and life. On that same night, 75 planes were sent to Cologne and 55 to Mannheim, but the latter was not bombed at all, whereas in Cologne the damage consisted of two houses and five civilians. Bad weather helped to make the mission a fiasco: in all nearly 1 plane in 10 was lost.[49] The results were poor largely because the RAF was constrained by shoddy aircraft, inadequate navigational aids, and a lack of skilled airmen (figure 6.5).

During 1941 the authorities invested heavily in both hardware and personnel, and the policy shift away from purely military targets toward carpet-bombing (or *area* bombing) around industrial sites in cities coincided with the increased capacity of the RAF. It did not originate with Arthur Harris, who was put in charge of Bomber Command in February 1942: Churchill's scientific adviser Frederick Lindemann had been arguing for area bombing since the summer of 1941, and Harris's superior, Chief of the Air Staff Charles Portal, was also in favor of it, as was Prime Minister Churchill. The likelihood that area bombing would increase civilian casualties would not be a constraint; indeed, Directive 22 from the British Air Ministry to RAF Bomber Command on February 14, 1942, which shifted the strategy from precision to area bombing, regarded the impact on "the morale of the enemy civil popula-

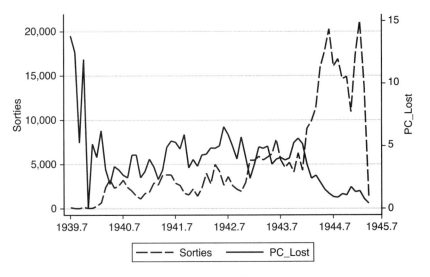

FIGURE 6.5. RAF Bomber Command sorties and losses, 1939–45

tion and in particular the industrial workers" as a bonus. Skeptics within the government cited the economic cost, not the cost in German civilian lives. Portal and Lindeman prevailed, and dehousing the civil population became a policy objective. In a memo dated March 30, Lindemann advised his chief that making one-third of Germany's population homeless would "break the spirit of the people." Implicit in all this was what Trenchard had described as "the difference between the German and British mentality": British morale had survived the Blitz unscathed, but Germany would react "very badly."[50]

The deficiencies that constrained the RAF in 1940–41 had been largely remedied by the time Sir Arthur Harris took over. Harris was an enthusiastic cheerleader for the shift toward more intensive bombing, famously proclaiming that "the Nazis entered this war under the rather childish delusion that they were going to bomb everyone else, and nobody was going to bomb them. . . . They sowed the wind, and now they are going to reap the whirlwind."[51] And how right he would prove to be: whereas the Germans dropped a total of 18,800 tons of bombs on London during the Blitz and 2,000 tons on Liverpool, Britain's second-most heavily bombed city, the Allies dropped 68,000 tons on Berlin between 1940 and 1945 and another 350,000 tons on the next twelve most heavily bombed cities.[52] Carpet saturation bombing entailed the use of incendiary bombs and ascertaining where such bombing would be most effective. In a much-quoted passage, Harris interpreted this as a directive that future attacks should be unambiguously stated [as] the destruction of German cities, the killing of German workers, and the disruption of civilised life throughout Germany. It should be emphasised that the destruction of houses, public utilities, transport and lives, the creation of a refugee problem on an unprecedented scale, and the breakdown of morale both at home and at the battle fronts by fear of extended and intensified bombing, are accepted and intended aims of our bombing policy. They are not by-products of attempts to hit factories.[53]

However, the shift to the incendiary bombing of civilian targets was neither as immediate nor as determined as implied by Harris's remarks. True, under Harris the bombing increased in intensity, but its main focus during 1942 and the first half of 1943—and, for the most part, even later—was on industrial and communications targets rather than on civilians, and the number of civilian casualties was relatively small. The raid on the Renault truck-making factory in Boulogne-Billancourt west of Paris on March 3, 1942, was the RAF's most ambitious thus far, involving 235 aircraft. It was a success, but nearly 400 civilians housed near the factory died. The raids that followed on Essen (repeatedly in March 1942), Lübeck (March 28–29, 1942), Rostock (April 24 and 27, 1942), Cologne (May 30, 1942), Essen again (June 1–2, 1942), and Bremen (June 25–26, 1942) did not result in major civilian casualties, even though the last three of these were massive *thousand-bomber raids*. Lübeck was chosen less for its shipyards than its combustibility, its location, and its weak defenses; although one-third of its built-up area was destroyed, only 300 civilians lost their lives. The raid on Cologne inflicted massive damage on built-up areas but killed fewer than 400 civilians. A further raid targeting the Krupp plant in Essen on March 5–6, 1943, set a new record for the number of civilians killed (about 482), but this was still small compared to what was to follow. Bomber Harris coined the term "to Essenise" as an answer to the Luftwaffe's *coventrieren*.[54] On August 17, Bomber Command was ordered to destroy the site of Germany's V-1 and V-2 rocket-building program at Peenemünde on the Baltic coast. The attack was a success. It destroyed the facility and "as a kind of bonus 250 scientific workers of various degrees of importance . . . lost their lives in the attack,"[55] but it also destroyed a neighboring forced labor camp, killing 500–600 people. The operation delayed the production of the rockets by three months; the first V-1 landed on England on June 13, 1944, and the first V-2 on September 8, 1944.

The firebombing of Wuppertal, another important industrial center, in May–June 1943 was probably the first operation to produce four-digit casualty figures. The sustained attacks on the port city of Hamburg, Germany's second largest, between July 24 and August 3, 1943, a combined RAF-USAAF operation code-named Gomorrah, were in a different league, killing an estimated 37,000 civilians and forcing 1.2 million Hamburgers to leave the city. Most of the deaths were due to a firestorm on the night of July 27, 1943, which, unlike those in Japan in 1945, had not been planned.[56] On a warm, bone-dry night, densely populated working-class districts with multistory apartments were the worst hit. Fires caused by the bombs linked and competed for oxygen; thousands died from asphyxiation from carbon monoxide as the air was sucked out of where they were sheltering. The firestorm lasted for three hours, until virtually everything had been burnt to cinders. Eighty years later Adam Tooze characterized the attack on Hamburg as "a point of culmination . . . on the ascending curve . . . that started in earnest in Guernica . . . an important way-station en route to Hiroshima and Nagasaki."[57] Three months later, on October 22–23, 1943, Kassel, an important industrial center with a population of 0.2 million, suffered a similar fate. The firestorm there killed 10,000 civilians and injured and dehoused thousands more.

In the campaign against Germany, a clear distinction is often made between the roles of the RAF's Bomber Command and the USAAF's 8th Air Force, with the former concentrating on nighttime area bombing against civilian targets and the latter focusing mainly on daytime attacks on pinpoint military-industrial targets. With few exceptions, both political and military leaders chafed at bombing civilians. The distinction is broadly valid, though in the case of Dresden about one-ninth of the area bombing was carried out by American B-17s.[58]

In a half-forgotten work, *Fire and the Air War* (1946), incongruously published by the U.S. National Fire Protection Association, a group of American and British experts described the planning that went into the firebombing campaigns in Germany and Japan. They were, effect, describing a "new science." One contributor described how aerial photographs of cities were analyzed by fire-protection engineers in order to assess vulnerability to attack. A major consideration was whether the roof was combustible. Another explained how the RAF and the USAAF used a combination of high-explosive and incendiary bombs for maximum effect; the damage inflicted by the explosives made the incendiaries more effective and made firefighting difficult by blocking streets and reducing water supplies. A third described how proper urban planning might limit the damage done by future attacks.[59]

The German capital was bombed repeatedly during the war, first by RAF Bomber Command and from 1943 onward in joint operations with the USAAF. At the outset Berlin was barely within the range of British aircraft, targeting was poor, and losses were heavy. The arrival of the Avro Lancaster bomber changed that, but it was not until 1943 that the attacks on the German capital intensified. What Bomber Command dubbed the Battle of Berlin began in November 1943, with Harris predicting that it would cost the RAF "between 440 and 500 aircraft . . . [but] it will cost Germany the war." Massed nightly attacks by hundreds of aircraft became the norm. The raids on November 22 and 23, 1943, resulted in big firestorms in residential areas and 3,000 deaths. Bomber Command reckoned that 175,000 people were "bombed out." By Christmas 1943 one-quarter of Berlin's housing stock had been rendered uninhabitable. But these raids were costly in terms of planes and crew lost, and the cumulative loss rate of 5.8 percent per sortie was deemed unsustainable. A final raid on March 24–25, 1944 ("the night of the strong winds") resulted in the loss of a disastrous 8.9 percent of the fleet. The official verdict on this phase of the assault on Berlin is that "in an operational sense the Battle of Berlin was more than a failure, it was a defeat." Thereafter, to the chagrin of Bomber Command, Operation Overlord diverted aerial resources to France, and sustained attacks on Berlin did not resume until February 3, 1945, when fifteen hundred American bombers attacked the city's railway system. The ensuing fires lasted for four days. Still, the death toll was less than 3,000, with up to 20,000 injured. In total the raids on Berlin cost, according to a recent reckoning, about 20,000 lives,[60] considerably less than the estimated 37,000 killed in Operation Gomorrah in Hamburg.

Nearly half of all bombs dropped by Bomber Command fell between mid-August 1944 and May 1945.[61] Most of them were directed at cities that would have been deemed conventional military targets. Kiel (July 24, 1944) was an important naval base and shipbuilding center; Friedrichshafen (July–August 1944) produced aircraft, tank engines, and tank gearboxes; Kaiserslautern (August 11 and September 28, 1944) had extensive railway marshalling yards; Darmstadt (September 11–12, 1944) contained extensive chemical works; Bochum, attacked by seven hundred bombers on November 4, 1944, was a major center of steel production; Ulm (December 17), where over 700 civilians died and thousands were left homeless, had two large truck factories, as well as other industries; and so on. Hanover, an important railway junction and manufacturing center, was bombed repeatedly throughout the war. Nearly a million bombs, mostly incendiaries, were dropped on it. On the night of October 9, 1943, in the heaviest raid of all, over five hundred RAF bombers dropped 3,000 explosives and 260,000 incendiary bombs on Hanover, killing 1,245 people and leaving 250,000 homeless. By the time the bombing stopped in late March 1945, Hanover had been virtually flattened, with only 5 percent of its dwellings still intact. Yet cumulative civilian casualties were fewer than 5,000. The toll would have been much heavier had half the population not been evacuated or fled the city during the war.

In 1944–45 Bomber Command prepared maps of the most vulnerable areas in several cities and of the areas in which housing had been rendered uninhabitable.[62] These maps offered a foretaste of the series of photographs of seemingly deserted, bombed-out cities taken by the American photojournalist Margaret Bourke-White and published just after the end of the war in Europe in *Life Magazine*. Her images ushered in the genre known as *rubble photography* (or *Trümmerfotografie* in German). Several examples, of which the most emblematic is probably that taken from the tower of Dresden's city hall in February 1945, are reproduced in figure 6.6. But for fear of misunderstanding, Bourke-White pointed out that despite the wreckage "civilian casualties were light."[63] For the most part, this was true until late in 1944, and moreover, most of the places targeted were important contributors to the German war effort. But cities such as Freiburg-im-Breisgau (November 27, 1944), Dresden (February 13–14, 1945), Pforzheim (February 23, 1945), and Würzburg (March 16–17, 1945) were different. Freiburg, a university town, was a secondary railway hub but contained no worthwhile industries.[64] Pforzheim had the misfortune of being one of three towns with a population of less than 100,000 to be included in the RAF's first list of towns to be destroyed in September 1941. In the attack, Pforzheim, a small city in the southwest of Germany, lost nearly a quarter of its population. An RAF Bomber Command memo had described it in June 1944 as "one of the centres of the German jewellery and watch making trade and is therefore likely to have become of considerable importance to the production of precision instruments." Indeed, it did contain plants producing submarine components and a tube-rolling plant, but it was really "of insignificant importance to the war effort."[65] A later report more accurately described it as a soft target. Würzburg was better known for its hospitals than its industry. "According to the British ministry of economic warfare, it had only one potential target, a power switching station."[66] The East Prussian capital of

FIGURE 6.6. Rubble photography

FIGURE 6.6. (*continued*)

FIGURE 6.6. (*continued*)

FIGURE 6.6. (*continued*)

Königsberg (today's Kaliningrad) was remote and contained no industries of strategic military importance. It thus was not included in the Ministry of Economic Warfare's original (1943) *Bomber's Baedeker*, but on the night of August 29, 1944, its historic center was flattened, causing over four thousand deaths, the displacement of tens of thousands, and the partial or total destruction of two-fifths of all buildings in the city.[67]

Dresden's fate was sealed at a meeting of Allied air leaders in Malta, which led to revised directives, including targeting "Berlin, Leipzig, Dresden and associated cities where heavy attack will cause confusion in civilian evacuation from the east and hamper reinforcements."[68] That directive worried USAAF commander Henry "Hap" Arnold, who protested that he would not accept "the promiscuous bombing of German cities of the purpose of causing civilian confusion." But Dresden was a joint USAAF and RAF operation, and to claim that the USAAF concentrated on the city's marshalling yard and that most of the civilian deaths were caused by the RAF was disingenuous.[69] Bomber Command put the cost in lives of the carpet-bombing of Dresden as "greater than the 40,000 who died in the Hamburg firestorm," adding "the Dresden figure may have exceeded 50,000." Initial reports put it even higher. Nearly a year after the bombing, the *Irish Times* put the death toll at "more than 200,000 persons," and later, thanks to the notorious Holocaust denier David Irving's *The Destruction of Dresden* (1966), a figure of 135,000 was widely circulated, prompting a reaction from one of those involved in the clearing-up operation in Dresden in 1945: "Soon after the attack we heard in the radio Joseph Goebbels reporting on the attack on Dresden. He spoke of 300,000 deads. In your book you mention the figure of 135,000. My records at the Clearing Staff showed 30,000 corpses. If you assume that the amount of deads completely burnt etc would reach 20%, the total figure of victims will not exceed 36,000. Still this figure—two full divisions—is terrible enough." Jörg Friedrich put the toll at 40,000 in his best-selling *Der Brand: Deutschland im Bombenkrieg, 1940–1945* (*The Fire: Germany in the Bombing War, 1940–1945*); the consensus nowadays among specialist historians is that 25,000 lives perished.[70]

The bombing of Dresden was somewhat of a defining moment, and there are many accounts of it. One survivor described it as follows:[71]

> As the incendiaries fell, the phosphorus clung to the bodies of those below, turning them into human torches. The screaming of those who were being burned alive was added to the cries of those not yet hit. There was no need for flares to lead the second wave of bombers to their target, as the whole city had become a gigantic torch. It must have been visible to the pilots from a hundred miles away. Dresden had no defences, no anti-aircraft guns, no search lights, nothing.

It was on Churchill's insistence that Bomber Command chose Dresden and a few other cities as "especially attractive targets." But in the wake of Dresden, the prime minister drafted a much-cited note stating that "it seems to me that the moment has come when the question of bombing of German cities simply for the sake of increasing the terror, though under other pretexts, should be reviewed."[72] Harris, however, was unrepentant: "The feeling, such as there is, over Dresden, could be easily explained by any psychiatrist. It is connected with German bands and Dresden shepherdesses. Actually, Dresden was a mass of munitions works, an intact government centre, and a key transport point to the East. It is now none of those things."[73]

The fates of Hamburg, Kassel, and Dresden were the exception rather than the rule. Yet the postwar era would not be kind to Arthur Harris: unlike other British wartime commanders, he was not ennobled, and his Bomber Command never received the official recognition of a campaign medal. A three-meter statue of Harris erected in 1992 outside Saint Clement Danes in London, the central church of the RAF, has been the target of sporadic attacks since. On a more ironic note, Rev. John Collins, chaplain at Bomber Command Headquarters from mid-1944, was so horrified by his experience there that he would become an antiwar activist and one of the founders of the Campaign for Nuclear Disarmament. Both in a postwar memoir and late in life, an embittered Harris would seek to justify his actions with the (false) assertion that "all major wars are always and have always been against the civil population," pointing to the 800,000 deaths (his figure) caused by the naval blockade of Germany during World War I.[74]

Italy also endured aerial bombardment throughout the war, with the RAF responsible for most of the bombing in the North and the USAAF for the South. The British hit industrial targets located near civilian populations as a means of testing and reducing morale.[75] The Italians had no effective defense against aerial bombing, and indeed, Mussolini's advice in the wake of the first major raids in northern Italy was civilian evacuation. British bombing in northern Italy would ultimately force hundreds of thousands to move out of the cities. Harris recalled the bombing of Turin in late autumn 1942:

> The effect on Italian morale was enormous and out of all proportion to the weight of the attack and to the extent of the damage. Three hundred thousand people, half the population, fled from Turin after our second attack on the city that autumn and there was as great, and probably greater, panic after the daylight attack on Milan by less than one hundred Lancasters.[76]

Churchill telegraphed Roosevelt on November 18, 1942, to the effect that "all the [Italian] industrial centres should be attacked in an intense fashion, every effort being made to render them uninhabitable and to terrorize and paralise [*sic*] the population."[77] But this was still a far cry from Berlin, Dresden, or Tokyo. The official reckoning is that aerial bombing in Italy killed 4,558 military personnel and 59,596 civilians, but these numbers are underestimates. A careful analysis based on disaggregated data suggests that the true figure is higher; a guesstimate of 80,000 seems reasonable.[78] Naples, which the Allies bombed relentlessly until they occupied it in October 1943, probably suffered most. The main targets were the port and transport and manufacturing facilities, but civilian casualties have been put at 20,000–25,000. In a notorious incident in the Milanese district of Gorla on October 20, 1944, USAAF bombers, having missed their intended targets, dropped their bombs on a residential area and killed almost 200 young schoolchildren.[79]

As in Italy most of the civilian dead and injured in France were victims of Allied bombing. Most perished in operations linked to the Allied landings in Normandy in June 1944. In the weeks before Operation Overlord, Churchill and his war cabinet agonized over the risks of the Allied bombing of France's communications infrastructure on civilian lives and worried particularly about a confidential memo predicting 80,000–160,000 civilian casualties, one-quarter of them fatal. On April 26, they agreed to a plan envisaging only attacks that would kill no more than 150 civilians each. Eisenhower was adamant that such a constraint would "emasculate" the role of airpower and increase the risks of the invasion. On May 3, Churchill asked whether the plan could be implemented at a cost of fewer than 10,000 (civilian) dead. Four days later he informed Roosevelt of the British government's concern over the "slaughter" of French civilians, which might "leave a legacy of hate behind them." Roosevelt was adamant: "However regrettable the attendant loss of civilian lives is, I am not prepared to impose from this distance any restriction on military action by the responsible commanders that in their opinion might militate against the success of 'Overlord' or cause additional loss of life to our Allied forces of invasion."[80] Churchill gave in and, fortunately, pre–D-Day attacks on railways and bridges proved less lethal than feared, resulting in about 5,750 deaths. The killing would not end there, however. In the following months in Normandy, thousands died in attacks supporting troops on the ground in cities such as Caen, Lisieux, Saint-Lô, and Le Havre. Nobel laureate Samuel Beckett, who worked as a volunteer in the Irish hospital in Saint-Lô for some months after its liberation, described how "when we got there, there was nothing at all. The whole of Saint-Lô was blotted out."[81] The post–D-Day bombing of France cost about sixty thousand civilian lives, yet it has received short shrift from historians; Victor Bisson-nette, whose doctoral thesis analyzes the "silence" surrounding the bombing, points to a one-thousand-page history of World War II that devoted a single paragraph to the bombardment of the Renault plant in the Paris suburb of Boulogne-Billancourt and another to the pre–D-day bombing of Normandy while the "disastrous bombardment" of Caen on July 6 received only a brief mention.[82]

Aerial bombing killed about 18,000 civilians in Belgium and 10,000 in the Netherlands. In Belgium most of the deaths were caused by either German V-2 rockets toward the end of the war or Allied bombardments in preparation for and in the wake of D-Day. Earlier, on May 5, 1943, a botched raid on Mortsel near Antwerp, home to a plant housing Luftwaffe aircraft, killed 936 people. Allied efforts at destroying strategic rail links from March 1944 on also resulted in high civilian casualties. It was estimated after the war that the V-2s killed about 6,000 people, mostly in and around Liège and Antwerp. The 567 who died in a direct hit on the Cinema Rex in downtown Antwerp on the afternoon of December 16, 1944, included 296 Allied troops on leave and about seventy children.[83]

In the Netherlands the most lethal raids were those on Rotterdam in mid-May 1940 by the Luftwaffe and on Nijmegen in February 1944 by U.S. aircraft, each of which cost about 800 lives. The Luftwaffe attacks on Rotterdam were part of the five-day battle for the city. On May 14, 1940, as the Dutch sought to negotiate a surrender, heavy incendiary bombing by a fleet of ninety Heinkel He 111s destroyed twenty-five thousand homes, but the mass evacuation of the city before the Germans arrived kept civilian deaths down to about 900. Capitulation on May 15 saved the Netherlands' other major cities from a similar fate. The costliest RAF raid in terms of civilian lives in the Netherlands was an attack on a V-2 rocket launching site out-side Den Haag on March 31, 1945, in which 520 civilians died because RAF intelligence "mixed up the horizontal and vertical coordinates of one of the aiming points." Allied planes were responsible for most bombing deaths, and most of those were due to planes being off target. The Nijmegen incident infuriated Churchill, and repeated mistakes by Allied planes led to protests by the Dutch government-in-exile; on one occasion the latter even tried to warn citizens of an upcoming attack.[84]

Estimates of aerial bombing victims in eastern Europe and the Balkans are elusive. The Luftwaffe bombing of Belgrade on April 6–7, 1941, caused up to 5,000–10,000 deaths (2,271 according to official data), but we have no solid estimate of civilian casualties in Yugoslavia as a whole. Five thousand civilians were killed by the Allied bombing of Bucharest in 1944 and 2,000 more in the Bulgarian capital, Sofia.[85]

Roughly how many civilians died from aerial bombardments in Europe during World War II? Comprehensive data for several countries are lacking. The latest estimates for individual countries in Europe and elsewhere are reported in table 6.2. It indicates that the European total is about 650,000, more than half in Germany.

Civilians suffered from bombings in Asia too. Setting aside Japan, estimates of 71,105 ("official statistics") and 335,934 (an unofficial count) have been cited for China, but these numbers are very shaky indeed: "There are no figures for the total number of Chinese killed by bombs, but given that bombing went on until late in the war, the figure must be in the hundreds of thousands." About 4,000 died of asphyxiation in Chongqing in the wake of Japanese bombing on August 5, 1941, one of many attacks on that city, which served as a nationalist capital during the war. The cost of Allied bombing in Thailand has been put at "8,711" and in Taiwan at "3,000." The Battle of Manila in February 1945 exacted a huge cost in civilian lives (100,000 at a minimum, compared to U.S. military losses of 1,010 men out of a force of 35,000), but most of these deaths were due to massacres by the Japanese and the indiscriminate use of heavy artillery by the Americans rather than aerial bombing.[86]

The use of the chemical weapon napalm in aerial bombardment is associated first and foremost with the U.S. campaigns in Japan in 1945 and Vietnam in the 1960s and 1970s.[87] Napalm, a "thickened oil incendiary agent," was invented on July 4, 1942, by Harvard scientist Louis Fieser for the National Defense Research Committee. It was put to military use for the first time in Sicily in August 1943 and on December 15, 1943, in Papua New Guinea, but in flamethrowers on battlefields rather than from the air. Its first aerial use was on February 15, 1944, on the Micronesian island of Pohnpei; it was used again a few weeks later in an attack on Berlin on March 6, 1944, and on Königsberg on August 29, 1944, by U.S. bombers. Napalm was used liberally in the carpet-bombing of Tokyo on March 9–10, 1945.[88]

Of all the aerial bombing campaigns, that waged by the USAAF against Japan was the most lethal. At the outset Arnold stated that the USAAF was "committed to a strategy of high-altitude, precision bombing of military objectives. . . . Use of incendiaries against cities is contrary to our national policy of attacking only military objectives,"[89] and, for the most part, it stuck to that policy in Europe. Such reservations about carpet-bombing were cast aside insofar as Japan was concerned.

Right from the start, the Office of Strategic Services (formed in June 1942) embarked on preparing the intelligence for a campaign of incendiary bombing of densely populated urban areas of Japan. Even Secretary of War Henry Stimson, who had held deep reservations about the morality of carpet-bombing, turned a blind eye to his air force's actions in Japan and in the end sanctioned and stoutly defended the dropping of the atomic bomb.[90] By the fall of 1943, the intelligence section of the Army Air Forces had already produced maps classifying neighborhoods in Japanese cities by their vulnerability to incendiary attacks, and Standard Oil was researching the most effective way of destroying by fire "small dwellings and tenement type construction which represent the largest portion of roof area in industrial Japan."[91] But prior to March 1945, USAAF air attacks on Japan consisted of attempts aimed at military-industrial rather than civilian targets. By and large, such attacks had proved ineffective, for which the dispersed location of Japanese manufacturing plants, unreliable aircraft, and the weather were blamed.

But with V-E looming, the Americans sought to bring the war against Japan to an end quickly and thereby avert the need for a land invasion. This led to Brigadier General Curtis LeMay, the U.S. version of Bomber Harris, being brought over from China in January 1945 as chief of XXI Bomber Command, based in the Mariana Islands. LeMay's early efforts proved no more successful than those of his predecessor, so in March 1945, on his own initiative, he switched to a campaign of low-altitude nighttime carpet-bombing using incendiaries.[92] On March 9, 1945, in an operation code-named Meetinghouse, 1,667 tons of incendiary bombs were dropped on Tokyo by 325 B-29 Superfortresses (figure 6.7). "You're going to deliver the biggest firecracker the Japanese have ever seen," LeMay told his airmen, and sure enough, LeMay described the attack on Tokyo in his diary as "the most devastating raid in the history of aerial warfare."[93] Tokyo, a city virtually built of wood, was highly vulnerable to attack. Fires left one million people homeless. Most of the bombs were cluster bombs that released smaller fire-creating bomblets weighing less than three kilograms but full of napalm, at an altitude of 750 meters:[94]

Dropped in loose clusters of 14, or "amiable" clusters of 38, the finless oil-bombs are exploded by a time fuse four or five seconds after landing. Thereupon M-69s become miniature flamethrowers that hurl cheesecloth socks full of furiously flaming goo for 100 yards. . . . Anything these socks hit is enveloped by clinging, fiery pancakes, each spreading to more than a yard in diameter. Individually, these can be extinguished as easily as a

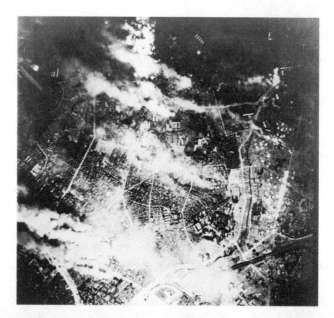

FIGURE 6.7. Firebombing Tokyo, 1945

magnesium bomb. But a single oil-bomb cluster produces so many fiery pancakes that the problem for fire fighters, like that of a mother whose child has got loose in the jam pot, is where to begin.

So intense was the heat that Tokyo's waterways came to a boil, and columns of heat brought down several B-29s.[95] Forty square kilometers of its most densely populated areas were razed to the ground, with an estimated loss of 100,000 civilian lives and another 40,000 injured, mainly in the downtown Shitamachi District. The death toll did not quite match that of Hiroshima and Nagasaki combined, but Operation Meetinghouse was probably the deadliest single bombing raid in history. LeMay would reminisce two decades later: "We knew we were going to kill a lot of women and kids when we burned that town. Had to be done . . . to worry about the morality of what we were doing. Nuts!"[96] Over the following nine days, 1,435 low-altitude sorties would rain 9,401 tons on Tokyo, Nagoya, Osaka, and Kobe, by which time "the generally destructive effect of incendiary attacks against Japanese cities had been demonstrated." By March 18 the campaign had resulted in 93,000–116,000 deaths, eighty-three square miles burned, and 528,000–598,000 homes destroyed.[97] Yet the monthly tonnage of bombs dropped increased thereafter from 13,800 in March to 42,700 in July, concentrating more on military and industrial targets, and would have reached 115,000 tons had the Japanese not surrendered. A postwar U.S. appraisal reckoned that by the end two-fifths of the built-up area in Japan's sixty-six biggest cities and towns had been destroyed and that 30 percent of the "entire urban population of Japan" had lost their homes. The survey estimated that eight months of bombing, including Hiroshima and Nagasaki, had resulted in 806,000 casualties, of which 330,000 were fatal.[98]

Given the intensity of the U.S. bombing campaign, what is surprising is that aside from Tokyo and Osaka (where over ten thousand died on March 13, 1945, in the Great Osaka Air Raid), civilian casualties in other cities numbered fewer than ten thousand.[99] This must have owed more to the attempts of Japanese civil defense to reduce casualties by creating firebreaks through tearing down buildings than to antiaircraft defenses. U.S. strategy consisted in part of convincing the Japanese military that it was no longer capable of protecting its civilian population.

According to the U.S. Strategic Bombing Survey (USSBS), between 1939 and 1945 Allied planes dropped 3.4 million tons of bombs on Axis powers, 2.7 million on continental Europe and the remainder on Japan. Of the European share, half was dropped on Germany, 21.8 percent on France, and 13.7 percent on Italy. The RAF and the USAAF divided the work more or less equally between them, at 45.8 and 54.2 percent, respectively. Allied aircraft dropped 656,000 tons of bombs on Japanese targets. Of this, 160,800 tons, or 24 percent, were dropped on the home islands of Japan, and 147,000 tons of the total were from B-29s.

Although quicker off the mark, the Luftwaffe's bombing offensive was paltry by comparison. It dropped 74,172 tons of ordnance on the United Kingdom during World War II, nearly four-fifths of that in 1940–41. A further one-eighth of German bombs were dropped in the V-weapon (Vergeltung-swaffe, or revenge weapon) offensive of 1944–45, the Third Reich's last-ditch effort at staving off defeat in western Europe. The first V-1 landed in Clapham on June 13, 1944, while the first V-2 rocket struck on September 8, 1944. Ten thousand of the former were aimed at London, but they were relatively easy to intercept, and only one in four reached its target, killing over six thousand people in all. The V-2s were technologically much more sophisticated and potentially much more dangerous. No conventional defense against them existed; the only strategy available was bogus intelligence that sought to divert attacks away from the city. This strategy worked. As a result the number of deaths caused by V-2s was limited to two thousand in England and a further fifteen hundred in Antwerp.

German bombs killed 60,595 British civilians. An early official estimate put the number of civilians killed by Allied bombing raids on Germany at 635,000, and a figure of 600,000 was widely circulated in the 2000s, thanks to Jörg Friedrich's *Der Brand*. The true figure was much lower, however. Although Air Vice Marshall Charles Portal had chillingly predicted in November 1942 that the RAF could kill 0.9 million Germans in eighteen months and seriously injure another million, it is now reckoned that 350,000–400,000 German civilians died in Allied air raids,[100] while in France and Italy the tolls were about 70,000 and 80,000, respectively. In terms of their lethality, Allied raids against the Nazis in France, Italy, and Germany were the least effective in terms of loss of life per ton. The Luftwaffe raids on Britain took over 60,000 civilian lives for 74,000 tons of bombs, while the RAF and USAF killed up to 0.4 million with 1.4 million tons of bombs. Overall, in terms of killing rates per thousand population, the Allied air forces were much more effective, if not more efficient, than the Luftwaffe, in the sense that they killed more people per ton dropped. A quick comparison between the Luftwaffe's attacks on London and the combined RAF-USAF campaign against Berlin may be helpful here. The former (which lasted from September 7, 1940 to May 11, 1941) cost 28,556 lives, whereas the latter cost about 20,000. The Luftwaffe dropped 16,593 tons of bombs on London, while Allied bombers dropped 67,600 tons on Berlin, mainly in 1943–45. But while the Luftwaffe relied on single-engine dive-bombing Stukas (Junker Ju 87s), effective against ground targets but very vulnerable to fighter planes, the latter used the heavy four-engine Avro Lancaster and Handley Page Halifax (RAF) and the Boeing B-17 Flying Fortress (USAF). The two-man Stuka's cruising speed was 250 kilometers per hour and its bomb load, 250 kilograms; the Avro Lancaster's, 370 kilometers per hour and 15,000 kilograms, respectively;

TABLE 6.3. Civilian deaths from aerial bombardment during World War II

Place	Estimate (1,000s)	Source
Germany	353	Overy 2014: 476–77
Austria	24	Austrian Press and Information Service 2000
Romania	5	https://adevarul.ro/stiri-locale/bucuresti/mari-dezastre-bombardarea-bucurestilor-in-44-mii-1369935.html, last accessed February 3, 2024
France	69	(plus 100,000 injured); Florentin 1997)
Belgium	10	Overy 2013: 603–4; Wikipedia
Netherlands	10	van Esch 2011: 4–5
UK	61	43,000 (+139,000 wounded) in Blitz, plus 18,000 others; GovUK, accessed January 28, 2023, https://history.blog.gov.uk/2015/01/19/air-raid-casualties-in-the-first-world-war/.
Italy	80	Gioannini and Massobrio 2007
USSR	51	Overy 2013: 225 (plus 136,425 injured)
Warsaw	20	Overy 2014: 6–34
Belgrade	5–10	See text. Compare *The Mainichi*, https://history.army.mil/books/wwii/balkan/20_260_2.htm.
EUROPE	c. 700	
Japan	387 +	*The Mainichi*, "387,000 Deaths Confirmed in WWII Air Raids in Japan; Toll Unknown in 15 Cities: Survey," August 23, 2020, https://mainichi.jp/english/articles/20200821/p2a/00m/0na/018000c.
Korea	70	Clodfelter 2017: 525 ("in allied air raids, merchant ship sinkings, or in Japanese military units")
China	70–350	Clodfelter 2017: 367; Rummel 1991: table 6A; Lary 2010: 24.
Burma, Mandalay	5	Clodfelter 2017: 501
Total	1.3–1.6 million	

the Halifax's, 400 kilometers per hour and 7,000 kilograms; and the B-17's 300 kilograms per hour and 2,700 kilograms. The Allies had both more bombs and bigger aircraft to fit them in. In this sense the least effective were the bombs dropped by the Allies on France and Italy, but in those cases, most of the victims were civilians killed by "friendly fire" (see table 6.2).

Table 6.3 is an attempt at summarizing casualty estimates across the globe. Those for Europe may be taken to be reasonably accurate. The figure for the Soviet Union is based on contemporary monthly data produced by the Main Directorate of Local Air Defence (MPVO); it is far more reliable than the half a million later claimed in propagandistic publications. MPVO data suggest that over half of the casualties occurred in areas of heavy fighting in 1942.[101] In both Leningrad and Moscow, many lives were saved by effective air defenses. The figures for Japan are from a recent Japanese source, while those for China can only be guessed at. Together they imply that well over one million civilians died from aerial bombing during World War II. They accounted for about 2 percent of all World War II victims and 3–4 percent of civilian victims.

Hiroshima and Nagasaki

The U.S.-led Manhattan Project was largely conceived with Nazi Germany in mind, but Germany had already been defeated before the first nuclear detonation in New Mexico, on July 6, 1945. While the technology was new, the atomic bombing of Hiroshima and Nagasaki nevertheless represented a continuum from incendiary bombing rather than a clean break. In the words of LeMay: "Nothing new about death, nothing new about deaths caused militarily. We scorched and boiled and baked to death more people in Tokyo on that night of 9–10 March than went up in vapor at Hiroshima and Nagasaki combined." LeMay was broadly correct, even if he implicitly exaggerated the death toll in Tokyo.[102] The horrors of the new warfare of indiscriminate bombing reached a peak in those cities (figure 6.8).

The impacts of the firebombing of Tokyo and the A-bombing of Hiroshima and Nagasaki were comparable, yet distinct. Being burned alive by napalm in Tokyo was perhaps worse than dying instantaneously in Hiroshima and Nagasaki, but the A-bomb imposed its own added burden on survivors who lived in fear from cancer from radiation.[103] Here are three survivors' accounts:

> [1] Tokyo 9–10 March 1945: The police were there and the powerless fireman who tried for a while to control the fleeing crowds, directing them towards blackened potholes left by earlier incendiaries. In the few places where the fire hoses worked firemen doused those fleeing with jets of water to let them to cross the most raging flames without getting burnt. . . . Hundreds of people gave up trying to escape and crawled into the holes that served as shelters, with or without their precious bundles; their carbonized bodies were found after the raid. . . . Wherever there was a canal, people hurled themselves into the water; where it was shal-

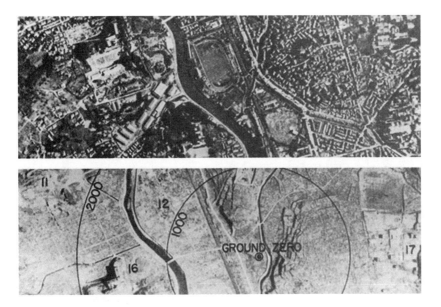

FIGURE 6.8. Nagasaki before and after the bombing

low, people waited, half sunk in filthy slime, mouths just above the surface of the water. Hundreds of them were later found dead, not from drowning but suffocated by the scorching heat and the surrounding fumes. In other places, the heat of the water rose and quickly became intolerable, and the unfortunate bathers perished; their boiled corpses were found later. Some canals flowed directly into the Sumida; as the tide rose, those in them lost their footing and drowned.[104]

[2] The day after the U.S. dropped an atomic bomb on Nagasaki, 11-year-old Yashiro Yamawaki went out in search of his father, who had failed to return from a shift at the local power station. On the way to the factory, Yamawaki and two of his brothers saw unspeakable horrors, including corpses whose "skin would come peeling off just like that of an over-ripe peach, exposing the white fat underneath"; a young woman whose intestines dragged behind her in what the trio at first thought was a long white cloth belt; and a 6- or 7-year-old boy whose parasitic roundworms had come "shooting out" of his mouth post-mortem.

The boys soon arrived at the power station, which was situated near the bomb's hypocenter and had been reduced to little more than a pile of scorched metal. Spotting three men with shovels, they called out, "Our name is Yamawaki. Where is our father?" In response, one of the men pointed toward a demolished building across the street and simply said, "Your father is over there."[105]

[3] 29-year-old Tsutomu Yamaguchi was walking to the shipyard when a "great flash in the sky" rendered him unconscious. Upon waking up, Yamaguchi told the *Times*' Richard Lloyd Parry, he saw "a huge mushroom-shaped pillar of fire rising up high into the sky. It was like a tornado, although it didn't move, but it rose and spread out horizontally at the top. There was prismatic light, which was changing in a complicated rhythm, like the patterns of a kaleidoscope."

The blast ruptured Yamaguchi's eardrums and burned his face and forearms. But after reuniting with two co-workers—Akira Iwanaga and Kuniyoshi Sato—the trio managed to retrieve their belongings from a dormitory and start making their way to the train station. On the way, "We saw a mother with a baby on her back," Yamaguchi recalled. "She looked as if she had lost her mind. The child on her back was dead and I don't know if she even realized."

Sato, who along with Iwanaga also survived both bombings, lost track of his friends on the train ride back to Nagasaki. He ended up sitting across from a young man who spent the journey clasping an awkwardly covered bundle on his lap. Finally, Sato asked what was in the package. The stranger responded, "I married a month ago, but my wife died yesterday. I want to take her home to her parents." Beneath the cloth, he revealed, rested his beloved's severed head.[106]

How much U.S. scientists knew before Hiroshima and Nagasaki about the impact of ionizing radiation on the health of survivors is the focus of a study by Sean Malloy.[107] He claims that while "understanding of radiation among Manhattan Project scientists was far from perfect, that the bomb would produce lingering and lethal effects was suggested as early as 1940" and that although scientists learned much during the war, neither President Truman nor his close advisers were ever told of the bomb's long-term effects on the health of survivors. Teams of researchers from Japan and the United States began intensive investigations of the impact of radiation on the health of survivors of Hiroshima and Nagasaki almost immediately after the bombings. In 1946 the Atomic Bomb Casualty Commission was created to run laboratories in Hiroshima and Nagasaki as cooperative research agencies, on the basis that a "detailed and long-range study of the biological and medical effects upon the human being [was] of the utmost importance to the United States and mankind in general."[108]

Because surviving women who conceived or gave birth in the wake of the bombings were more likely to have miscarriages and because babies irradiated in utero were more likely to have malformations, children born in the fol-

TABLE 6.4. Adverse pregnancy outcomes (%), 1948–53
(number of births in parentheses)

Mother's radiation dose (Gy)	Father's radiation dose (Gy), N and percentage affected		
	<0.01	0.01–0.49	≥0.50
<0.01	5.0 (45,234)	5.0 (1,614)	5.7 (506)
0.01–0.49	4.8 (5,445)	4.6 (1,171)	4.5 (133)
≥0.50	6.1 (1,039)	4.1 (73)	8.0 (88)

Source: Radiation Effects Research Foundation, https://www.rerf.or.jp/en/programs
/roadmap_e/health_effects-en/geneefx-en/birthdef/.

lowing years were a particular focus of study.[109] Nearly all pregnancies and births in the two cities between 1948 and 1953 were closely monitored and information on stillbirths, birth weights, gender, neonatal mortality, and birth defects collected. The outcomes, summarized in tables 6.4 and 6.5, suggest no consistent link between adverse outcome and parental exposure to radiation. In table 6.5, adverse outcomes include stillbirths, malformations, and neonatal death within two weeks of birth. The most common malformations were anencephaly, cleft palate, cleft lip with or without cleft palate, clubfoot, polydactyly (an additional finger or toe), and syndactyly (the fusion of two or more fingers or toes), which together accounted for three-quarters of the total.

Ad hoc research in the 1940s gave way to more formal cohort studies, in particular the Life Span Study of A-bomb survivors, which was intended to identify later health effects of radiation, including cancer. The Life Span Study divided subjects by proximity to ground zero (within 2 kilometers, 2 to less than 2.5 kilometers, 2–5 to less than 10 kilometers, and greater than 10 kilometers). The database contains 82,214 survivors from Hiroshima and 38,107 from Nagasaki; 50,175 males and 70,146 females. These subjects have been followed through from 1950.[110] Leukemia and cancer were particular concerns from the beginning. It was found that survivors had a four- to fivefold increase in the risk of developing leukemia for a decade or so after the bombing, with the risk falling off thereafter. But leukemia is a rather rare disease, so the number succumbing to it was modest, about three hundred. The evidence for an increased incidence of cancer among survivors is overwhelming. The increase in the risk of cancer, which averaged 10 percent for all survivors, depended on age, closeness to ground zero, and gender. The rise in cancer deaths began to be noticed around 1960; such deaths continued to rise until the new millennium, when they reached a plateau. The rise applied to most kinds of cancer.

TABLE 6.5. Stillbirths and malformations by exposure conditions

STILLBIRTHS

Mother's exposure	Father's exposure and percentage of stillbirths (number of births in parentheses)		
	None	Low/middle	High
None	1.3 (31,559)	1.6 (4,455)	1.7 (528)
Low/middle	1.6 (17,452)	1.8 (7,881)	2.1 (608)
High	1.6 (1,656)	1.3 (457)	1.4 (144)

MALFORMATIONS

Mother's exposure	Father's exposure and percentage of malformations diagnosed within two weeks (number of births in parentheses)		
	None	Low/middle	High
None	0.92 (31,904)	0.89 (4,509)	1.10 (534)
Low/middle	0.82 (17,616)	0.99 (7,970)	0.81 (614)
High	1.10 (1,676)	1.30 (463)	0.70 (145)

Source: Radiation Effects Research Foundation, https://www.rerf.or.jp/en/programs/roadmap_e/health_effects-en/geneefx-en/birthdef/.

Additionally, in 2002–06 possible links between exposure and diabetes/ hypertension were investigated, but the outcome was negative. Again, the caveat about the relative youth of the subjects in the 2000s should be noted.

A more recent analysis using the Life Span Study panel of survivors finds that survivors exposed to low doses of radiation have a higher life expectancy than control subjects not exposed to radiation.[111] This finding supports the controversial hypothesis of radiation *hormesis* (from the Greek for "to set in motion")—the hypothesis that very low doses of ionizing radiation might yield adaptive responses that prove beneficial. However, it bears noting that the hormesis hypothesis is very much a minority view among scientists and that eminent bodies such as the United Nations (UN) Scientific Committee on the Effects of Atomic Radiation reject it, insisting that all doses of radiation, no matter how small, are harmful. Alternative explanations for Sutuo's finding, such as that A-bomb survivors received better medical care than the population at large, need to be considered.[112]

Yet another study assessed the impact of radiation exposure on the health of over 75,000 children of A-bomb survivors sixty-two years after the event.[113]

The children were born between 1946 and 1984, and 5,183 had already died; the mean age at assessment of the remainder was fifty-four years. The study identified no link between the degree of maternal or paternal exposure and the risk of dying of either cancer or noncancer diseases. Similarly, genetic studies reveal no significant association between parental exposure to radiation and the frequency of genetic abnormalities among children conceived after the exposure. From the health examination program, the prevalence of multifactorial diseases, including hypertension, hypercholesterolemia, diabetes mellitus, angina pectoris, myocardial infarction, and stroke has, so far, not been associated with parental radiation exposure. A limiting factor here is that the cohort of A-bomb survivors' children is still relatively young; it may be too soon to detect pathologies associated with late adulthood.[114] In sum, although the A-bomb inflicted catastrophic horrors on innocent civilians in the two cities, the outcome with regard to health outcomes for the postbomb generation is somewhat reassuring.

Both the military benefits and the morality of dropping Little Boy and Fat Man remain controversial.[115] The USSBS took the position in its summary report on the Pacific War that the nuclear option might not have been necessary. The report, published less than a year after the Japanese surrender, noted that "certainly prior to December 31, 1945, and in all probability prior to November 1, 1945, Japan would have surrendered even if the atomic bombs had not been dropped, even if Russia had not entered the war, and even if no invasion had been planned or contemplated."[116] Certainly, the Japanese economy and military were on their knees. Relentless bombing had reduced Japan's ingot steel production from a 1943 peak of 7.8 million tons per annum to 2.9 million tons by mid-1945, and production even at that level could not have been maintained thereafter.[117] Coal imports had dwindled to zero, and production plus imports in the first half of 1945 were less than a third of their levels on the eve of the war. There was virtually no aluminum or oil. Bombing had destroyed nearly nine-tenths of the shipping stock, and some of what remained was laid up for the lack of oil. By June 1945 oil tanks were being recycled for scrap and refineries shut down.[118] As already discussed in chapter 1, the food availability situation had become critical before the end of the war, with starvation looming; a further 10 percent reduction in the rice ration in Tokyo was planned for August 11. The lack of bauxite and aluminum had seriously constrained aircraft production and would have reduced it to zero by the autumn. Tellingly, not a single one of the 747 B-29s involved in the XXI Bomber Command's last incendiary raid on August 14, 1945, was lost (figure 6.9).

FIGURE 6.9. Carnage
Source: Bundesarchiv, Bild 146-1970-050-31 / CC-BY-SA 3.0 (*this page, top*);
Deutsche Fotothek of the Saxon State Library / State and University Library
Dresden (SLUB) (*this page, bottom*)

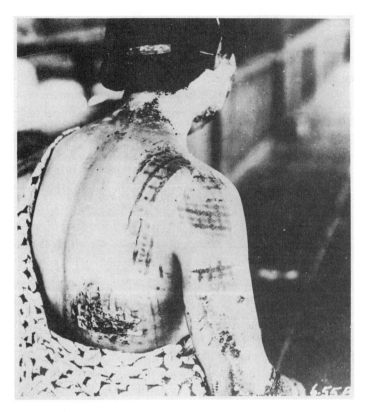

FIGURE 6.9. (*continued*)

Would the Japanese have surrendered in any case? Why did the incendiary bombing, although more damaging cumulatively than the A-bombs and arguably even more obscene in terms of how it killed victims, fail to induce the Japanese to surrender prior to August 1945? Was the threat of a Soviet invasion of Korea in August an added trigger that forced the Japanese surrender? These remain controversial questions.[119]

Japan had effectively already lost the war, but supporters of the bombing have always focused on the military lives saved by forcing the Japanese to lay down arms. The counterfactual arithmetic can be traced back to President Truman's utterances and to Secretary of War Henry Stimson's lesser-of-two-evils apologia in *Harper's Magazine* in February 1947, which claimed that over 1 million American casualties (probably implying 200,000–250,000 lives) would have resulted from fighting that lasted another year. Stimson's estimate almost certainly exaggerated; secret estimates made at the time proposed a worst-case scenario of 220,000 casualties, 46,000 of them fatal.[120] His article spawned a controversy that has lasted to this day. The archival record convinced the influential Japanese American historian Tsuyoshi Hasegawa in 2005 that contrary to the conclusion of the USSBS, it was the Soviet attack on Japanese forces in Manchuria on August 9 that forced the emperor's hand. Hasegawa's claims have gained some traction since, but the debate continues.[121]

The Demographic Profile of Bombing Victims

What was the age and gender profile of civilians killed in the aerial bombings of World War II? On the one hand is a presumption that the victims of strategic bombing of centers of heavy industry were more likely to have been male. The evacuation of females and their children from at-risk areas (as in Britain during the Blitz) might also tilt the gender ratio toward males. On the other hand, carpet- or area bombing was perhaps more likely target females, particularly in places where a significant proportion of the male population was on the battlefront. Systematic research on the topic is lacking, so all we can offer here is a few snapshots.

In Britain in 1941–42, 53 percent of the adults killed and 57 percent of those injured in bombing raids were males. Might this reflect the fact that the Luftwaffe's main targets were strategic? An analysis of the Civilian War Dead Roll of Honour of victims in the northeast of England offers some detail on ages, showing that one civilian casualty in four was under twenty years of age and one in five over sixty (figure 6.10).[122] But taking into account the age

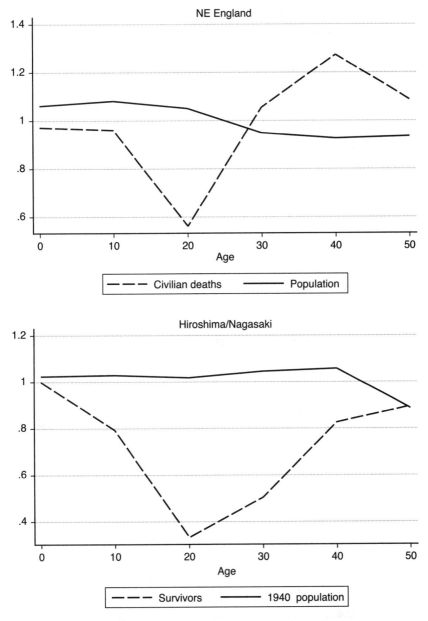

FIGURE 6.10. Gender ratios in the northeast of England and Hiroshima/Nagasaki. In Japan, 1940 population refers to Hiroshima Province; in England, population refers to north rural.
Source: United Kingdom data taken from the Commonwealth War Dead website. It includes only those buried in the United Kingdom. https://www.cwgc.org/find -records/find-war-dead/

and gender distribution of the population, those most at risk were the older adults, and those least at risk were children and adolescents. The plight of the older people is not surprising, but the reason why the young were less vulnerable is because many of them were moved out of harm's way to rural areas. It comes as no surprise that men in their twenties were also hugely underrepresented among the civilian dead, but note, too, the overrepresentation of men aged thirty and above (figure 6.10).

The USSBS concluded that a majority of the victims of the firebombing of Tokyo on March 9–10, 1945, "were the most vulnerable: women, children and the elderly." The database of survivors compiled by the Hiroshima-Nagasaki Life Span Study (LSS) offers more precision. Its total of 50,175 males and 70,146 females is probably a good measure of the demographic composition of those who perished in the two cities.[123] Far more females died because they represented a higher share of the cities' populations. The massive underrepresentation of males in their twenties and thirties is remarkable but unsurprising, given wartime mobilization.

Law, Public Opinion, and Aerial Bombing

From the very beginning, there was an element of make-believe about international treaties aimed at protecting civilians from aerial attack. Acceptance of the 1899 prohibition against the use of projectiles from balloons was predicated on the presumption that such attacks would not be very effective in any case, and limiting the prohibition to five years was enough to satisfy signatories who would not be bound by laws against making the most of innovations in aerial technology.[124] And when the Germans justified their Zeppelin raids in 1915–16 as retaliation for an illegal blockade against innocent civilians, the British merely retaliated in kind with their own aircraft.

Revulsion against attacking civilians from the air and viewing it as immoral made a comeback after the war, and Article 22 of The Hague Rules prohibited aerial attacks "for the purpose of terrorizing the civilian population, of destroying or damaging private property not of a military character, or of injuring non-combatants."[125] But for all the indignation at the aerial bombing of innocents in Spain and China in the 1930s, both sides during World War II came to regard civilians in the cities as legitimate and important bombing targets. In October 1940 British public opinion was still split down the middle on the morality of "bombing the civilian population of Germany," but by April 1941, 55 percent approved, while only 36 percent

TABLE 6.6. British responses to *"What are your feelings when you hear that there has been a heavy air raid on a German city?"* in July 1943

Response	%
Very pleased, increase the bombing	35
Satisfied, got to be done, smashes their production, brings end nearer	9
Justice, getting their deserts	15
Indifference, don't mind	4
Mixed feelings	5
Pity but it's necessary, they deserve it	11
Sorry for the Germans	12
Scared of reprisals	1
Sorry for the lost airmen	2
Miscellaneous and don't know	6

Source: Cantril 1951: 1069.

disapproved, and when questioned about their feelings on hearing about a heavy air raid on a German city in July 1943, most people expressed their satisfaction (table 6.6).[126] During and in the wake of the war, American public opinion had no qualms about the morality of bombing civilians or of using the A-bomb. In the wake of Pearl Harbor, two-thirds of the population were in favor of the indiscriminate bombing of Japanese cities.[127]

Table 6.7 describes U.S. public opinion seven months later. Whereas half of those surveyed favored a "friendly attitude" toward German civilians after the war, 10 percent supported the "extermination" of Japanese civilians and another 10 percent, punishment and torture.

In an editorial published in the wake of President Truman's announcement of the Hiroshima bombing, the Vatican's *Osservatore Romano* took the high moral ground, turning its thoughts to a story about Leonardo da Vinci:

He planned a submarine, but he feared that man would not apply it to progress, namely to the constructive uses of civilisation, but to its ruin. He destroyed that possible instrument of destruction. . . . Leonardo chose the path of vanquishing death by thought, the only ideal of life. The road of men who have not his Christian charity must defeat death only with death.[128]

Such sentiments cut no ice in the United States at the time. Some months after the use of the A-bomb against Japan, the National Opinion Research

TABLE 6.7. U.S. responses to *"If you had your say, how would we treat the people who live in Germany/Japan after this war?"* in February 1944

Choice	Germany	Japan
Active assistance	6	3
Friendly attitude	50	26
Educate them	9	11
Put them on probation	5	5
Unfriendly attitude—isolation	7	18
Supervise government, industry, finance	14	14
Police them, military government	6	6
Punishment, torture	6	10
Extermination	2	10
Other	1	2
Disarmament	10	8
Don't know	5	6
Total	121*	119*

Source: Cantril 1951: 1115, 1118 (surveys by NORC, February 1944).

Note: * Percentages add to more than 100 because some respondents gave more than one answer.

Center [NORC] asked a sample of Americans: "If you had been the one to decide whether or not to use the atomic bomb against Japan, which one of these things do you think you would have done?"

The breakdown of answers was as follows (percentages):

Bombed one city at a time	44
Wiped out cities	23
Bombed where there were no people	26
Refused to use	4
Don't know	2

In another poll carried out by Gallup in the wake of the bombing of Hiroshima (on August 8, 1945), 85 percent of Americans approved of the action.[129] Have opinions softened since? Yes, if the 2015 Sagan poll, which found that only 46 percent of Americans still approved of the bombing, can be relied upon. But Sagan and Valentino add a sobering gloss to this finding, arguing that if Americans today faced a wartime threat similar to that of 1945, a clear majority would no longer feel constrained by the nuclear taboo.[130]

They used a survey experiment involving a hypothetical war between the United States and Iran to gauge opinions and found that the principle of civilian immunity went out the window in face of "the pressures of war." A clear majority—three-fifths or respondents—would approve of going nuclear in such circumstances, and an even higher proportion would approve of a bombing campaign like that against Tokyo in March 1945.[131]

Still, article 51(2) of Additional Protocol I to the Fourth Geneva Convention (1949) stated that "the civilian population as such, as well as individual civilians, shall not be the object of attack. Acts or threats of violence, the primary purpose of which is to spread terror among the civilian population, are prohibited." Almost half a century later (in 1993), the UN Security Council declared that the convention had become customary international law, binding even those states that had not signed the convention. In 1980 Protocol III of the UN Convention on Certain Conventional Weapons took another step in the same direction, declaring the use of napalm against civilian targets a war crime. The United States used a form of napalm by another name against military targets for the last time in Iraq in 2003. President Obama signed the treaty on his first full day in office (January 21, 2009), although his signature was subject to the caveat that the prohibition may be set aside when use can save civilian lives.

Such legislation, and Obama's reservation, supports the plea that American political scientist Michael Waltzer made in *Just and Unjust Wars* (1977) for civilian immunity in warfare as a basic human right. But Waltzer also proposed an exceptional category that he called "a supreme emergency," when the traditional *jus in bello* norms of a just war no longer apply. He defined a supreme emergency as a situation in which the danger of defeat was imminent and its consequences "literally beyond calculation" and "unimaginably horrific." For Waltzer, a prime example of a supreme emergency was the situation facing the United Kingdom between the British retreat from Dunkirk (May 26–June 4, 1940) and the Japanese attack on Pearl Harbor (December 7, 1941). Waltzer's definition is designedly very narrow: in his view, as soon as the United States entered the war the supreme emergency was past, and the United Kingdom was subject again to legal and moral constraints. But during the window between Dunkirk and Pearl Harbor, Waltzer saw the area bombing of German cities as a justifiable last resort. The irony is that, as we have seen, the RAF was incapable of the kind of bombing that Waltzer envisaged during the period he reckoned to be a supreme emergency. As late as two months before Pearl Harbor, so inaccurate were RAF bombers that "on any given night only about one in five crews put bombs within five miles of their target." They were really effective only from 1943 on, when the existential threat was over. Waltzer found that the dropping of atomic bombs on Hiroshima and Nagasaki and indeed the indiscriminate firebombing of cities in Germany and Japan in early 1945 did not meet his criterion of a supreme emergency.[132]

7

Migration, Displacement, and Ethnic Cleansing

They are the Refugees. It is impossible to be with them and not
be stirred to the depth of your soul. On the faces of all is the same
expression, a look of mingled hopelessness and bewilderment: how
have they come, why have they come, whither are they going, what
will they do?

—"THE REFUGEES AT KIEV," 1915

I remember going across in a car. On the other side was hot food. As a
small boy the journey was so long. I was sure at one point my mother
had died in the car. . . . Men and women were terrified going along
that road because of the shelling.

—A LENINGRAD EVACUEE, 1942

Warfare constrains migration, yet throughout history wars have been associated with civilians fleeing or being displaced. The war in Ukraine, which
caused an exodus of over six million and the internal migration of many
more in its first year,[1] is a stark reminder. In economic terms such migration
differs from ordinary emigration in several ways. First, whereas voluntary
migrants typically choose their time of departure and destination with some
forethought, forced migrants are more likely to end up suddenly and perhaps
penniless in places where the facilities are lacking and their prospects are

few. The selection effects are accordingly likely to be very different. In the case of Ukraine in 2022, for example, the migrants consisted overwhelmingly of women and children, and whereas older people migrate internally, younger women and their children are more likely to migrate abroad. Second, forced migration tends to be concentrated in time and to occur during emergencies and so places tremendous pressures on the people and resources at the destination. This can create resentment, with accusations that the refugees are carriers of disease, idlers who place a strain on public services, and so on. The refugees may also be less committed to integrating in their new homes, which they regard as transitional and temporary. Third, the burden of such sudden, unplanned inflows may fall disproportionately on the poor and the civic-minded in the receiving country.

Thanks largely to the world wars, when it was barely half over the twentieth century was dubbed "the century of the homeless man."[2] During World War I and World War II, individuals and households migrated in order to escape from famine (as they did from cities in the Soviet Union during World War I and from Leningrad during World War II) and to avoid military conflict and the threat of conscription (as in the Soviet Union, Belgium, France, and many other places during World War I). The world wars also witnessed many examples of other more sinister forms of migration: the forced removal of targeted groups and minorities (such as Jews, Roma, Armenians, Greeks, and Turks) and the drafting of labor in occupied territories as substitutes for those in uniform and, in extremis, genocide (as in Germany, Austria, and elsewhere just before and during the Holocaust). A minority died in the attempt to escape. Also common, if far less traumatic, was the temporary movement of children and others, mainly the older adults and women with children, out of harm's way in cities at risk of aerial bombing.

World War I

World War I provoked massive movements of civilians between countries: of Belgians to France, the Netherlands, and Great Britain; of Germans out of Russian-occupied East Prussia; of non-Russian minorities from border regions to the Russian interior; and, most cataclysmically of all, beginning in July 1915, of Armenians out of their homes in eastern Anatolia to death camps in the Syrian desert. That latter migration, described in some detail in chapter 4, resulted in the deaths of a million or more through a combination of violence, dehydration, disease, and starvation. World War I also led to the mass movement of internally displaced persons (IDPs)—the very

TABLE 7.1. Refugees and IDPs during World War I and its aftermath

Country	Numbers displaced (millions)
Belgium	1.5
France	2
Italy[a]	0.8
Germany	1
Austro-Hungary	2
Russia	7
Serbia	0.2
Greece	1.2
Ottoman Empire	1
Total	17

Source: Totals as discussed in the text.

[a] The total includes the 0.2 million expelled in 1914 (see p. 286 below).

term dates from that era.[3] The IDPs included huge numbers of French, Italians, Russians, and Serbs. Most of those forced to move eventually returned home; the Armenians expelled from Anatolia, the Pontic Greeks expelled from Asia Minor, and the Turks expelled from Greece are glaring exceptions. Such movements are inherently difficult to measure, but it is reckoned that those who fled and those who were forced to move during World War I numbered at least seventeen million, nearly half of them in Russia (see table 7.1 and figure 7.1).[4]

"Brave Little Belgium" paid a high price for not allowing the German invader to advance through its territory unhindered.[5] The illegal invasion, accompanied by atrocities where it met resistance, prompted a mass exodus of civilians. The Netherlands, initially the main destination of Belgian refugees, contained more than a million of them, mostly Dutch speakers, by November 1914. In the early months of the war, another 200,000 escaped to England (where there were still 125,000 in November 1918) and nearly 250,000 to France. In all about 1.5 million Belgians out of a total of 6.5 million became refugees at some point, with about 0.6 million of them spending most or all of the war abroad.

The migration began with the flight of about one hundred thousand people from the provinces of Limburg and Flemish Brabant in the first weeks of the war but became an exodus during the German siege and bombardment of Antwerp in early October 1914. That caused the populations of the towns and cities of the southern Netherlands to double or triple almost

FIGURE 7.1. Photographic images of World War I refugees
Source: Státní okresní archiv Rychnov nad Kněžnou (Galician refugee, *bottom, p. 281*)

FIGURE 7.1. (*continued*)

overnight. Those who fled north from Antwerp and its hinterland spanned the socioeconomic spectrum, from refined aristocrats to farmers and farm servants and from rich professionals to artisans, factory workers, and clerks. At the outset the refugees were warmly welcomed by Dutch civil society, but given the strain imposed by their numbers, the euphoria did not last. By October 11, the day after the loss of Antwerp, Amsterdam contained fourteen thousand refugees, and the authorities declared that the city was full, pleading with the railway station master in Roosendaal by the Belgian border not to send any more to the city. In the southern city of Breda (pop. thirty thousand), local charities found shelter for some in public buildings, more on shop and factory floors. In the small town of Hulst (pop. five thousand), streets were covered with straw as sleeping accommodations.[6]

The burden on the Dutch was unsustainable, and soon a combination of *zachte drank* (soft pressure), the lack of employment, and the bleak prospect of being confined indefinitely to uncomfortable and unhealthy camps pressured most of the refugees into returning home.[7] Besides, partly for diplomatic reasons but also because it feared that refugees in the Netherlands might be mobilized by the Belgian government-in-exile, the Germans sought to hasten their return. Two days after capturing Antwerp, it issued a proclamation guaranteeing the safety of returnees. Only 0.2 million remained in the Netherlands at the end of 1914 and 0.1 million in May 1915.

Those keenest to return home to Belgium were farmers fearful for their land and wealthy individuals worried about the threat of taxation and the confiscation of property belonging to those who had not returned by March 1, 1915. Most likely to stay were the utterly destitute. In the Netherlands the refugees came to be resented both as a threat to Dutch workers and as a welfare burden. There was xenophobia and resentment at refugees' complaints about being housed like vagrants. The very length of the war played its part too. Most of those who stayed were housed for the duration of the war in five remote refugee camps spread across the Netherlands. Some refugees headed for England instead of home: skilled metal workers were in short supply in Britain.

The refugees from *la petite Belgique* were welcomed in France and in Britain as emblems of the atrocities inflicted by the Germans on civilians. In France their number rose more or less continuously since returning across German lines was impossible and reached 0.5 million in early 1915 and 1.0 million by the end of 1916. It rose further in the wake of German advances in early 1918, reaching a maximum of 1.85 million in September 1918. At that time France's Nord département contained 311,000 Belgians; Pas-de-Calais, 321,000; Somme, 173,000; and Aisne, 163,000.

The presence of Belgian refugees in Britain throughout World War I is rarely mentioned today, but it was headline news at the time.[8] Belgians began arriving in Britain in August 1914, and nearly 100,000 had crossed the English Channel by the end of the year. By mid-1915 the total in Britain had reached a maximum of about 175,000, of whom about 29 percent were children. The aggregate inflow may have exceeded 250,000; some did not stay long, and nearly all were gone again by mid-1919. Most of the refugees were from Flanders and two-fifths of them from the province of Antwerp. At the outset, "Everyone was Belgian mad."[9] The euphoria did not last, but at least in Britain and in France, where work was more readily available, the pressure to repatriate Belgians was not as strong as in the Netherlands. In January 1918 Britain's munitions factories employed over 32,000 Belgians, most of whom were women.

On the southern front, the heavy defeat of Italian forces at Caporetto in October 1917 led to the disorganized and chaotic flight of a demoralized army accompanied by over half a million civilians. The refugees were disproportionately older people, women, and children. Ernest Hemingway's narrator in *A Farewell to Arms*,[10] Frederick Henry, did not exaggerate by much when he exclaimed, "After a while we came on the main channels of the retreat and walked all night toward the Tagliamento [river]. I had not realized how gigantic the retreat was. The whole country was moving, as well as the army." The state sought to find accommodation for those who could not afford it; others fended for themselves. The cost of relief was not trivial. It absorbed 1.5 percent of all government spending in 1918–19.[11]

Although many refugees from the Northeast found themselves in make-shift accommodations in rural areas where there was no work or health-care facilities, most were located in provinces not too far from where they had fled. Table 7.2 describes the place of origin of the refugees by province and the place of destination by region. Over one-fifth of the inhabitants of Udine, Treviso, Venezia, and Vicenza fled. Nearly half of those from Treviso and Vicenza found refuge elsewhere within their own region of Veneto, whereas half of the refugees from Udine and Padova were forced to bypass Veneto and settle in Lombardy, Tuscany, or Emilia. Fearing the spread of "defeatist" rhetoric, the authorities tended to keep them out of the main cities. Nearly two-thirds of the refugees were relocated in the northern and central regions of Lombardy, Veneto, Emilia, and Tuscany, where on average they briefly constituted over 2 percent of the population.

Only one-fifth of those displaced were sent further afield than Tuscany or Lombardy. Sicily received over twenty thousand refugees, but they represented only 0.5 percent of its population. The further south, the worse the conditions: the town commissioner and the parish priest of Enego in the province of Vicenza, visiting refugees in Calabria four months after the exodus, found that most of them were still sleeping on the ground or in dirty and unhealthy ground-floor rooms, and they came across instances of malaria.

TABLE 7.2. The origins and destinations of Italian refugees

Destination (region)	Province of origin							Pop. 1911 (1,000s)	Refugees (% regional population)
	Belluno	Padova	Treviso	Udine	Venezia	Vicenza	Total		
Piedmont	2,384	1,292	8,806	12,410	8,542	8,537	42,021	3,424	1.2
Liguria	1,246	1,420	4,245	8,356	8,155	2,073	25,495	1,197	2.1
Lombardy	4,811	1,913	17,041	20,802	13,517	13,439	71,523	4,790	1.5
Veneto	13,091	362	52,728	5,746	11,711	37,732	121,370	3,527	3.4
Emilia	3,046	1,600	14,194	19,906	24,851	4,053	67,650	2,681	2.5
Tuscany	3,669	2,353	11,261	35,437	14,136	2,058	68,914	2,695	2.6
Marche	315	235	2,452	3,864	7,603	1,181	15,650	1,093	1.4
Umbria	338	125	1,185	3,159	1,601	290	6,698	687	1.0
Lazio	695	861	2,548	5,381	3,308	321	13,114	1,302	1.0
Abruzzi/Molise	308	1,423	3,999	1,868	4,799	903	13,300	1,431	0.9
Campania	498	241	5,933	4,903	5,431	2,735	24,241	3,312	0.7
Puglia	151	50	2,897	1,576	1,719	257	6,650	2,130	0.3
Basilicata	68	12	57	268	833	88	1,326	474	0.3
Calabria	221	37	1,035	1,942	976	327	4,538	1,402	0.3
Sicily	460	138	9,968	4,641	3,366	2,282	20,855	3,672	0.6
Sardinia	4	5	38	57	33	12	149	852	0.0
Total	31,305	12,067	138,387	134,816	110,581	76,338	503,494	36,671	1.4
Pop. 1911	192,793	194,521	491,166	628,081	466,752	263,089	2,236,402		
Refugees/population(%)	16.2	6.2	28.2	21.6	23.7	29.0	22.5		

Sources: Ceschin 2006: 241–48; Mitchell 1975: 63.

The refugee death rate was higher than that of the rest of the population.[12] The refugees included Anna Buliani, a young mother from Treppo Carnico in Udine who pleaded with a committee of the Veneto Parliament that she had been sent eight hundred kilometers to the most miserable place in Campania Province. Hygiene and sanitation were deplorable, and the lack of employment forced most refugees to leave. In the preceding months, in the commune where she was staying, a woman with puerperal fever had been charged ten lire by a midwife.[13] At least exile did not last long; repatriation was virtually complete by 1920.

The number of civilians displaced by war in France exceeded those in Italy and in Belgium. The French authorities put the total at 0.5 million by the end of 1914, 1 million by the end of 1916, and 1.85 million in September 1918. A majority of the refugees were adult women (37 percent) or children (44 percent).[14] The refugees had lived in ten départements in northern and eastern France, half of them in Nord, Pas-de-Calais, and Somme. Naturally, they wanted to be relocated as near to home as possible, but for the authorities "as possible" meant dispersal far from the front lines. Those from regions where migration to industrial hubs such as Paris was already common were at an advantage. The first to leave tended to be those who had somewhere to go and who could tap into communal social capital;[15] refugees from the Ardennes, for example, could call on the Fraternelle Ardennoise, a mutual support organization in existence since 1889.

Paris was the first port of call for most refugees from the war zones. Many stayed in the capital; others moved on, supported by the state and by private philanthropy. Many would end up in the South of France, where integration with the host population was most challenging and where the refugees faced growing hostility as the war wore on. There was petty criminality by some refugees; according to a Maine-et-Loire weekly, "*Les provinces martyres ne produisent pas que des saints.*"[16] There were accusations that the newcomers were gaming the system, and suspicion that young women among them had been socializing with German troops before they became refugees escalated tensions. Some even referred to the refugees as "*les Boches du Nord*" (the Huns of the North). Nicolas Charles notes than in many diaries kept by women during the war, bitterness was the prevalent theme: that of being forced to leave one's loved ones and property in the enemy's grasp and, even more so, facing unwelcoming compatriot strangers who did not appreciate their situation.[17] The refugee problem did not vanish immediately at the end of 1918, but by the mid-1920s, the populations of the affected départements were close to their 1911 levels again.[18]

Neutral Switzerland offered a safe passage, if not a haven, to French civilians evacuated from war zones by Germany and to Italian, German, and Austrian refugees expelled by France at the outbreak of hostilities in August 1914. These included nearly 0.2 million Italians; a year later several thousand Austrian and German civilians in Italy took their turn at taking the same route in reverse.[19]

Forced migrations during World War I, mainly of ethnic minorities, were far more numerous on the Eastern Front. They involved citizens of the Russian, Austro-Hungarian, and Ottoman Empires, as well as of Germany and several Balkan countries. Early Russian gains on the Eastern Front in 1914–15 caused about 1 million East Prussians, or half the population of East Prussia, to flee westward and also led to the displacement of hundreds of thousands of Turks from eastern Anatolia. Some returned as the Russians were repulsed during the spring of 1915. The final German offensives in 1918 forced another 0.2 million people to move.[20] As often happens during wartime, the loyalty of minorities was in question, and indeed, some minorities availed of the opportunity to advance their claims of self-determination. In Russia the number of internally displaced—Germans, Jews, Poles, Latvians, Gypsies, Belarusians, Kazakhs, Bulgarians—reached at least 3 million and probably double that by the time the Bolsheviks took over. Local authorities, charities, and patriotic societies improvised with regard to accommodations and provided first aid and clothing; societies representing the various nationalities were also very active. The government created a Special Council for Refugees in August 1915. After the Treaty of Brest-Litovsk (March 3, 1918), several hundred thousand refugees returned home, but further displacement followed as the Russian Civil War intensified. About 1.5 million left Russia for new homes in Europe and further afield. A Bolshevik victory in 1921 led to another phase of repatriation, including that of 1.3 million Poles.[21]

World War I led to the internal displacement of up to 2 million people in the Austro-Hungarian Empire.[22] Francesco Frizzera puts their number at 1.1 million by mid-1915, including 360,000 Jews, 130,000 Poles, 300,000 Ruthenians (Rusyn- and Ukrainian-speaking inhabitants of the empire), 145,000 Italians, 70,000 Slovenians, and 7,000 Croatians.[23] Most of them fled or were moved to safe havens in present-day Austria and the Czech Republic. As in the Russian case, fears of disloyalty and treason, rather than imminent physical danger from attack, motivated the transfer of many of the refugees. The authorities housed most of them in purpose-built camps. In some cases, mortality from infectious diseases and malnutrition was high; of the 0.2 million

25 JUIN 1916
JOURNÉE SERBE

FIGURE 7.2. French poster marking the anniversary of the Battle of Kosovo and the exodus that ensued

housed in Gmünd camp in Lower Austria, one of the largest, 30,000 died there. Austria and Czechoslovakia still contained 0.3 million refugees at the end of the war, whom the authorities refused citizenship.

Population displacements in the Balkans were widespread during World War I and the bloody local wars that preceded it (figure 7.2). There were forced movements of ethnic Greeks, Bulgarians, Serbs, Albanians, and Turks and of Muslims, Christians, and Jews. In relative terms, the Serbs (whose fate has already been described in chapter 2) and the Greeks probably suffered the most. In the initial phases of the Greek-Turkish War of 1919–20, hundreds of thousands more Turks were forced eastward by Greek forces. When the Bulgarian army occupied Eastern Macedonia, its thirty-six thousand Greek inhabitants were deported to Bulgaria. At the end of the war, the survivors— seventeen thousand—returned home.[24] The impact of displacements on the population of Greek Macedonia and of Eastern and Western Thrace may be inferred from tables 7.3 and 7.4. At the outset these were ethnically diverse regions, populated mainly by Greeks and Turks. The Muslims included not

TABLE 7.3. The population of Greek Macedonia by ethnicity, 1904–24 (1,000s)

	1904	1913	1914	1918	1920	1924
Greeks	513	528	678	659	577	1,277
Bulgars	119	104	104	104	104	77
Muslims	475	465	350	350	350	2
Other	98	98	96	90	91	91
All	1,205	1,195	1,228	1,203	1,122	1,447

Source: Pallis 1925: 330.

TABLE 7.4. The populations of Eastern and Western Thrace by ethnicity/religion, 1904–24 (1,000s)

WESTERN THRACE

	1902	1915	1920	1924
Greeks	87	17	68	189
Bulgarians	35	35	35	23
Muslims	111	84	84	84
Other	4	4	4	8
All	237	140	191	304

EASTERN THRACE

	1912	1915	1920	1924
Greeks	235	138	186	0
Bulgarians	50	1	1	1
Muslims	223	300	300	370
Armenians	24	24	7	0
Other	19	19	19	19
All	569	482	513	390

Source: Pallis 1925: 330.

just Turks but Pomaks (Bulgarian-speaking Muslims), Albanians, Valaades (a small Greek-speaking Muslim community, numbering perhaps seventeen thousand in the early twentieth century), and Muslim Gypsies. Only Muslims of Albanian origin were exempted from population exchanges. The others included Jews, Romanized Vlachs (Balkan Romance speakers), Uniates (Eastern Catholics), Albanians, and foreigners. Eastern Thrace lost all its Greeks and Armenians, while Greek Macedonia lost all its Muslims.

During World War I, Germany relied on forced foreign labor from two occupied areas: (1) Belgium and northern France and (2) Poland and the area known as Ober Ost (the Upper East) along the Baltic coasts of Latvia and Lithuania. Some of the former were forced into going by destitution and unemployment, but from mid-1916 Germany relied increasingly on forcibly conscripted foreign labor. During the summer of 1916, over 20,000 women and children from southern Belgium were drafted for summer harvest work across the border. In October, as the shortage of manpower intensified, General Erich Ludendorff, by then Germany's chief policymaker, ordered the authorities in occupied Belgium to draft "work-shy" labor in Belgium and to a lesser extent in Poland and Ober Ost. Over 60,000 Belgian workers were sent to workplaces in Belgium and another 60,000, to Germany. Housing and work conditions were dismal and nutrition inadequate. Of the 120,000, over 2,000 died.[25] The experiment proved a costly failure. It led to an outcry, both internationally and among progressives in Germany, and in February 1917 the Germans switched from deportations from Belgium to a (much more successful) reliance on voluntary enrollment. As in Belgium, the use of forced labor from the East began in October 1916. But most forced labor in Germany during World War I—2.5 million out of 3 million—was prisoner-of-war (POW) labor, more than half of it Russian. The high death rates of POWs are consistent with harsh treatment. Ironically, those captured early on, disproportionately Russians, were less likely to die than those captured toward the end of the war, but that was partly because the former were more likely to be employed on the land, whereas the latter tended to work in less healthy industrial settings.[26] The German occupiers also conscripted civilians to work locally. A contemporary estimate put the number of forced workers in Lithuania during World War I at 130,000.[27]

World War II

In a survey funded by the International Labor Office, sociologist Eugene Kulischer estimated in 1943 that more than 30 million Europeans had been "transplanted or torn" from their homes since the outbreak of war in 1939.[28] That estimate may be on the low side,[29] and Kulischer believed that allowing for the movement of Germans and Italians recently displaced by war would bring the total up to 40 million for 1939–1943. Of Kulischer's 30 million, 10 million had fled Soviet territory occupied by Germany and Romania; 6.5 million were foreign workers employed in Germany; 2.5 million were Germans who had moved abroad; 1.5 million had fled the western parts of

Belarus and Ukraine; 1 million had fled the coastal areas of Belgium and of France, where northern départements were virtually emptied of their civilian populations; and the rest was made up of many smaller movements. Wendy Goldman and Donald Filtzer note that estimates of the number of evacuees and refugees in the Soviet Union in 1941–43 range from 12 million to 25 million, while Mark Harrison puts the total number of Soviet citizens displaced by World War II at 16.5 million.[30] Much of the Soviet displacement was linked to the wholesale evacuation of industrial plant and hardware, and accompanying labor, out of the reach of invading German forces in the wake of Operation Barbarossa, which began on June 22, 1941, and the creation of a new improvised war economy in the East in 1941, an operation unprecedented in human history. In the months following Barbarossa, over 1,500 manufacturing plants, mainly large ones, and the labor required to man them were moved by rail from Ukraine, Belarus, and the Moscow region to the Volga and Ural regions, to Siberia, and to central Asia. A second wave followed in 1942.[31]

Ethnic cleansing was a recurrent feature. In 1941–42 the Germans transferred about 55,000 ethnic Slovenians deemed *nicht-eindeutschungfähig* (incapable of becoming German) from Lower Styria to Serbia, Croatia, and Germany, while 10,000 or so ethnic Germans from Bessarabia and South Tyrol were resettled in Slovenia (some against their will).[32] The German conquest of western Poland in September 1939 led to the expulsion of 1.5 million Poles from areas incorporated into the Reich to the so-called General Government. At the same time, the Soviet invasion of Poland on September 17, 1939, led to the expulsion of several hundred thousand Poles from conquered Polish territory, while the German occupation of Soviet-occupied Poland in 1941 led to the eastward flight of a further 1.2 million Poles.[33] The German retreat after Stalingrad led to the expulsion of hundreds of thousands more Poles from areas that would become part of Soviet Ukraine and of the entire ethnic Ukrainian population from lands that became Polish. These transfers resulted in over 0.1 million deaths and 1.4 million displaced Poles and Ukrainians; meanwhile, practically the entire Jewish population of both areas was annihilated.[34]

If the westward exodus of 12 million ethnic German refugees in 1945 and 1946 is added, the number involved in war-induced migrations in Europe quickly reaches 50 million.[35] In the wake of the war, 0.4 million Karelian Finns were transferred from the Soviet Union to Finland, 0.6 million Ukrainians were transferred from southeastern Poland to Ukraine, and 1.5 million Poles were transferred west from territory ceded to the Soviet Union.

There were smaller population transfers between Slovakia and Hungary; the Slovak capital Bratislava was entirely cleansed of Hungarians. Outside Europe, famine migration out of the Chinese province of Henan in 1942–43 has been put at 4 million, but that represented only a small fraction of Chinese migration between 1937, when the Japanese attacked, and 1945. As explained below, reliable data are unavailable, but allowing another 50 million for migrations outside Europe is probably being conservative. Thus, World War II may have spawned a migration of 100 million globally, about six times that of World War I.[36]

Leaving Leningrad

Located to the east of the city across the southern part of Lake Lagoda, its official name was the Military Automobile Highway No. 101. The construction of the improvised 130-kilometer Doroga Zhizni (Road of Life) or Ice Road, as it was universally known, in late 1941 led to what was perhaps the most spectacular and dramatic mass migration of World War II. Building the road involved estimating the lake's layers of ice and the impact of heavy traffic on the ice so that the best route might be chosen. The first convoy of sixty trucks carrying flour made the journey from Soviet-occupied territory to Leningrad across the lake on November 22, 1941. Three months later the road was employing "about 15,200 people, over 4,200 vehicles, 140 tractors and 540 horses." It resulted in the evacuation of nearly 0.5 million *blokadniki*, mainly women, children, and wounded soldiers, before the ice began to melt in mid-April 1942. Another 0.8 million would follow before the land blockade ended in early 1943. The route was treacherous. German aircraft sought to melt the ice with oil bombs and demolition bombs and to disrupt traffic with small white-painted butterfly bombs. Traffic was also strafed by gunfire from low-flying fighters. And those who made it safely to the other side risked dying from eating the food they were offered too quickly. One survivor remembered "a doctor running along the banks of the lake yelling, 'Do not feed them! Do not feed them!' ['*Ne kormi! Ne kormi!*']" (figure 7.3).[37]

The ice road was also used to bring out some of the city's most valuable cultural artifacts and to bring back food, equipment, and ammunition. Between 1941 and 1943, the road delivered 1.6 million tons of supplies to Leningrad. In January 1943 a major Soviet offensive, Operation Iskra, opened a land corridor to the city, and within weeks a railway link was built to Shlisserburg, thirty-five kilometers east of Leningrad at the head of the

FIGURE 7.3. The Road of Life, 1941–43

Neva River, making the ice road redundant. Although aspects of the evacu-ation have been criticized, it was nevertheless an amazing achievement. For the refugees, the Ice Road was only the beginning. Most were sent on to the Urals or to cities in central Asia. On arrival in Chuvashia, a republic in cen-tral European Russia where her grandmother lived, one refugee found her shirt "alive with lice." The discovery cheered her as "lice could not survive in Leningrad."[38]

Reichsdeutsche and Volksdeutsche

Between 1944 and March 31, 1952, when the transfers came to an official end, about 12 million ethnic Germans were expelled or displaced from their former homes in eastern Europe, mostly from Poland and Czechoslovakia, with Yugoslavia accounting for 0.4 million and Hungary about 0.2 million.[39] Most of the substantial German communities in eastern Europe fled or were expelled from their former homes in three distinct phases. The first, organized by retreating German forces as Operation Hannibal (*Unternehmen Hannibal*) and given the green light by Admiral Karl Dönitz, head of the German navy, on January 23, 1945, was the most ambitious naval evacuation—and perhaps the biggest—in history. The second consisted of the so-called wild expulsions of Germans from Poland and Czechoslovakia during the first half of 1945. That phase, engineered by the authorities in both countries, was linked to numerous atrocities. The third phase refers to movements in the wake of the Potsdam Conference of July–August 1945, which legitimized orderly transfers. It was nonviolent but also entailed hardship and death.

Operation Hannibal was a plan to evacuate army personnel and civilians from East Prussia by sea, combining two aims: (1) the strategic retreat of troops and hardware to German soil and (2) the ferrying by sea to Germany of refugees and prisoners. A week after it began, on January 30, 1945, the military transport ship MV *Wilhelm Gustloff* (originally a liner for the Nazi leisure organization Kraft durch Freude) was sunk by a Soviet submarine in the Baltic Sea with the loss of ninety-six hundred lives, mostly civilians. As the ship was also carrying naval personnel and equipment, it was a legitimate target. The loss of the virtually defenseless *Wilhelm Gustloff*, which represented the biggest loss of life from a ship sinking in history, is a central theme in Günter Grass's 2002 novella *Im Krebsgang* (*Crabwalk*). Grass claimed that he had written the book to annoy the far Right in Germany: "They said the tragedy of *Wilhelm Gustloff* was a war crime. It wasn't. It was terrible, but it was a result of war, a terrible result of war."[40] In the following weeks, the *Steuben*, carrying mainly wounded German soldiers, and the MV *Goya*, carrying both military personnel and civilians, suffered the same fate. Those on board the SS *Cap Arcona*, an improvised floating prison, were in a different category. They had been mainly political prisoners held in a grim concentration camp in Neuengamme near Hamburg. Tragically, because intelligence about those on board had not been processed, the *Cap Arcona* was destroyed by Royal Air Force fighter-bombers on the day before the Nazis surrendered, resulting in about 7,000 deaths.[41] In all about 30,000 passengers, mostly civilians, were lost during Operation Hannibal. A horrific number, but it bears noting that those deaths represented a relatively small fraction of the total evacuated. Between January 23, 1945, and the Nazi surrender fifteen weeks later, hundreds of ships of all shapes and sizes were used to ferry 0.8–0.9 million civilians and 0.35 million military personnel across the Baltic from Danzig/Gdańsk, Gdynia, and Hela to Germany and

Denmark. When all ports and shores used are included, a total of over 2 million refugees, military personnel, and prisoners were evacuated.[42]

Article XII of the Potsdam Agreement sanctioned the "orderly and humane" transfer to Germany of the ethnic German populations and citizens from several eastern European countries, most of them from former East Prussia, Poland, and Czechoslovakia.[43] These two distinct groups were referred to as *Volksdeutsche* and *Reichsdeutsche* in the Third Reich. Given what had happened in those areas during the war, expulsions were an inevitable outcome. The transfer represented what must be the greatest forced displacement of populations in history. Those who were forced out were disproportionately older adults, female, or very young. Before the mass flight westward beginning in early 1945, about eleven million Germans lived east of the Oder-Neisse line; after it, few remained. Figure 7.4 describes the distribution of *Volksdeutsche* and *Reichsdeutsche* at the end of October 1946.

German-speaking Czechs and Slovaks accounted for more than half the refugees living in West Germany in 1950 (table 7.5). The expulsion of these *Sudetendeutsche* had been planned by the Czech government-in-exile since 1941.[44] In the 1920s a majority of Sudetenland voters voted for parties committed to active participation in the new Czechoslovakian state, but the onset of the Great Depression, perceived and real discrimination, and the lure of Nazi ideology converted most of Sudetenland into enthusiastic backers of the pro-Nazi Sudetendeutsche Partei.[45] While expulsion was linked to the welcome Hitler had received in Czechoslovakia in March 1939, some supporters traced German perfidy to long before the Nazis; getting rid of the ethnic Germans would "correct errors that go back very far in our history, to the times of the *Pfemyslids* [the first Czech dynasty] when Germans were invited *en masse* to develop our towns and industry and subsequently destroyed the Slav character and culture of our land, with time becoming a danger and a threat to the very existence of the Czech people."[46] The Czech authorities pronounced ethnic Germans collectively guilty of supporting the Nazis and incapable of being integrated into postwar Czech society, and so about 2.4 million were expelled in quite ruthless and brutal fashion. "We can't complain," one refugee wearily explained. "We brought it on ourselves."[47] About 2 million were expelled during the "wild times" (*divoky odsun*) from Czechoslovakia and Poland before the Potsdam agreement. They included the forced expulsion of the German population of Brno on May 30, 1945, which resulted in the deaths of several hundred people. This period also witnessed several other local massacres of ethnic Germans.

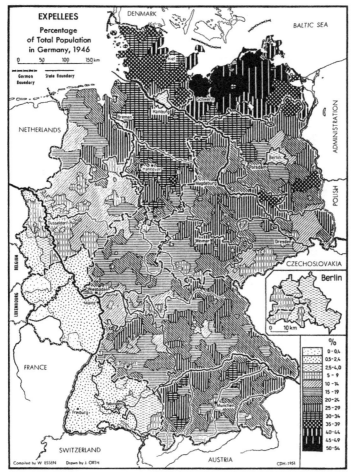

FIG. 1. Expellee Percentage of Total Population of Germany, Census of October 29, 1946. (Reproduced by permission of Werner Essen and the Institut für Raumforschung, Bonn, from *Das deutsche Flüchtlingsproblem, Sonderheft der Zeitschrift für Raumforschung*, p. 11.)

FIGURE 7.4. *Reichsdeutsche* and *Volksdeutsche* as a percentage of the population, 1946
Source: Werner Essen and the Institut für Raumforschung, Bonn, from *Das deutsche Flüchtlingsproblem, Sonderheft der Zeitschrift für Raumforschung*, p. 11

Germans living in the areas ceded to Poland in 1945—parts of Pomerania and Silesia—also suffered severely. Before the war the Pomeranian port city of Stettin (present-day Szczecin), which had been a Nazi stronghold in the last free elections of 1933 (figure 7.5*d*), contained 0.4 million inhabitants. Many fled at the approach of the Soviet army in early 1945, and when the Soviets arrived in April 1945, the city was in ruins and contained only about 20,000

TABLE 7.5. Expellees in the two Germanys (1,000s)

Province/country of origin	Federal Republic 1950	Soviet Zone 1946
Former Germany	4,469	2,274
East Prussia	1,347	
Silesia	2,053	
Pomerania	891	
Brandenburg	131	
Saar	47	
Ethnic Germans	3,407	1,327
Czechoslovakia	1,912	841
Poland	410	246
Hungary	178	.
Danzig	225	.
Romania	149	57
Yugoslavia	147	.
USSR	51	57
Baltic states	59	.
Memel	48	.
Other Europe	207	.
Overseas	21	.
Not specified	.	126
Refugees from Soviet Zone and East Berlin	*1,555*	.
Displaced Persons	*249*	.
Neorefugees	*200*	.
TOTAL	9,860	3,601

Source: Harris and Wülker 1953: tables 1 and 2.

people. Thereafter some returned, and in September 1945 Germans still made up nearly three-quarters of the 85,000 inhabitants of the now Polish city of Szczecin. By the end of 1946, however, only 17,000 Germans were left versus 100,000 Poles. The war had reduced the population of Breslau/Wrocław in Silesia from 650,000, of whom no more than a few thousand were Polish, to slightly over 0.2 million, of whom 17,000 were Polish, in August 1945. Today ethnic Germans account for about 1,000 of its population of 650,000.

In the months before the end of the war, over 30,000 ethnic Germans were transported from Hungary to the Donbas in eastern Ukraine as a form of war reparations; about 1 in 10 died there. Compared to the treatment of

Germans expelled from Poland and Czechoslovakia, Hungarian Germans were treated relatively well by the majority population. In line with the Potsdam agreements, the Hungarian government began to expel Germans who had been identified with Nazi organizations or who had declared themselves as German in the 1941 census. Those with a clean political record or useful skills were allowed to stay, yet the vast majority left all the same. By 1949 only 22,445 who self-identified as German were left in Hungary, but many more self-identified as Hungarian.

Of all the *Volksdeutsche*, those still in Yugoslavia at the end of the war fared worst of all. Most of the 0.5 million living there escaped before the end of the war. The 0.2 million or so who did not join them included—again these numbers are fallible—7,000 shot by partisans, 167,000 sent to concentration camps, and 13,000 abducted to Soviet labor camps in lieu of reparations. Forty-eight thousand of the camp internees and 2,000 of those shipped to the Soviet Union perished.[48]

The aggregate death toll resulting from the expulsion of the Germans is still disputed. Early estimates of the aggregate death toll linked to Czech ethnic cleansing were very high—0.2 million to 0.3 million—but in 1996 a joint Czech-German committee of historians agreed on a much lower death toll: about 10,000 murdered and another 5,000–6,000 deaths from other causes. That does not include the suicides of about 3,400 deportees. Expulsions from the Czech lands in the wake of the Potsdam Agreement were much more orderly.

Hans Schoenberg reckoned that in 1950 about 2.2 million ethnic Germans were not accounted for either in Germany or "in or near their homes [and that] many of them probably perished during the exodus," while the German Historical Museum proposes the toll of 0.6 million advocated by German historians Rüdiger Overmans and Inge Haar, rejecting the estimates of 2 million current in the 1950s. Overmans claimed that the 2 million figure included soldiers and refugees of non-German origin, and his 0.6 million has become the accepted wisdom.[49]

Whereas a revanchist memory of the *Vertreibung* (expulsion) had been kept alive by the dwindling population of survivors, Grass's best-selling work heightened awareness of it among the population at large over half a century after the event. Commemorating it remained a delicate issue, however. In 2008 the German government permitted the creation of a permanent exhibition of the exodus within the *Haus der Geschichte* (House of History) in Berlin (figure 7.5).[50]

In 1950, 12.5 million *Heimatvertriebene* (literally, "homeland expellees") lived in the two Germanys. Ten million had settled in the Federal

FIGURE 7.5. German refugees from the East in 1944–45
a. Fleeing from Łódź to Berlin
b. Being evacuated from Kurland, 1944 (*Source:* Bundesarchiv, Bild 183-1985-0531-500 / CC-BY-SA 3.0)

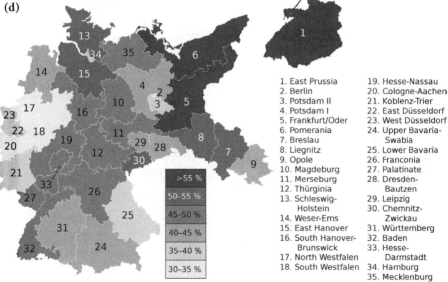

1. East Prussia
2. Berlin
3. Potsdam II
4. Potsdam I
5. Frankfurt/Oder
6. Pomerania
7. Breslau
8. Liegnitz
9. Opole
10. Magdeburg
11. Merseburg
12. Thürginia
13. Schleswig-
    Holstein
14. Weser-Ems
15. East Hanover
16. South Hanover-
    Brunswick
17. North Westfalen
18. South Westfalen
19. Hesse-Nassau
20. Cologne-Aachen
21. Koblenz-Trier
22. East Düsseldorf
23. West Düsseldorf
24. Upper Bavaria-
    Swabia
25. Lower Bavaria
26. Franconia
27. Palatinate
28. Dresden-
    Bautzen
29. Leipzig
30. Chemnitz-
    Zwickau
31. Württemberg
32. Baden
33. Hesse-
    Darmstadt
34. Hamburg
35. Mecklenburg

>55 %
50–55 %
45–50 %
40–45 %
35–40 %
30–35 %

FIGURE 7.5. (*continued*)
c. Fleeing from the Russians, 1945 (*Source:* Bundesarchiv, Bild 146-1985-021-09 /
Unknown author / CC-BY-SA 3.0)
d. Votes for the National Socialist German Workers' (Nazi) Party, March 5, 1933
(*Source:* Korny78)

FIGURE 7.5. (*continued*)
e. Refugee family in northwest Germany (*Source:* Bundesarchiv, Bild 183-W0911-501 / CC-BY-SA 3.0)
f. Refugee with her son in a forest near Potsdam, Germany, 1945 (*Source:* Hilmar Pabel)

TABLE 7.6. Distribution of the displaced by region

State	Population (1,000s)	Expellees/ others (1,000)	% Pop.	Pop. 1961/ 1964
West (excl. Berlin)	47,696	9,431	19.8	
Schleswig-Holstein	2,595	991	38.2	2,317
Hamburg	1,606	184	11.5	1,832
Lower Saxony	6,797	2,121	31.2	6,641
Nordrhein-Westfalen	13,196	1,711	13.0	15,902
Bremen	559	70	12.5	706
Hesse	4,324	886	20.5	4,814
Baden-Württemberg	6,430	1,106	15.7	7,759
Bavaria	9,126	2,155	23.6	9,515
Rheinland-Pfalz	3,005	199	6.6	3,417
East (excl. Berlin)	17,198	4,442	25.8	16,006
Saxony	5,945	989	16.6	5,486
Saxony-Anhalt	3,637	1,062	29.2	3,254
Thuringia	2,694	681	25.3	2,530
Brandenburg	2,669	723	27.1	2,674
Mecklenburg	2,253	987	43.8	2,062
Berlin	3,336	130	3.9	3,278

Source: Harris and Wülker 1953: table 3; Mitchell 1975: 62.

Republic—4.5 million inhabitants of areas in the Third Reich no longer German (*Reichsdeutsche*), 3.4 million ethnic Germans (*Volksdeutsche*), 1.6 million from the Soviet Zone and East Berlin, and 0.4 million others (table 7.5). At the outset the arrivals, 1 in 6 of the total population, were very unevenly dispersed across Germany (table 7.6).[51] Geography and the refusal of the French to accept refugees in the zone under their control in the southwest of Germany influenced the spread. Large concentrations of refugees settled, at first at least, in Mecklenburg and Saxony-Anhalt in the East and in Schleswig-Holstein, Lower Saxony, and Bavaria in the West. In 1950 refugees still accounted for 35 percent of the population (and over half of those unemployed) in Schleswig-Holstein and 26 percent of that in Lower Saxony. Note that four of those provinces (Bavaria being the exception) were to lose population in the 1950s as the refugee burden became spread more evenly. Czech Germans were more likely to settle in Bavaria, while 71 percent of those settled in Schleswig-Holstein were *Reichdeutsche* from either East Prussia or Pomerania. Geography and politics were thus important factors. The availability of housing in rural areas—since most of the cities (e.g., Bremen and Hamburg) were in ruins—and the lack of planning were added issues. Allied advances in the months after D-Day also produced migration, though on a lesser scale (figure 7.6).[52]

The increase of one-fifth in the labor force represented a huge shock for the West German economy. At the outset the refugees faced serious problems of accommodation and employment. In 1950 66.6 percent lived as subtenants and another 11 percent in temporary housing, though that situation improved rapidly so that by 1956 those proportions were 30.5 and 6.6 percent, respectively.[53] Unemployment was high where refugee settlement was high. Lüttinger and Bauer et al. offer mildly negative appraisals of the economic integration of the immigrants in the immediate postwar decades.[54] Lüttinger found big differences between natives and newcomers in terms of occupational status in 1971, with the newcomers still overrepresented in low-paid occupations and more unlikely to own their own businesses. Bauer et al. found that arriving as refugees after the war had big and negative effects on the economic conditions of the *Heimatvertriebene*.[55] The outcome cannot have been due to adverse characteristics of the displaced because the differences between them and the nondisplaced were minor; thus, years of education were 10.5 and 10.4, respectively, for males and 9.4 and 9.2, respectively, for females. The displaced were more likely to have come from a farming background (18.9 and 12.5 percent for males displaced and not displaced, respectively) and marginally more likely to be out of the labor force (11.1 percent and 10.1 percent), but all in all the differences on the eve of the war were minor. Despite favorable economic conditions for bettering themselves, the immigrants were still significantly behind their co-Germans twenty-five years after arriving. Bauer et al. conclude that the policies to integrate the *Aussiedler* (expelled ethnic Germans) were not as successful as perceived. A possible caveat here is that the newcomers may have been on a par in 1939 but not necessarily in 1945. They started life in the West in camps, not in places of their own choosing.

On the other hand, Michael Wyrwich argues that although adversely selected in terms of age and gender, the expellees integrated quickly and constituted a boon to the German economy.[56] In an analysis of the impact of the expulsions on population growth in Germany, he shows that subsequent population growth in the French sector, which barred immigrants, grew much slower than in the American-United Kingdom and Soviet sectors that accepted them. The result stands after other factors that might influence the

FIGURE 7.6. Refugees on the Western Front, 1944–45
a. Troops and refugees, Belgium, 1940
b. German women leaving heavily bombed Aachen, October 1944 (*Source:* Bundesarchiv, Bild 183-H26814 / CC-BY-SA)

outcome are controlled for; moreover, it has persisted. A second study of German Aussiedler focused not on demography but on economic activity and productivity.[57] It found that the impact of the immigrants on economic outcomes in the 1950s and 1960s was positive by several different measures and also stronger in the long run than in the short run.

The refugees tended to settle initially in poorer *Länder* and in places spared aerial bombing. In the 1950s about three million moved on, some with state assistance, to more prosperous or economically dynamic areas such as North Rhine Westphalia and Baden-Württemberg. The newcomers were twice as mobile as the original population.[58] Yet in 1970 they were still overrepresented in poorer *Länder* (figure 7.7).

The refugees' gradual integration was also reflected in electoral politics. At the outset both the occupying powers and local elites sought to deny the newcomers associational and political representation. But in July 1950, the newly founded All-German Bloc/League of Expellees and People Deprived of Rights (Gesamtdeutscher Block/Bund der Heimatvertriebenen und Entrechteten, or GB/BHE)—a right-wing coalition of newcomers and nationalists—won 23.4 percent of the vote in a state election in Schleswig-Holstein. It won a respectable 5.7 percent of the vote in the federal elections of 1953, but note that at that time refugees accounted for almost one-fifth of the population. It performed best in states with big refugee populations—Bavaria, Lower Saxony, and Schleswig-Holstein—where it won 8.2, 10.8, and 11.6 percent of the vote, respectively. But its 4.6 percent in the federal election of 1957 was below the 5 percent threshold necessary for representation. Thereafter it was weakened by internal divisions and by voters deserting to the Christian Democrats (i.e., the Christlich Demokratische Union Deutschlands [CDU] and their Christlich-Soziale Union [CSU] allies in Bavaria). Even though the GB/BHE merged with another right-wing party to form the Gesamtdeutsche Partei in an attempt to enter Parliament in 1961, its 2.8 percent of the vote was not enough. Thereafter it was restricted to participation in *Länder* parliaments. By 1961 only 15 percent of newcomers voted for parties purporting to represent them, down from 34 percent in 1953. Still, voting patterns among the immigrants from the East remained distinctive; they continued to be more likely to vote for those parties of the Right and extreme Right who articulated their grievances. In Austria, too, migration had an enduring impact on political choices; provinces such as Upper Austria that attracted the largest number of Nazis relative to population remain bastions of hard-right politics in the form of the Freiheitliche Partei Österreichs (Austrian Freedom Party). Conversely, left-leaning ethnic Germans

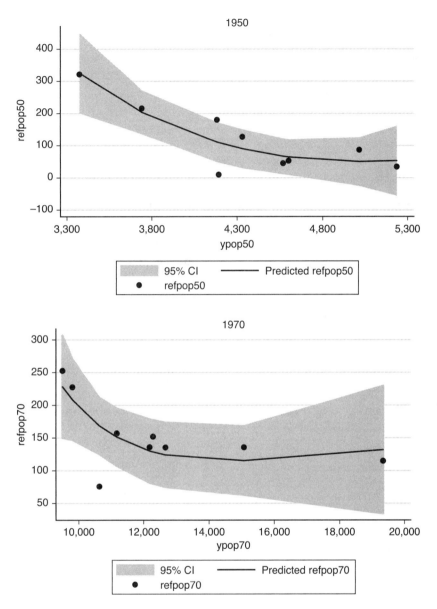

FIGURE 7.7. Refugees/population (refpop) and GDP per capita (ypop50) across eight *Länder* in 1950 and 1970

who were allowed to stay on in Czechoslovakia after the great majority were expelled seem to have left a contrasting footprint. The more numerous they were, the stronger left-wing politics and social policies are today.[59] Like voting patterns, shifting marriage patterns in Germany also imply integration. By 1960 the newcomers were much more likely to marry out than a decade earlier; and by 1954 they were less than half as likely be unemployed as in 1950 (3.1 versus 6.5 percent).[60]

The German expellees fared poorly compared to the Poles expelled from territory ceded to the Soviet Union in 1945 and transplanted in areas formerly occupied by *Volksdeutsche* (most of Pomerania, East Brandenburg, German Silesia, and part of East Prussia, including the war-devastated cities of Szczecin, Gdańsk, and Wrocław). The 1.5 million Polish migrants from the East were overwhelmingly rural and poor, and they lost most of the little they possessed in transit. While that loss "deeply influenced the expellees' attitude toward the societies and the governments already existing in the territories to which they came,"[61] in terms of human capital these Poles fared much better, and so did their dependents, than the Poles who were not displaced. Becker et al. (2020) argue that migration shifted the preferences of the displaced Poles toward more investment in human capital relative to physical capital or consumption.

A much smaller expulsion campaign, code-named Operation Black Tulip, was launched in the Netherlands in September 1946. The original aim was to deport all Germans in the country, starting with those who had arrived after 1940. The earliest to be expelled, mainly likely ex-Nazis from the Amsterdam area, were allowed a maximum of fifty kilograms of luggage and one hundred guilders each, with the rest of their household belongings confiscated by the Dutch state. Most of the remainder were interned, along with tens of thousands of Dutch collaborators. But the Allies in Germany were strongly opposed to a wholesale expulsion, and public opinion in the Netherlands gradually softened, with the Catholic Church and the press increasingly calling for leniency. In the end only 15 percent—3,691—of Germans with a suspected "brown" past were deported.[62]

FINLAND

Finland also hosted displaced people after the war. About 410,000 Finns (12 percent of Finland's population) living in Finnish Karelia, which was ceded to the Soviet Union in 1945, settled in Finland. Sarvimäki et al. use a 10 percent anonymized sample of the 1950 census linked to the 1970 census, as well as 1971 tax records data on income, occupation, and residence, to study the economic status of Finns who were moved from Karelia.[63] A unique feature of this scheme is that the authorities tried to resettle people in a setting as close as possible to what they had left behind, with a holding proportional to what they had whether in farming or in other monetary compensation, and with the same neighbors. They show that these migrants were more likely to move out of agriculture than the settled population, which explains why their incomes were higher in 1971. The settled population was more likely to stay put, not because they were *adscriptus glebae* but because they were more attached to their homes. It could be argued that this was not market failure—that both groups were maximizing their welfare, given the setting they found themselves in. Or perhaps that smacks of tautology. Either way, forced migration increased the migrants' incomes, if not their welfare.

GREECE

During World War II, Greece, too, had its IDPs and refugees. Though few at the outset, the number of refugees aided by the Greek Red Cross in the wake of the Allied bombing of Piraeus on January 11, 1944 (which killed 700 people) reached 181,000 in January and February 1944. As the crisis subsided, the number relieved dropped to 32,000 by the end of 1944.[64]

ASIA

Outside Europe, migration also operated powerfully wherever fighting occurred. According to Muscolino,[65] famine in the Chinese province of Henan in 1942 forced 3 to 4 million people to leave in a quest for food, with news that harvests elsewhere in Northwest China were good prompting an exodus to Shaanxi in particular. But that was only the tip of the iceberg. In *Thunder out of China* (1946), Anna Lee Jacoby and Theodore White describe the Chinese westward exodus of Chinese refugees in the wake of the Japanese attack of 1937:

> Through the long months of 1938, as the Chinese armies were pressed slowly back toward the interior, they found their way clogged by moving people. The breathing space of winter had given hundreds of thousands time to make their decision, and China was on the move in one of the greatest mass migrations in human history. It is curious that such a spectacle has not been adequately recorded by a Chinese writer or novelist. Certainly the long files of gaunt people who moved west across the roads and mountains must have presented a sight unmatched since the days of nomad hordes; yet no record tells how many made the trek, where they come from, where they settled anew.

Mass movements of people continued throughout the war, often triggered by aerial bombing. Those in a position to settle permanently elsewhere tended to be the better off; the poor lacked the means to do so.[66] Estimates of the aggregate size of this migration from 1937 to 1945 tell their own story. They range from three million to over ninety million. White and Jacoby mention estimates of from three million to twenty-five million caused by the Japanese invasion, while Peter Gatrell has put the total at forty-five million at least. In 1946 a Guómíndǎng source put the number of "wartime refugees and homeless people" between the Japanese attack and these years at over ninety-five million. That total is most likely inflated, if only because it involves the double counting of those who fled more than once and includes an unknown number who were not refugees but merely civilians who had lost their homes for one reason or another. Here we opt for an estimate of fifty million. In terms of percentages of provincial populations, the share ranged from just below 10 percent in coastal Fujian and Jiangxi to over 40 percent in Shanxi, Hunan, and Henan in the interior.[67]

World War II also led to the mass migration of Indians living in Burma. Burma's Indian minority, relatively privileged, educated, and urban, faced a dilemma. An unloved minority fearing mistreatment by both Burmese and Japanese, they felt compelled to leave but, loyal to the empire, were also reluctant to disregard official entreaties to remain. The exodus began with the departure of perhaps 15,000 in the wake of the Japanese bombing of Rangoon in late 1941. Another 70,000 traveled to India by ship, reaching Madras and Calcutta before Rangoon fell to the Japanese. But a prohibition of travel on deck excluded all but the affluent. Only when the arrival of the Japanese was imminent did the authorities encourage the remainder to move. Then another 0.3 million headed north on foot and by mule and cart, mostly for the coastal village of Ton-up, a distance of 270 kilometers. From there they traveled by boat to Akia (present-day Sittwe) and then on to relative safety in Chittagong. According to the local head of the British administration in Burma, by March 9, 1942, Rangoon seemed to be "completely empty of Indians,"[68] but most of the refugees still had a long road ahead. Still, casualties on the way were light, proportionately speaking.[69] The Japanese invasions of the Philippines and the Dutch East Indies also generated many forced migrants, though numbers are lacking.

Famines also forced people to move. The situation in Leningrad has already been described. Migration between the Greek island of Chios and neighboring Asia Minor in 1942–43 also operated as a form of famine relief, although on a much smaller scale. This migration tended to tear families apart because the young were much more likely to leave, abandoning the older adults.[70] The Great Bengal Famine of 1943 led to the migration of tens of thousands of rural smallholders and laborers to Calcutta. Elsewhere in South Asia, such as in Java and Vietnam, the search for food and relief led to major migrations both into and out of cities. In Africa, famine in Ruanda-Urundi (today's Rwanda and Burundi), mainly due to prolonged drought but exacerbated by wartime exactions, led to mass migration to the neighboring Belgian Congo in 1943–44.[71]

VOLGA GERMANS, CHECHENS, AND OTHERS IN THE SOVIET UNION

In the mid-eighteenth century, some 30,000 ethnic Germans settled in Russia, many of them in colonies in the then sparsely populated Volga region of southeastern Russia. They had been recruited as immigrants on the orders of Czarina Catherine II and granted certain privileges as enticements. The settlements, mostly in European Russia but also found in Ukraine, Crimea, Kazakhstan, and central Asia, thrived and grew. In the nineteenth century, the diminution of their civil rights and vigorous Russification caused many of the Volga Germans to emigrate, and the communities suffered severely during the Russian Civil War. Still, on the eve of World War II the settlements contained about 0.8 million German speakers, about 0.5 million of whom lived in what had been declared in 1924 the Volga German Autonomous Soviet Socialist Republic, with its capital city named after Friedrich Engels. On August 28, 1941, the Volga Germans' republic was abolished, and four days later the mass evacuation of all ethnic Germans to Siberia and Kazakhstan was announced. The forced transfers were completed by the end of September and the evacuees subjected to forced labor. Perhaps 3–4 percent died in transit.[72] After the war the migrants were prohibited from returning home, and about 0.2 million ethnic Germans who had survived the war in the German-occupied territory were in turn forced east.

In 1943–44 the Soviets also forcibly expelled whole nations suspected of collaboration with the enemy, including Kalmyks, Karachai, Chechens, Ingush, Balkars, and Meshketians from the Caucusus, as well as Crimean Tatars, numbering in total over one million, to remote locations in Kazakhstan, Uzbekistan, Kirghizia, Siberia, and elsewhere. The pretext in all cases was suspected collaboration, for which there was limited evidence. Over one-fourth of the Chechens had perished either in transit or in confinement by 1949. The number of Crimean Tatar victims remains highly contentious:

TABLE 7.7. Percentages of population by ethnicity before and after World War II

	Year	Poles	Ukrainians	Jews	Russians	Lithuanians	Others
Lvov/Lviv	1931	50.4	15.9	31.9	0.2	..	1.6
	1950	10.3	49.9	6.4	31.2	..	2.2
	1979	1.8	74.0	2.7	19.3	..	2.2
Vilna	1931	65.9	..	28.0	3.8	0.8	1.5
	1951	21	..	3.1	33.3	30.8	11.8
	1970	18.6	..	4.4	24.5	42.8	10

Source: Wikipedia, citing reputable sources.

an official source stated that forty-five thousand, or 20 percent of the total, perished in 1944–45, but the true figure could be as high as 30 percent.[73] The dramatic impact of these displacements and of the Holocaust are reflected in the populations of Lviv and Vilna in 1930–31 and 1950–51 (table 7.7).

Forced Civilian Labor during World War II

Germany relied on forced foreign civilian labor to a much greater extent during World War II than World War I (12 million as opposed to 3 million). By May 1943 the Germans were already employing 6 million foreign civilian laborers on what was then German soil; by September 1944 that figure had reached 7.4 million, augmented by 0.5 million concentration camp inmates (table 7.8). In 1944 two-thirds of the total had been sent from occupied lands in central and eastern Europe (mainly the Union of Soviet Socialist Republics and Poland) and most of the remainder, from western Europe (half of them from France). They included 0.5 million from the Netherlands and 0.6 million supplied by the Vichy regime through the Service de travail obligatoire.[74] Much more numerous were forced workers from Russia and Poland, who arrived in transit camps on closed trains and were then allocated to German contractors. Their employers ranged from family farms and small workshops to manufacturing giants like I. G. Farben and Krupp. Toward the end of the war, foreign workers, some voluntary but most forcibly conscripted, and prisoners of war made up one-quarter of Germany's labor force. About half of the men worked in agriculture; women were more likely to be employed as servants and factory workers.

Workers from western Europe and from Allied countries were better treated than those from the East; Nazi ideology was not only anti-Semitic

TABLE 7.8. The labor force of the Third Reich during World War II (including Austria, Sudetenland, and Memel/Klaipėda) (millions)

Date	Drafted (cumulative)	German workers		Foreign civilians	POWs	Camp inmates	Total
		Male	Female				
May 1939	1.4	24.5	14.6	0.3			39.4
May 1940	5.5	19.7	13.7	2.6	0.0		36.0
May 1941	7.4	18.3	13.4	2.9	1.4		36.0
May 1942	9.4	16.2	13.7	4.0	1.5		35.4
May 1943	11.2	14.8	14.1	6.1	1.6		36.6
May 1944	12.4	13.5	14.1	7.0	1.9		36.5
Sept. 1944	13.0	12.8	14.2	7.4	1.5	c. 0.5	36.4

Source: Spoerer 2015: table 6.1.

but also anti-Slavic. In principle, all workers were entitled to the same wages and conditions as German workers, but in practice only a small minority, those from Allied Italy, Slovakia, and Croatia, were treated as such. Mark Spoerer and Jochen Fleischhacker have divided the rest into three groups; tables 7.8 and 7.9 are based on their work. The first included "forced" western Europeans and Balts who lacked the right to leave but were granted some agency over working conditions; the second were effectively "slave" workers from Poland and other occupied parts of the Soviet Union with no civil rights but a good chance of surviving their ordeal. Their third category, "less-than-slaves," consisted of concentration camp inmates, mainly Jews and Poles, whose lives were expendable. As defeat approached, the conditions faced by workers from the West worsened and in the end approached that of slave labor. A decree of July 7, 1944, sanctioned the killing of those no longer fit for work by lethal injection, "rationaliz[ing] a practice of murdering East European civilian labourers that had evolved in the preceding fifteen months," and it may be assumed that many more died of starvation and overwork than from injections.[75] In 1944–45 the Wehrmacht "released" some 220,000 French, 460,000 Italian, and 205,000 POWs from their POW status and "transformed" them into forced civilian laborers, with or without their consent.[76]

After the war the shoe was on the other foot. At the Yalta conference of February 1945, Stalin and the Soviets made plain their intention of using forced German labor as a form of reparations after the war. As they moved west, they interned able-bodied ethnic Germans in the territories they conquered. Nearly two million Germans were forced to work as laborers in

TABLE 7.9. Total foreign labor in Germany during World War II and survival rate to mid-1945

	Total (1,000s)	Survival rate (%)
Civilian laborers	8,435	94
POWs	4,575	70
CC inmates	1,550	31
"Working Jews"	55	55
Total	13,480	82
Privileged laborers	1,070	99
Forced laborers	4,820	98
Slave laborers	5,170	89
Less-than-slave laborers	3,555	41
Total	11,025	82

Source: Spoerer 2020: table 7.4.

eastern Europe as a form of war reparation. They were cruelly exploited and suffered a high mortality rate (table 7.10).

Throughout the war the Japanese also relied heavily on forced laborers, euphemistically referred to as *rōmusha* (a Japanese word meaning an unskilled temporary construction worker). Many laborers were lured by false promises of short contracts and high wages; many more were press-ganged. Up to a million were exploited in this way in Japanese-occupied northern China. Hundreds of thousands of Koreans and tens of thousands of Chinese toiled as *rōmusha* in Japanese factories or as miners and construction workers. The Japanese occupiers also made widespread use of the system in Southeast Asia. About 250,000–300,000 *rōmusha* and 60,000 POWs were involved in the construction of the notorious 400-kilometer-long Burma-Thailand "death railway" in 1942–43. The former were mainly Burmese, Malayan, and Thai but also included Chinese, Javanese, and Vietnamese workers. Again, the number of dead is contested. One calculation reckons that 21 percent of the POWs died and 36 percent of the rōmusha, indicating about 12,000 and 90,000 deaths, respectively, mainly from disease and malnutrition. Another puts the number of *rōmusha* dead at 70,000–90,000. Those estimates broadly tally with a British estimate of 41 percent mortality among the 78,204 Malays sent to work on the railway in 1943.[77] A further 100,000 mainly Javan *rōmusha* and several thousand POWs worked in 1943–44 on building the railway line linking the towns of Muaro

TABLE 7.10. German forced labor and expulsions (1,000s)

Country	Deported	Deaths
Germany (1937 borders)	400	160
Poland (1939 borders)	112	40
Danzig	10	5
Czechoslovakia	30	4
Baltic States	19	8
Hungary	30	10
Romania	89	33
Yugoslavia	40	10
USSR	980	310
Total	*1,780*	*580*

Source: Reichling [1986] 1995: 33, 36 (as cited in Wikipedia).

ª The total includes the 0.2 million expelled in 1914.

and Pekanbaru in Sumatra. The completed line, traversing 270 kilometers of very difficult terrain, was an engineering wonder but a humanitarian disaster. Fewer than one-fifth of the rōmusha and four-fifths of the POWs who built it survived.

Gregg Huff puts the death toll of Javanese *rōmusha* during the Japanese occupation at a minimum of 0.4 million lives. The bombing of Rangoon by the Japanese in December 1941 prompted a flight towards India by the local Indian and Anglo-Burmese population which within nine months had involved 0.6 million leaving Burma, and the deaths of 80,000 of them (figure 7.8).[78] Allowing for the deaths of Chinese, Koreans, Thai, Burmese, Malay, and Vietnamese *rōmusha* would bring that figure to 1 million and, conceivably, 1.5 million. That would still mean a lower death toll than implied by table 7.9 for Germany.

Evacuation during the Hunger Winter

Another evacuation that doubtless saved many lives was that of about forty thousand children from famine-afflicted areas during the Dutch Hunger Winter of 1944–45. In early 1945 the Interkerkelijk Bureau voor Noodvoed-selvoorziening (Interdenominational Bureau for Emergency Nutrition; IKB) organized the evacuation outside the famine zone of about sixteen thousand children and of other smaller church groups composed of another 2,000. The

FIGURE 7.8. Burmese refugees fleeing along the Prome Road into India, January 1942
Source: Bundesarchiv, Bild 183-H26814 / CC-BY-SA)

National Socialist welfare organization Nederlandse Volksdienst evacuated another eight thousand and other corporate, municipal, and private initiatives, six thousand. And about eight thousand so-called wild children, some orphaned or deserted, sought refuge outside the famine zone themselves. In sum, nearly one in ten of all children aged four to fifteen years in the affected urban areas were evacuated.

The evacuation relied on preexisting religious and political institutions and networks. Some foster parents were eager to volunteer, while others did so more reluctantly under pressure from their local churches or elites. Presumably, this had some impact on child welfare. Nor was matching children and foster parents always straightforward. There was an excess supply of young boys, and some evacuees felt distinctly unwanted. But on the whole, the impact on the health of the evacuees was considerable.[79]

Fleeing Aerial Bombing

A major factor in averting deaths from aerial bombardment in all countries at war was the transfer of nonessential civilians—particularly unaccompanied schoolchildren and mothers with younger children—away from places most at risk. In most places at risk—in urban areas in the United Kingdom, Germany, and Japan—the evacuations followed a similar pattern.[80]

BRITAIN

Long before the summer of 1939, the authorities in Britain had been preparing for the likelihood of air raids. The thirty-eight million gas masks issued during 1938 were part of this. During the buildup to war, the United Kingdom's Air Ministry had been assessing the likely damage from aerial bombing. With little evidence to build on, a daily quota of seven hundred tons of bombs was expected, with an average of seventy-two casualties per ton dropped.[81] Operation Pied Piper—a rather unfortunate choice of code name for a child evacuation campaign—began on September 1, 1939, two days before the outbreak of war. Over three days a total of 1.5 million schoolchildren and mothers with younger children were evacuated by the authorities from areas deemed at immediate risk from bombing to the countryside. The children were moved as school units with their teachers.[82]

The number evacuated was far lower than the four million originally anticipated by the authorities but excludes two million or so who moved on their own resources. In the heavily industrial Northwest and in London, half or more of the eligible schoolchildren left, but in cities like Birmingham, Edinburgh, Nottingham, and Sheffield, the proportion was only half that. Richard Titmuss surmised that the poverty of the sending area probably affected the proportion leaving;[83] a survey of evacuees in Edinburgh showed that children in large families were more likely to be sent.

GERMANY

In Germany the authorities estimated that up to 9 million people had moved or been evacuated in response to the increased threat from bombing from 1942 onward. These included nearly 3 million children sent to stay with rural families or else to *Kinderlandverschickung* (KLV; Children's Transfer to the Countryside) camps run by the Hitler Youth and located mainly to the east and the south.[84] The Allied bombing had forced the conversion of the KLV, a charitable organization providing holidays in the countryside for city children, into an emergency wartime evacuation program; the number of children transported rose from under 0.4 million in early 1941 to a peak of 1 million by the end of 1943.

The middle classes and parents with rural connections preferred to evacuate their children privately; the KLV catered overwhelmingly to children from working-class and lower-middle-class backgrounds. In Berlin, for example, by the end of 1943 only 32,000 schoolchildren had been moved by the KLV; 85,000 were still in the city while 132,000 had been sent to rural relatives.[85]

FRANCE

In France the Blitzkrieg of May–June 1940 led to the displacement of at least 3 million from northern and eastern France, mostly to places south of the Loire, but most of those had returned home by March 1941. Still, a census of consumers carried out in April 1941 suggests that several départements close to the German border had not yet recovered their prewar numbers; the worst affected was Ardennes, which had declined over 50 percent since 1936. The Allied landings of June 1944 led to further displacement, doubling the million or so evacuees in France before it; the population of Calvados fell from 405,000 to 380,000 between January 1944 and January 1945.[86]

FINLAND

In Finland children were also evacuated out of harm's way during World War II, about sixty-five thousand to Sweden and four thousand to Denmark. They were sent in two waves during the Winter War of 1939–40 and again in early 1944 when the fighting intensified during the so-called Continuation War. They were young—aged six years on average—and most were from exposed frontier areas or cities at risk from Soviet bombing. About five thousand of the "war children" were sick on departure; others had lost a father in the war. Most stayed in private homes and built close bonds with their foster parents; almost one in four remained in Sweden after the war and one in ten in Denmark.[87] The evacuation prompted research into its impact on physical and mental well-being. There is no consensus on outcomes. Alastalo et al. found a higher prevalence of type 2 diabetes and heart disease and Räikkönen et al. a higher risks of mental diseases among evacuees in late middle age. However, Santavirta et al. studied the impact of evacuation on mental health in adulthood by comparing the proportions of samples of evacuated and nonevacuated children born between 1933 and 1944 who were admitted to a hospital for psychiatric disorders between 1971 and 2011.[88] They found that taking men and women together, there was no difference in the outcomes for evacuees and their nonevacuated siblings. Indeed, for evacuated men the risk of admission was lower, while for women there was no difference except in the case of admissions for mood disorders. In an interview-based study with evacuees who had stayed on in Sweden, Andersson et al. found that "despite the hardships connected with the migration, [they] had successfully lived a good life in Sweden. Such subjects such as these is bedevilled by two issues: [1] the likelihood that the children evacuated were ill or poor or from troubled families; and [2] shocks in later life which could not be controlled for."[89]

JAPAN

In Japan, U.S. air raids led to the evacuation of up to 8.5 million civilians[90]— mostly children, women, and older people—from all the main cities in 1943–45. At the outset the authorities merely encouraged people to join friends and relatives in the countryside, and many needed no encouragement; later, whole schools were moved to rural areas where hotels, temples, and other buildings were converted to accommodate them. Many households were moved to facilitate the creation of firebreaks in the cities. In the final months of the war, American propaganda also encouraged people to evacuate. As the bombing intensified, the Japanese evacuation became "one of history's great migrations."[91] The evacuees included one-third of Hiroshima's population of 360,000.

Later . . .

The issue of how war refugees who did not return fared in the long run materially is addressed in the growing literature on the economics of forced migration. One notable example studies the long-term impact of the redrawing of the borders of Poland in the wake of World War II on those forced to move from lands in the East, ceded to the Soviet Union, to lands in the West, formerly part of Germany.[92] Finding that the descendants of migrating Poles are much better educated than the rest of the Poles, they argue that this stems from a shift in preferences among migrants away from fixed assets to more mobile human capital. This finding supports the disputed *uprootedness hypothesis*, whereby a discriminated or highly mobile group places a high value on liquid and portable assets.[93]

Although the outcome would have been of little consolation to the Greeks displaced in 1922, in the longer run their descendants also fared well. A recent study by Elie Murard and Seyhun Orcan Sakalli shows that people living today in locations with a disproportionate share of refugees in 1923 are richer and more educated than Greeks as a whole, after controlling for initial levels of development before the migration.[94] Murard and Sakalli attribute this to the scale economies generated by bigger increases in the workforce and the resultant specialization and to the human capital imported by refugees. A related paper by Muradi focuses on the acculturation of the refugees and their descendants. It shows high rates of intermarriage between native and newcomer and high levels of political and cultural engagement and suggests that initial efforts to facilitate immigration paid dividends in due course.[95]

8

No quieren

RAPE DURING WORLD WAR I
AND WORLD WAR II

> Muffled by the wall—a groan:
> I find the mother still alive.
> Were there many on the mattress?
> A company? A platoon? What's the difference!
> The daughter, still a child, dead.
> All in accord with the slogans
> DO NOT FORGET! DO NOT FORGIVE!
> BLOOD FOR BLOOD! A tooth for a tooth!
> —ALEKSANDR SOLZHENITSYN, *PRUSSIAN NIGHTS*

Modern scholarship considers *The Rape of the Sabine Women* (*Sabinae raptae*) of Roman mythology to really be about mass abduction or kidnapping rather than sexual assault.[1] Throughout history, however, as Goya's famous etching reminds us, "raping" and "pillaging" have been synonymous with war, although inferring numbers or trends from the available accounts is impossible (figure 8.1). There is no straightforward answer either to a question prompted by the sadistic atrocities that French troops committed on Italian women near Monte Casino in 1944: "What is it that turns an ordinary decent Moroccan peasant into the most terrible of sexual psychopaths as soon as he becomes a soldier?" Factors mentioned in the literature range from the innate depravity

FIGURE 8.1. *No quieren* (*They Don't Like It*) by Francisco Goya
Source: Plate 9 from the series *Los Desastres de la Guerra* (1810–15)

of the enemy (the "Hun" in Belgium in 1914–1915) to the victor's desire for revenge (Soviet troops in Berlin in 1945) to "the sadistic consequence of the aggressive virility fostered in soldiers by the brutalization of civilized values and the stresses of military life (generally)" to military propaganda that sells war as "an erotic adventure" (U.S. troops in France in 1944–45).[2]

Rapes, sometimes systematic and more often due to indiscipline, were a feature of both world wars, but reliable numbers are invariably lacking. Existing estimates are contested and prone to both exaggeration and underreporting, not least because girls and women, for very understandable reasons, were not eager to report rape. Moreover, many were raped several times, and it is likely that soldiers who raped once raped again, while others refrained. Reliable estimates are inherently difficult not only for these reasons: the numbers often emerge and are recycled in fraught contexts in which nonacademic agendas, ranging from political disputes to compensation claims, loom large. Therefore, in what follows new estimates of the number of rapes committed or women raped are not attempted, and the focus is more on why widely cited estimates must be treated with skepticism.

Accounts of rape feature prominently in the rival propagandistic inquiries conducted by the warring parties.[3] Belgian and French women being

FIGURE 8.2. Sexual violence and war, 1914–18

raped by invading German troops in the early weeks of World War I, particularly in August and September 1914, became a key feature of Allied propaganda (figure 8.2). That such rapes occurred is indisputable.[4] On the Western Front, they tended to be random acts committed by individual German soldiers, with the clear exception of "mass rapes" amid sustained violence over several days in the town of Aarschot, east of Leuven, in August 1914.[5] Though rapes were far fewer than on the Eastern Front during World War I or in Germany in 1945, thousands of them still occurred in German-occupied France and Belgium. Estimates range widely. Ruth Harris's informed guess is of "hundreds . . . in the early weeks of the war." Antoine Rivière extrapolates from the 403 infants registered by *special decision* (a category discreetly reserved for infants born to "victims of enemy violence") as wards of the state in the département of Seine between 1915 and 1920 to infer an aggregate estimate of one thousand to five thousand births due to rapes by German troops in occupied France during the same period. The first such registration on May 1, 1915, referred to the child of a seventeen-year old Belgian refugee; the infant died three weeks later. Rivière's range is lower than the figure of ten thousand *naissances allemandes* circulated in French newspapers at the time. How many rapes did such "German births" entail? Assuming an intercourse-to-conception rate of one-tenth and few abortions or self-induced miscarriages and noting that most, but not all, births in this category were the outcome of rape, Rivière's numbers are consistent with ten thousand to fifty thousand rapes. But here again we are in the realm of highly speculative "dark figures."[6]

German atrocities against civilians in Belgium in the early weeks of World War I, notably in Leuven, Dinant, Aarschot, Tamines, and Liège are, as noted above, well documented. The evidence supports some of the claims made in the propagandistic *Report of the Committee on Alleged German Outrages Appointed by His Majesty's Government* (1915), widely known as the *Bryce Report* after its chairman, Lord Bryce.[7] However, the accounts of rape in the *Bryce Report* rely on secondhand evidence or hearsay and are, overall, unpersuasive. In particular, two witness statements refer to mass rapes in Liège on August 20–21, 1914; one to "the rape in open day of 15 or 20 women on tables" in a public square, another to "a story, very circumstantial in its details, of how women were publicly raped in the market-place of the city, five young German officers assisting." Such statements find no support in a recent account of horrific events on those days in Liège, which offers graphic details of German reprisals against alleged snipers and others but makes no mention of rapes. Nor, as the *Bryce Report* implicitly concedes, is there evidence that the German authorities approved of their soldiers engaging in sexual violence. It cites the fate of a drunken soldier who pursued a young girl in Leuven and who was shot immediately after the girl appealed to a German officer. Another witness described how "an officer of the 32nd Regiment of the Line was led out to execution for the violation of two young girls, but reprieved at the request or with the consent of the girls' mother."[8] As the Irish antiwar activist Jim Roche pointed out on the centenary of the Belgian atrocities, the sad irony about the propaganda they spawned is that "actual cases of multiple raping of women and the severing of children's hands, the latter actually recorded in photos, were . . . carried out by the agents of King Leopold 2 of Belgium as part of his rape and plunder of the African Congo over 20 years previously."[9]

In Italy in the aftermath of the defeat at Caporetto toward the end of the war, reports of rape against local women by occupying Habsburg troops were widespread. A few years later a Royal Commission of Inquiry into Acts of Violence Committed against People by the Enemy documented, often in graphic detail, 165 complaints in which victims and circumstances were identified and 570 more in which details were lacking.[10] The numbers are small relative to World War II, even allowing for the likely reluctance of victims to provide evidence. Two reports from Oderzo (in the province of Treviso) describe in starkly different terms what is most likely the same incident. The first describes how 200 refugee girls from Ormelle were violently locked up in a room of a field hospital by order of the local Austrian command and "subjected to ignominious visits by the director of that hospital" for eight consecutive days "on the pretext that these women were syphilitic." Sinister as this may sound, a second account based on folk memory substitutes "the group rape of 180 mostly displaced women" for the hospital director's visits and links the group rape to "the births of forty children." To consider the former account the more reliable is not to rule out the guilt of the inspector.[11]

Sexual violence, like other atrocities, was certainly more common on the Eastern Front during World War I. Still, German investigations of civilian casualties in the wake of the Russian invasion of East Prussia in 1914–15 fail to support claims of "countless . . . bestial rapes" of women of all ages. Information from local officials implies "a minimum of 338" sexual assaults perpetrated by Russian troops during the invasion[12]—horrific but again small compared to estimates of rapes committed at the end of World War II. At much greater risk, particularly from Cossack troops, were Jewish women in Galicia and Russia itself. In some places the violence was concerted and took on the character of a pogrom, as in the Belarusian town of Glubokoe (today's Hlybokaye), where "according to some witnesses, all the women were raped, whereas according to others the number of those raped reached a hundred"—note again the fragility of the evidence—and in Bogemlja in Minsk governorate where the arrival of Cossack detachments caused "the entire female Jewish population" to leave.[13] But for the most part, rapes were neither systematic nor officially sanctioned, with the possible exception of occupied Serbia, where Bulgarian troops stood accused of concerted mass rapes against Serbian and Greek women.[14]

Contemporary references to sexual violence against women during the Armenian genocide in forms ranging from abduction and forced marriages to rape and prostitution were commonplace, but again, numbers were never given. While the rapes were orchestrated by the Young Turks, three of the four mentions in Bryce and Toynbee's *Blue Book* refer to Kurds as the perpetrators.[15]

John Horne has recently pointed out that, setting aside the genocidal campaign against the Armenians in 1915–16, more rapes were perpetrated in the wake of World War I than during it. Sexual violence was an important component of the extreme violence inflicted by nationalist and Communist forces on enemy civilians in conflicts in central and eastern Europe, in Russia, and in Turkey.[16]

Tens of thousands of women were raped during World War I, yet these numbers are fewer than implied by contemporary propaganda and far fewer than during World War II. An abiding image of the final weeks of World War II is what ex-soldier and military historian Antony Beevor has dubbed the "greatest phenomenon of mass rape in history"—that carried out by a rampaging Soviet "army of rapists" in Germany in 1944–5. The atrocities began further east, with those in the East Prussian village of Nemmersdorf in October 1944 and in Metgethen, then a suburb of Königsberg (present-day Kaliningrad), in February 1945 achieving special notoriety (figure 8.3). The second image in figure 8.3 is captioned as "Close-up of the two women and the three children in the Jodeit home, Metgethen, Horst Wesselweg 23."[17]

The phenomenon is not in doubt and has been described in detail by Beevor, Ian Buruma, and others. Some see it as a product of the brutalization of Soviet troops caused by the German offensive and/or the hate propaganda of the widely read Soviet journalist Ilya Ehrenburg, of whose inflammatory articles it was said that "army commanders forbade soldiers to use old newspapers with Ehrenburg's publications for kindling or making hand-rolled cigarettes." Ehrenburg's 1942 propagandistic poem "Retribution" foreshadowed his bloodcurdling exhortations of 1944–45 ("If you leave a German alive, the German will hang a Russian and rape a Russian woman"):[18]

> She lay beside the bridge. The German troops had reckoned
> To cheapen her by this. Instead, her nakedness
> Was like an ancient statue's unadorned perfection,
> Was like unspotted Nature's loveliness and grace.
> We covered her and carried her. The bridge, unsteady,
> Appeared to palpitate beneath our precious load.
> Our soldiers halted there, in silence stood bare-headed,
> Each transformed, acknowledging the debt he owed.
> Then Justice headed westward. Winter was a blessing,
> With hatred huddled mute, and snows a fiery ridge.
> The fate of Germany that murky day was settled
> Because of one dead girl, beside a shaky bridge.

Others blame the Soviet authorities for turning a blind eye to the atrocities, if not condoning them outright. For Mark Edele and Filip Slaveski,

FIGURE 8.3. Murdered rape victims in East Prussia, 1945
Source: CC 3.0: Bundesarchiv, Bild 101I-464-0383I-26 / Kleiner / CC-BY-SA 3.0
(*top*)

however, it was the inability of the Soviets and their supporters to control loosely organized groups of violent men at war's end that allowed the latter to act with impunity against defenseless women and others.[19] Whatever the origin of the atrocities, they are not easily quantified. Rapes were not only commonplace; many women were raped several times. According to Soviet military historian Geoffrey Roberts, "estimates . . . range from tens of thousands to the low millions. The true figure probably lies somewhere in between, with the vast majority of rapes taking place in the city of Berlin, a city that was by 1945 largely a city of women." Richard Bessel, a specialist on Nazi Germany, refers to "hundreds of thousands." But it is Beevor's estimate of 2 million that has stuck. It is based on the work of the statistician Gerhard Reichling, who collaborated with film director Helke Sander and Barbara Johr on the documentary *Befreier und Befreite* (*Liberators Take Liberties*). The figure was made up of estimates of 110,000 rapes in Berlin alone and a further 1.9 million in the occupied Soviet Zone (the future German Democratic Republic) and former German territory in present-day Poland and Russia.[20]

Since quantification is an important aspect of the present study, it is important to make clear that Reichling's calculations—and, therefore, Beevor's figure of two million rapes—rest on shaky foundations. Nor is the claim that in Berlin "some 10,000 died as a result, mostly from suicide" corroborated by the official statistics for Berlin, which recorded 3,996 female suicides in 1945, compared to 2,108 in 1938 and 1,884 in 1946.[21] Reichling's calculation began with the 34 births fathered by Russians out of a total of 804 births (or 4.2 percent) in the Kaiserin Auguste Victoria Haus children's hospital in Berlin's inner city between September 1, 1945 and December 31, 1946. Treating this 4.2 percent ratio, rounded up to 5 percent, as the product of a random sample, Reichling reckoned that 5 percent, or 1,156, of all 23,124 births (both live and stillborn) across the city between September 1945 and August 1946 were *Russenkinder* (Russian children) and that all had been born of women who had been raped. He then assumed that 20 percent of rapes resulted in pregnancies and that 90 percent of pregnancies were aborted.[22] All these assumptions are contestable. On the one hand, the births-to-rapes ratio seems high,[23] but on the other, the 90 percent figure for pregnancies terminated is not supported by data from another well-known Berlin institution, the Charité women's clinic, where terminations made up 40 out of 118 (34 percent) of pregnancies due to rape.

Setting such caveats aside, Reichling's assumptions would imply $(1,156) \times (5) \times (10)$ or 57,800 rapes to women of childbearing age, of whom there were about 600,000, a rate of 9.5 percent. If, in the spirit of Beevor's assertion that "they raped every female from eight to 80," one applies the same rate of 9.5 percent to the 800,000 women aged between fourteen and eighteen years and over forty-five years in Berlin at the time, that would imply a further 73,300 rapes. Alternatively, using half that rate would imply 36,650. These calculations lead to Reichling's assertion that between 94,450 and 131,100 women were raped by Soviet troops in Berlin, or between 6.7 and 9.4 percent of the 1.4 million women living in Berlin at the time. The estimate of 1.9 million rapes outside Berlin assumed that 7.5 percent of deportee and refugee women from the East and of the minority left behind were raped.[24] The implied average of about 1 rape per Russian soldier conceals both serial rapists and those who raped nobody.

Though routinely quoted, Reichling's figure of two million rapes, sensationally recycled by Beevor and now common currency, does not deserve to be taken seriously. As noted, other reputable scholars favor lower numbers, while in his landmark study of the Soviet occupation Norman Naimark wisely despaired of ever knowing how many German women were raped during the occupation—a laudably cautious approach.[25] German historian Miriam Gebhardt (on whom more is said below) has also argued for a lower number and has questioned Reichling's assumption that women outside Berlin were at almost the same risk as those in the capital. She has also noted that whereas the Soviet army in Berlin was an army of occupation, only a portion of troops on the move before the fall of the capital could have been in any particular region at one time. Moreover, they would have been almost constantly engaged in heavy fighting, making contact with the civilian population less likely.[26]

All estimates of rapes in Germany in 1945 are contestable. Accusing filmmaker Sander of the "virtual fetishization of statistical clarity," a very angry Atina Grossmann wondered

> whether or not the focus on numbers has something to do with precisely a competitiveness about the status of victim (*ein Verbrechen mit dem anderen aufgerechnet*), so sensitive in the context of WWII, that Sander claims to resist in her work; it even suggests a lust for generally portraying women as victims that seems central to her particular historical and feminist agenda.[27]

Grossmann, an eminent historian of Nazi and Jewish Germany, was echoing a concern common in mainstream Germany at the time: that categorizing the raped women (much like the civilians killed by Allied bombing or the *Volksdeutsche* evicted from their homes in the East) as victims was a means of offsetting Nazi crimes. In her view Sander's "eagerness to integrate German women into the international transhistorical sisterhood of victims of male violence leads to historical slippage and displacement," something "highly problematic in the contest of the general German unwillingness to acknowledge responsibility for the misery they endured and the crimes that they perpetrated."[28]

According to military historian Vojin Majstorović, Soviet troops also "wreaked havoc" in other countries they conquered, raping "hundreds of thousands of women" in Romania, Hungary, and Austria during the last year and a half of World War II, while in "brotherly" countries they liberated— Yugoslavia, Bulgaria, and Czechoslovakia—their behavior "had more in common with the behavior of other contemporary allied militaries." The suggestion that rape was subject to some agency on the part of soldiers would support higher rates of rape in Germany. But in this case, too, precise numbers are impossible: Majstorović's estimated range for Yugoslavia is between 2,420 and 24,380 women. In Romania, by comparison, extrapolating from data for the counties of Arad and Iași to the country as a whole and applying Lilly's formula for underreporting, Majstorović puts the number of women raped between September 14 and October 19, 1944, at "more than 355,200." Allowing for rapes before and after those dates, he deems a total of "at least half a million" conservative. Estimates for Hungary and Austria are even more fallible, but they all imply sexual violence on a huge scale; in Vienna alone a range of 70,000–100,000 rapes has been suggested, while James Mark cites a claim that 1 in 10 women in Budapest (pop. about 1 million in 1945) were raped. All these numbers can be questioned but are probably sufficient to justify Majstorović's claim that the Red Army behaved less brutally in Yugoslavia than elsewhere. It is also probably safe to say that in all these countries, estimates and memories of rapes by Soviet troops reflect, at least in part, "the political debate and conflicts . . . within society."[29]

The issue of rape by German troops in France during World War II has received relatively little attention. One recent study, noting the relatively low number recorded—514, including 200 cases in which the victim was named, mostly in the later stages of the war—mentioned the understandable reluctance of victims to report rape and cited an old U.S. study suggesting that only 1 in every 20 rapes was reported and a more recent study of violence against women in France proposing 1 in 11.[30] Accounts of German troops committing sexual violence on the Eastern Front have been rather overshadowed by controversies over Soviet troops raping German women in 1945. While the mass rape of German women is often put down to motives of revenge and hate, German sexual atrocities in the East have been variously ascribed to a sense of racial superiority, stress on the battlefield in the wake of the defeat at Stalingrad, and lax discipline.[31] Nobody has attempted to quantify rapes by German troops; in her valuable dissertation on the topic

Wendy Jo Gertejanssen ventures no further than saying "sexual violence during World War II was a reality for hundreds of thousands, if not millions of people, primarily women and girls, on the eastern front."[32]

The Wehrmacht and the SS sought to minimize the spread of venereal disease through the use of soldiers' brothels. They also established brothels (*Lagerbordelle*) in ten concentration camps (Mauthausen, Theresienstadt, Neuengamme, Flossenbürg, Auschwitz, Sachsenhausen, Dachau, Dora-Mittelbau, Gusen, and Buchenwald) using visits as carrots for the most productive and cooperative workers. The original idea seems to have come to Himmler during a visit to Mauthausen; the first camp brothel was established there in 1941.[33] Some of the women who worked in the brothels were former prostitutes. Some were political prisoners or those whom the Nazis referred to as antisocial (*asozial*) prisoners, lured into the service on the basis of false promises of an early release. Gertjejanssen describes the decision of female prisoners to volunteer for work as camp prostitutes as "another layer of victimhood" that tends to get ignored in the literature.[34] Civilian labor camps in Germany were not, except for a few months in 1942, closed or guarded. In some cities with many foreign workers, the German authorities also operated *Ausländerbordelle* (brothels for foreigners).

Sexual Violence in Western Zones

In 1995 the American historian Norman Naimark made the point that "rape became a part of the social history of the Soviet Zone in ways unknown to the Western zones" and that it was "important to establish the fact that women in the Eastern zone—both refugees from further East and inhabitants of the towns, villages and cities of the Soviet Zone—shared an experience for the most part unknown in the west."[35] Naimark's assessment still broadly holds. Yet according to Richard Bessel, French troops stationed in Baden-Württemberg, Germany, did not behave much better than the Soviets while Canadian historian Perry Biddiscombe refers to "a considerable spate of raping by French and American forces, particularly during April and May 1945," and Joanna Bourke has noted "a tendency . . . to ignore or downplay the fact that British, American and Australian troops have also periodically engaged in orgies of sexual violence." Mark Jones makes the same point about French troops in occupied German territory in 1923.[36] Particularly shocking were the actions of French colonial troops in Magstadt, then a small town west of Stuttgart, on the evening of April 20, 1945, where they left 260 medically diagnosed cases of rape in their wake. Worse was to follow in Stuttgart in the following days when the same troops carried out another 1,200 or so officially verified cases of rape. The rapes were firmly denied by the French and U.S. authorities, even though twelve soldiers were executed for them. According to the *New York Times*, most victims were "attacked in their homes by turbaned Moroccan troops who broke down the doors in looting forays. Four women were killed, and four others committed suicide after being raped. . . . In one other case, it said, a husband killed his wife who had been attacked, and then killed himself." One disgusted U.S. soldier stationed in Stuttgart at the time wrote home to his parents: "By the way did you hear about Stuttgart? I was ashamed at what we allowed them (i.e. the French) to do there. It'd make your hair stand on end."[37]

American troops were not entirely blameless either. Accounts of the involvement of Western troops gain further corroboration in Robert Lilly's *Taken by Force* (2007), Marie-Louise Roberts's *What Soldiers Do* (2013), and Miriam Gebhardt's *Als die Soldaten kamen* (2015), translated as *Crimes Unspoken* (2017). Those studies and related work have tilted the spotlight away from Beevor's "army of rapists" and toward Western soldiers and their victims. Lilly's *Taken by Force* invoked evidence from courts martial not only to document rape by American GIs but to highlight how the judicial process discriminated against Black soldiers, an issue also discussed by Roberts. And not only has Gebhardt challenged the Reichling/Beevor aggregate figure of two million rapes by Russian troops, which had attained quasi-universal currency, she has also questioned the view that Russian troops alone were culpable. In *Crimes Unspoken* she reckons that of the "at least 860,000" women raped between 1945 and 1955, "190,000 of them, perhaps even more, were assaulted by US soldiers, others by British, Belgian or French."[38] These numbers have been uncritically recycled by some but rejected out of hand by others.

Like Reichling's estimates, Gebhardt's are built on very weak foundations. Her starting point is data produced by the Federal Statistics Office in 1956 reporting that sixty-eight thousand "occupation children" were born to women in the German Federal Republic and West Berlin between the above dates. More than half of those were fathered by GIs, 15 percent by French troops, 13 percent by British, 5 percent by Soviet, and 3 percent by Belgian troops. The vast majority of these children were born of consensual unions; according to the mothers, about thirty-two hundred, or 5 percent, of those children were born of rapes. Assuming that one in four rape victims were married and their children raised as if they were conceived with their husbands, then the total number of "rape children" becomes forty-three hundred. Gebhardt next assumes—arbitrarily, it must be said—that there were "at least" as many victims in the future German Democratic Republic, yielding eighty-six hundred "rape children" in all. And assuming a multiplier of one hundred—that is, a conception rate of 10 percent and an abortion rate of 90 percent[39]—she arrives at her total of 860,000 rapes, of whom she attributes 190,000 to American GIs and 50,000 to French troops.

Gebhart's and Reichling's estimates, both built on a series of highly contestable extrapolations, are unreliable, and the actual number of rapes likely lies beyond the reach of historians. While Gebhardt's account does not claim that the behavior of British and Americans replicated the "mass rape and vengeful wanton destruction that accompanied the Soviet advance into Germany,"[40] it tilts the narrative away from one of the Russians intent on rape, while the Americans "got everything they wanted with a Lucky Strike." The most that can be said for Gebhardt's estimate is that her downward revision of Soviet rapes seems more convincing than her 0.2 million blamed on Western troops. To argue, as one reviewer has put it, that it "provides a sense of the scale of the phenomenon and puts the often harrowing analysis of motives, experiences, and outcomes in a meaningful context" and that it "describes attacks by American soldiers that in both scale and violence rival those committed by the Soviets" is going too far.[41] In *Crimes Unspoken*, Gebhardt acknowledges that many of the rape victims were "at least potential perpetrators" (i.e., Nazi activists or sympathizers) but called for an "empathetic approach" that did not deny "their status as victims because they belonged to the aggressor nation." Although her book received generally favorable reviews, Lilly accurately predicted that it would be resisted for relativizing (*relativieren*) by scholars who "think it will make the war crimes committed by the Germans less bad."[42]

Predictably and rightly, Gebhardt's numbers have been contested. A hostile reviewer in the *Times Literary Supplement* lambasted her for "touting" them as a publicity stunt and then later "back-pedalling" on them. Even before reading her book, Beevor dismissed her estimates on the basis that any inferences from illegitimate children were "ludicrous" and that "there was a huge amount of voluntary sex. There were vast numbers of cases of genuine fraternisation. Many young women were hanging around outside the gates of American camps."[43] Alas, while Gebhardt's numbers are shaky, Beevor's "huge," "vast," and "many" are no substitutes for them. Naimark was also skeptical of Gebhardt's calculations, which he described as a misplaced attempt to relativize the rapes in postwar U.S. and Soviet Zones. Noting that the number of children born of rape in the Soviet Zone cannot be verified, he proposed that her calculations "are far too low for the east (and probably not particularly accurate for the west)." Robert Lilly, who had earlier put the number of rapes by U.S. troops by November 1945 at 11,000, was kinder. Overgenerously, he deemed Gebhardt's much higher estimates "plausible" even though "no exact number could ever be known because of a lack of records." The most recent attempt at estimating what the authors call "the dark number" of rapes by U.S. troops is explicit about how sensitive the outcome is to the underlying assumptions. The estimates, covering the period of May 1945–June 1946, are based on the number of rapes reported. They range from 8,146 (13 percent reported) to 105,900 (1 percent reported). The 5 percent reported rate assumed by Lilly for France would mean 21,180 rapes; a rate of 2.5 percent, possibly providing "a modern facsimile of the strained conditions in post-war Germany," yields 42,360. Again, it is a matter of take your pick—or, better, don't.[44]

From the beginnings of the invasion of Sicily to the aftermath of the Battle of Monte Cassino in the spring of 1944, Allied, and particularly French, troops were involved in sexual violence against local women. The situation in Naples as depicted by Norman Lewis and Curzio Malaparte makes the lines between consensual, trade, and forced sex seem very blurred.[45] Singled out for special opprobrium were the *goumiers* (from the Arabic *qum*, a band), former colonial police recruited in Morocco, who formed part of the French expeditionary force in Italy. Two-thirds of that force were North Africans, and twelve thousand were Moroccans. In both contemporary accounts and popular memory, these troops were deemed mainly responsible for the rapes, known in Italian as *marocchinate* (acts perpetrated by Moroccans). During the Allied advance through Sicily, resistance and vengeance kept the number of rapes down. In one case in the village of Capizzi, the rape of some local women led to the killing of some fifteen Moroccans, a reaction that tellingly provoked no reaction from the authorities. That rapes were numerous is not in doubt; in one instance concerning six villages in the province of Frosinone between June 2 and 5, 1944, the local police informed the prime minister's office that Moroccan troops had perpetrated 418 rapes, including 3 on men, and 29 murders. An inquiry into these incidents by the Italian Senate in 1966 found that General Juin's Moroccan troops raped over two thousand women and six hundred men in these villages; medical tests later established that one-fifth of the women had contracted syphilis.[46] Given the duration of the invasion and occupation and the wide area affected, historian Tommaso Baris has described the figure of 12,000 rapes proposed by the anti-Fascist Unione Donne Italiane as "credible." Baris also notes that many

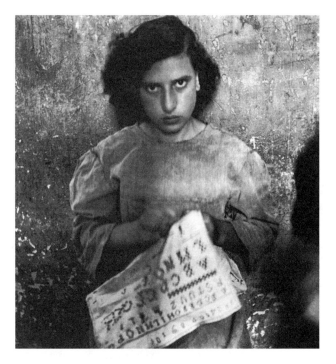

FIGURE 8.4. Teenage rape victim in Naples

of the rapes perpetrated by the goumiers were mass rapes—in contrast, say, to those committed by U.S. troops, which were for the most part individual acts. An imposing statue commemorating the victims was erected in Castro dei Volsci in 1964. It depicts an unnamed mother (*la Ciociara*) who sought to protect her daughter against rape by French colonial troops in the wake of the Battle of Monte Cassino. The incident inspired the eponymous 1957 novel by Alberto Moravia and, three years later, a very popular film starring Sophia Loren (figure 8.4).[47]

Japan

Sexual violence by soldiers against civilians during World War II began not in 1939 but in the wake of the Japanese Rape of Nanjing in December 1937. The Tokyo War Crimes Tribunal put the number of rapes in Nanjing at "approximately 20,000 . . . during the first month of occupation," without any supporting documentation, although a recent dissection of the available evidence suggests that this estimate may be of the right order.[48] Toward the end of the war, Japanese troops were also involved in systematic rapes during the Rape of Manila in February 1945.[49]

In the early stages of World War II, the Japanese military authorities, fearful of the spread of venereal disease in occupied territories and eager to maintain troop morale, recruited prostitutes for army use by conventional means. Indeed, the practice dates back to 1932, when the first *comfort houses* were set up in Shanghai in the wake of atrocities committed by Japanese troops. At the outset the women were Japanese prostitutes recruited by private agents on behalf of the authorities. After the supply of voluntary recruits in Japan dried up, thousands more, mainly Korean, Taiwanese, or Chinese, were sourced. Some were tricked or coaxed into prostitution, some were sold by their parents, and more were forcibly trafficked or captured. Estimates of the total number taken vary—an article in the *New Yorker* in 2021 noted that estimates "have ranged widely, from tens of thousands to hundreds of thousands"[50]—but the expert consensus is somewhere between eighty thousand and one hundred thousand women, a range based on the (arbitrary) assumption of one prostitute per forty troops (figure 8.5).

There were "comfort stations" wherever Japanese troops were stationed. Somewhere between five hundred and six hundred and three thousand women worked as "comfort women" on the occupied island of New Britain, off mainland New Guinea, at some point between early 1942 and the end of 1943 when it was occupied by about one hundred thousand Japanese troops. A memoir written by an English internee in New Britain describes the women used by the officer class as Japanese, but "in Chinatown and along the harbour most of the women at the end of the queues meeting men from the ranks were Koreans." The memoirist was informed by an "irate Korean" that the latter "were supposed to come south for the purpose of working in factories and on cacao and coffee plantations. Only on their arrival in Rabaul did they discover the real nature of their employment." They had been "regimented to amuse the troops; black-birded into prostitution; or perhaps it might be better termed Victims of the Yellow Slave trade. At any rate they were said to be pressed into service, not knowing to what they were coming." These women reportedly "handled" twenty-five to thirty-five clients per diem.[51] An August 1944 report by a U.S. "psychological warfare team" in Burma containing interviews with twenty captured Korean comfort girls noted how in May 1942 Japanese recruiters arrived in Korea for the purpose of finding women to serve in Southeast Asia:[52]

FIGURE 8.5. U.S. Army personnel interrogating three captured comfort women in August 1944

The nature of this "service" was not specified but it was assumed to be work connected with visiting the wounded in hospitals, rolling bandages, and generally making the soldiers happy. The inducement used by these agents was plenty of money, an opportunity to pay off the family debts, easy work, and the prospect of a new life in a new land—Singapore. On the basis of these false representations many girls enlisted for overseas duty and were rewarded with an advance of a few hundred yen.

The majority of the girls were ignorant and uneducated, although a few had been connected with "the oldest profession on earth" before. The contract they signed bound them to Army regulations and to work for the "house master" for a period from six months to a year depending on the family debt for which they were advanced.

The treatment of the prostitutes, euphemistically described as "comfort women" by the Japanese, has been contested since the end of the war, punctuated by Japanese denials and apologies. Revisionist Japanese commentary likened the treatment of comfort women to that of Japanese prostitutes held in brothels for U.S. troops after the war, but in 2015 the Japanese government paid 1 billion yen ($8.3 million) as compensation to surviving South Korean victims. Japanese prime minister Shinzo Abe expressed Japanese remorse "to all the women who underwent immeasurable and painful experiences and suffered incurable physical and psychological wounds as comfort women."[53] That did not prevent Harvard law professor Mark Ramseyer from echoing earlier revisionist Japanese claims when he argued in 2020 that the prostitution was contractual and voluntary. Ramseyer's findings attracted considerable notoriety and were forcefully dismissed by other scholars, whereupon the *International Review of Law and Economics* (IRLE), the Elsevier journal in which they were published, speedily issued an "expression of concern." Even so, Ramseyer's was the IRLE's most downloaded paper in the final quarter of 2021.[54] In the wake of the controversy surrounding his article, Ramseyer conceded that he could not locate any Korean prostitution contracts that would support his case, which he had built on evidence of contracts involving Japanese women in the prewar era.[55]

Japanese historian Toshiyuki Tanaka's claim that "from the day they landed" occupying American troops raped Japanese women on a scale "comparable to that of any other force during the war" is also highly controversial.[56] True, rapes of women by U.S. troops on the island of Okinawa in 1945 are well documented, and high numbers of rapes for Japan as a whole have been cited. In *Year Zero: A History of 1945*, Ian Buruma reports a rate of forty women raped per day during the second half of 1945.[57] However, hard evidence of American troops committing rape on a mass scale during the Occupation of Japan is lacking. Indeed, U.S. and Japanese records reveal that while there was a good deal of criminality at the outset, ranging from not paying bills for food or alcohol to carjacking, there is little evidence of more violent crimes like rape and murder. The headline of an article in Tokyo's mass-circulation *Asahi shinbun* on September 11, 1945, "No Violence against Women," is striking.[58] A scrupulous analysis of the judicial evidence in a PhD dissertation by Brian Walsh finds that while rapes occurred, a mass sexual rampage by U.S. troops on arrival just did not materialize. Walsh estimates that there were 1,312 cases of rape during the Occupation, which translates to about 200 a year. However, those numbers refer to reported cases; the number of unreported cases remains moot but should not be neglected. Walsh nonetheless concludes strongly on a defiant note: "Stories of mass rape and organized sexual exploitation during the Occupation are better understood as metaphoric expressions of the humiliation of defeat, occupation and continuing diplomatic subordination, than as history."[59]

Worried that U.S. troops would, in effect, replicate the behavior of Japanese troops in China led the Japanese authorities to create the Recreation and Amusement Association (RAA) at the so-called comfort women meeting of the Japanese cabinet on August 21, 1945. The aim was to build a female "floodwall against the raging waves, helping to defend and nurture the purity of our race." In the context of the near-apocalyptic desperation and starvation then facing Japan, recruiting women to "comfort" soldiers was relatively easy. The RAA's first brothel, *Komachien* (the Babe Garden), opened for business in a Tokyo suburb on August 27, 1945. That night, "500 or 600 soldiers" stood in line outside and were issued tickets and condoms for fifteen yen each (half the cost of a packet of cigarettes).[60] In the weeks that followed, the RAA procured thousands of women to work in its network of brothels, although the frequently recycled number of seventy thousand, like that of eighty thousand to one hundred thousand Korean comfort women mentioned above, seems to have no empirical basis.[61] The U.S. authorities became worried when RAA brothels were identified as sources of venereal disease and sex trafficking, and declared the brothels off-limits for troops. That led to the winding up of the RAA in March 1946. But prostitution on a mass scale continued while the Occupation lasted.[62]

Hierarchies of Victimhood

Many wartime rapes, which nearly always target civilians, go unreported; others are invented. This is why much of the preceding discussion of rape during World War I and World War II has been about the virtual impossibility of quantifying this aspect of civilian suffering. The flimsy underpinnings of widely recycled numbers bear highlighting. This is particularly true in the case of what Atina Grossmann has dubbed "The Big Rape": the rapes perpetrated by Soviet troops in occupied Germany in 1945. Grossmann's own summary illustrates:

> The numbers reported for these rapes vary wildly, from as few as 20,000 to almost one million, or even two million altogether as the Red Army pounded westward. A conservative estimate might be about 110,000 women raped, many more than once, of whom as many as 10,000 died in the aftermath; others suggest that perhaps one out of every three of about 1.5 million women in Berlin fell victim to Soviet rapes.[63]

The notoriety of these rapes is due in part to their scale, but it is also linked to their context: the defeat of the Third Reich and the start of the Cold War.

After Nazi Germany's defeat, those raped could be seen as supporters of the Nazi regime, while the Cold War made it easier to describe the perpetrators as "an army of rapists." However, the context also brings us back to some of the troublesome ambiguities raised in the introduction to this book.

Wartime rape is a fraught topic. Some victims receive less sympathy than others. In the long poem *Prussian Nights* (an excerpt from which forms the epigraph at the beginning of this chapter), Aleksandr Solzhenitsyn, who fought on the Belorussian front during World War II as captain of an artillery battery, dwelt on the mayhem inflicted by Soviet troops in East Prussia in early 1945 and in particular on the sexual violence inflicted on women, old and young. Although outraged at the vengeance wreaked on civilians, he did not pass judgment on the troops. And perhaps, according to some critics, he had his own reasons for not doing so. They hint that the fictionalized Sergei Nerzhin who apologizes at the end of *Prussian Nights* to the young woman he has raped was the poet himself.[64] Given what civilians of the Soviet Union had suffered, Solzhenitzyn's humanitarianism would have seemed excessive to many, like the female army telephone operator who confided to Svetlana Alexievich: "Now I feel shame, but I did not feel shame back then. . . . Do you think it was easy to forgive [the Germans]? We hated to see their clean undamaged white houses. With roses. I wanted them to suffer. I wanted to see their tears. . . . Decades had to pass until I started feeling pity for them."[65]

More than once, historian Atina Grossmann has echoed the sentiment that at least those women who had supported the Nazi regime got what they deserved. Neither the "farmer's daughter who was a Hitler Maiden and took delight in trying to prove the Russians were second-class human beings" nor "Poor Frau Graubach (who) when she had voted *ja*, had not bargained for this" was an innocent rape victim. When Grossmann insisted that German women "as a group" were not only victims but also "agents, collaborators, or beneficiaries" of Nazism and that Soviet troops would have seen them in that light, she made a valid point that continues to resonate, even if this tars all German victims with the same brush. But in denying or minimizing these women's suffering, she surely went too far.[66]

The Lasting Impact of Sexual Violence

Could it be that German women in 1944–45 suffered less than rape victims in other times and places because "the modernist *Sachlichkeit* of Weimar culture" and the loosening of sexual mores in wartime reduced their pain and trauma? This, Grossmann suggests, was reflected in their "bravado," "sang-froid," "self-preserving sexual cynicism," "gallows humour," and "matter-of-fact tone," all of which also attenuated their status as victims.[67] Grossmann cites the well-known example of a rape victim in Berlin in 1945, later identified as Marta Hillers, who survived by "sleeping for food" with a Ukrainian officer. Hillers kept an account of her ordeal and her will to survive, which was released anonymously as *Eine Frau in Berlin* and published in English as *A Woman in Berlin* in 1954. A highly articulate and well-educated woman in her thirties whose identity was not revealed until after her death, Hillers experienced the horrors of rape and learned to live with them: "Slowly but surely we're starting to view all the raping with a sense of humour—gallows humour," she wrote, adding that "we have ample grounds for doing so too." But there were times when humor was found wanting, and just thinking about the serial rapes of a friend "makes me gag all over again." And Hiller's ordeal led to her boyfriend Gerd, "who used to mean everything to me," leaving her.[68]

Two later survivor narratives also reveal a resilience of sorts. Gabriele Köpp from Schneidermühl in the former province of West Prussia-Posen (present-day Piła in northwest Poland) became a physics professor, while Leonie Biallas from western Silesia "got over it because I had a happy childhood, . . . my mother was always by my side and . . . I had always found friends and also my husband who accepted the silence." Still, for long afterward Köpp suffered from headaches and had a fear of men in uniform, and half a century later Biallas still could not bear to describe what happened directly.[69] Both were raped at a young age, and both wrote memoirs published in 2010; the former, *Warum war ich bloss ein Mädchen?* (*Why Did I Have to Be a Girl?*) and the latter, *"Komm, Frau, raboti": Ich war Kriegsbeute* (*"Come, Woman, Work": I Was War Booty*). Two or three trees do not a forest make, but it would be difficult to argue from these memoirs that *Sachlichkeit* or loose morals helped their authors to endure rape with equanimity.

Grossmann's claim has been contested, and indeed, there is ample qualitative documentation, too, of pain, depression, enduring physical injury, impaired sex life, traumatization, anxiety, shame, and even suicide.[70] One does not have to take far-fetched assertions that one rape victim in ten took her own life literally to accept that many German victims attempted or committed suicide.[71] The evidence on rape survivors elsewhere is more plentiful and bleaker but uncertain and contradictory, with examples of both trauma and resilience. If inferences from more recent conflicts are permitted, a 2017 review of twenty studies of the consequences of sexual violence during military conflicts, mainly in Africa, reported prevalence rates ranging from 3 to 76 percent for what is categorized as "post-traumatic stress disorder" (PTSD), from 7 to 75 percent for "anxiety disorders," and from 9 to 76 percent for "depression." The authors blame the high variability in outcomes, from modest to huge, on methodological and nonmethodological factors. That does not get us very far, but it explains why this section must end on a somewhat agnostic note, accepting that enduring trauma followed rape without attempting to quantify its extent or severity.[72]

9

Atrocities and Other
Horrors of War

What is war? I believe that half the people that talk about war have not the slightest idea of what it is. In a short sentence it may be summed up to be the combination and concentration of all the horrors, atrocities, crimes, and sufferings of which human nature on this globe is capable.

—JOHN BRIGHT, ENGLISH PARLIAMENTARIAN, 1853

The innocent bystanders hitherto discussed have ranged from those who were unintended "collateral damage" (e.g., the Frenchmen and French-women killed by Allied actions during the fighting in Normandy or the Dutch killed by Allied bombings) to the victims of willful exterminations and genocides. Most were in one form or another victims of modern technological capabilities and improved state capacity, the two telltale signs of modernization. But there were horrors, too, as old as war itself, and most of the war crimes discussed in this chapter and chapter 10 were more conventional, like twentieth-century versions of those painted by Jacques Callot in the seventeenth century and Francisco Goya in the nineteenth but still horrific in their own way.

World War I

World War I was hardly a week old when reports began to emerge of atrocities by German troops against Belgian civilians, soon followed by news of more atrocities by Habsburg, Prussian, and Russian troops on the Eastern Front. The worst of the Belgian *massacres de 1914*, carried out in the wake of an unquestionably illegal invasion of a small neutral country, resulted in the deaths of over 6,000 civilians during the second half of August 1914.[1] They included the murder of nearly 700 in Dinant, a town next to the French border in southern Wallonia, on August 23; 383 in Tamines, a small town halfway between Namur and Charleroi, on the previous day; and 248 in the university city of Leuven (Louvain) on August 25.

Like some of the atrocities committed by German (and Austrian) troops in the East, much of the killing in Belgium in August 1914 was attributed to paranoia, widespread in the German ranks, about being fired on by civilian or partisan snipers ("*die Zivilisten haben geschossen*").[2] That the victims of the atrocities were mainly adult men lends some support to this view. Nonetheless, although military technology certainly allowed for the possibility of effective sniping, *none* of the thousands shot by the Germans in August 1914 was identified as a civilian sniper, or franc-tireur.[3] As John Horne and Alan Kramer explain in their classic study, this paranoia probably had its origins in the Franco-Prussian War of 1870–71, when attacks by a small number of French sharpshooters dressed as civilians led to panic. Horne and Kramer cite the confession of a German soldier captured by the French:[4]

> We were given the order to kill all civilians shooting at us, but in reality the men of my regiment and I myself fired at all civilians we found in the houses from which we suspected there had been shots fired; in that way we killed women and even children.

While the atrocities committed by German troops in those first weeks offered an echo of events in 1870–71 for some historians, for others they were a foretaste of what was to come during World War II.[5] The latter reading is stretching it: the atrocities committed by German troops on the Western Front at the start of the war were not repeated and paled in comparison with those committed by Austro-Hungarian and Russian troops in the East. Indeed, after the autumn of 1914 the Western Front was depopulated and civilian casualties therefore relatively few, which has led some historians to argue that the atrocities of August 1914 were the product of mobile warfare and confusion among soldiers, rather than attitudes deeply embedded in the German army since 1870–71.[6] There were further German excesses of a different kind against Belgium, however. The German occupation was accompanied by the requisitioning of property, higher taxation, and the conscription of tens of thousands of workers, to the extent that Belgium was brought to the brink of starvation by 1915. Only the intervention of U.S. businessman (and future president) Herbert Hoover and his Commission for Relief in Belgium saved it from a worse fate.[7]

Meanwhile, from the outset of World War I the Austro-Hungarian army treated Serbian civilians harshly: if the assassination of the Habsburg heir Archduke Franz Ferdinand by a Bosnian Serb nationalist was an obvious pretext for—or proximate cause of—such treatment, old enmities doubtless fueled it too. During the first fortnight of their invasion, Habsburg troops massacred up to four thousand civilians, burning houses, using women as human shields, employing collective punishment, and executing hostages. Provoked in part by the actions of *komitadji* (partisans) and soldiers in civilian dress, they tended to treat the entire Serb population as soldiers in plain clothing. Still, a table describing the age and gender of about thirteen hundred civilians killed by Austro-Hungarian troops in the early weeks of the war suggests that males were much more likely to be singled out, with middle-aged or older men aged between 45 and 64 accounting for over half of all males shot. According to the Swiss forensic scientist Rudolph Reiss, whose findings, accompanied by gruesome photographic evidence, were published for their propaganda value by the Serbs in 1918, Hungarian and Croatian troops were the worst perpetrators, "though the men were incited by their officers to commit atrocities."[8] The war seemed to turn ancient bilateral resentments into slaughter.

Estimates of the number of Serb civilians executed without trial during World War I by the Habsburg army range from ten thousand to thirty thousand. That figure would include several thousand Serbs murdered by Bulgarian forces in 1916–17; these were mostly civil servants, ex-soldiers, priests, and teachers who had remained behind in the wake of defeats in 1915 or had returned to Serbia. The most notorious of these atrocities against Serb civilians was the mass murder of an estimated two thousand to three thousand males who were "taken to Sofia" at Surdulica in southern Serbia in late 1916 and early 1917 (figure 9.1).[9]

Austro-Hungarian atrocities did not end there. Initial Habsburg defeats in Serbia were followed by further reverses and more atrocities in Galicia (a historical region now divided between southeastern Poland and western Ukraine) in 1914 and 1915, where Habsburg troops massacred twenty-five

FIGURE 9.1. Remains of Serbian civilians murdered on display at Surdulica, 1926

thousand to thirty thousand Ruthenians (Transylvanian Slavs belonging to the Uniate or Eastern Rite Catholic Churches), whom they suspected of being Russophiles and traitorous. The Russian invasions of East Prussia also brought their share of atrocities: rape, deportations, arson, murder, summary executions, and hostage-taking.[10] The Russians targeted ethnic Germans and Poles, as well as Jews, as disloyal. An internal Russian general staff headquarters memorandum, dated as early as October 15, 1914, urged that "not a single German or Austrian subject alive can or should be considered harmless. All must be investigated, and this will be expensive for the government and likely unsuccessful. . . . The only solution is deportation without exceptions."[11] In 1914–15 at least a quarter of Galicia's Jewish community—probably between 0.2 and 0.3 million—fled west toward Austria, where they received a cold welcome. Disliked and widely suspected of spreading disease, they were entering territories with long histories of anti-Semitism. Nearly 0.1 million of the fleeing Galician Jews sought refuge in Vienna and many more in the Czech lands. As communal tensions grew,

Habsburg solidarity collapsed. Many Jews who remained in the East were relocated away from the front.[12] German and Austro-Hungarian armies, for their part, repaid in kind the atrocities committed by the Russians. As elsewhere, some of the violence stemmed from armed partisan resistance that blurred the distinction between soldier and civilian.

Outside Europe, African civilians were not spared the violence of World War I. Soon all the imperial powers saw the conflict as a means of making territorial gains. Atrocities were committed against native peoples in Portuguese East Africa (modern Mozambique),[13] in the Belgian Congo (notorious for atrocities right from its colonial beginnings in the 1880s), in German East Africa, and in South Africa. There were no formal counts, but it is reckoned that 0.1 million or so people recruited or conscripted as porters or carriers in South Africa succumbed to malnutrition, exhaustion, and disease, while about half that number died in East Africa. In the Belgian Congo, a postwar estimate put the number of porters who died, mainly from maltreatment and disease, at 24,975.[14] Altogether, as many as 0.2 million native porters and carriers may have perished during the war in Africa.

The Italian conquest of Ethiopia in 1935–36 and the Spanish Civil War also deserve mention here. Both foreshadowed World War II and were associated with mass atrocities against civilians.[15] In both cases the numbers are disputed. Thousands died in Ethiopia through a combination of deaths by bombing, the destruction of villages, deportation to concentration camps, and revenge killings in February 1936 in the wake of the attempted assassination of the Italian general Rodolfo Graziani. Mussolini's secret authorization to Graziani, his viceroy in Ethiopia, "to initiate and systematically conduct a policy of terror and extermination" allowed Italian troops and civilians to act with impunity.[16] Ethiopian sources later claimed that thirty thousand died in the Yekatit 12 (February 19 in the Western calendar) massacres following the attempt on Graziani, but contemporary newspapers reported four–digit figures, while a 2017 study of the massacres suggests a toll of nineteen thousand.[17]

The Spanish Civil War was also particularly brutal and its toll in civilian deaths high. Both so-called Red (republican) and White (nationalist) terrors were responsible for tens of thousands of civilian lives; how many of the excess deaths were due to hunger remains uncertain. Estimates of the civilian toll remain controversial and span a wide range. Taking an indirect demographic approach, Ortega and Silvestre put excess mortality between 1936 and 1939 due to a combination of war and famine of those aged over

TABLE 9.1. Excess mortality and missing births in Spain, 1936–39

Year	Excess female	Excess male	Total excess	"Lost" births
1936	−3,565	37,716	34,151	−16,523
1937	19,302	68,917	88,219	−61,334
1938	35,842	80,343	116,185	−117,968
1939	30,116	77,263	107,379	−201,535
1936–39	*81,695*	*264,239*	*345,934*	*−397,360*
1940	10,339	42,262	52,601	10,901
1941	32,903	77,243	110,146	−106,588
1942	8,069	22,639	30,708	−83,209
1940–42	*51,311*	*142,144*	*193,455*	*−178,896*
1936–42	*133,006*	*406,584*	539,389	*−576,256*

Source: Ortega and Silvestre 2006: tables 8 and 9. Deaths refer to those aged >1.

one year at 346,000, or including lost births—that is, births prevented by a combination of malnutrition, dislocation, and postponed marriages[18]—at 396,000 (table 9.1). The mortality includes both civilians and military. An estimate of 140,000 for military deaths and a compromise figure of 150,000 for executions and murders implies a residual of about 56,000 civilian deaths attributable to other causes (mainly famine) during the war years.[19]

The huge drop in births in 1939 to only two-thirds of the norm is particularly noteworthy, indicating that malnutrition and famine deaths are likely to have peaked in 1938. But the dying and the killing in Spain did not cease with the end of the civil war. Table 9.1 puts total excess deaths in 1940–42 at 193,000 and the births deficit at 179,000. While the huge drop in biomass daily consumption per capita—from twenty-nine hundred kilocalories in 1933 to twenty-two hundred kilocalories in 1940 with no subsequent recovery in the 1940s[20]—points to a role for malnutrition, the very high percentage of male deaths points to the extent of postwar repression. Still, the estimates of lost births imply that 1940 and 1941 were worse than 1939. The data also imply, making allowance for violent deaths, that the ratio of losses from famine relative to those from lost births was probably higher after the civil war than during it. Clearly, no definitive estimate of deaths from hunger and famine is possible; here a figure of 0.2 million is proposed with due caution, about as many as were murdered by death squads and vigilantes during and in the immediate wake of the war.[21]

Atrocities against Civilians during World War II

Civilian victims of violence during World War II greatly outnumbered those during World War I. The worst of the violence was in eastern Europe and beyond, but western Europe was not spared either. German atrocities under the Nazis dwarfed those carried out by the kaiser's troops in Belgium and France and on the Eastern Front, and it bears noting that with the exception of Soviet killings in Poland and the Baltic, most of the atrocities during World War II were caused by Axis (German and Japanese) forces.

The most heinous atrocities of World War II were linked to the Holocaust. Two of the most notorious against non-Jewish civilians occurred in Lidice, a mining village about twenty kilometers northwest of Prague, on June 9–10, 1942, and in the hamlet of Ležáky, located about 150 kilometers east of Prague, a fortnight later. Lidice was razed to the ground and all its two hundred or so adult males murdered in retaliation for the assassination of senior Nazi Reinhart Heydrich, one of the main architects of the Holocaust and chief of the intelligence wing of the SS, as well as acting *Reichsprotektor* of Bohemia-Moravia. Heydrich's assassins were members of the Czech and Slovak resistance. Lidice's women and children were first sent to a nearby town and from there to Ravensbrück concentration camp in northern Germany; many of them perished there. A small number of the children were selected for Germanization and the rest murdered. In Ležáky all adults were shot; two of the children were selected for Germanization as part of the *Lebensborn* program (on which more below), and the remaining eleven perished in Chełmno extermination camp. Lidice and Ležáky, obliterated on the pretext of responsibility by association for the assassination of Heydrich, became global symbols of Nazi brutality, but they were just two of many.[22]

On June 10, 1944, a similar fate befell the village of Oradour-sur-Glane near Limoges, site of by far the biggest atrocity against non-Jewish civilians in France. Indeed, the death toll in Oradour was double that in Lidice and Ležáky. SS troops from the *der Führer* regiment burned the village to the ground after killing about 640 of its inhabitants in retaliation, it was said, for the capture of a German officer the previous day. The villagers were gathered together on the pretext of an identity check, but none was carried out: in the words of its last survivor, this was a *crime gratuit*. A month later, in an extensive operation against the local maquis in the Vercor massif in southeastern France, the dead included not only over 600 resistance fighters but also about 200 civilians.[23]

In Italy between July 1943 and May 1945, 25,000 civilians were killed by the SS and the Wehrmacht, sometimes assisted by Fascist troops, in both large-scale massacres and smaller actions against civilians, mainly in central and northern Italy. The massacres were often reprisal actions for partisan attacks against the Wehrmacht on its retreat northward. For an army vulnerable to attack by an invisible enemy, those massacres had their own diabolical wartime logic. But there were many—thousands—of small-scale murders too, seemingly unrelated to partisan activity, implying that much of the killing was indiscriminate. The most notorious major actions against civilians, all in 1944, included those in the Ardeatine caves on the outskirts of Rome (March 24, 335 victims), in the Tuscan villages of Civitella in Val di Chiana (June 29, 146 victims), in Sant'Anna di Stazzema (August 12, 560 victims), in San Terenzo Monti (August 17–19, 159 civilian victims), in Padule di Fucecchio (August 23, 174 victims), in Strage di Cavriglia in the province of Arezzo (July 4–11, 192 victims), and at Monte Sole near the village of Marzabotto in the hills south of Bologna (early October, 770 victims). Unlike most of the numbers cited below, these estimates are likely to be reasonably accurate. The killings in the Ardeatine caves were systematic and planned by the SS, while most of the others were carried out as reprisal killings by Wehrmacht units. All those killed in the Roman caves were male; 75 were Jewish, most of them selected simply because they were Jewish, while most of the remainder were members of the resistance, many of them Communists or Socialists. Several of the other massacres occurred in June–August 1944, a period when Wehrmacht troops were encouraged by their commander in chief, Albert Kesselring, to act with impunity. In Civitella in Val di Chiana and Strage di Cavriglia, nearly all the victims were also males, but in Marzabotto, Sant'Anna di Stazzema, Padule di Fucecchio, and San Terenzo Monti half or more were either women or children (figure 9.2).[24]

German troops also committed many atrocities against Greek civilians for alleged collaboration with partisans. On August 16, 1943, over 300 inhabitants of the village of Kommeno in northwestern Greece died in one such action. Operation Kalavryta, revenge for the murder of seventy-eight captured German soldiers by Greek partisans, resulted in the killings of nearly 700 mainly male Greek civilians on December 13, 1943. On August 22, 1944, another operation in the Amari valley in Crete resulted in the deaths of 164 Greeks, mainly civilians. In the village of Chortiatis on September 2, 1944, 146 civilians, nearly all women, children, and older men, were killed in retaliation for partisan activity. And there were many more. Such atrocities closely mirrored those in Italy. Aggregate numbers in Greece can only be guessed

FIGURE 9.2. Memorials

a. Oradour-sur-Glane (Haute-Vienne): A massacre site frozen in time (*Source:* CC 4.0: Wikimedia user Davdavlhu)

b. Sant'Anna di Stazzema in northern Tuscany

at; the Wehrmacht may have killed up to 20,000 in total, while their Bulgarian allies may have murdered or expelled even more in occupied Thrace, significant proportions of whom were innocent civilians.[25] Italian troops also engaged in bloody reprisals. In Domenikon, a village in central Greece, on February 16–17, 1943, Italian troops shot over 150 male civilians as a reprisal for a partisan attack. Other lesser atrocities followed.

Italian troops also committed atrocities—reprisals, summary executions, displacement, incarceration in concentration camps—against the civilian populations of Yugoslavia. Some thousands of ethnic Italians, on the other hand, were the victims of massacres carried out by Yugoslav partisans in Istria and Dalmatia by the Adriatic coast. Some of these killings involved throwing victims into *foibe* (sinkholes); they later came to be known as the *foibe massacres* (figure 9.3). The *infoibati* numbered 3,000–4,000. Some accounts treat their deaths as a form of brutal ethnic cleansing, others as anti-Fascist reprisals.[26] Atrocities by Croats (allies of Germany) against ethnic Serbs in the puppet Independent State of Croatia, particularly in the notorious Jasenovac complex of extermination camps, resulted in tens of thousands of civilian deaths. Most of those who died in Jasenovac between late 1941 and April 1945 were ethnic Serbs, but they also included Jews, Roma, and Croat opponents of the pro-Nazi regime. In the wake of World War II, the death toll was put at 0.7 million, but nowadays it is accepted that the truth lies somewhere between 80,000 and 100,000.[27]

The civilian casualties of World War II also include an estimated 0.7 million patients with mental disabilities or illnesses murdered in Germany and Austria. In Germany they were targeted first by the program dubbed Aktion T4 (after the address, Tiergartenstrasse 4, of a building in Berlin associated with the program), which began in September 1939 and was suspended in August 1941, after the Holy See and in particular Clemens von Galen, the Catholic bishop of Münster, condemned the killings. Most of the victims were killed by gassing, and most of the executions took place in Germany itself. After August 1941 the killings continued on a lesser scale, using lethal injections and pills.[28] A further 0.2 million asylum inmates died of malnutrition after the suspension of the program in August 1941.[29] The Germans also shot or poisoned thousands of psychiatric patients in Poland and the Soviet Union. In Latvia, for example, over 2,000 chronic psychiatric patients were killed by shooting between August 1941 and October 1942, whereas in Poland about 20,000 died, mainly by gassing. Some of the techniques developed in the course of Aktion T4 were later applied in the death camps:[30]

FIGURE 9.3. Entrance to a *foibe* discovered in Friuli after World War II

Once the Germans learned that gas was a cheap and effective method of killing, they constructed special gas chambers on trucks so that patients could be killed while being transported to their place of burial. Vans with chambers lined with brass sheets, insulated inside by felt moved, like symbols of death, throughout the district of Warta.[31] On each there was a drawing of a coffee pot and an inscription: *Kaisers Kaffee-Geschaft* (Kaiser's Coffee Shop) meant to calm the patients. The procedure was strictly routinized. Patients were forced into the truck under supervision of SS escorts. Sometimes they received sedatives beforehand. Then the convoy proceeded to the preselected place of burial. During the procession, the patients were gassed to death. They were buried in forests, in mass graves, which were then camouflaged by grass and small trees. Considerable evidence exists that the van killings first started in November 1939 at the psychiatric hospital in Owinska. After all the patients were murdered, the hospital served as barracks for the SS.

As already noted in chapter 2, the toll of those with mental disabilities during World War II also included tens of thousands of inmates of psychiatric institutions who died of malnutrition in Vichy France, Greece, the Netherlands, southern Italy, and elsewhere.[32]

Apart from those who perished in the carpet bombings of 1944–45, the main German civilian victims of atrocities during World War II were the *Volksdeutsche* and *Reichsdeutsche* expellees during World War II (see chapter 7). The resultant death toll is still contested. Estimates by the West German government have consistently exceeded 2 million ("ca. *zwei Millionen—immerhin etwa ein Sechstel—ums Leben gekommen sind*" [c. two million—about one-sixth of the total—perished]), but that number is certainly far too high, and others have argued for a much lower figure of 0.5–0.6 million. In 2006 a spokesman for the German government sought, without too much conviction, to reconcile such estimates by claiming that the latter included only those who were killed on the spot, while the former included all those who died of hunger, exposure, disease, and air raids on their way to Germany.[33]

Atrocities against civilians were more widespread and systematic in the East. The massacre of nearly 3,000 civilians in the Ukrainian village of Kortelisy by German troops, assisted by local police, and the destruction of the village, was one of many such atrocities across Ukraine and Belarus. The Belarusian village of Katyn is best known for the mass murder of thousands of Polish officers and members of the intelligentsia in April–May 1940 by the Soviets (see below); the villagers of similarly sounding Khatyn were almost all (about 150 people) exterminated by German forces in a smaller, unrelated action on March 22, 1943. Elsewhere in areas that would become part of western Ukraine, the nationalist Ukrainian Insurgent Army (UPA)—then allied to Germany—murdered about 50,000-100,000 ethnic Polish civilians as part of what some see as an ethnic cleansing exercise, and others as an act of genocide, in 1943.[34]

Long-term Nazi planning for its occupied eastern territories envisioned the forced expulsion or starvation of millions of civilians. The colonization project known as *Generalplan Ost* (General Plan for the East), a byproduct of Hitler's *Lebensraum* ideology, proposed that occupied Poland, the Baltic states, Belarus, and much of Ukraine and the occupied Soviet Union should be ethnically cleansed of most of their populations over a period of two or three decades and replaced by ethnic Germans. The plan evolved between 1940 and 1942. Its last version covered territory that was home to about forty-five million people, of whom about two-thirds (thirty million) would be shifted east toward Siberia; the entire Jewish population of about five million would be murdered, and the remaining ten million or so would be employed as unskilled underlings or, at worst, worked or starved to death.

Separately, the Hunger Plan devised by Herbert Backe, as outlined in chapter 2, envisaged transfers of food on such a scale from civilians in the East as to constitute a genocide involving the deaths of millions of people. Some German actions during the occupation, such as the mass starvation imposed on Leningrad and parts of Ukraine and the resettlement of about 0.5 million ethnic Germans in what the Nazis called Reichsgau Warthel-and, formed from Polish lands annexed in 1939, offered foretastes of these plans, but both were effectively aborted when the Wehrmacht began its long retreat after Stalingrad. Nevertheless, by inferring war-related deaths from a comparison of estimated total deaths and what might be considered normal peacetime mortality, World War II is believed to have led to a total of 25 million deaths in the Soviet Union, of whom fewer than 9 million were military (although that excludes about 3 million prisoners of war [POWs] and partisans). The Russian Academy of Science put the number of civilian deaths under German occupation due to direct violence (shootings, bomb-ings, etc.) at 7.4 million (including about 2 million Jews); famine and disease were responsible for a further 4.1 million and slave labor in Germany for 2.2 million. The last figure is almost certainly too high but that for famine and disease, probably too low. The Academy of Science data exclude war deaths in areas that remained under Soviet control, including those of ethnic minor-ities, prison-camp inmates, and victims of the Leningrad siege-famine. These could easily have accounted for another 2 million. Most of the atrocities that lay behind those statistics were carried out in blood-soaked Belarus and Ukraine, occupied in whole or in part by the Wehrmacht between mid-1941 and August 1944. Of the deaths due to direct violence, about 2.5 million were Jewish.[35] Some of the latter are documented in Ilya Ehrenburg and Vasily Grossman's *Complete Black Book of Russian Jewry* (1944), a compilation of evidence collected by Jewish war correspondents accompanying the Soviet army on its advance westward through areas containing traces of the Nazi genocide against the Jews, while Nobel laureate Svetlana Alexievich's *Last Witnesses: An Oral History of the Children of World War II* (2019) describes the wartime memories and suffering of child survivors in Belarus. According to Christian Gerlach, 1 million civilians out of a total of 9 million Belarusians perished during the war: 500,000–550,000 Jews and 100,000 from other ethnic groups and 345,000 victims of antipartisan actions.[36]

Estimates of the number of civilians murdered in Poland during World War II range between 4.5 and 6 million. From the outset the German invad-ers arrested and deported members of the educated Polish elite, includ-ing politicians, public servants, intellectuals, clergy, nobility, high school teachers, and university academics. This was part of the policy to make a colony of Poland; indeed, tens of thousands of Poles had been identified by the Gestapo in the *Sonderfahndungsbuch Polen* (*Special Prosecution Book-Poland*) as targets for such treatment in the two years or so before the invasion.[37] Just a week after the invasion of Poland, Heydrich instructed SS units following the troops: "The leading stratum of the population in Poland should be rendered as harmless as possible. . . . We want to protect the little people, but the nobility, the priests and the Jews must be killed."[38] The *Intelligenzaktionen* (campaigns against the intelligentsia), in which thousands of the Polish intellectual and white-collar elite were murdered, followed. The killing was done by SS death squads, with help from members of the local German minority militia. By the end of 1939, perhaps 40,000 had been murdered in these *Intelligenzaktionen*. By the end of 1941, about 0.2 million ethnic Poles had been killed by the Nazis.

Meanwhile, while the Molotov-Ribbentrop pact was in operation (August 23, 1939– July 30, 1941) the Soviets murdered tens of thousands more ethnic Poles in the territories they annexed, similarly targeting the elite. Their most notorious action was the secret mass shooting of about twenty thousand Poles, mainly military officers, landlords, businessmen, senior civil servants, and clergymen, by the NKVD at Katyn forest near Smolensk and elsewhere in the spring of 1940. The shootings followed in the wake of a memo from the NKVD's Lavrentii Beriia to Stalin in early March 1940.[39] The site at Katyn was discovered by the Wehrmacht in late 1942 and put to gruesome propagandistic use by the Nazis (figure 9.4). Other mass graves at Kharkiv and Bykivnia (Ukraine) and Mednoye (Russia) were discovered later. Subsequent Soviet attempts to blame the Germans lacked conviction. In 1952 a U.S. congressional report found that the massacre was a Soviet action intended to eliminate "the flower of Poland's intelligentsia," but for half a century the Soviet authorities denied all involvement in the Katyn massacre. Katyn was just part of a much broader "Polish operation" conceived by the NKVD in 1937–38 that would ultimately involve the murder of tens of thousands of Poles.[40] In general, civilians from poorer backgrounds suffered more than their share during World War II, but in the case of Poland, thanks to the anti-intelligentsia campaigns of both the Germans and the Soviets, the opposite may have been true. At particular risk in Poland were medical practitioners, lawyers, Catholic priests, state employees, and academics.[41]

In 1947 the Polish Bureau of War Damages put the number of civilian deaths at 6 million, of whom half were Jewish. The 5.1 million proposed by

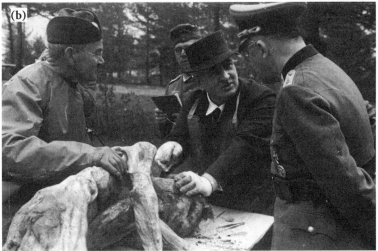

FIGURE 9.4. Katyn, March 1943

a second official estimate in 1951 included 550,000 military deaths. An estimate published in a specialist journal in 1987 put the total number of Polish war dead, including military, at 6 million. There have been many competing estimates since but with numbers converging to somewhat under 2 million gentile Poles. These would include the 0.1 million or so murdered by the UPA in Volhynia (a historic region now an integral part of Ukraine) and eastern Galicia, as mentioned above. In 2016 the Polish Parliament pronounced the murders a genocide. That the killings occurred is not in doubt, though others describe them as the product of ethnic cleansing rather than genocide. The most recent estimate of Polish deaths, 5,219,053, is at the core of a campaign by the former Law and Justice Party government for compensation for the losses inflicted by Germany in 1939–1945. Curiously, while the report notes that the 5.2 million total includes 150,000 regular military deaths, the majority share of 2.9–3 million Jewish deaths (see Table 5.2 above) in the remaining 5 million receives no mention.[42]

The Baltic states were subjected to three rounds of violent occupation: first the Soviets (June 1940–June 1941), then the Germans (June 1941–October/November 1944), and thereafter the Soviets again. Reliable numbers are lacking for casualties. An account of the situation in Estonia claims that "roughly 12–14 percent of the population thus fell victim to Soviet persecution and four percent lost its life due to unbearable conditions or was executed," adding that data are available on a few mass killings and three thousand death penalty cases, "but the majority of deaths can be traced to criminal neglect in the camps, prisons or special settlements." Such figures are within the realm of possibility, but they are not hard data, and *Encyclopedia Britannica* reports an estimate of 90,000, significantly lower than that implied above. Local estimates of the demographic losses in Lithuania average 0.4–0.5 million for the period up to January 1945. These include nearly 0.2 million Holocaust victims and do not distinguish between military and civilian victims among the remainder, though civilians would have been in the majority. Latvia's non-Holocaust World War II victims, about 0.1 million, numbered fewer than half Lithuania's.[43] In Finland, in addition to nearly 20,000 POWs who perished "due to camp conditions and the poor basic supply of food, shelter, clothing, and health care," 4,361 civilian internees died in camps in East Karelia.[44]

Estimates of Chinese civilians killed by Japanese forces between the mid-1930s and 1945 are far more uncertain. In his *Statistics of Democide*, R. J. Rummel estimated the number of Japanese killings in World War II at between "near 3,000,000 to over 10,000,000 people, most probably almost 6,000,000 Chinese, Indonesians, Koreans, Filipinos, and Indochinese, among others, including Western prisoners of war," whereas Werner Gruhl's *Imperial Japan in World War 2* places the total number of civilian deaths at 20,365,000. Rummel allows only 0.25 million deaths from "democidal famine," but the combined estimates of famine deaths in Vietnam and Indonesia, for which the Japanese were mainly responsible, range from 2.3 to 3.4 million. Gruhl's estimate of 4.5 million civilian deaths in Indochina and

Indonesia includes famine victims.[45] One probably cannot improve on Rummel's best-guess estimate of 6 million, which largely avoids double counting famine victims, but that does not mean it should be taken literally. These deaths would also include the victims of the floods following the deliberate breach of dikes on the Yellow River on June 5–7, 1936, by the Chinese army in an effort to stop the advance of Japanese forces. This action led to the inundation of thousands of square kilometers of prime farmland in Henan, Anhui, and Jiangsu. The toll in lives lost is controversial, but the most recent scholarship suggests that between 0.3 million and 0.5 million died.[46] Millions of Vietnamese, Javanese, Malays, Koreans, and Filipinos also died at the hands of the Japanese, through famine, forced labor, and other atrocities. The famines in Vietnam, Java, and Indonesia have already been described in chapter 2; a 1947 UN report put the number killed by the Japanese "or who had died of hunger, disease and lack of medical attention . . . at 3,000,000 for Java alone, and 1,000,000 for the Outer Islands."[47]

Graphic depictions of the atrocities committed by Japanese troops against Filipino civilians during the Battle of Manila in February–March 1945 survive, and such atrocities were not confined to Manila. Filipino civilians were also killed in the tens of thousands by American artillery and mortars, in part because of General Douglas MacArthur's dictum that "good generals don't have casualties." One of MacArthur's subordinates boasted: "Our bombers have done some pretty alteration work on the appearance of Berlin and Tokyo. Just the same, I wish they could see what we did with our little artillery on the Jap strongholds in Manila. . . . So much for Manila. It is a ruined city. . . . Let us thank God our cities have been spared such a fate." The precise number of civilian victims will never be known, but an aggregate toll of 100,000 civilian deaths in Manila (a city of 0.6 million in 1939) has been cited in a reputable source.[48]

Cannibalism

Skeptics may doubt the authenticity of repeated accounts of survivor cannibalism in the Old Testament and during medieval crusades, but there is no doubting well-authenticated episodes linked to the ill-fated Donner Party in the Sierra Nevada in 1846–47, the Franklin Canadian Arctic expedition of 1845, or the Uruguayan Air Force Flight 571 in 1972. Recent research has conclusively shown that some of the first English colonists in America engaged in one of "those things wch seame [*sic*] incredible" during the "starving time" of winter 1609–10, and we even know the names of some of the perpetrators and victims of cannibalism during the Chinese Great Leap Famine of 1959–61.[49] All these cases mainly involved survival cannibalism—that is, seeking to subsist on the remains of those who had already died. Famines and the risk of starvation, however, also give rise to the more sinister exocannibalism, an aggressive form of cannibalism directed at victims with the objective of consuming their remains. Russian may be the only language with words that distinguish between the two: *trupoyedstvo*, which refers to survivor cannibalism, and *lyudoyedstvo*, which involves killing victims in order to consume them.

Although the aggregate number of victims was certainly small, cannibalism was a feature of several World War I and World War II famines. There is anecdotal evidence of cannibalism in Mount Lebanon in 1916, with people's names added for rhetorical effect:[50]

> By the Sanayi' School, two children picked sesame seeds from piles of excrement; in Harat Huraiq, men, women, and children competed to rob an anthill of grain; in the village of Bait Shabab, a child by the name of Nasri Sa'id Murad Ghibril stole seeds from ants near the church; in Hadath, a young man died after gorging himself on lemon peels; in Riyaq, after the Germans had disposed of a horse which had died of some disease—so foul that even the wolves were repulsed—a group of forty people ate the carcass from head to hoof and died from that disease; in Damur, Kattar Shahdan al-Salafani ate three human corpses; in Mitn, Helena bint Salibi 'Abd ate the corpse of her nephew, Najib Salibi 'Abd. And she was not the only one who ate a corpse. In Tripoli, four women cannibalized four children.

The evidence is much firmer for the Soviet Union, where World War I and World War II cast their dark shadows until 1922 and 1947, respectively. In the wake of World War I, the famine of 1921–22 became notorious for its links to cannibalism:

> In the Russian famine of 1921–22 there were many rumors of cannibalism and some of them were tracked down. . . . Eating of dead bodies was apparently rather common in all districts. Professor Frank of Kharkov University was able to establish the authenticity of 26 cases in which human beings were killed and eaten by their murderers. In 7 cases murder was committed and the flesh, disguised in sausages, was sold on the open market. In Orenburg a notorious case resulted in an order by the city authorities forbidding the sale of meat balls and all forms of ground and

chopped meats. . . . In many areas the cemeteries had to be guarded to prevent the exhumation of freshly buried corpses.[51]

Far from denying the presence of cannibalism, the Bolshevik leadership used it as propaganda. The persistence of famine after they had won the civil war reconciled them to a combination of restoring a free market in food-stuffs and accepting the aid provided by Herbert Hoover's American Relief Administration, the International Committee of the Red Cross (ICRC), and other charities.[52]

Cannibalism was also a reality in Leningrad during World War II. The first case recorded in mid-November 1941 involved a woman "who strangled her one and a half month old daughter in order to feed three children." Soon the Leningrad NKVD were reporting to Zhdanov about both murders and the theft of corpses for the purpose of selling them under the guise of animal meat. On December 26 the NKVD reported the case of "V.F. Vorobyov, 18, unemployed, [who had] killed his grandmother Maksimova, 68, with an axe. He chopped the body into pieces, liver and lungs, boiled and ate them. Body parts were found during a search of the apartment. Vorobyov testified that he had committed the murder out of hunger. An expert assessment found that Vorobyov was sane."[53] In all about two thousand cases were recorded. At the height of the blockade, reports of cannibalism led to widespread panic. "Don't leave the child unattended," a nurse advised the mother of a sick child in one of the city's clinics. "We've had cases of children being kidnapped." One seven-year-old boy lured away by a strange woman promising "bread, sweets and other treats" as he waited for his aunt outside a bakery was res-cued just in time. The police arrested the stranger and once they established her motive, shot her on the spot. Sixty years after the blockade, blokadnik Natalia Velezhova told oral historian James Clapperton: "I had to do every-thing. Go out and collect water and so on. My mother was a large lady. She could not go out because those people that were engaged in cannibalism might spot her. . . . Yes, the blockade is about cold, hunger and darkness but the absolute worst thing about it was the cannibalism." People paid in bread to have their relatives buried deep so that cannibals could not get at their corpses.[54] The authorities created a special investigative unit consisting of detectives and, interestingly, psychiatrists. Between early December 1941 and mid-February 1942, 886 people were tried for unspecified crimes relat-ing to cannibalism; the number of cases declined thereafter, and none were reported in 1943 or 1944. In meting out punishment, the authorities dis-tinguished between those who sought to survive on the remains of those who predeceased them and those who murdered for human food: imprisonment or clemency for the former, summary execution for the latter.[55] Later, survivors claimed that no cannibals survived the war. As Clapperton learned from his informants, "The possibility that former cannibals could have survived the blockade was too disturbing a reality for these *blokadniki* to countenance."[56]

In 1946–47, cases of cannibalism were reported from Moldova and adjoining parts of Ukraine. The authorities were aware of the practice and sought to stamp it out. Soviet premier Nikita Khrushchev admitted as much in his memoirs, and Alexei Kosygin, future prime minister of the Soviet Union, was confronted with evidence of cannibalism on a visit from Moscow to investigate the famine in February 1947. On his tour of villages near Chisinau, he visited a house that contained a body ready for consumption. There were even stories of murder cannibalism, including one of a peasant woman who had killed two of her children and another of a peasant who killed a visiting grandson and ate him. Archival sources provide evidence of as many as 150 cases in Moldova.[57] And in the occupied East Prussian city of Königsberg (soon to be incorporated into the Soviet Union as Kaliningrad) in early 1946 were rumors that meat and meatballs for sale on the black market consisted of human flesh. There was also unsubstantiated talk that a butcher operating in the city's ruins lured victims to his shop where he killed them and processed their flesh for sale.[58]

During World War II, Japanese troops in remote areas of New Guinea and the Philippines sanctioned or engaged in cannibalism. Their victims were fellow soldiers, enemy soldiers, POWs, and the civilian population. For the most part, the cannibalism was confined to near the end of the war, after troops were not allowed to surrender and were cut off from food supply chains. The abandonment of Japanese forces in New Guinea by the Imperial Headquarters led to the death by starvation of thousands of soldiers.[59] Accounts of some of what ensued can be found in Japanese memoirs, in literary works such as Oaka Shohei's 1951 prize-winning novel *Fires on the Plain*, in Kazuo Hara's documentary *The Emperor's Naked Army Marches On*, and in the records of postwar military tribunals in Australia and the United States. Yuki Tanaka,[60] who has studied the evidence in detail, believes that such cannibalism "was extensive," part of an "organized process," and "a systematic and organised strategy," although again neither the aggregate number of victims, nor the civilian share, is known. Some of the victims of cannibalism in New Guinea were Indian troops who had refused to join the pro-Japanese Indian National Army after the fall of Singapore. They had been sent to concentration camps in New Guinea, where they were subjected to extreme ill-treatment. Several Indians testified to incidents of cannibalism after they were rescued.[61] Several of the perpetrators were found guilty by postwar tribunals and executed.

Ronaldo Esteban has carefully documented the case of Japanese troops in Bukidnon Province in northern Mindanao in the Philippines, where some resorted to cannibalism, and thirty-three survivors of a group of two hundred surrendered to Philippine police on February 16, 1947. Unable to plant food or to use their guns to hunt for fear of detection, they relied on an inadequate diet of "pumpkins, camotes [sweet potatoes], and other vegetables, and the meat of birds, cats, pigs, and rats." They also tried to pillage from local farmers, but over a year and a half, their total booty consisted of "a carabao [water buffalo], a horse, a pig, and two cats and kittens." Several died of starvation. Protein and salt deficiencies led to deaths from malaria and starvation. Cannibalism followed. In the words of their leader, Lieutenant Hajime Ainoda, a medical doctor, "Since it was extremely difficult to obtain animal meat such as pigs and cattle, etc., we began eating human flesh. It was not mere diversion which provoked this act; desperate necessity was the reason for this." The human flesh was that of Filipinos: a total of three adults and five children were killed in July–August 1945. Several others were killed thereafter, sometimes accompanied by torture and rape. There were also cases of consuming the remains of fellow soldiers and others. Seventeen ex-soldiers were eventually tried for war crimes, including murder and the "prevention of honorable burial." Ten were sentenced to execution by hanging in September 1949.[62]

Finally, the first to resort to cannibalism in the Nazi concentration camps of World War II were probably starving Soviet POWs.[63] Bergen-Belsen concentration camp was another grim theater of famine cannibalism in the weeks before its liberation by British troops in April 1945.[64] The only British survivor of Bergen-Belsen described in his claim for a disability allowance that toward the end "jungle law reigned among the prisoners; at night you killed or were killed; by day cannibalism was rampant." Prison doctors told of fleshless bodies with "the liver, kidneys, and heart . . . knifed out." And an Irish chaplain serving with the British troops who helped liberate Bergen-Belsen wrote in his diary: "Many of the bodies showed signs of cannibalism, with their livers removed."[65] Several survivors also referred later in oral testimonies to witnessing cannibalism in Mauthausen concentration camp in Upper Austria, in Kaufering (a subcamp of Dachau), in Nordhausen (a subcamp of Dora-Mittelbau concentration camp in Thuringia), in Camp

Pechora in Romania, in Stutthof near Danzig, and elsewhere.[66] No estimate of the number of victims is available, however.

Femmes á Boches, Tyskerpiger, and Moffenmeiden

This discussion ends with a few paragraphs on a much milder form of war-related violence: the punishment of women targeted in 1918 in France and Belgium, and more generally in occupied Europe in 1944–45, for befriending or for sleeping with the enemy. In northern France during World War I were criticisms of *femmes à boches* (women who consorted with German troops), with assessments ranging from "relations between Frenchwomen and German men and actually were very limited" to claims that they were ubiquitous. An example of the latter is the charge by a policeman from Comines in the Nord département that eight in ten women in the locality had been socializing with Germans before British bombardment forced the civilian population to leave in 1917. They included middle-class women who had fewer excuses than those who could use their precarious economic situation as an excuse. It was said, too, that returning French soldiers felt anger and betrayal, both as men and as soldiers.[67]

Again, reliable hard numbers are lacking. One way of addressing the issue is through estimates of the number of children with German fathers born during or soon after the war. In 1925 French historian Georges Gromaire extrapolated from some local data to argue that about ten thousand Frenchwomen had given birth to children fathered by Germans. More recently, Emmanuel Debruyne has inferred a minimum of 6,000 such births in Belgium and between 10,000 and 20,000 in France during World War I. Of course, those numbers do not distinguish between children born to prostitutes and those born of relationships, casual or other, between local women and German soldiers. In the case of Belgium, 6,000 would represent only 1.5 percent of the 0.4 million or so conceptions occurring during the occupation. In the case of the areas of France occupied by Germany, however, a birth rate of 12 per 1,000 over four years is consistent, with German fathers responsible for a much higher proportion—one-tenth or more—of all births. But these are just very fallible guesses for others to disprove or improve on.[68]

After World War I, the authorities interned hundreds of "bad French-women," mostly prostitutes, on suspicion of spying, but there was little of the savage popular outrage that followed liberation in 1944.[69] In 1944–45 an estimated twenty thousand Frenchwomen had their heads shaved in public in what came to be known as *La Grande Tonte* (the Great Mowing), part punishment for "horizontal" or other forms of collaboration with German troops. Such women would have represented only a minority of those guilty of consorting with the enemy since estimates of the number of *enfants blonds* or *enfants de Boches* fathered by German soldiers range from "several tens of thousands" to two hundred thousand; although really, no definitive figure is possible. The figure of eighty thousand quoted by Grieg would imply that about 3 percent of all French wartime births were in this category The images reproduced in figure 9.5 show a Frenchwoman in the département of Drôme having her hair shaven for befriending the enemy and three Dutch young collaborators, the girls with heads shaven, being marched through the streets of the city of Deventer.[70]

Many decades later, the behavior and treatment of the women who befriended or consorted with German troops remains controversial. That is in part because of the relativization issues addressed above; in part because they are a reminder of broader questions about collaboration in wartime France; and in part because of the ensuing stigma extended to the children of such unions. The women, though hardly their children, belong in a small corner of Primo Levi's "grey zone." In the words of French foreign minister Bernard Kitchner in 2008:

> I am talking about those war children known in France by that awful name *enfants de Boches*. . . . Rejects of damned mothers and forgotten fathers, these children, now adults, ask us six decades later to be recognised for their worth, their life, above all their identity. . . . This identity, a product of war and suffering, or loves and hates, is also the identity of Europe.[71]

In Norway an officially funded research project revealed that 10,000 to 12,000 children were born of unions between local women and German soldiers, about half of them in special *Lebensborn* (fountain of life) homes for "racially valuable children." Norway had nine such homes. Given that the population of Norway was about 4 million at the time and the birth rate 17 per 1,000, "10,000 to 12,000" (if correct) is a nonnegligible number: 5 to 6 percent of all 0.2 million or so births during the five-year occupation. Analysis of the data generated by the research suggested that the children suffered from "poorer health, higher suicide rates, less education and income than other Norwegians from the same age cohort."[72] Such children and their mothers were ostracized after the war, and some of the women were consigned to internment camps or deported to Germany with their children. Seventy years later, attitudes had softened. In 2018, Norway's prime minister

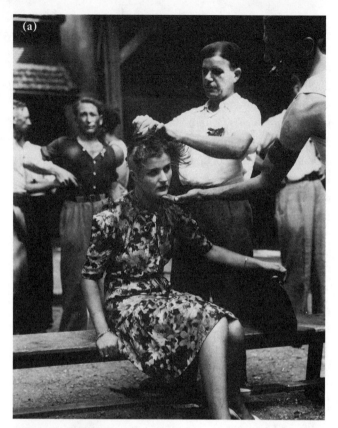

FIGURE 9.5. *Femmes à boches, moffenmeiden, tyskerpiger*
a. Woman having her head shaved, Montelimar, France, August 29, 1944
b. Collaborators and shaven *moffenmeiden*, Deventer, the Netherlands, April 11, 1945 (*Source:* Willem van de Poll, CC BY-SA 3.0 NL <https://creativecommons.org /licenses/by-sa/3.0/nl/deed.en>, via Wikimedia Commons)

apologized for the treatment the mothers and their children had received, and startlingly, a historian representing the Centre for Holocaust and Minorities Studies denied that "women who had personal relations with German soldiers were helping the German war effort." Their crime, he claimed, was "breaking unwritten rules and moral standards."[73]

In Denmark, too, also occupied between 1940 and 1945, the German authorities encouraged liaisons between troops and local women presumed to be "of good blood." Such liaisons resulted in nearly six thousand children born during or just after the war being registered as having a German father, but "the real total is far higher—probably 10,000," implying a proportion of total wartime births comparable to Norway's. Anette Warring has interpreted the lower estimate of children fathered by a German soldier in Denmark as suggesting that at least fifty thousand Danish women had liaisons with soldiers. If true, that would represent a sizeable 8 percent of all Danish women aged fifteen to thirty-four in 1940. Warring's study of the girls and women, known as *tyskerpiger* or *tyskertøser* (Germans' girls), describes them as a "complex group" in sociological terms but with a considerable overrepresentation of "socially badly situated young women out of the direct control of the family"—perhaps not what the Nazi proponents of *Lebensborn* had in mind. Warring finds that although few of the *tyskerpiger* were active collaborationists, nevertheless their behavior signaled an acceptance of the occupation and thus constituted a form of collaboration. The tyskerpiger were widely reviled and harshly treated after liberation.[74]

In the Netherlands and in Belgian Flanders, the occupiers also encouraged relations between soldiers and Dutchwomen. It is reckoned that 130,000–150,000 Dutchwomen had affairs with German troops and that 12,000–15,000 children were conceived of such relationships during the war.[75] Again, 130,000–150,000, if even roughly accurate, would have represented a nonnegligible share of all 1.8 million Dutchwomen aged fifteen to thirty-nine years in 1940. In the Low Countries, the women involved in "sentimental collaboration" were likely to be younger and from a working-class background. But not all fitted that stereotype; women accused of unacceptable behavior included mature and divorced women and widows. *Moffenmeiden* (Krauts' girls) suspected of liaisons with German troops were humiliated or worse in the wake of liberation.[76] A high number of births involving German fathers relative to all births—20,000–40,000 of about 0.6 million—has been cited for Belgium, but, again, hard data are lacking.[77]

Civilian Internees

Another group of civilians mistreated during the two wars should not be forgotten. At the outbreak of hostilities in both 1914 and 1939, fear and panic led to the widespread practice of interning "enemy aliens" as a security threat. The United Kingdom passed the Aliens Restriction Act, demanding that all foreign nationals register with the police, just a day after the start of World War I. Initially, enemy aliens were merely subjected to a range of restrictions, such as not being allowed to own maps and carrier pigeons or live in specified high-security areas. In 1915 growing anti-German feeling forced the authorities' hand, however, and most foreign enemy nationals were interned. Canada interned 9,000 German, Habsburg, and Ottoman subjects during World War I, while the United States arrested thousands of Germans and interned over 2,000—a small proportion of the 250,000 German nationals in the United States at the time—for the duration of the war. France created about fifty internment camps for foreign enemy nationals, all located in remote locations far from the front, such as l'île d'Yeu off the Vendée coast, which held several hundred German and Austrian internees. In the West, civilians interned by Germany fared the worst: Germany initially interned large numbers of Belgian and French civilians and later transported thousands of them to Germany as forced laborers. According to ICRC estimates, about 100,000 Belgian and French internees were deported in this fashion. One of the most notorious internment camps was Thalerhof in Graz, then a city in the Habsburg Empire. The authorities interned up to 10,000 civilian males deemed Russophiles in Thalerhof, where they were brutally mistreated; about 2,000 died there before it was closed in 1917. It is believed that internees in Russia accounted for half of the total of up to 400,000 in internment camps during World War I.[78]

Of about 80,000 Germans and Austrians in Britain at the outbreak of World War II, a small number (about 600) were immediately interned as security risks, and 6,500 were subject to restrictions and surveillance. The remainder, mostly Jewish refugees, were unaffected. As the "phony war" phase came to an end in early 1940, fears of fifth columnists and a German invasion rose. At the end of April 1940, the social researchers of Mass-Observation found that "it is becoming the socially done thing to be anti-refugee." Security became much tighter, and thousands of Germans, Italians and Austrians, including many German Jewish refugees, were interned in improvised camps. Overcrowding led to over 7,000 of these being deported to Canada and Australia during the summer of 1940. In one highly publicized tragedy, over 700 of those bound for Canada on the SS *Arandora Star*, a passenger liner, perished when it was torpedoed in July 1940. That led to complaints in Parliament at the treatment of innocent internees, and by December 1940 about 8,000 internees had been let go, leaving 19,000 still in camps in Britain, Canada, and Australia. Most of those were freed by 1942, when about 5,000 remained, mainly in camps on the Isle of Man. Meanwhile, in the United States the authorities interned over 110,000 Japanese Americans and several thousands more of German birth or ancestry in "relocation centers" for the duration of the war. In the Far East, the Japanese interned 130,000 enemy aliens, a majority of whom were Dutch nationals living in the Netherlands East Indies. Over 1 in 10 died in captivity, mainly of disease and malnutrition. The Germans interned 2,000 civilians from the Channel Islands in Germany in 1942, while on the Continent they interned Allied civilians in internment camps (*Internierungslager*) in the areas they occupied. In Australia, soon after the outbreak of World War II about 5,000 Italian residents were interned as enemy aliens.[79]

10

Panic and Morale, Trauma and Resilience

We can count the deaths and devastated buildings in Ukraine, but Putin's bombs rain down emotional terror too.
—OLHA ZAIARNA, *THE GUARDIAN*, JUNE 26, 2023

War wounds are not just physical. Over the last century or so, researchers have increasingly focused on the impact of wars on the mental health of those involved in them, first on combatants and later on both combatants and civilians. During the two world wars, all sides tried to control the effect of bad news at home through censorship and to strike fear and despair into enemy civilians through propaganda or, more directly, by cutting off food supplies and employing the new strategy of aerial bombing. The objective was to hasten victory by boosting morale at home and by breaking the will of civilians abroad to resist. A related concern is the potential result of extreme violence on the mental health of victims in the longer run. Wars are not over when they are over. Survivors of the Holocaust are an important case in point. So are victims of sexual assault in wartime. These issues are the subject of the present chapter.

Panic and Morale

During World War I, the impact of heavy artillery bombardment on the mental health of soldiers on the Western Front was obvious from the beginning. The term *shell shock*, apparently first used in print in January 1915,[1] quickly became the catchall term for symptoms affecting combatants. As medical practitioners diagnosed patients and struggled to find cures, military commanders fretted about malingerers and were anxious to get men back into the trenches as quickly as possible.[2]

The mental health of civilians was not a concern in 1914–18, but their morale was, although to a much lesser extent than during World War II. Thanks mainly to the parts played by the aerial bombing of heavily populated urban areas, the state of civilian morale was an abiding preoccupation during World War II. Aerial bombing counted for little during World War I, but it still unsettled civilians, as did malnutrition by blockade in some places. In public the authorities everywhere claimed that morale on the home front was high; in private, they worried about it and sought ways to monitor and improve it.[3] They did so directly by controlling the press and censoring private correspondence, by using all available means of propaganda (film, music, radio, drama, and so on), by surveying and spying on public opinion and behavior, by punishing those suspected or accused of reducing morale and rewarding those capable of raising it, and by seeking to protect those at risk by minimizing hunger and homelessness. But morale is a woolly concept, distinct from mental health and trauma, harder to define and measure than to recognize. During World War I, low or declining morale might express itself through anger and resentment: examples included women protesting against food shortages (as in Berlin in 1916–18) and men striking for higher wages (as in Paris in May 1918 and Germany in January 1918) or betraying an increasing reluctance to enlist (as in Ireland from 1917 on). Sometimes it expressed itself through fear and panic, and sometimes it led to war-weariness as the fighting continued despite increasing privation and massive carnage.[4] For the authorities, low civilian morale compromised the war effort. For civilians, the hurt and the anxiety associated with low morale imposed an added psychic cost—and all the more so during long wars like World War I and World War II.

As described in chapter 6, aerial warfare did not count for much during World War I. Still, how civilians reacted to aerial attacks and the prospect of them was a concern from early on. In England, once Zeppelin dirigibles began their sporadic attacks in early 1915, the official line was that German bombs "appear to cause wonderfully little panic at the moment of murder, and no permanent panic afterwards. Their effect is, not a demand for peace, but a demand of the whole nation to help in the war."[5] According to a report in the *Weekly Dispatch* in October 1916 on the lack of accounts of "hysterical women," "there are no such descriptions because there were no such women. The most extraordinary feature of each of the recent raids has been the calm with which they were faced by women and children."[6] But scenes in London of tens of thousands of people rushing for shelter in underground subways as soon as darkness set in, "whether raids were made or not," blocking passages, and ignoring the pleas of railway officials, did not inspire confidence. Therefore, "it was arranged that the Prime Minister should see the editors of the leading newspapers and ask them to cease to publish descriptive accounts and pictures of air-raid destruction." It was feared, too, that the nightly treks to safer spaces would lead to significant losses of output in munitions factories and elsewhere.[7] Not just in London, but everywhere bombs were dropped, there was anger at the inadequate warnings of raids, at the lack of shelter, and at the ineffectiveness of antiaircraft defenses. Production was interrupted and men and equipment were diverted to counter the attacks. In France, too, media reports of "perfect calm" contrasted with police intelligence describing "mass exoduses" and the "nervousness of the masses."[8] However, nowhere was there a formal attempt at analyzing or measuring morale during World War I.

What civilians feared is what the Italian strategist Giulio Douhet banked on as a means of winning wars. For Douhet, targeting ordinary people specifically by means of bombs, incendiary devices, and poisonous gases could largely replace relying on traditional armies, and in addition, it could shorten the duration of wars:[9]

> No longer can there be places where life can continue in complete safety and relative tranquility, nor can the battlefield be confined to the combatants. It will be limited only by the borders of the countries at war: everyone becomes a combatant because everyone is subject to direct attack by the enemy; there can no longer be a division between combatants and non-combatants. . . . Just imagine the reaction of the civilian population of inhabited centers, when the news spread that the centers targeted by the enemy were completely destroyed, leaving no escape for anyone.[10]

Douhet (1869–1930) had first made the case for aerial bombing over Libya in 1911 after Italy declared war on the Ottoman Empire. This was the first time airplanes were involved in warfare, and the experience led

Douhet to argue for aerial bombing as the primary use of aircraft in war. During World War I, his loud entreaties in favor of aerial bombing against the Austrians were ignored, and indeed, he was sentenced to a year in jail for insubordination. Returning to duty in the wake of the disastrous defeat of Caporetto, he served briefly as head of the Italian General Aviation Director-ate before retiring from the army at the end of the war. In 1921 he wrote *Il dominio dell'aria* (*The Command of the Air*), in which he made the case for the potential impact of airpower on enemy morale. Douhet, for whom morale was everything, claimed that the outcome of World War I had turned, not on the military defeat of Germany but on the war-weariness of its civilians, and the next war would be won by the side using its "command of the air" to destroy civilian morale. In a posthumously published study, *The War of—*, he described a future war between Germany and a French-led alliance, in which the powerful German air force, despite suffering significant losses, forces the enemy into surrendering after just two days. The victory is due to the collapse in civilian morale caused by indiscriminate bombing.[11]

The destructive power of war from above expanded by leaps and bounds in the interwar era. Before World War II, predictions of panic and hysteria in the wake of aerial bombing were widespread, and during the war civilian morale would be a key preoccupation. By the 1920s there were proponents of aerial bombing other than Douhet, such as Sir Hugh Trenchard in Britain and Brigadier General Billy Mitchell in the United States, who highlighted the impact of attacks, or even the threat of an attack, on civilian morale. Some invoked the reaction of civilians to zeppelins and Gotha raids during World War I in their support. For British prime minister Stanley Baldwin, the sense that "the bomber will always get through" meant that in future wars "the only defence is in offence, which means that you have got to kill more women and children more quickly than the enemy if you want to save yourselves."[12]

The emotional stress on civilians during World War II was far greater than during World War I. In Britain, where images of the aerial damage from Guernica and China were still fresh in people's minds, the fear of aerial bombardment by Germany was widespread from the start. This was reflected in a strange and unusual outcome in London: the slaughter of hundreds of thousands of domestic cats and dogs during the first week or so of the war. Just before the outbreak of hostilities, the National Air Raid Precautions Committee had issued a pamphlet warning that pets would not be allowed into air-raid shelters and advising owners to move their cats and dogs to the countryside. Failing that, it suggested that it would be "really kindest to have them destroyed." The pamphlet contained an advertisement for a stun gun for humane killing. The first sirens—a false alarm, as it turned out—resulted in the mass panic of pet owners seeking to have their animals destroyed. Cats and dogs were abandoned in the corridors of veterinary practices or released to roam the streets in the thousands. In all about 0.4 million pets were put down in London alone in the first week of the war.[13]

A start at gauging civilian morale in the United Kingdom during World War II was made by the survey organization Mass-Observation (M-O), founded in 1937 by a trio of left-leaning intellectuals to study public opinion in working-class urban England.[14] M-O was contracted by the Ministry of Information in late 1940 to report on the impact of the Blitz on civilian morale. In its research M-O combined evidence gathered from casual observation and diaries with more systematic inquiries by trained surveyors. Its research was criticized for sometimes failing to transcend pub-talk stereotypes of plucky northerners and dour southerners, as in "Southampton has deeper social roots than Coventry or Stepney. There is a certain tradition of local toughness, partly associated with the docks and the sea." However, many of its findings were plausible, such as that the impact of the bombing of city centers on collective morale was severe and that institutions such as the public house, the music hall, and community networks were helpful in raising morale. One survey of a pub in Plymouth found that "the talk of raids decreased from 80 percent to 40 percent as more alcohol was consumed"![15]

Although the overall tenor of M-O's confidential findings was positive, their account of the effect of raids on a series of cities in December 1940 and January 1941 gave cause for official concern. Nina Masel, who worked in London's East End for M-O, did not share the positive spin sought by the home office. A week into the Blitz, she recorded from Stepney:[16]

> Continual alarms are playing on people's nerves. Everyone is listening for warnings and guns. Faces this morning are grim and tired. There is a lot of talk about casualties: How many? Anyone I know? There is also bewilderment and a kind of hopelessness about shelters. "What are we going to do? They've admitted that they won't always sound the siren—have we got to sit in our shelters all day, waiting for it?" This is the general feeling, particularly because several people in Cephas Avenue are said to have been killed because they were walking about when the bomb dropped. The warning hadn't gone then. Lack of confidence in shelters growing fast.
>
> "All we do is eat, sleep, and go to the shelters" (25-year old woman)

"It doesn't feel real to me," said one woman, "it's like some sort of vague dream that you can't realise is on somehow."

This is a pretty general feeling—one which I also share. No one is talking about anything except the bombing. There is a strong demand for Berlin bombing, and a very deep personal hatred of Hitler, which is spreading to the German people as a whole.

Chronic cases of psychiatric breakdown may have been rare during the Blitz, but there was plenty of evidence of "the terrors and miseries of ordinary people under the bombs and the depressing failure of the authorities to rise to the (admittedly enormous) human problems that followed the raids."[17] M-O reports contained references to "open signs of hysteria, terror, neurosis" (Coventry), "low morale" (Bristol), and "considerable private opinion of real depression and despair" (Manchester).[18] The strain and disorientation were particularly tough on older adults.

A common reaction to the Blitz was the "new air-raid problem" of masses of people trekking from at-risk areas to outlying villages and the countryside. The following contemporary account from "the port of A . . . a legitimate enough target" describes:[19]

By July a matter-of-fact nightly routine had been established, workable at least so long as mild weather and long evenings continued. A census taken by the Bus Company gave at that time a nightly total migration of 15,000, of whom no more than a third travelled by rail, the remainder by bus, private car, cycle or on foot. The procession began as early as 4 P.M., long queues forming without pause till the last bus left at 8.30 P.M., but until well on to midnight, cars, cyclists and walkers continued their northward trend, together with many commercial vans dispersing to safety outside the city, bearing the drivers' families and friends with the owners' full approval. . . . [The] trekkers from A. represented a true cross-section of the community. . . . An incredibly early return to the city was universal and by 6 A.M. most of the huge fleet of double-deckers had roared their way up the long hill and returned, loaded to capacity.

Chaotic mass evacuation from an ill-prepared Belfast (not surveyed by M-O) in the wake of intense bombing in April–May 1941 was interpreted at the time as evidence of a collapse of morale, with some witnesses making invidious comparisons with reactions elsewhere. A visiting senior Presbyterian clergyman from Scotland sensed that "the reaction . . . was braver in Scotland," and local friends confessed to him that "they did not think Ulster had stood up well to the ordeal," while a government minister conceded that "blitz-quitters" were more numerous in proportion to population in Belfast than any other city in the United Kingdom.[20] In the same vein, an American working on secondment at the Short Brothers' aerospace factory in Belfast wrote home scathingly about the reaction of his fellow workers:

> You have heard how tough the Irish are—well all I can say is that the tough Irish must come from the South of Ireland because the boys up in Northern Ireland are a bunch of chicken shit yellow bastards—90% of them left everything and ran like hell. Short and Harland's the Aircraft factory that builds Sterling here had 300 Volunteer fire fighters in the plant, after the raid they were lucky to get 90 of them.[21]

While some of Belfast's better-off citizens left nightly by car and returned in the morning, thousands more engaged in what was known locally as "ditching"—trekking out to the suburbs and beyond for the duration of any likely attack. A critic of the government claimed in Parliament that "Catholics and Protestants were leaving the city together, were sleeping in the hedges together, and talking to each other and all saying the same thing—that the Government is no good,"[22] but in truth, the routes and destinations chosen by the ditchers were mainly defined by religion.

During April and May 1941, the attendance at the nightly confraternity prayers in Clonard monastery in west Belfast plummeted because "the whole city has been disorganised. . . . Nine-tenths of the people . . . go the country . . . and spend the night on the roads and fields." That proportion is a huge exaggeration, but the *Irish Times* reckoned in mid-May 1941 that "in one district 20,000 people were sleeping out at night." That a false air-raid alert in Belfast at 2 A.M. on June 23, 1941, could prompt an estimated thirty thousand people to flee the city by any means available must have compounded fears of the impact the Blitz was having on civilian morale. Even in the town of Enniskillen, although never bombed and 150 kilometers from Belfast, in early June 1941 people were still heading to the countryside nightly.[23]

The impact of a raid on August 24, 1940, on the English coastal town of Ramsgate in Kent (pop. thirty-five thousand), which had a strong collective memory of being bombed during World War I, was also disquieting. A disused network of underground tunnels had been prepared as a municipal shelter on the eve of World War II. When the town was hit, the number of casualties was modest, but thousands headed for the tunnels and some—up to a thousand people—lived/slept underground throughout the war. The fear that caused people to remain underground in unhealthy conditions in

Ramsgate and elsewhere concerned the authorities. It not only implied low morale and discomfort but also meant that people could not work.

Initial studies of the impact of aerial bombing on the mental health of civilians in Britain was reassuring.[24] To reassure the United States that Britain had not lost its resolve in the face of German air raids, in April 1941 the authorities sought advice from the Medical Research Council and on its suggestion sought reassurance from Aubrey Lewis, a noted psychiatrist. Lewis's brief was to provide a report on the incidence of neurosis "for propaganda's sake if for nothing else." Based on information and data culled from general practitioners' records and admissions to casualty and mental health units, Lewis's report, a version of which was published in the *Lancet* in 1942, was a mélange of the analytical and the discursive. If found no significant increase in psychiatric morbidity and concluded that most of those who broke down after bombing raids had a history of vulnerability to stress:

> From all of this it follows that a severe neurosis hardly occurs as a war phenomenon except in people who had been neurotic before the war; and that when neurosis develops or is aggravated during the war, war stress had not been responsible for this in a quarter of the previously healthy, and in a fifth of those with previous neurotic history.[25]

But Lewis tried too hard to produce the outcome the authorities wanted. In his hands the "boundaries between the social and the professional had vanished within a narrative of resistance, patriotism, and commitment to maintain the morale of the nation."[26] In another effort at eliciting reassuring results, in January 1942 the government commissioned biologist Solly Zuckerman and physicist J. D. Bernal to direct a systematic investigation of the impact of bombing on morale and output.[27] The project had its origin in earlier exchanges between Zuckerman and Churchill's chief scientific adviser Frederick Lindemann (made Lord Cherwell in 1941 and known as "the Prof" in official circles). But Lindemann's primary interest in the project was in the potential impact of Royal Air Force bombing on German civilian morale. Zuckerman later noted that

> we discussed the possibilities of finding a more objective basis for the strategy of a bomber offensive than was implied by the simple belief that Germany could be bombed into submission. The idea I put to him was that what was needed was a survey of the overall effects of bombing on some English cities. I suggested that we choose for study Hull and Birmingham, first because the Bomb Census had an almost complete tally

of the bombs that had fallen on them, and second because they could be regarded as typical of manufacturing and port towns. The Prof agreed the job was worth doing.[28]

In other words, the Bernal-Zuckerman study would serve two purposes: first, it would provide a sense of morale on the home front and, second, offer a guide to the likely success of area bombing German cities. Hull had attracted attention because of the large number of "trekkers" who left the city nightly during the Blitz for fear of raids. Finding that over half of their Hull sample of over seven hundred revealed no symptoms, while 20 percent of men and 53 percent of women showed signs of slight to moderate neuroses, Bernal and Zuckerman concluded that reports of low morale in Hull had been overdone. "Hull today looks like a badly blitzed town," they found, "but a visitor is not impressed by any peculiarities of the population." While some of the individual case reports prepared by the team's psychiatrists make for harrowing reading, that may have been a fair summary of the evidence insofar as collective morale was concerned and also the kind of finding sought by the ministry. In comparing the impact of bombing on the two cities, Bernal and Zuckerman found that Birmingham displayed "an inner buoyancy . . . while Hull was . . . torpid and apathetic." Still, what mattered is that there was no mass panic in Hull: even the "trekking," which had attracted the authorities' attention to the city, was a rational response to the inability of air defenses to protect them, not born of panic. One of the Hull schoolgirls described it very differently, however. Recalling that "we thought every minute was our last," she wrote: "I do know everyone was afraid to stop in the town at night. They used to run away anywhere to get away from the town of Hull, even if it was to sleep in an open field they were so frightened. I was one of those who went out to sleep."[29] Bernal and Zuckerman also initially intended to include the results of a survey of schoolchildren's experiences, and ten-to-fourteen-year-olds in fourteen schools in Hull and two in Birmingham participated, producing two thousand essays, but the resultant material was never processed.

Bernal and Zuckerman's main finding was that bombing would not lead to a collective collapse of morale. If anything, they tended to downplay the impact of aerial bombardment on the public: "There is no evidence of breakdown of morale from the intensities of the raids experienced by Hull or Birmingham." That was a reassuring result, and confirmation bias may have played a role in it. Yet Bernal and Zuckerman also intended the report to put to rest the idea of winning a war by bombing a country into a collective nervous breakdown. "We are not yet in a position," Zuckerman reported, "to state what intensity of raiding would result in the complete breakdown of the life and work of a town, but it is probably of the order of 5 times greater than any that has been experienced in this country up till now."[30]

Lindemann, however, effectively turned the report's findings upside down in order to underline the benefits of "area bombing" aimed at German civilians.[31] On March 30, 1942, before the Bernal-Zuckerman report was submitted, he twisted its message in his "dehousing memorandum" to Churchill:[32]

> Investigation seems to show that having one's house demolished is most damaging to morale. People seem to mind it more than having their friends or even relatives killed. At Hull, signs of strain were evident, though only one-tenth of the houses were demolished. On the above figures we should be able to do ten times as much harm to each of the 58 principal German towns. There seems to be little doubt that this would break the spirit of the people.

Zuckerman would seek to set the record straight in his memoirs, protesting that "although the Prof used the results of our study to claim that bomber raids of the intensity that Hull and Birmingham had experienced were most damaging to morale, this was the very reverse of what we had stated."[33]

State-sponsored research into civilian morale did not end there. Further analysis used measures including absenteeism and sickness from work, destruction of houses, content analysis of newspaper reports and population surveys.[34] The contrasts between the rather pessimistic reports from M-O during the Blitz, on the one hand, and Zuckerman and Bernal's more upbeat assessments in its wake, on the other, are clear. That the impact of the deaths of 60,595 civilians during the Blitz was not greater is perhaps what is surprising. One reason may be that the mortality rate remained relatively low given the size of the urban population and the length of the conflict. London's 29,890 deaths represented 0.3 percent of the capital's population. The highest death rates were in Plymouth and Coventry, where in both towns 0.5 percent of residents were killed.[35]

A number of psychiatrists argued that the health effects of the conflict might not be revealed until the return of peace. Indeed, Aubrey Lewis warned that the full effect of "war-related stress" might be delayed and that "the evil harvest may be reaped afterwards."[36] But Britain's stoic "stiff-upper-lip" culture and a desire not to appear defeatist may also have deterred people from reporting traumatic illness. A national survey of mental health services conducted in 1943 by psychiatrist and eugenicist C. P. Blacker found that many directors of psychiatric clinics believed that "latent neurosis" existed in the civilian population. Whether this developed into overt psychological or psychosomatic disorders after the war was dependent on "the social and economic conditions . . . and the moral atmosphere which prevailed."[37] The availability of employment and positive attitudes toward work were considered important mediators in helping people to manage the long-term effects of air raids.[38]

The impact of the aerial bombing on civilian morale continued to be disputed after the war. Official histories tended to argue for resilience—that Blitz spirit of "never say die"—while revisionist accounts pointed to trauma. Terence O'Brien's official history of civil defense during World War II, published in 1955, argued that there had been little panic; Richard Titmuss, who covered social policy, found that the health of the nation actually improved during wartime while allowing for the possibility that the "indignities of war [may] have left wounds which will take time to heal and infinite patience to understand." O'Brien noted that both the official and unofficial exodus of urban dwellers during the Blitz occurred without panic, though conceding that in 1944 the V2 rockets caused an increase in absenteeism and a reduction in working hours caused by "loss of sleep and anxiety."[39] Jones et al. reviewed the impact of bombing by looking at the evidence on hospital admissions for formal mental illness and concluded that civilians proved more resilient than either planners had predicted or revisionist historians would claim. One of the latter, historian and whistleblower Clive Ponting, maintained that the "Blitz spirit" owed more to government propaganda and a censored media than to reality. While conceding that the Allied bombing campaign failed to destroy German resistance, Richard Overy has also emphasized the impact of the Blitz in terms of physical and psychological damage.[40]

The issues raised by research into Hull and elsewhere during the war have also been discussed both by the victors in the wake of the war and by historians and commentators since.[41] In its appraisal of the impact of the bombing campaign in Europe, the U.S. Strategic Bombing Survey (USSBS) concluded that it had seriously reduced the morale of German civilians. Those bombed were more resigned to surrendering or less hopeful of victory than those not bombed. However, the survey also found that bombing, like most things, was subject to diminishing returns: the biggest contrasts were between unbombed towns and those only lightly bombed. It also stressed that reduced morale did not necessarily affect military capacity much:

despite all the assembled evidence of feelings of "defeatism, fear, hopeless-ness, fatalism, and apathy," the Nazi war effort had "kept up amazingly" until near the end.[42] A later study of interviews carried out by the USSBS in the city of Darmstadt, heavily bombed in 1944, broadly corroborates this, find-ing that while the destruction led to anguish, nervous collapse, and even despair at the individual level, it also, perhaps paradoxically, led people to support each other and "helped create the social bond that Nazi ideology had striven in vain to achieve."[43] A cautious reading of the evidence would sug-gest that while aerial bombing rarely achieved the kind of result Lindemann or Douhet anticipated, urban populations at risk nevertheless paid a price in terms of panic and anxiety and, for some, nervous collapse. But amid the claims and counterclaims, it would be foolhardy to attempt to estimate the resultant psychic cost with any great precision.

The literature on the aftershock of war on survivors, which we address next, is much more voluminous than that on the contemporaneous impact of aerial bombing on civilian morale and mental health. It is also more con-tentious. We focus first on the long-term impact of Holocaust survivors and then on that of aerial bombing, sexual violence, and displacement.

Trauma and Resilience

More than once, Italian Holocaust survivor Primo Levi credited fellow Piemontese Lorenzo Perrone (1904–1952) with saving his life in Aus-chwitz.[44] Perrone was in Auschwitz in 1944–45, not as an inmate like Levi but as a laborer at the Buna-Werke plant on the site. Little is known about the bricklayer from the town of Fossano beyond what Levi discloses. Levi's description of him as a sensitive man of few words—*un muradur di poche parole*—is echoed in the plaque in his memory in Fossano. In Auschwitz he had already helped a Pole and a Frenchman before coming to Levi's aid, bringing him food on a regular basis, recycling an old shirt, and sending messages to Italy on his behalf. Their last meeting in Auschwitz was in the wake of an Allied air raid that burst one of Perrone's eardrums. Back in Fos-sano after liberation, Perrone no longer worked as a bricklayer but made a precarious living as a dealer in *ferrivecchi*, or scrap metal. Sharing a home with five siblings and selling his scrap without an overcoat in midwinter, he developed a serious drinking problem and seemingly lost his will to live. Levi went to see him in Fossano, where they visited his local riverside tavern. On a later visit, Levi's entreaties were greeted coldly with "life isn't worth it, I drink because I prefer to be drunk than sober." Levi had him hospitalized in Savigliano, not far from Fossano; later he was found inebriated and in a dying state next to a canal. Lorenzo Perrone was buried in a common grave, "awaiting a new location."

In Levi's account Perrone was deeply traumatized by what he had seen and lived through; he was "not an Auschwitz survivor but . . . died as if he were." Perrone's story fits a Holocaust narrative whereby survivors were so scarred by their experiences that they never recovered. Yet he remains an enigma. Did his personality or the conditions he faced once back in Fossano, about which little is known, predispose him toward his sad end? How typical was Perrone? The impact of their experiences on the mental health of Holocaust survivors, refugees, survivors of air raids, and other abused and terrified civilians remains controversial. The topic is a fraught and delicate one. It is easy to believe that enduring the horrors of the Holocaust would leave a permanent scar on all survivors. Studies supporting such an outcome highlight survivors' syndrome, "depression, disturbances in cognition and memory, tendency to isolation, sense of guilt, low psychological well-being, and difficulties in emotional expression."[45] For Primo Levi there was no cure:

> The injury cannot be healed: it extends through time, and the Furies, in whose existence we are forced to believe, not only rack the tormentor (if they do rack him, assisted or not by human punishment), but perpetuate the tormentor's work by denying peace to the tormented.[46]

Both Levi and others have discussed the impact that his own experience in Auschwitz had on his life. Even the circumstances of his death in 1987 are disputed; the official verdict of suicide has been vehemently contested by several who knew him.[47] There is much in Levi's life after Auschwitz to support both the claim that he carried the trauma with him to the grave and the counterclaim that, while never forgetting what he suffered and what he witnessed, he found a way to cope and recover.

More generally, there are two competing views on Holocaust trauma. The first holds that the damage inflicted on victims was permanent and universal. In recent years, support for such an outcome has been extended to, or sometimes replaced by, the claim that the trauma is passed on to the next generation, as in "Many Holocaust Survivors Thrived—but Have Their Children Inherited the Trauma?"[48] The second view asserts that no matter how extreme the trauma in the aftermath of the Holocaust, survivors' innate resilience helped many, if not most, to live fulfilling lives in due course.

It is clear that there must be room for a range of outcomes. On the one hand, it is not implausible that victims like Lorenzo Perrone, a vulnerable "loner," were less likely to recover. On the other, it might matter that wartime trauma is, to some extent at least, shared and recognized as such, that its victims are mostly adults, and that the enemy is known and hated (in the sense of Prime Minister Winston Churchill's image of "a whole nation suffering and fighting together"). Such factors open up possibilities for help and compassion not readily available to sufferers from abuses that go unrecognized, such as domestic violence in adulthood or neglect and sexual abuse in childhood by trusted adults.

Trauma, Neuroses, and Depression

According to a character in one of the Irish playwright Brian Friel's *Translations*, "to remember everything is a form of madness." So is forgetting a cure? The answer is yes in the psychological subfield of autobiographical memory, where it is argued that the memories of healthy people are subject to *fading affect bias* (FAB), in the sense that their negative memories are more likely to recede than their positive ones.[49] Crucially, however, the problem is less one of forgetting traumatic or tragic events—one never forgets, in the literal sense, the death of a loved one or a debilitating accident—than preventing those events from constantly intruding and preying on one's mind and disrupting one's normal life.[50] From this perspective trauma does not cause amnesia; on the contrary, "forgetting" is a healthy and natural way of coping with potentially traumatic memories.[51] But the ability to forget is not universal, and surely it is undeniable that shocks and tragedies like those described in this book can have a long-lasting traumatic effect on the minority who lack it. The issue then becomes *which* survivors were traumatized and whether their experiences continued to traumatize them for the rest of their lives.

In recent decades an influential strand in the literature on the long-term impact of tragic events such as bereavement, debilitating illness, divorce, and unemployment on mental health claims that most people—though certainly not all—who are subjected to them recover from, or at least manage to cope with, the trauma. This is attributed to an inbuilt ability to recover from adversity. Much of the research has focused on how much is "most" and how long recovery takes. An important pioneering study in this vein is George Bonanno's influential *The Other Side of Sadness*. Bonanno's analysis of bereaved spouses found few signs of "shock, despair, anxiety, or intrusive thoughts (the hallmark symptoms of acute grief)" in half of his subjects after six months. As for the remainder, about 15 percent still showed significant signs of loneliness at six months that had virtually disappeared a year later. One in ten still faced serious difficulties over a longer period. The remaining quarter or so consisted of two groups. Half or so had suffered from depression before their partner died and the depression persisted. And, for a variety of reasons, the other half were happier in the wake of their partner's death. For Bonanno and like-minded psychologists, the most common outcome after potentially traumatic events is "a stable trajectory of healthy functioning or resilience."[52]

What has become known as the *resilience hypothesis* is controversial; in the present context an obvious concern is that it can be weaponized to minimize the impact of militarization and war.[53] One might raise questions, too, about what counts as "recovery" or "normal." Some seemingly resilient and successful people might simply be adept at concealing their true state. Yet the hypothesis has been tested against a variety of data on events ranging from terrorist acts and military combat to school shootings, divorce, and parental loss, with broadly similar outcomes. For example, losing a child is the worst tragedy that can befall a parent, yet a 2017 study in this tradition, using a rich Swedish database, finds that the average impact on parental health and well-being is dramatic in the year of the death and the following year but small and statistically indistinguishable from zero thereafter. Such findings are corroborated in a 2018 metastudy of research on trauma victims of "mass shootings, spinal cord injuries, things like that," which found that "two-thirds were found to be resilient [and] were able to function very well in a short period of time."[54]

For those who believe in psychological resilience, issues such as what proportion of people recover of their own accord and what innate characteristics and medical and other interventions speed the recovery continue to be debated. All agree that although reactions to a shock vary across subjects, a majority—again not all—recover rather quickly from acute grief and in time betray few or no symptoms at all. In this view, resilience is the default, not an anomaly. A key feature of the research is its focus on how and why resilience varies from person to person and the roles for personality and biology, demography (older males are more resilient, or at least they claim to be), and economics (education helps), as well as social networks.[55] Concentrating on the *average* impact of a traumatic shock ignores the variation across individuals in the size and duration of the shock. This rather undermines the familiar notion of collective trauma, equally shared by all, and makes it less likely that trauma is passed from one generation to the next.

The Holocaust: Trauma and Resilience

For survivors of the Jewish Holocaust, those Primo Levi dubbed *gli salvati* (the saved), being saved was far from a happy ending. They had not only endured and been traumatized by the unendurable but faced an uncertain and challenging future. Few wanted to return to the place from which they had come. The first choice of most was emigration, either to Palestine—part of which the United Nations (UN) recognized as Israel in 1949—or to the United States, but that was not easy before 1948 when the U.S. Displaced Persons Act precipitated a significant Jewish immigration to America (eighty thousand by 1952). That there was trauma in the wake of liberation is certain, but what of its impact in the longer run? In what follows we offer a glimpse of a large specialist literature on trauma among Holocaust survivors.

At the outset the consensus was that the psychic scars—the trauma—caused by the camps were widespread and long-lasting, and many still support that view.[56] A group of researchers led by the Israeli sociologist Aaron Antonovsky was among the first (in 1971) to point toward a different possibility: an ability of Holocaust survivors to adapt and recover. This influential study criticized an earlier literature that focused only on patients undergoing psychiatric care or lacked appropriate controls. Antonovsky's data consisted of 287 women aged forty-five to fifty-four years in an unidentified midsized Israeli city, 77 of whom had been in a death camp during World War II. While, on the whole, Antonovsky found "camp survivors to be more poorly-adjusted than the controls," he was really surprised that "a not-inconsiderable number of concentration camp survivors were found to be well-adapted." Antonovsky coined a term to describe this ability to adapt: *salutogenesis* (as distinct from pathogenesis). He offered three possible explanations for it: "An initial underlying strength, a subsequent environment which provided opportunities to re-establish a satisfying and meaningful existence, and a 'hardening' process which allows the survivor to view current stresses with some equanimity."[57] These insights, anticipating the resilience literature described above, have had broad resonance far beyond the field of Holocaust studies. In addition, in the case of the Holocaust there was selection: the very fact that one survived indicated some added inner strength and resilience.

Several subsequent studies of Holocaust survivors have gone further than Antonovsky, arguing that resilience was the rule rather than the exception. An early example compared an admittedly small number (fifty-two) of "concentration camp and other survivors of World War II" to a control group of twenty-nine others of similar backgrounds and then to forty-seven and sixteen children, respectively, from the two groups. It could find no psychological differences between the survivor and control groups at either the first- or second-generation level. This led the authors to reject "notions of survivor guilt, the manifestation of emotional blunting in the survivors, and the extremely maladaptive psychological influence of their parents' experiences on the children of survivors."[58]

An interview-based analysis in the 1990s of 133 Holocaust survivors—two-thirds of them women—found that the overwhelming majority were resilient and had lived long and productive lives.[59] Those who suffered life-long trauma were very exceptional. According to lead author Roberta Green, "there is growing evidence that, regardless of their great loss, survivors and their families show remarkable resilience."

William Helmreich's study of Holocaust survivors similarly found that the traits that enabled victims to survive their experience, like adaptability, initiative, and tenacity, may also account for their later success. He attributed the contrast between his finding that most survivors adapted successfully and previous research that claimed the opposite to selection: that earlier research, he argued, suffered from selection bias by relying too much on "the more troubled among the survivors of the Holocaust." His subjects were more likely to remain married (83 versus 62 percent) and to be successful and less likely to engage in crime than Jews of the same age who had arrived in the United States before World War II. They were also far less likely to have consulted a psychiatrist than comparable American Jews (18 and 31 percent, respectively), and Helmreich notes that this finding raises a question about studies based on those who had undergone therapy. Finally, Helmreich noted that the more successful survivors were better able to distance themselves from their past, an example of the FAB described above.[60]

Many more studies have been conducted in the same vein. For example, two studies that compare Holocaust survivors with their older Israeli and Canadian neighbors find that suicide rates among Holocaust survivors were lower than among reference groups and also link the finding to resilience.[61] Another study of older Holocaust survivors and other older Canadians and Israelis found that Holocaust survivors, instead of "compartmentalizing bitter memories" of the past, "integrat[e] those memories as part of a coherent life narrative."[62] As such, survivors "are not victims of the past, but symbols of endurance and survival." Such survivors attain levels of life satisfaction on a par with the rest of the population. Indeed, another group of researchers, using the same database, go further, arguing that "it may be that [Holocaust survivors] report high life satisfaction not despite, but because of, experiencing early life trauma, juxtaposing early years with the comparatively good conditions of their lives today."[63]

A limitation of the above studies is the small size of their samples or databases. However, a 2010 meta-analysis by a team of Israeli scholars compared 71 samples with 12,746 Holocaust survivors to elucidate "the long-term psychiatric, psychosocial, and physical consequences of the Holocaust for survivors."[64] The survivors were compared to sample groups with no Holocaust background "on physical health, psychological well-being, posttraumatic stress symptoms, psychopathological symptomatology, cognitive functioning, and stress-related physiology." The study found that although Holocaust survivors "showed substantially more posttraumatic stress symptoms," they "did not lag . . . much behind their comparisons in several other domains of functioning (i.e., physical health, stress-related physical measures, and cognitive functioning) and showed remarkable resilience."

A second Israeli study by Haim Knobler et al. offers a seven-decadal perspective on the evolving literature on Holocaust survivors. It notes the sharp shift in the specialist literature from an early emphasis on persistent survivor trauma to "the underscoring of their resilience including new findings of their surprising longevity and the low rate of their current post-traumatic symptomatology." The shift may reflect changes over time in the condition of survivors. Whereas it is not surprising to find that at the outset practitioners who treated survivors found them post-traumatic, perhaps it is not so surprising either that later researchers would discover the survivors served "as a model for post traumatic growth, resilience, and an inspiration for Antonovsky's salutogenic theory." Finally, this study notes that recent data reveal that Holocaust survivors live longer than others and have fewer post-traumatic symptoms.[65]

Second-Generation Trauma?

Although the Canadian clinical psychiatrist Vivian Rakoff seems to have been one of the first to claim in print, in 1966, that Holocaust trauma could be transferred to the children of survivors, the so-called second generation, this view had already been widely shared by psychoanalysts and other therapists since the 1950s.[66] By 2001 the number of publications on the transgenerational transmission of Holocaust trauma had already reached almost four hundred.[67] On the whole, however, meta-analytic studies have found little evidence of such transmission.

A 1998 survey of "a rich body of empirical literature" focused on "psychopathological symptoms, personality traits, cognitive and defensive styles, and family interactions and communication patterns" and concluded that "on the whole, no evidence was obtained for psychopathology." A 2001 analysis of thirty-five comparative studies found that "this extensive research indicates rather conclusively that the non-clinical population of children of Holocaust survivors does not show signs of more psychopathology than others do." In the psychopathological sense, the second generation performed well, and the research implies that differences between the mental state of offspring of survivors and others are "small." These rather striking findings were corroborated in meta-studies by van IJzendoorn et al., who analyzed thirty-two "adequately designed clinical studies" with over four thousand participants and found no evidence to support the hypothesis of transgenerational traumatization in Holocaust survivor families: "Secondary traumatization emerged only in studies on clinical participants, who were stressed for other reasons." The failure of academic researchers to find any significant differences between the second generation and comparable groups clashed with reports from psychotherapists of the persistence of distress. Inferences from a population of patients are subject to clear selection bias: such patients sought help precisely because they had "a predisposition to PTSD, various difficulties in separation-individuation and a contradictory mix of resilience and vulnerability when coping with stress."[68]

This continues to be a very fraught subject. The tension between findings based on clinical case studies that linked the explanation for patients' psychopathology and maladjustment exclusively to a parent's exposure to the Holocaust and findings reliant instead on studies of Holocaust survivors in general, which found that most of them "were able to recover their ego capacities, integrate their traumas, and function well," has not abated. In a recent article, psychoanalyst-cum-sociologist Robin Gomolin claims that the case study approach described subjects who "were imprisoned within the perceptions and beliefs of the clinicians who were treating them" and accused clinicians of a reductionism that always related symptoms to "the Nazi aggressor."[69] Gomolin's skepticism led to her surmise that second-generation trauma is merely a way of memorializing the Holocaust "by creating a theoretical framework in which the trauma lives on in collective memory for future generations" and to a backlash of indignant counterclaims.[70] In the context of Holocaust suffering, this "war" between different schools of thought about trauma is a minefield. It should not distract us from the demonic horrors of the Holocaust.

Aerial Bombing: Dresden, Hiroshima, and Nagasaki

For several decades after World War II, researching the impact of air raids on survivors in Germany was constrained by legitimate concerns about moral equivalence. Perhaps as a result, the literature on the ethics of such research dwarfed research on the issue itself. One early, small-sample ($N = 47$) study of the impact of the bombing of Dresden found that although its subjects had vivid recollections of February 13, 1945, they betrayed "a relatively low level of PTSD symptomatology." Another much more ambitious study ($N = 33,534$) analyzing the link between strategic bombing in eighty-nine German cities and the mental health of survivors found that those living in the more heavily bombed cities were less prone to depression and other mental illnesses, an outcome unaffected by the addition of controls for a variety of economic factors and social structures. This rather puzzling finding was interpreted as evidence that the stress related to bombing made communities more resilient in the long run.[71] The outcome of more recent work, relying on a shrinking population of survivors, is mixed. For example, a 2022 study of the delayed impact of Allied bombing links its intensity to the mental status of Germans between their late fifties and their seventies and finds that the mental health of those born during or immediately before the war was significantly affected.[72] Given the shrinking pool of survivors, whether such contradictory outcomes can be reconciled at this point is moot.

Research on both the short- and long-term impact on survivors in Japan is much more plentiful. One of the earliest studies, John Hersey's long essay "Hiroshima," created a sensation when it appeared in the *New Yorker* in July 1946. Republished as a short monograph within two months, it has never been out of print since. Hersey's essay began an unending debate about the morality of weapons of mass destruction. It brought their impact home to American readers through the experiences of six survivors as recollected less than a year after the event. The bomb made a cripple of twenty-year-old Toshiko Sasaki, who had worked as a clerk, and an invalid of Wilhelm Kleinsorge, a thirty-eight-year-old Jesuit missionary. War widow Hatsuya Nakamura was left penniless, and physician Masakazu Fujii lost his private hospital, and neither Terufumi Sasaki, another medic, nor Kiyoshi Tanimoto, a Methodist clergyman, had recovered their strength when Hersey met them.

Nearly four decades later, Hersey returned to Hiroshima to see how his six subjects had coped, and he published his impressions in the *New Yorker* in July 1985. To what extent had the six managed to lead full lives? Hersey found that Toshiko Sasaki had become a nun and been put in charge of a retirement home. In 1978 she had been presented with a trip to the Vatican as a retirement gift. Kleinsorge, the Jesuit priest, had died in 1977; although he had suffered from radiation sickness for the rest of his life, he had become a parish priest and a Japanese citizen. For many years life had been extremely hard for widow Nakamura and her children, but eventually she had found her way; later she was made a member of the Bereaved Family Association and traveled the world as a witness. Fujii, an extrovert bon viveur, had successfully rebuilt his medical practice; he died of cancer in 1973. Dr. Sasaki, the most traumatized of the six interviewees, had sought to cope by also setting up his own medical practice and, in Hersey's words, "liv[ing] enclosed in the present tense." Tanimoto, a fluent English speaker, continued to preach in Japan and to go on speaking tours abroad.

Although "Hiroshima" has been widely studied in academia since, Hersey had no academic pretensions. His choice of interviewees was informal and his narrative, while utterly compelling, was impressionistic rather than analytical. One of the first non-Japanese scholarly analyses of the longer-term impact of bombing on civilian survivors to be published outside Japan, Irving Janis's *Air War and Emotional Stress: Psychological Studies of Bombing and Civilian Defense* appeared in 1951. It had been commissioned by the RAND corporation for the U.S. Air Force, and its message that aerial bombing did not result in lasting chronic psychological damage was presumably what the U.S. Air Force wanted to hear. However, as an analysis of the psychological impact of the atomic bomb (A-bomb) on its victims in Hiroshima, *Air War and Emotional Stress* was hardly compelling. Janis did not conduct any fieldwork; instead he based his analysis on interviews with civilians conducted in the immediate wake of the Japanese surrender by the USSBS. While not dismissing "the more transient symptoms of emotional shock," he claimed that a mere three months after the bombing most uninjured survivors were focused on the economic challenges that faced them and how to overcome them. The proportion of uninjured Hiroshima interviewees who said they were worse off than before the war barely exceeded that of all Japanese civilians.[73] But the evidence underpinning Janis's report precluded any analysis of longer-lasting trauma.

The next well-known study in English of the impact of the A-bomb on survivors, Robert Jay Lifton's *Death in Life: Survivors of Hiroshima* (1967), while enormously important, might also not, like Janis's, pass muster as rigorous analysis today. Unlike Janis, Lifton conducted his own casework; *Death in Life* is based on in-depth interviews with seventy-five Hiroshima *hibakusha* (A-bomb survivors). And in direct contradiction of Janis, it highlighted the persistence of the "raw pain of that experience" through feelings of survivor guilt, low self-esteem, and recurrent anxieties about the impact of radiation on one's physical health and that of one's children. Only through "psychic numbing" about deaths they have witnessed could survivors live ordinary lives. Such numbing may be seen as a costly coping mechanism because it involves a "cessation of feeling." Still, Lifton found that survivors often had the resilience "to recover from their ordeal and reclaim their lives."[74] The evidence in *Death in Life* is compelling and influential; what it lacks is any formal content analysis of that evidence, in terms of the proportion of interviewees who were traumatized and how the impact of bombing varied across victims.

In Japan itself, while studies of the long-term impact of the bomb on morbidity and life expectancy have been plentiful, studies of its psychological impact are fewer. The very first, a study of fifty randomly selected inpatients in Nagasaki, reported two suffering from neurosis and one from depression three months after the event. A 1956 study of over seven thousand victims found symptoms of neurosis in 7.3 percent, with those suffering from radiation sickness much more likely to display neurotic symptoms (9.7 versus 3.9 percent). Four decades later a Japanese team of psychiatrists led by Yasuyuki Ohta analyzed the responses of nearly four thousand Nagasaki survivors to a popular questionnaire for detecting psychological distress and to a prepared set of interview questions. Comparing their responses to those of a control group, over one-third of the survivors scored over the cutoff point compared to one-eighth of the controls, indicating that one-fifth of survivors were mentally scarred by the bomb. The interviews revealed that the most powerful influence on psychological status was a fear that exposure to the bomb had led to health problems (presumably, such as radiation sickness and cancer). Curiously, perhaps, this study also found that while symptoms such as anxiety and depression were milder among survivors in Nagasaki than the control group, those related to social interaction and the capacity to enjoy life were more severe.[75]

More recent studies also point to enduring health issues. Several have identified a link between exposure and anxieties about radiation effects later in life.[76] A possible limitation here is that correlation does not mean causation: poor mental health could have led to such anxieties. Overall, these Japanese studies seem to point to two important findings. First, the impact of the bomb on the mental health of survivors was significant and enduring but by no means universal. Second—and this distinguishes the victims of nuclear bombing from those of conventional bombing—the impact on mental health was closely linked to fears of radiation and its effect on one's own health and that of one's children. The potential costs of radiation in terms of foregone earnings and medical expenses were a further source of worry.

Displacement Trauma

The impact of displacement on refugees has been widely studied. Whether displacement always qualifies as a traumatic event is debatable: today, according to the United Nations High Commissioner for Refugees senior medical officer, most refugees respond with "normal distress" to displacement, whereas 15–20 percent have mental issues "on the mild part of the spectrum," and 3–4 percent "suffer serious disorders."[77] But these numbers refer to the immediate impact of displacement, not its long-term consequences. Inevitably, the suffering of the millions of refugees of World War I and World War II left its mark on them, for a while at least. Homesickness is a form of trauma, but it tends not to last. What, then, of the longer run?

Studies of the impact of displacement on the mental health of German refugees from the East argue for a negative long-run impact. A group of researchers led by Philipp Kuwert found that displacement in the wake of World War II was linked to higher levels of anxiety and lower levels of resilience and life satisfaction, though not higher levels of depression, six decades later.[78] Kuwert and his associates recognize some limitations of their study. In particular, the displaced in their sample may have differed systematically from the displaced in ways not controlled for in the analysis. In a 2013 study, Simone Freitag and her colleagues sounded an equally negative note.[79] Their analysis of a representative sample of older Germans [$N = 1,659$, of whom 206 were displaced] found that displaced Germans from the East were more likely to display symptoms of PTSD and somatic symptom disorder in later life, though (again) not depressive disorders. However, in Freitag et al.'s estimation, the impact of displacement fell after current household income bands were added as controls, and it packed a statistical punch only in the case of those aged seventy-five and above. Note too—and this point also applies to Kuwert et al.—that if the displaced were poorer than the rest at the time of the study, they were likely to have been poorer still when they arrived. These studies do not control for any independent impact tougher life conditions in the interim would have had on mental health. The case for a robust link between displacement and mental health in late adulthood, after other relevant factors have been fully taken into account, remains to be made.

Finally, during World War II about seventy thousand Finnish children aged between one and ten years were evacuated to neutral Sweden and (to a much lesser extent) to Denmark, where they stayed with local foster families until repatriated in 1945–47. Most of the children were from working-class backgrounds, and they stayed an average of two years. The Wikipedia entry on these *sotalapset*, or "war children," echoes a widespread perception that evacuation inflicted enduring psychiatric damage on the evacuees. Some never returned, and there is evidence that some parents did not want others back. However, an impressive interdisciplinary 2015 study compares the risks of psychiatric disorders among evacuees in later life with nonevacuated siblings. Using admission to a hospital for a psychiatric condition as a measure, it finds that evacuation resulted in no long-term adverse effects for either male or female children. Indeed, male evacuees were somewhat less likely to enter a psychiatric hospital for treatment than nonevacuee siblings.[80]

Let us sum up. This chapter has pointed to a rather neglected aspect of the two world wars: how they imposed additional costs on the mental health of civilian victims, both in terms of panic and anxiety while they lasted and lasting trauma long after they ended. The concept of psychic trauma was still in its infancy during and in the wake of World War I, but it was central to the discussion of survivors' well-being after World War II. Several very different categories of potential victims have been considered here: civilians fearful of aerial bombing and survivors of aerial bombing; survivors of the Holocaust and the atomic bombing of Hiroshima and Nagasaki, in a different league in terms of suffering; and victims of displacement and forced exile. The specialist literature invoked here suggests that those costs were unevenly borne and that, in aggregate, they were greater in the short run and perhaps lower in the long run than often claimed in the past.

11

A Conclusion without an End

If the people really knew [the truth] the war would be stopped tomorrow. But of course they don't know, and can't know.
—UK PRIME MINISTER LLOYD GEORGE, 1916

They kill my children and my father, and then talk of rules of war and magnanimity to foes. . . . War is not courtesy but the most horrible thing in life.
—LEO TOLSTOY, WAR AND PEACE, 1863

Over 60 Million Civilian Dead

Counts of civilian deaths caused by the two world wars will always be approximate at best. Not surprisingly, in the case of World War I the earliest stab at estimating mortality in "civil populations of the belligerent countries" did not get very far beyond "it must be reckoned in millions." Perhaps more surprisingly, one of the latest estimates proposes three sets of numbers, dubbing them all "but suppositions." Excluding Russia/the Soviet Union, where the data are incomplete, these numbers range from 4.6 million to 7.4 million.[1]

In the case of World War II, over three decades ago Mark Mazower cautiously proposed a combined toll of "approximately forty million" for combatants and civilians, far more than "even the millions killed in the First World War and the Russian Civil War." More recent calculations suggest that Mazower's estimate is much too low. However, it is certainly closer to the truth than what must be the most farfetched estimate in circulation for World War II: "More than 150 million died; more than half were civilians."[2] A key aim of this book has been to show that one can do better, even with suspect numbers accompanied by doubts and warnings and worries about the dangers of moral relativization (see chapter 1).[3] One can search for biases and omissions and guard against prejudiced exaggeration and evasion. Ballpark approximations of lives lost are important, even at the risk of some statistical numbing and the inevitable hand-waving.

Estimates of military deaths (and injuries), unlike those of civilian deaths, serve an immediate military purpose. They are therefore recorded and are usually much more reliable than those of civilian deaths. Often, the latter can be estimated, if at all, only as a residual. For example, the civilian toll in the Soviet Union during World War II is obtained by subtracting military deaths from an estimate of total deaths, inferred from estimates of those living in the Soviet Union on the eve of Barbarossa and in mid-1945, after allowing for net migration. An estimate of 26–27 million excess deaths, less 10 million military deaths,[4] entails a residual of 16–17 million civilian deaths.[5] This residual, in turn, consists of deaths from the range of causes discussed in previous chapters of this book. Determining their relative importance is the next step. If one allows for 7–8 million deaths from famine (chapter 2), 1.4 million Holocaust deaths (chapter 5), and perhaps 0.2 million deaths of would-be ethnic German refugees,[6] that still leaves a large residual of 6.4–8.4 million for deaths from other unidentified causes.

Considerable uncertainty also surrounds Russian/Soviet civilian deaths during World War I. Rough but reputable estimates of famine mortality (8 million) and total excess civilian mortality (11.4 million) in the Soviet Union between 1915 and 1923 (see chapter 2) leave 3.4 million deaths due to violence against civilians and to the global influenza pandemic. The epidemic accounts for most of these 3.4 million. The most recent estimate for flu deaths in the Soviet Union in 1918–19 is 2.8 million.[7] That leaves 0.6 million unaccounted for. Note that the proximate cause of most of the 8 million famine deaths would have been infectious diseases (chapter 3).

The biggest remaining uncertainty concerns China between 1937 and 1945. Dividing a very speculative figure of 14 million Chinese deaths between 3.5 million military and 10.5 million civilians and allowing 5 million for hunger and famine leaves 5.5 million for the Nanjing Massacre, the Yellow River inundation, and other unidentified causes.[8] We allow a figure of 4 million for nonfamine civilian deaths in Southeast Asia, Europe, and elsewhere. Taken together, these guesses add up to 16 to 18 million from "other causes." The tens of thousands of seamen in the merchant navies of both sides—about 30,000 British lives were lost in that way—and the tens of thousands more passengers and refugees who perished at sea in the attempt to escape would not make much of a dent in that total. They would also include the million or so non-Jewish Poles murdered on the orders of Hitler and Stalin, a million or so German expellees from eastern Europe and other refugees, the 0.4 to 0.5 million deemed "unfit" for society by the Nazis in Germany and elsewhere, the 0.1 million or so murdered by the Ukrainian Insurgent Army, and the hundreds of thousands of Belarusians murdered in antipartisan actions by the Wehrmacht and the SS. With more detailed knowledge, some of those deaths might be more appropriately included under genocide.

All this tedious demographic arithmetic, built on material described in some detail in chapters 2–7, leads to the estimates of aggregate excess civilian mortality by broad proximate cause, as reported in table 11.1. The outcome suggests an overall death toll of about 90 million from both wars, with World War I costing in the region of 10 million military and 16 million civilian lives and World War II 20 million military and 45 million civilian lives. Note that civilian casualties far exceeded military in both wars.[9] We can only underline once more that our estimates are approximations, subject to debate and revision. The weakest components concern data for the Soviet Union in both wars and for China in 1937–45.

These figures imply that, between them, the two world wars cost about 60 million civilian lives, or double the cost in military lives (about 30 million). Most of World War I's civilian casualties—roughly 12.5–13 million—died from hunger, famine, and disease and perhaps 3–3.5 million from other causes (including the Armenian genocide but not the flu pandemic).[10] There are greater uncertainties about the causes of death in World War II, with one-third attributed to "other causes." Civilian deaths during World War II were double those during World War I, with deaths from hunger and famine, genocide, and, especially, "other causes" accounting for most of the difference.[11] In relative terms, civilians were more vulnerable during World War II than World War I. When military casualties are added on, the World War II range proposed here is even higher than the "ballpark" 60 million proposed by Richard Bessel and Gerhard Weinberg.[12]

About three-fifths of the civilian deaths of World War I and World War II were caused by famine and hunger-related diseases and close to one-fifth by genocide (mainly the Jewish Holocaust of World War II and the Armenian genocide of World War I). Aerial bombardment accounted for 1.3–1.6 million, and the remainder—the most difficult to count—were the victims of other

TABLE 11.1. Civilian deaths during World War I and World War II: Main causes (millions)

Causes	World War I	World War II
Famine	12.5 to 13	20 to 21
Genocide	2	6.5
Aerial bombing	Few	1.3 to 1.6
Other causes	1.6	16 to 18
Total	16 to 16.5	43.8 to 47.1

military actions and atrocities. In both wars, Russia and the Soviet Union suffered most; they accounted for close to half of all deaths, military and civilian, and civilians made up two-thirds of Russian/Soviet deaths. Moreover, the number of those wounded or maimed by aerial bombing probably matched the number killed. For example, a table prepared by the U.S. Strategic Bombing Survey (USSBS) put the numbers killed in Hiroshima, Nagasaki, and Tokyo at 70,000–80,000, 35,000–40,000, and 83,600, respectively, and the numbers injured at 70,000, 40,000, and 102,000. The numbers injured in the attacks on Britain during World War II also approximated the numbers killed.[13] In addition, the wars inflicted further costs in terms of trauma, sexual violence, physical injuries, and bereavement. We do not minimize those, but they cannot be quantified with any precision.

Our data make no allowance for the impact of World War I on the spread of the Spanish influenza pandemic of 1918–19 and therefore on mortality. The pandemic could be considered part of our story, for a double reason. First, it is often claimed that the war facilitated its spread through the movement of clusters of infected soldiers and sailors. Second, it was recognized at the time that wartime priorities constrained public health measures that would have reduced mortality. Indeed, just two days after the end of World War I Great Britain's most senior public health official, Sir Arthur Newsholme, declared that troop movements had been "responsible on a large scale" for the increased virulence of the flu and that wartime priorities had ruled out taking measures that would have curbed its spread. And, using an expression more usually associated with the home front in England during World War II, he added:[14]

I did in my official capacity in July prepare a memorandum for public use, but on the balance of considerations, its distribution was not considered expedient at that time. There are national circumstances in which the major duty is to "carry on," even when risk to life and health is involved.

This duty has arisen as regards influenza among the belligerent forces, both our own and of the enemy, milder cases being treated in the lines; it has arisen among nutrition workers and other workers engaged in work of urgent national importance; it has arisen on a gigantic scale in connexion with the transport during 1918 of many hundreds of thousands of troops to this country and to France from overseas. In each of the cases cited some lives might have been saved, spread of infection diminished, great suffering avoided, if the known sick could have been isolated from the healthy; if rigid exclusion of known sick and drastic increase of floor space for each person could have been enforced in factories, workplaces, barracks and ships; if overcrowding could have been prohibited. But it was necessary to "carry on."

Given that the flu was responsible for tens of millions of deaths globally, attributing even a modest share of them to the war would increase World War I's civilian death toll considerably. But there is no consensus among historians and epidemiologists on the issue,[15] and nobody yet has sought to estimate the size of any likely impact. I have opted, accordingly, to err on the side of caution and refrain from including an estimate of war-induced pandemic deaths.[16]

"There Are No Innocent Civilians"

In both wars, belligerents highlighted the civilian deaths caused by the enemy but showed little empathy or concern for civilians on the other side.[17] In the early days of World War I, an impulsive and histrionic Kaiser Wilhelm II confided to his Austrian counterpart:[18]

> My soul is torn, but everything must be put to fire and sword; men, women and children and old men must be slaughtered and not a tree or house be left standing. With these methods of terrorism, which are alone capable of affecting a people as degenerate as the French, the war will be over in two months, whereas if I admit considerations of humanity it will be prolonged for years. In spite of my repugnance I have therefore been obliged to choose the former system.

Soon, however, the kaiser was addressing "a solemn protest" to U.S. president Wilson about the (alleged) use of dumdum bullets by British troops in France and having misgivings about using zeppelins to bomb English cities.[19] In time, Wilhelm would shed his scruples about aerial bombing, but as we have seen, the number of civilian deaths caused by German airpower during World War I was modest. And purely in terms of the number of civilian deaths, the slow deaths caused by the Allied blockades of the Central Powers during and in the wake of World War I far outnumbered those due to the atrocities committed by Wilhelm's troops against innocent Belgian and French civilians. Moreover, the concession by both sides at the height of World War I to allow Herbert Hoover's Commission for Relief in Belgium to assist a neutral, starving country offered "a remarkable example of humanitarian intervention" in the absence of any formal international law to protect civilians.[20] On the Eastern Front during World War I, as outlined earlier, the brutality against civilians was in a different league.

During World War II, the warring parties came closer to adopting the kaiser's "methods of terrorism." Civilians had fewer places to hide, and most civilian deaths—apart from the genocidal murders of the Holocaust—can be attributed to armies making the most of the possibilities offered by military technologies. That was because separating civilian from military targets was either undesirable or too costly and because only rarely did the fear of retaliation in kind constrain military action.[21] Toward the end of World War II, George Orwell declared that "war is not avoidable at this stage in history, and since it has to happen it does not seem to me a bad thing that others should be killed besides young men. . . . The immunity of civilians, . . . has been shattered. . . . I don't regret that."[22] Orwell was almost certainly reflecting majority public opinion at the time in May 1944, just before D-Day.[23] It is sad to reflect that when it came to targeting rather than sparing innocent enemy civilians in western Europe, there was little to choose between George Orwell and Bomber Harris. Neither would have been interested in technologies that distinguished between civilian and legitimate military targets, had they been available at the time. But it was mainly the greater brutality against civilians in the killing fields of Poland, Russia, Belarus, Ukraine, China, and Southeast Asia, coupled with the pressures on already low living standards due to occupation and mobilization, that made World War II the more lethal of the two wars.

"What Ifs" and "Might Have Beens"

Silent enim leges inter arma.[24]
CICERO, *PRO MILONE*, 52 B.C.

Was there a connection between death tolls in the two wars? Probably, in the "what if" sense that the prolongation of World War I made World War II more likely. What if the secret negotiations brokered by U.S. president Woodrow

Wilson involving Germany, the United Kingdom, and the United States, which lasted between August 1916 and January 1917, had yielded at least a ceasefire?[25] What if the warring parties had heeded Pope Benedict XV's "Peace Note"[26] of August 1, 1917, and opted for a peace based broadly on letting bygones be bygones and a return to the status quo ante? Neither was going to happen, and more is the pity. Even considering Benedict's plea might have delayed or prevented a Bolshevik Revolution, and it is difficult to imagine a Joseph Stalin without Lenin. An earlier negotiated peace would also have created a world without Mussolini and Hitler and their disgruntled followers. And without World War II, the Holocaust would not have happened, just as without World War I the Armenian genocide might have been mitigated, if not avoided. Most accounts agree that, although the Young Turk leadership was already hostile to the Armenians before 1914, World War I and fears that the Armenians represented a fifth column are what radicalized them to the point of engineering a genocide.[27] But wars rarely end in stalemates or draws. Once havoc had been cried and the dogs of war let slip, there was no effective way of preventing tens of millions of civilian deaths.

Since the end of World War II, international law has offered some protection to civilians against the horrors of total war. Might that protection have made a difference had it been enacted earlier? The Rome Statute that created the International Criminal Court (July 17, 1998, in force since July 1, 2002) outlaws all intentional killing of civilians. Article 8, for example, explicitly defines war crimes as "intentionally using starvation of civilians as a method of warfare by depriving them of objects indispensable to their survival"; "intentionally directing attacks against the civilian population as such"; and "committing rape, sexual slavery, enforced prostitution." Clearly, had military choices been constrained by the Rome Statute, World War I and World War II would have been very different wars, lasting perhaps somewhat longer and creating more military deaths but causing far fewer civilian casualties.

International humanitarian law attempts to impose rules that limit the horrors of war by protecting both civilians and combatants removed from the fighting from being captured or wounded. In reacting to the atrocities of past wars, it seeks to temper the barbarity of future wars. In so doing it seeks a balance between military considerations and the principle of humanity— allowing for killing on an organized basis while regulating this as far as possible in order to spare persons and properties taking no part in the fight. In theory, international law might have played a role in protecting civilians during World War I and World War II. In practice, alas, the history of efforts to shield civilians in wartime through binding international agreements is, by and large, one of good intentions before the event and duplicity and broken treaties during it. World War I was still young when the first zeppelins struck on British soil, clearly a breach of the Second Hague Convention of 1907. Germany justified the attacks on the grounds that the British blockade against Germany, which targeted and threatened civilian lives, was also in breach of international law. By the time Britain mounted a full-blown blockade against Germany in 1916, the aspirations of The Hague and the London agreements of 1907 and 1909 were dead letters. In the absence of credible commitments by all warring parties to international laws prohibiting certain stipulated actions, all resorted to aerial bombardment and attacking unarmed ships from neutral countries. In the memorable words of a recent study of blockades:[28]

> Overall, . . . one might well hope that the delegations to the 1856, 1907, and 1908–09 conferences were entertained with good food, drink, and parties. Clearly, their efforts to provide a legal set of rules to govern blockades came to nought; each side violated any rule with which it disagreed. It is a well-known fact that without an effective method of enforcement no law, domestic or international, has much chance of success.

The International Criminal Court in The Hague has been active since 2002, with a remit to charge suspects of the crimes listed in the Rome Statute. The refusal of four key players—the United States, Russia, China, and India—to join has not made its work easier. Nevertheless, it has to be said that its hefty annual budget (€170 million in 2023) and sizeable staff (over nine hundred in 2023[29]) dwarf the number of convictions to date (ten, all African). Perhaps it is still too soon to pass verdict on the court. In the meantime, civilians continue to be killed in wars big and small, particularly in Africa and the Middle East, as well as in Ukraine.

Epilogue

Yeah, that's why all these institutions were set up after World War II,
to see to it that it didn't happen again.

—US PRESIDENT JOSEPH R. BIDEN JR., NOVEMBER 2023

Civilians continue to be killed in wars, big and small, declared and unde-
clared. Much of this book was written during the COVID-19 pandemic, when
there was still no hint of the horrors that would unfold in Ukraine, Israel,
Gaza, and, largely ignored by the media, Sudan. Although "more of the
same" analogies are certainly inappropriate, some of the resonances with
World War I and World War II, as well as the humanitarian initiatives to
protect the civilians that followed them, are strong.

Russia's "special military operation" against Ukraine began on February 24, 2022. Nearly two years later, in November 2023, the United Nations
(UN) put the number of civilian casualties there at a minimum of 10,000,
"including 560 children . . . and more than 18,500 injured." That number,
though probably an underestimate, implies that the proportion of children
among the civilian dead was very low; older people were overrepresented,
presumably because it was not as easy for them to move to safer locations
as it was for the parents, most especially the mothers, of the young.[1] Heavy
artillery and missile attacks on built-up areas caused most of the deaths; by
comparison with the two World Wars, deaths from malnutrition and infectious disease were, at most, very few.

In 2022–23, military deaths in Ukraine were far more numerous than civilian deaths, though estimates are contested. In late April 2023, the US Defense Intelligence Agency put the numbers of Russian and Ukrainian troops killed at 35,500–43,000 and 15,500–17,500, respectively. By mid-August 2023, US officials were proposing totals of 120,000 and 70,000. Three months later, a civic group in Kyiv proposed a much lower estimate of Ukrainian deaths—30,000—based on an analysis of open sources. That bears comparing with a Ukrainian Ministry of Defence estimate, not independently verified, of "about 326,440" Russian military casualties (killed and wounded) to November 28, 2023.[2] The Russia-Ukraine war, then, has exacted a heavy toll in military lives, and military realities and calculations are more likely to bring it to an end than condemnation by much of the international community or the threat of any sanctions imposed by international law. In the meantime, the ratio of civilian to military dead in Ukraine as of December 2023 was, thankfully, low. A cautious guess might be 10,000 to 0.2 million, or 1 civilian per 20 military deaths. That is very low compared to either World War or, indeed, most wars since.

The civilian-to-military ratio is probably much higher in the underreported Sudanese conflict, which began as a power struggle between generals in Khartoum in April 2023 but descended thereafter into a series of atrocities carried out by Arab militias against non–Arab-speaking communities in the west and south of the country. The conflict, which has led, if UN data are to be credited, to the internal displacement of nearly 6 million people and the forced emigration of 1.5 million (meaning that 15 percent of the entire population of Sudan became refugees within seven or eight months), more closely resembles the "new wars" described at the beginning of this book, in which civilians are very vulnerable.[3]

Purely in terms of the number of civilian casualties relative to population, the Israel-Hamas war has been in a different league. The "action" that started it on October 7, 2023, brought back memories of the worst Nazi atrocities against non-Jewish civilians during World War II, like those in Oradour-sur-Glane, Lidice, and Sant'Anna di Stazzema. Those murdered by Hamas militants on that day included about 800 civilians, 368 members of the Israeli Defence Forces (IDF), 59 police officers, and 10 agents of the Shin Beit (Israeli intelligence). Among the civilian dead were 260 attendees, mostly young adults, at an all-night dance festival near a kibbutz close to the border with Gaza; the other civilian victims included over 30 young children and many older people. Most of the victims were Jewish Israelis, some with dual citizenship, but they also included dozens of Negev Bedouin, 33 Thai farm workers, and 10 Nepalese students on a visit to a kibbutz. Several women were raped before being murdered. In addition, Hamas kidnapped and forcibly moved 240 Israelis and others to Gaza.[4]

In terms of civilian lives lost, much worse was to come. Relative to population, the civilian death toll in Gaza quickly became an outlier, even by the horrific standards of the two World Wars. By the end of 2023, reports from Gaza were placing the cumulative toll at well over twenty thousand (or 1 percent of the entire population), of whom over two-thirds were women and children. In addition, three-fifths of the territory's housing stock had been damaged or destroyed, and access to basic needs such as food and emergency health care was sorely compromised. And to make matters worse, by early 2024 the lack of access to food and medical supplies was making "the entire population highly food insecure and at risk of Famine."[5]

Again, a controversy over numbers ensued. As reports of civilian casualties mounted, US president Biden at first discounted them: "I have no notion that the Palestinians are telling the truth about how many people are killed. I'm sure innocents have been killed, and it's the price of waging a war. . . . But I have no confidence in the number that the Palestinians are using." Biden soon apologized, however, and others argued subsequently that the numbers, if anything, are underestimates since they exclude some thousands missing since the war began.[6] Given the lack of information on Hamas casualties, the ratio of military-to-civilian dead cannot be estimated with any accuracy; on the basis of an analysis of data covering the first three weeks, the Israeli sociologist Yagil Levy reckoned that up to that point 4,594 of the 6,747 dead (or over three-fifths) were civilians. In early November, a senior Israeli official told reporters that one-third of the dead were enemy soldiers and that the data issued by the Gaza authorities were "more or less" correct.[7] The war also led to the displacement of most of the population of 2.2 million and made much of Gaza uninhabitable. The failure of the IDF to provide adequate safe havens for fleeing Gazans has been an abiding issue.[8]

All three wars involved breaches of international law. The Russian invasion of Ukraine plainly contravened the UN charter that prohibits the "use of force against the territorial integrity or political independence of any state." Moreover, both Russia and Ukraine breached the 2008 Convention on Cluster Munitions.[9] The International Criminal Court (ICC) has also accused Russia of the unlawful kidnapping of Ukrainian children.[10] More controversially, a statement released by Amnesty International in August 2022 accused both sides in Ukraine of failure to protect civilians. The statement was heavily—and correctly—criticized for making exaggerated and unsubstantiated claims against the victim in the conflict, Ukraine. Yet although Russia's failure to protect civilians was much more clear-cut, Ukrainian forces were not entirely blameless. An international panel of experts accepted the "principal factual finding" of the Amnesty International report that "in the various locations surveyed, Ukrainian armed forces placed themselves in civilian objects in the proximity of civilians who remained in these areas, including hospitals and abandoned schools."[11] But whether the threat of sanctions imposed by international law has influenced the course of the war in Ukraine—or in Sudan, where previous interventions by the ICC have been ineffective—remains doubtful.[12]

The savagery of Hamas's surprise attack on Israeli civilians caused widespread outrage. Outrage at the enormous toll of civilian deaths in Gaza was even greater, if not universally shared, with much criticism centering on the "proportionality" of the Israeli response. It was claimed that the IDF bombed power targets (*matarot otzem*) in Gaza so that civilians would pressure Hamas to surrender, rather like Bomber Command had hoped to do in Germany in 1944–45. Whether such a military strategy existed remains moot. Claims that Hamas has used sections of the Gazan population as human shields by, for instance, constructing tunnels for military personnel directly below civilian infrastructure are more firmly grounded.[13] Accusations that both sides have breached international law are commonplace and plausible.

But it is to "proportionality" that even the gentlest critics of Israel return. Article 8(2)(b)(iv) of the Rome Statute makes it unlawful for a country at war to launch an attack intentionally while knowing that it would cause a loss of civilian lives out of proportion to the military advantage gained. The ratio implied in this statement—with the military advantage as a denominator and the loss of civilian lives as a numerator—is a fuzzy one.[14] Even so, there is a strong case for considering, say, the civilian carnage of Dresden or of Hiroshima/Nagasaki during World War II as war crimes since the Allies would have soon won regardless. Gaza was different. Given the population density and the lack of escape routes, the military goal of eradicating Hamas meant a "proportional" response was next to impossible: the collateral cost in civilian lives would be great. Yet evidence, based on the satellite imagery of craters, that the IDF used huge low-precision bombs in areas where civilians had been advised to move for safety points to feasible precautions not taken. And so, within weeks of the initial onslaught, even Israel's closest allies had joined the call for it to "abide by international law," noting that "the number of casualties are too high" and accusing the Israelis of "indiscriminate bombing."[15] In the end the proportionality underpinning the Rome Statute lost its meaning in Gaza. Its civilians continue to be the victims of a long-standing failure of politics, not least those of Hamas, and the consequent failure to prevent the war that engulfed them.

Samuel Moyn, eminent historian of international law and human rights, has argued that efforts to humanize war,[16] no matter how well-intentioned, may serve only to make it more acceptable to the public and therefore more likely. That may be so: boxing gloves were intended to protect the boxers, but only ended up making boxing bloodier. Moyn's point recalls President Barack Obama's promise in Stockholm in 2009, as the recipient of the Nobel Peace Prize, not to abstain from future wars but to "remain a standard bearer in the conduct of war." Obama highlighted his decision to stop the policy of torturing suspects and his (undelivered) promise to close down the US detention camp at Guantánamo Bay. It was an interesting aspiration, given the United States' record in selectively ratifying international weapons treaties and the decision,[17] fourteen years later, of another US president to supply Ukraine with cluster bombs in its war against Russia. So, might the wars in Ukraine, Gaza, and Sudan have been waged any differently in the absence of what President Biden has referred to as "all these institutions" set up after World War II "to see to it that it didn't happen again"? Current evidence suggests that, as in the past, when push comes to shove, attempts to spare civilians by humanizing war fall terribly short. Sherman's words still ring true: "War is cruelty, and you cannot refine it . . ."

ACKNOWLEDGMENTS

Is olc an ghaoth nach séideann do dhuine éigin (It's an ill wind that doesn't help someone). This book has its origins in a paper about the famines of the First and Second World Wars intended for a conference aborted by COVID-19. The paper then morphed into a COVID-19 project in 2020–2021, when social distancing restrictions in Ireland were severe.

The two world wars gave rise to many famines, some even in relatively well-off places, and my attempts at calculating their death tolls suggested that existing estimates of civilian casualties during the wars were on the low side. That prompted my curiosity about civilian casualties more generally and led to investigations of causes of death ranging from atrocities to aerial bombing, and from infectious diseases to genocide. It also led to considerations of the psychic damage caused by fear, exile, and sexual violence. Five years later, the resultant book combines discussions of the data (and their limitations) with narrative accounts of the events that gave rise to them.

Given the constraints on travel and working in physical archives during COVID, I relied heavily on sources available through the libraries at University College Dublin, on online publications and archival sources, and on the generosity of friends and colleagues near and far. So I am extremely grateful to the librarians at UCD and also to the republic of online research repositories which make their material freely available to scholars. These include Wikipedia, Wikimedia, and JSTOR. I have used such sources wherever possible, steering clear where possible of predatory journal publishers. I also wish to thank those institutions and individuals who freely allowed me to use images in their possession.

Joel Mokyr bears much of the responsibility for persuading me to attempt the book and for unflinching support along the way. I am also grateful to many friends and colleagues for their help. Breandán Mac Suibhne, Michael Laffan, Antoin Murphy, Fionn Ó Gráda, and Mark Spoerer read earlier versions of most or all of it, and their suggestions and encouragement were extremely helpful. Tyler Anbinder, Matthias Blum, Joe Dunne, Ingrid de

Zwarte, John FitzGerald, Robert Gerwarth, Andreas Hess, John Horne, Hendrik Jürges, Morgan Kelly, Liam Kennedy, Saeunn Kjartansdottir, Haim Knobler, Chihua Li, Bertie Lumey, Dave Madden, Anil Menon, Ida Milne, William Mulligan, Máire Ní Chiosáin, Ruadhán Ó Gráda, Sadhbh Ní Ghráda, Rüdiger Overmans, Xavier Silvestre, Peter Solar, Paul Sweeney, Stephen Wheatcroft, Mark Wynne, and Zhou Xun offered useful comments on different sections or helped in other ways.

I am grateful to Princeton University Press for taking the book on board, and for including it in the Princeton Economic History of the Western World series. The referees were extremely helpful, and it was a pleasure to be guided through the production process by Emma Wagh, Joe Jackson, Wendy Lawrence, and Angela Piliouras.

Cormac Ó Gráda
Dublin, March 2024

NOTES

Introduction

Epigraph 1: As cited in Berg 2016: 34.

Epigraph 3: Royal Air Force Centre for Air Power Studies, "Interview with Sir Arthur Harris," July 1977, https://www.youtube.com/watch?v=UCWK-O7cKvc, quotation at 1.16:52.

1. Prost 2014a: 588; Bessel 2015: 258; Clemens and Singer 2000.

2. Harrison 2003a: 943; *Encyclopaedia Britannica* online, "World War II: Costs of the War," accessed December 20, 2023, https://www.britannica.com/event/World-War-II/Costs-of-the -war; estimates for China, all speculative, are discussed in chapters 2 and 9.

3. Including the Taiping Rebellion (1851–64), which has been described as "perhaps the most bloody and genocidal religious insurrection in world history" (Corfield 2011).

4. George Orwell, "As I Please," *Tribune*, May 19, 1944.

5. Proctor 2010; Gatrell 1999, 2014a, 2014b.

6. As cited in Paula Mahar, "All Eyes on Antietam: The Bloodiest Day in American History," accessed December 20, 2023, https://www.argunners.com/antietam-bloodiest-day-american -history/; John F. Marszalek, "Sherman's March to the Sea: Scorched Earth," *Hallowed Ground Magazine*, fall 2014, accessed December 20, 2023, https://www.battlefields.org/learn/articles /shermans-march-sea.

7. James McPherson also suggested, by way of contrast, that "probably twice as many civilians as soldiers in Europe died as a direct result of the Napoleonic Wars." McPherson 1988: 619fn53; McPherson, personal communication, March 25, 2009, as cited in Jewell et al. 2018: 384; Hacker 2011. On the Lieber Code, see Carnahan 1998.

8. Ronald Reagan in 1983, as cited in Flora Lewis, "Foreign Affairs: The Nuclear Apple," *New York Times*, November 25, 1983. In 1916 in a well-known study, the Austrian military historian Gaston Bodart proposed, on the basis of very little evidence, that armies rather than civilians had been the main victims in most past wars.

9. Keisinger 2015: 344; Barros and Martin 2022; Winter 2022.

10. Eckhardt 1989: 90.

11. Michael Kulikowski, "A Very Bad Man," *London Review of Books* 42, no. 12 (June 18, 2020): n.p.; Thucydides, *History of the Peloponnesian War*, chap. 17, https://www.mtholyoke.edu/acad /intrel/melian.htm.

12. Parker 1984; Outram 2001; Hanlon 2012; Wilson 2017 (on the Thirty Years' War); Moreira, Reis, and Martins de Sousa 2021; Prados de la Escosura and Santiago Caballero 2018 (on the Napoleonic Wars).

13. Following Ó Gráda 2017: 167.

14. Gellately and Kiernan 2003: 56.

15. Little 2014.

16. Carnegie Commission on Preventing Deadly Conflict 1997: 11; UN Development Programme, *Human Development Report 1998*, pp. 35–36, accessed December 20, 2023, https:// www.un-ilibrary.org/content/books/9789210576871c005; Kaldor 1999: 100. Pérouse de Montclos (2016a) and Jewell et al. (2018) note that such claims lack "evidentiary support."

17. Kaldor 1999: 8; Roberts 2010; Burkle 2019; Goldhagen 2009: 517; Kaldor 2019; Gerwarth 2014. Compare Edele and Slaveski 2016. Less plausible is the "brutalization thesis" associated with Mosse (1990), which posited that the levels of violence experienced on and off the battlefields during World War I paved the way for worse to come during World War II.

18. On Vietnam, see Jewell et al. 2018: 388. On Afghanistan, see https://watson.brown.edu /costsofwar/costs/human/civilians/afghan, accessed December 20, 2023. On Iran-Iraq and Syria, see the sources cited in Wikipedia. Compare Khorram-Manesh 2021. On Ukraine and Gaza, see the epilogue.

19. Tabeau and Bijak 2005; Khorram-Manesh 2021.

20. Mann 2018: 55.

21. As cited in Lawson and Lawson 1996: 79.

22. Léon Daudet, "Une guerre totale: Eux ou nous," *Action Française*, March 11, 1916.

23. "Activity Flares on the Western Front," *New York Times*, January 31, 1940; "M. Daladier s'adresse à 'ceux' de l'arrière," *Feuille d'avis de Neuchatel*, January 30, 1940. Goebbels's speech is available at the Internet Archive, https://archive.org/details/WolltIhrDenTotalenKrieg/mode /2up, accessed March 4, 2022.

24. *Guardian* (Manchester), December 23, 1914 ("war effort"); *Sunday Review* (Decatur, IL), September 6, 1914; *Times* (London), May 1, 1917 ("rationing"); *Times* (London), November 9, 1916 ("propaganda film"); *Times* (London), April 11, 1917 ("home front"). Dates and sources are from the *Oxford English Dictionary* online.

25. Bourodon 1936: 210.

26. Using Stephen Daggett, "Costs of Major U.S. Wars," U.S. Congressional Research Service, June 29, 2010, https://sgp.fas.org/crs/natsec/RS22926.pdf, table 1. The cost of the World Wars was calculated using a range of sources, including Broadberry and Harrison (2005) and Daniel et al. (2014– 19; contributions of Fabio Degli Esposti [Italy], Felix Butschek, and Agnes Pogány [Austria-Hungary]).

27. In terms of the mobilization of manpower, the United States seems to have been a partial outlier. The enlistment rate during the American Civil War (3.2 million out of a male population of about 15.5 million) exceeded that reached in the United States in 1917–18 (4.7 million out of a male population of over 50 million) and almost matched that of 1941–45 (16 million out of a male population of 66 million).

28. Nurick 1945: 680.

29. As cited in Michelle Zancarini-Fournel, "Travailler pour la patrie," *Combats de femmes, 1914–1918*, 2004, 32, https://www.cairn.info/resume.php?ID_ARTICLE=AUTRE_MORIN_2004 _01_0032.

30. *House of Commons Debates*, vol. 364, col. 1160, August 20, 1940.

31. Tanaka and Young 2009: 119; LeMay, as cited in Sherry 1987: 408.

32. Margalit 2007: 126; compare Grossman 1995. Herzog, as cited in Isaac Chotiner, "The Humanitarian Catastrophe in Gaza," *New Yorker*, October 15, 2023.

33. Wollacott 1994: 18–19, 31; Histoires 14–18: Les "munitionnettes" des usines d'armement (citing Joffre), accessed December 31, 2023, https://france3-regions.francetvinfo.fr/hauts-de -france/histoires-14-18-munitionnettes-usines-armement-1108159.html; Welskopp 2015.

34. Giddens 1985: 230.

35. As cited in Physicians for Social Responsibility, *Body Count: Casualty Figures after Ten Years of the War on Terror*, 2015, accessed December 6, 2021, https://www.psr.org/wp-content /uploads/2018/05/body-count.pdf.

36. Rachel VanLandingham and Geoffrey Corn, "The Emphasis on Counting Civilian Casualties Ends Up Helping the Islamic State," *Washington Post*, September 8, 2016; John Bates Clark, introduction to Bodart 1916, v.

37. Maier 2005: 441.

38. *Times* (London), October 23, 1945, as cited in Perkins 2002: 162.

39. Grossmann 1995: 47, 48; Krimmer 2015: 97–98.

40. Edward Luttwak, "Opportunity Costs," *London Review of Books* 39, no. 2 (November 21, 2013); see also Christian Schütze, "Speaking the Unspeakable," *London Review of Books*, August 27, 2003.

41. Wikipedia, "List of Wars by Death Toll," accessed November 11, 2021, https://en.wikipedia.org/wiki/List_of_wars_by_death_toll. At that time it is reckoned that the population of China was about fifty million.

42. In a review in the *Journal of Economic History* 69, no. 4 (2009): 1156–61. Compare Greenhill 2010; Aranson 2013.

43. For example, Winter 2010.

44. Vad Yashem, "FAQ: How Many Jews Were Murdered in the Holocaust?," accessed December 7, 2021, https://www.yadvashem.org/holocaust/faqs.html.

45. Lewi 2000: 221–22; United States Holocaust Memorial Museum (hereafter USHMM), Holocaust Encyclopedia, accessed December 20, 2023, https://encyclopedia.ushmm.org/content/en/article/genocide-of-european-roma-gypsies-1939-1945.

46. On Vietnam and Java, see chapter 2. Genocide historian Ben Kiernan claims that Japanese aggression in Asia caused up to 20 million deaths between 1931 and 1945, while democide historian R. J. Rummell estimates that between 1937 and 1945 the Japanese military murdered from nearly 3 million to over 10 million people. His best guess is 6 million, including prisoners of war. Rummel relies heavily on Iris Chang, *The Rape of Nanking* (Perseus Books, 1997) for his Nanjing numbers. Kiernan (2007: 455) relies on Werner Gruhl, "The Great Asian-Pacific Crescent of Pain: Japan's War from Manchuria to Hiroshima, 1931 to 1945," in Li 2003: 243, 250. Sokolov (2009: 438–39) "conditionally" chooses a figure of 2.5 million, equivalent to estimated military losses, but given the famine mortality in Henan (see chapter 2) and an estimated 0.3 million civilian deaths in Hong Kong alone (Banham 2019), this seems much too low.

47. USSBS 1947a: 1–2; *Mainichi*, "387,000 Deaths Confirmed in WWII Air Raids in Japan; Toll Unknown in 15 Cities: Survey," August 23, 2020, https://mainichi.jp/english/articles/20200821/p2a/00m/0na/018000c.

48. See Tomasevic (2001: 718–50) on "alleged and true population losses."

49. For a good discussion of the difficulties, see Pérouse de Montclos 2016b.

50. Naimark 1998: 45–46 (citing Nawratil 1987: 71).

51. Overy 2013: 395; Buettner 1950: 732; Susan Sontag, "Looking at War: Photography's View of Devastation and Death," *New Yorker*, December 1, 2002.

52. Royal Air Force Centre for Air Power Studies, interview with Sir Arthur Travers Harris, July 1977, https://www.youtube.com/watch?v=UCWK-O7cKvc.

53. As discussed in chapter 7.

54. Grossman 1946: 393.

55. Letter from William T. Sherman to James M. Calhoun, mayor of Atlanta, and two others, September 12, 1864, as cited in, e.g., Mackubin Owens, "William Tecumseh Sherman and Total War," accessed December 21, 2023, https://billofrightsinstitute.org/essays/william-tecumseh-sherman-and-total-war.

56. Overy 2021.

57. Winter's book is part of The Greater War Series, in recognition of World War I's "greater chronological dimension."

Chapter 1: Mobilization, Relief, and Famine

1. Ó Gráda 2009: 4.

2. Ted Widmer, "Lenin and the Russian Spark," *New Yorker*, April 20, 2017.

3. Fallible data are the most likely cause, although collapses in GDP and the depletion of stocks produced in previous years to be recycled into military use would have increased the ratios. We rely here on Roser and Nagdy 2020.

4. Broadberry and Harrison 2005; Eloranta and Harrison 2010; Harrison 1998; Feinstein 1972: T15–T16.

5. Stephen Daggett, "Costs of Major U.S. Wars," *Congressional Research Service*, June 29, 2010; O'Brien 2017.

6. Boehnke and Gay 2020.

7. Wollacott 1994: 18–19; see also Dewey 1987, 1984; Mitchell and Deane 1975: 62–63.

8. "L'emploi des femmes dans les usines Renault de Billancourt," *14–18: Le Magazine de la Grande Guerre*, no. 1, April–May 2001.

9. Collingham 2012: 156–60; Tooze 2006: 361.

10. "Employment of Women in War Production," *[U.S.] Social Security Bulletin*, July 1942, p. 4; Blum, Eloranta, and Osinsky 2014.

11. Farrar 1972; Strachan 2001: 1005–14; Kronenbitter 2007; Stevenson 2014.

12. Borchert 1948.

13. Milward 1970: 259, 261, 262.

14. Lyautey and Elie 2019: 109.

15. Suhara 2017.

16. G. Jones 1920: 419.

17. Starling 1920: 234; Lee 1975: 232–33.

18. Boldorf 2015: 18–19.

19. Starling 1920: 232.

20. Blum 2011.

21. Cundy 2015: 230, 20 (citing Lord Beveridge and French prime minister Clemenceau, respectively).

22. Cundy 2015: 2.

23. Sallagar 1974: 1, 2, 52.

24. Davis and Engerman 2006: 334–35 (data), 375 (quotation).

25. Gerhard 2009.

26. Grant 2014, 2017; Little 2014; Patenaude 2002.

27. Its first use in the *Irish Times* was in 1916.

28. Bonn 1916: 126; Edgeworth 1916: 224. For another example, see Anderson 1917: 886.

29. Weitzman 1977.

30. Anonymous 1945: 882–99 (at 887).

31. Yarov 2017: 43–52.

32. Griffiths 2002: 826.

33. Laurent Nesly, "Rationnement et réquisition sous le siège et la commune de Paris," March 24, 2016, https://wikicollection.fr/?p=36028.

34. As cited in Goodman 2018: 213.

35. With connotations of *Kartoffelbrot* (potato bread) and *Kriegsbrot* (war bread).

36. Offer 1989: 69–70.

37. Davis and Engerman 2006: 204.

38. Offer 1989: 54.

39. *Beds and Herts Saturday Telegraph*, December 8, 1917 (as cited at http://www.world war1luton.com/blog-entry/queues-food-shortages-bite).

40. Scriba 2014, citing *Berliner Tageblatt*, May 9, 1916. More generally, Allen 1998; Davis 2000.

41. Karau 2015: 63.

42. Blum 2013b.

43. Davis 2000.

44. Several other countries had already done so in April 1916. See "Early Adoption in Law," Daylight Saving Time, accessed December 13, 2023, http://www.webexhibits.org/daylightsaving/e.html.

45. Lynch 2012.

46. One hundred grams of white bread contains about 250 kilocalories.

47. V. I. Lenin, "On the Famine: A Letter to the Workers of Petrograd," May 24, 1918, https://www.marxists.org/archive/lenin/works/1918/may/22b.htm.

48. Gatrell and Harrison 1993; Wheatcroft 1997.

49. Compare Gazely and Newell 2013.

50. Johnston 1953: 170; Barber and Harrison 1991: 80.

51. Pavlov 1965: 136–37; compare Hass 2011: 935.

52. Salisbury 1969: 474–81; Yarov 2017: 23–26, 29–30, 71–72.

53. Collingham 2012: 378–83.

54. The claim that German consumers had it easy during World War II thanks to the exploitation of occupied lands to both Germany's east and west is a key theme in Götz Aly's *Hitler's Volksstaat* (2005), translated as Aly (2008), but it is widely agreed nowadays that Aly overargued his case. See Mark Spoerer, "Review of Aly, Götz: *Hitlers Volksstaat. Raub, Rassenkrieg und nationaler Sozialismus*," *H-Soz-Kult*, May 26, 2005, www.hsozkult.de/publicationreview/id/reb-7448; Adam Tooze, "Economics, Ideology and Cohesion in the Third Reich: A Critique of Goetz Aly's *Hitlers Volksstaat*," accessed March 15, 2022, https://adamtooze.com/wp-content/uploads/2017/01/Tooze-Review-of-Aly-for-Dapim-2005-.pdf; Overy 2018.

55. Spicknall 1943.

56. Zierenberg 2015; Kochanowski 2017: 41–42; Lutjens 2019: 93–96.

57. Gruchmann 1992; Sven Felix Kellerhoff, "Verschwenderisch ließ es sich die NS-Elite schmecken," *Die Welt*, March 28, 2018.

58. As cited in Weinreb 2012: 64.

59. Bessel 2009: 345–53; Collingham 2011: 467–68.

60. Jürges 2013.

61. Weinreb 2012: 53.

62. Cantril 1951: 729, 45; Zweiniger-Barbielowska 2000: 73; Collingham 2012: 376.

63. Zweiniger-Barbielowska 2000: 45.

64. Mills and Rockoff 1987: 207.

65. Mills and Rockoff 1987; Roodhouse 2013: 253–54.

66. Cited in Mazower 1993: 54.

67. Hionidou 2004, 2006: 104–8; League of Nations 1946: 38; Klemann and Kudryashov 2012: 391–93.

68. Kochanowski 2018; *Polish Fortnightly Review*, "How the Germans Are Starving Poland," December 15, 1942 (citing Robert Ley), http://www.holocaustresearchproject.org/nazioccupation/polandstarved.html; Polish rations as cited in Wikipedia, "Commission for Polish Relief"; Kochanowski 2018 (quotation on p. 30).

69. Goldman and Filtzer 2015: 46–47, 55.

70. Much of this paragraph is based on Anonymous 1945: 887–88.

71. For a brilliant account of the workings of the black market in the Soviet Union during World War II, see Goldman and Filtzer (2021). The quotation is from Richard Bidlack, "Review of Goldman and Filtzer," in *Slavic Review* 75, no. 4 (2015): 1044–45. According to Simonov (1996), in the 1920s expectations of future war were also a trigger for collectivization. On the trade in ration cards, see Ironside 2016: 661.

72. Diarist Esfir' Levina, as cited in Peri 2011: 180; Ironside 2016.

73. Montefiore 2004: 391ff.

74. Peri 2011: 179–80.

75. Salisbury 1969: 450; Belozerov 2005.

76. Hass 2011: 941.

77. Mouré 2010: 271; Bidlack 2000: 101.

78. Mouré 2010.

79. Grenard 2019: 92; Tönsmeyer 2021: 1151.

80. Taylor 1997: 164–65, 171.

81. Grenard 2019: 93.

82. Mouré 2010: 279; Tönsmeyer et al. 2021: 198.

83. Mouré 2010; Grenard 2019.

84. As cited in Lynch 2012: 236–27.

85. Anonymous 1945: 890; Calussi and Salvador 2018: 104.

86. For an excellent documentary on the tragedy, see Rai Storia, "Balvano: Il titanic ferroviario," March 8, 2015, https://www.youtube.com/watch?v=8jimaPXAzwA.

87. Anonymous 1945.

88. Johnston 1953: 163–64, 268–69, 276; USSBS 1946: 20–21; Kagawa et al. 2011; Aldous 2010.

89. USSBS 1946: 21.

90. Simon Partner, "The WWII Home Front in Japan," *Duke Today*, 2003, https://today.duke.edu/2003/03/japan_lecture0321.html. See also Masland 1946; Wright 2012; Garon 2017.

91. Johnston 1953: 202.

92. Griffiths 2002: 831–32; Shizume 2018.

93. Griffiths 2002: 828–34.

94. USSBS 1947a.

95. Blum 2013a: 288.

96. Beccatini and Bellanca 1986: 21; Bignon 2009: 21

97. Acemoglu and Robinson 2001.

98. Thompson 1971; Bohstedt 2010: 33–34, 89.

99. Morelon 2018; Engel 1997; Stadsarchief Amsterdam, *Amsterdam en de Eerst Wereldoorlog: Aarappeloproer*, accessed December 21, 2000, https://www.amsterdam.nl/stadsarchief/stukken/eerste-wereldoorlog/aardappeloproer/; Davis 2000: 51–53, 80–86, 212; Naert 2018.

100. Vrints 2011.

101. *New York Times*, "Vichy Rushes Food to Subdue Rioters," January 29, 1942; *New York Times*, "6 Sentenced to Die for Riot in Paris," June 27, 1942; "One Killed, Nine Hurt in Rioting in Paris," August 3, 1942.

102. Taylor 2000, quotation on p. 1; Schwartz 1999: 41.

103. *New York Times*, "Housewives Riot on Prices in Rome," December 8, 1944; *New York Times*, "Food Riots Reach Rome Areas," December 9, 1944; Stefania Conti, "Donne e resistenza: A Roma 'fucilate' per il pane," March 8, 2018, https://fondazionenenni.blog/2018/03/08/donne-e-resistenza-a-roma-fucilate-per-il-pane-2/.

104. *New York Times*, "60 Reported Killed in Vienna Food Riot," October 4, 1944.

Chapter 2: Hunger and Famine

Epigraph 1: From J. J. Graham's 1873 translation, book 6, chap. 13, https://clausewitz.com/readings/OnWar1873/BK6ch13.html.

Epigraph 2: Cited in The Hague Online, "UN Security Council Votes Unanimously on Dutch Initiative to Ban Starvation as a Weapon of War," May 25, 2018.

1. Shirinian 2017: 13–14.

2. Wheatcroft 2017: 218; Harrison and Markevich 2011: 679. For a higher estimate, see Adamets 2002: 163–64. On food rioting, see Engel 1997.

3. Smith 1980: 186, 453; Koenker 1984.

4. Wheatcroft 2017.

5. League of Nations, *Report on Economic Conditions in Russia: With Special Reference to the Famine of 1921–22 and the State of Agriculture* (Geneva: League of Nations, 1922), 1.

6. Wheatcroft 1997.

7. Wheatcroft 2024.

8. Wheatcroft 2017; Patenaude 2002: 26–27; V. I. Lenin, *The Tax in Kind: The Significance of the New Policy and Its Conditions*, 1921, https://www.marxists.org/archive/lenin/works/1921/apr /21.htm; League of Nations, *Report on Economic Conditions in Russia*, 16 (citing Lenin).

9. E.g., "Russia Pleads for Famine Relief," *New York Times*, July 19, 1921; Patenaude 2002.

10. Starling 1920: 230.

11. A point emphasized by Harrison 2016.

12. Lee (1975: 237) cites Georg Froehlich (1912) on the dangers, which the authorities ignored.

13. Albrecht Ritschl, "The Pity of Peace," 2003, table 13 (citing Skalweit 1927: 235–39); Davis and Engerman 2006: 201.

14. Cribb 2019: 45; Watson 2014; Herwig 2002: 168–70.

15. Osborne 2004: 1; compare Offer 1989; Davis and Engerman 2006: 201–38.

16. See, e.g., Janicki 2014; Siney 1963.

17. Letter of February 4, 1917, as cited in Offer 1989: 29 and Zeller 2018: 17. The source is Cooper and Denholm 1982: 144.

18. "Feed me . . . ," as cited in Weinreb 2017: 34; Kramer 2010a: 195. See also Kramer 2014c: 156–57.

19. Estimated from Mitchell 1975: 254, 270.

20. Roessle 1925: 175, figure 6.

21. Keys et al. 1950: 15.

22. Weinreb 2017: 25.

23. As quoted in Howard 1993: 183.

24. Offer 1989: 75–76; Davis and Engerman 2006: 206; "Germans Fearful of Terrors to Come," *New York Times*, April 11, 1919.

25. Howard 1993; Cundy 2015: 194; Kramer 2010a: 195; 2014c: 461. The data exclude Alsace-Lorraine and the provinces ceded to Poland.

26. Winter and Cole 1993; Kramer 2010a: 196.

27. As cited in Cundy 2015: 95–96.

28. Aly 2007; Occhino et al. 2008. For a measured critique of Aly's calculations, see Richard J. Evans, "Parasites of Plunder? Review of Götz Aly, Hitler's Beneficiaries: Plunder, Racial War, and the Nazi Welfare State," *Nation* 284, no. 2 (January 8, 2007): 23–28.

29. Kay 2006: 89 (citing Hitler); Arnold and Lübbers 2007; Prieml 2015; Klemann and Kudryashov 2012: 381–82.

30. Healy et al. 2015.

31. As cited in Healy 2004: 157.

32. Schmied-Kowarcik 2016.

33. Watson 2014 (citing Loewenfeld-Russ, *Regelung der Volksvernährung*, p. 354).

34. Note, though, that this decline is small compared to those reported in Leningrad in 1941–43 and in Amsterdam in 1945 (on which more is discussed below).

35. Schmied-Kowarcik 2016; Grebler and Winkler 1940: 147, as cited in Downes 2008: 87; Schultze 2005; Sked 2014; Healy 2004; Ward 1988: 222. Schmied-Kowarzik put the number

of excess civilian deaths in the empire at 465,000 (351,000 in Austria, 82,000 in Hungary, and 32,000 in Bosnia), which is uncannily close to Grebler and Winkler's estimate of 467,000 deaths. However, the latter includes influenza deaths, whereas the former does not.

36. Healy 2004: 41–86, 305.

37. Olbrechts 1926: 40, as cited in Majerus and Roekens 2017: 26.

38. Vrints 2014; Scholliers and Daelemans 1988: 143.

39. Hersch 1927: 65–70; Hamlin 2009.

40. See Erik Sass, "Serbian 'Great Retreat' Begins," *Mental Floss*, November 19, 2015, https://www.mentalfloss.com/article/71469/wwi-centennial-serbian-great-retreat-begins; Radivojević and Penev 2014: 47; Hersch 1927: 65–70; Notestein et al. 1944.

41. Hamlin 2009: 470; Hersch 1927: 80, 81.

42. Anonymous 1939: 233; Davies 2005: 132; Toynbee 1916; Blobaum 2018.

43. Mortara 1925: 68–106.

44. Mortara 1925: 81.

45. Sister Maria Agnese Zanderigo Rosolo, "Vita di paese durante l'occupazione austriaca," accessed December 22, 2023, http://www.comelicocultura.it/pdf/storia/la_grande_guerra/1917-1918.pdf.

46. Mortara 1925: 100–103.

47. Mortara 1925: 250–51.

48. Scolè 2015.

49. Fornasin et al. 2018. Kramer's claim (2007: 130) that the civilian "excess mortality rate" was at least 50 percent higher in Italy than in Germany does not allow for flu deaths.

50. My thanks to Giovanni Grazioli of Belluno's public library for this information.

51. "1914–1922 War Victims in Finland," accessed December 28, 2023, http://vesta.narc.fi/cgi-bin/db2www/sotasurmaetusivu/main?lang=en; Tepora and Roselius 2014: 113; Mikko Myrskylä and Torsten Santavirta, "Look at Your Old Men Dying: Long-Run Effect of Civil War on Mortality," unpublished, 2023, https://tsantavirta.com/wp-content/uploads/2023/11/Myrskyla_Santavirta_short.pdf.

52. Schatkowski Schilcher 1992: 229, 234; Brand 2023. Brand's work is the first comprehensive study of the famine in English. More are in train.

53. As cited in Aksakal 2014: 31.

54. Bozarslan 2010: 496–97; Bas 2017.

55. Maddox 1990, citation on p. 184.

56. Paice 2007; Lunn 2015 (citing data by Vadim Erlichman); Murphy 2015; Ngongo, Piret, and Tousignant 2018; Michael Vogel, "The Hungry War: German East Africa in World War I," Warfare History Network, accessed February 16, 2023, https://warfarehistorynetwork.com/article/the-hungry-war-german-east-africa-in-world-war-i/.

57. Dunsterville 1920: 124, 135.

58. Majd 2003; Bharier 1968; Atabaki 2016.

59. League of Nations 1946: 6.

60. Tomasevic 2001: 712.

61. Roland 1992: 99–104.

62. Archer 1944: 197 (entry for April 28, 1941).

63. Valaoras 1946: 216; Antoniou and Moses 2018: 2; Hionidou 2006: 25.

64. Mazower 1993: 37–41; Hionidou 2006: 158–89.

65. Helder 1949: 11.

66. Helder 1949: 26; Hionidou 2006: 68–81.

67. Helder 1949: 32, 33; Tönsmeyer et al. 2021: 437, 582.

68. Helder 1949: 13.

69. Helder 1949: 237.

70. Helder 1949: 598–600.

71. Valaoras 1946.

72. Cundy 2015: 196–99 (on Save the Children).

73. Black 1992: 15–16.

74. See, e.g., Lumey and van Poppel 2013. The impact of malnutrition on adult health is discussed briefly in chapter 3.

75. Ekamper et al. 2017. Due to worsening wartime conditions, mortality in the Netherlands was already rising before the famine, which makes estimating excess famine mortality tricky.

76. The best account of this famine is de Zwarte 2020. See also Banning 1946; Dols and van Arcken 1946; Tönsmeyer et al. 2021: 1311. For an interesting local perspective, see Online Museum de Bilt, "Hongertochten vanuit De Bilt," February 24, 2020, https://onlinemuseumdebilt .nl/hongertochten-vanuit-de-bilt/.

77. Stein et al. 1975: 244–46.

78. Banning 1946; Human Mortality Database; Ekamper et al. 2017; Trienekens 2000.

79. Online Museum De Bilt, evidence of Margreet Barkmeijer, accessed December 22, 2023, https://www.onlinemuseumdebilt.nl/hongertochten-vanuit-de-bilt/.

80. Rollet and De Luca 2005.

81. Daniele and Ghezzi 2019: figure 5; League of Nations 1946: 5; Collingham 2012: 366; Calussi and Salvador 2018.

82. Lewis 1978: 28–29; Daniele and Ghezzi 2019.

83. Anonymous 1945: 890.

84. Luzzatto-Fegiz 1946b: 326.

85. As cited in von Bueltzingloewen 2005: 17.

86. As explained in chapter 2.

87. The Soviet microbiologist Zinaida Ermolyeva independently synthesized penicillin for the Soviet military during World War II. It was first used in Soviet hospitals in 1943.

88. Klinsberg 2010.

89. Vallin et al. 2012; Cherepenina 2005: 61–64; Suhara 2017: 38; Goldman and Filtzer 2015, 2021; Barber and Harrison 1991: 87–88; Iris Morley, "Moscow a City of Allotment Holders," *Observer*, June 4, 1944.

90. Wikipedia, "World War II Casualties of the Soviet Union," accessed December 22, 2023, https://en.wikipedia.org/wiki/World_War_II_casualties_of_the_Soviet_Union.

91. Compare Goldman and Goldman 2021; Ellman and Maksudov 1994; Harrison 2003a; Andreev et al. 2002.

92. Filtzer 2015: 267–70.

93. Katkoff 1950: 212; Charon Cardona and Markwick 2019: table 1.

94. Katkoff 1950: 212.

95. Charon Cardona and Markwick 2020: table 1.

96. Forrest 1947: 319.

97. Remarks by Timothy Snyder at the conference "Germany's Historical Responsibility towards Ukraine" (Deutschen Historischen Verantwortung für die Ukraine), German Bundestag, Berlin, June 20, 2017, https://www.youtube.com/watch?v=5FnpkClVfWk. On Kiev, see Berkhoff 2004: 164–86.

98. Aldous 2010; Collingham 2011: 467–74.

99. Jürges and Kopetsch 2021.

100. Herbert Hoover, *The President's Economic Mission to Germany and Austria, Report No. 1: German Agricultural Food Requirements*, press release, February 28, 1947, p. 8. Farquharson (1985: 237–38) indicates, however, that the incidence of malnutrition was exaggerated.

101. Slaveski 2013: 99–101.

102. "The Great Mortality in Königsberg," August 17, 2021, https://holocaustcontroversies
.blogspot.com/2021/08/the-great-mortality-in-konigsberg.html.

103. Ellman 2000: 611–17; Ganson 2009; Vallin et al. 2012: 70; Wheatcroft 2012; Filtzer 2008:
347. Slaveski (2013: 115) surmised that "probably 1 million died directly from the famine, and about
4 million deaths resulted from related diseases, though this distinction is by no means fixed."

104. Forrest 1947: 326, 329, 331.

105. Suhara 2017: table 3.3.

106. Forrest 1947: 322–23.

107. Ellman 2000.

108. Casu 2010: 45.

109. Wheatcroft 2012 (quote at p. 1004).

110. Ganson 2009: 95–116.

111. Cherepenina 2005: 40–46.

112. Peri 2011: 134.

113. Cited in M. Jones 2008: 244.

114. "April 15, 1942 Blockade Tram. The Start of the Tram in Leningrad as a Symbol of Victory,"
accessed December 21, 2023, https://rosinka173.ru/en/15-aprelya-1942-goda-blokadnyi-tramvai
-pusk-tramvaya-v-blokadnom-leningrade.html.

115. Dzeniskevich 2005: 114–29; Peeling 2010: 192–93.

116. Chirsky 2005: 169.

117. Moscoff 1990: 198–99.

118. Roland 1992; Longacre et al. 2015; Ó Gráda 2009: 109–23; Hionidou 2006: 212–19; de
Zwarte 2020: 49–52; Manley 2015; Magaeva 2005: 131–33.

119. Salisbury 1969: 450–52; Simmons and Perlina 2002: 32; Peri 2011: 190, 192; Manley 2015.

120. Georgy Manaev, "7 Things from the Siege of Leningrad That Speak Louder than Words,"
Russia Beyond, January 27, 2019, https://www.rbth.com/history/329898-7-things-from-siege-of
-leningrad; Bidlack 2001; Goldman and Filtzer 2015: 18.

121. Frolov 2005; Goldman and Filtzer 2021.

122. On the blockade, see del Arco Blanco 2023; on mortality, see Ortega and Silvestre 2006.

123. Tawney 1964: 6; Huff 2019b; Dũng 1995. On FAD, see Ellman 2000: 621.

124. Sen 1981: 76.

125. The following account draws on Ó Gráda 2009: 159–94 and Ó Gráda 2015: 38–91. See
also Mukerjee 2014.

126. Ó Gráda 2015: 74; *Amrita Bazar Patrika*, August 20, 1943.

127. Das 1949: iii.

128. Ó Gráda 2015: 38–91; Tauger 2009.

129. Ó Gráda 2015: 38.

130. Ashley Jackson, "Defend Lanka Your Home: War on the Home Front in Ceylon, 1939–
1945," *War in History* 16, no. 2 (April 2009): 213–38.

131. Sarkar 2020.

132. Maharatna 1996.

133. Maharatna 1996: 227; Tauger 2009; Pria 2014; Balasubramanian 2023.

134. These data are from van der Eng 2008.

135. Anonymous 1946a: 81–82; Department of Economic Affairs, Batavia 1947: 10; van der
Eng 2008: 197. I am grateful to Gregg Huff for these references.

136. Brennan et al. 2017: 26; van der Eng 1998.

137. Van der Eng 2008, 2024; Brennan, Heathcote, and Lucas 2017; Huff 2019a, 2019b, 2020.

138. Marr 1995: 96–100.

139. Ó Gráda 2009: 94; Marr 1997: 104; Huff 2019a: 3, 17.

140. Assuming 360 calories per 100 grams of rice (FAO).

141. Marr 1997: 96–100; Smith 2015: 210.

142. Marr 1997: 100; Gunn 2011; Huff 2019a.

143. Huff 2019a: 9; van der Eng 2008: 74. In the case of Vietnam, the analysis omits Thai Nguyen "because its figure of a 69 per cent increase of output is too large . . . to be sensible" (Huff 2019: 11).

144. Ó Gráda 2015: 87.

145. Cui Fandi and Zhang Yuying, "China Marks Anniversary of War against Japanese Aggression: Sirens Howl across Nation to Remind People of History, Cherish Peace," *Global Times*, September 18, 2023. For an account of the incident, see Ferrell 1955. I am grateful to Zhou Xun for these references.

146. Edgerton-Tarpley 2014; Muscolino 2011; Lary 2001.

147. Garnaut 2013; Baker 2018.

148. Baker 2018: 97.

149. Baker typescript.

150. Baker typescript.

151. "The Desperate Urgency of Flight," *Time Magazine*, October 26 1942; "Until the Harvest Is Reaped," *Time Magazine*, March 22, 1945.

152. Devereux 2000: 6.

153. Lary 2010: 124–26; White and Jacoby 1946: 176.

154. E.g., *New York Times*, "Kwantung Fears Another Famine," November 1, 1943; "Famine and Cholera Kill 1,000,000 Chinese," February 1, 1944. On Hebei, see Li 2007: 338.

155. "Harrison Forman Diary, China, October 1943–May 1944," University of Wisconsin Milwaukee, accessed December 21, 2023, https://collections.lib.uwm.edu/digital/collection/forman/id/40/rec/6.

156. Winter 1977. See also Gazeley and Newell 2013.

157. Hilton 2021: 214.

158. Majerus and Roekens 2017: 126.

159. Offer 1989: 38; Cox 2019: 243; Winter and Cole 1993; Harrison 2016; Davis 2000: 184; Seeman 2006–07: 6, 8; Engwall 2005: 6 (citing a German source for the estimate of seventy thousand deaths), 11–12.

160. Mitchell 1975: 115, 121; von Bueltzingsloewen 2002, 2007: 34–36.

161. Masson and Azorin 2006–07; Chapireau 2007.

162. Von Bueltzingloewen 2007. See also Valérie Di Chiappari, "Handicap et Seconde Guerre mondiale: Le documentaire *La Faim des fous* en accès libre sur faire-face.fr," May 6, 2022, https://www.faire-face.fr/2022/05/06/handicap-seconde-guerre-mondiale-faim-des-fous-acces-libre/.

163. Gietema and aan de Stegge 2017 (data on causes of death in the Willem Arntsz Hoeve on p. 254); aan de Stegge 2022.

164. Buchheim and Futselaar 2020.

165. Buchheim and Futselaar 2023: 113–15; Lucie Beaufort, "Meer en Bosch," in de greep van het nationaalsocialisme, *Historiek.net*, October 8, 2022, https://historiek.net/meer-en-bosch-in-de-greep-van-het-nationaalsocialisme/151657/.

166. Buchheim and Futselaar 2023: 214–16, 285–88 (quotation on p. 286, translation mine).

167. Aan de Stegge (2019: 110), citing data in H. Oosterhuis and M. Gijswijt-Ofstra, *Verward van geest en ander ongerief: Psychiatrie en geestelijke gezondheidszorg in Nederland (1870–2005)*, 3 vols., 5 pts. (The Netherlands: Nederlands Tijdschrift voor Geneeskunde/Bohn Stafleu van Lochum, 2008), pt. 3, p. 1437.

168. Gietema and aan de Stegge 2017; aan de Stegge 2019: 110. One might also mention the 1,023 Jewish patients who were deported from the Het Apeldoornsche Bosch, a Jewish institution, in January 1943, along with 45 of the staff, who would be included in the number of Dutch Holocaust victims given in chapter 5.

169. In the postwar years, Vipeholm hospital was the locus of highly controversial dental experiments carried out on over four hundred of its adult patients.

170. Tzavaras, Ploumbidis, and Asser 2007–008.

171. Ørnulv Ødegard, "The Excess Mortality of the Insane," *Acta psychiatrica et neurologica Scandinavica* 27 (1952): 353–67; B. Ekblom and M. Frisk, "On Changes in the Death-Risk in Mental Hospitals in Finland during the Years 1920–1955," *Acta psychiatrica Scandinavica* 36, no. 2 (1961): 300–324, as cited in Chapireau 2007: 6. See also Engwall 2005 and the special issue of *International Journal of Mental Health* 35, no. 4 (2006), on "Starving the Mentally Ill," particularly the contributions on Finland (Ilkka Taipale and Ari-Pekka Blomberg), Greece (Athenassios Douzenis), and Italy (Paolo Francesco Peloso).

172. As cited in Maureen Murphy 2015: 152.

173. Greenough 1982: 219.

174. Peri 2011; Yarov 2017.

175. Yarov 2017: 268.

176. Clapperton 2006: abstract and *passim*.

177. Peri 2011: 81–86.

178. Dalya Alberge, "'Only Skeletons, Not People': Diaries Shed New Light on Siege of Leningrad," *Guardian*, December 24, 2016; Van Buskirk 2010: 281 (citing Ginsburg).

179. De Zwarte 2020.

180. Peri 2011: 85.

181. Das 1949: 9.

Chapter 3: The Demography of World War Famines

1. Ó Gráda 2009: 108–21.

2. Wheatcroft 1983: 340. On the role of infectious diseases, particularly typhus and malaria, in Lebanon in 1915–17, see Brand 2023: 128–46.

3. MacArthur 1956: 268.

4. Manley 2015: 206–8.

5. Snyder 1947.

6. MacPherson 1921: 140.

7. Wheatcroft 1983; Patterson 1993; Strong 1920.

8. Patterson 1993; V. I. Lenin, address to the Seventh All-Russia Congress of Soviets, December 5–9, 1919, https://www.marxists.org/archive/lenin/works/1919/dec/05.htm.

9. Patterson 1993: 375.

10. Rudnytskyi et al. 2020.

11. Blobaum 2018: 97, 99; Zavadivker 2020.

12. Pennington 2019.

13. Linton 2010: 612.

14. This account relies on Linton 2010.

15. Das Gupta and Siddons 1945.

16. Tanielian 2017: 155–58; Maharatna 1996: 217–19.

17. Stone et al. 2020. For a more ambiguous verdict, see Roland 2014: 78–79.

18. Cited in Longacre et al. 2015: 300. On medics and typhus, see Offer 2012: 473. On resistance to typhus in the ghettos generally, see Baumslag and Shmookler 2014.

19. Roland 1992, 2014; Longacre et al. 2015; Ó Gráda 2009: 109–23; Hionidou 2006: 212–19; de Zwarte 2020: 49–52; Manley 2015; Magaeva 2005: 131–33; on *Łódź*, see Tushnet 1963.

20. Bayne-Jones et al. 1964: 231.

21. Snyder 1947.

22. Compare Mokyr and Ó Gráda 2002.

23. Hionidou 2006: 190–219.

24. Malaria was more serious elsewhere: see Gardakas 2008. More generally, see Hionidou 2006: 190–219.

25. CBRs refer to the annual number of births/deaths divided by population, unadjusted for the age structure of the population. Here we use birth/death rate and CBR/CDR interchangeably.

26. Drolet 1945; Blobaum 2014: 42. See also Murray 2015.

27. Daniels 1949.

28. Ó Gráda 2009: 98–102. Compare, e.g., Mohanty 2022: 205–40; Rudnytskyi et al. 2015: 66.

29. Hionidou 2006: 165–78; Helder 1949: 619; Maharatna 1996: 165–73; Cherepenina 2005: 60; Filtzer 2015: 302–4.

30. de Zwarte 2020: 47–49; Cherepenina 2005: 60–61; Maharatna 1996: 168–69.

31. Hionidou 2018.

32. The underlying data are taken from Andreev et al. 1992; see also Livi-Bacci 2020: 109.

33. Offer 1989: 37; Voth 1995; Winter and Cole 1993: 245–46.

34. Antonov 1947: 252. The Leningrad data come from a medical practitioner in one of the city's clinics during the siege. Seventy-nine of all 1,323 births in the city during the second half of 1942 were in his clinic.

35. Regressing the recovery in 1946 on the fall in 1945 across all eleven provinces yields:
$RECOVERY = 5.13 + 1.81FALL$
(0.39) (0.21)
$N = 11$
$F (1, 9) = 72.11$
Adjusted $R^2 = 0.877$
Standard errors in parentheses

36. Valaoras 1946; Helder 1949: 620.

37. Markowitz 1955: 269–70.

38. Markowitz 1955.

39. Brainerd 2010; Daniele and Ghezzi 2019: 126; Markowitz 1955: 262; Liczbinska et al. 2017.

40. Fishman 2008: chap. 2.

41. Schneider, Ogasawara, and Cole 2021.

42. This section is based on ongoing research with Chihua Li and Bertie Lumey.

43. Almond and Currie 2011: 153.

44. Stein et al. 1975; Almond and Currie 2011.

45. The case for malnutrition in utero increasing the risk of type 2 diabetes later in life is supported by evidence from twentieth-century Austria, although the estimated increases are smaller. There, being born in 1919–21 increased the risk of males developing diabetes by 13 percent compared to those born in either 1918 or 1922. For those born in another crisis year, 1938, the increase was 9 percent, while for those born in 1946–47, the increase was 3 percent. The percentages for females were 16, 8, and 3, respectively. Moreover, the risks were much higher for those born in the poorer parts of Austria (Thurner et al. 2013).

46. Lumey and van Poppel 2013; see also Lumey et al. 2011.

47. "Birthweight Link to Lifelong Health," BBC News, August 22, 2011, accessed April 22, 2023, https://www.bbc.com/news/health-14576961; Diamond 2000: 5.

48. Zimmet et a. 2018: 738–46. "World War II Dutch Famine Babies' Brains 'Aging Faster,'" BBC News, September 14, 2010; "Brief Famine May Boost Cancer Risk," *Science News*, April 9, 2004; "How Famines Make Future Generations Fat," *Daily Beast*, May 11, 2014.

49. Ó Grada, Li, and Lumey 2023.

50. The details are explained in Ó Gráda, Li, and Lumey 2023.

51. Neelsen and Stratman 2013; Vågerö et al. 2013; Stanner and Yudkin 2001; Kesternich et al. 2014; compare Havari and Perocchi 2019.

52. Guven et al. 2021.

53. Schneider et al. 2021.

54. Vågerö et al. 2013; Allais, Fagherazzi, and Mink 2021.

55. Jürges and Kopetch 2021.

56. *Statistical Abstract 1951* (Dublin: Stationery Office, 1952), table 195.

57. This paragraph and the following draw on Ó Gráda and O'Rourke 2022.

Chapter 4: The Genocides of World War I

1. As cited in Dadrian 1991: 562. See also Winter 2022: 97–98.

2. Redzik 2017: 19; Lemkin 2013, as cited in Jacobs 2019: 33.

3. Kramer 2006: 442.

4. As cited in Ball 2011: 10.

5. Michael Ignatieff, "The Unsung Hero Who Coined the Term 'Genocide,'" *New Republic*, September 22, 2013. For an excellent introduction to Lemkin's life and thoughts, see Elder 2005. See also Sandes 2016, *passim*.

6. See https://www.un.org/en/genocideprevention/genocide.shtml, accessed December 26, 2023.

7. On the United States delay in ratifying, see Power 2002.

8. Ignatieff, "Unsung hero."

9. McDonnell and Moses 2005; John Docker, "Raphael Lemkin's History of Genocide and Colonialism," accessed December, 26, 2023, https://www.ushmm.org/m/pdfs/20040316-docker-lemkin.pdf.

10. Morris and Ze'evi 2019.

11. Mayersen 2018: 161–62; Bloxham 2005: 51.

12. On the role of economic crises in boosting extremist politics, see de Bromhead et al. 2013; Galofré-Vilà et al. 2017; Straumann 2019. On Turkey, see Bloxham 2003; Emin 1930: 218–19; Üngör 2015.

13. Dominian 1915.

14. Akçam 2012, 2019. Bloxham (2003) provides an excellent account of the genocide.

15. For overviews of Armenian suffering, see Gilbert 2003; Kiernan 2007: 395–415; Rogan 2015: 159–84.

16. Bryce and Toynbee 2020; Tusan 2012: 126, 128.

17. *The Treatment of Armenians in the Ottoman Empire, 1915–16: Documents Presented to Viscount Grey of Fallodon, Secretary of State for Foreign Affairs, by Viscount Bryce* (London, 1916), p. 645; Tehlirian, cited in Gatrell 2014b.

18. Bloxham 2003: 180–83.

19. Akçam 2012: 197–240.

20. According to Bloxham (2003: 141), "at least one million Armenians died, more than two-thirds of those deported." See also Rogan 2015: 183–84; Bas 2017; Kieser and Bloxham 2014: 610; Gilbert 2003: 19.

21. "Million Armenians Killed or in Exile," *New York Times*, December 15, 1915.

22. Shirinian 2017: 14 (dispatch dated June 30, 1915).

23. Morgenthau 1918: 309.

24. Akçam 2012: chap. 8, *passim*. John Kifner, "Armenian Genocide of 1915: An Overview," *New York Times*, accessed December 26, 2023, https://archive.nytimes.com/www.nytimes.com/ref/timestopics/topics_armeniangenocide.html?module=inline.

25. Tusan 2012: 130.

26. Kieser 2018: 181–314; Morgenthau 1918: 326; Gaunt, Atto, and Barthoma 2017: 1–2.

27. Toynbee 1922.

28. Toynbee 1922: 262; Winter 2022: 67–71.

29. Naimark 1998: 20, citing Venzopoulos; Morgenthau 1929: 48–49.

30. R. J. Rummel, "Statistics of Turkey's Democide Estimates, Calculations, and Sources," table 5.1, accessed December 26, 2023, https://www.hawaii.edu/powerkills/sod.chap5.htm; Morris and Ze'evi 2019.

31. Klapsis 2014: 625–36; Murard and Sakalli 2018; Salvanou 2017.

32. Toynbee, as cited in Tusan 2012: 158; Toynbee 1922.

33. Shaller and Zimmerer 2009: 1–3.

34. Heifetz 1921 (quotation on p. 1); Veidlinger 2021; Abigail Green, "It All Fell Apart," *London Review of Books*, July 21, 2022, pp. 23–24; Jean-Jacques Marie, "En Ukraine, des pogroms dont l'Occident se lavait les mains," *Le Monde diplomatique*, December 2019, pp. 20–21. Referring to 1919 alone, Heifetz (1921: 180) states, "If we assume that 120,000 deaths were due directly to the pogroms, we shall not be guilty of exaggeration." See also Johnson 2012.

Chapter 5: The Jewish Holocaust

1. Churchill to Sir Anthony Eden, as cited in Rubinstein 1997: 13.

2. In 2019 the U.S. Library of Congress catalogue contained sixteen thousand under the heading "Holocaust" (Hayes 2017: xiii).

3. Levi 1988: 3–4. Levi also cites Norbert Bobbio on the Nazi death camps as "not *one of the* events, but *the* monstrous, perhaps unrepeatable event of human history" (1988: 122).

4. On the Soviet Union, see Klier 2004.

5. As cited in Kiernan 2007: 437.

6. Browning 2004: 37, 195–96.

7. Levi 1988: 131–32.

8. Levi 1988: 134.

9. Laqueur 2001: 217.

10. Browning 1985: 15.

11. Wischnitzer 1940; Strauss 1980; Matthaeus 2015: 166–67; Rubinstein 1997: 18–19.

12. Laqueur 2001: 191–93.

13. Ritschl 2019; Meinl and Zwilling 2004: 40–43; Wikipedia, "Reich Flight Tax," accessed December 26, 2023, https://en.wikipedia.org/wiki/Reich_Flight_Tax.

14. Spitzer 2001; José Arturo Cárdenas, "Bolivia's Schindler Saved 10 Times as Many Jews from Holocaust," *Yahoo! News*, October 27, 2018.

15. Bartrop 2018.

16. Witschnitzer 1940: 39.

17. "Continental Britons: Jewish Refugees from Nazi Europe," Jewish Museum, 2002, p. 8, https://web.archive.org/web/20120414203729/http://www.ajr.org.uk/documents/cb_continental_britons_full.pdf.

18. Eber 2018.

19. Rosenthal 1944: 244, 249; Rubinstein 1997: 18; Hertzstein 1998.

20. Sonneck, Hirnsperger, and Mundschütz 2012.

21. Offenberger 2017: 31–67.

22. Caestecker and Moore 2010: 245–46; Pauley 1992: 273, 294; Offenberger 2017: chapter 8.

23. Botz 1987; Offenberger 2017; Jewish Telegraph Agency Archive, accessed December 26, 2023, https://www.jta.org/1940/12/30/archive/122000-jews-emigrated-from-austria-since -anschluss.

24. Offenberger 2017: chapter 8.

25. Adolf Eichmann to Herbert Hagen, May 8, 1938, https://www.jewishvirtuallibrary.org /adolf-eichmann-takes-control-of-jewish-life-in-austria-may-1938.

26. Ritschl 2019.

27. Caestecker 2014.

28. Compare Kushner 1989; London 1989; Dawidowicz 1992; Rubinstein 1997; Hertzstein 1998.

29. De Waal 2010: 264, 268.

30. Goeschel 2008: 27.

31. Brade 2017: 79; Herman 1969: 191.

32. Pimentel 2020; Jennings 2002; Kaplan 2013, 2020.

33. Blum and Rei 2018.

34. Blum and Rei 2018.

35. Buggle et al. 2020.

36. Becker, Lindenthal, Mukand, and Waldinger 2021.

37. USHMM, "Polish Jewish Refugees in Lithuania, 1939–40," accessed March 7, 2022, https:// encyclopedia.ushmm.org/content/en/article/polish-jewish-refugees-in-lithuania-1939-40.

38. Schatkes 1991; USHMM, "Polish Jews in Lithuania: Escape to Japan," accessed December 26, https://encyclopedia.ushmm.org/content/en/article/polish-jews-in-lithuania-escape-to -japan.

39. Mike Lanchin, "SS St. Louis: The Ship of Jewish Refugees Nobody Wanted," BBC World Service, May 13, 2014, accessed March 7, 2022, https://www.bbc.com/news/magazine-27373131; USHMM, "Voyage of the St. Louis," accessed December 23, 2023, https://encyclopedia.ushmm .org/content/en/article/voyage-of-the-st-louis. The story of the *St. Louis* also features in the well-known novel *Herejes/Heretics* (2013/2017) by Cuban author Leonardo Padura.

40. The sources for the figures are as follows: MS *St. Louis*, http://search.archives.jdc.org /multimedia/Documents/Names%20Databank/St%20Louis/Additional%20Links/Complete _StLouis_Passengers.pdf; Vilna, http://search.archives.jdc.org/multimedia/Documents /Names%20Databank/Vilna%20Refugees/Additional%20Links/Complete_Vilna_AR33-44 _00876.pdf; Kobe, accessed December 26, 2023, http://search.archives.jdc.org/multimedia /Documents/Names%20Databank/Japan%20Emigration%20Lists/Set%20III/Additional%20 Links/CompleteJapanSetIII.pdf.

41. https://www.bundesarchiv.de/gedenkbuch/directory.html.en?result#frmResults, accessed December 26, 2023.

42. The data are available online at holocaust.cz.

43. As Spoerer and Fleishhacker (2002b: 176) note: "To call the most ill-treated foreign laborers *slaves* is almost euphemistic: Soviet and Jewish Polish POWs were less-than-slave laborers."

44. Anders and Dubrovskis 2003: 131–32.

45. Levi 1988: 63. See also Ellis and Rawicki 2012.

46. Levi 1960.

47. Welch 2020.

48. Bělín et al. 2023.

49. Tammes 2018.

50. Tammes 2019a. See also Tammes 2007.

51. Croes 2012; see, too, Croes 2006, 2008; Croes and Tammes 2006.

52. Nagy 2016.

53. Mariot and Zalc 2017.

54. Pinchuk 1978: 145; Edele and Warlik 2017: 123; Goldlust 2017: 79. The "well over one hundred thousand Polish Jews" mentioned by Adler (2020: 282) seems too low. See also Ruth Franklin, "The Lucky Ones," *New York Review of Books*, October 21, 2021.

55. As cited in Jokusch and Lewinsky 2010: 392; Edele and Warlik 2017: 123, citing the story of Adam Broner.

56. Eglitis and Bērziņš 2018; Levin 1995: 15.

57. Eber 2018.

58. Ferenc Piotrowska 2018.

59. Tushnet 1963: 71; Dobroszycki 1984; Leah Preiss, "Women's Health in the Ghettos of Eastern Europe," Shalvi-Hyman Encyclopedia of Jewish Women, accessed December 26, 2023, https://jwa.org/encyclopedia/article/womens-health-in-ghettos-of-eastern-europe. More generally, several of the essays in Grodin (2014) discuss the heroic efforts of medics in the ghettos of Warsaw, Shavli, Kovno, Vilna, and elsewhere.

60. Winick 1979.

61. Ferenc Piotrowska 2018: 143–46. This gender calculation excludes children.

62. USHMM, "Documenting Numbers of Victims of the Holocaust and Nazi Persecution," last accessed December 26, 2023, https://encyclopedia.ushmm.org/content/en/article/documenting -numbers-of-victims-of-the-holocaust-and-nazi-persecution; Hayes 2017: 137.

63. USHMM, "Escapes and Reports," July 23, 2019, http://auschwitz.org/en/history /resistance/escapes-and-reports; https://www.dw.com/en/auschwitz-last-survivor-of-the-first -convoy-dies/a-49722157.

64. *Trials of War Criminals before the Nuernberg Military Tribunals under Control Council Law* 4, no. 10 (October 1946–April 1949): 40.

65. The images are available at USHMM, "Mizocz," accessed May 29, 2023, https://www .ushmm.org/search/results/?q=mizocz.

66. "Dr Saulius Sužiedėlis Explains Why Gas Chambers Weren't Used in Lithuania," August 2, 2018, https://www.lzb.lt/en/2018/02/08/dr-saulius-suziedelis-explains-why-gas-chambers -werent-used-in-lithuania/.

67. The numbers are from Wawrzeniuk 2018.

68. Ben-Naftali 2016; Arad 2002: 5–6.

69. Quoted in Arad 2002: 5.

70. Arad 2002: 5.

71. The SD was an intelligence wing of the SS.

72. The numbers are from Wawrzeniuk 2018.

73. Lower 2011; Finder and Prusin 2004; Katchanovski 2019; Karel Berkhoff, "Auxiliary Administration and Police," European Holocaust Research Infrastructure Online Course in Holocaust Studies, accessed December 26, 2023, https://training.ehri-project.eu/auxiliary -administration-and-police.

74. Dumitru 2011.

75. Hilberg 1961; Nuremberg Trial Proceedings, December 14, 1945, https://avalon.law.yale .edu/imt/12-14-45.asp; Pohl 2004; USHMM, "Documenting the Numbers of Victims . . . ," https://encyclopedia.ushmm.org/content/en/article/documenting-numbers-of-victims-of-the -holocaust-and-nazi-persecution; Yad Vashem, "How Many Jews Were Murdered in the Holo- caust?," accessed December 26, 2023, https://www.yadvashem.org/holocaust/faqs.html. Accord- ing to Hilberg, "When you segment these losses by country, you find that the major difference

between my count and those who say six million . . . is the Soviet Union" (as cited by D. D. Gutenplan, "The War on Truth," *Guardian*, March 12, 2001).

76. Edward van Woolen, "Ashkenazi Jews in Amsterdam," accessed December 26, 2023, https://web.archive.org/web/20070929090929/http://www.jhm.nl/jhm/documenten/InleidingEvV%20cd.eng.pdf. Of the 400,000 Jews who had left Germany or Austria by September 1939, 288,000 had gone to the United States, the United Kingdom, Palestine, Latin America, or China. Most of those still in Nazi-occupied Europe perished. Data from USHMM, "German Jewish Refugees, 1933–1939," accessed December 26, 2023, https://encyclopedia.ushmm.org/content/en/article/german-jewish-refugees-1933-1939. See also the map in the Anne Frank House, "The (Im)possibilities of Escaping. Jewish Emigration, 1933–1942," accessed December 26, 2023, https://www.annefrank.org/en/anne-frank/go-in-depth/impossibilities-escaping-1933-1942/.

77. On the role of Wannsee, the key sources remain Gerlach 1997, 1998.

78. Holmila, Silvennoinen, and Geverts 2011; Levine 1996; Silvennoinen 2013.

79. Griffioen and Zeller 2011, as cited by Tammes 2019b.

80. https://www.jewishvirtuallibrary.org/survivors-of-the-nazi-extermination-camps, accessed December, 2023.

81. Griffioen and Zeller 2006.

82. Brustein and King 2004a: 42.

83. Brustein and King 2004a; Gerlach 2016. See also Richard S. Levy, review of *Roots of Hate*, *German Studies Review* 29, no. 1 (2006): 203–4.

84. I am grateful to Mark Spoerer for pointing this out to me.

85. For a useful overview of the historiography of the Roma genocide, see Weiss-Wendt 2013.

86. Niewyk and Nicosia 2000: 422; USHMM, "Genocide of European Roma (Gypsies), 1939–1945," accessed December 26, 2023, https://encyclopedia.ushmm.org/content/en/article/genocide-of-european-roma-gypsies-1939-1945.

87. Ley 2000: 221–22.

88. Kenrick and Puxon 1972.

89. On the poor quality of data on Yugoslav Romam, see Jevtic 2004: 143.

90. Compare Jevtic 2004: 97.

91. Achim 1998.

92. The above paragraphs are based on Yad Vashem, *Report of the International Commission on the Holocaust in Romania*, 2004, chap. 8, https://www.yadvashem.org/docs/international-commission-on-romania-holocaust.html.

93. Steven Bowman (1986) reckons that over ten thousand Jews were saved by Greek interventions. Still, there were communal tensions, particularly between the "new" Greek refugees from Turkey (see chapter 6) and the Jewish community in Thessaloniki, where two-thirds of Greek Jews lived on the eve of the war. The occupiers did their best to exacerbate those tensions by, for example, transferring Jewish housing to homeless Greeks.

94. Fleming 2018: 361–70.

95. Mazower 1993: 257–61; Bowman 1986: 57; Bowman 2009.

96. While many Christians sympathized with their Jewish neighbors, that sympathy was lacking in professional and business circles. The president of the city's chamber of commerce, who would have known many in the Jewish business community and indeed spoke Ladino, did nothing to help. Municipal politicians and the local Orthodox archbishop were more concerned with the danger of the Germans allowing the Bulgarian army to enter the city than with intervening on behalf of the Jewish community (Mazower 2004: 440–42).

97. Mazower 2004: 442.

98. McElligott 2018.

99. Ikonomopoulos 2003: 96, as cited in Gikopoulou 2014: 100–102. See, too, Tzavaras, Ploumbidis, and Asser 2007–08: 62, table 5.

100. Stone 2019; Arad 1987.

101. Browning 2017: 133–42, 240. The extent of the acquiescence and collaboration of non-Jewish Poles in the virtual extermination of the Jewish population remains controversial, as do the motivations and feelings of the German soldiers responsible. The "central thesis" of Szymańska-Smolkin (2017: 6, 214) is that "participation of the Polish police facilitated the German implementation of the Holocaust in Poland." The police, she argues, were "guided by greed, contempt for Jewish lives, and fear of repression from the Germans in case they refused to follow orders and existing laws." On the *mentalités* of German soldiers, Browning 1992 is a classic source; compare Klier (2004: 279) on the Soviet Union.

102. Arendt 2006: 184; Anonymous, "Jewish History of Yugoslavia," accessed December 26, 2023, http://www.porges.net/JewishHistoryOfYugoslavia.html.

103. Tomasevich 1975: 606–7, https://www-fulcrum-org.ucd.idm.oclc.org/epubs/8k71nh39w ?locale=en#/6/1252[xhtml00000626]!/4/4/1:0.

104. Acemoglu, Hassan, and Robinson 2011: 897 (invoking Maksudov 2001); USHMM, "Jewish Losses during the Holocaust by Country," accessed December 26, 2023, https://encyclopedia .ushmm.org/content/en/article/jewish-losses-during-the-holocaust-by-country?parent =en%2F11652; Timothy Snyder, "Holocaust: The Ignored Reality," *Eurozine*, June 25, 2006, https//www.eurozine.com/holocaust-the-ignored-reality/; Klier 2004: 279.

105. Pinchuk 1980; Arad 2009: 77, 82–86.

106. Sužiedėlis 2004.

107. Zalkin 2010: 152.

108. Fitzpatrick 2017b: 44–46.

109. Weiss-Wendt 1998, 2013.

110. Katz 2016. See, too, Dovid Katz, "Why Is the US Silent on 'Double Genocide'?," *Guardian*, December 21, 2010; compare Timothy Snyder: "The Germans' anti-Semitic equation of Jews with Soviet rule allowed Lithuanians (and others) to find a scapegoat for their own humiliation and suffering under Soviet rule. It also provided an escape route for many who had collaborated with the prior Soviet regime," accessed December 26, 2023, https://www.nybooks.com/daily /2011/07/25/neglecting-lithuanian-holocaust/.

111. Radchenko 2013; Browning 2017: 135–36; Berkhoff 2004: 69.

112. Lower (2011) cites estimates ranging from twelve thousand to thirty thousand for murders in pogroms in that area, including three thousand to four thousand in its largest city, L'viv.

113. Finder and Prusin 2004; Katchanovski 2019; Mick 2011; Karel Berkhoff, "Auxiliary Administration and Police," EHRI Online Course in Holocaust Studies, accessed December 26, 2023, https://training.ehri-project.eu/auxiliary-administration-and-police.

114. Dumitru 2011.

115. Lucy Dawidowicz's estimate of two-thirds of the 375,000 Jews living in Belarus on the eve of World War II refers to Soviet Belarus, whereas the 751,861 deaths claimed in a 2009 estimate based on archival research refer to modern Belarus. *EHRI Online Course*, https://ehri-project.eu /content/genocide-jewish-population-belarus-republic-during-wwii.

116. Epstein 2008.

117. Rudling 2013: 61.

118. Wikipedia; USHMM, "The Holocaust in Bohemia and Moravia," accessed December 26, 2023, https://encyclopedia.ushmm.org/content/en/article/the-holocaust-in-bohemia -and-moravia.

119. Kless 1988. See also Saerens 2012.

120. Griffioen and Zeller 1999.

121. Croes 2012: 123–24.

122. Ungváry 2016: 145.

123. Braham 2016.

124. Rubinstein 1997: 191–97.

125. Bruland and Tangestuen 2011; Levin 2013.

126. Brustein and Ronnqvist 2002.

127. *Report of the International Commission on the Holocaust in Romania*, 2004.

128. Ragaru 2017; Sage 2017; Vassilev 2010.

129. Browning 2016.

130. Sémelin 2013, 2018; Browning 2016: 229–31; Griffioen and Zeller 2006; Robert O. Paxton, *Vichy France* (London: Barrie and Jenkins, 1972), p. 183. For an interesting recent regional study, see Dallaire 2020.

131. Lammers 2011; USHHM, "Denmark," accessed December 26, 2023, https://encyclopedia.ushmm.org/content/en/article/Denmark; BBC News, "The Tip-Off from a Nazi That Saved My Grandparents," October 21, 2018, https://www.bbc.com/news/stories-45919900.

132. Silvennoinen 2013; Holmila and Silvennoinen 2011.

Chapter 6: Civilian Deaths by Aerial Bombing

Epigraph 1: Bilbrough 2014: 182, 200.

Epigraph 2: Douhet 2012 (n.p.; my translation).

Epigraph 3: Colby 1925: 705.

1. Andrew Johnston, "Libya 1911: How an Italian Pilot Began the Air War Era," BBC News, May 10, 2011, https://www.bbc.com/news/world-europe-13294524.

2. Maurer 1978: 92.

3. "The Ascension of Count Zeppelin's Airship," *Scientific American* 83, no. 6 (August 11, 1900): 88.

4. On January 9, 1915, the kaiser ruled that raids "be expressly restricted to shipyards, arsenals, docks, and military establishments generally, and that London itself was not to be attacked" (Goss 1948a: 11).

5. Brock and Brock 2014: 68.

6. "Bombarding a Defense with Dirigibles," *Scientific American* 109, no. 1 (July 5, 1913): 2.

7. *Teeside Mercury*, September 29, 1915.

8. On his way back from an earlier raid on Hull, Mathy wrote to his wife that "they've shot at me and it's a nasty fire, and yet fighting submarines is nicer than setting towns on fire. But we'll always give them all we have, the harder [we attack] the earlier they will crumble," as cited in https://www.bbc.com/news/live/uk-england-humber-32920960, accessed December 20, 2023.

9. Grayzel 2006: 596, 609; Goss 1948a: 29 fn82.

10. Mortara 1925: 62; Harvey 2000.

11. Geinitz 2000: 212. Barros (2009) argues that the French followed a policy of strategic restraint during World War I.

12. Lord Weir, secretary of state for air, to Hugh Trenchard, chief of the air staff, September 10, 1918, as cited in John H. Morrow Jr., "The War in the Air," in Horne 2010: 167.

13. Anonymous, "Bombing Germany: General Trenchard's Report of Operations of British Airmen against German Cities," *New York Times Current History* 10, no. 1 (1919): 152.

14. Gallagher 2013: 73.

15. Lawson and Lawson 1996: 223.

16. Geinitz 2000: 212.

17. Cited in Geinitz 2000: 213.

18. Goss 1948a: 12; Feinstein 1972: T104.

19. Goss 1948a: 38; Anonymous 1919: 151–56.

20. U-Boat.net, "Für Kaiser und Reich: His Imperial German Majesty's U-boats in WW1," pt. 6, accessed December 5, 2023, https://uboat.net/history/wwi/part6.htm.

21. General Sherman Miles (1882–1966). See Miles (1926–27).

22. As cited in Jones et al. 2004.

23. Biddle 2002: 46 (citing Weir); E. Jones 2015; Bellamy 2008: 47.

24. Overy 1984: table 1.

25. Castelli 1908; Vagts 2000: 35.

26. Killingray 1984.

27. Clodfelter 2017: 379.

28. As cited in Satia 2006.

29. Goss 1948b: 178 (citing *Time* 29 [March 29, 1937]: 21.

30. Corum 1996: 98.

31. These are discussed in chapter 7.

32. Goss 1948a: 107–13.

33. Goss 1948a: 138–39 (citing Hsu 1941: 265).

34. As cited in *U.S. Congressional Record-Proceedings and Debates of the Senate*, February 3, 1938, p. 1358. The same source contains several other protests at the Chinese actions.

35. Lippman 2002: 13.

36. White and Jacoby 1946: 3.

37. White and Jacoby 1946: 12.

38. Yale Law School, "The Laws of War," accessed December 26, 2023, https://avalon.law.yale.edu/subject_menus/lawwar.asp.

39. http://www.dannen.com/decision/int-law.html#d, accessed December 20, 2023.

40. As cited in Harmon 1991: 5, accessed December 20, 2023, https://digital-commons.usnwc.edu/newport-papers/1/.

41. As cited in Downes 2008: 132; Davis and Engerman 2006: 323.

42. As cited in Sahr 2014. Compare Wellerstein 2020b. Nine years later the English moral philosopher Elizabeth Anscombe would protest against the award of an honorary University of Oxford degree to Truman, whom she considered a mass murderer. Here is a link to her *Mr. Truman's Degree*: https://projectintegrity.files.wordpress.com/2015/07/mr_trumans_degree.pdf, accessed December 20, 2023.

43. Baldwin, as cited in Mackay 2002: 20; Titmuss 1950: 4–6, 9, 12–13.

44. Wikipedia, "Bombing of Wieluń"; Instytut Pamieci Narodowej, Oddzialowa Komisja w Lodzi, "Śledztwa zakończone wydaniem postanowienia o umorzeniu" (Institute of National Remembrance, Lodz branch, "Investigations concluded with the issuance of a decision on discontinuance"), para. 19, May 2020; Norman Davies, "We Must Not Forget the Real Causes of the War," *Independent*, August 29, 2009.

45. Oleg Hoeffding, "German Air Attacks against Industry and Railroads in Russia, 1941–1945," RAND Corporation Memorandum RM-6206-PR, March 1970, p. v.

46. Atkinson 2017.

47. MacLeod 2011; The Blitz on Clydeside, "Population Statistics," http://web.archive.org/web/20121008234036/http://www.glasgow.gov.uk/en/Residents/Libraries/Collections/Blitz/Clydebank/Theaftermath/populationstatsclydebank.htm?content=2, accessed December 20, 2023.

48. Caroline Le Marechal, "Bristol Blitz: Recalling the Bombing, 75 Years On," BBC News, November 24, 2015, https://www.bbc.com/news/uk-england-bristol-34857868; Jones 2016.

49. Overy 2014: 278.

50. Cited in Biddle 1999: 635; Lindemann, as cited in Alexander 2014: 326; Trenchard, as cited in Biddle 2002: 194.

51. Cited in Robin Cross, *Fallen Eagle* (London: Wiley 1995), p. 78.

52. Derived from Overy 2014: 472.

53. Harris to the undersecretary of state, Air Ministry, Sir Arthur Street. Writing to Street, October 25, 1943 (as cited in, e.g., Biddle 2002: 220; ter Haar 2018). See also Leo McKinstry, "The Revenger's Tragedy," *New Statesman*, December 17, 2009; Hohn 1994.

54. Iredale 2021: chap. 11.

55. National Archives London, accessed December 6, 2021, https://www.nationalarchives
.gov.uk/education/resources/british-response-v1-and-v2/source-4/.

56. Chasseaud 2015: 155–58. For a useful database on the Allied bombing of Germany, see
https://ww2db.com/battle_spec.php?battle_id=55, accessed December 20, 2023. For a higher
estimate of civilian casualties in Hamburg, see Frankland and Webster 1961: 260–61.

57. Adam Tooze, "Burning Hamburg 1943," *Chartbook 230*, July 29, 2023, https://adamtooze
.substack.com/p/chartbook-230-burning-hamburg-1943?publication_id=192845&post_id
=135539839&isFreemail=true.

58. John T. Correll, "The Allied Rift on Strategic Bombing," *Air and Space Forces Magazine*,
May 4, 2022; Overy 2014: 395.

59. Bond 1946. Compare Friedrich 2006: 9; Overy 2013: 330. For some interesting autobiographical meditations on the aerial bombing of civilians during World War II, see Joyce 2021:
chaps. 6–7.

60. Rürup 1995: 13.

61. Based on Fahey 2004: chap. 1.

62. Chasseaud 2015.

63. Fuchs 2012: 30–42. Bourke-White is cited on p. 31.

64. Wikipedia, "Operation Tigerfish," accessed January 2, 2024, https://en.wikipedia.org
/wiki/Operation_Tigerfish.

65. Hohn 1994: 220; *DW*, "Pforzheim: The Dresden Nobody Knows About," February 23,
2015, https://www.dw.com/en/pforzheim-the-dresden-nobody-knows-about/a-18274739.

66. Richard Norton-Taylor, "Allied Bombers Chose 'Easy' German Targets," *Guardian*,
August 23, 2001.

67. Hohn 1994: 222, 224; Wieck 2003: 96–102.

68. As cited in Crane 2002: 234.

69. Crane 2002: 234–36.

70. Muller, Schonherr, and Widera 2008; https://webarchive.nationalarchives.gov.uk
/20070706054419/http://www.raf.mod.uk/bombercommand/dresden.html, accessed December 20, 2023; *Irish Times*, "Thousands Still Buried in Ruined Dresden," January 3, 1946; Fuchs
2012: 6. See *the.local.de*, "Official Report: Dresden Bombing Killed 25,000," March 17, 2010,
https://www.thelocal.de/20100317/25945; Theo Miller (member of Dresden Aufräumungsstab), as
cited in "The Nizkor Prokect, XI: Justification: The Bombing of Dresden," accessed December 20,
2023, http://www.nizkor.com/hweb/people/i/irving-david/judgment-11-01.html.

71. Victor Gregg, "I Survived the Bombing of Dresden and Continue to Believe It Was a War
Crime," *Guardian*, February 15, 2013. Fitzpatrick (2017b: 94–111) contains an eyewitness account
of the bombing of Dresden. Compare Malaparte (2013: 106–9) on the bombing of Hamburg.

72. Biddle 2002: 256; https://www.nationalarchives.gov.uk/education/heroesvillains
/transcript/g1cs3s3t.htm, accessed December 20, 2023.

73. Probert 2020.

74. Compare Harris 1947: 176; Royal Air Force Centre for Air and Space Power Studies (RAF
CASPS) Historic Interview, 1977, https://www.youtube.com/watch?v=UCWK-O7cKvc.

75. Evangelista 2023.

76. Cited in Smith 1998: 25.

77. As cited in Smith 1998: 7.

78. Gioannini and Massobrio 2007.

79. Centro Studi Federici, "20 ottobre 1944: la strage di Gorla," accessed December 20, 2023,
https://www.centrostudifederici.org/20-ottobre-1944-la-strage-di-gorla/ (where the victims'
names and ages are given).

80. Davis 2006: 252.

81. As cited in Gaffney 1999: 23.

82. Bissonette 2020: 19; John Laurenson, "D-Day Anniversary: France's Forgotten Blitz," BBC News, June 5, 2014, https://www.bbc.com/news/world-europe-27703724.

83. Derek Blyth, "Hidden Belgium: Cinema Rex," *Brussels Times*, December 19, 2021, https://www.brusselstimes.com/news/art-culture/198403/hidden-belgium-cinema-rex; Overy 2013: 603–4.

84. Van Esch 2011: 46, 50, 55.

85. "World War 2: Bombardments of Belgrade," accessed December 20, 2023, https://stalnapostavka.arhiv-beograda.org/en/chapters/20th-century-century-of-mass-suffering/world-war-ii.html; adevarl.ro, "Mari dezastre: Bombardarea Bucureştilor în '44: Mii de morţi şi sute de clădiri făcute praf," accessed December 20, 2023, https://adevarul.ro/stiri-locale/bucuresti/mari-dezastre-bombardarea-bucurestilor-in-44-mii-1369935.html; discovered through https://en.wikipedia.org/wiki/Bombing_of_Bucharest_in_World_War_II#; Gigova 2011: 132.

86. Clodfelter 2017: 367; Lary 2010: 24 (quotation); Ricardo Morales, "The Americans Destroyed Manila in 1945," *Rappler*, February 4, 2015, accessed February 23, 2023, https://www.rappler.com/newsbreak/iq/82850-americans-destroyed-manila-1945/.

87. The word is a compound of naphthenic and palmitic acids, its two main components.

88. Neer 2013; Guillaume 2016.

89. As cited in Ralph 2006: 498.

90. Stimson 1947.

91. Standard Oil Development Company, *Design and Construction of Typical German and Japanese Test Structures at Dugway Proving Grounds*, Utah, 1943, as cited by Fedman and Karacas 2012: 314.

92. Downes 2008: 128–29; Crane 2002: 238–39.

93. As cited in Neer 2013: 82; Ralph 2006.

94. *DW*, accessed December 20, 2023, https://www.dw.com/en/tokyo-firebombing-survivors-recall-most-destructive-air-raid-in-history/a-18300080; Lily Rothman, "Behind the World War II Fire Bombing Attack of Tokyo," *Time Magazine*, March 9, 2015, citing a contemporary report, https://time.com/3718981/tokyo-firebombing-1945/.

95. *Time Magazine*, March 27, 2012, https://nation.time.com/2012/03/27/a-forgotten-horror-the-great-tokyo-air-raid/.

96. As cited in Ralph 2006.

97. USSBS 1946: 17; Downes 2008: 118.

98. SBS 1946: 20, 143.

99. The *Mainichi* (August 23, 2020) reports that another twenty-eight cities suffered deaths toll of over a thousand people.

100. Sperling 1956 (as cited in Overy 2018: 243); Werrell 1986: 709; Luke Harding, "Germany's Forgotten Victims," *Guardian*, October 22, 2003; Ian Buruma, "The Destruction of Germany," *New York Review of Books*, October 21, 2004; Overy 2014: 476–77. The USSBS (1945a: 15) put the death toll at 305,000, plus 780,000 wounded; von Benda-Beckmann (2015: 9) at 380,000.

101. Overy 2015: 225–26.

102. Cited in Crane 1993: 143. See also Hasegawa 2009: 120; Gordin 2007. On the numbers, see Wellerstein 2020a; "387,000 Deaths Confirmed in WWII Air Raids in Japan; Toll Unknown in 15 Cities: Survey," accessed December 20, 2023, https://mainichi.jp/english/articles/20200821/p2a/00m/0na/018000c.

103. The trauma is discussed in chapter 9.

104. Guillain 1947: 209.

105. Solly 2020.

106. Solly 2020.

107. Malloy 2012.

108. Lindee 1994: 32.

109. Compare William C. Broad, "The Black Reporter Who Exposed a Lie about the Atom Bomb," *New York Times*, August 9, 2021, https://www.nytimes.com/2021/08/09/science/charles-loeb-atomic-bomb.html.

110. Tomonaga 2019.

111. Sutou 2018.

112. Sutou 2018.

113. Grant et al. 2015.

114. Fujiwara et al. 2008; Grant et al. 2015; Ozasa et al. 2018; Jordan 2016.

115. Julian Borger, "Hiroshima at 75: Bitter Row Persists over US Decision to Drop the Bomb," *Guardian*, August 5, 2020.

116. SBS 1946: 26.

117. Parish 1956: 380; Krause 1968: 4.

118. Cohen 1946.

119. Pelopidas and Egeland 2020; Garon 2020. See also *New York Times*, "70 Years after Nagasaki Bombing, Atomic Debate Yields Little Consensus," August 8, 2015.

120. Bernstein 1999.

121. E.g., Stimson 1947; Sallagar 1974: 58; Martin 1985: 199; Pape 1993; Hasegawa 2005; H-Diplo 2006; Wilson 2007.

122. Pears and Nutbrown 2013.

123. Ozasa et al. 2018.

124. Lippman 2002: 6 (citing Kuhn 1910: 109, 118).

125. As cited in Lippman 2002: 11.

126. Cantril 1951: 1067–69.

127. Crane 2002: 221.

128. *New York Times*, "Vatican Deplores Use of Atom Bomb," August 8, 1945.

129. Cantril 1951: 20.

130. Sagan and Valentino 2017.

131. Compare Pew Research Center, "70 Years after Hiroshima Opinions Have Shifted on Use of Atomic Bomb," 2015, accessed December 20, 2023, https://www.pewresearch.org/fact-tank/2015/08/04/70-years-after-hiroshima-opinions-have-shifted-on-use-of-atomic-bomb/; Dill et al. 2019.

132. Waltzer 1977; Cook 2007; Biddle: 2002: 1. Compare Best 1980: 280–83.

Chapter 7: Migration, Displacement, and Ethnic Cleansing

Epigraph 1: John Pollock, "The Refugees at Kiev," *Fortnightly Review* 98 (1915): 476.

Epigraph 2: As cited in Clapperton 2006: 390.

1. United Nations High Commissioner for Refugees, "Ukraine Refugee Situation," accessed December 27, 2023, https://data.unhcr.org/en/situations/ukraine.

2. Rees 1957.

3. See https://www-oed-com.ucd.idm.oclc.org/view/Entry/98068#eid92471938, accessed December 27, 2023. The first uses of the term in the *Irish Times* were on September 30 and October 16, 1989.

4. Compare Gatrell 2013a: 25–31.

5. Amara 2008. See also Michael Amara, "Les Belges en exil durant la Premiere Guerre mondiale," accessed December 27, 2023, http://docum1.wallonie.be/DOCUMENTS/CAHIERS/CN89/SPW1154_CN89_05_Amara.pdf.

Much in the following two paragraphs is based on information in P.–A. Tallier, *Archives de la Guerre. Série d'inventaire 5. Fonds d'archives relatifs aux réfugiés belges aux Pays-Bas durant la première guerre mondiale*, 1924, https://search.arch.be/en/?option=com_rab_findingaids&view =findingaid&format=pdf&eadid=BE-A0510_002071_002401_FRE.

6. Abbenhuis 2006: 97; Piercy 2016: 151–54.

7. Cammaert 1916.

8. Declercq 2020.

9. Purseigle 2007: 441.

10. Hemingway 1998: 198.

11. Ceschin 2006; Ermacora 2007: 455.

12. Ceschin 2006: 130–31, 153.

13. Ceschin 2006: 164.

14. Charles 2019.

15. Charles 2018.

16. As cited in Nivet 2004: 356.

17. Charles 2019; see also Nivet 2004: *passim*, and especially chaps. 2 and 3.

18. Nivet 2004: 533.

19. Cristophe Vuilleumier, "Réfugiés de guerre, les Italiens in 1914," accessed December 27, 2023, https://blog.nationalmuseum.ch/fr/2019/02/refugies-de-guerre-les-italiens-en-1914/.

20. Gatrell 1999, 2013a, 2014a, 2017.

21. Gatrell 2017.

22. Thorpe 2011.

23. Frizzera 2016; see also Stibbe 2014: 494.

24. Gatrell 2014b; McCarthy 1999; Pallis 1925: 318.

25. Spoerer 2006: 129.

26. Spoerer 2006.

27. Liulevicius 2000: 74.

28. Kulischer 1943: 163.

29. E.g., Adelman (2013: 168) claims that in the wake of the defeat of France in 1940, "eight million people took to the road"; Gatrell (2013a: 89) mentions a total of forty million.

30. Kulischer 1943: 114–15; Goldman and Filtzer 2021. The text of Kulischer is available at https://ia801608.us.archive.org/21/items/in.ernet.dli.2015.34228/2015.34228.Displacement-Of -Population-In-Europe_text.pdf, accessed December 27, 2023.

31. Goldman and Filtzer (2021) provide a masterly account of this operation, largely based on unfamiliar archival material. See also Manley 2013; Lieberman 1983: 90–91; Harrison 1985: 71–72; Manley 2007: 495.

32. Harriman 1973: 172–74.

33. Kulischer 1943: 48–49; Polian 2003: 117.

34. Snyder 2003.

35. Malcolm Proudfoot (1957: 21) put the European total at sixty million.

36. Gatrell 2014a.

37. Weal 2001: 63; Clapperton 2006: 384–86. Clapperton's valuable account is based mainly on survivor narratives; the quotes are taken from it.

38. Muscolino 2015; Bidlack 2000: 88; Sputnik News 2017.

39. Tomasevic 2001: 731.

40. Alan Riding, "Still Intrigued by History's Shadows: Günter Grass Worries about the Effects of War, Then and Now," *New York Times*, April 8, 2003. Compare Niven 2008.

41. The episode is discussed in detail in Long 2018.

42. Bessel 2009: 75.

43. *Potsdam Agreement Protocol of the Proceedings*, August 1, 1945, https://www.nato.int /ebookshop/video/declassified/doc_files/Potsdam%20Agreement.pdf.

44. Benes 1941: 154; see also Douglas 2012: 21.

45. In the May 1938 communal elections, the pro-Nazi Sudetendeutsche Partei won 88 percent of the ethnic German vote.

46. As cited in Glassheim 2000: 475.

47. Anonymous 2005: 300.

48. Prauser and Rees 2004.

49. Schoenberg 1970: 32; German Historical Museum, *Die Flucht der deutschen Bevölkerung, 1944/45*, dhm.de; Douglas 2012. The Wikipedia entry "1944–50 Flight and Expulsion of Germans" is very informative.

50. Kift 2010; see also Moeller 2003.

51. Braun 2017: figure 1.

52. Connor 1986, 2006, 2007; Harris and Wülker 1953; Braun and Dwenger 2017.

53. Connor 2007: 140.

54. Lüttinger 1986, 1989; Bauer et al. 2013.

55. Bauer et al. 2019. Bauer, Thomas K., Matthias Giesecke, and Laura M. Janisch.

56. Wyrwich 2020.

57. Peters 2022.

58. Grosser 2000.

59. Menon 2022; Ochsner and Roesel 2020; Grossman et al. 2021.

60. Grosser 2000: table 2.

61. Ther 1996: 787.

62. Bongaarts 1981; Schrover 2015.

63. Sarvimäki et al. 2022; see also Sarvimäki et al. 2009.

64. Helder 1949: 307.

65. Muscolino 2011: 302, citing Edward J. Wojniak.

66. Lary 2010: 25.

67. MacKinnon 2008: 44; White and Jacoby 1946: 55, 60; Lary 2010: 175–76; Gatrell 2000; MacKinnon 2001: 120–22 (citing data from a 1946 Guómíndǎng survey by Ch'i His-sheng). See also MacKinnon 2008.

68. Tinker 1975: 6.

69. Tinker 1975.

70. Hionidou 2021.

71. Thibon 2004: 83–122; Huff and Huff 2014.

72. Pohl 2016: 292.

73. Kreindler 1986; Campana 2008; Pohl 1999.

74. Spoerer 2006: table 1; de Zwarte 2020: 36; Spoerer 2015: 74–75.

75. Spoerer 2020: 146. The term "less-than-slave" comes from Ferencz 1979. Compare B. W. Patch, "Labor Reparations," *Editorial Research Reports*, vol. 1, 1945, accessed December 27, 2023, http://library.cqpress.com/cqresearcher/cqresrre1945060200.

76. Spoerer and Fleischhacker 2002a, 2002b.

77. David Boggett, "Notes of the Thai-Burma Railway, Part II: Asian Romusha; the Silenced Voices of History," pp. 160–66 (available online), citing economic historian Peter N. Davies, *The Man behind the Bridge: Colonel Toosey and the River Kwai* (London: Athlone Press, 1991), p. 196; and Australian prisoner of war Hugh V. Clarke, *A Life for Every Sleeper: A Pictorial Record of the Burma-Thailand Railway* (Crows Nest, Australia: Allen and Unwin, 1986), p. 49; Melber 2016: 169 (Malay deaths).

78. Huff 2020; Bayley and Harper 2004: 167.

79. de Zwarte 2020: 231–56. In addition, another thirty thousand Dutch children were sent abroad in 1945–46 to recover from the war. For a contemporary video, see "Orphans–Dutch Children Arrive aka Orphans of the Storm" 1945, https://www.youtube.com/watch?v=9MxOrKuNuwk.

80. Garon 2016.

81. Titmuss 1950: 4–6, 13–14.

82. Elcock 1999; Gärtner 2011: 11; The History Press, "The Evacuation of Children during the Second World War," accessed December 27, 2023, https://www.thehistorypress.co.uk/articles/the-evacuation-of-children-during-the-second-world-war/.

83. Titmuss 1950: 104.

84. Torrie 2010: 2; Hermand 1997.

85. Gärtner 2011: 165, citing Evans 2009: 451.

86. Bunle 1947; Torrie 2010: 2, 40.

87. Korppi-Tommola 2008.

88. Alastalo et al. 2009; Räikkönen et al. 2011; Santavirta et al. 2015.

89. Andersson et al. 2019; Alastalo et al. 2009.

90. Havens (1975: 932) puts the number at "at least ten million." See also Havens (1978: 154–73) for an excellent account of the evacuation.

91. Havens 1978: 167.

92. Becker et al. 2020.

93. Brenner and Kiefer 1981; Borjas 1982; Ayal and Chiswick 1983.

94. Murard and Sakalli 2018.

95. Murard 2022.

Chapter 8: *No quieren*

Epigraph: My translation from the German version, *Ostpreußische Nächte. Eine Dichtung in Versen* (in Russian and German), trans. Nikolaus Ehlert (Darmstadt and Neuwied: Luchterhand, 1976), p. 35.

1. The National Gallery (London), "The Rape of the Sabine Women: Peter Paul Rubens," accessed December 28, 2023, https://www.nationalgallery.org.uk/paintings/peter-paul-rubens-the-rape-of-the-sabine-women.

2. Lewis 1978: 130–32; Roberts 2013; Costello 1985: 140; Jennifer Schuessler, "The Dark Side of Liberation," *New York Times*, May 20, 2013. See also Horne and Kramer 2001: 197.

3. Strazza 2010: 35–36.

4. Strazza (2010: 21–34) offers a good summary of the literature on Belgium and France.

5. Horne and Kramer 2001: 198; Kramer 2007: 246; Lipkes 2007: 162–5.

6. Gullace 1997; Rivière 2012: 354–55; Rivière 2015; Harris 1993: 170. On sexual liaisons more generally, see Connelly 2018.

7. *Report on German Outrages* (London: H. M. Stationery Office, 1915).

8. *Report on German Outrages*, p. 30; Bechet, 2014: 7–18. An attempt by Jeff Lipkes (2007) to defend the *Bryce Report* and view the atrocities as a foretaste of what was to come during World War II has been met with skepticism. Compare, e.g., Herwig 2009; Vrints 2010; de Schaepdrijver 2009; Abbenhuis 2008.

9. Jim Roche, "Fog of War: The Lies That Lay behind WW1," *Irish Examiner*, August 23, 1914.

10. Palumbo 2017; Strazza 2010: 43–47; Ceschin 2013.

11. Strazza 2010: 59; Palumbo 2017.

12. Watson 2014: 796–97.

13. Strazza 2010: 38–43.

14. Pissari 2013.

15. Bryce and Toynbee 2020: 92, 165, 544, 579; Akçam 2012: 312–16.

16. John Horne, "Rape in Wartime, 1911–1923: Myths and Realities," keynote address presented at the workshop on "War Crimes and Sexual Violence in World War One and Beyond," University of Vienna, June 15, 2023. I am very grateful to Professor Horne for sharing a copy of his lecture. Compare Hagen 2005; Astashkevich 2018; Bodo 2011: 156.

17. de Zayas 1986: 35–63. These villages became Mayakovskoye and Imeni Alexandra Kosmodemyanskogo in Kalinigrad Oblast after 1945.

18. Valeria Paikova, "Ten Moving Soviet Poems about World War II," accessed December 28, 2023, https://www.rbth.com/arts/333537-moving-soviet-wwii-poems. The translation is by Gordon McVay.

19. Andrew Roberts, "Stalin's Army of Rapists: The Brutal War Crime That Russia and Germany Tried to Ignore," *Daily Mail*, October 24, 2008; Edele and Slaveski 2016; Rubinstein 2002. See also Naimark 2012.

20. On the rapes, generally, see Beevor 2002b; Buruma 2013. On estimates, see Roberts 2006: 263; Bessel 2009: 167; Beevor 2002b; Beevor, as cited in *Sydney Morning Herald*, "An Orgy of Denial in Hitler's Bunker," May 17, 2003.

21. Beevor, "The Russian Soldiers"; Kershaw 2011: 357.

22. The data may be found in Barbara Johr, "Die Ereignisse in Zahlen," in *Befreier und Befreite*, edited by Sander and Johr, p. 54 (as cited in Helke Sander and Stuart Liebman, "Remembering/Forgetting," *October* 72 (1945); *War and Rape*, "Liberators Take Liberties," Spring 1995, pp. 15–26.

23. Compare Allen J. Wilcox et al., "Likelihood of Conception with a Single Act of Intercourse: Providing Benchmark Rates for Assessment of Post-Coital Contraceptives," *Contraception* 63 (2001): 211–15; C. Kruttschnitt, W. D. Kalsbeek, and C. C. House, eds., *Estimating the Incidence of Rape and Sexual Assault*, Panel on Measuring Rape and Sexual Assault in Bureau of Justice Statistics Household Surveys, Committee on National Statistics, Division of Behavioral and Social Sciences and Education (Washington, DC: National Academies Press, 2014), https://www.hoplofobia.info/wp-content.

24. Johr 1992.

25. Naimark 1995: 132–33.

26. Compare Bourke 2007: 360.

27. Grossmann 1995: 46–47.

28. Grossmann 1995: 49, 58.

29. Majstorović 2016: 398; Mark 2005: 133–61; Roberts 2006: 263.

30. Virgili 2016.

31. Burds 2009: 37; Tönsmeyer 2021, "Letter from a Smolensk Physician, Written after the Liberation of the City, Detailing the Situation in the City's Hospitals and German Atrocities in the Area," p. 1020.

32. Gertjejanssen 2004: 1, 30, 204; Mühlhäuser 2012.

33. Wachsmann 2015: 411–14; Sommer 2009.

34. Gertjejanssen 2004: 226–62, 364–65, "The Forgotten History of Sexual Crimes in World War 2," 2019, https://wendygphd.com/forgotten-history-of-sexual-crimes-in-wwii/; Levi 1960: 29, 91.

35. Naimark 1995: 132–33.

36. Bessel 2009: 116, 158–61; Bourke 2007: 360; Biddiscombe 2001: 614, also 635fn27; M. W. Jones 2023.

37. Karlheinz Reichert, "Die Marokkaner kannten keine Gnade: 260 Verwaltigungen in der Nacht vom 20. bis 21. April 1945 in Magstadt," *zeitreise bb*, https://zeitreise-bb.de/kr_end/; Thomas Faltin, "Ende des Zweiten Weltkriegs in Stuttgart: Drei furchtbare Tage im April,"

Stuttgarter zeitung (digital), April 18, 2015; *New York Times*, "Rape Story Unsupported, 6th Army Group Says Stuttgart Inquiry Finds No Basis for It," July 7, 1945, p. 4; *New York Times*, "Rape Story Dispute Grows in Stuttgart," August 11, 1945, p. 10; Lawlor 2021; Bill Taylor to his parents, May 20, 1945, as cited in Lawlor 2021. See also Marks 1983.

38. Gebhardt 2016: 2.

39. Two widely cited studies of the proportion of rapes resulting in pregnancy in the United Staes ca. 1990 reported figures of 5 and 7.5 percent. See Holmes et al. 1996; Stewart and Trussell 2000.

40. Bessel 2009: 152, 161.

41. Lockenour 2019.

42. Gebhardt 2017: 163, 199; Emma Anderson, "Allies Raped Almost 1m Germans: Academic" (citing Lilly), *Local*, March 5, 2015.

43. Jane Yager, "Rubble Women: On Rape in Germany at the End of the War," *Times Literary Supplement*, April 14, 2017; Naimark 2015; *Daily Telegraph*, March 7, 2015; David Charter, "Allied Troops Raped 860,000 Germans," *Times*, March 7, 2015 (citing Lilly). Compare Klaus Wiegrafe, "Postwar Rape: Were Americans as Bad as the Soviets?," *Der Spiegel International*, March 2, 2015, https://www.spiegel.de/international/germany/book-claims-us-soldiers-raped-190-000-german-women-post-wwii-a-1021298.html.

44. Kehoe and Kehoe 2017: 390–93.

45. Lewis 1978; Malaparte 2013.

46. Senato della Repubblica, XIII Legislatura, "Norme in favore delle vittime di violenze carnali in tempo di Guerra," July 25, 1996, https://www.senato.it/service/PDF/PDFServer/BGT/00001012.pdf.

47. Baris 2007; Strazza 2010: 104, 118.

48. International Military Tribunal for the Far East, *Judgement*, p. 1012, accessed December 28, 2023, http://www.ibiblio.org/hyperwar/PTO/IMTFE/IMTFE-8.html; Walsh 2016: 50–55.

49. Connaughton, Pimlott, and Anderson 1995: 1145–21; Satoshi Nakano, "The Death of Manila in World War II and Postwar Commemoration," August 2019, https://www.researchgate.net/publication/324079142_The_Death_of_Manila_in_World_War_II_and_Postwar_Commemoration.

50. Jeanie Suk Gersen, "Seeking the True Story of the Comfort Women," *New Yorker*, February 25, 2021.

51. Nelson 2007.

52. U.S. Office of War Information, India-Burma Theater, *Japanese Prisoner of War Interrogation Report No. 49* (Washington, DC: Office for Emergency Management, 1944).

53. Lary 2010: 25; BBC News, "Japan and South Korea Agree World War II 'Comfort Women' Deal," December 28, 2015, https://www.bbc.com/news/world-asia-35188135.

54. Ramseyer 2020; Stanley et al. 2021. Compare Tadashi Wakabayashi 2003; Gersen, "Seeking the True Story."

55. Ramseyer, as cited by Gersen in "Seeking the True Story."

56. Tanaka 2008: 115; Tanaka and Young 2019; Calvin Sims, "3 Dead Marines and a Secret of Wartime Okinawa," *New York Times*, June 1, 2000. Tanaka (2008) extrapolates from the number recorded in Kanagawa Prefecture.

57. Ian Buruma 2013: 38, as cited in Walsh 2016: 8.

58. As cited in Walsh 2016: 25.

59. Walsh 2016: 45–46, iv. See also Walsh 2018.

60. Kramm 2017: 603; NBC News, "U.S. Troops Used Japanese Brothels after WWII," April 27, 2007, https://www.nbcnews.com/id/wbna18355292.

61. Walsh 2016: 193.

62. Nicholas D. Kristof, "Fearing G.I. Occupiers, Japan Urged Women into Brothels," *New York Times*, October 27, 1995.

63. Grossmann 2011: 137.

64. de Zayas 1978; Congden 2017: 29–30.

65. Svetlana Alexievich 2017, *War's Unwomanly Face*, 386.

66. Grossmann 2011; Grossmann 1995: 49.

67. Grossmann 2011: 138–40; 1995: 49–50; 2007: 51–55. *Sachlichkeit* might be translated as "blasé matter-of-factness."

68. Published in the United Kingdom as *A Woman in Berlin* (Anonymous 2005). The quotes are on pp. 146, 162, 307.

69. Deutschlandfunk, "Leonie Biallas in Conversation with Sandra Schultz," May 5, 2015, https://www.deutschlandfunk.de/zweiter-weltkrieg-das-thema-massenvergewaltigung-1945-war -100.html; Schwartz 2021: 48.

70. Kuwert et al. 2014; Le Bonhomme 2015, 2016; Krimmer 2015: 97–98.

71. Beevor's (2002) speculation that "one doctor deduced that out of approximately 100,000 women raped in Berlin, some 10,000 died as a result, mostly from suicide" has been widely recycled as the "fact" that one-tenth of raped women committed suicide.

72. Schwartz and Tatjana Takševa 2020; Eichhorn and Kuwert 2011; Koos 2018. On African-based research, see Zraly and Nyirazinyoye 2010; Ba and Bhopal 2017.

Chapter 9: Atrocities and Other Horrors of War

1. *Annuaire Statistique de la Belgique et du Congo Belge, 1915–1919*, Brussels, 1922, p. 100. Another 17,700 died in prison, were deported, or were the victims of German court martials, etc.

2. Horne and Kramer 2001: 132. Van Essen (1917) contains repeated references to francs-tireurs—e.g., pp. 89, 158, 190.

3. Lipkes 2007: 16.

4. Horne and Kramer 2001: 162–64.

5. Horne and Kramer 2006; Kramer 2014b: 17; Lipkes 2007.

6. I am grateful to William Mulligan for this point.

7. Best 1980: 226–28.

8. Reiss 1916: 36 (quotation), 136–39, 142; Horne and Kramer 2001; Horne 2014: 572; Gumz 2009; Kramer 2017.

9. Pissari 2013: 378 (citing W. Drayton, "Report on Bulgarian Atrocities in Serbia," in *Rapport de la Commission interalliée sur les violations des Conventions de la Haye et le Droit International en général, commises de 1915–1918 par les Bulgares en Serbie occupée. Documents* [Paris 1919], vol. 1, doc. 41, 192).

10. Lohr 2003; Watson 2014.

11. Lohr 2003: 126.

12. Lohr 2001; Watson 2014.

13. Meneses and Gomes 2015.

14. Kramer 2014: 159–62; Crowder 1985; Ngongo et al. 2018; Strachan 2003, pp. 641, 568.

15. The bloody Italian reprisals, mainly against civilians, in Libya in October 1911 in which four hundred women and four thousand men were killed, offer a pre–World War I parallel. See Wilcox 2021: 34–35.

16. Mussolini to Graziani, July 8, 1936, as cited in Campbell (2022: 125fn17).

17. Campbell 2022: 31fn44.

18. The number of recorded marriages in Spain was 138,710 in 1936, 143,339 in 1937, and 113,020 in 1938 (Ortega and Silvestre 2006: 70).

19. Salas Larrazábal 1977; *Annexo: Mortalidad en la Guerra civil española, por inscription en juzgados*, November 28, 2022, https://es.wikipedia.org/wiki/Anexo:Mortalidad_en_la_guerra _civil_espa%C3%B1ola,_por_inscripci%C3%B3n_en_juzgados.

20. Manuel González Molina, David Soto, Juan Infante, and Antonio Herrera, "Agricultural Crisis and Food Crisis in Early Francoism: Hunger Seen through the Lens of Biophysics," in del Arco Blanco 2021: 36–56.

21. Preston 2012.

22. USHMM, "Lidice," accessed December 20, 2023, https://encyclopedia.ushmm.org /content/en/article/lidice.

23. Neil Genzlinger, "Robert Hebras, Last Survivor of a 1944 Massacre in France, Dies at 97," *New York Times*, February 26, 2023; Ashdown 2015 (on the Vercors); Thomas Fontaine, "Chronology of Repression and Persecution in Occupied France, 1941–44" (entry for July 21, 1944), *Mass Violence and Resistance Research Network*, Sciences Po, November 19, 2007 (available online).

24. Costalli, Moro, and Ruggeri 2020; Bertazzini and Giorcelli 2023; "La memoria," http://www.santannadistazzema.org/default.asp; "L'eccidio di Padula di Fucecchio," http:// www.eccidiopadulefucecchio.it/; Andrew Lawless, "Who's to Blame? The Fosse Ardeatine and the Struggle over Memory in Modern Italy," accessed December 20, 2023, https://www .threemonkeysonline.com/whos-to-blame-the-fosse-ardeatine-and-the-struggle-over-memory -in-modern-italy/. The Wikipedia entries on the massacres mentioned in the text contain many useful links to the massacres themselves and their aftermaths. On the "logic" of Marzabotto, see Mazower 2009: 501.

25. Kotzageorgi and Kazamias 1994; Knopp 2009: 93 (as cited in Wikipedia).

26. Santarelli 2004; Chris Hedges, "In Trieste, Investigation of Brutal Era Is Blocked," *New York Times*, April 20, 1997; Francesco Boscarol, "Foibe, fascisti e comunisti: Vi spiego il Giorno del ricordo: Parla lo storico Raoul Pupo," *Post Internazionale*, February 10, 2019, https://www.tpi .it/news/foibe-giorno-del-ricordo-fascisti-comunisti-20190210248565/.

27. USHMM, "Jasenovac," accessed January 10, 2022, https://encyclopedia.ushmm.org /content/en/article/jasenovac.

28. Spoerer 2020: 144–46.

29. Based on the claim in Knittel (2010, 125) that "according to the latest studies, approximately three hundred thousand disabled and mentally ill people were murdered."

30. Osterloh, Schulte, and Steinbacher 2022; Tuters and Viksna 2006: 72–74; Nasierowski (2006): 50–61 (citation on pp. 52–53). See also "German War Crimes against Soviet Civilians," Everybody Wiki, last modified July 25, 2020, https://en.everybodywiki.com/German_war_crimes _against_Soviet_civilians.

31. A small town in central Poland.

32. Masson and Azorin 2006–07; Chapireau 2009.

33. *Bundeszentrale für politische Bildung*, "Die Vertreibung der Deutschen aus den Gebieten jenseits von Oder und Neisse," April 6, 2005; Ingo Haar, "Hochgerechnetes Unglück, Die Zahl der deutschen Opfer nach den Zweiten Weltkrieg wird übertrieben," *Süddeutsche Zeitung*, November 14, 2006; Wordisk, "Flight and Expulsion of Germans (1944–1950)," fn250, https://worddisk .com/wiki/Flight_and_expulsion_of_Germans_(1944–1950)/.

34. Snyder 2001.

35. Ellman and Maksudov 1994; Harrison 2003a; Barber and Harrison 2006. The Academy of Science data have been conveniently reproduced in Wikipedia, "World War II Casualties of the Soviet Union."

36. Rudling 2008.

37. A digitized version of this source is available online at https://www.sbc.org.pl/dlibra /publication/27260/edition/24330/content, accessed December 28, 2023.

38. As cited in Wildt 2002.

39. Ciencala 2001; Ciencala, Lebedeva, and Materski 2008.

40. "The Katyn Indictment," *New York Times*, December 24, 1952; "Moscow's Statement on Katyn," *New York Times*, September 15, 1992; Werth 2012, 232; Piotr H. Kosicki, "The Katyn Massacres of 1940," *SciencesPo Mass Violence and Resistance Research Network*, December 8, 2008, https://www.sciencespo.fr/mass-violence-war-massacre-resistance/en/document/katyn-massacres-1940.html.

41. I owe this point to Mark Spoerer. See too Wnęk 2023: 128-30.

42. Earlier estimates are summarized in (https://en.wikipedia.org/wiki/World_War_II_casualties_of_Poland, last accessed, February 5 2024); Wnęk 2023: Table 2.2.

43. Mertelsmann and Rahi-Tamm 2009: 308, 311, and *passim*; Wikipedia, "German Occupation of Lithuania during World War II," reports details from four separate Lithuanian-language estimates; Britannica, "Baltic States," accessed December 28, 2023, https://www.britannica.com/place/Baltic-states/Independent-statehood.

44. Westerlund 2008: 8–9.

45. Rummel, *Statistics of Democide*, chap. 3, accessed January 24, 2024, https://www.hawaii.edu/powerkills/SOD.CHAP3.HTM. Rummel puts POW deaths at 139,000, a small proportion of the total. See also Werner 2007, as cited in Wikipedia; Arnaud Doglia, "Japanese Mass Violence and Its Victims in the 'Fifteen Years' War' (1931–45)," October 7, 2011, https://www.sciencespo.fr/mass-violence-war-massacre-resistance/en/document/japanese-mass-violence-and-its-victims-fifteen-years-war-1931-45.html; Bessel 2015: 254–57.

46. Lary 2001; Muscolino 2014; Bessel 2015: 255.

47. As cited in Bessel 2015: 257.

48. Connaughton et al. 1995: 174–76. See pp. 179–81, 183–84 of this reference for discussion of MacArthur's obsession with taking Manila.

49. Joseph Stromberg, "Starving Settlers in Jamestown Colony Resorted to Cannibalism," *Smithsonian Magazine*, April 30, 2013; Zhou 2012: 60–71.

50. al-Qattan 2014 (citing a contemporary source), October 9, 2014, https://www.cambridge.org/core/journals/international-journal-of-middle-east-studies/article/when-mothers-ate-their-children-wartime-memory-and-the-language-of-food-in-syria-and-lebanon/F9B59F8A788BE59114D6E8466A9BC5FA; Tanielian 2012: 62; Brand 2014: 259–60.

51. Keys et al. 1950: 7.

52. Suhara 2017: 35; Wheatcroft 2017: 229; Patenaude 2002: 262–70.

53. "О каннибализме в блокадном Ленинграде," March 9, 2019, https://5rim.ru/text-news/o-kannibalizme-v-blokadnom-leningrade/.

54. Clapperton 2006: 280, 289–90; Mikael Kai Zhakarov, "'Bread in Those Days was like Gold!' A Survivor's Account of the Siege of Leningrad," History Workshop Online, November 28, 2018, https://www.historyworkshop.org.uk/bread-in-those-days-was-like-gold-a-survivors-account-of-the-siege-of-leningrad/.

55. Kochina 1990: 72, 92; Salisbury 1969: 474–81; Belozerov 2005: 223–24; Clapperton 2006: 44, 54, 106; Peri 2011: 99–101.

56. Clapperton 2006: 291–92.

57. Khruschev 1970: 234, 240; Ó Gráda 2015: 13–14; Council of Europe Parliamentary Committee, *Report Commemorating the Victims of the Great Famine (Holodomor) in the Former USSR*, March 1, 2010. I owe the figure of 150 to Igor Casu.

58. Wieck 2003: 187.

59. Tanaka 2008: 147; Ó Gráda 2015: 17.

60. Tanaka 2008: 123–48.

61. Manimugdha S. Sharma, "Japanese Ate Indian PoWs, Used Them as Live Targets in WWII," *Times of India*, August 11, 2014.

62. Esteban 2016. The quotations are all taken from this source.

63. Wachsmann 2015: 282.

64. On Belsen in the wake of liberation, see "Richard Dimbleby Describes Belsen," originally broadcast on the BBC on April 19, 1945, https://www.bbc.co.uk/archive/richard-dimbleby-describes-belsen/zvw7cqt.

65. Ó Gráda 2015: 16–17; "Death for Jap Who Practiced Cannibalism," *Canberra Times*, April 17, 1946; "Cannibalism in Prison Camp: British Medical Officer's Visit to 'Most Horrible Place,'" *Guardian*, April 19, 1945; Paul Peachey, "Cannibalism 'Rampant' at Nazi Concentration Camp, New Documents Reveal," *Independent*, March 31, 2016; Coates 2016; *the.journal.ie*, "'The Most Harrowing Work I've Had to Do': The Irish Priest among the Liberators at Bergen-Belsen," April 15, 2017; National Archives, transcript of description of conditions at the camp on April 16, 1945, WO 235/19/76008, https://nationalarchives.gov.uk/documents/education/belsen.pdf.

66. Many oral testimonies on the USHHM contain accounts of cannibalism in Bergen-Belsen and elsewhere. See https://www.ushmm.org/search/results/?q=cannibalism, accessed May 5, 2023. On Strutthof, see Olivia Land, "Cannibalism at Camp Stutthof: Holocaust Survivor Testifies to Life of 'Hell,'" *New York Post*, August 21, 2022.

67. Connelly 2018: 37–66 (quotation from Becker 2010: 240–41, on p. 38); Le Naour 2000: 152. On "children of war" more generally, see Grieg 2001.

68. Gromaire 1925: 475–77, as cited in Debruyne 2014; Fabienne Pasau, "On les appelait 'les femmes à boches': Que sont devenus leurs enfants?," *rtbf.be*, July 22, 2019, https://www.rtbf.be/article/on-les-appelait-les-femmes-a-boches-que-sont-devenus-leurs-enfants-10138375. The population of the occupied parts of France dropped from 2,235,467 in 1915 to 1,663,340 in mid-1918 (Wikipedia, "German Occupation of North-East France during WW1").

69. Le Naour 2000.

70. Anne Mah, "This Picture Tells a Tragic Story of What Happened to Women after D-Day," *Time*, June 6, 2018 (citing Buruma 2014); Yves Denechere, "Des adoptions d'État: Les enfants de l'occupation française en Allemagne, 1945–1952," *Revue d'histoire moderne et contemporaine* 57 (2): 159–79; Maurin Picard, "200,000 enfants de soldats allemands seraient nés en France," *Le Figaro*, November 30, 2009; Grieg 2001: 8 (citing an article in *Aftenposten* [Oslo], July 4, 2001). The figure of 200,000 was proposed by Picaper and Norz (2004).

71. "Kouchner pour la reconnaissance des 'enfants de Boches,'" *Libération*, April 25, 2008.

72. Mochmann, Lee, and Stelzl-Marx 2009 (citing Dag Ellingsen, *En registerbasert undersokelse*, Statistics Norway, Rapport Nr. 2004/19, 2004). See also Mochmann and Larsen 2008.

73. Iliana Magra, "Norway Apologizes, 70 Years Later, to Women Who Had Relationships with WWII Germans," *New York Times*, October 19, 2018; *Guardian*, "Norway Apologises to Women Punished for Relationships with German Soldiers," October 17, 2018.

74. Anette Warring, "German-Girls during Occupation and Post War Purge," summary of dissertation published as *Tyskerpiger—under besættelse og retsopgør* (Copenhagen: Gyldendal, 2019), https://web.archive.org/web/20120204061753/http://www.krigsboern.dk/artikler/anette_warring.htm. The ten thousand figure is given at the (excellent) Aarhus Occupation Museum, accessed January 20, 2024, https://www.besaettelsesmuseet.dk/, hence the quote. Hansen (2009) provides an interesting account of fraternization between teenage girls and German troops in Ejsberg in western Jutland.

75. Monika Diederichs, "'Moffenkinder': Kinder der Besatzung in den Niederlanden," *Historical Social Research/Historische Sozialforschung* 34, no. 3 (2009): 304–20.

76. Fabian de Bont, "Liefde of 'seksueel collaboreren'?," accessed January 20, 2024, https://www.tweedewereldoorlog.nl/onderzoekuitgelicht/liefde-in-tijden-van-oorlog/liefde-of-seksueel-collaboreren/; Machteld de Metsenaere and Sophie Bollen, "Schandelijke liefde: Sentimentele collaboratie en haar bestraffing in Belgie na de tweede wereld oorlog," *Wetenschappelijke tijdingen* 5016 (2007): 228–59.

77. Hushion 2015: 190.

78. Matthew Stibbe, "Enemy Aliens and Internment," in Daniel et al. 2014; Stibbe 2006, 2009, 2014; Heather Jones, "Prisoners of War (Belgium and France)," in Daniel et al. 2015; Roman Senkus, "Thalerhof," *Encyclopedia of Ukraine*, vol. 5, 1993, accessed October 15, 2023, https://www.encyclopediaofukraine.com/display.asp?linkpath=pages%5CT%5CH%5CThalerhof.htm; Speed 1990: 187 (source of the estimate of the number of internees).

79. BBC, WW2 People's War, "Fact File: Civilian Internment, 1939–1945," October 15, 2014, https://www.bbc.co.uk/history/ww2peopleswar/timeline/factfiles/nonflash/a6651858.shtml; Denness 2012: 240–41 (citing Mass-Observation); Imperial War Museum, "A Short History of Civilian Internment Camps in the Far East," accessed December 28, 2023, https://www.iwm.org.uk/history/a-short-history-of-civilian-internment-camps-in-the-far-east; Mia Spizzica, "When Ethnicity Counts: Civilian Internment in Australia during WW2," *Conversation*, September 20, 2012; Roger Kershaw, "Collar the Lot! Britain's Policy of Internment during the Second World War," *National Archives Blog*, July 2, 2015, https://blog.nationalarchives.gov.uk/collar-lot-britains-policy-internment-second-world-war/.

Chapter 10: Panic and Morale, Trauma and Resilience

1. *Oxford English Dictionary*, s.v. "shell shock," citing the *British Medical Journal*, January 30, 1915 ("Only one case of shell shock has come under my observation. A Belgian officer was the victim. A shell hellburst near him without inflicting any physical injury. He presented practically complete loss of sensation in the lower extremities and much loss of sensation").

2. Winter 2000; Jones and Wessely 2014.

3. Grayzel 2006. Naturally, the authorities worried more about soldiers' morale (compare Watson 2008).

4. Ermacora 2015; Horne 2014.

5. F. H. Manners, *Times* (London), September 10, 1915 (editorial written by Manners, private secretary of the lord of the Admiralty).

6. M. Ryan, "The Women's Splendid Courage in the Raided Areas. How They Met Frightfulness from the Sky Alone and Unprotected," *Weekly Dispatch*, October 1, 1916 (as cited in Linden 2021).

7. Goss 1948a: 13, 22–23, citing Jones (1931: 13, 89–90) and Charlton (1936: 91).

8. Grayzel 2006: 599–601.

9. Kovacs 1943: 28fn14; Hippler 2013: 28.

10. Douhet (1921) 2012: n.p. (my translation).

11. Meilenger 1997: 19.

12. *HC Debates*, November 10, 1932, vol. 270, col. 632 (Baldwin).

13. Kean 2018.

14. Hinton 2013.

15. Beaven and Griffiths 1999. See also Beaven and Thoms 1996.

16. *Mass-Observation Teaching Booklet No. 1: The Blitz*, University of Sussex, 1987, p. 7, http://www.massobs.org.uk/images/booklets/Blitz.pdf.

17. Mackay 2002: 6.

18. Beaven and Griffiths 1999; Jones et al. 2004: 470–71.

19. Lister 1941: 80–81.

20. Barton 1989: 164; *Irish Times*, "20,000 Sleeping in the Fields," May 14, 1941.

21. As cited in "Extracts from an Article on the Belfast Blitz, 1941. By Jonathan Bardon," c. 2013, accessed December 28, 2023, http://www.joeoloughlin.co.uk/belfast-blitz/.

22. *Irish Press*, "M.P. Urges 40,000 Huts for Belfast," May 14, 1941.

23. *Irish Times*, May 14, 1941.

24. Hemphill 1941 and the sources cited there.

25. As cited in Casper 2008: 341.

26. Casper 2008.

27. On Bernal, see Brown 2005.

28. Zuckerman 1978: 140.

29. Jones et al. 2004; Atkinson 2017; "Till We Hear the Last All Clear: Gender and the Presentation of Self in Young Girls' Writing about the Bombing of Hull during the Second World War," accessed December 27, 2023, http://eprints.lincoln.ac.uk/id/eprint/14793/1/14793%20Till%20We%20Hear%20the%20Last%20All%20Clear%20J%20Greenhalgh%202014.pdf.

30. As cited in Burney 2012: 66. For more on Hull, see M. Jones 2008; Atkinson 2017.

31. Kirby and Capie 1997; Burney 2012.

32. As cited in Hastings 1979: 127–28. See also Overy 2014: 288.

33. Zuckerman 1978: 145–46.

34. Overy 2014: 169–72.

35. For a good overview, see Imperial War Museum, "The Blitz around Britain," accessed January 2, 2024, https://www.iwm.org.uk/history/the-blitz-around-britain.

36. Lewis 1943: 27.

37. Blacker 1946: 175.

38. Jones 2016.

39. O'Brien 1955; Titmuss 1950: 538.

40. Jones et al. 2004; Ponting 1990; Overy, "Why the Cruel Myth of the 'Blitz Spirit' Is No Model for How to Fight Coronavirus," *Guardian*, March 19, 2020.

41. E.g., Tim Luckhurst, "Lessons from Britain's Blitz Shows Bombing Civilians Strengthens Defiance—Suggesting Russia Doomed to Fail," *Independent*, November 3, 2022.

42. USSBS 1947a: 1, 53; Pape 1996: 273; Overy 2014: 616–17.

43. Schreiter 2017: 374.

44. Levi paid tribute to Perrone in Levi (1960) and elsewhere.

45. Fridman et al. 2011.

46. Levi (1960: 24–25).

47. Compare Romano 2019; McCord 1995: 255–56.

48. This is the title of a piece by Luke Mintz in the *Telegraph*, February 1, 2020.

49. Walker and Skowronski 2009.

50. At the opposite end of the spectrum to FAB is highly superior autobiographical memory (HSAM)—or *hyperthymesia*. People with HSAM remember almost everything, even the most trivial detail, in their lives. One might consider this a gift, but not so: HSAM is regarded as a unique neurological condition that prevents people from living a normal life. People with HSAM—a very rare condition, with only a handful of sufferers identified so far—are prone to depression and find it hard to escape tragedies and embarrassments in their past. According to neuroscientist James McGaugh, who first identified HSAM, "The overall summary of all of this is that they're bad forgetters" (McRobbie 2017).

51. Bonanno 2004; Kihlstrom 2005.

52. Bonanno, Westphal, and Mancini 2012.

53. Bourke and Schott 2022.

54. Van den Berg et al. 2017; Eilene Zimmerman, "What Makes Some People More Resilient than Others," *New York Times*, June 18, 2020. The study in question is Galatzer-Levy et al. 2018.

55. Bonanno and Manzini 2012; Bonanno 2021.

56. Levav 1998.

57. Antonovsky et al. 1971.

58. Leon et al. 1981.

59. Greene et al. 2012.

60. Daniel Goleman, "Holocaust Survivors Had Skills to Prosper," *New York Times*, October 6, 1992; Helmreich 1996.

61. Levine et al. 2016; Levav and Klomet 2018.

62. Canham et al. 2017.

63. Bachner et al. 2017; compare Kagansky et al. 2019 (who, however, focus more on physical resilience).

64. Barel et al. 2010.

65. Knobler et al. 2018. Compare Ayalon 2005.

66. Rakoff et al. 1966; Sigal et al. 1973. I owe the caveat to Haim Knobler.

67. Kellerman 2001. There is much in this vein also in the context of the Northern Ireland Troubles; compare the website of the Commission for Victims and Survivors, Northern Ireland, https://www.cvsni.org/, accessed January 2, 2024.

68. Rieck 1994; Felsen 1998; Kellerman 2001: 36; Van IJzendoorn et al. 2003. See also Lindert et al. 2017, who note that "studies investigating random samples of genocide survivors did not find an impact of genocides on health of children of survivors."

69. Gomolin 2004, 2019.

70. Gerson 2019; see also five responses and a rejoinder by Gomolin in the same issue of *Psychological Quarterly* 88, no. 3 (2019). This does not rule out a possibly behavioral transmission mechanism: a traumatized parent may be a poor or even abusive role model for children.

71. Maercker and Haerrle 2003; Obschonka et al. 2017. On the controversies surrounding moral equivalence in this context, compare Heins and Langenohl 2011.

72. Akbulut-Yuksel et al. 2022.

73. As cited in Suedfeld 1997: 855.

74. Robert Jay Lifton, "Hiroshima and the World: The Wisdom of Survivors," *Chugoku shinbun*, January 3, 2009, https://www.hiroshimapeacemedia.jp/?p=19659. See also Lifton, "The Bomb," *New York Review of Books*, February 1, 1963 ("Most survivors recover from the experience and lead more or less normal lives").

75. Ohta et al. 2000.

76. E.g., both Honda et al. 2002 and Kim et al. 2011 highlight the long-term impact of the Nagasaki bombing on mental well-being.

77. Tim Gaynor and Pieter Ventevogel, "Q&A: Far from Being Traumatized, Most Refugees Are 'Surprisingly Resilient,'" January 3, 2017, https://www.unhcr.org/news/latest/2017/1/586b78de4/qa-far-traumatized-refugees-surprisingly-resilient.html. In a metastudy of child refugees, Tol et al. (2013) find they "support a perspective of resilience as a complex dynamic process."

78. Kuwert et al. 2009.

79. Freitag et al. 2013.

80. Santavirta et al. 2015. Compare Wikipedia, "Finnish War Children," https://en.wikipedia.org/wiki/Finnish_war_children, accessed January 2, 2024; Korppi-Tommola 2008. Santavirta (2012) investigated whether the socioeconomic status of the fostering family influenced the subsequent educational outcomes and found that those fostered with better-off families were more likely to attend secondary school or college.

Chapter 11: A Conclusion Without an End

Epigraph 1: As cited in Roy Greenslade, "First World War: How State and Press Kept Truth off the Front Page," *Guardian*, July 23, 2014.

Epigraph 2: As translated by Louise and Aylmer Maude (1922–23), May 18, 2017, https://archive.org/details/war-peace/page/n2/mode/1up?q=play, pp. 1272, 1273.

1. Vedel-Petersen 1923, editor's preface, p. 133; Prost 2014b, table 3.

2. Mazower 1999: 212–23; Withuis and Mooij 2010: 1, 107.

3. Grossmann 1995; Götz Aly, "The Logic of Horror," June 12, 2006 (translation of an article in *Die Zeit*, June 1, 2006), http://www.signandsight.com/features/800.html.

4. The 10 million figure for military deaths is a compromise between the 8.7 million suggested by Ellman and Maksudov (1994) and the 11 million proposed in other places. The Wikipedia entry "World War II Casualties of the Soviet Union," accessed January 5, 2023, https://en.wikipedia.org /wiki/World_War_II_casualties_of_the_Soviet_Union, provides a useful overview.

5. Ellman and Maksudov 1994; Harrison 2003a, 2019. Both Harrison (2019) and Ellman and Maksudov (1994), as well as several Russian scholars, put the aggregate death toll at twenty-six to twenty-seven million.

6. Schoenberg 1970: 32.

7. Markevich and Harrison 2011; Wheatcroft 2017: 229; Athukorala and Athukorala 2022.

8. Mitter 2013: 397 (based on a compromise between a range of sources).

9. Here I differ from Bessel (2015: 274) because I attribute post-1918 deaths in the Soviet Union to World War I.

10. These totals rely on Harrison (2003a) for the Soviet Union and Mitter (2013) for China and on *Encyclopaedia Britannica Online*, accessed January 4, 2024, https://www.britannica.com /topic/casualties-of-World-War-II-2231003, for the rest of the World War II deaths. Prost (2014a: 588) has put World War I military deaths at ten million.

11. Scott Slovic and Paul Slovic, "The Arithmetic of Compassion," *New York Times*, December 4, 2015.

12. Bessel 2015: 252; Weinberg 2005: 895.

13. USSBS, "The Effects of the Atomic Bombings of Hiroshima and Nagasaki, June 19, 1946," President's Secretary's File, Truman Papers, http://www.trumanlibrary.org/whistlestop /study_collections/bomb/large/documents/index.php?pagenumber=42&documentid =65&documentdate=1946-06-19. The USSBS put the number killed in Germany at just over 300,000 and the number wounded at 780,000. *Summary Report (European War)*, p. 15, accessed January 5, 2024, https://www.anesi.com/ussbs02.htm#tc.

14. Newsholme 1918–19.

15. Compare World War I historian Jay Winter's insistence in 1988 that the pandemic "was neither caused by the first World War, nor can its victims be counted among the victims of the conflict" with pandemic historian Phillips's claim that "in effect, the H1N1 virus was globalized by World War I which systematically turned a local outbreak in one continent into a world pandemic" (Winter 1988: 23; Phillips 2014). See also Prost 2014b: 6.

16. See, however, Ó Gráda (2023) and the sources described there.

17. "There are no innocent civilians."—Curtis LeMay.

18. George Orwell, "As I Please," *Tribune*, July 14, 1944; William Adams, "The American Peace Commission and the Punishment of Crimes Committed during War," *Law Quarterly Review* 39 (1923): 248 (quoting a letter from Kaiser Wilhelm to Austrian kaiser Franz Joseph).

19. "Kaiser Wilhelm II's Letter to President Wilson regarding Belgian Use of Dum-Dum Bullets," September 7, 1914, https://www.firstworldwar.com/source/kaiserdumdumbullets.htm.

20. Best 1980: 231.

21. And some commentators on all sides, as already noted, would have questioned the desirability of sparing civilians on the grounds that the distinction between combatant and noncombatant was already anachronistic by 1914 (Jourdain 1918).

22. Orwell, "As I Please," May 19, 1944.

23. Harmon 1991: 26.

24. In times of war, the laws are silent.

25. These negotiations are described in Zelikow 2021.

26. Pope Benedict XV, "Apostolic Exhortation: *Dès le début*," August 1, 1917, https://www
.vatican.va/content/benedict-xv/it/apost_exhortations/documents/hf_ben-xv_exh_19170801_des
-le-debut.html; Melloni, Cavagnini, and Grossi 2020. On another pope's more recent interventions in the same direction, see Matthew Schmitz, "The Pope of Peace," *First Things*, August/
September 2023.

27. Gatrell 2013b.

28. Davis and Engerman 2006: 426.

29. International Criminal Court, "About the Court," accessed January 5, 2024, https://www
.icc-cpi.int/about/the-court.

Epilogue

Epigraph: "Biden Takes a Tougher Stance on Israel's 'Indiscriminate Bombing' of Gaza," PBS
NewsHour, December 12, 2023.

1. United Nations, "Ukraine: Civilian Casualties Mount as War Enters Second Winter," November 21, 2023, https://www.ungeneva.org/en/news-media/news/2023/11/87722/ukraine-civilian
-casualties-mount-war-enters-second-winter.

2. Guy Faulconbridge, "Ukraine War, Already with Up to 354,000 Casualties, Likely to Last
Past 2023—US Documents," *Reuters Report*, April 12, 2023; Helen Cooper, Thomas Gibbons-Neff,
Eric Schmitt, and Julian E. Barnes, "Troop Deaths and Injuries in Ukraine War Near 500,000, US
Officials Say," *New York Times,* August 18, 2023; Reuters, "Ukrainian Group Says More than 30,000
Troops Have Died in Russia's Invasion," November 15, 2023; https://www.reuters.com/world
/europe/ukrainian-group-says-more-than-30000-troops-have-died-russias-invasion-2023-11-15/;
Ministry of Defence of Ukraine, "The Total Combat Losses of the Enemy from 24.02.2022 to
28.11.2023," November 28, 2023, https://www.mil.gov.ua/en/news/2023/11/28/the-total-combat
-losses-of-the-enemy-from-24-02-2022-to-28-11-2023/.

3. Alex de Waal and Abdul Mohammed, "The War the World Forgot," *New York Times*, December 4, 2023.

4. Wikipedia, "Casualties of the 2023 Israel-Hamas War," accessed November 19, 2023; Aaron
Boxerman, "What We Know about the Death Toll in Israel from the Hamas-Led Attacks," *New York
Times*, November 12, 2023; Jeffrey Gettleman, Adam Sella, and Anat Schwartz, "What We Know
about Sexual Violence during the Oct. 7 Attacks on Israel," *New York Times*, December 4, 2023.

5. Lauren Leatherby, "Gaza Civilians, under Israeli Barrage, Are Being Killed at Historic Pace,"
New York Times, November 25, 2023; UN, "Hostilities in the Gaza Strip and Israel: Reported
Impact," December 18, 2023, https://www.ochaopt.org/sites/default/files/Gaza_casualties_info
-graphic_18_Dec_2023.pdf; Integrated Food Security Phase Classification, "Gaza Strip: Acute
Food Insecurity Situation for 24 November–7 December 2023," December 21, 2023, https://
ipcinfo.org/ipc-country-analysis/details-map/en/c/1156749/?iso3=PSE.

6. Yasmeen Serhan, "Biden Cast Doubt on Gaza's Death Toll. Palestinian Officials Responded
with 6,747 Names," *Time Magazine*, October 26, 2023. See also Zeina Jamaluddine, Francesco
Checchi, and Oona M. R. Campbell, "Excess Mortality in Gaza," *Lancet* 402 (November 26, 2023):
2189-90.

7. Yigal Levy, "The Israeli Army Has Dropped the Restraint in Gaza, and the Data Shows
Unprecedented Killing," *Haaretz*, December 9, 2023; Ali Sawafta and Maggie Fick, "How Many
Palestinians Have Died in Gaza? Death Toll Explained," Reuters, December 9, 2023, https://www
.reuters.com/world/middle-east/how-many-palestinians-have-died-gaza-war-how-will-counting
-continue-2023-12-06/; Nancy Youssef and Jared Malsin, "US Officials Have Growing Confidence
in Death Toll Reports from Gaza: Reliance on the Palestinian Data Is a Partial Shift by the Biden
Administration," *Wall Street Journal*, November 11, 2023.

8. Anushka Patil and Thomas Fuller, "Displaced Gazans in the South Facing Dangers They Had Sought to Escape," *New York Times*, December 29, 2023.

9. Eric Schmitt, "Ukraine Starts Using American-Made Cluster Munitions in Its Counteroffensive, US Officials say," *New York Times*, July 19, 2023; James I. Rogers, "Remembering the Terror the Luftwaffe's Butterfly Bombs Brought to the North," *Guardian*, June 21, 2013.

10. ICC, "Statement by Prosecutor Karim A. A. Khan KC on the Issuance of Arrest Warrants against President Vladimir Putin and Ms Maria Lvova-Belova," March 17, 2023.

11. Report of the legal review panel, published April 28, 2023, of the Amnesty International press release concerning Ukrainian fighting tactics, August 4, 2022, accessedhttps://www.amnesty.org/en/documents/org60/6731/2023/en/.

12. ICC, "31 Cases," accessed December 31, 2023, https://www.icc-cpi.int/cases?page=0.

13. Robin Stein et al., "A Times Investigation Tracked Israel's Use of One of Its Most Destructive Bombs in South Gaza," *New York Times*, December 21, 2023.

14. Steven Erlanger, "Under Rules of War, 'Proportionality' in Gaza Is Not about Evening the Score," *New York Times*, December 13. 2023; Michael D. Shear, "Biden Warns Israel It Is 'Losing Support' over War," *New York Times*, November 13, 2023.

15. James Landale, "David Cameron Warns Israel over Gaza Civilian Casualties," BBC News, November 24, 2023, https://www.bbc.com/news/uk-politics-67518614.

16. Samuel Moyn, *Humane: How the United States Abandoned Peace and Reinvented War* (New York: Farrar, Straus, and Giroux, 2021).

17. Wikipedia, "List of Treaties Unsigned or Unratified by the United States," last modified March 5, 2023, https://en.wikipedia.org/wiki/List_of_treaties_unsigned_or_unratified_by_the_United_States. See Mark Tran et al., "Humble Obama Accepts Nobel prize," *Guardian*, December 10, 2009; Downes 2008.

BIBLIOGRAPHY

aan de Stegge, Cecile. 2019. "Excess Mortality and Causes of Death in Dutch Psychiatric Institutions." In Bailer and Wetzel 2019: 97–126.

Abbenhuis, Martje M. 2006. "Fugitives of War: Refugees and Internees." In *The Art of Staying Neutral: The Netherlands in the First World War, 1914–1918*, pp. 95–115. Amsterdam: Amsterdam University Press.

———. 2008. "Review of Lipkes (2007)." *American Historical Review* 113 (3): 930–31.

Abramitzky, Ran, and Hanna Halaburda. 2020. "Were Jews in Interwar Poland More Educated?" *Journal of Demographic Economics* 86 (3): 291–304.

Acemoglu, Daron, and James A. Robinson. 2001. "A Theory of Political Transitions." *American Economic Review* 91 (4): 938–63.

Achim, Viorel. 1998. *The Roma in Romanian History*. Budapest: Central European University Press. https://books.openedition.org/ceup/1532.

Adamets, Serguei. 2002. "Famine in Nineteenth- and Twentieth-Century Russia: Mortality by Age, Cause, and Gender." In *Famine Demography: Perspectives from the Past and Present*, edited by Tim Dyson and C. Ó Gráda, pp. 158–80. Oxford: Oxford University Press.

Adelman, Jeremy. 2013. *Worldly Philosopher: The Odyssey of Albert O. Hirschman*. Princeton, NJ: Princeton University Press.

Adena, M., R. Enikolopov, M. Petrova, and H.-J. Voth. 2020. "Bombs, Broadcasts, and Resistance: Allied Intervention and Domestic Opposition to the Nazi Regime during World War II." Centre for Economic Policy Research Discussion Paper No. 15292.

Adler, Eliyana. 2020. *Survival on the Margins: Polish Jewish Refugees in the Wartime Soviet Union*. Cambridge, MA: Harvard University Press.

Afflerbach, Holger, and David Stevenson, eds. 2007. *An Improbable War? The Outbreak of World War I and European Political Culture before 1914*. New York: Berghahn.

Ager, Philip, Katherine Eriksson, Ezra Karger, Peter Nencka, and Melissa A. Thomasson. 2020. "School Closures during the 1918 Flu Pandemic." National Bureau of Economic Research Working Paper No. 28,246, December.

Akbulut-Yuksel, Mevlude, Erdal Tekin, and Belgi Turan. 2022. "World War II Blues: The Long-Lasting Mental Health Effect of Childhood Trauma." National Bureau of Economic Research Working Paper No. 30284.

Akçam, Taner. 2006. *A Shameful Act: The Armenian Genocide and the Question of Turkish Responsibility*. New York: Metropolitan Books.

———. 2012. *The Young Turks' Crime against Humanity: The Armenian Genocide and Ethnic Cleansing in the Ottoman Empire*. Princeton, NJ: Princeton University Press.

———. 2019. "When Was the Decision to Annihilate the Armenians Taken?" *Journal of Genocide Research* 21 (4): 457–80.

Aksalal, Mustafa. 2014. "The Ottoman Empire." In *Empires at War, 1911–1923*, edited by Robert Gerwarth and Erex Manela, pp. 17–33. Oxford: Oxford University Press.

Alastalo, Hanna, Katri Räikkönen, Anu-Katriina Pesonen, Clive Osmond, David J. P. Barker, Eero Kajantie, Kati Heinonen, Tom J. Forsén, and Johan G. Eriksson. 2009. "Cardiovascular Health of Finnish War Evacuees 60 Years Later." *Annals of Medicine* 41 (1): 66–72. https://doi .org.10.1080/07853890802301983.

Aldous, Chris. 2010. "Contesting Famine: Hunger and Nutrition in Occupied Japan, 1945–1952." *Journal of American-East Asian Relations* 17 (3): 230–56.

Alexander, John D. 2014. "Justice in Warfare: The Ethical Debate over British Area Bombing of German Cities in World War II." PhD diss., School of Theology, Boston University. https:// core.ac.uk/download/pdf/142063659.pdf.

Alexievich, Svetlana. 2017. *The Unwomanly Face of War: An Oral History of Women in World War II.* London: Penguin.

Alfani, G., and C. Ó Gráda. 2017. *Famine in European History since the Middle Ages.* Cambridge: Cambridge University Press.

———. 2018. "The Timing and Causes of Famine in Europe." *Nature Sustainability* 1:283–88.

Allais, Olivier, Guy Fagherazzi, and Julia Mink. 2021. "The Long-Run Effects of War on Health: Evidence from World War II in France." *Social Science and Medicine* 276:113812.

Allen, Keith. 1998. "Sharing Scarcity: Bread Rationing and the First World War in Berlin, 1914– 1923." *Journal of Social History* 32 (2): 371–93.

Almond, Douglas. 2006. "Is the 1918 Influenza Pandemic Over? Long-Term Effects of *in Utero* Influenza Exposure in the Post-1940 U.S. Population." *Journal of Political Economy* 114 (4): 672–712.

Almond, Douglas, and Janet Currie. 2011. "Killing Me Softly: The Fetal Origins Hypothesis." *Journal of Economic Perspectives* 25 (3): 153–72.

Al-Qattan, Najwa. 2014. "When Mothers Ate Their Children: Wartime Memory and the Language of Food in Syria and Lebanon." *International Journal of Middle East Studies* 46 (4): 719–36.

Aly, Götz. 2008. *Hitler's Beneficiaries: Plunder, Racial War, and the Nazi Welfare State.* London: St. Martin's Press.

Amara, Michael. 2008. *Des Belges à l'epreuve de l'exil: Les réfugiés de la Premiere Guerre mondiale.* Brussels: Éditions de l'Université de Bruxelles.

Anderson, Margaret Lavinia. 2004. "A German Way of War?" *German History* 22 (2): 254–58.

———. 2006. "How German Is It?" *German History* 24 (1): 122–26.

Andreasen, N. C. 2000. "Schizophrenia: The Fundamental Questions." *Brain Research Reviews* 31:106–12.

Andreev, E. M., L. E. Darski, and T. L. Kharkova. 1992. "L'histoire de la population de l'URSS, 1920–1955." *Annales de démographie historique*, 61–150.

———. 2002. "Population Dynamics: Consequences of Regular and Irregular Changes." In *Demographic Trends and Patterns in the Soviet Union before 1991*, edited by Wolfgang Lutz, Sergie Scherbov, and Andrei Volkov, pp. 423–40. London: Routledge.

Angelucci, Enzo. 2001. *Illustrated Encyclopedia of Military Aircraft.* Edison, NJ: Chartwell.

Anonymous. 1919. "Bombing Germany: General Trenchard's Report of Operations of British Airmen against German Cities." *Current History (1916–1940)* 10 (1): 151–56.

Anonymous. 1923. "The Fate of the Civilian in Future Wars." *British Medical Journal* 1 (3246): 480–81.

Anonymous. 1939. "Demographic Problems of Poland." *Population Index* 5 (4): 233–38.

Anonymous. 1945. "Price Control and Rationing in Foreign Countries during the War." *Monthly Labor Review* 61 (5): 882–99.

Anonymous. 1946a. "De rijstpositie van Nederlandsch–Indie" (The Rice Situation in the Dutch Indies). *Economisch Weekblad voor Nederlandsch-Indië* 12, no. 11 (May 25): 81–82.

Anonymous. 1946b. "Die wirtschafliche Lage des Österreichs am Ende des ersten Nachkriegjahres." *Monatsberiche des Österreichischen Institutes für Wirtschaftsforschung* 19 (July 31): n.p.

Anonymous. 2005. *A Woman in Berlin*. London: Virago Press.

Antoniou, Giorgos, and A. Dirk Moses. 2018. *The Holocaust in Greece*. Cambridge: Cambridge University Press.

Antonov, A. N. 1947. "Children Born during the Siege of Leningrad in 1942." *Journal of Pediatrics* 30 (3): 250–59.

Antonovsky, A. B. Moaz, N. Dowty, and H. Wijsenbeek. 1971. "Twenty-Five Years Later: A Limited Study of the Sequelae of the Concentration Camp Experience." *Social Psychiatry* 6:186–93.

Anders, Edward, and Juris Dubrovskis. 2003. "Who Died in the Holocaust? Recovering Names from Official Records." *Holocaust and Genocide Studies* 17 (1): 114–38.

Anderson, Frank F. 1917. "Fundamental Factors in War Finance." *Journal of Political Economy* 25 (9): 857–87.

Anderson, Truman. 1999. "Incident at Baranivka: German Reprisals and the Soviet Partisan Movement in Ukraine." *Journal of Modern History* 71 (3): 585–623.

Andersson, Yvonne, Rolf Holmqvist, and Doris Nilsson. 2019. "Child Evacuations during World War II: This Should Not Happen Again." *Journal of Loss and Trauma* 24:3, 213–25. https://doi.org.10.1080/15325024.2018.1549198.

Arad, Yitshak. 2002. "The Holocaust in Lithuania as Reflected in Jewish Sources: Diaries, Memories, Testimonies." Paper presented to Holocaust Conference, Vilnius, September 23–25.

———. 2009. *The Holocaust in the Soviet Union*. Lincoln: University of Nebraska Press.

———. 2011. "Social Structure and Development: A Legacy of the Holocaust in Russia." *Quarterly Journal of Economics* 126, no. 2 (May): 895–946.

Archer, Laird. 1944. *Balkan Journal*. New York: W. W. Norton.

Arendt, Hannah. 2006. *Eichmann in Jerusalem*. New York: Penguin.

Arnold, Klaus Jochen, and Gert C. Lübbers. 2007. "The Meeting of the Staatssekretäre on 2 May 1941 and the Wehrmacht: A Document Up for Discussion." *Journal of Contemporary History* 42 (4): 613–26.

Aronson, J. D. 2013. "The Politics of Civilian Casualty Counts." In Seybolt, Aronson, and Fischhoff 2013: 29–50.

Ashdown, Paddy. 2015. *The Cruel Victory: The French Resistance, D-Day and the Battle for the Vercors*. London: Collins.

Astashkevich, Irina. 2018. *Gendered Violence: Jewish Women in the Pogroms of 1917 to 1921*. Boston: Academic Studies Press.

Atabaki, Touraj. 2016. "Persia/Iran." In Daniel et al. 2014–19.

Athukorala, Prema-chandra, and Chaturica Athukorala. 2022. *The Great Influenza Pandemic of 1918–20: An Interpretative Survey in the Time of COVID-19*. Cambridge: Cambridge University Press.

Atkinson, D. 2017. "Trauma, Resilience and Utopianism in World War II Hull." In *Hull: Culture, History, Place*, edited by D. Starkey, D. A. Atkinson, B. McDonagh, S. McKeon, and E. Salter, pp. 238–69. Liverpool: Liverpool University Press.

Austrian Press and Information Service. 2000. "The Unloved Democracy of the Interwar Period." Accessed February 3, 2024. https://web.archive.org/web/20060420214655/http://www.austria.org/history_rep.shtml.

Ayal, Eliezer B., and Barry R. Chiswick. 1983. "The Economics of the Diaspora Revisited." *Economic Development and Cultural Change* 31 (4): 861–75.

Ayalon, Liat. 2005. "Challenges Associated with the Study of Resilience to Trauma in Holocaust Survivors." *Journal of Loss and Trauma* 10:347–58.

Ba, I., and R. S. Bhopal. 2017. "Physical, Mental and Social Consequences in Civilians Who Have Experienced War-Related Sexual Violence: A Systematic Review (1981–2014)." *Public Health* 142:121–35.

Bachner, Yaacov, Sara Carmel, and Norm O'Rourke. 2017. "The Paradox of Well-Being and Holocaust Survivors." *Journal of the American Psychiatric Nurses Association* 24 (1): 45–52.

Bailer, Brigitte, and Julianne Wetzel, eds. 2019. *Mass Murder of People with uerrase n and the Holocaust*. Berlin: Metropol Verlag.

Bajohr, F. 2001. *"Aryanisation' in Hamburg: The Economic Exclusion of Jews and the Confiscation of Their Property in Nazi Germany*. New York: Berghahn.

Baker, Mark. 2018. "The Slow, the Quick and the Dead: Environment, Politics and Temporality in the Henan Famine, 1942–43." *International Review of Environmental History* 4 (2): 93–109.

Balasubramanian, Aditya. 2023. "A Forgotten Famine of '43? Travancore's Muffled 'Cry of Distress.'" *Modern Asian Studies* 57:1495–529.

Baldoli, Claudia, and Marco Fincardi. 2009. "Italian Society under Allied Bombs: Propaganda, Experience, and Legends, 1940–1945." *Historical Journal* 52 (4): 1017–38.

Ball, Howard. 2011. *Genocide: A Reference Guide*. Santa Barbara: ABC-CLIO.

Bandeira, Mário Leston. 2009. "A sobremortalidade de 1918 em Portugal: Análise demográfica." In *A pandemia esquecida: Olhares comparados sobre a pneumónica, 1918–1919*, edited by José Manuel Sobral et al., pp. 131–54. Lisboa: Institute of Social Sciences, University of Lisbon.

Banham, Tony. 2019. "Hong Kong's Civilian Fatalities of the Second World War." *Journal of the Royal Asiatic Society (Hong Kong)* 59:31–50.

Banning, C. 1946. "Food Shortage and Public Health, First Half of 1945." *Annals of the American Academy of Political and Social Science* 245:93–110.

Banse, Ingo E. 1975. "The Bomber Menace, 1917–1933: The Evolution of the First Ultimate Weapon and the Inability to Cope with It." Master's diss., Western Michigan University. https://scholarworks.wmich.edu/masters_theses/2435.

Barber, John, and Andrei Dzeniskevich, eds. 1991. *The Soviet Home Front, 1941–1945: A Social and Economic History of the USSR in World War II*. London: Longman.

———. 2005. *Life and Death in Besieged Leningrad, 1941–44*. London: Palgrave Macmillan.

Barber, John, and Mark Harrison. 2006. "Patriotic War, 1941–1945." In *The Cambridge History of Russia: Vol. 3, The Twentieth Century*, edited by Ronald Grigor Suny, pp. 217–42. Cambridge: Cambridge University Press.

Barel, Efrat, Marinus H. Van Ijzendoorn, Abraham Sagi-Schwartz, and Marian J. Bakermans-Kranenburg. 2010. "A Meta-analysis of the Long-Term Sequelae of a Genocide." *Psychological Bulletin* 136 (5): 677–98.

Baris, Tommaso. 2007. "Le corps expéditionnaire français en Italie: Violences des 'libérateurs' en Italie durant l'été 1944." *Vingtième siècle: Revue d'histoire* 93:47–61.

Barker, D. J. 1995. "Fetal Origins of Coronary Heart Disease." *British Medical Journal* 311 (6998): 171–74.

Barker, D. J., and C. N. Martyn. 1992. "The Maternal and Fetal Origins of Cardiovascular Disease." *Journal of Epidemiology and Community Health* 46:8–11.

Barker, D. J., and C. Osmond. 1986. "Infant Mortality, Childhood Nutrition, and Ischaemic Heart Disease in England and Wales." *Lancet* 327 (8489): 1077–81.

Barros, Andrew. 2009. "Strategic Bombing and Restraint in 'Total War,' 1915–1918." *Historical Journal* 52 (2): 413–31.

Barton, Brian. 1989. *The Blitz: Belfast in the War Years*. Belfast: Blackstaff.

Bartrop, Paul R. 2018. *The Evian Conference of 1938 and the Jewish Refugee Crisis*. London: Palgrave Macmillan.

Bas, Mehmet Fatih. 2017. "War Losses (Ottoman Empire/Middle East)." In Daniel et al. 2014–19.

Bauer, Thomas K., Sebastian Braun, and Michael Kvasnicka. 2013. "The Economic Integration of Forced Migrants: Evidence for Post-War Germany." *Economic Journal* 123 (571): 998–1024.

Bauer, Thomas K., Matthias Giesecke, and Laura M. Janisch. 2019. "The Impact of Forced Migration on Mortality: Evidence from German Pension Insurance Records." *Demography* 56 (1): 25–47.

Baumslag, Naomi, and Barry M. Shmookler. 2014. "Typhus Epidemic Containment as Resistance to Nazi Genocide." In Grodin 2014: 39–48.

Bayly, Christopher, and Tim Harper. 2004. *Britain's Asian Empire & The War with Japan.* London: Allen Lane.

Bayne-Jones, Stanhope, Henry S. Fuller, et al. 1964. *Preventive Medicine in World War 2:* Vol. 7, *Communicable Diseases.* Washington, DC: Office of the Surgeon General.

Beaven, Brad, and John Griffiths. 1999. "The Blitz, Civilian Morale and the City: Mass-Observation and Working-Class Culture in Britain, 1940–41." *Urban History* 26 (1): 71–88.

Beaven, Brad, and D. Thoms. 1996. "The Blitz and Civilian Morale in Three Northern Cities, 1940–42." *Northern History* 32:195–203.

Beccatini, Giacomo, and Nicolò Bellanca. 1986. *Economia di uerra e mercato nero: Note e riflessioni sulla Toscana, Italia contemporanea* 165:5–28.

Becher, Heiko, Oliver Razum, Catherine Kyobutungi, Judit Laki, Jördis Jennifer Ott, Ulrich Ronellenfitsch, and Volker Winkler. 2007. "Mortality of Immigrants from the Former Soviet Union: Results of a Cohort Study." *Deutsches Aertzeblatt* 104 (23): 1655–61.

Bechet, Cristophe. 2014. "Les massacres du 20 août 1914 à Liège." *Bulletin du Centre Liégeois d'Histoire et d'Archéologie Militaires,* no. 137:7–18.

Becker, Annette. 2010. *Les Cicatrices rouges 14–18: France et Belgique occupées.* Paris: Fayard.

———. 2019. "Against Civilians: Atrocities, Extermination, and Genocide from One World War to Another, 1942/44–1914." In *A World at War, 1911–1949: Explorations in the Cultural History of War,* edited by Catriona Pennell and Filipe Ribeiro de Meneses, pp. 161–80. Leiden: Brill.

Becker, Sascha O., Irene Grosfeld, Pauline A. Grosjean, Nico Voigtländer, and Ekaterina Zhuravskaya. 2020. "Forced Migration and Human Capital: Evidence from Post-WWII Population Transfers." *American Economic Review* 110 (5): 1430–63.

Becker, Sascha O., Volker Lindenthal, Sharun Mukand, and Fabian Waldinger. 2021. "Persecution and Escape: Professional Networks and High-Skilled Emigration from Nazi Germany." IZA Working Paper No. 14,120.

Beevor, Antony. 2002a. *Berlin: The Downfall, 1945.* London: Viking Penguin.

———. 2002b. "They Raped Every German Female from Eight to 80." *Guardian,* May 1.

Beiner, Guy. 2006. "Out in the Cold and Back: New-Found Interest in the Great Flu." *Cultural and Social History* 3:496–505.

Bělín, Matěj, Tomáš Jelínek, and Štěpán Jurajda. 2023. "Preexisting Social Ties among Auschwitz Prisoners Support Holocaust Survival." *Proceedings of the National Academy of Sciences* 120 (29): e2221654120.

Bellamy, Alex J. 2008. "The Ethics of Terror Bombing: Beyond Supreme Emergency." *Journal of Military Ethics* 7 (1): 41–65.

Belozerov, Boris. 2005. "Crime during the Siege." In Barber and Dzeniskevich 2005: 213–28.

Benes, E. 1941. "The New Order in Europe." *Nineteenth Century and After* 130:150–55.

Ben-Naftali, Aya. 2016. "Collaboration and Resistance: The Ninth Fort as a Test Case." Typescript. https://yivo.org/cimages/9th_fort_as_a_test_case_ben-naftali.pdf.

Berche, Patrick. 2012. *Faut-il encore avoir peur de la grippe? Histoire des pandémies.* Paris: Odile Jacob.

Berg, Joseph. 2016. "De iniustitia belli: Violence against Civilians in the Thirty Years War." Honors thesis, Loyola Marymount University. https://digitalcommons.lmu.edu/cgi/viewcontent.cgi?referer=&httpsredir=1&article=1124&context=honors-thesis.

Bergner, L., and M. W. Susser. 1970. "Low Birth Weight and Prenatal Nutrition: An Interpretative Review." *Pediatrics* 46:946–66.

Bergs, Christoph. 2017. "The History of the US Air Force in World War 1." https://www.centenaire.org/en/autour-de-la-grande-guerre/aviation/history-us-air-service-world-war-i.

Berkhoff, Karel C. 2004. *Harvest of Despair: Life and Death in Ukraine under Nazi Rule*. Cambridge, MA: Harvard University Press.

Bernstein, Barton. 1999. "Reconsidering Truman's Claim of 'Half a Million American Lives' Saved by the Atomic Bomb: The Construction and Deconstruction of a Myth." *Journal of Strategic Studies* 22 (1): 54–95.

Bertazzini, Mattia, and Michela Giorcelli. 2023. "The Economics of Civilian Victimization: Evidence from World War II Italy." Working paper. Accessed December 28, 2023. https://papers .ssrn.com/sol3/papers.cfm?abstract_id=4248228.

Bessel, Richard. 2009. *Germany, 1945: From War to Peace*. London: Simon and Schuster.

———. 2015. "Death and Survival in the Second World War." In Geyer and Tooze 2015: 252–76.

Best, Geoffrey. 1980. *Humanity in Warfare: The Modern History of the International Law of Armed Conflict*. London: Weidenfeld and Nicolson.

Beveridge, Sir William. 1939. *Blockade and the Civilian Population*. Oxford Pamphlets on World Affairs. Oxford: Oxford University Press.

Bharier, Julien. 1968. "A Note on the Population of Iran, 1900–1966." *Population Studies* 22 (2): 273–79.

Biddiscombe, Perry. 2001. "Dangerous Liaisons: The Anti-fraternization Movement in the U.S. Occupation Zones of Germany and Austria, 1945–1948." *Journal of Social History* 34 (3): 611–47.

Biddle, Tami Davis. 1999. "Bombing by the Square Yard: Sir Arthur Harris at War, 1942–1945." *International History Review* 21 (3): 626–64.

———. 2002. *Rhetoric and Reality in Air Warfare: The Evolution of British and American Ideas about Strategic Bombing, 1914–1945*. Princeton, NJ: Princeton University Press.

Bidlack, Richard. 2000. "Survival Strategies in Leningrad during the First Year of the Soviet-German War." In *The People's War: Responses to World War II in the Soviet Union*, edited by R. W. Thurston and B. Bonwetsch, pp. 84–108. Chicago: University of Illinois Press.

Bignon, Vincent. 2009. "Cigarette Money and Black-Market Prices during the 1948 German Miracle." EconomiX Working Paper No. 2009-2, University of Paris Nanterre.

Bilbrough, Ethel. 2014. *My War Diary, 1914–1918*. London: Ebury Books.

Bissonnette, Victor. 2020. 'Mémoires sous silence: La France bombardée par les allies 1940–2014." PhD diss., Université de Québec à Montréal.

Black, Maggie. 1992. *A Cause for Our Times: Oxfam the First Fifty Years*. Oxford: Oxfam and Oxford University Press.

Blau, Bruno. 1950. "The Jewish Population of Germany, 1939–1945." *Jewish Social Studies* 12 (2): 161–72.

Blobaum, Robert. 2014. "A City in Flux: Warsaw's Transient Populations during World War I." *Polish Review* 59 (4): 21–43.

———. 2018. *A Minor Apocalypse: Warsaw during the First World War*. Ithaca, NY: Cornell University Press.

Bloxham, Donald. 2003. "The Armenian Genocide of 1915–1916: Cumulative Radicalization and the Development of a Destruction Policy." *Past and Present* 181:141–91.

———. 2005. *The Great Game of Genocide: Imperialism, Nationalism, and the Destruction of the Ottoman Armenians*. Oxford: Oxford University Press.

Bloxham, Donald, and Hans-Lukas Kieser. 2014. "'Genocide.'" In Winter and Stille 2014: 1:585–614.

Blum, Matthias. 2011. "Government Decisions before and during the First World War and the Living Standards in Germany during a Drastic Natural Experiment." *Exploration in Economic History* 48 (4): 556–67.

———. 2013a. "Der deutsche Lebensstandard während des Ersten Weltkrieges in historischer Perspektive: Welche Rolle spielten Konsumentenpräferenzen?" *Vierteljahrschrift für Sozial- und Wirtschaftsgeschichte* 100 (3): 273–91.

———. 2013b. "War, Food, Rationing and Socioeconomic Inequality in Germany during the First World War." *Economic History Review* 66 (4): 1063–83.

Blum, Matthias, J. Eloranta, and P. Osinsky. 2014. "Organization of War Economies." In Daniel et al. 2014–19.

Blum, Matthias, and Claudia Rei. 2018. "Escaping Europe: Health and Human Capital of Holocaust Refugees." *European Review of Economic History* 22 (1): 1–27.

Bodart, Gaston. 1916. *Losses of Life in Modern Wars: Austro-Hungary: France*. Oxford: Oxford University Press. https://archive.org/details/lossesoflifeinmo00bodauoft/page/n7.

Bodo, Bela. 2011. "The White Terror in Hungary, 1919–1921: The Social Worlds of Paramilitary Groups." *Austrian History Yearbook* 42:133–63.

Boehnke, Jörn, and Victor Gay. 2020. "The Missing Men: World War I and Female Labor Force Participation." https://www.iast.fr/sites/default/files/IAST/wp/wp_iast_102.pdf.

Bohstedt, John. 2010. *The Politics of Provisions: Food Riots, Moral Economy, and Market Transition in England, c.1550–1850*. Farnham, UK: Ashgate.

Boldorf, Marcel. 2015. *European Economies under National Socialist Rule*. London: Routledge.

———. 2016. "European Economies under National Socialist Rule." In Boldorf and Okazaki 2015: 7–23.

Boldorf, Marcel, and Tetsuji Okazaki, eds. 2015. *Economies under Occupation: The Hegemony of Nazi Germany and Imperial Japan in World War II*. London: Taylor and Francis.

Bonanno, George A. 2004. "Loss, Trauma, and Human Resilience." *American Psychologist* 59 (1): 20–28. https://doi.org/10.1037/0003-066X.59.1.20.

———. 2009. *The Other Side of Sadness: What the New Science of Bereavement Tells Us about Life after Loss*. New York: Basic Books.

———. 2021. *The End of Trauma: How the New Science of Resilience Is Changing How We Think about PTSD*. New York: Basic Books.

Bonanno, George A., and Anthony D. Mancini. 2012. "Beyond Resilience and PTSD: Mapping the Heterogeneity of Responses to Potential Trauma." *Psychological Trauma: Theory, Research, Practice and Policy* 4, no. 1 (December): 74–83.

Bonanno, George A., Maren Westphal, and Anthony D. Mancini. 2011. "Resilience to Loss and Potential Trauma." *Annual Review of Clinical Psychology* 7:511–35.

Bond, Horatio, ed. 1946. *Fire and the Air War*. Boston: National Fire Protection Association.

Bongaarts, M. D. 1981. "'Weg met de Moffen' De uitwijzing van Duitse ongewenste vreemdelingen uit Nederland na 1945." *BMGN—Low Countries Historical Review* 96 (2): 334–51.

Bonn, Moritz. 1916. "The Fall in German Exchange." *Quarterly Journal of Economics* 31 (1): 108–27.

Bonzon, Thierry. 2006. "Consumption and Total Warfare in Paris." In *Food and Conflict in Europe in the Age of Two World Wars*, edited by F. Trentman and F. Just, pp. 49–64. London: Palgrave Macmillan.

Borchert, John R. 1948. "The Agriculture of England and Wales, 1939–1946." *Agricultural History* 22 (1): 56–62.

Borjas, George J. 1982. "Earnings of Male Hispanic Immigrants in the United States." *Industrial and Labor Relations Review* 35 (3): 343–53.

Botticini, Maristella, and Zvi Eckstein. 2005. "Jewish Occupational Selection: Education, Restrictions, or Minorities?" *Journal of Economic History* 65 (4): 922–48.

Botz, Gerhard. 1987. "The Jews of Vienna from the 'Anschluß' to the Holocaust." In *Jews, Antisemitism and Culture in Vienna*, edited by Gerhard Botz, Ivar Oxaal, and Michael Pollak, pp. 185–204, 276–82. London: Routledge and Kegan Paul.

Bourke, Joanna. 2007. *Rape: A History from 1860 to the Present Day*. London: Virago.

Bourke, Joanna, and Robin May Schott, eds. 2022. *Resilience: Militaries and Militarization*. London: Palgrave Macmillan.

Bournova, E., and M. Dimitropoulou. 2015. "Stratification socioprofessionnelle de la capitale, 1860–1940." *Athens Social Atlas*. Edited by T. Maloutas and S. Spyrellis. http://www.athenssocialatlas.gr/fr/.

Bourodon, Jean. 1936. "Levées et pertes d'hommes en France de 1792 à 1815 comparées à celles de 1914 à 191." *Journal de la société statistique de Paris* 77:207–15.

Bowman, Steven B. 1986. "Jews in Wartime Greece." *Jewish Social Studies* 48 (1): 45–62.

———. 2009. *The Agony of Greek Jews, 1940–1945*. Stanford, CA: Stanford University Press.

Bozarslan, Hamit. 2010. "The Ottoman Empire." In Horne 2010: 494–507.

Brade, Laura. 2017. "Networks of Escape: Jewish Flight from the Bohemian Lands, 1938–1941." PhD diss., University of North Carolina, Chapel Hill.

Braham, Randolph L. 2016. *The Politics of Genocide: The Holocaust in Hungary*. New York: Columbia University Press.

Brainerd, Elizabeth. 2010. "Reassessing the Standard of Living in the Soviet Union: An Analysis Using Archival and Anthropometric Data." *Journal of Economic History* 70 (1): 83–117.

Brand, Aaron Tylor. 2014. "Lives Darkened by Calamity: Enduring the Famine of World War I in Lebanon and Western Syria." PhD diss., American University of Beirut.

Brand, Tyler. 2023. *Famine Worlds: Life amid Suffering in World War I Lebanon*. Stanford, CA: Stanford University Press.

Brassley, Paul. 2012. "International Trade in Agricultural Products, 1935–1955." In Brassley et al. 2012: 33–51.

Brassley, Paul, Yves Segers, and Leen Van Molle, eds. 2012. *War, Agriculture, and Food: Rural Europe from the 1930s to the 1950s*. New York: Routledge.

Bräu, Ramona. 2016. "The Economic Consequences of German Occupation Policy in Poland." In *Paying for Hitler's War: The Consequences of Nazi Hegemony for Europe*, edited by Jonas Schermer and Eugene N. Whited, pp. 427–49. Cambridge: Cambridge University Press.

Braun, Sebastian T. 2017. "Integrating Forced Migrants: Evidence from the Displacement of Germans after World War II." *ifo DICE Report* 15:3–5.

Braun, Sebastian, and Nadja Dwenger. 2019. "Settlement Location Shapes Refugee Integration: Evidence from Post-War Germany." IZA Discussion Paper No. 12741, November.

Braun, Sebastian, and M. Kvasnicka. 2014. "Immigration and Structural Change: Evidence from Post-War Germany." *Journal of International Economics* 93:253–69.

Braun, Sebastian, and T. O. Mahmoud. 2014. "The Employment Effects of Immigration: Evidence from the Mass Arrival of German Expellees in Postwar Germany." *Journal of Economic History* 74 (1): 69–108.

Brennan, Lance, Les Heathcote, and Anton Lucas. 2017. "War and Famine around the Indian Ocean during the Second World War." In *Ethics in the Global South*, edited by Michael Schwartz, Howard Harris, and Debra C. Comer, pp. 5–70. Bingley, UK: Emerald.

Brenner, Reuven, and Nicholas M. Kiefer. 1981. "The Economics of the Diaspora: Discrimination and Occupational Structure." *Economic Development and Cultural Change* 29 (3): 517–34.

Britain, Vera. 1944. *Seed of Chaos: What Mass Bombing Really Means*. London: New Vision (for the Bombing Restriction Committee).

British Parliamentary Papers (BPP). 1919. *Forty-Eighth Annual Report of the Local Government Board. Supplement to the Report of the Medical Department for 1918–1919*. Vol. 24, cmd. 462.

Broadberry, S., and M. Harrison, eds. 2005. *The Economics of World War I*. Cambridge: Cambridge University Press.

———. 2018. *The Economics of the Great War: A Centennial Perspective*. A VoxEU book. London: Centre for Economic Policy Research Press.

Brock, Michael, and Eleanor Brock. 2014. *Margot Asquith's Great War Diary, 1914–1916*. Oxford: Oxford University Press.

Brown, Andrew. 2005. *J. D. Bernal: The Sage of Science*. Oxford: Oxford University Press.

Brown, Felix. 1941. "Civilian Psychiatric Air-Raid Casualties." *Lancet* 237 (6144): 686–91.

Browning, Christopher R. 2004. *Ordinary Men: Reserve Police Battalion 101 and the Final Solution in Poland*. New York: HarperCollins.

———. 2007. *The Origins of the Final Solution: The Evolution of Nazi Jewish Policy, September 1939–March 1942*. Lincoln: University of Nebraska Press.

———. 2016. "From Humanitarian Relief to Holocaust Rescue: Tracy Strong Jr., Vichy Internment Camps, and the Maison des Roches in Le Chambon." *Holocaust and Genocide Studies* 30 (2): 211–46.

———. 2017. *Ordinary Men: Reserve Police Battalion 101 and the Final Solution in Poland*. New York: HarperCollins. First published in 1992.

Brownmiller, Susan. 1975. *Against Our Will: Men, Women and Rape*. London.

Bruland, Bjarte, and Mats Tangestuen. 2011. "The Norwegian Holocaust: Changing Views and Representations." *Scandinavian Journal of History* 36 (5): 587–604.

Brulard, Benjamin. 2018. "La grippe espagnole en Belgique occupée (1918–1919): Analyse épidémiologique et étude de l'imaginaire et de la perception de l'épidémie a travers les carnets de guerre.'" PhD thesis, Université Catholique de Louvain. https://dial.uclouvain.be/memoire/ucl/fr/object/thesis%3A16082.

Brustein, William I. 2003. *Roots of Hate: Anti-Semitism in Europe before the Holocaust*. Cambridge: Cambridge University Press.

Brustein, William I., and Ryan D. King. 2004a. "Anti-Semitism in Europe before the Holocaust." *International Political Science Review* 25 (1): 35–53.

———. 2004b. "Anti-Semitism as a Response to Perceived Jewish Power: The Cases of Bulgaria and Romania before the Holocaust." *Social Forces* 83 (2): 691–708.

Brustein, William, and Amy Ronnkvist. 2002. "The Roots of Anti-Semitism: Romania before the Holocaust." *Journal of Genocide Research* 4 (2): 211–35.

Bryce, James, and Arnold Toynbee. 2020. *The Treatment of Armenians in the Ottoman Empire, 1915–1916: Documents Presented to Viscount Grey of Falloden by Viscount Bryce*. Facsimile ed. Princeton, NJ: Gomidas Institute. Originally published as a Blue Book in 1916.

Buchheim, Eveline, and Ralf Futselaar. 2020. "De verkelijkheid was heus al erg genoeg! De psychiatrische inrichting Dennenoord in Zuidlaren tijdens de Tweede Wereldoorlog." *Nieuwe Drentse Volksalmanac: Jaarboek voor geschiedenis en archeologie* 137:15–22.

———. 2023. *Uit Zorg Verdreven: Het Nederlandse Krankzinnigenwezen tijdens de Tweede Wereldoorlog*. Amsterdam: Boom.

Buettner, Konrad. 1950. "Effects of Extreme Heat on Man: Protection of Man against Conflagration Heat." *JAMA* 144 (9): 732–38.

Buggle, Johannes, Thierry Mayer, Seyhun Orcan Sakalli, and Mathias Thoenig. 2020. "The Refugee's Dilemma: Evidence from Jewish Migration out of Nazi Germany." http://people.unil.ch/mathiasthoenig/files/2020/02/BMST_7_February_2020.pdf.

Bukey, Evan B. 2020. "Review of *The Jews of Nazi Vienna, 1938–1945: Rescue and Destruction* by Ilana Fritz Offenberger." *Antisemitism Studies* 4 (1): 207–210.

Bunle, Henri. 1947. "La population de la France depuis 1939: De 1939 à 1945." *Revue d'économie politique* 57 (5): 816–63.

Burds, Jeffrey. 2009. "Sexual Violence in Europe in World War II, 1939–1945." *Politics and Society* 37 (1): 35–74.

Burkle, Frederick M. 2019. "Revisiting the Battle of Solferino: The Worsening Plight of Civilian Casualties in War and Conflict." *Disaster Medicine and Public Health Preparedness*, 837–41. doi:10.1017/dmp.2019.77.

Burney, Ian. 2012. "War on Fear: Solly Zuckerman and Civilian Nerve in the Second World War." *History of the Human Sciences* 25 (5): 49–72.

Buruma, Ian. 2013. *Year Zero: A History of 1945*. London: Penguin.

Butschek, Felix. 2016. "Organization of War Economies (Austria-Hungary)." In Daniel et al. 2014–19.

Caestacker, Frank. 2014. "Review of Insa Meinen and Ahlrich Meyer." *Verfolgt van Land zu Land. Juedishe Fluechtlinge in Westeuropa, 1938–1944.* H-Migration, H-Net Reviews. https:// networks.h-net.org/node/8382/reviews/11468/caestecker-insa-meinen-verfolgt-von-land -zu-land-j%C3%BCdische-fl%C3%BCchtlinge.

Caestecker, Frank, and Bob Moore, eds. 2010. *Refugees for Nazi German and the Liberal European States.* New York: Berghahn.

Caffarena, Fabio. 2014. "Air Warfare (Italy)." In Daniel et al. 2014–19.

Calder, A. 1969. *The People's War: Britain, 1939–45.* London: Jonathan Cape.

———. 1991. *The Myth of the Blitz.* London: Jonathan Cape.

Calussi, J., and A. Salvador. 2018. "The Black Market in Occupied Italy and the Approach of Italian and German Authorities (1943–1945)." In Tönsmeyer et al. 2018: 99–117.

Cameron, E., M. Spagat, and M. Hsiao-Rei Hicks. 2009. "Tracking Civilian Casualties in Combat Zones Using Civilian Battle Damage Assessment Ratios." *British Army Review* 147:87–93.

Cammaert, C. A. 1916. "Over typhoied en typhoiedenting in het vluchtoord te Hontenisse" (Typhoid among Belgian refugees in Holland). *Nederlandsch Tijdschrift v. Geneeskunde,* no. 10 (March 4): n.p.

Campana, Aurélie. 2008. "Sürgün: The Crimean Tatar's Deportation and Exile." *Sciences-Po: Violence de masse et résistance: réseau de recherche.* https://www.sciencespo.fr/mass-violence -war-massacre-resistance/fr/document/suerguen-crimean-tatars-deportation-and-exile .html.

Campbell, Bruce. 2016. *The Great Transition: Climate, Disease and Society in the Late-Medieval World.* Cambridge: Cambridge University Press.

Campbell, Ian L. 2022. "Italian Atrocities in Ethiopia: An Enquiry into the Violence of Fascism's First Military Invasion and Occupation." *Journal of Genocide Research* 24 (1): 119–33.

Canham, Sarah L., Hagit Peres, Norm O'Rourke, David B. King, Annette Wertman, Sara Carmel, and Yaacov G. Bachner. 2017. "Why Do Holocaust Survivors Remember What They Remember?" *Gerontologist* 57 (6): 1158–65.

Cantril, Hadley. 1951. *Public Opinion, 1943–1946.* Princeton, NJ: Princeton University Press. https://ia601603.us.archive.org/2/items/in.ernet.dli.2015.128827/2015.128827.Public -Opinion-1935-1946_text.pdf.

Carbonetti, Adrián. 2010. "Historia de una epidemia olvidada. La pandemia de gripe española en la argentina, 1918–1919." *Desacatos (Mexico),* no. 32 (January–February). http://www.scielo .org.mx/scielo.php?script=sci_arttext&pid=S1607–050X2010000100012.

Cardona, Euridice C., and Roger D. Markwick. 2019. "The Kitchen Garden Movement on the Soviet Home Front, 1941–1945." *Journal of Historical Geography* 64:47–59.

Carmel, Sara, David B. King, Norm O'Rourke, and Yaakov G. Bachner. 2017. "Subjective Well-Being: Gender Differences in Holocaust Survivors-Specific and Cross-National Effects." *Aging and Mental Health* 21 (6): 668–75.

Carnahan, Burrus M. 1998. "Lincoln, Lieber, and the Laws of War: The Origins and Limits of the Principle of Military Necessity." *American Journal of International Law* 92 (213): 213–31.

Carnegie Commission on Preventing Deadly Conflict. *1997 Final Report: Preventing Deadly Conflict.* Accessed November 10, 2021. https://www.carnegie.org/publications/preventing-deadly -conflict-final-report/.

Casper, Stephen T. 2008. "The Origins of the Anglo-American Research Alliance and the Incidence of Civilian Neuroses in Second World War Britain." *Medical History* 52:327–46.

Castelli, Giulio. 1908. "Il dominio dell'aria." *Rivista Internazionale di Scienze Sociali e Discipline Ausiliarie* 47 (187): 315–23.

Casu, Igor. 2010. "Stalinist Terror in Soviet Moldavia, 1940–1953." In *Stalinist Terror in Eastern Europe: Elite Purges and Mass Repression*, edited by Kevin McDermott and Matthew Stibbe, pp. 39–56. Manchester: Manchester University Press.

Ceschin, Daniele. 2006. *Gli esuli di Caporetto: I profughi in Italia durante la grande guerra*. Rome: Laterza.

———. 2013. "Dopo Caporetto: L'invasione, l'occupazione, la violenza sui civili." *Annali della Fondazione Ugo La Malfa* 28:167–85.

Chapireau, François. 2007. "La mortalité des maladies mentaux hospitalisés en France pendant la deuxième guerre mondiale." *L'Encéphale* 35 (2): 121–28.

Charles, Nicolas. 2018. "Accueillir les réfugiés ardennais a Paris entre 1914 and 1918." https://hal .archives-ouvertes.fr/hal-01722249/document.

———. 2019. "Les 'Boches du Nord': Ces femmes françaises exilées et leur image en France entre 1914 et 1918." *Revue de l'Institut des langues et cultures d'Europe, Amérique, Afriques, Asie et Australie*. Vol. 34. https://doi.org/10.4000/ilcea.5764.

Charlton, L. E. O. 1936. *War over England*. London: Longmans Green.

Charters, Erica, Eve Rosenhaft, and Hannah Smith, eds. 2017. *Civilians and War in Europe, 1618–1815*. Liverpool: Liverpool University Press.

Chasseaud, Peter. 2015. *Mapping the Second World War*. London: Collins.

Checchi, Francesco. 2010. "Comment: Estimating the Number of Civilian Deaths from Armed Conflicts." *Lancet* 375 (9,711): 255–57.

Cherepenina, Nadezhda. 2005. "Assessing the Scale of Famine and Death in the Besieged City." In Barber and Dzeniskevich 2005: 28–70.

Childers, Thomas. 2005. "'Facilis descensus averni est': The Allied Bombing of Germany and the Issue of German Suffering." *Central European History* 38 (1): 75–105.

Chirsky, Vadim. 2005. "The Work of Civilian and Military Pathologists." In Barber and Dzeniskevich 2005: 160–73.

Ciencala, Anna M. 2001. "Poles and Jews under German and Soviet Occupation, September 1 1939–June 22 1941." *Polish Review* 46 (4): 391–402.

Ciencala, Anna M., Natalia S. Lebedeva, and Wojciech Materski. 2008. *Katyn: A Crime without Punishment*. New Haven, CT: Yale University Press.

Clapperton, James. 2006. "The Siege of Leningrad and the Ambivalence of the Sacred: Conversations with Survivors." PhD diss., University of Edinburgh.

Clark, Gemma. 2020. "Violence against Women in the Irish Civil War, 1922–3: Gender-Based Harm in Global Perspective." *Irish Historical Studies* 44 (165): 75–90.

Clemens, Walter, and J. David Singer. 2000. "The Human Cost of War: Modern Warfare Kills More Civilians than Soldiers." *Scientific American* 282 (6): 56–57.

Clodfelter, Michael. 2017. *Warfare and Armed Conflicts: A Statistical Encyclopedia of Casualty and Other Figures, 1492–2015*. 4th ed. Jefferson, NC: McFarland.

Coates, Sarah. 2016. "Belsen, Dachau, 1945: Newspapers and the First Draft of History." PhD diss., Deakin University. http://dro.deakin.edu.au/eserv/DU:30088987/coates-belsendachau -2016A.pdf.

Cohen, A. A., J. Tilinghast, and V. Canudas-Rono. 2010. "No Consistent Effects of Prenatal or Neonatal Exposure to Spanish Flu on Late-Life Mortality in Developed Countries." *Demographic Research* 22 (20): 579–634.

Cohen, Dara Kay. 2016. *Rape during Civil War*. Ithaca, NY: Cornell University Press.

Cohen, Jerome B. 1946. "The Japanese War Economy: 1940–1945." *Far Eastern Survey* 15, no. 24 (December 4): 361–70.

———. 1949. *Japan's Economy in War and Reconstruction*. Minneapolis: University of Minnesota Press.

Colby, Elbridge. 1925. "Aërial Law and War Targets." *American Journal of International Law* 19 (4): 702–15.

Collet, Dominik, and Daniel Krämer. 2016. "Germany, Switzerland, and Austria." In Alfani and Ó Gráda 2017: 73–100.

Collingham, Lizzie. 2012. *The Taste of War and the Battle for Food*. London: Penguin.

Congden, Lee. 2017. *Solzhenitsyn: The Historical-Spiritual Destinies of Russia and the West*. De Kalb: Northern Illinois University Press.

Connaughton, Richard, John Pimlott, and Duncan Anderson. 1995. *The Battle for Manila*. Novato, CA: Presidio.

Connelly, James E. 2018. *The Experience of Occupation in the Nord, 1914–18: Living with the Enemy in First World War France*. Manchester: Manchester University Press.

Connor, Ian D. 1986. "The Bavarian Government and the Refugee Problem, 1945–50." *European History Quarterly* 16:131–53.

———. 2006. "German Refugees and the SPD in Schleswig-Holstein, 1945–50." *European History Quarterly* 36 (2): 173–99.

———. 2007. *Refugees and Expellees in Post-War Germany*. Manchester: Manchester University Press.

Conway-Lanz, Sahr. 2014. "The Ethics of Bombing Civilians after World War II: The Persistence of Norms against Targeting Civilians in the Korean War." In *The American Way of Bombing: Changing Ethical and Legal Norms, from Flying Fortresses to Drones*, edited by Matthew Evangelista and Henry Shue, pp. 47–63. Ithaca, NY: Cornell University Press.

Cook, Martin L. 2007. "Michael Walzer's Concept of 'Supreme Emergency.'" *Journal of Military Ethics* 6 (2): 138–51.

Cooper, Caroline Ethel, and Decie Denholm. 1982. *Behind the Lines: One Woman's War, 1914–1918: The Letters of Caroline Ethel Cooper*. London: Collins.

Corfield, Justin. 2011. "Taiping Rebellion." In *The International Encyclopedia of Revolution and Protest*. Wiley Online Library. https://onlinelibrary.wiley.com/doi/abs/10.1002/9781405198073 .wbierp1432.pub2.

Cormier, David. 2020. "Ces épidémies qu'a connues Brest." *Le télégramme*, April 19. https://www .letelegramme.fr/finistere/brest/ces-epidemies-qu-a-connues-brest-19–04–2020–12541150 .php.

Cornwall, Mark. 1997. "Morale and Patriotism in the Austro-Hungarian Army, 1914–1918." In Horne 1997: 173–91.

Corum, James S. 1996. "From Biplanes to Blitzkreig: The Development of German Air Doctrine between the Wars." *War in History* 3 (1): 85–101.

Costalli, Stefano, Francesco Niccolò Moro, and Andrea Ruggeri. 2020. "The Logic of Vulnerability and Civilian Victimization: Shifting Front Lines in Italy (1943 1945)." *World Politics* 72 (4): 679–718.

Costello, John. 1985. *Love, Sex, and War: Changing Values, 1939–1945*. London: Collins.

Cox, Mary Elizabeth. 2019. *Hunger in War and Peace: Women and Children in Germany, 1914–1924*. Oxford: Oxford University Press.

Crammer, J. L. 1992. "Extraordinary Deaths of Asylum Inpatients during the 1914–1918 War." *Medical History* 36:430–41.

Crane, Conrad C. 1993. *Bombs, Cities, and Civilians: American Airpower Strategy in World War II*. Lawrence: University of Kansas Press.

———. 2002. "'Contrary to Our National Ideals': American Strategic Bombing of Civilians in Word War 2." In Grimsley and Rogers 2002: 219–50.

Cribb, Julian. 2019. *Food or War*. Cambridge: Cambridge University Press.

Croes, Marnix. 2006. "The Holocaust in the Netherlands and the Rate of Jewish Survival." *Holocaust and Genocide Studies* 20 (3): 474–99.

———. 2008. "Pour une approche quantitative de la survie et du sauvetage des juifs." In *La résistance aux genocide: De la pluralité des actes de sauvetage*, edited by Jacques Sémelin, Claire Andrieu, and Sarah Gensburger, pp. 83–97. Paris: Presse de Sciences Po.

———. 2012. "Facteurs de survie face a la Shoah: Le cas de la province néerlandaise d'Overijssel, 1942–1945." *Le Genre Humain*, no. 52:121–45.

Croes, Marnix, and Peter Tammes. 2006. *"Gif laten wij niet voortbestaan": Een onderzoek naar de overlevingskansen van joden in de Nederlandse gemeenten, 1940–45*. Amsterdam: Aksant. Summary in English, pp. 593–608. http://webdoc.ubn.kun.nl/mono/c/croes_m/gif_lawin.pdf.

Crosby, Alfred. *Epidemic and Peace, 1918*. Westport, CT: Greenwood Press.

Crowder, Michael. 1985. "The First World War and Its Consequences in Africa." In Vol. 7, *General History of Africa*. Paris: UNESCO.

Cundy, Alyssa. 2015. "A 'Weapon of Starvation': The Politics, Propaganda, and Morality of Britain's Hunger Blockade of Germany, 1914–1919." PhD diss., Wilfred Laurier University. https://scholars.wlu.ca/etd/1763.

Dadrian, Vahakn N. 1991. "The Documentation of the World War I Armenian Massacres in the Proceedings of the Turkish Military Tribunal." *International Journal of Middle East Studies* 23 (4): 549–76.

Dallaire, Adrien. 2020. "Explaining Survival: The Hierarchy of Persecution and the Jews of the Department of Vaucluse, 1933–1945." PhD diss., University of Ottawa.

Daly, Gavin. 2017. "Plunder on the Peninsula: British Soldiers and Local Civilians during the Peninsular War, 1808–1813." In Charters, Rosenhaft, and Smith 2017: 209–24.

Daniel, Ute. 1997. *The War from Within: German Working-Class Women in the First World War*. Oxford: Oxford University Press.

———. 2002. "Zweierlei Heimatfronten: Weibliche Kriegserfahrungen 1914 bis 1918 und 1939 bis 1945 im Kontrast." In *Erster Weltkrieg, Zweiter Weltkrieg. Ein Vergleich. Krieg, Kriegserlebnis, Kriegserfahrung in Deutschland*, edited by Burno Thoß and Hans-Erich Volkmann, pp. 391–409. Paderborn, Germany: F. Schöningh.

Daniel, Ute, Peter Gatrell, Oliver Janz, Heather Jones, Jennifer Keene, Alan Kramer, and Bill Nasson, eds. 2014–19. *International Encyclopedia of the First World War*. Berlin: Freie Universität Berlin.

Daniele, Vittorio, and Renato Ghezzi. 2019. "The Impact of World War II on Nutrition and Children's Health in Italy." *Investigaciones de Historia Economica* 15 (2): 119–31.

Daniels, Marc. 1949. "Tuberculosis in Europe during and after the Second World War." *British Medical Journal* 2, no. 4636 (November 12): 1065–72.

Darmon, Pierre. 2000. "Une tragédie dans la tragédie: La grippe espagnole en France (Avril 1918–Avril 1919)." *Annales de Démographie Historique*, 153–75.

Das, Tarakchandra. 1949. *Bengal Famine (1943) as Revealed in a Survey of the Destitutes of Calcutta*. Calcutta: University of Calcutta.

Das Gupta, B. M., and L. B. Siddons. 1945. "The Parasitology of Malaria among Destitutes in Calcutta during and after the Bengal Famine of 1943." *Indian Medical Gazette*, March, 160–64.

Daugherty, William, Barbara Levi, and Frank Von Hippel. 1986. "Casualties Due to the Blast, Heat, and Radioactive Fallout from Various Hypothetical Nuclear Attacks on the United States." In *The Medical Implications of Nuclear War*, edited by Institute of Medicine of the National Academy of Sciences, pp. 207–32. Washington, DC: National Academy Press.

Dawidowicz, Lucy S. 1992. *What Is the Use of Jewish History?* New York: Knopf.

Davies, Norman. 2005. *God's Playground: A History of Poland:* Vol. 2, *1795 to the Present*. Oxford: Oxford University Press.

Davis, L. E., and S. L. Engerman. 2006. *Naval Blockades in Peace and War: An Economic History since 1750*. Cambridge: Cambridge University Press.

Davis, Belinda. 2000. *Home Fires Burning: Food, Politics, and Everyday Life in World War I Berlin.* Chapel Hill: University of North Carolina Press.

Davis, David John. 1917. "Bacteriology and the War." *Scientific Monthly* 5 (5): 385–99.

Davis, Richard G. 2006. *Bombing the European Axis Powers: A Historical Digest of the Combined Bomber Offensive, 1939–1945.* Maxwell Air Force Base, AL: Air University Press.

Dean, Martin. 2004. "Local Collaboration in the Holocaust in Eastern Europe." In Stone 2004: 120–40.

de Bromhead, Alan, Barry Eichengreen, and Kevin H. O'Rourke. 2013. "Political Extremism in the 1920s and 1930s: Do German Lessons Generalize?" *Journal of Economic History* 73 (2): 371–406.

Debruyne, Emmanuel. 2014. "Les "femmes à Boches' en Belgique et en France occupées: 1914–1918." *Revue du Nord* 96 (404–5): 157–86.

Declercq, Christophe. 2017. "Belgian Refugees in Britain: A Short Summary." https://blogs.kent.ac.uk/rtwbelgians/belgian-refugees-in-britain-a-short-summary/#.

———. 2020. "Making Home in Limbo: Belgian Refugees in Britain during the First World." In *Refuge in a Moving World: Tracing Refugee and Migrant Journeys across Disciplines*, edited by Elena Fiddian-Qasmiyeh, pp. 74–93. London: UCL Press. https://www.jstor.org/stable/j.ctv13xprtw.12.

Degli Esposti, Fabio. 2015. "War Finance (Italy)." In Daniel et al. 2014–19.

Degli Esposti, Fabio, and Peter Anderson, eds. 2021. *Franco's Famine: Malnutrition, Disease and Starvation in Post-Civil War Spain.* London: Bloomsbury.

del Arco Blanco, Miguel Ángel. 2023. "Building an Empire and Bringing about a Famine: The Allied Blockade of Spain during the Second World War (1939–1945)." *Contemporary European History.* Published online ahead of print. doi:10.1017/S0960777322000959.

de Metsenaere, Machteld, and Sophie Bollen. 2007. "Schandelijke liefde: Sentimentele collaboratie en haar bestraffing in Belgie na de tweede wereld oorlog." *Wetenschappelijke tijdingen* 5016: 228–59.

Denechere, Yves. 2010. "Des adoptions d'État: Les enfants de l'occupation française en Allemagne, 1945–1952." *Revue d'histoire moderne et contemporaine* 57 (2): 159–79.

Denness, Zoë Andrea. 2012. "A Question of Which Affects Our Prestige as a Nation: The History of British Civilian Internment, 1899–1945." PhD diss., University of Birmingham.

Department of Economic Affairs, Batavia. 1947. "Rice Production in Indonesia." *Economic Review of Indonesia* 1 (1): 9–12.

de Schaepdrijver, Sophie. 2009. "Review of Lipkes (2007)." *English Historical Review* 124 (509): 1002–3.

Devereux, Stephen. 2000. "Famine in the Twentieth Century." University of Sussex, Institute of Development Studies Working Paper No. 105.

Devos, Isabelle, M. Bourguignon, E. Debruyne, Y. Doignon, T. Eggerickx, H. Greefs, and T. Soens. 2021. "The Spanish Flu in Belgium, 1918–1919: A State of the Art." *Historical Social Research* 33 (suppl.): 251–83. https://doi.org.10.12759/hsr.suppl.33.2021.251–283.

de Vries, E. 1947. "Vital Statistics under the Japanese Occupation." *Economic Review of Indonesia* 1:18–19.

de Waal, Edmund. 2010. *The Hare with Amber Eyes: A Hidden Inheritance.* London: Chatto and Windus.

Dewey, Peter E. 1975. "Agricultural Labour Supply in England and Wales during the First World War." *Economic History Review* 28 (1): 100–112.

———. 1984. "Military Recruiting and the British Labour Force during the First World War." *Historical Journal* 27 (1): 199–223.

de Zayas, Alfred-Maurice. 1978. "Prussian Nights." *Review of Politics* 40 (1): 154–56.

———. 1986. *A Terrible Revenge: The Ethnic Cleansing of the East European Germans, 1944–1950*. New York: St. Martin's Press.

de Zwarte, Ingrid. 2020. *The Hunger Winter*. Cambridge: Cambridge University Press.

Diamond, Jared. 2000. "War Babies." In *The Nature-Nurture Debate: The Essential Readings*, edited by S. J. Ceci and W. M. Williams, pp. 14–22. New York: Wiley-Blackwell.

Dieckman, Christoph, and Saulius Sužiedėlis. 2006. *The Persecution and Mass Murder of Lithuanian Jews during Summer and Fall of 1941*. Vilnius: Margi Raštai. https://www.yivo.org/cimages/persecution_and_mass_murder_2006_cdss.pdf.

Dill, Janina, Scott D. Sagan, and Benjamin A. Valentino. 2019. "The Bomb beyond Borders: Public Opinion on the Nuclear Taboo and Non-combatant Immunity Norms in the United States, the United Kingdom, France, and Israel." Typescript, July 9. https://ndisc.nd.edu/assets/333578/dill_sagan_valentino_public_opinion_on_the_nuclear_taboo.pdf.

Dobroszycki, Lucjan, ed. *The Chronicle of the Łódź Ghetto, 1941–1944*. New Haven, CT: Yale University Press.

Dols, M.J.L., and D.J.A.M. van Arken. 1946. "Food Supply and Nutrition in the Netherlands during and Immediately after World War II." *Milbank Memorial Fund Quarterly* 24 (4): 319–58.

Dominian, Leon. 1915. "The Peoples of Northern and Central Asiatic Turkey." *Bulletin of the American Geographical Society* 47 (11): 832–71.

Dorney, John. 2012. "War and Famine in Ireland, 1580–1700." The Irish Story. https://www.theirishstory.com/2012/01/03/war-and-famine-in-ireland-1580-1700/#.XjlXMC2cY8Z.

Douglas, R. M. 2012. *Orderly and Humane: The Expulsion of the Germans after the Second World War*. New Haven, CT: Yale University Press.

Douhet, Giulio. (1921) 2012. *Il Dominio dell'Aria*. Torazzo Piemonte, Italy: Amazon Italia Logistica.

Downes, Alexander B. 2008. *Targeting Civilians in War*. Ithaca, NY: Cornell University Press.

Drolet, Godias J. 1945. "World War I and Tuberculosis." *American Journal of Public Health* 35:689–97.

Dumas, Samuel, and Knud Otto Vedel-Petersen. 1923. *Losses of Life Caused by War*. Oxford: Clarendon Press.

Dumitru, Diana. 2011. "Attitudes towards Jews in Odessa: From Soviet Rule through Romanian Occupation, 1921–1944." *Cahiers du monde russe* 52 (1): 133–62.

Dũng, Bùi Minh. 1995. "Japan's Role in the Vietnamese Starvation of 1944–45." *Modern Asian Studies* 29 (3): 573–618.

Dunsterville, Lionel Charles. 1920. *The Adventures of Dunsterforce*. London: E. Arnold.

Dwyer, Philip G. 2013. "Violence and the Revolutionary and Napoleonic Wars: Massacre, Conquest and the Imperial Enterprise." *Journal of Genocide Research* 15 (2): 117–31.

Dyson, Tim. 2018. *A Population History of India*. Oxford: Oxford University Press.

Dzeniskevich, A. 2005. "Medical Research Institutes during the Siege." In Barber and Dzeniskevich 2005: 86–122.

Eber, Irene, ed. 2018. *Jewish Refugees in Shanghai, 1933–1947: A Selection of Documents (Archiv Judischer Geschichte Und Kultur)*. Göttingen: Vandenhoeck and Ruprecht.

Eckhardt, William. 1989. "Civilian Deaths in Wartime." *Bulletin of Peace Proposals* 20 (1): 89–98.

Edele, Mark, Sheila Fitzpatrick, and Atina Grossmann, eds. 2017. *Shelter from the Holocaust: Rethinking Jewish Survival in the Soviet Union*. Detroit: Wayne State University Press.

Edele, Mark, and Filip Slaveski. 2016. "Violence from Below: Explaining Crimes against Civilians in the Soviet Space, 1943–1947." *Europe-Asia Studies* 68 (6): 1020–35.

Edele, Mark, and Wanda Warlik. 2017. "Saved by Stalin? Trajectories and Numbers of Polish Jews in the Soviet Second World War." In Edele, Fitzpatrick, and Grossmann 2017: 95–131.

Edgerton-Tarpley, K. 2014. "From 'Nourish the People' to 'Sacrifice for the Nation': Changing Responses to Disaster in Late Imperial and Modern China." *Journal of Asian Studies* 73 (2): 447–69.

Edgeworth, F. Y. 1916. "Review of the Economy and Finance of the War by A. C. Pigou." *Economic Journal* 26 (102): 223–27.

Eichengreen, Barry, and Timothy Hatton. 1988. "Interwar Unemployment in International Perspective: An Overview." In *Interwar Unemployment in International Perspective,* edited by Eichengreen and Hatton, pp. 1–59. Amsterdam: Kluwer.

Eglitis, Daina S., and Didzis Bērziņš. 2018. "Mortal Threat: Latvian Jews at the Dawn of Nazi Occupation." *Nationalities Papers* 46 (6): 1063–80.

Eichhorn, Svenja, and Philipp Kuwert. 2011. *Das Geheimnis unserer Großmütter: Eine empirische Studie über sexualisierte Kriegsgewalt um 1945.* Gießen, Germany: Psychosozial-Verlag.

Ekamper, Peter, Govert Bijwaard, Frans van Poppel, and L. H. Lumey. 2017. "War-Related Excess Mortality in the Netherlands, 1944–45: New Estimates of Famine- and Non- famine-Related Deaths from National Death Records." *Historical Methods: A Journal of Quantitative and Interdisciplinary History* 50 (2): 113–28.

Elcock, Audrey Anne. 1999. "Government Evacuation Schemes and Their Effect on School Children in Sheffield during the Second World War." PhD diss., University of Sheffield. https://etheses.whiterose.ac.uk/14455/1/301006.pdf.

Elder, Tanya. 2005. "What You See before Your Eyes: Documenting Raphael Lemkin's Life by Exploring His Archival Papers, 1900–1959." *Journal of Genocide Research* 7 (4): 469–99.

Ellis, Carolyn, and Jerry Rawicki. 2012. "More than Mazel? Luck and Agency in Surviving the Holocaust." *Journal of Loss and Trauma* 19 (2): 99–120. https://www.tandfonline.com/doi/pdf/10.1080/15325024.2012.738574?needAccess=true.

Ellman, Michael. 2000. "The 1947 Soviet Famine and the Entitlement Approach to Famines." *Cambridge Journal of Economics* 24 (5): 603–30.

Ellman, Michael, and S. Maksudov. 1994. "Soviet deaths in the Great Patriotic War: A Note." *East-West Studies* 46(4): 671–80.

Eloronta, Jari, and Mark Harrison. 2010. "War and Disintegration, 1940–1950." In Vol. 2, *The Cambridge History of Modern Europe*, edited by S. Broadberry and M. Harrison, pp. 133–55. Cambridge: Cambridge University Press.

Emin, Ahmed. 1930. *Turkey in the World War.* New Haven, CT: Yale University Press.

Engel, Barbara Alpern. 1997. "Not by Bread Alone: Subsistence Riots in Russia during World War I." *Journal of Modern History* 69 (4): 696–721.

Engwall, Kristina. 2005. "Starved to Death? Nutrition in Asylums during the World Wars." *Scandinavian Journal of Disability Research* 7 (1): 2–22.

Epstein, Barbara. 2008. *The Minsk Ghetto, 1941–1943: Jewish Resistance and Soviet Internationalism.* Berkeley: University of California Press.

Ermacora, Matteo. 2007. "Assistance and Surveillance: War Refugees in Italy, 1914–1918." *Contemporary European History* 16 (4): 445–59.

———. 2015. "Civilian Morale." In Daniel et al. 2014–19.

Esteban, Ronaldo. 2016. "Cannibalism among Japanese Soldiers in Bukidnon, Philippines, 1945–47." *Asian Studies: Journal of Critical Perspectives on Asia* 52 (1): 63–102.

Evangelista, Matthew. 2023. *Allied Air Attacks and Civilian Harm in Italy, 1940–1945: Bombing among Friends.* London: Routledge.

Evans, R. J. 2009. *The Third Reich at War: How the Nazis Led Germany from Conquest to Disaster.* London: Penguin.

Evdokimov, Rostislav, ed. 1995. *Human Losses of the USSR during the Second World War: A Collection of Articles* (in Russian). Moscow: Russian Academy of Sciences.

Eyler, John M. 1997. *Sir Arthur Newsholme and State Medicine, 1885–1935.* Cambridge: Cambridge University Press.

Fahey, John T. 2004. "Britain 1939–1945: The Economic Cost of Strategic Bombing." PhD diss., University of Sydney. https://ses.library.usyd.edu.au/bitstream/handle/2123/664/adt-NU20050104.11440202whole.pdf?sequence=2&isAllowed=y.

Farquharson, John E. 1985. *The Western Allies and the Politics of Food: Agrarian Management in Postwar Germany*. Oxford: Berg.

Farrar, L. L. Jr. 1972. "The Short-War Illusion: The Syndrome of German Strategy, August–December, 1914." *Militärgeschichtliche Zeitschrift* 2: 39–52.

Fearon, Peter. 1984. "The Growth of Aviation in Britain." *Journal of Contemporary History* 20 (1): 21–40.

Federico, Giovanni, and Antonio Tena-Junguito. 2022. "How Many People on Earth? World Population, 1800–1938." Typescript.

Fedman, David, and Cary Karacas. 2012. "A Cartographic Fade to Black: Mapping the Destruction of Urban Japan during World War II." *Journal of Historical Geography* 38: 306–28.

Feinstein, C. H. 1972. *Statistical Tables of National Income, Expenditure, and Output of the UK, 1855–1965*. Cambridge: Cambridge University Press.

Felder, Björn. 2019. "Starvation, Mass Murder, and Experimentation: Nazi 'Euthanasia' in the Baltics, 1944–1944." In Bailer and Wetzel 2019: 175–200.

Felsen, Irit. 1998. "Transgenerational Transmission of Effects of the Holocaust." In *International Handbook of Multigenerational Legacies of Trauma*, edited by Y. Danieli, pp. 43–68. Boston: Springer.

Ferenc Piotrowska, Maria. 2018. "'Isle of Death': The Demographic Grounds of Social Changes in the Warsaw Ghetto." *Annales de démographie historique*, no. 136:137–58.

Ferencz, Benjamin B. 1979. *Less than Slaves: Jewish Forced Labor and the Quest for Compensation*. Cambridge, MA: Harvard University Press.

Ferrell, Robert H. 1955. "The Mukden Incident: September 18–19, 1931." *Journal of Modern History* 27: 66–72.

Filtzer, Donald A. 2008. "The 1947 Food Crisis and Its Aftermath." In *A Dream Deferred: New Studies in Russian and Soviet Labour History*, edited by Donald A. Filtzer and Wendy Z. Goldman, et al., pp. 343–83. Bern: Peter Lang.

———. 2015. "Starvation Mortality in Soviet Home-Front Industrial Regions during World War Two, Hunger and War." In Goldman and Filtzer 2015: 265–337.

Finder, Gabriel N., and Alexander V. Prusin. 2004. "Collaboration in Eastern Galicia: The Ukrainian Police and the Holocaust." *East European Jewish Affairs* 34 (2): 95–118.

Fishman, Sarah. 2008. *La bataille de l'enfance: Délinquance et justice des mineurs en France pendant la Seconde Guerre mondiele*. Rennes, France: Presses Universitaires de Rennes.

Fisk, Robert. 1990. *Pity the Nation: Lebanon at War*. Oxford: Oxford University Press.

Fitzpatrick, Sheila. 2017a. "Annexation, Evacuation, and Antisemitism in the Soviet Union, 1939–1946." In Edele, Fitzpatrick, and Grossmann 2017: 133–61.

———. 2017b. *Mischka's War: A Story of Survival from War-Torn Europe to New York*. London: I. B. Taurus.

Fleming, Katherine E. 2018. "Grey Zones." In *The Holocaust in Greece*, edited by Giorgos Antoniou and Dirk Moses, pp. 361–70. Cambridge: Cambridge University Press.

Florentin, Eddy. *Quand les Alliés bombardaient la France*. Perrin, Paris, 1997.

Ford, John C. 1944. "The Morality of Obliteration Bombing." *Theological Studies* 5:261–309.

Ford, Joseph H. 1927. *The Medical Department of the US Army in the WW*: Vol. 2, *Administration American Expeditionary Forces*. Washington, DC: U.S. Government Printing Office.

Fornassin, Alessio, Marco Breschi, and Matteo Manfredini. 2018. "Spanish Flu in Italy: New Data, New Questions." *Le Infezioni in Medicina* 26 (1): 97–106.

Forrest, William P. 1947. "Nutrition in the Ukrainian S.S.R." *Milbank Memorial Fund Quarterly* 25 (4): 319–33.

Frankland, Noble, and Charles Webster. 1961. *The Strategic Air Offensive against Germany, 1939–1945:* Vol. 2, *Endeavour.* Part 4. London: Her Majesty's Stationery Office.

Freitag, Simone, Elmar Braehler, Silke Schmidt, and Heide Glaesmer. 2013. "The Impact of Forced Displacement in World War II on Mental Health Disorders and Health-Related Quality of Life in Late Life—a German Population-Based Study." *International Psychogeriatrics* 25 (2): 310–19.

Freud, Anna, and Dorothy T. Burlingham. 1974. *Infants without Families: Reports on the Hampstead Nurseries, 1939–1945.* London: Hogarth Press.

Fridman, Ayala, Marian J. Bakermans-Kranenburg, Abraham Sagi-Schwartz, and Marinus H. Van IJzendoorn. 2011. "Coping in Old Age with Extreme Childhood Trauma: Aging Holocaust Survivors and Their Offspring Facing New Challenges." *Aging and Mental Health* 15:2, 232–42. https://doi.org.10.1080/13607863.2010.505232.

Friedrich, Jörg. 2006. *The Fire: The Bombing of Germany, 1940–1945.* New York: Columbia University Press. First published in German in 2002.

Frizzera, Francesco. 2016. "Refugees (Austria-Hungary)." In Daniel et al. 2014–19.

Frizzera, Francesco, and Marco Mondini. 2017. "Beyond the Borders. Displaced Persons in the Italian Linguistic Space during the First World War." In Gatrell and Zhvanko 2017: 177–96.

Froehlich, Georg. 1912. "Deutsche Volksernährung im Kriege." *Schmollers Jahrbuch* 36:575–94.

Frolov, Mikhail. 2005. "Evacuation from Leningrad to Kostroma." In Barber and Dzeniskevich 2005: 71–85.

Frounfelker, Rochelle, Stephen E. Gilman, Theresa S. Betancourt, Sergio Aguilar-Gaxiola, Jordi Alonso, Evelyn J. Bromet, Ronny Bruffaerts, et al. 2018. "Civilians in World War II and DSM-IV Mental Disorders: Results from the World Mental Health Survey Initiative." *Social Psychiatry and Psychiatric Epidemiology* 53:207–19.

Fuchs, Anna. 2012. *After the Dresden Bombing: Pathways of Memory, 1945 to the Present.* London: Macmillan.

Fujiwara, Saeko, Akihiko Suyama, John Cologne, et al. 2008. "Prevalence of Adult-Onset Multifactorial Disease among Offspring of Atomic Bomb Survivors." *Radiation Research* 170 (4): 451–57.

Futselaar, Ralf. 2008. *Lard, Lice and Longevity: The Standard of Living in Occupied Denmark and the Netherlands, 1940–1945.* Amsterdam: Aksant.

Gaertner, Niko. 2012. *Operation Pied Piper: The Wartime Evacuation of Children from Lond and Berlin, 1938–46.* Charlotte: Information Age.

Gaffney, Phyllis. 1999. *Healing amid the Ruins.* Dublin: A. and A. Farmar.

Galatzer-Levy, Isaac R., Andy H. Huang, and George A. Bonanno. 2018. "Trajectories of Resilience and Dysfunction Following Potential Trauma: A Review and Statistical Evaluation." *Clinical Psychology Review* 63:41–55.

Galbraith, John K. 1981. *A Life in Our Times: Memoirs.* Boston: Houghton Mifflin.

Gallagher, Tom. 2013. *Outcast Europe: The Balkans, 1789–1989: From the Ottomans to Milosevic.* London: Taylor and Francis.

Galofré-Vilà, Gregori, Christopher M. Meissner, Martin McKee, and David Stucker. 2017. "Austerity and the Rise of the Nazi Party." National Bureau of Economic Research Working Paper No. 24106. Revised April 2019.

Ganson, Nicholas. 2009. *The Soviet Famine of 1946–1947 in Global and Historical Perspective.* London: Palgrave Macmillan.

Gardakas, Katarina. 2008. "Relief Work and Malaria in Greece, 1943–1947." *Journal of Contemporary History* 43 (3): 493–508.

Garnaut, Anthony. 2013. "A Quantitative Description of the Henan Famine of 1942." *Modern Asian Studies* 47 (6): 2007–45.

Garon, Sheldon. 2016. "Defending Civilians against Aerial Bombardment: A Comparative/Transnational History of Japanese, German, and British Home Fronts, 1918–1945." *Asia-Pacific Journal* 14 (2): 1–20.

———. 2017. "The Home Front and Food Insecurity in Wartime Japan: A Transnational Perspective." In *The Consumer on the Home Front: Second World War Civilian Consumption in Comparative Perspective*, edited by Hartmut Berghoff, Jan Longemann, and Felix Romer, pp. 29–53. Oxford: Oxford University Press.

———. 2020. "On the Transnational Destruction of Cities: What Japan and the United States Learned from the Bombing of Britain and Germany in the Second World War." *Past and Present* 247: 235–71.

Gärtner, Niko. 2011. "Operation Pied Piper: Wartime Evacuation of Schoolchildren from London and Berlin 1938–1946." PhD diss., Institute of Education, University of London. https://discovery.ucl.ac.uk/id/eprint/10019989/2/GAERTNER,%20N_Redacted.pdf.

Gatrell, Peter. 1999. *A Whole Empire Walking: Refugees in Russia during WW1*. Bloomington: Indiana University Press.

———. 2000. "Forced Migration during the Second World War: An Introduction." In *Refugees, Relief, and Resettlement*, edited by Peter Gatrell, n.p. Farmington Hills, MI: Gale. https://www.gale.com/intl/essays/peter-gatrell-forced-migration-second-world-war-introduction.

———. 2013a. *The Making of the Modern Refugee*. Oxford: Oxford University Press.

———. 2013b. "Review Essay." *European Review of History* 20 (5): 903–6.

———. 2014a. "Refugees." In Daniel et al. 2014–19.

———. 2014b. "Resettlement." *International Encyclopedia of the First World War*, 1914–1918. August 10. https://encyclopedia.1914–1918-online.net/article/resettlement?version=1.0.

———. 2017. "War, Refugeedom, Revolution: Understanding Russia's Refugee Crisis, 1914–1918." *Cahiers du monde russe* 58 (1–2): 123–46.

Gatrell, Peter, and Mark Harrison. 1993. "The Russian and Soviet Economies in Two World Wars: A Comparative View." *Economic History Review* 46 (3): 425–52.

Gatrell, Peter, and Lyubov Zhvanko, eds. 2017. *Europe on the Move: Refugees in the Era of the Great War*. Manchester: Manchester University Press.

Gaunt, David, Naures Atto, and Soner O. Barthoma. 2017. *Let Them Not Return: Sayfo—the Genocide against the Assyrian, Syriac, and Chaldean Christians in the Ottoman Empire*. New York: Berghahn.

Gazeley, Ian, and Andrew Newell. 2013. "The First World War and Working-Class Food Consumption in Britain." *European Review of Economic History* 17 (1): 71–94.

Gebhardt, Miriam. 2016. *Crimes Unspoken: The Rape of German Women at the End of the Second World War*. Cambridge: Polity.

Geinitz, Christian. 2000. "The First War against Noncombatants: The Strategic Bombing of German Cities in World War 1." In *Great War, Total War: Combat and Mobilization on the Western Front, 1914–1918*, edited by Roger Chickering and Stig Foerster, pp. 207–25. Cambridge: Cambridge University Press.

Gellately, Robert, and Ben Kiernan, eds. 2003. *The Specter of Genocide: Mass Murder in Historical Perspective*. Cambridge: Cambridge University Press.

Gentile, Gian P. 1997. "A-Bombs, Budgets, and Morality: Using the Strategic Bombing Survey." *Air Power History* 44 (1): 18–31.

Geppert, Dominik, William Mulligan, and Andreas Rose, eds. 2015. *The Wars before the Great War: Conflict and International Politics before the Outbreak of the First World War*. Cambridge: Cambridge University Press.

Gerhard, Gesine. 2009. "Food and Genocide: Nazi Agrarian Politics in the Occupied Territories of the Soviet Union." *Contemporary European History* 18 (1): 45–65.

Gerhardt, Miriam. 2019. *We Children of Violence: How Women and Families Are Still Suffering Today from the Aftermaths of Mass Rape at the End of the War.* New York: Random House.

Gerlach, Christian. 1997. "Die Wannsee-Konferenz, das Schicksal der deutschen Juden und Hitlers politische Grundsatzentscheidung, alle Juden Europas zu ermorden." *WerkstattGeschichte* 18:7–44.

———. 1998. *Krieg, Ernährung, Völkermord: Forschungen zur deutschen Vernichtungspolitik im Zweiten Weltkrieg.* Hamburger: Hamburger Edition.

———. 2016. *The Extermination of the European Jews.* Cambridge: Cambridge University Press.

Gerson, Sam. 2019. "The Enduring Psychological Legacies of Genocidal Trauma: Commentary." *Psychological Quarterly* 88 (3): 501–11.

Gertjejanssen, Wendy Jo. 2004. "Victims, Heroes, Survivors: Violence on the Eastern Front during World War II." PhD diss., University of Minnesota.

Gerwarth, Robert. 2014. "The Continuum of Violence." In Winter and Stille 2014: 2:638–62.

Geyer, Michael, and Adam Tooze, eds. 2015. *The Cambridge History of the Second World War:* Vol. 3, *Total War: Economy, Society, and Culture.* Cambridge: Cambridge University Press.

Giannuli, Dimitra. 2010. "Greeks or 'Strangers at Home': The Experiences of Ottoman Greek Refugees during Their Exodus to Greece, 1922–1923." *Journal of Modern Greek Studies* 13 (2): 271–87.

Giddens, Anthony. 1985. *The Nation-State and Violence.* Cambridge: Polity.

Gietema, Marco, and Cecile aan de Stegge. 2017. *Vergeten slachtoffers: Psychiatrische inrichting de Willem Arntsz Hoeve in de Tweede Wereldoorlog.* Amsterdam: Boom.

Gigova, Irina. 2011. "Sofia Was Bombed? Bulgaria's Forgotten War with the Allies." *History and Memory* 23 (2): 132–71.

Gikopoulou, Paraskevi. 2004. *The Holocaust in Greece: Occupation, Nationalism and Legacy.* PhD diss., University of Warwick. http://wrap.warwick.ac.uk/66498/1/WRAP_THESIS _Gikopoulou_2014.pdf.

Gilbert, Martin. 2003. "Twentieth-Century Genocides." In Winter 2003a: 9–35.

Gioannini, Maro, and Giulio Massobrio. 2007. *Bombardate l'Italia: Storia della guerra di distru- zione aerea, 1940–1945.* New York: Rizzoli.

Glassheim, Eagle. 2000. "National Mythologies and Ethnic Cleansing: The Expulsion of Czecho- slovak Germans in 1945." *Central European History* 33 (4): 463–86.

Glausiusz, Josie G. 2014a. "Doubts Arising about Claimed Epigenetics of Holocaust Trauma." *Haaretz*, April 30.

———. 2014b. "Searching Chromosomes for the Legacy of Trauma: The Daughter of a Holocaust Survivor Narrates Her Own Participation in a Study of Epigenetic Inheritance." *Nature*, June 11. https://www.nature.com/news/searching-chromosomes-for-the-legacy-of-trauma-1.15369.

Glei, Dana, Silvia Bruzzone, and Graziella Caselli. 2005. "Effects of War Losses on Mortality Estimates for Italy: A First Attempt." *Demographic Research* 13:363–88.

Glover, E. 1942. "Notes on the Psychological Effects of War Conditions on the Civilian Popula- tion." *International Journal of Psychoanalysis* 23:17–37.

Goeschel, Christian. 2008. "Suicides of German Jews in the Third Reich." *German History* 25 (1): 22–45.

Goldhagen, Daniel J. 2009. *Worse than War: Genocide, Eliminationism, and the Ongoing Assault on Humanity.* New York: Public Affairs.

Goldlust, John. 2017. "A Different Silence: The Survival of More than 200,000 Polish Jews in the Soviet Union during World War II as a Case Study in Cultural Amnesia." In Edele, Fitzpatrick, and Grossman 2017: 29–94.

Goldman, Wendy Z., and Donald Filtzer, eds. 2015. *Hunger and War: Food Provisioning in the Soviet Union during World War II*. Bloomington: Indiana University Press.

———. 2021. *Fortress Dark and Stern: Life, Labor, and Loyalty on the Soviet Home Front during World War II*. Oxford: Oxford University Press.

Gomolin, Robin P. 2004. "Ideological Artifacts in Social Science Research: The Case of Rachel and the Theory of Intergenerational Transmission of Trauma." Typescript, University of Massachusetts Boston.

———. 2019. "The Intergenerational Transmission of Holocaust Trauma: A Psychoanalytic Theory Revisited." *Psychoanalytic Quarterly* 88 (3): 461–500.

Goodman, Sam. 2018. "Unpalatable Truths: Food and Drink as Medicine in Colonial British India." *Journal of the History of Medicine and Allied Sciences* 73 (2): 205–22.

Gordin, Michael D. 2007. *Five Days in August: How World War II Became a Nuclear War*. Princeton, NJ: Princeton University Press. E-book.

Goss, Hilton P. 1948a. *Civilian Morale under Aerial Bombardment, 1914–1939*. Part I. Maxwell Air Force Base, AL: U.S. Air University. https://apps.dtic.mil/dtic/tr/fulltext/u2/a953063.pdf.

———. 1948b. *Civilian Morale under Aerial Bombardment 1914–1939*. Part II. Maxwell Air Force Base, AL: U.S. Air University. https://apps.dtic.mil/dtic/tr/fulltext/u2/a953064.pdf.Grant, Eric J., Kyoji Furukawa, Ritsu Sakata, et al. 2015. "Risk of Death among Children of Atomic Bomb Survivors after 62 Years of Follow-Up: A Cohort Study." *Lancet Oncology* 16 (13): 1316–23. https://pubmed.ncbi.nlm.nih.gov/26384241/.

Grant, Peter. 2014. *Philanthropy and Voluntary Action in the First World War: Mobilizing Charity*. London: Routledge.

———. 2017. "Philanthropy in Britain during the First World War." *Tocqueville Review/La Revue Tocqueville* 38 (2): 37–51.

Grayling, A. C. 2006. *Among the Dead Cities*. London: Bloomsbury.

Grayzel, Susan R. 2006. "'The Souls of Soldiers': Civilians under Fire in First World War France." *Journal of Modern History* 78 (3): 588–622.

———. 2012. *At Home and Under Fire: Air Raids and Culture in Britain from the Great War to the Blitz*. Cambridge: Cambridge University Press.

Grebler, Leo, and Wilhelm Winkler. 1940. *The Cost of the World War to Germany and to Austria-Hungary*. New Haven, CT: Yale University Press.

Greene, R. R., S. Hantman, A. Sharabi, and H. Cohen. 2012. "Holocaust Survivors: Three Waves of Resilience Research." *Journal of Evidence Based Social Work* 9 (5): 481–97.

Greenhill, Kelly M. 2010. "Counting the Cost: The Politics of Numbers in Armed Conflicts." In *Sex, Drugs, and Body Counts: The Politics of Numbers in Global Crime and Conflict*, edited by Peter Andreas and Kelly M. Greenhill, pp. 127–58. Ithaca, NY: Cornell University Press.

Greenough, Paul R. 1982. *Prosperity and Misery in Modern Bengal: The Famine of 1943–1944*. Oxford: Oxford University Press.

Grenard, Fabrice. 2019. "The Black Market is a Crime against Humanity . . ." In Tönsmeyer et al. 2018: 83–97.

Grieg, Kai. 2001. *The War Children of the World, War and Children Identity Project*. Bergen: War and Children Identity Project.

Griffioen, Pim, and Ron Zeller. 1999. "La persécution des Juifs en Belgique et aux Pays-Bas pendant la Seconde Guerre mondiale: Une analyse comparative." *Cahiers d'Histoire du Temps présent-Bijdragen tot de Eigentijdse Geschiedenis*, no. 5:73–132.

———. 2006. "Anti-Jewish Policy and Organization of the Deportations in France and the Netherlands, 1940–1944: A Comparative Study." *Holocaust and Genocide Studies* 20 (3): 437–73.

———. 2011. *Jodenvervolging in Nederland, Frankrijk en België, 1940–1945: Overeenkomsten, verschillen, oorzaken*. Amsterdam: Boom.

Griffiths, Owen. 2002. "Need, Greed, and Protest in Japan's Black Market, 1938–1949." *Journal of Social History* 35 (4): 825–58.

Grimsley, Mark, and Clifford J. Rogers, eds. 2002. *Civilians in the Path of War*. Lincoln: University of Nebraska Press.

Grip, Lina, and John Hart. 2009. "The Use of Chemical Weapons in the 1935–36 Italo-Ethiopian War." SIPRI Arms Control and Non-proliferation Programme. https://www.sipri.org/sites /default/files/Italo-Ethiopian-war.pdf.

Grodin, Michael A., ed. 2014. *Jewish Medical Resistance in the Holocaust*. New York: Berghahn.

Gromaire, Georges. 1925. *L'Occupation allemande en France (1914–1918)*. Paris: Payot.

Grosser, Thomas. 2000. "The Integration of Deportees into the Society of the Federal Republic of Germany." *Journal of Communist Studies and Transition Politics* 16:1–2, 125–47. https://doi .org/10.1080/13523270008415434.

Grossman, Vassili. 1946. *The Years of War, 1941–45*. Moscow: Foreign Languages.

Grossmann, Atina. 1995. "A Question of Silence: The Rape of German Women by Occupation Soldiers." *October* 72:42–63.

———. 2007. *Jews, Germans, and Allies: Close Encounters in Occupied Germany*. Princeton, NJ: Princeton University Press.

———. 2011. "The 'Big Rape': Sex and Sexual Violence, War, and Occupation in Post-World War II Memory and Imagination." In *Sexual Violence in Conflict Zones from the Ancient World to the Era of Human Rights*, edited by Elizabeth D. Heineman, pp. 137–51. Philadelphia: University of Pennsylvania Press.

Grossmann, Jakub, Stepan Jurajda, and Felix Roesel. 2021. "Forced Migration, Staying Minorities, and New Societies: Evidence from Post-War Czechoslovakia." CESifo Working Paper No. 8950.

Gruchmann, Lothar. 1992. "Korruption im dritten Reich: Zur 'Lebensmittelversorgung' der NS-Führerschaft." *Vierteljahrshefte fuer Zeitgeschichte* 42 (4): 571–93.

Gruhl, Werner. 2007. *Imperial Japan's World War Two, 1931–1945*. Piscataway, NJ: Transaction.

Guillain, Robert. 1947. *Le peuple japonais et la guerre: Choses vues, 1939–1946*. Paris: Julliard, 1947.

Guillaume, Marine. 2016. "Napalm in US Bombing Doctrine and Practice, 1942–1975." Online Encyclopedia of Mass Violence. http://bo-k2s.sciences-po.fr/mass-violence-war-massacre -resistance/en/document/napalm-us-bombing-doctrine-and-practice-1942-1975.

Guimbeau, Amanda, Nidhiya Menon, and Aldo Musacchio. 2020. "The Brazilian Bombshell? The Long-Term Impact of the 1918 in Pandemic the South American Way." National Bureau of Economic Research Working Paper No. 26929.

Guinnane, T.W. 2007. "Returns, Regrets and Reprints." *Field Day Review* 3:247–57. http://fieldday .ie/wp-content/uploads/sites/136/2014/12/Timothy-W.-Guinnane.pdf.

Gullace, Nicoletta F. 1997. "Sexual Violence and Family Honor: British Propaganda and International Law during the First World." *American Historical Review* 102 (3): 714–47.

Gumz, Jonathan. 2009. *The Resurrection and Collapse of Empire in Habsburg Serbia, 1914–1918*. Cambridge: Cambridge University Press.

Gunn, Geoffrey. 2011. "The Great Vietnamese Famine of 1944–45 Revisited." 東南アジア研究年報 *Annals of Southeast Asian Studies* 52:81–105. https://core.ac.uk/download/pdf/58754237.pdf.

Guven, Cahit, Trung Hoang, Muhammad H. Rahman, and Mehmet A. Ulubaşoğlu. 2021. "Long-Term Effects of Malnutrition on Early-Life Famine Survivors and Their Offspring: New Evidence from the Great Vietnam Famine, 1944–45." *Health Economics* 30 (7): 1600–1627.

Haber, Ludwig Fritz. 2002. *The Poisonous Cloud: Chemical Warfare in the First World War*. Oxford: Oxford University Press.

Hacker, David J. 2011. "A Census-Based Estimate of the Civil War Dead." *Civil War History* 57:306–47.

Hagen, William W. 1996. "Before the 'Final Solution': Toward a Comparative Analysis of Political Anti-Semitism in Interwar Germany and Poland." *Journal of Modern History* 68 (2): 351–81.

———. 2005. "The Moral Economy of Ethnic Violence: The Pogrom in Lwów." *Geschichte und Gesellschaft* 31 (2): 203–26.

Hamlin, David. 2009. "'Dummes Geld': Money, Grain, and the Occupation of Romania in WWI." *Central European History* 42:451–71.

Hanlon, Gregory. 2012. "Wartime Mortality in Italy's Thirty Years War: The Duchy of Parma, 1635–1637." *Histoire, Économie et Société* 31 (4): 3–22.

Hansen, Lulu Anne. 2009. "'Youth off the Rails': Teenage Girls and German Soldiers—a Case Study in Occupied Denmark, 1940–1945." In *Brutality and Desire War and Sexuality in Europe's Twentieth Century*, edited by Dagmar Herzog, pp. 135–67. London: Palgrave Macmillan.

Hardach, Gerd. 1977. *The First World War, 1914–1918*. London: Allen Lane.

Harmon, Christopher C. 1991. *"Are We Beasts?" Churchill and the Moral Question of World War II "Area Bombing."* Newport, RI: Naval War College.

Harriman, Helga Horniak. 1973. "The German Minority in Yugoslavia, 1941–1945." PhD diss., Oklahoma State University, Stillwater, 1973.

Harris, Arthur. 1947. *Bomber Offensive*. Toronto: Stoddart.

Harris, Chauncy D., and Gabriele Wülker. 1953. "The Refugee Problem of Germany." *Economic Geography* 29 (1): 10–25.

Harris, Ruth. 1993. The "'Child of the Barbarian': Rape, Race and Nationalism in France during the First World War." *Past and Present* 141:170–206.

Harrison, Mark. 1985. *Soviet Planning in Peace and War, 1938–1945*. Cambridge: Cambridge University Press.

———. 1998. Introduction to *The Economics of World War 2: Six Great Powers in International Comparison*. Cambridge: Cambridge University Press.

———. 2003a. "Counting Soviet Deaths in the Great Patriotic War: Comment." *Europe-Asia Studies* 55 (6): 939–44.

———. 2003b. "War Communism." In *The Encyclopedia of Soviet Communism*, edited by James R. Millar, pp. 1660–61. New York: Macmillan.

———. 2016. "Myths of the Great War." In *Economic History of Warfare and State Formation*, edited by Jari Eloranta, Eric Golson, Andrei Markevich, and Nikolaus Wolf, pp. 135–56. London: Springer.

———. 2019. "Counting the Soviet Union's War Dead: Still 26–27 Million." *Europe-Asia Studies* 71 (6): 1036–47. doi:10.1080/09668136.2018.1547366 ISSN 0966–8136.

———. 2020. "Economic Warfare in Twentieth-Century History and Strategy." CAGE Working Paper No. 468.

Harrison, Mark, and Andrei Markevich. 2011. "Great War, Civil War, and Recovery: Russia's National Income, 1913 to 1928." *Journal of Economic History* 71 (3): 672–703.

Harrison, Mark, and Nikolaus Wolf. 2012. "The Frequency of Wars." *Economic History Review* 65:1055–76.

Harvey, A. D. 2000. "Bombing and the Air War on the Italian Front, 1915–1918." *Air Power History* 47 (3): 34–39.

Hasegawa, Tsuyoshi. 2009. "Were the Atomic Bombings of Hiroshima and Nagasaki Justified?" In Tanaka and Young 2009: 97–134.

Hass, Jeffrey K. 2011. "Norms and Survival in the Heat of War: Normative versus Instrumental Rationalities and Survival Tactics in the Blockade of Leningrad." *Sociological Forum* 26 (4): 921–49.

Hastings, Max. 1979. *Bomber Command: The Myths and Realities of the Strategic Bombing Offensive, 1939–1945*. New York: Dial Press.

Haukka, J., J. Suvisaari, M. Sarvimäki, and P. Martikainen. 2017. "The Impact of Forced Migration on Mortality: A Cohort Study of 242,075 Finns from 1939–2010." *Epidemiology* 28 (4): 587–93.

Havari, Enkelejda, and F. Perocchi. 2019. "Growing Up in Wartime: Evidence from the Era of Two World Wars." *Economics and Human Biology* 25:9–32.

Havens, Thomas R. H. 1975. "Women and War in Japan, 1937–45." *American Historical Review* 80 (4): 913–34.

———. 1978. *Valley of Darkness: The Japanese People and World War Two*. New York: W. W. Norton.

Hayes, Peter. 2017. *Why? Explaining the Holocaust*. New York: W. W. Norton.

H-Diplo Roundtable. 2006. "Roundtable on Tsuyoshi Hasegawa's *Racing the Enemy*." https://issforum.org/roundtables/PDF/Maddux-HasegawaRoundtable.pdf.

He, Ping, Gong Chen, Chao Guo, and Xu Wen. 2020. "Long-Term Effect of Prenatal Exposure to Malnutrition on Risk of Schizophrenia in Adulthood: Evidence from the Chinese Famine of 1959–1961." *European Psychiatry* 51:42–47.

Healy, Maureen. 2004. *Vienna and the Fall of the Habsburg Empire: Total War and Everyday Life in World War I*. Cambridge: Cambridge University Press.

Healy, Maureen, Dana Bronson, and Musa Jemal. 2015. "Social Conflict and Control, Protest and Repression (Austria-Hungary)." In Daniel et al. 2014–19.

Heifetz, Elias. 1921. *The Slaughter of the Jews in the Ukraine in 1919*. New York: Thomas Selzer.

Heinrichs, R. W. 2003. "Historical Origins of Schizophrenia: Two Early Madmen and Their Illness." *History of the Behavioral Sciences* 39 (4): 349–63.

Helder, Bent. 1949. *Ravitaillement de la Grèce pendant l'occupation 1941–1944 et pendant les premiers cinq mois après la libération: Rapport final*. Athens: Imprimerie de la Société hellenique d'éditions. https://library.icrc.org/library/docs/DIGITAL/DOC_00111.pdf.

Helmreich, William B. 1996. *Against All Odds: Holocaust Survivors and the Successful Lives They Made in America*. New York: Simon and Schuster.

Hemingway, Ernest. 1998. *A Farewell to Arms*. London: Random House. First published in 1929.

Hemphill, R. E. 1941. "The Influence of the War on Mental Disease: A Psychiatric Study." *Journal of Mental Science* 87 (367): 170–82.

Henryot, Fabienne. 2013. "Guerre et charité: L'action de Vincent de Paul en Lorraine (1637–1649)." In *Religion et piété au défi de la guerre de Trente Ans, actes du colloque de Lyon (27 septembre 2013) et Neuchâtel (17–18 janvier 2014)*, edited by Bertrand Forclaz and Philippe Martin, pp. 141–56. Rennes, France: Presses Universitaires de Rennes.

Herman, Jan. 1969. "The Development of Bohemian and Moravian Jewry, 1918–1938." *Proceedings of the World Congress of Jewish Studies* 5:191–206.

Hermand, Jost. 1997. *A Hitler Youth in Poland: The Nazis' Program for Evacuating Children during World War II*. Evanston, IL: Northwestern University Press.

Hersch, Liebman. 1927. "La mortalité causée par la guerre mondiale: La mortalité cause indirectement par la guerre." *Metron: The International Review of Statistics* 7 (1): 3–82.

Hersey, John. 1946. "Hiroshima." *New Yorker*, August 31.

Herwig, Holger. 2002. "The Immorality of Expediency: The German Military from Ludendorff to Hitler." In Grimsley and Rogers 2002: 111–1335.

———. 2009. "Review of Lipkes (2007)." *International History Review* 31 (1): 153–55.

Hilberg, Raul. 1961. *The Destruction of the European Jews*. London: W. H. Allen.

Hilton, Claire. 2021. *Civilian Lunatic Asylums during the First World War: A Study of Austerity on London's Fringe*. London: Palgrave Macmillan.

Hinton, James. 2013. *The Mass Observers: A History, 1937–1949*. Oxford: Oxford University Press.

Hionidou, Violetta. 2004. "Black Market, Hyperinflation, and Hunger: Greece 1941–1944." *Food and Foodways* 12:107–36.

———. 2006. *Famine and Death in Occupied Greece, 1941–1944*. Cambridge: Cambridge University Press.

———. 2013. "Relief and Politics in Occupied Greece, 1941–4." *Journal of Contemporary History* 48 (4): 761–83.

———. 2018. "'Choosing' between Children and the Elderly in the Greek Famine (1941–1944)." In Tönsmeyer et al. 2018: 203–22.

———. 2021. "'If We Hadn't Left . . . We Would Have All Died': Escaping Famine on the Greek Island of Chios, 1941–44." *Journal of Refugee Studies* 34 (1): 1101–20.

Hippler, Thomas. 2013. *Bombing the People: Giulio Douhet and the Foundations of Air-Power Strategy, 1884–1939*. Cambridge: Cambridge University Press.

Hobsbawm, Eric. 1994. "Barbarism: A User's Guide." *New Left Review*, July—August.

Hohn, Uta. 1994. "The Bomber's Baedeker—Target Book for Strategic Bombing in the Economic Warfare against German Towns 1943–45." *GeoJournal*, special issue on "Military Geography: The Changing Role of the Military," 34 (2): 213–30.

Holmes, M. M., H. S. Resnick, D. G. Kilpatrick, and C. L. Best. 1996. "Rape-Related Pregnancy: Estimates and Descriptive Characteristics from a National Sample of Women." *American Journal of Obstetrics and Gynecology* 175 (2): 320–24.

Holmila, Antero, and Oula Silvennoinen. 2011. "The Holocaust Historiography in Finland." *Scandinavian Journal of History* 36 (5): 605–19.

Holmila, Antero, Oula Silvennoinen, and Karin Kvist Geverts. 2011. "On Forgetting and Rediscovering the Holocaust in Scandinavia: Introduction to the Special Issue on the Histories and Memories of the Holocaust in Scandinavia." *Scandinavian Journal of History* 36 (5): 520–35.

Honda, Sumihisa, Yoshisada Shibata, Mariko Mine, et al. 2002. "Mental Health Conditions among Atomic Bomb Survivors in Nagasaki." *Psychiatry and Clinical Neuroscience* 56 (5): 575–83.

Honigsbaum, Mark. 2008. *Living with Enza: The Forgotten Story of Britain and the Great Flu Pandemic of 1918*. London: Palgrave Macmillan.

———. 2013. "Regulating the 1918–19 Pandemic: Flu, Stoicism and the Northcliffe Press." *Medical History* 57 (2): 165–85.

Horne, John, ed. 1997. *State, Society, and Mobilization in Europe during the First World War*. Cambridge: Cambridge University Press.

———, ed. 2010. *A Companion to World War I*. Oxford: Blackwell.

———. 2014. "Atrocities and War Crimes." In Winter and Stille 2014: 1:561–84.

Horne, John, and Alan Kramer. 2001. *German Atrocities, 1914: A History of Denial*. New Haven, CT: Yale University Press.

———. 2006. "German Atrocities in the First World War 1: A Response." *German History* 24 (1): 118–21.

Howard, N. P. 1993. "The Social and Political Consequences of the Allied Food Blockade of Germany, 1918–1919." *German History* 11 (2): 161–88.

Hsu, Shuhsi. 1941. *A New Digest of Japanese War Conduct*. Shanghai: Kelly and Walsh.

Huff, Gregg. 2019a. "Causes and Consequences of the Great Vietnam Famine, 1944–5." *Economic History Review* 72 (1): 286–316.

———. 2019b. "The Great Second World War Vietnam and Java Famines." *Modern Asian Studies* 54 (2): 1–36.

———. 2020. *World War II and Southeast Asia: Economy and Society under Japanese Occupation*. Cambridge: Cambridge University Press.

Huff, Gregg, and Gillian Huff. 2014. "Urbanization in Southeast Asia during the World War II Japanese Occupation and Its Aftermath." University of Oxford Discussion Paper in Economic and Social History No. 128.

Hughes, Laura A. E., Piet van den Brandt, Andiaan P de Bruine, et al. 2009. "Early Life Exposure to Famine and Colorectal Cancer Risk: A Role for Epigenetic Mechanisms." *PLoS One* 4 (11): e7951.

Hull, Isabel. 2014. *A Scrap of Paper: Breaking and Making International Law during the Great War.* Ithaca, NY: Cornell University Press.

Hushion, Stacy. 2015. "Intimate Encounters and the Politics of German Occupation in Belgium, 1940–44/45." PhD diss., University of Toronto. file:///Users/cormacograda/Downloads/Hushion_Stacy_201506_PhD_thesis.pdf.

Hußlein, H. 1947. "Geburtsgewicht in Mangelzeiten." *Wiener klinische Wochenschrift* 59 (34/35): 586–88.

Ikonomopoulos, Marcia Haddad. 2003. "The Story behind the Statistics: Variables Affecting the Tremendous Losses of Greek Jewry during the Holocaust." *Journal of the Hellenic Diaspora* 32 (1/2): 89–109.

Iredale, Will. 2021. *The Pathfinders: The Elite RAF Force That Turned the Tide of WWII.* London: Penguin.

Ironside, Kirsty. 2016. "Stalin's Doctrine of Price Reductions during the Second World War and Postwar Reconstruction." *Slavic Review* 75 (3): 655–77.

Jacobs, Steven L. 2019. "The Complicated Cases of Soghomon Tehlirian and Sholem Schwartzbard and Their Influences on Raphael Lemkin's Thinking about Genocide." *Genocide Studies and Prevention* 13 (1): 33–41.

Janicki, David A. 2014. "The British Blockade during World War I: The Weapon of Deprivation." *Inquiries Journal* 6 (6): 1–5.

Janis, I. L. 1951. *Air War and Emotional Stress: Psychological Studies of Bombing and Civilian Defence.* New York: McGraw Hill.

Jennings, Eric. 2002. "Last Exit from Vichy France: The Martinique Escape Route and the Ambiguities of Emigration." *Journal of Modern History* 74 (2): 289–324.

Jevtic, Elizabeta. 2004. "Blank Pages of the Holocaust: Gypsies in Yugoslavia during World War II." Master's diss., Brigham Young University. https://scholarsarchive.byu.edu/etd/149.

Jewell, Nicholas P., Michael Spagat, and Britta L. Jewell. 2018. "Accounting for Civilian Casualties: From the Past to the Future." *Social Science History* 42 (3): 379–410.

Jockusch, Laura, and Tamara Lewinsky. 2010. "Paradise Lost: Postwar Memory of Polish Jewish Survival in the Soviet Union." *Holocaust and Genocide Studies* 24 (3): 373–99.

Johns, Robert, and Graeme A. M. Davies. 2019. "Civilian Casualties and Public Support for Military Action: Experimental Evidence." *Journal of Conflict Resolution* 63 (1): 251–81.

Johnson, Kelly. 2012. "Sholem Schwarzbard: Biography of a Jewish Assassin." PhD diss., Harvard University. Accessed December 26, 2023. http://nrs.harvard.edu/urn-3:HUL.InstRepos:9830349.

Johnston, Bruce F. 1953. *Japanese Food Management in World War II.* Stanford, CA: Stanford University Press.

Johr, Barbara. 1992. "Die Ereignisse in Zahlen." In *Befreier und Befreite: Krieg, Vergewaltigung, Kinder,* edited by Helke Sander and Barbara Johr, pp. 54–59. Munich: Fischer.

Jones, H. A. 1931. *The Great War in the Air.* Vol. 5. Oxford: Clarendon Press.

Jones, Derry. 2008. "Hull Blitz, Scientific Surveys and City Bombing Campaigns: 1941–42 Surveys of Morale in Much-Bombed Hull." *East Yorkshire Historian* 9:27–36.

Jones, Edgar. 2015. "Air-Raid Casualties in the First World War." *History of Government* (blog), January 19. https://history.blog.gov.uk/2015/01/19/air-raid-casualties-in-the-first-world-war/.

———. 2016. "Air Raids and the Crowd—Citizens at War." *Psychologist,* May 9. Accessed December 20, 2023. https://www.bps.org.uk/psychologist/air-raids-and-crowd-citizens-war.

Jones, Edgar, and Simon Wessely. 2014. "Battle for the Mind: World War 1 and the Birth of Military Psychiatry." *Lancet* 384:1708–14.

Jones, Edgar, Robin Woolvem, Bill Durodie, and Simon Wessely. 2004. "Civilian Morale during the Second World War: Responses to Air Raids Re-examined." *Social History of Medicine* 17 (3): 463–79.

Jones, Grinnell. 1920. "Nitrogen: Its Fixation, Its Uses in Peace and War." *Quarterly Journal of Economics* 34 (3): 391–431.

Jones, Mark William. 2023. *1923: The Crisis of German Democracy in the Year of Hitler's Putsch.* New York: Basic Books.

Jones, Michael. 2008. *Leningrad: Stage of Siege.* London: John Murray.

Jordan, B. R. 2016. "The Hiroshima/Nagasaki Survivor Studies: Discrepancies between Results and General Perception." *Genetics* 203 (4): 1505.

Jordan, Douglas. 2019. "The Deadliest Flu: The Complete Story of the Discovery and Reconstruction of the 1918 Pandemic Virus." Centers for Disease Control and Prevention, December 19. https://www.cdc.gov/flu/pandemic-resources/reconstruction-1918-virus.html.

Jorland, Gérard. 2011. "La variole et la guerre de 1870." *Les tribunes de la santé*, no. 33: 25–30. https://www.cairn.info/revue-les-tribunes-de-la-sante1-2011-4-page-25.htm.

Jourdain, Margaret. 1918. "Air Raid Reprisals and Starvation by Blockade." *International Journal of Ethics* 28 (4): 542–53.

Joyce, Patrick. 2021. *Going to My Father's House.* London: Verso.

Jürges, Hendrick. 2013. "Collateral Damage: The German Food Crisis, Educational Attainment and Labor Market Outcomes of German Post-War Cohorts." *Journal of Health Economics* 32 (1): 286–303.

Jürges, Hendrick, and Thomas Kopetsch. 2021. "Prenatal Exposure to the German Food Crisis 1944–1948 and Health after 65 Years." *Economics and Human Biology* 40:100952.

Kagansky, Nadya, Hilla Knobler, Marina Stein-Babich, Hillary Voet, Adi Shalit, Jutta Lindert, and Haim Y. Knobler. 2019. "Holocaust Survival and the Long-Term Risk of Cardiovascular Disease in the Elderly." *Israeli Medical Association Journal* 21 (4): 241–45.

Kagawa, Masaharu, Yasuaki Tahara, Kazuhiko Moji, Rieko Nakao, Kiyoshi Aoyagi, and Andrew P. Hills. 2011. "Secular Changes in Growth among Japanese Children over 100 Years (1900–2000)." *Asia Pacific Journal of Clinical Nutrition* 20 (2): 180–89.

Kaldor, Mary. 1999. *New and Old Wars: Organized Violence in a Global Era.* Cambridge: Polity.

———. 2019. *Peacemaking in an Era of New Wars.* Brussels: Carnegie Europe. Accessed December 28, 2023. https://carnegieeurope.eu/2019/10/14/peacemaking-in-era-of-new-wars-pub-80033.

Kane, Eileen. 1986. "Stereotypes and Irish Identity: Mental Illness as a Cultural Frame." *Studies: An Irish Quarterly Review* 75 (300): 539–51.

Kaniewski, David, and Nick Marriner. 2020. "Conflicts and the Spread of Plagues in Pre-industrial Europe." *Humanities and Social Sciences Communications* 7:162. https://doi.org/10.1057/s41599-020-00661-1.

Kaplan, Marion. 2013. "Lisbon Is Sold Out! The Daily Lives of Jewish Refugees in Portugal During World War II." New York University, Tikvah Working Paper No. 01/13. http://www.law.nyu.edu/sites/default/files/TikvahWorkingPapersArchive/WP1Kaplan.pdf.

———. 2020. *Hitler's Jewish Refugees: Hope and Anxiety in Portugal.* New Haven, CT: Yale University Press.

Karau, Mark D. 2015. *Germany's Defeat in the First World War.* New York: Praeger.

Katchanovski, Ivan. 2019. "The OUN, the UPA, and the Nazi Genocide in Ukraine." In *Mittäterschaft in Osteuropa im Zweiten Weltkrieg und im Holocaust/Collaboration in Eastern Europe during World War II and the Holocaust*, edited by Peter Black, Béla Rásky, and Marianne Windsperger, pp. 67–93. Vienna: New Academic Press.

Katkoff, V. 1950. "Soviet Grain Production: 1940–1950." *Land Economics* 26 (3): 207–21.

Katz, Dovid. 2016. "Is Eastern European 'Double Genocide' Revisionism Reaching Museums?" *Dapim: Studies on the Holocaust* 16 (3): 191–220.

Kay, Alex J. 2006. "Germany's Staatsekretäre, Mass Starvation and the Meeting of 2 May 1941." *Journal of Contemporary History* 41 (4): 685–700.

———. 2012. "The Purpose of the Russian Campaign Is the Decimation of the Slavic Population by Thirty Million: The Radicalization of German Food Policy in Early 1941." In *Nazi Policy on the Eastern Front, 1941: Total War, Genocide, and Radicalization*, edited by Alex J. Kay, Jeff Rutherford, and David Stahel, pp. 101–29. Rochester: University of Rochester Press.

Kean, Hilda. 2017. *The Great Cat and Dog Massacre: The Real Story of World War Two's Unknown Tragedy*. Chicago: University of Chicago Press.

Kehoe, Thomas J., and E. James Kehoe. 2016. "Crimes Committed by U.S. Soldiers in Europe, 1945–1946." *Journal of Interdisciplinary History* 47 (1): 53–84.

———. 2017. "A Reply to Dykstra's 'Evident Bias in Crimes Committed by U.S. Soldiers in Europe, 1945–1946.'" *Journal of Interdisciplinary History* 47 (3): 385–96.

Keisinger, Florian. 2015. "Uncivilised Wars in Civilised Europe? The Perception of the Balkan Wars 1912–1913 in English, German and Irish Newspapers and Journals." In *The Wars before the Great War: Conflict and International Politics before the Outbreak of the First World War*, edited by D. Geppert, W. Mulligan, and A. Rose, pp. 343–58. Cambridge: Cambridge University Press.

Kellerman, N. P. 2001. "Psychopathology in Children of Holocaust Survivors: A Review of the Research Literature." *Israeli Journal of Psychiatry and Related Sciences* 38 (1): 36–46.

Kenrick, Donald, and Grattan Puxon. 1972. *The Destiny of Europe's Gypsies*. New York: Basic Books.

Kershaw, Ian. 2011. *The End: The Defiance and Destruction of Hitler's Germany, 1944–1945*. London: Penguin.

Kesternich, Irish, Bettina Siflinger, James P. Smith, and Joachim K. Winter. 2014. "The Effects of World War II on Economic and Health Outcomes across Europe." *Review of Economics and Statistics* 96 (1): 103–18.

Keys, Ancel, Josef Brožek, Austin Henschel, Olaf Mickelsen, and Henry Longstreet Taylor. 1950. *The Biology of Human Starvation*. Vol. 1. Minneapolis: University of Minnesota Press.

Khorram-Manesh, Amir, Frederick M. Burkle, Krysztof Goniewicz, and Yohan Robinson. 2021. "Estimating the Number of Civilian Casualties in Modern Armed Conflicts—a Systematic Review." *Frontiers in Public Health* 9:765261.

Khruschev, Nikita S. 1970. *Khruschev Remembers*. Boston: Little, Brown.

Kiernan, Ben. 2007. *Blood and Soil: A World History of Genocide and Extermination from Sparta to Darfur*. New Haven, CT: Yale University Press.

Kieser, Hans-Lukas. 2018. *Talaat Pasha: Father of Modern Turkey, Architect of Genocide*. Princeton, NJ: Princeton University Press.

Kieser, Hans-Lukas, and Donald Bloxham. 2014. "Genocide." In Winter and Stille 2014: 1:585–614.

Kift, Dagmar. 2010. "Neither Here nor There? Memorialization of the Expulsion of Ethnic Germans." In *Memorialization in Germany since 1945*, edited by Bill Niven and Chloe Paver, pp. 78–90. London: Palgrave Macmillan.

Kihlstrom, John F. 2005. "Dissociative Disorders." *Annual Review of Clinical Psychology* 1 (1): 227–53.

Killingray, David. 1984. "'A Swift Agent of Government': Air Power in British Colonial Africa, 1916–1939." *Journal of African History* 25 (4): 429–44.

Kim, Yoshiharu, Atsuro Tsutsumi, Takashi Izutsu, Noriyuki Kawamura, Takao Miyazaki, and Takehiko Kikkawa. 2011. "Persistent Distress after Psychological Exposure to the Nagasaki Atomic Bomb Explosion." *British Journal of Psychiatry* 199: 411–16.

Kind-Kovács, Friederike. 2015. "The 'Other' Child Transports: World War I and the Temporary Displacement of Needy Children from Central Europe." *Revue d'histoire de l'enfance "irrégulière."* https://journals.openedition.org/rhei/3474).

Kirby, M., and R. Capey. 1997. "The Area Bombing of Germany in World War II: An Operational Research Perspective." *Journal of the Operational Research Society* 48 (7): 661–77.

Kirschenbaum, Lisa A. 2017. "The Meaning of Resilience: Soviet Children in World War II." *Journal of Interdisciplinary History* 47 (4): 521–35.

Klapsis, Antonis. 2014. "Violent Uprooting and Forced Migration: A Demographic Analysis of the Greek Populations of Asia Minor, Pontus and Eastern Thrace." *Middle Eastern Studies* 50 (4): 622–39.

Klee, Ernst, Willi Dressen, and Volker Riess. 1991. *"The Good Old Days": The Holocaust as Seen by Its Perpetrators and Bystanders.* New York: MacMillan.

Klemann, Hein A. M., and Sergei Kudryashov. 2012. *Occupied Economies: An Economic History of Nazi-Occupied Europe, 1939–1945.* London: Bloomsbury. E-book.

Kless, Shlomo. 1988. "The Rescue of Jewish Children in Belgium during the Holocaust." *Holocaust and Genocide Studies* 3 (3): 275–87.

Klier, John. 2004. "The Holocaust and the Soviet Union." In Stone 2004: 276–95.

Klingberg, Marcus. 2010. "An Epidemiologist's Journey from Typhus to Thalidomide, and from the Soviet Union to Seveso." *Journal of the Royal Medical Society* 103 (10): 418–23.

Knell, Herman, 2003. *To Destroy a City: Strategic Bombing and Its Human Consequences in World War 2.* Cambridge, MA: Perseus.

Knittel, Susanne. 2010. "Remembering Euthanasia: Grafeneck in the Past, Present, and Future." In *Memorialization in Germany since 1945*, edited by Bill Niven and Chloe Paver, pp. 124–32. London: Palgrave Macmillan.

Knobler, Haim Y., Moshe Z. Abramowitz, and Jutta Lindert. 2018. "Survival and Resilience versus Psychopathology: A Seven-Decade Perspective Post-Holocaust." In *Multidisciplinary Perspectives on Genocide and Memory*, edited by J. Lindert and A. Marsoobian, pp. 103–13. New York: Springer.

Knopp, Guido. 2009. *Die Wehrmacht: Eine Bilanz.* Munich: Goldmann.

Kochanowski, Jerzy. 2017. *Through the Back Door: The Black Market in Poland, 1944–1989.* New York: Peter Lang.

———. 2018. "Black Market in the General Government, 1939–1945: Survival Strategy or (Un) official Economy?" In Tönsmeyer et al. 2018: 27–47.

Kochina, Elena. 1990. *Blockade Diary: One Woman's Harrowing Diary of the German Blockade of Leningrad.* Ann Arbor: Ardis.

Koenigsberg, Ruth Davis. 2011. "Grief, Unedited." *New York Times*, February 14.

Koenker, Diane. 1985. "Urbanization and De-urbanization in the Russian Revolution and Civil War." *Journal of Modern History* 57 (3): 424–50.

Koos, Carlo. 2018. "Decay or Resilience? The Long-Term Social Consequences of Conflict-Related Sexual Violence in Sierra Leone." *World Politics* 70 (2): 194–238.

Korppi-Tommola, Aura. 2008. "War and Children in Finland during the Second World War." *Paedagogica Historica* 44 (4): 445–55.

Kotzageorgi, Xanthippi, and Georgios A. Kazamias. 1994. "The Bulgarian Occupation of the Prefecture of Drama (1941–1944) and Its Consequences on the Greek Population." *Balkan Studies* 35 (1): 81–112.

Kovacs, A. F. 1943. "Military Origins of the Fall of France." *Military Affairs* 7 (1): 25–40.

Kramer, Alan. 2006. "The First Wave of International War Trials: Istanbul and Leipzig." *European Review* 14 (4): 441–55.

———. 2007. *Dynamic of Destruction: Culture and Mass Killing in the First World War.* Oxford: Oxford University Press.

———. 2010a. "Atrocities, Massacres, and War Crimes." In Horne 2010: 188–201.

———. 2010b. "Ethnische Säuberungen vom Ersten Weltkrieg zum Nationalsozialismus." In *Nationalsozialismus und Erster Weltkrieg*, edited by G. Krumeich, pp. 323–45. Essen, Germany: Klartext.

———. 2014a. "Blockade and Economic Warfare." In Winter and Stille 2014: 2: 460–89.

———. 2014b. "Recent Historiography of the First World War: Part I." *Journal of Modern European History* 12 (1): 5–28.

———. 2014c. "Recent Historiography of the First World War: Part II." *Journal of Modern European History* 12 (2): 155–74.

———. 2017. "Atrocities." In Daniel et al. 2014–19.

Kramm, Robert. 2017. "Haunted by Defeat: Imperial Sexualities, Prostitution, and the Emergence of Postwar Japan." *Journal of World History* 28 (3/4): 587–614.

Krause, Richard Lee. 1968 "The Iron and Steel Industry in Wartime Japan." Master's diss., Oklahoma State University.

Kravis, Irving. 1948. "Prices and Wages in the Austrian Economy, 1938–47." *Monthly Labor Review* 66, no. 1 (January): 20–27.

Kreindler, Isabelle. 1986. "The Soviet Deported Nationalities: A Summary and an Update." *Soviet Studies* 38 (3): 387–405.

Krimmer, Elizabeth. 2015. "Philomela's Legacy: Rape, the Second World War, and the Ethics of Reading." *German Quarterly* 81 (1): 82–103.

Kronenbitter, Guenther. 2007. "The German and Austro-Hungarian General Staffs and Their Reflections on an 'Impossible' War." In Afflerbach and Stevenson 2007: 149–60.

Kuber, Johannes. 2019. "'Frivolous Broads' and the 'Black Menace': The Catholic Clergy's Perception of Victims and Perpetrators of Sexual Violence in Occupied Germany, 1945." In *War and Sexual Violence: New Perspectives in a New Era*, edited by Sarah K. Danielsson, pp. 183–208. Paderborn, Germany: Verlag Ferdinand Schöningh.

Kuhn, Arthur K. 1910. "The Beginnings of an Aerial Law." *American Journal of International Law* 4:109–32.

Kulischer, Eugene M. 1943. *The Displacement of Population in Europe*. Montreal: International Labour Organization.

Kulrestha, Sujay. 2010. "Wartime Rationing during World War II and the Effect of Public Opinion in Great Britain and Austria." *Inquiries* 2 (12): 1. http://www.inquiriesjournal.com/articles/339 /wartime-rationing-during-world-war-ii-and-the-effect-of-public-opinion-in-great-britain -and-austria.

Kushner, Tony. 1989. *Persistence of Prejudice: Antisemitism in British Society during the Second World War*. Manchester: Manchester University Press.

Kushner, Tony, and Katharine Knox. 1999. *Refugees in an Age of Genocide: Global, National and Local Perspectives during the Twentieth Century*. London: Routledge.

Kuwert, Philipp, Elmar Braehler, Heide Glaesmer, Harald J. Freyberger, and Oliver Decker. 2009. "Impact of Forced Displacement during World War II on the Present-Day Mental Health of the Elderly: A Population-Based Study." *International Psychogeriatrics* 21 (4): 749–53. https:// www.ncbi.nlm.nih.gov/pubmed/19426574/.

Kuwert, Philipp, Heide Glaesmer, Svenja Eichhorn, Elena Grundke, et al. 2014. "Long-Term Effects of Conflict-Related Sexual Violence Compared with Non-sexual War Trauma in Female World War II Survivors: A Matched Pairs Study." *Archives of Sexual Behavior* 43:1059–64.

Kuwert, Philipp, Carsten Spitzer, Jenny Rosenthal, and Harald J. Freyberger. 2008. "Trauma and Post-Traumatic Stress Symptoms in Former German Child Soldiers of World War II." *International Psychogeriatrics* 20:1–5.

Lacina, B., and N. P. Gleditsch. 2005. "Monitoring Trends in Global Combat: A New Dataset of Battle Deaths." *European Journal of Population* 21:145–66. http://dx.doi.org/10.1007/s10680-005-6851-6.

Lafont, Max. 2000. *L'Extermination douce: La mort de 40 000 malades mentaux dans les hôpitaux psychiatriques en France, sous le Régime de Vichy.* Lormont, France: Bord de l'eau.

Lahaie, Olivier. 2011. "L'épidémie de grippe dite "espagnole" et sa perception par l'armée française (1918–1919)." *Revue historique des armées,* no. 262:102–9.

Lamb, Christina. 2020. *Our Bodies Their Battlefield: What War Does to Women.* London: William Collins.

Lammers, Karl Christian. 2011. "The Holocaust and Collective Memory in Scandinavia: The Danish Case." *Scandinavian Journal of History* 36 (5): 570–86.

Langthaler, Ernst. 2016. "Food and Nutrition (Austria-Hungary)." In Daniel et al. 2014–19.

Laqueur, Walter. 2001. *Generation Exodus: The Fate of Young Jewish Refugees from Nazi Germany.* Waltham: Brandeis University Press.

Lardas, Mark. 2019. *Japan, 1944–45: LeMay's B-29 Strategic Bombing Campaign.* Oxford: Osprey.

Larson, Eric V., and Bogdan Savych. 2006. *Misfortunes of War: Press and Public Reactions to Civilian Deaths in Wartime.* Santa Monica: RAND.

Lary, Diana. 2001. "Drowned Earth: The Strategic Breaching of the Yellow River Dyke, 1938." *War in History* 8 (2): 191–207.

———. 2010. *The Chinese People at War: Human Suffering and Social Transformation, 1937–1945.* Cambridge: Cambridge University Press.

Lawson, Eric, and Jane Lawson. 1996. *The First Air Campaign: August 1914–November 1918.* Cambridge, MA: Da Capo Press.

League of Nations. 1946. *Food, Famine and Relief, 1940–46.* Geneva: League of Nations.

Le Bonhomme, Fanny. 2015. "Viols en temps de guerre, psychiatrie et temporalités enchevêtrées: Expériences de femmes violées par les soldats de l'Armée Rouge entre la fin de la Seconde Guerre mondiale et le début de la période de paix (République démocratique allemande, 1958–1968)." *Guerres mondiales et conflits contemporains,* no. 257:53–74.

———. 2016. "Psychiatrie et société en République démocratique allemande: Histoires de patients de la clinique psychiatrique et neurologique de la Charité (Berlin-Est, 1960–1968)." PhD diss., Université Rennes/Universität Postdam.

Lee, Joseph. 1975. "Administrators and Agriculture: Aspects of German Agricultural Policy during the First World War." In *War and Economic Development: Essays in Memory of David Joslin,* edited by Jay Winter, pp. 229–38. Cambridge: Cambridge University Press.

Leitenberg, M. 2006. "Deaths in War and Conflicts in the 20th Century." Cornell University Peace Studies Program Occasional Paper 29. 3rd ed.

Lemkin, Raphael. 2013. *Totally Unofficial: The Autobiography of Raphaël Lemkin.* Edited by Donna-Lee Frieze. New Haven, CT: Yale University Press.

Le Naour, Jean-Yves. 2000. "Femmes tondues et répression des 'femmes à boches' en 1918." *Revue d'Histoire Moderne et Contemporaine* 47 (1): 148–58.

Leon, Gloria L., J. N. Butcher, M. Kleinman, Almagor M. Goldberg, and Moshe Almagor. 1981. "Survivors of the Holocaust and Their Children." *Journal of Personality and Social Psychology* 41 (3): 503–16.

Levav, Itzhak. 1998. "Individuals under Conditions of Maximum Adversity: The Holocaust." In *Adversity, Stress, and Psychopathology,* edited by Bruce P. Dohrenwend, pp. 13–33. New York: Oxford University Press.

Levav, Itzhak, and Anat Brunstein Klomek. 2018. "A Review of Epidemiologic Studies on Suicide before, during, and after the Holocaust." *Psychiatry Research* 261: 35–38.

Levi, Primo. 1960. *If This Is a Man.* Translated by Stuart Woolf. London: Bodley Head.

———. 1988. *The Drowned and the Saved*. Translated by Raymond Rosenthal. London: Michael Joseph.

Levin, Dov. 1995. *The Lesser of Two Evils: Eastern European Jewry under Soviet Rule, 1939–1941*. Philadelphia: Jewish Publications Society.

———. 2000. *The Litvaks: A Short History of the Jews in Lithuania*. Jerusalem: Yad Vashem.

Levin, Irene. 2013. "Oslo: The Escape from Norway." In *Civil Society and the Holocaust: International Perspectives on Resistance and Rescue*, edited by Anders Jerichow and Cecilie Felicia Stokholm Banke, pp. 162–75. New York: Humanity in Action Press.

Levine, Paul A. 1996. *From Indifference to Activism: Swedish Diplomacy and the Holocaust, 1938–1944*. Uppsala: Acta Universitatis Upsaliensis.

Levine, Stephen Z., Itzhak Levav, Rinat Yoffe, Yifat Becher, and Inna Pugachova. 2016. "Genocide Exposure and Subsequent Suicide Risk: A Population-Based Study." *PLos One* 11 (2): e0149524. https://www.ncbi.nlm.nih.gov/pmc/articles/PMC4763158/.

Levitt, Martin L. 1995. "The Psychology of Children: Twisting the Hull-Birmingham Survey to Influence British Aerial Strategy during World War 2." *Psychologie und Geschichte* 7(1): 44–59.

Lewis, Aubrey. 1942. "Incidence of Neuroses in England under War Conditions." *Lancet* 2:175–83.

———. 1943. "Mental Health in Wartime." *Public Health* 57 (3): 27–30.

Lewis, Norman. 1978. *Naples '44: A World War II Diary of Occupied Italy*. London: Collins.

Lewy, Guenter. 2000. *The Nazi Persecution of the Gypsies*. Oxford: Oxford University Press.

Li, Chihua, L. H. Lumey, and C. Ó Gráda. 2023. "Horrors of Famine: Explaining the Long Run and Short Run Costs." Under review.

Li, Lillian. 2007. *Fighting Famine in North China: State, Market, and Environmental Decline, 1690s–1990s*. Stanford: Stanford University Press.

Li, Peter, ed. 2003. *Japanese War Crimes*. New Brunswick, NJ: Transaction.

Liczbinska, Graxyna, Zbigniew Czapla, Robert M. Malina, and Janusz Piontek. 2017. "Body Size of Young Adult Polish College-Age Women Born before, during, and after WWII." *American Journal of Human Biology* 29 (6). https://onlinelibrary.wiley.com/doi/full/10.1002/ajhb.23040.

Lieberman, Sandford R. 1983. "The Evacuation of Industry in the Soviet Union during World War." *Soviet Studies* 35 (1): 90–102.

Lifton, Robert Jay. 1963. "Psychological Effects of the Atomic Bomb in Hiroshima: The Theme of Death." *Daedalus* 92 (3): 462–97.

———. 1968. *Death in Life: Survivors of Hiroshima*. New York: Random House.

Lindeboom, Martin, and Reyn van Ewijk. 2015. "Babies of the War: The Effect of War Exposure Early in Life on Mortality throughout Life." *Biodemography and Social Biology* 61:2, 167–86.

Lindee, Susan. 1994. *Suffering Made Real: American Science and the Survivors at Hiroshima*. Chicago: University of Chicago Press.

Linden, Stefanie Caroline. 2021. "When War Came Home: Air-Raid Shock in World War I." *History of Psychiatry*. https://doi.org/10.1177/0957154X21998217.

Lindert, Jutta, Haim Y. Knobler, Ichiro Kawachi, et al. 2017. "Psychopathology of Children of Genocide Survivors: A Systematic Review on the Impact of Genocide on Their Children's Psychopathology from Five Countries." *International Journal of Epidemiology* 46 (1): 246–57.

Linton, Derek S. 2010. "'War Dysentery' and the Limitations of German Military Hygiene during World War I." *Bulletin of the History of Medicine* 84 (4): 607–39.

Lipkes, Jeff. 2007. *Rehearsals: The German Army in Belgium, August 1914*. Leuven: Leuven University Press.

Lippman, Matthew. 2002. "Aerial Attacks on Civilians and the Humanitarian Low of War: Technology and Terror from World War I to Afghanistan." *California Western Law Journal* 33 (1): 1–67.

Lister, J. C. 1941. "The War and the People, No. 2: The Nightly Trekker." *Social Work* 2 (2): 79–91.

Little, Brandon. 2014. "An Explosion of New Endeavours: Global Humanitarian Responses to Industrialized Warfare in the First World War Era." *First World War Studies* 5 (1): 1–16.

Litz, B. T. 2014. "Resilience in the Aftermath of War Trauma: A Critical Review and Commentary." *Interface Focus* 4:20140008. http://dx.doi.org/10.1098/rsfs.2014.0008.

Liulevicius, Vejas. 2000. *War Land on the Eastern Front*. Cambridge: Cambridge University Press.

Livi-Bacci, Massimo. 2020. *I traumi d'Europa. Natura e politica al tempo delle guerre*. Madrid: Il Mulino.

Lockenour, Jay. 2019. "Review of Gebhardt, 'Crimes Unspoken.'" *American Historical Review* 124 (2): 769–70.

Lohr, Eric. 2001. "The Russian Army and the Jews: Mass Deportation, Hostages, and Violence during World War I." *Russian Review* 60 (3): 404–19.

———. 2003. *Nationalizing the Russian Empire: The Campaign against Enemy Aliens during World War I*. Cambridge, MA: Harvard University Press.

London, Louise. 1989. "British Government Policy and Jewish Refugees, 1933–45." *Patterns of Prejudice* 23 (4): 26–43.

———. 2003. *Whitehall and the Jews, 1933–1948: British Immigration Policy, Jewish Refugees and the Holocaust*. Cambridge: Cambridge University Press.

Long, Daniel. 2018. "A Disaster in Lübeck Bay: An Analysis of the Tragic Sinking of the Cap Arcona, 3 May 1945." PhD diss., Nottingham Trent University.

Longacre, Mckenna, Solon Beinfeld, Sabine Hildebrandt, Leonard Glantz, and Michael A. Grodin. 2015. "Public Health in the Vilna Ghetto as a Form of Jewish Resistance." *American Journal of Public Health* 105 (2): 293–301.

Lower, Wendy. 2011. "Pogroms, Mob Violence and Genocide in Western Ukraine, Summer 1941: Varied Histories, Explanations and Comparisons." *Journal of Genocide Research* 13:3, 217–46.

Lumey, L. H., and Alexander Vaiserman, eds. 2013. *Early Life Nutrition and Adult Health and Development*. New York: Nova Science.

Lumey, L. H., and F.W.A. van Poppel. 2013. "The Dutch Famine of 1944–45 as a Human Laboratory: Changes in the Early Life Environment and Adult Health." In Lumey and Vaiserman 2013: 59–76.

Lunn, Joe Harris. 2015. "War Losses (Africa)." In Daniel et al. 2014–19.

Lutjens, Richard N. Jr. 2019. *Submerged on the Surface: The Not-So-Hidden Jews of Nazi Berlin, 1941–1945*. New York: Berghahn.

Lüttinger, P. 1986. "Der Mythos der schnellen Immigration: Eine empirische Untersuchung zur Integration der Vertriebenen und Flüchtlinge in der Bundesrepublik Deutschland bis 1971." *Zeitschrift für Soziologie* 15 (1): 20–36.

———. 1989. *Die Integration der Vertriebenen: Eine empirische Analyse*. Frankfurt am Main: Campus Verlag.

Luzzatto-Fegiz, Pierpaolo. 1946a. "Nuove ricerche sui bilanci familiari." *Giornale degli Economisti e Annali di Economia* 5 (3/4): 197–207.

———. 1946b. "Nuove ricerche sui bilanci familiari." *Giornale degli Economisti e Annali di Economia* 5 (5/6): 320–30.

Lyautey, Margot, and Marc Elie. 2019. "German Agricultural Occupation of France and Ukraine, 1940–1944." *Comparativ. Zeitschrift für Globalgeschichte und vergleichende Gesellschaftsforschung (Leipzig)* 29 (3): 86–117.

Lynch, Eduard. 2012. "Food Stocks, the Black Market, and Town and Country Tensions in France during Two World Wars and Beyond." In Brassley, Segers, and Van Molle 2012: 229–44.

MacArthur, W. A. 1956. "Medical History of the Famine." In *The Great Famine: Essays in Irish History*, edited by Edwards and Williams, pp. 263–315. Dublin: Browne and Nolan.

Mackay, Robert. 2002. *Half the Battle: Civilian Morale in Britain during the Second World War.* Manchester: Manchester University Press.

MacKinnon, Stephen. 2001. "Refugee Flight at the Outset of the Anti-Japanese War." In *The Scars of War: The Impact of Warfare on Modem China*, edited by Diana Lary and Stephen MacKinnon, pp. 118–35. Vancouver: UBC Press.

———. 2008. *Wuhan, 1938: War, Refugees, and the Making of Modern China.* Berkeley: University of California Press.

MacLeod, John. 2011. *River of Fire: The Clydebank Blitz.* Rev. ed. Glasgow: Birlinn.

MacPherson, Sir W. G., et al. 1921. *History of the Great War Based on Official Documents: Medical Services Disease of the War.* Vol. 1. London: His Majesty's Stationery Office.

Maddox, Gregory. 1990. "Mtunya: Famine in Central Tanzania, 1917–1920." *Journal of African History* 31:181–97.

Maercker, Andres, and Johannes Herrle. 2003. "Long-Term Effects of the Dresden Bombing: Relationships to Control Beliefs, Religious Belief, and Personal Growth." *Journal of Traumatic Stress* 16 (6): 579–87.

Magaeva, Svetlana. 2005. "Physiological and Psychosomatic Prerequisites for Survival and Recovery." In Barber and Dzeniskevich 2005: 123–59.

Maharatna, Arup. 1996. *The Demography of Famines: An Indian Historical Perspective.* Delhi: Oxford University Press.

———. 2014. "Food Scarcity and Migration: An Overview." *Social Research* 81 (2): 271–98.

Maier, Charles S. 2005. "Targeting the City: Debates and Silences about the Aerial Bombing of World War II." *International Journal of the Red Cross* 87 (859): 429–44.

Majd, Mohammad Gholi. 2003. *The Great Famine and Genocide in Iran, 1917–1919.* Lanham, MD: University Press of America.

Majerus, Benoît, and Anne Roekens. 2017. "Deadly Vulnerabilities: The Provisioning of Psychiatric Asylums in Occupied Belgium (1914–1918)." *Journal of Belgian History* 47 (4): 19–47.

Majstorović, Vojin. 2016. "The Red Army in Yugoslavia, 1944–1945." *Slavic Review* 75 (2): 396–421.

———. 2017. "Ivan Goes Abroad: The Red Army in the Balkans and Central Europe, 1944–1945." PhD diss., University of Toronto.

Maksudov, Sergei. 2001. "The Jewish Population Losses of the USSR from the Holocaust." In *The Holocaust in the Soviet Union: Studies and Sources on the Destruction of the Jews in the Nazi-Occupied Territories of the USSR, 1941–1945*, edited by L. Dobroszycki and J. S. Curock, pp. 207–14. Armonk, NY: M. E. Sharpe.

Malaparte, Curzio. 2013. *The Skin.* New York: New York Review of Books (originally published as *La Pelle* in 1949).

Malloy, Sean L. 2012. "'A Very Pleasant Way to Die': Radiation Effects and the Decision to Use the Atomic Bomb against Japan." *Diplomatic History* 36 (3): 515–45.

Manley, Rebecca. 2007. "The Perils of Displacement: The Soviet Evacuee between Refugee and Deportee." *Contemporary European History* 16 (4): 495–509. https://doi.org.10.1017/s0960777307004146.

———. 2013. *To the Tashkent Station: Evacuation and Survival in the Soviet Union at War.* Ithaca, NY: Cornell University Press.

———. 2015. "Nutritional Dystrophy: The Science and Semantics of Starvation in World War 2." In Goldman and Filtzer 2015: 206–64.

Mann, Michael. 2018. "Have War and Violence Declined?" *Theory and Society* 47:37–60.

Margalit, Gilad. 2007. "Dresden and Hamburg: Official Memory and Commemoration of the Victims of Allied Air Raids in the Two Germanies." In *A Nation of Victims? Representations of German Wartime Suffering from 1945 to the Present*, edited by Helmut Schmitz, pp. 124–40. Leiden: Brill.

Mariot, Nicolas, and Claire Zalc. 2017. "Reconstructing Trajectories of Persecution: Reflections on a Prosopography of Holocaust Victims." In *Microhistories of the Holocaust*, edited by Claire Zalc and Tal Bruttman, pp. 85–112. New York: Berghahn.

Mark, Ethan. 2018. *Japan's Occupation of Java in the Second World War: A Transnational History.* London: Bloomsbury.

Mark, James. 2005. "Remembering Rape: Divided Social Memory and the Red Army in Hungary, 1944–1945." *Past and Present* 188:133–61.

Markevich, Andrei, and Mark Harrison. 2011. "Great War, Civil War, and Recovery: Russia's National Income, 1913 to 1928." *Journal of Economic History* 71 (3): 672–703.

Markowitz, S. D. 1955. "Retardation in Growth of Children in Europe and Asia during WW2." *Human Biology* 27:258–71.

Marks, Sally. 1983. "Black Watch on the Rhine: A Study in Propaganda, Prejudice and Prurience." *European Studies Review* 13 (3): 297–334.

Márquez Morfin, Lourdes, and América Molina del Villar. 2010. "El otono de 1918: Las repercusiones de la pandemia de gripe en la ciudad de México." *Desacatos: Revista de Ciencias Sociales* 32:121–44 (available online).

Marr, David G. 1995. *Vietnam 1945: The Quest for Power.* Berkeley: University of California Press.

Martin, Berndt. 1985. "Agriculture and Food Supply in Japan during the Second World War." In *Agriculture and Food Supply in the Second World War*, pp. 181–205. Ostfildern: Scripta Mercaturae Verlag. https://freidok.uni-freiburg.de/fedora/objects/freidok:2035/datastreams /FILE1/content.

Marushiakova, Elena, and Vesselin Popov. 2001. "The Bulgarian Gypsies (Roma) during World War II." In *Remembering the Future*, edited by J. K. Roth, pp. 456–65. London: Palgrave Macmillan.

Masland, John W. 1946. "Neighbourhood Associations in Japan." *Far Eastern Survey* 15(23): 355–58.

Masson, Marc, and Jean-Michel Azorin. 2006–07. "The French Mentally Ill in World War II: The Lesson of History." *International Journal of Mental Health* 35 (4): 26–39.

Matthaeus, Juergen. 2015. "Nazi Genocides." In *The Cambridge History of the Second World War: Vol. 2, Politics and Ideology*, edited by Richard J. B. Bosworth and Joseph A. Maiolo, pp. 162–80. Cambridge: Cambridge University Press.

Maurer, Maurer. 1978. *The US Air Service in World War I.* Vol. 2. Washington, DC: U.S. Air Force. Accessed February 22, 2023. https://media.defense.gov/2010/Oct/13/2001329758/-1/-1/0 /us_air_service_ww1-vol1–2.pdf.

Mayersen, Deborah. 2018. "The 1895–1896 Armenian Massacres in Harput: Eyewitness Account." *Études arméniennes contemporaines* 10:161–83.

Mazower, Mark. 1993. *Inside Hitler's Greece.* New Haven, CT: Yale University Press.

———. 1999. *Dark Continent: Europe's Twentieth Century.* New York: Knopf.

———. 2004. *Salonica, City of Ghosts: Christians, Muslims, and Jews, 1430–1950.* London: HarperCollins.

———. 2009. *Hitler's Empire: How the Nazis Ruled Europe.* New York: Penguin.

McCaa, Robert. 2003. "Missing Millions: The Demographic Costs of the Mexican Revolution." *Mexican Studies/Estudios Mexicanos* 19 (2): 367–400.

McCance, R. A., and E. M. Widdowson. 1951. *Studies of Undernutrition, Wuppertal, 1946–49.* Cambridge: Cambridge University Press.

McCarthy, Justin. 1999. *Death and Exile: The Ethnic Cleansing of Ottoman Muslims, 1821–1922.* Princeton, NJ: Darwin Press.

McCord, Janet Schenk. 1995. "A Study of the Suicides of Eight Holocaust Survivor/Writers." PhD diss., Boston University. ProQuest Dissertations. https://www.proquest.com/docview /304167746/fulltextPDF.

McDonnell, Michael A., and A. Dirk Moses. 2005. "Raphael Lemkin as Historian of Genocide in the Americas." *Journal of Genocide Research* 7 (4): 501–29.

McElligott, Anthony. 2018. "The Deportation of the Jews of Rhodes, 1944: An Integrated History." In Antoniou and Moses 2018: 58–86.

McKittrick, David, Seamus Kelters, Brian Feeney, and Chris Thornton. 1999/2001. *Lost Lives: The Stories of the Men, Women and Children Who Died as a Result of the Northern Ireland Troubles.* Edinburgh: Mainstream.

McPherson, James. 1988. *The Battle Cry of Freedom: The Civil War Era.* New York: Oxford University Press.

McRobbie, Linda Rodriguez. 2017. "An Extremely Rare Condition May Transform Our Understanding of Memory." *Guardian*, February 8.

Meilinger, Phillip S. 1997. "Giulio Douhet and the Origins of Airpower Theory." In *The Paths of Heaven: The Evolution of Airpower Theory*, edited by Phillip Meilinger, pp. 1–40. Maxwell Air Force Base, AL: Air University Press.

Meinhof, Renate. 2005. *Das Tagebuch der Maria Meinhof: April 1945 bis März 1946 in Pommern—eine Spurensuche.* Hamburg: Hoffman und Campe.

Meinl, Susanne, and Jutta Zwilling. 2004. *Legalisierter Raub: Die Ausplünderung der Juden im National sozialismus durch die Reichsfinanzvertung in Hessen.* Frankfurt: Campus Verlag.

Melber, Takuma. 2016. "The Labour Recruitment of Local Inhabitants as *Rōmusha* in Japanese-Occupied South-East Asia." *International Review of Social History* 61 (S24): 165.

Melloni, Alberto, Giovanni Cavagnini, and Giulia Grossi, eds. 2020. *Benedict XV: A Pope in the World of the "Useless Slaughter" (1914–1918).* Turnhout, Belgium: Brepols.

Meneses, Maria Paula, and Margarida Gomes. 2015. "Secrets, Lies, Silences and Invisibilities: Unveiling the Participation of Africans on the Mozambique Front during World War I." In *Eurocentrism, Racism and Knowledge*, edited by Marta Araújo and Sílvia Maeso, pp. 154–77. London: Palgrave Macmillan.

Menon, Anil. 2022. "The Political Legacy of Forced Migration: Evidence from Post-WWII Germany." Unpublished manuscript.

Mertelsmann, Olaf, and Aigi Rahi-Tamm. 2009. "Soviet Mass Violence in Estonia Revisited." *Journal of Genocide Research* 11 (2–3): 307–22.

Michels, Eckard. 2010. "Die 'Spanische Grippe' 1918/19 Verlauf, Folgen und Deutungen in Deutschland im Kontext des Ersten Weltkriegs." *Vierteljahrshefte für Zeitgeschichte* 58 (1): 1–33.

Mick, Christoph. 2011. "Incompatible Experiences: Poles, Ukrainians and Jews in Lviv under Soviet and German Occupation, 1939–44." *Journal of Contemporary History* 46 (2): 336–63.

Miles, Sherman. 1926–27. "War in the Third Dimension." *North American Review* 223 (833): 594–605.

Mills, Geofrey, and Hugh Rockoff. 1987. "Compliance with Price Controls in the United States and the United Kingdom during World War II." *Journal of Economic History* 47 (1): 197–213.

Milward, Alan S. 1970. *The New Order and the French Economy.* Oxford: Oxford University Press.

Mitchell, Brian R. 1975. *European Historical Statistics.* London: Macmillan.

Mitchell, Brian R., and Phyllis Deane. 1971. *Abstract of British Historical Statistics.* Cambridge: Cambridge University Press.

Mitter, Rana. 2013. *China's War with Japan, 1937–1945: The Struggle for Survival.* London: Allen Lane.

Mochmann, Ingvill C., and Stein Ugelvik Larsen. 2008. "Children Born of War: The Life Course of Children Fathered by German Soldiers in Norway and Denmark during WWII—Some Empirical Results." *Historical Social Research/Historische Sozialforschung* 33 (1): 347–63.

Mochmann, Ingvill C., Sabine Lee, and Barbara Stelzl-Marx. 2009. "The Children of the Occupations Born during the Second World War and Beyond—an Overview." *Historical Social Research/Historische Sozialforschung* 34 (3): 263–82.

Moeller, Robert G. 2003. "Sinking Ships, the Lost Heimat and Broken Taboos: Günter Grass and the Politics of Memory in Contemporary Germany." *Contemporary European History* 12 (2): 147–81.

———. 2006. "On the History of Man-Made Destruction: Loss, Death, Memory, and Germany in the Bombing War." *History Workshop Journal* 61:103–34.

Mohanty, Bidyut. *A Haunting Tragedy: Gender, Caste and Class in the 1866 Famine of Odisha.* Delhi: Manohar, 2022.

Mokyr, J., and C. Ó Gráda. 2002. "What Do People Die of during Famines?" *European Review of Economic History* 6:339–63.

Montefiore, Simon Sebag. 2004. *Stalin: The Court of the Red Tzar.* London: Phoenix.

Moreira, Cristina, Jaime Reis, and Rita Martins de Sousa. 2021. "Portugal's French Wars: Cost, Loss, Missed Opportunities?" In *The Crucible of Revolutionary and Napoleonic Warfare and European Transitions to Modern Economic Growth,* edited by Patrick K. O'Brien, pp. 203–49. Leiden: Brill.

Morelon, Claire. 2018. "Social Conflict." In Daniel et al. 2014–19.

Morgenthau, Henry. 1918. *Ambassador Morgenthau's Story.* New York: Doubleday.

———. 1929. *I Was Sent to Athens.* New York: Doubleday.

Morozova, Olga, Tatiana I. Troshina, Elena N. Morozova, and Aleksandr N. Morozov. 2021. "The Spanish Flu Pandemic in 1918 in Russia: Questions a Hundred Years Later" (in Russian). *Journal of Microbiology, Epidemiology, and Immunobiology* 98 (1): 113–24.

Morris, Benny, and Dror Ze'evi. 2019. *The Thirty-Year Genocide: Turkey's Destruction of Its Christian Minorities, 1894–1924.* Cambridge, MA: Harvard University Press.

Mortara, Giorgio. 1925. *La salute pubblica in Italia durante e dopo la Guerra.* Bari, Italy: Laterza; New Haven, CT: Yale University Press. https://archive.org/stream/lasalutepubblica00mort?ref=ol#page/100/mode/2up.

Moscoff, William. 1990. *The Bread of Affliction: The Food Supply in the USSR during WW2 II.* Cambridge: Cambridge University Press.

Mosse, George L. 1990. *Fallen Soldiers: Reshaping the Memory of the World Wars.* Oxford: Oxford University Press.

Mougel, Nadège. 2011. "World War One Casualties." REPERES. Module 1–0. Accessed December 30, 2023. https://www.census.gov/history/pdf/reperes112018.pdf.

Mouré, Kenneth. 2010. "Food Rationing and the Black Market in France (1940–1944)." *French History* 24 (2): 262–82.

Mourelos, Yiannis. 1985. "The 1914 Persecutions and the First Attempt at an Exchange of Minorities between Greece and Turkey." *Balkan Studies* 26 (2): 389–413.

Moyn, Samuel. 2021. *Humane: How the United States Abandoned Peace and Reinvented War.* New York: Farrar, Straus, and Giroux.

Mudge, George Alfred. 1970. "Starvation as a Means of Warfare." *International Lawyer* 4 (2): 228–68.

Mühlhäuser, Regina. 2012. "The Unquestioned Crime: Sexual Violence by German Soldiers during the War of Annihilation in the Soviet Union, 1941–45." In *Rape in Wartime,* edited by Raphaëlle Branche and Fabrice Virgili, pp. 34–46. London: Palgrave Macmillan.

Mukerjee, Madhusree. 2014. "Bengal Famine of 1943: An Appraisal of the Famine Inquiry Commission." *Economic and Political Weekly* 49 (11): 71–75.

Muller, Robert, Nicole Schonherr, and Thomas Widera. 2008. *Die Zerstorung Dresdens 13. bis 15. Februar 1945: Gutachten und Ergebnisse der Dresdner Historikerkommission zur Ermittlung der Opferzahlen.* Dresden: Hannah-Arendt-Institut: Berichte und Studien.

Mulligan, William. 2000. "Total War: A Review." *War in History* 15 (2): 211–21.

Mulvey, Stephen. 2019. "The Long Echo of WW2 Trauma." BBC, June 8. https://www.bbc.com/news/stories-48528841.

Murard, Eli. 2022. "Long-Term Effects of the 1923 Mass Refugee Inflow on Social Cohesion in Greece." World Bank Policy Research Working Paper No. 9912.

Murard, Eli, and Seyhun Orcan Sakalli. 2018. "Mass Refugee Inflow and Long-Run Prosperity: Lessons from the Greek Population Resettlement." IZA Discussion Paper No. 11613.

Murphy, Mahon. 2015. "Carrier Corps." In Daniel et al. 2014–19.

Murphy, Maureen O'Rourke. 2015. *Compassionate Stranger: Asenath Nicholson and the Great Irish Famine.* Syracuse: Syracuse University Press.

Murray, Christopher, et al. 2002. "Armed Conflict as a Public Health Problem." *British Medical Journal* 324:346–49.

Murray, John F. 2015. "Tuberculosis and World War I." *American Journal of Respiratory and Critical Care Medicine* 192 (4): 411–14.

Muscolino, Micah S. 2011. "Violence against People and the Land: The Environment and Refugee Migration from China's Henan Province, 1938–1945." *Environment and History* 17:301–2

———. 2015. *The Ecology of War in China: Henan Province, the Yellow River and Beyond, 1938–1950.* Cambridge: Cambridge University Press.

Naert, Jan. 2018. "'Ventre affamé n'a pas d'oreilles': Une histoire sociale de l'approvisionnement par les autorités locales dans les territoires occupés en Belgique et en France (1914–1918)." *Guerres mondiales et conflits contemporains*, no. 272:35–50.

Nagy, Péter Tibor. 2016. "The Sociology of Survival: The Presence of the Budapest Jewish Population Groups of 1941 in the 1945 Budapest Population." In *The Holocaust in Hungary: Seventy Years Later*, edited by Randolph L. Braham and András Kovács, pp. 183–93. Budapest: Central European University Press.

Naimark, Norman M. 1995. *The Russians in Germany: A History of the Soviet Occupation.* Cambridge, MA: Harvard University Press.

———. 1998. *Ethnic Cleansing in Twentieth-Century Europe.* Donald Treadgold W. Papers, University of Washington. Accessed December 28, 2023. https://digital.lib.washington.edu/researchworks/bitstream/handle/1773/35339/Treadgold_No19_2000.pdf?sequence=1&isAllowed=y.

———. 2012. "The Russians and Germans: Rape during the War and Post-Soviet Memories." In *Rape in Wartime*, edited by Raphaëlle Branche and Fabrice Virgili, pp. 201–19. London: Palgrave Macmillan.

———. 2015. Review of Gebhardt, *Als die Soldaten kamen, FranciaRecensio,* issue 3].

Nasierowski, Tadeusz. 2006."In the Abyss of Death: The Extermination of the Mentally Ill in Poland during World War II." *International Journal of Mental Health* 35 (3): 50–61.

Nawratil, Heinz. 1987. *Vertriebungsverbrechen an Deutschen.* Munich: Ullstein.

Neelsen, Sven, and Thomas Stratmann. 2013. "Early-Life Famine Exposure and Later-Life Outcomes: Evidence from Survivors of the Greek Famine." In Lumey and Vaiserman 2013: 109–22.

Neer, Robert. 2013. *Napalm: An American Biography.* Cambridge, MA: Belkap Press.

Nef, John U. 1950. *War and Human Progress.* Cambridge: Cambridge University Press.

Neff, Stephen C. 2018. "Disrupting a Delicate Balance: The Allied Blockade Policy and the Law of Maritime Neutrality during the Great War." *European Journal of International Law* 29 (2): 459–75.

Nelson, Hank. 2007. "The New Guinea Comfort Women, Japan and the Australian Connection: Out of the Shadows." *Asia-Pacific Journal* 5 (5): article ID 2426.

Newsholme, Arthur. 1918–19. "Discussion on Influenza." *Proceedings of the Royal Society of Medicine* 12 (1): 1–18.

Ngongo, Engika, Bérengère Piret, and Nathalie Tousignant. 2018. "The Forgotten: African Soldiers and Porters of the Belgian Colonial Forces in the First World War." *Journal of Belgian History* 48 (1–2): 14–33.

Niewyk, David L., and Francis R. Nicosia. 2003. *Columbia Guide to the Holocaust*. New York: Columbia University Press.

Niven, Bill. 2008. "The Good Captain and the Bad Captain: Joseph Vilsmaier's Die Gustloff and the Erosion of Complexity." *German Politics and Society* 89 (4): 82–98.

Nivet, Philippe. 2004. *Les réfugiés français de la Grande Guerre (1914–1920): Les "boches" du nord.'* Paris: Economica.

Nolan, Mary. 2005. "Germans as Victims during the Second World War." *Central European History* 38 (1): 7–40.

Notestein, F. W., Irene Taeuber, Dudley Kirk, Ansley J. Coale, and Louise K. Kiser. 1944. *The Future Population of Europe and the Soviet Union: Population Projections, 1940–1970*. Series of League of Nations Publications. Geneva: Economic, Financial and Transit Department, League of Nations.

Nurick, Lester. 1945. "The Distinction between Combatant and Noncombatant in the Law of War." *American Journal of International Law* 39 (4): 680–97.

O'Brien, Patrick K. 2017. "The Contribution of Warfare with Revolutionary and Napoleonic France to the Consolidation and Progress of the Industrial Revolution." LSE Economic History Working Paper 264, London School of Economics.

Obschonka, Martin, Michael Stuetzer, P. Jason Rentfrow, Jeff Potter, and Samuel D. Gosling. 2017. "Did Strategic Bombing in the Second World War Lead to 'German Angst'? A Large-Scale Empirical Test across 89 German Cities." *European Journal of Personality* 31 (3): 234–57.

Occhino, F., K. Oosterlinck, and E. N. White. 2008. "How Much Can a Victor Force the Vanquished to Pay? France under the Nazi Boot." *Journal of Economic History* 68:1–45.

Ochsner, Christian, and Felix Roesel. 2020. "Migrating Extremists." *Economic Journal* 130 (628): 1135–72.

Offenberger, Ilana. 2017. *The Jews of Nazi Vienna, 1938–1945: Rescue and Destruction*. London: Palgrave Macmillan.

Offer, Avner. 1989. *The First World War: An Agrarian Interpretation*. Oxford: Oxford University Press.

Offer, Miriam. 2012. "Ethical Dilemmas in the Work of Doctors and Nurses in the Warsaw Ghetto." *Polin* 25:467–92.

Ó Gráda, C. 2009. *Famine: A Short History*. Princeton, NJ: Princeton University Press.

———. 2011. "Fetal Origins, Childhood Development, and Famine: A Bibliography and Literature Review." University College Dublin, School of Economics Working Paper No. 2011/28.

———. 2015. *Eating People Is Wrong and Other Essays on the Past and Future of Famine*. Princeton, NJ: Princeton University Press.

———. 2017. "Ireland." In Alfani and Ó Gráda 2017: 166–84.

———. 2023. "World War 1 and the Spanish Flu." University College Dublin School of Economics Working Paper (available online).

Ó Gráda, C., Chihua Li, and L. H. Lumey. 2023. "How Much Schizophrenia Do Famines Cause?" *Schizophrenia* 9 (90). https://doi.org/10.1038/s41537-023-00416-2.

Ó Gráda, C., and Kevin H. O'Rourke. 2022. "The Irish Economy during the Century after Partition." *Economic History Review* 75:336–70.

Ohta, Yasuyuki, Mariko Mine, Masako Wakasugi, Etsuko Yoshimine, Yachiyo Himuro, Megumi Yoneda, Sayuri Yamaguchi, et al. 2000. "Psychological Effect of the Nagasaki Atomic Bombing on Survivors after Half a Century." *Psychiatry and Clinical Neurosciences* 54 (1): 97–103.

Olbrechts, Raymond. 1926. "La population." In *La Belgique restaurée: Étude sociologique*, edited by Ernest Mahaim, n.p. Bruxelles: Lamertin.

O'Neill, G. 1999. *My East End: Memories of Life in Cockney London*. London: Penguin.

Oren, Laura E. 2008. "Children and Disasters: Child Evacuation in World War II and Public Policy." In *Children and Disasters: What Have We Learned from the Hurricanes of 2005?*, edited by Howard Davidson, Ellen Marrus, and Laura Oren. SSRN Product and Services. https://ssrn.com/abstract=1586026.

O'Rourke, Norm, Yaacov G. Bachner, Philippe Cappeliez, and Sara Carmel. 2015. "Reminiscence Functions and the Health of Israeli Holocaust Survivors as Compared to Other Older Israelis and Older Canadians." *Aging and Mental Health* 19 (4): 335–48.

Ortega, José Antonio, and Javier Silvestre. 2006. *Las consecuencias demográficas*. In *La economía de la guerra civil*, edited by Pablo Martín Aceña and Elena Martin Ruiz, pp. 53–106. Madrid: Marcial Pons.

Orwell, George. 1945. "As I Please." *Tribune*, May 19, 1944.

Osborne, Eric W. 2004. *Britain's Economic Blockade of Germany, 1914–1919*. London: Frank Cass.

Osterloh, Jörg, Jan Erik Schulte, and Sybille Steinbacher, eds. 2022. *"Euthanasie"—Verbrechen inm besetzten Europa: Zur Dimension des nationalsozialistischen Massenmords*. Göttingen: Wallstein Verlag.

Outram, Quentin. 2001. "The Socio-economic Relations of Warfare and the Military Mortality Crises of the Thirty Years' War." *Medical History* 45 (2): 151–84.

Overy, R. J. 1984. "German Air Strength, 1933 to 1939: A Note." *Historical Journal* 27 (2): 465–71.

———. 1995. *Why the Allies Won*. New York: W. W. Norton.

———. 2013. *The Bombing War: Europe, 1939–1945*. London: Allen Lane.

———. 2014. *The Bombers and the Bombed: Allied Air War over Europe, 1940–1945*. New York: Viking.

———. 2015a. "Making and Breaking Morale: British Political Warfare and Bomber Command in the Second World War." *Twentieth Century British History* 26 (3): 370–99.

———. 2015b. *The Oxford Illustrated History of World War Two*. Oxford: Oxford University Press.

———. 2015c. "'Why We Bomb You': Liberal War-Making and Moral Relativism in the RAF Bomber Offensive." In *Liberal Wars: Anglo-American Strategy, Ideology and Practice*, edited by A. Cromartie, pp. 22–37. London: Routledge.

———. 2018. "The German Home Front under the Bombs." In *A Companion to Nazi Germany*, edited by Shelley Baranowski, Armin Nolzen, and Claus-Christian W. Szejnmann, pp. 231–46. Chichester: Wiley Blackwell.

———. 2021. *Blood and Ruins: The Great Imperial War, 1931–1945*. London: Penguin.

Ozasa, Kotaro, Eric J. Grant, and Kazunori Kodama. 2018. "Japanese Legacy Cohorts: The Life Span Study Atomic Bomb Survivor Cohort and Survivors' 'Offspring.'" *Journal of Epidemiology* 28 (4): 162–69.

Paice, Edward, 2007. *Tip and Run: The Untold Tragedy of the Great War in Africa*. London: Phoenix.

Pal, Radhabinod. 1953. *International Military Tribunal for the Far East*. Calcutta: Sanyal.

Pallis, A. A. 1925. "Racial Migrations in the Balkans during the Years 1912–1924." *Geographical Journal* 66 (4): 315–31.

Palmer, C. T., L. Sattenspiel, and C. Cassidy. 2007. "Boats, Trains and Immunity: The Spread of the Spanish Flu on the Island of Newfoundland." *Newfoundland and Labrador Studies* 22 (2): 474–504.

Palumbo, Valeria. 2017. "La Caporetto delle donne: Il dramma taciuto degli stuprie dei 'figli della Guerra.'" *Corriere della Sera*, October 24.

Paneth, Nigel. 2016. "Commentary: The Origins of Fetal Origins." *International Journal of Epidemiology* 45 (2): 319–20. https://doi.org/10.1093/ije/dyw066.

Pape, Robert A. 1993. "Why Japan Surrendered." *International Security* 18 (2): 154–201.

———. 1996. *Bombing to Win: Air Power and Coercion in War*. Ithaca, NY: Cornell University Press.

Parish, John B. 1956. "Iron and Steel in the Balance of World Power." *Journal of Political Economy* 64 (5): 369–88.

Parker, Geoffrey. 1984. *The Thirty Years War*. London: Routledge.

Patenaude, Bertrand M. 2002. *The Big Show in Bololand: The American Relief Expedition to Soviet Russia in the Famine of 1921*. Stanford, CA: Stanford University Press.

Patterson, K. David. 1993. "Typhus and Its Control in Russia, 1870–1940." *Medical History* 37:361–81.

Pauley, Bruce F. 1992. *From Prejudice to Persecution: A History of Austrian Anti-Semitism*. Chapel Hill: University of North Carolina Press.

Pavlov, D. V. 1965. *Leningrad 1941: The Blockade*. Translated by John Clinton Adams. Chicago: University of Chicago Press.

Pears, Brian, and Carl Nutbrown. 2013. "Index to the 'Civilian War Dead Roll of Honour' for Northumberland, Durham and Yorkshire." https://www.genuki.org.uk/big/eng/Indexes/NE _WarDead/.

Peeling, Siobhan. 2010. "'Out of Place' in the Postwar City: Experiences and Representations of Displacement during the Resettlement of Leningrad at the End of the Blockade." PhD thesis, University of Nottingham. http://eprints.nottingham.ac.uk/11700/1/OUT_OF_PLACE.pdf.

Peet, Jessica L., and Laura Sjoberg. 2020. *Gender and Civilian Victimization in War*. London: Routledge. https://books.google.ie/books?hl=en&lr=&id=6BTADwAAQBAJ&oi =fnd&pg=PT8&ots=JZq1P3m1Is&sig=6_1hPG8nfm5ZwveJfaQs8iJdE64&redir_esc=y#v =onepage&q&f=false.

Pelopidas, Benoît, and Kjølv Egeland. 2020. "What Europeans Believe about Hiroshima and Nagasaki—and Why It Matters." *Bulletin of the Atomic Scientists*, August 3.

Pennington, Hugh. 2019. "The Impact of Infectious Disease in War Time: A Look Back at WW1." *Future Microbiology* 14 (3): 165–68.

Peri, Alexis Jean. 2011. "Minds under Siege: Rethinking the Soviet Experience inside the Leningrad Blockade, 1941–45." PhD Diss., University of California, Berkeley. https://escholarship .org/uc/item/6qq1w925.

———. 2015. "Queues, Canteens, and the Politics of Location in Diaries of the Leningrad Blockade." In Goldman and Filtzer 2015: 158–205.

Perkins, Ray Jr. 2002. *Yours Faithfully, Bertrand Russell: A Lifelong Fight for Peace, Justice, and Truth in Letters to the Editor*. Chicago: Open Court.

Pérouse de Montclos, Marc-Antoine. 2016a. "General Introduction: Armed Conflicts and the Body Count: An Issue for Population Studies and Development." In Pérouse de Montclos et al. 2016: 1–22.

———. 2016b. "Numbers Count: Dead Bodies, Statistics, and the Politics of Armed Conflicts." In Pérouse de Montclos et al. 2016: 47–59.

Pérouse de Montclos, Marc-Antoine, Elizabeth Minor, and Samrat Sinha, eds. 2016. *Violence, Statistics, and the Politics of Accounting for the Dead*. Heidelberg: Springer.

Peters, Michael. 2022. "Market Size and Spatial Growth: Evidence from Germany's Post-War Population Expulsions." *Econometrica* 90 (2): 2357–96.

Phillips, Howard. 2014. "Influenza Pandemic." In Daniel et al. 2014–19.

Picaper, Jean-Paul, and Ludwig Norz. 2004. *Enfants Maudits*. Paris: des Syrtes.

Piercey, Nicholas. 2016. *Four Histories about Early Dutch Football, 1910–1920*. London: UCL Press.

Pimentel, Irene. 2020. "Jewish Refugees and Anti-Nazis among the Portuguese during the Second World War." In *As diásporas dos judeus e cristãos-novos de origem ibérica entre o mar mediterrâneo e o Oceano Atlântico: Estudos*, edited by J.A.R.S. Tavim, H. Martins, A. P. Ferreira, Â.S.B. Coutinho, and M. Andrade, pp. 351–70. Lisbon: Centro de História da Universidade de Lisboa.

Pinchuk, Ben-Cion. 1978. "Jewish Refugees in Soviet Poland, 1939–1941." *Jewish Social Studies* 40 (2): 141–58.

———. 1980. "Was There a Soviet Policy for Evacuating the Jews? The Case of the Annexed Territories." *Slavic Review* 39 (1): 44–55.

Pinker, Steven. 2011. *The Better Angels of Our Nature: A History of Violence and Humanity.* London: Penguin.

Pissari, Milovan. 2013. "Bulgarian Crimes against Civilians in Occupied Serbia during the First World War." *Balcanica* 44:357–90.

Pogány, Ágnes. 2014. "War Finance (Austro-Hungary)." In Daniel et al. 2014–19.

Pohl, J. Otto. 1999. *Ethnic Cleansing in the USSR, 1937–1949.* Westport, CT: Greenwood Press.

———. 2016. "The Persecution of Ethnic Germans in the USSR during World War II." *Russian Review* 75 (2): 284–303.

Poitras-Raymond, Chloé. 2019. "Fabriquer la victim": Crimes sexuels en Allemagne dans les procès de la Cour martiale américaine, février-juin 1945." *Histoire, Idées, Sociétés.* https://revuehis .uqam.ca/non-classe/fabriquer-la-victime-crimes-sexuels-en-allemagne-dans-les-proces-de -la-cour-martiale-americaine-fevrier-juin-1945/.

Polian, Pavel. 2003. *Against Their Will: The History and Geography of Forced Migrations in the USSR.* Budapest: Central European University Press.

Pollock, John. 1915. "The Refugees at Kiev." *Fortnightly Review* 585:476–79.

Ponting, Clive. 1990. *1940: Myth and Reality.* London: Hamish Hamilton.

Power, Samantha. 2002. *A Problem from Hell: America and the Age of Genocide.* New York: Basic Books.

Pozzi, Lucia. 2002. "La population italienne pendant la Grande guerre." *Annales de démographie historique* 1:121–42.

Prados de la Escosura, Leandro, and Carlos Santiago-Caballero. 2021. "The Napoleonic Wars: A Watershed in Spanish History?" In *The Crucible of Revolutionary and Napoleonic Warfare and European Transitions to Modern Economic Growth,* edited by P. K. O'Brien, pp. 171–204. Leiden: Brill.

Prauser, Steffen, and Arfon Rees, eds. 2004. *The Expulsion of the "German" Communities from Eastern Europe at the End of the Second World War.* European University Institute Working Paper HEC No. 2004/1.

Preston, Paul. 2012. *The Spanish Holocaust: Inquisition and Extermination in Twentieth-Century Spain.* London: HarperPress.

Prieml, Kim Christian. 2015. "Occupying Ukraine: Great Expectations, Failed Opportunities, and the Spoils of War, 1941–1943." *Central European History* 48 (1): 31–52.

Primoratz, Igor, ed. 2010. *Terror from the Sky: The Bombing of German Cities in World War II.* New York: Berghahn.

Prinzing, Friedrich. 1916. *Epidemics Resulting from Wars.* Oxford: Clarendon Press.

Priya, P. 2014. "Malabar Famine of 1943: A Critique of War Situation in Malabar (1939–45)." *Proceedings of the Indian History Congress* 75:628–38.

Probert, Henry. 2020. *Bomber Harris: His Life and Times.* London: Frontline Books.

Proctor, Tammy M. 2010. *Civilians in a World War, 1914–1918.* New York: New York University Press.

Prost, Antoine. 2014a. "The Dead." In Winter and Stille 2014: 3:561–91.

———. 2014b. "War Losses." In Daniel et al. 2014–19.

Proudfoot, Malcolm. 1957. *European Refugees: 1939–52. A Study in Forced Population Movement.* London: Faber and Faber.

Purseigle, Pierre. 2007. "'A Wave on to Our Shores': The Exile and Resettlement of Refugees from the Western Front, 1914–1918." Theme Issue: World Wars and Population Displacement in the Twentieth Century. *Contemporary European History* 16 (4): 427–44.

Radchenko, Yuri. 2013. "Accomplices to Extermination: Municipal Government and the Holocaust in Kharkiv, 1941–1942." *Holocaust and Genocide Studies* 27 (3): 443–63.

Radivojević, Biljana, and Goran Penev. 2014. "Demographic Losses of Serbia in the First World War and Their Long Term Consequences." *Economic Annals (Belgrade)* 59 (203): 29–54. https://doi.org.10.2298/EKA1403029R.

Ragaru, Nadège. 2017. "Contrasting Destinies: The Plight of Bulgarian Jews and the Jews in Bulgarian-Occupied Greek and Yugoslav Territories during World War Two." *Violence de masse et Résistance—Réseau de recherche.* Sciences Po, March 15. https://www.sciencespo.fr/mass-violence-war-massacre-resistance/fr/node/3338.html.

Räikkönen, K., M. Lahti, K. Heinonen, A.-K. Pesonen, et al. 2011. "Risk of Severe Mental Disorders in Adults Separated Temporarily from Their Parents in Childhood: The Helsinki Birth Cohort Study." *Journal of Psychiatric Research* 45 (3): 332–38. https://doi.org.10.1016/j.jpsychires.2010.07.003.

Rakoff, V. M. 1966. "Long Term Effects of the Concentration Camp Experience." *Viewpoints* 1:17–22.

Ralph, Willliam W. 2006. "Improvised Destruction: Arnold, LeMay, and the Firebombing of Japan." *War in History* 13 (4): 495–522.

Ramseyer, J. Mark. 2021. "Contracting for Sex in the Pacific War." *International Review of Law and Economics* 105985 (online).

Rasmussen, Ann. 2014. "The Spanish Flu." In Winter and Stille 2014: 3:334–57.

Redzik, Adam. 2017. *Rafał Lemkin (1900–1959) Co-creator of International Criminal Law: Short Biography.* Warsaw: Oficyna Allerhanda. https://depot.ceon.pl/handle/123456789/15408.

Rees, Elfan. 1957. *Century of the Homeless Man.* International Conciliation No. 515. Self-published by author.

Reichling, Gerhard. (1986) 1995. *Die deutschen Vertriebenen in Zahlen.* Pt. 1. Bonn: Kulturstiftung der deutschen Vertriebenen.

Reinisch, Jessica, and Elizabeth White, eds. 2011. *The Disentanglement of Populations: Migration, Expulsion and Displacement in Post-War Europe, 1944–9.* New York: Springer.

Reiss, Rudolf Archibald. 1916. *Report upon the Atrocities Committed by the Austro-Hungarian Army during the First Invasion of Serbia Submitted to the Serbian Government.* London: Simkin.

Ribeiro de Meneses, F. 2004. *Portugal, 1914–1926: From the First World War to Military Dictatorship.* Bristol: Hispanic, Portuguese, and Latin American Monographs.

Rieck, Miriam. 1994. "The Psychological State of Holocaust Survivors' 'Offspring': An Epidemiological and Psychodiagnostic Study." *International Journal of Behavioral Development* 17 (4): 649–67.

Riley, Denise. 1979. "War in the Nursery." *Feminist Review* 2:82–108

Ritschl, Albrecht. 2019. "Fiscal Destruction: Confiscatory Taxation of Jewish Property and Income in Nazi Germany." In *Dispossession: Plundering German Jewry, 1933–1945,* edited by C. Kreutzmüller and J. Zatlin. Ann Arbor: University of Michigan Press. https://eh.net/eha/wp-content/uploads/2019/06/Ritschl.pdf.

Rivière, Antoine. 2012. "La Misère et la faute: Abandon d'enfants et mères abandonneuses à Paris (1876–1923)." PhD diss., Université Paris-Sorbonne. https://hal.science/tel-03836224/document.

———. 2015. "Rape." In Daniel et al. 2014–19.

Roberts, Adam. 2010. "Lives and Statistics: Are 90% of War Victims Civilians?" *Survival* 52 (3): 115–36. https://weblearn.ox.ac.uk/access/content/user/1044/Survival_Jun-Jul_2010_-_AR_on_lives___statistics_-_non-printable.pdf.

Roberts, Geoffrey. 2006. *Stalin's Wars from World War to Cold War, 1939–1953.* New Haven, CT: Yale University Press.

Roberts, Mary Louise. 2013. *What Soldiers Do: Sex and the American GI in World War II France.* Chicago: University of Chicago Press.

Roessle, E. 1925. "The Mortality in Germany, 1913–1921: The Effects of War Casualties and Famine on Mortality." *Journal of the American Statistical Association* 20 (150): 163–78.

Rogan, Eugene. 2015. *The Fall of the Ottomans: The Great War in the Middle East.* New York: Basic Books.

Rohrbasser, Jean-Marc, and Martine Rousso-Rossmann. 2015. *1939–1945: Une démographie dans la tourmente.* Paris: Institut national d'études demographiques.

Roland, Charles G. 1992. *Courage under Siege: Starvation, Disease and Death in the Warsaw Ghetto.* New York: Oxford University Press.

———. 2014. "Courage under Siege: Starvation, Disease and Death in the Warsaw Ghetto." In Grodin 2014: 59–92.

Rollet, Catherine, and Virginie de Luca. 2005. "La vulnérabilité des enfants: Les crises de mortalité de 1940 et 1945." In *Morts d'inanition: Famines et exclusions en France sous l'Occupation,* edited by Isabelle von Bueltzingsloewen, pp. 263–79. Rennes, Presses universitaires de Rennes.

Rollo, Maria Fernanda, Ana Paula Pires, and Filipe Ribeiro de Meneses. 2017. "Portugal." In Daniel et al. 2014–19.

Romano, Carlin. 2019. "Primo Levi's Work Outshines His Murky Death." *Moment Magazine,* November–December. https://momentmag.com/primo-levis-work-outshines-his-murky -death/.

Roodhouse, Mark. 2013. *Black Market Britain: 1939–1955.* Oxford: Oxford University Press.

Rosenthal, Erich. 1944. "Trends of Jewish Population in Germany, 1910–1939." *Jewish Social Studies* 6:233–74.

Roser, Max, and Mohamed Nagdy. 2020. "Military Spending." OurWorldInData.org. https:// ourworldindata.org/military-spending.

Rubinstein, W. H. 1997. *The Myth of Rescue: Why the Democracies Could Not Have Saved More Jews from the Nazis.* London: Routledge.

Rubinstein, Joshua. 2002. "Ilya Ehrenburg—between East and West." *Journal of Cold War Studies* 4 (1): 44–65.

Rudling, Per Anders. 2013. "The Invisible Genocide: The Holocaust in Belarus." In *Bringing the Dark Past to Light: The Reception of the Holocaust in Postcommunist Europe,* edited by John-Paul Himka and Joanna Beata Michlic, pp. 59–82. Lincoln: University of Nebraska Press.

Rudnytskyi, Omelian, Stanislav Kulchytskyi, Oleksandr Gladun, and Natalia Kulyk. 2020. "The 1921–1923 Famine and the Holodomor of 1932–1933 in Ukraine: Common and Distinctive Features." *Nationalities Papers* 48 (3): 549–68.

Rudnytskyi, Omelian, Nataliia Levchuk, Oleh Wolowyna, Pavlo Shevchuk, and Alla Kovbasiuk. 2015. "Demography of a Man-Made Human Catastrophe: The Case of Massive Famine in Ukraine, 1932–1933." *Canadian Studies in Population* 42 (1–2): 53–80.

Rummel, R. J. 1991. *Statistics of Democide.* Accessed May 1, 2023. https://www.hawaii.edu /powerkills/SOD.CHAP3.HTM#TOP.

Rürup, Reinhard. 1995. *Berlin 1945: A Documentation.* Berlin: Verlag Willmuth Arenhövel.

Rusby, James S. M., and Fiona Tasker. 2009. "Long-Term Effects of the British Evacuation of Children during World War 2 on Their Adult Mental Health." *Aging and Mental Health* 13 (3): 39–404.

Saerens, Lieven. 2012. "Insa Meinen: The Persecution of the Jews in Belgium through a German Lens." *Journal of Belgian History* 42 (4): 200–7.

Sagan, Scott D., and Benjamin A. Valentino. 2017. "Revisiting Hiroshima in Iran: What Americans Really Think about Using Nuclear Weapons and Killing Noncombatants." *International Security* 42 (1): 41–79.

Sage, Steven F. 2017. "The Holocaust in Bulgaria: Rescuing History from 'Rescue.'" *Dapim: Studies on the Holocaust* 31:2, 139–45.

Sagi-Schwartz, Abraham, Marian J. Bakermans-Kranenberg, Shai Linn, and Marinus H. van IJzendoorn. 2013. "Against All Odds: Genocidal Trauma Is Associated with Longer Life-Expectancy of the Survivors." *PLoS One* 8 (7): e69179. https://www.ncbi.nlm.nih.gov/pmc/articles/PMC3722177/.

Salas Larrazábal, Ramón. 1977. *Pérdidas de la guerra*. Barcelona: Planeta.

———. 2005. "El mito del millón de muertos: Demografía contra leyenda." *La Tribuna de la Guerra*. http://www.generalisimofranco.com/mitos/009.htm.

Salisbury, Harrison E. 1969. *The 900 Days: The Siege of Leningrad, 1969*. London: Secker and Warburg.

Sallagar, Frederick M. 1974. *Lessons from an Aerial Mining Campaign (Operation "Starvation"): A Report Prepared for the United States Air Force Project Rand*. Santa Monica: RAND.

Salvanou, Emilia. 2017. "The First World War and the Refugee Crisis: Historiography and Memory in the Greek Context." *Historein* 16 (1/2): 120–38.

Sandes, Philippe. 2016. *East West Street: On the Origins of "Genocide" and "Crimes Against Humanity."* New York: Knopf.

Santavirta, Torsten. 2012. "How Large Are the Effects from Temporary Changes in Family Environment: Evidence from a Child-Evacuation Program during World War II." *American Economic Journal: Applied Economics* 4 (3): 28–42.

Santavirta, Torsten, N. Santavirta, Theresa S. Betancourt, and S. E. Gilman. 2015. "Long Term Mental Health Outcomes of Finnish Children Evacuated to Swedish Families during the Second World War and Their Non-evacuated Siblings: Cohort Study." *British Medical Journal* 350:g7753. https://doi.org.10.1136/bmj.g7753.

Sarkar, Abhijit. 2020. "Fed by Famine: The Hindu Mahasabha's Politics of Religion, Caste, and Relief in Response to the Great Bengal Famine, 1943–1944." *Modern Asian Studies* 54 (6): 2022–86.

Sarvimäki, Matti, Roope Uusitalo, and Markus Jantti. 2009. "Long-Term Effects of Forced Migration." IZA Discussion Paper No. 4003.

———. 2022. "Habit Formation and the Misallocation of Labor: Evidence from Forced Migrations." *Journal of the European Economic Association* 20 (6): 2497–539.

Satia, Priya. 2006. "The Defense of Inhumanity: Air Control and the British Idea of Arabia." *American Historical Review* 111 (1): 16–51.

Schaffer, Ronald. 1980. "American Military Ethics in World War II: The Bombing of German Civilians." *Journal of American History* 67 (2): 318–34.

———. 1985. *Wings of Judgment: American Bombing in World War II*. Oxford: Oxford University Press.

Schaller, Dominik J., and Jürgen Zimmerer, eds. 2008. *Late Ottoman Genocides: The Dissolution of the Ottoman Empire and Young Turkish Population and Extermination Policies*. London: Routledge.

Schatkes, Pamela. 1991. "Kobe: A Japanese Haven for Jewish Refugees, 1940–1941." *Japan Forum* 3 (2): 257–73.

Schatkowski Schilcher, Linda. 1992. "The Famine of 1915–1918 in Greater Syria." In *Problems of the Modern Middle East in Historical Perspective*, edited by John Spagnolo, pp. 229–58. Reading: Ithaca Press.

Schmied-Kowarcik, Anatol. 2016. "War Losses (Austria-Hungary)." In Daniel et al. 2014–19.

Schneider, Eric, Kota Ogasawara, and Tim J. Cole. Forthcoming 2021. "Health Shocks, Recovery, and the First Thousand Days: The Effect of the Second World War on Height Growth in Japanese Children." *Population and Development Review* 47 (4): 1075–105.

Schoenberg, Hans W. 1970. *Germans from the East: A Study of Their Migration, Resettlement and Subsequent Group History since 1945*. The Hague: Nijhoff.

Scholliers, Peter, and Frank Daelemans. 1988. "Standards of Living and Standards of Health in Wartime Belgium." In *The Upheaval of War*, edited by Richard Wall and Jay Winter, pp. 139–57. Cambridge: Cambridge University Press.

Schreiter, Katrin. 2017. "Revisiting Morale under the Bombs." *Central European History* 50 (3): 347–74.

Schrover, Marlou. 2015. "The Deportation of Germans from the Netherlands, 1946–1952." *Immigrants and Minorities* 33 (3): 250–78.

Schultz, Theodore W. 1964. *Transforming Traditional Agriculture*. New Haven, CT: Yale University Press.

Schultz Vento, Carol. *Hidden Legacy of World War II: A Daughter's Journey of Discovery*. Boiling Springs, PA: Sunbury Press.

Schultze, Max-Stephan. 2005. "Austria-Hungary's Economy in World War I." In *The Economics of World War I*, edited by Stephen Broadberry and Mark Harrison, pp. 77–111. Cambridge: Cambridge University Press.

Schwartz, Agatha. 2021. "Trauma, Haunting, and the Limits of Narration in Gabi Köpp's *Warum war ich bloß ein Mädchen*, Leonie Biallas's *'Komm, Frau, raboti': Ich war Kriegsbeute*, and Renate Meinhof's *Das Tagebuch der Maria Meinhof*. *Seminar: A Journal of Germanic Studies* 57 (1): 41–60.

Schwartz, Agatha, and Tatjana Takševa. 2020. "Between Trauma and Resilience: A Transnational Reading of Women's Life Writing about Wartime Rape in Germany and Bosnia and Herzegovina." *Aspasia* 14 (1): 124–43.

Schwartz, Paula. 1999. "The Politics of Food and Gender in Occupied Paris." *Modern and Contemporary France* 7 (1): 35–45.

Scianna, Bastian Matteo. 2019. "A Predisposition to Brutality? German Practices against Civilians and Francs-Tireurs during the Franco-Prussian War 1870–1871 and Their Relevance for the German 'Military Sonderweg' Debate." *Small Wars and Insurgencies* 30:4–5, 968–93.

Scolè, Pierluigi. 2015. "War Losses (Italy)." In Daniel et al. 2014–19.

Scriba, Arnulf. 2014. "Berlin in the 1914–1918 War." *Cahiers Bruxellois/Brussels Cahiers* 46 (1): 173–88.

Seeman, Mary V. 2006–07. "What Happened after T4? Starvation of Psychiatric Patients in Nazi Germany." *International Journal of Mental Health* 35 (4): 5–10.

Selden, Mark. 2016. "American Fire Bombing and Atomic Bombing of Japan in History and Memory." *Asia-Pacific Journal* 14 (23): 4.

Sémelin, Jacques. 2013. *Persécutions et entraides dans la France occupée*. Paris: Éditions des Arènes.

———. 2019. *The Survival of the Jews in France, 1940–44*. Oxford: Oxford University Press.

Sen, Amartya K. 1967. "Surplus Labour in India: A Critique of Schultz's Statistical Test." *Economic Journal* 77 (305): 154–61.

———. 1981. *Poverty and Famines: An Essay on Entitlement and Deprivation*. Oxford: Oxford University Press.

Seybolt, Taylor B. 2013. "Significant Numbers: Civilian Casualties and Strategic Peacebuilding." In Seybolt, Aronson, and Fischhoff 2013: chapter 2.

Seybolt, Taylor B., Jay D. Aronson, and Baruch Fischhoff. 2013. *Counting Civilian Casualties: An Introduction to Recording and Estimating Nonmilitary Deaths in Conflict*. Oxford: Oxford University Press.

Shaller, Dominik J., and Jürgen Zimmerer, eds. 2009. *The Origins of Genocide: Raphael Lemkin as a Historian of Mass Violence*. London: Routledge.

Shaw, Earl. 1942. "Potato Fed Swine in Germany." *Economic Geography* 18 (3): 287–97.

Sherry, Michael. 1987. *The Rise of American Air Power: The Creation of Armageddon*. New Haven, CT: Yale University Press.

Shirinian, George N. 2017. "Starvation and Its Political Use in the Armenian Genocide." *Genocide Studies International* 11 (1): 8–37.

Shizume, Masato. 2018. "Black Market Prices during World War II in Japan: An Estimate Using the Hedonic Approach." Bank of Japan Institute for Monetary and Economic Studies Discussion Paper No. 2018-E-17.

Shternshis, Anna. 2014. "Between Life and Death: Why Some Soviet Jews Decided to Leave and Others to Stay in 1941." *Kritika: Explorations in Russian and Eurasian History* 15 (3): 477–504.

Sigal, J. J., Silver, D., Rakoff, V., and Ellin, B. 1973. "Some Second-Generation Effects of Survival of the Nazi Persecution." *American Journal of Orthopsychiatry* 43 (3): 320–27. https://doi.org/10.1111/j.1939-0025.1973.tb00801.x.

Silvennoinen, Oula. 2013. "Helsinki: On the Brink—Finland and the Holocaust Era." In *Civil Society and the Holocaust: International Perspectives on Resistance and Rescue*, edited by Anders Jerichow and Cecilie Felicia Stokholm Banke, 148–61. New York: Humanity in Action Press.

Simmons, Cynthia, and Nina Perlina. 2002. *Writing the Siege of Leningrad: Women's Diaries, Memoirs, and Documentary Prose*. Pittsburgh: University of Pittsburgh Press.

Simonov, N. S. 1996. "Strengthen the Defence of the Soviets: The 1927 'War Alarm' and Its Consequences." *Europe-Asia Studies* 48 (8): 1355–64.

Siney, Marion C. 1963. "British Official Histories of the Blockade of the Central Powers during the First World War." *American Historical Review* 68 (2): 392–401.

Skalweit, August. 1927. *Die Deutsche Kriegsernahrungswirtschaft*. Stuttgart: Berlin Deutsche Verlagsanstalt; New Haven, CT: Yale University Press.

Sked, Alan. 2014. "Austria-Hungary and the First World War." *Histoire@Politique*, no. 22:16–49. https://www.cairn.info/revue-histoire-politique-2014-1-page-16.htm#no73.

Skeoch, L. A. 1953. "Food Prices and Ration Scale in the Ukraine." *Review of Economics and Statistics* 35 (3): 229–35.

Skowronski, John J. 2009. "The Positivity Bias and the Fading Affect Bias in Autobiographical Memory: A Self-Motives Perspective." In *Handbook of Self-Enhancement and Self-Protection*, edited by Mark D. Alicke and Constantine Sedikides, pp. 211–30. New York: Guildford Press.

Slaveski, Filip. 2013. *The Soviet Occupation of Germany: Hunger, Mass Violence and the Struggle for Peace, 1945–1947*. Cambridge: Cambridge University Press.

Smith, Jenny Leigh. 2015. "The Awkward Years: Defining and Managing Famines, 1944–1947." *History and Technology* 31 (3): 206–19.

Smith, Philip A. 1998. "Bombing to Surrender: The Contribution of Airpower to the Collapse of Italy, 1943." Master's thesis, Air University Press, Maxwell Air Force Base, AL. https://media.defense.gov/2017/Dec/28/2001861681/-1/;1/0/t_0051_smith_bombing_to_surrender.pdf.

Smith, Stephen Anthony. 1980. "The Russian Revolution and the Factories of Petrograd, February 1917 to June 1918." PhD diss., University of Birmingham. Accessed December 22, 2023. https://etheses.bham.ac.uk/id/eprint/1411/1/Smith80PhD.pdf.

Smolar, Aleksander. 1987. "Jews as a Polish Problem." *Daedalus* 116 (2): 31–73.

Snyder, J. C. 1947. "Typhus Fever in the Second World War." *California Medicine* 66 (1): 3–10.

Snyder, Timothy. 2001. "To Resolve the Ukrainian Question Once and for All: The Ethnic Cleansing of Ukrainians in Poland, 1943–1947." Working paper, History Department, Yale University. Accessed December 28, 2023. http://cis.mit.edu/sites/default/files/documents/ToResolveTheUkrainianQuestion.pdf.

———. 2003. "The Causes of Ukrainian-Polish Ethnic Cleansing 1943." *Past and Present* 179:197–234.

Sokolov, Alexander. 2009. "How to Calculate Human Losses during the Second World War." *Journal of Slavik Military Studies* 22:435–78.

Solly, Meilan. 2020. "Nine Eyewitness Accounts of the Bombings of Hiroshima and Nagasaki." *Smithsonian Magazine*, August 5. https://www.smithsonianmag.com/history/nine-harrowing -eyewitness-accounts-bombings-hiroshima-and-nagasaki-180975480/.

Sommer, Robert. 2009. "Camp Brothels: Forced Sex Labour in Nazi Concentration Camps." In *Brutality and Desire: War and Sexuality in Europe's Twentieth Century*, edited by Dagmar Herzog, pp. 168–96. London: Palgrave Macmillan.

Sonneck, Gernot, Hans Hirnsperger, and Reinhard Mundschütz. 2012. "Suizid und Suizidpräven- tion 1938–1945 in Wien." *Neuropsychiatrie* 26:111–20. https://link.springer.com/content/pdf /10.1007/s40211–012–0032–8.pdf.

Soo, J., M. P. Webber, J. Gustave, R. Lee, et al. 2011. "Trends in Probable PTSD in Firefighters Exposed to the World Trade Center Disaster, 2001–2010." *Disaster Medicine and Public Health Preparedness* 5:S197-S203.

Speed, Richard B. III. 1990. *Prisoners, Diplomats, and the Great War*. New York: Greenwood Press.

Sperling, Hans. 1956. "Die Luftkriegsverluste während des zweiten Weltkriegs in Deutschland." *Wirtschaft und Statistik* 8:493–500.

Spicknall, Charles G. 1943. "The Diet in Germany and the Occupied Countries during the Second World War." *Public Health Reports* 58, no. 46 (November 12): 1669–81.

Spitzer, Leo. 2001. "Rootless Nostalgia: Vienna in La Paz, La Paz in Elsewhere." *Shofar* 19 (3): 6–17.

Spitzer, Yannay. 2018. "Pogroms, Networks, and Migration: The Jewish Migration from the Russian Empire to the United States, 1881–1914." Typescript. Hebrew University of Jerusalem, May 25. https://yannayspitzer.files.wordpress.com/2019/03/pogromsnetworksmigration_182505.pdf.

Spoerer, Mark. 2006. "The Mortality of Allied Prisoners of War and Belgian Civilian Deportees in German Custody during the First World War: A Reappraisal of the Effects of Forced Labour." *Population Studies* 60 (2): 121–36.

———. 2007. "Zwangsarbeitsregimes im Vergleich. Deutschland und Japan im Ersten und Zweiten Weltkrieg." In *Zwangsarbeit im Europa des 20. Jahrhunderts. Vergleichende Aspekte und gesell- schaftliche Auseinandersetzung*, edited by Klaus Tenfelde and Hans-Jürgen Seidel, pp. 187–226. Essen: Klartext.

———. 2010. "Forced Labor in the Third Reich." Norbert Wollheim Memorial Lecture. Frankfurt: J. W. Goethe-Universität.

———. 2015. "Forced Labour in Nazi-Occupied Europe." In Boldorf and Okazaki 2015: 73–96.

———. 2020. "The Nazi War Economy, the Forced Labor System, and the Murder of Jewish and Non-Jewish Workers." In *A Companion to the Holocaust*, edited by Simone Gigliotti and Hilary Earl, pp. 136–51. London: Wiley.

Spoerer, Mark, and Jochen Fleischhacker. 2002a. "The Compensation of Nazi Germany's Forced Labour Demographic Findings and Political Implications." *Population Studies* 55:5–21.

———. 2002b. "Forced Laborers in Nazi Germany: Categories, Numbers, and Survivors." *Journal of Interdisciplinary History* 33 (2): 169–204.

Sputnik News. 2017. "This Literal 'Road of Life' Helped Leningrad Withstand the 900 Day Nazi Siege." November 22.

Stanley, Amy, Hannah Shepherd, Sayaka Chatani, David Ambaras, and Chelsea Szendi Schie- der. 2021. "Contracting for Sex in the Pacific War: The Case for Retraction on Grounds of Academic Misconduct." *Asia-Pacific Journal* 19, no. 5 (March). https://apjjf.org/2021/5 /ConcernedScholars.html.

Stanner, S. A., K. Bulmer, C. Andrès, et al. 1997. "Does Malnutrition in Utero Determine Diabetes and Coronary Heart Disease in Adulthood? Results from the Leningrad Siege Study, a Cross- Sectional Study." *British Medical Journal* 315, no. 7119 (November 22): 1342–48.

Stanner, Sara A., and John S. Yudkin. 2001. "Fetal Programming and the Leningrad Siege Study." *Twin Research* 4 (5): 287–92.

Starling, Ernst H. 1920. "The Food Supply of Germany during the War." *Journal of the Royal Statistical Society* 83 (2): 225–54.

Statistisches Bundesamt. 1958. *Die deutschen Vertreibungsverluste: Bevölkerungsbilanzen für die deutschen Vertreibungsgebiete 1939/50*. Stuttgart: W. Kohlhammer.

Stauber, Roni, and Raphael Vago, eds. 2007. *The Roma: A Minority in Europe. Historical, Political and Social Perspectives*. Budapest: Central European University Press.

Stein, Zena, Mervyn Susser, Gerhart Saenger, and Francis Marolla. 1975. *Famine and Human Development: The Dutch Hunger Winter of 1944–1945*. New York: Oxford University Press.

Stevenson, David. 2014. "World War One and the 'Short-War Illusion.'" Sky News. https://news .sky.com/story/world-war-one-and-the-short-war-illusion-10394372.

Stewart, Felicia H., and James Trussell. 2000. "Prevention of Pregnancy Resulting from Rape: A Neglected Preventive Health Measure." *American Journal of Preventive Medicine* 19 (4): 228–29.

Stibbe, Matthew, 2006. "The Internment of Civilians by Belligerent States during the First World War and the Response of the International Committee of the Red Cross." *Journal of Contemporary History* 41 (1): 5–19.

———. 2009. "Civilian Internment and Civilian Internees in Europe, 1914–20." In *Captivity, Forced Labour and Forced Migration in Europe during the First World War*, edited by Matthew Stibbe, chapter 3. London: Routledge.

———. 2014. "Enemy Aliens, Deportees, Refugees: Internment Practices in the Habsburg Empire, 1914–1918." *Journal of Modern European History/Zeitschrift für moderne europäische Geschichte/ Revue d'histoire européenne contemporaine* 12 (4): 479–99.

Stimson, Henry L. 1947. "The Decision to Use the Atomic Bomb." *Harper's Magazine*, February.

Stocks, Percy. 1941. "Diphtheria and Scarlet Fever Incidence during the Dispersal of 1939–40." *Journal of the Royal Statistical Society* 104 (4): 311–45.

Stone, Dan, ed. 2004. *The Historiography of the Holocaust*. London: Palgrave Macmillan.

Stone, Lewi, Daihai He, Stephan Lehnstaedt, and Yael Artzy-Randrup. 2020. "Extraordinary Curtailment of Massive Typhus Epidemic in the Warsaw Ghetto." *Science Advances* 6 (30): eabc0927.

Strachan, Hew. 2003. *The First World War: Vol. 1, To Arms*. Oxford: Oxford University Press.

Straumann, Tobias. 2019. *1931: Debt, Crisis, and the Rise of Hitler*. Oxford: Oxford University Press.

Strauss, H. A. 1980. "Jewish Emigration from Germany: Nazi Policies and Jewish Responses (i)." *Leo Baeck Institute Year Book* 25 (1): 313–61.

———. 1981. "Jewish Emigration from Germany: Nazi Policies and Jewish Responses (ii)." *Leo Baeck Institute Year Book* 26 (1): 343–409.

Strazza, Michele. 2010. *Senza via di scampo: Gli stupri nelle guerre mondiali*. Villa d'Agri, Italy: Consiglio regionale della Basilicata.

Strong, Richard P. 1920. *Typhus Fever with Particular Reference to the Serbian Epidemic*. Cambridge, MA: Harvard University Press.

Sturgeon-Clegg, Imogen Sarah. 2007. "Long-Term Effects of Living through Both Evacuation and the Bombing of London during the Second World War as Perceived by Those Who Experienced Them: A Qualitative Study." PhD diss., University of London. https://openaccess .city.ac.uk/id/eprint/8599/1/Long-term_effects_of_living_through_both_evacuation_and _the_bombing_of_London_during_the_Second_World_War_as_perceived_by_those_who _experienced_them.pdf.

Suedfeld, Peter. 1997. "Reactions to Societal Trauma: Distress and/or Eustress." *Political Psychology* 18 (4): 849–61.

Suhara, Manubu. 2017. "Russian Agricultural Statistics." Working paper, Russian Research Center, Hitotsubashi University, Tokyo. http://www.ier.hit-u.ac.jp/rrc/Japanese/pdf/RRC_WP _No67.pdf.

Susser, E. S., and S. P. Lin. 1992. "Schizophrenia after Prenatal Exposure to the Dutch Hunger." *Arch Gen Psychiatry* 49 (12): 983–88.

Susser, E. S., R. Neugebauer, H. W. Hoek, A. S. Brown, S. P. Lin, D. Labovitz, and J. M. Gorman. 1996. "Schizophrenia after Prenatal Famine: Further Evidence." *Archives of General Psychiatry* 53 (1): 25–31.

Sutou, Shizuyo. 2018. "Low-Dose Radiation from A-bombs Elongated Lifespan and Reduced Cancer Mortality Relative to Un-irradiated Individuals." *Genes and Environment* 40:26. https://doi .org/10.1186/s41021–018–0114–3.

Sužiedėlis, Saulius. N.d. "The Historical Sources for Antisemitism in Lithuania and Jewish-Lithuanian Relations during the 1930s." Typescript, Millersville University of Pennsylvania. https://yivo.org/cimages/historical_sources_of_antisemitism.pdf.

———. 2004. "The Historical Sources for Antisemitism in Lithuania and Jewish-Lithuanian Relations during the 1930s. In *The Vanished World of Lithuanian Jews*, edited by Alvydas Nikzentaitis, Stefan Schreiner, and Darius Staliunas, pp. 119–54. Leiden: Brill.

———. 2018. "The International Commission for the Evaluation of the Crimes of the Nazi and Soviet Occupation Regimes in Lithuania: Successes, Challenges, Perspectives." *Journal of Baltic Studies* 49 (1): 103–16. https://yivo.org/cimages/the_international_commission_jbs _online_2014_routledge-ss.pdf.

Szymańska-Smolkin, Sylwia. 2017. "Fateful Decisions: The Polish Policemen and the Jewish Population of Occupied Poland, 1939–1945." PhD diss., University of Toronto. https://tspace.library .utoronto.ca/bitstream/1807/98749/1/Szymanska-Smolkin_Sylwia_201711_PhD_thesis.pdf.

Tabeau, Ewa, and Jakub Bijak. 2005. "War-Related Deaths in the 1992–1995 Armed Conflicts in Bosnia and Herzegovina: A Critique of Previous Estimates and Recent Results." *European Journal of Population* 21 (2/3): 187–215.

Tadashi Wakabayashi, Bob. 2003. "Comfort Women: Beyond Litigious Feminism." *Monumenta Nipponica* 58 (2): 223–58.

Tammes, Peter. 2007. "Survival of Jews during the Holocaust: The Importance of Different Types of Social Resources." *International Journal of Epidemiology* 36:330–35.

———. 2018. "Surviving the Holocaust: Socio-demographic Differences among Amsterdam Jews." *European Journal of Population* 33 (3): 293–318.

———. 2019. "Associating Locality-Level Characteristics with Surviving the Holocaust: A Multilevel Approach to the Odds of Being Deported and to Risk of Death among Jews Living in Dutch Municipalities." *American Journal of Epidemiology* 188:896–906.

Tanaka, Yuki. 2008. *Hidden Horrors: Japanese War Crimes in World War II*. 2nd ed. Lanham, MD: Rowman and Littlefield.

———. 2019. "War, Rape and Patriarchy: The Japanese Experience." *Asia-Pacific Journal* 18, no. 1 (December 31): article ID 5335.

Tanaka, Yuki, and Marilyn B. Young, eds. 2009. *Bombing Civilians: A Twentieth-Century History*. New York: New Press.

Tanielian, Melanie. 2012. "The War of Famine: Everyday Life in Wartime Beirut and Mount Lebanon (1914–1918)." PhD diss., University of California, Berkeley. https://escholarship.org/uc /item/4bs8383d.

———. 2017. *The Charity of War: Famine, Humanitarian Aid, and World War I in the Middle East*. Stanford, CA: Stanford University Press.

Tauger, Mark B. 2009. "The Indian Famine Crises of World War II." *British Scholar* 1 (2): 166–96.

Tawney, R. H. 1932. *Land and Labour in China*. London: Allen and Unwin.

Taylor, Lynne. 1997. "The Black Market in Occupied Northern France, 194–04." *Contemporary European History* 6 (2): 153–17

———. 2000. *Between Resistance and Collaboration: Popular Protest in Northern France, 1940–45*. London: Palgrave Macmillan.

Tepora, Tuomas, and Aapo Roselius. 2014. *The Finnish Civil War, 1918: History, Memory, Legacy*. Leiden: Brill.

ter Haar, Peter. 2018. "Bombing of Dresden, 13 and 14 February 1945." Traces of War. December 26, 2018. https://www.tracesofwar.com/articles/4476/Bombing-of-Dresden-13-and-14 -February-1945.htm.

Theien, Iselin. 2009. "Food Rationing during World War Two: A Special Case of Sustainable Consumption?" *Anthropology of Food*, S5, September. https://journals.openedition.org/aof/6383.

Ther, Philipp. 1996. "The Integration of Expellees in Germany and Poland after World War II: A Historical Reassessment." *Slavic Review* 55 (4): 779–805.

Ther, Phillip, and Ana Siljak, eds. 2001. *Redrawing Nations: Ethnic Cleansing in East-Central Europe, 1944–1948*. Lanham, MD: Rowman and Littlefield.

Thibon, Christian. 2004. *Histoire démographique du Burundi*. Paris: Karthala.

Thompson, E. P. 1971. "The Moral Economy of the English Crowd in the Eighteenth Century." *Past and Present* 50 (1): 76–136.

Thorpe, Julie. 2011."Displacing Empire: Refugee Welfare, National Activism and State Legitimacy in Austria-Hungary in the First World War." In *Refugees and the End of Empire*, edited by P. Panayi and P. Virdee. London: Palgrave Macmillan. https://doi.org/10.1057/9780230305700_5.

Thurner, Erika. 2007. "Nazi and Postwar Policy against Roma and Sinti in Austria." In Stauber and Vago 2007: 55–67.

Thurner, Stefan, Peter Klimeka, Michael Szella, et al. 2013. "Quantification of Excess Risk for Diabetes for Those Born in Times of Hunger, in an Entire Population of a Nation, across a Century." *Proceedings of the National Academy of Sciences* 110 (12): 4703–7.

Tinker, Hugh. 1975. "A Forgotten Long March: The Indian Exodus from Burma, 1942." *Journal of Southeast Asian Studies* 6 (1): 1–15.

Titmuss, Richard M. 1950. "Problems of Social Policy." In *History of the Second World War*, edited by W. K. Hancock. London: His Majesty's Stationery Office. https://www.ibiblio.org /hyperwar/UN/UK/UK-Civil-Social/UK-Civil-Social-21.html.

Tobin, James. 1952. "A Survey of the Theory of Rationing." *Econometrica* 20 (4): 521–53.

Todd, Nicolas, Sophie Le Fur, Pierre Bougnères, and Alain-Jacques Valleron. 2017. "Impact of Social Inequalities at Birth on the Longevity of Children Born 1914–1916: A Cohort Study." *PLOS One*, October 17, 1–13. https://doi.org/10.1371/journal.pone.0185848.

Todd, Nicolas, Alain-Jacques Valleron, and Pierre Bougnères. 2017. "Prenatal Loss of Father during World War One Is Predictive of a Reduced Lifespan in Adulthood." *Proceedings of the National Academy of Sciences* 114 (16): 4201–6.

Tol, Weitse A., Suzan Wong, and Mark J. D. Jordans. 2013. "Annual Research Review: Resilience and Mental Health in Children and Adolescents Living in Areas of Armed Conflict—a Systematic Review of Findings in Low- and Middle-Income Countries." *Journal of Child Psychology and Psychiatry* 54 (4): 445–60.

Tomasevic, Jozo. 2001. *War and Revolution in Yugoslavia, 1941–1945: Occupation and Collaboration*. Stanford, CA: Stanford University Press.

Tomic, Yves. 2010. "Massacres in Dismembered Yugoslavia, 1941–1945." Online Encyclopedia of Mass Violence. Accessed April 27, 2020. http://bo-k2s.sciences-po.fr/mass-violence-war -massacre-resistance/en/document/massacres-dismembered-yugoslavia-1941–1945.

Tomonaga, Masao. 2019. "The Atomic Bombings of Hiroshima and Nagasaki: A Summary of the Human Consequences, 1945–2018, and Lessons for Homo sapiens to End the Nuclear Weapon Age." *Journal for Peace and Nuclear Disarmament* 2 (2): 491–517.

Tönsmeyer, Tatjana, Peter Haslinger, Włodzimierz Borodziej, et al., eds. 2021. *Fighting Hunger, Dealing with Shortage: Everyday Life under Occupation in World War II Europe: A Source Edition*. Vol. 1. Brill: Leiden.

Tönsmeyer, Tatjana, Peter Haslinger, and Agnes Laba, eds. 2018. *Coping with Shortage under German Occupation in World War II*. London: Palgrave Macmillan.

Tooze, Adam. 2006. *The Wages of Destruction: The Making and Breaking of the Nazi Economy*. Cambridge: Cambridsge University Press.

Torrie, Julia Suzanne. 2010. *"For Their Own Good": Civilian Evacuations in Germany and France, 1939–1945*. Oxford: Berghahn.

Toynbee, Arnold. 1916. *The Destruction of Poland: A Study of German Efficiency*. London: T. Fisher Unwin.

———. 1922. *The Western Question in Greece and Turkey: A Study in the Contact of Civilisations*. London: Constable. http://louisville.edu/a-s/history/turks/WesternQuestion.pdf.

Travis, Hannibal. 2006. "Native Christians Massacred: The Ottoman Genocide of the Assyrians during World War I." *Genocide Studies and Prevention: An International Journal* 1 (3): 327–72.

Trienekens, Gerard. 2000. "The Food Supply in the Netherlands during the Second World War." In *Food, Science, Policy and Regulation in the Twentieth Century: International and Comparative Perspectives*, edited by David F. Smith and Jim Phillips, pp. 117–33. London: Routledge.

Trilla, Antoni, Guillem Trilla, and Carolyn Daer. 2018. "The 1918 'Spanish Flu' in Spain." *Clinical Infectious Diseases* 47 (5): 668–73.

Trumpener, Ulrich. 1975. "The Road to Ypres: The Beginnings of Gas Warfare in World War." *Journal of Modern History* 47 (3): 460–80.

Tusan, Michelle. 2012. *Smyrna's Ashes: Humanitarianism, Genocide, and the Birth of the Middle East*. Berkeley: University of California Press.

Tushnet, Leonard. 1963. "Health Conditions in the Ghetto of Lodz." *Journal of the History of Medicine and Allied Sciences* 18 (1): 64–73.

Tuters, Kaspars, and Arnis Viksna. 2006. "The Extermination of Psychiatric Patients in Latvia during World War II." *International Journal of Mental Health* 35 (3): 72–74.

Tzavaras, Athanase, Dimitris Ploumbidis, and Ariella Asser. 2007–08. "Greek Psychiatrie Patients during World War II and the Greek Civil War, 1940–1949." *International Journal of Mental Health* 36 (4): 57–66.

Üngör, Uğur Ümit. 2015. "Ottoman Diplomacy, the Balkan Wars and the Great Powers." In Geppert et al. 2015: 76–90.

Ungváry, Krisztián. 2016. "Master Plan? The Decision-Making Process behind the Deportations." In *The Holocaust in Hungary: Seventy Years Later*, edited by Randolph L. Braham and András Kovács, pp. 105–46. Budapest: Central European University Press.

USSBS (U.S. Strategic Bombing Survey). 1945a. *Effects of SB on the German War Economy*. Washington, DC: Government Printing Office.

———. 1945b. *Overall Report (European War)*. Washington, DC: Government Printing Office.

———. 1945c. *The United States Strategic Bombing Surveys: European War, Pacific War*. Washington, DC: Government Printing Office.

———. 1947a. *The Effects of Strategic Bombing on German Morale*. Vol. 1. Washington, DC: Government Printing Office.

———. 1947b. *Japanese Wartime Standard of Living and Utilization of Manpower*. Washington, DC: Government Printing Office.

Vågerö, Denny, Ilona Koupil, Nina Parfenova, and Pär Sparen. 2013. "Long-Term Health Consequences Following the Siege of Leningrad." In Lumey and Vaiserman 2013: 207–26.

Vagts, Detlev F. 2000. "The Hague Conventions and Arms Control." *American Journal of International Law* 94 (1): 31–41.

Valaoras, V. G. 1946. "Some Effects of Famine on the Population of Greece." *Milbank Memorial Fund Quarterly* 24, no. 3 (July): 215–34.

Valentino, Benjamin. 2014. "Why We Kill: The Political Science of Political Violence against Civilians." *Annual Review of Political Science* 17:89–103.

———. 2016. "Moral Character or Character of War? American Public Opinion on the Targeting of Civilians in Times of War." *Daedalus* 145 (4): 127–38.

Valentino, Benjamin, Paul Huth, and Sarah Croco. 2006. "Covenants without the Sword: International Law and the Protection of Civilians in Times of War." *World Politics* 58 (3): 339–77.

Vallin, Jacques, France Meslé, Serguei Adamets, and Serhii Pyrozhkov. 2002. "A New Estimate of Ukrainian Population Losses during the Crises of the 1930s and 1940s." *Population Studies* 56 (3): 249–64.

———. 2012. "The Consequences of the Second World War and the Stalinist Repression." In *Mortality and Causes of Death in 20th-Century Ukraine*, edited by Meslé and Vallin, pp. 39–74. New York: Springer.

van Besouw, Bram, and Daniel R. Curtis. 2022. "Estimating Warfare-Related Civilian Mortality in the Early Modern Period: Evidence from the Low Countries, 1620–99." *Explorations in Economic History.* 84:101–425.

Van Buskirk, Emily. 2010. "Recovering the Past for the Future: Guilt, Memory, and Lidiia Ginzburg's Notes of a Blockade Person." *Slavic Review* 69 (2): 281–305.

van den Berg, Gerard. J., A. Hammerschmid, J. C. Schoch, and K. Walliczek. 2015. "Disentangling Stress from Nutrition as Determinants of the Long Run Effects of Adverse Conditions around Birth on Economic and Health Outcomes Late in Life." Mimeo.

van den Berg, Gerard J., Petter Lundborg, and Johan Vikström. 2017. "The Economics of Grief." *Economic Journal* 127:1794–832.

van der Eng, Pierre. 1998. "Regulation and Control: Explaining the Decline of Food Production in Java, 1940–46." In *Food Supplies and the Japanese Occupation in Southeast Asia*, edited by Paul H. Kratoska, pp. 187–207. London: Macmillan.

———. 2008. "Food Supply in Java during War and Decolonisation, 1940–1950." Munich Personal RePEc Archive Paper No. 8852, table A.3.2. http://mpra.ub.uni-muenchen.de/8852/.

———. 2024. "Mortality from the 1944–1945 Famine in Java, Indonesia." Discussion Paper 2024–01, Center for Economic History, Research School of Economics, Australian National University.

van der Essen, Leon. 1917. *The Invasion and the War in Belgium from Liege to the Yser*. London: Fisher Unwin.

van der Kloot, William. 2003. "Ernst Starling's Analysis of the Energy Balance of the German People during the Blockade, 1914–1919." *Notes and Records of the Royal Society of London* 57 (2): 189.

van Esch, Maj Joris A. C. 2011. *Restrained Policy and Careless Execution: Allied Strategic Bombing on the Netherlands in the Second World War*. U.S. Army Command and General Staff College, Fort Leavenworth, Kansas. https://apps.dtic.mil/dtic/tr/fulltext/u2/a545115.pdf.van IJzendoorn M. H., M. J. Bakermans-Kranenburg, and A. Sagi-Schwartz. 2003. "Are Children of Holocaust Survivors Less Well-Adapted? A Meta-analytic Investigation of Secondary Traumatization." *Journal of Traumatic Stress* 16:459–69.

Vassilev, Rossen. 2010. "The Rescue of Bulgaria's Jews in World War II." *New Politics* 14 (4). https://newpol.org/issue_post/rescue-bulgarias-jews-world-war-ii/.

Vaughan, V. C., and G. T. Palmer. 1918. "Communicable Diseases in the National Guard and National Army of the United States during the Six Months from September 29, 1917, to March 29, 1918." *Journal of Laboratory and Clinical Medicine* 3:635–718. Google Scholar.

Vedel-Petersen, K. O. 2023. *Losses of Life Caused by War.* Part II, *The World War.* Oxford: Clarendon Press.

Veidlinger, Jeffrey. 2021. *In the Midst of Civilized Europe: The 1918–1921 Pogroms in Ukraine and the Onset of the Holocaust.* London: Picador.

Vemandere, Martine. 2016. "Van geliefde kitten tot ongewenste kat Belgische vluchtelingen in Engeland tijdens WO1." *FARO: Tijdschrift over cultereel erfgoed* 9 (2): 34–39.

Virgili, Fabrice. 2016. "Rapes Committed by the German Army in France (1940–1944)." *Vingtième Siècle. Revue d'histoire* 2 (130): n.p.

Vita A., S. Barlati, L. De Peri, G. Deste, and E. Sacchetti. 2016. "Schizophrenia." *Lancet* 388:1280.

von Benda-Beckmann, Bas. 2015. *German Historians and the Bombing of German Cities: The Contested Air War.* Amsterdam: University of Amsterdam Press.

von Bueltingsloewen, Isabelle. 2002. "Les 'aliénés' morts de faim dans les hôpitaux psychiatriques français sous l'Occupation.'" *Vingtime siècle: Revue d'histoire* 76 (4): 99–15.

———. 2005. "La difficile identification des victimes d'une famine sélective." In *"Morts d'inanition": Famine et exclusions en France sous l'Occupation,* edited by Isabelle von Bueltzingsloewen, pp. 11–19. Rennes, France: Presses Universitaires de Rennes.

———. 2007. *L'hécatombe des fous: La famine et les hôpitaux psychiatriques français sous l'Occupation.* Paris: Aubier.

von Hagen, Mark. 2007. *War in a European Borderland: Occupations and Occupation Plans in Galicia and Ukraine, 1914–1918.* Seattle: University of Washington Press.

Voth, Hans-Joachim. 1995. "Civilian Health during World War I and the Cause of German Defeat: A Re-examination of the Winter Hypothesis." *Annales de démographie historique,* 291–307.

Vrints, Antoon. 2010. "Review of Lipkes (2007)." *European History Quarterly* 40, no. 1: 358–59.

———. 2011. "Sociaal protest in een bezet land. Voedseloproer in België tijdens de Eerste Wereldoorlog." *Tijdschrift voor Geschiedenis* 124 (1): 30–47.

———. 2014. "Food and Nutrition (Belgium)." In Daniel et al. 2014–19.

Wachsmann, Nikolaus. 2015. *KL: A History of the Nazi Concentration Camps.* New York: Farrar, Brown, and Giroux.

Walker, W. Richard, and John J. Skowronski. 2009. "The Fading Affect Bias? What the Hell Is It For?" *Applied Cognitive Psychology* 23:1122–36.Walsh, Brian P. 2016. "The Rape of Tokyo: Legends of Mass Sexual Violence and Exploitation during the Occupation of Japan." PhD diss., Princeton University. Accessed April 29, 2022. https://dataspace.princeton.edu/handle/88435/dsp01qf85nd705.

———. 2018. "Sexual Violence during the Occupation of Japan." *Journal of Military History* 82 (4): 1199–230.

Walsh, Dermot. 1971. *The 1963 Irish Psychiatric Hospital Census.* Dublin: Medico-social Research Board.

Walzer, M. 1977. *Just and Unjust Wars: A Moral Argument with Historical Illustrations.* New York: Basic Books.

Ward, W. Peter. 1988. "Birth Weight and Standards of Living in Vienna, 1865–1930." *Journal of Interdisciplinary History* 19 (2): 203–29.

Watson, Alexander. 2008. *Enduring the Great War: Combat, Morale and Collapse in the German and British Armies, 1914–1918.* Cambridge: Cambridge University Press.

———. 2014. "Unheard-of Brutality: Russian Atrocities against Civilians in East Prussia, 1914–15." *Journal of Modern History* 86 (4): 780–825.

Waugh, Melinda J., Ian Robbins, Stephen Davies, and Janet Feigenbaum. 2007. "The Long-Term Impact of War Experiences and Evacuation on People Who Were Children during World War Two." *Aging and Mental Health* 11 (2): 168–74.

Wawrzeniuk, Piotr. 2018. "'Lwów Saved Us': Roma Survival in Lemberg, 1941–44." *Journal of Genocide Research* 20 (3): 327–50.

Weal, John. 2001. *Jagdgeschwader 54 "Grünherz."* Oxford: Osprey.

Weinberg, Gerhard. 2005. *A Word at Arms: A Global History of World War II.* 2nd ed. Cambridge: Cambridge University Press.

Weinreb, Alice. 2012. "For the Hungry Have No Past nor Do They Belong to a Political Party: Debates over German Hunger after World War II." *Central European History* 45 (1): 50–78.

———. 2017. *Modern Hungers: Food and Power in Twentieth-Century Germany.* Oxford: Oxford University Press.

Weiss-Wendt, Anton. 1998. "The Soviet Occupation of Estonia in 1940–41 and the Jews." *Holocaust and Genocide Studies* 12 (2): 308–25.

———. 2009. *Murder without Hatred: Estonians and the Holocaust.* Syracuse, NY: Syracuse University Press.

———, ed. 2013. *The Nazi Genocide of the Roma: Reassessment and Commemoration.* New York: Berghahn.

Weitzman, Martin L. 1977. "Is the Price System or Rationing More Effective in Getting a Commodity to Those Who Need It Most?" *Bell Journal of Economics* 8 (2): 517–24.

Welch, Susan. 2020. "Gender, Age, and Survival of Italian Jews in the Holocaust." *Genocide Studies and Prevention: An International Journal* 14 (3): 110–28.

Wellerstein, Alex. 2020a. "Counting the Dead at Hiroshima and Nagasaki." *Bulletin of the Atomic Scientists*, August 4. https://thebulletin.org/2020/08/counting-the-dead-at-hiroshima-and-nagasaki/.

———. 2020b. "The Kyoto Misconception: What Truman Knew, and Didn't Know, about Hiroshima." In *The Age of Hiroshima*, edited by M. D. Gordin and G. J. Ikenberry, pp. 34–55. Princeton, NJ: Princeton University Press.

Welskopp, Thomas. 2015. "Labor (Germany)." In Daniel et al. 2014–19.

Werrell, Kenneth P. 1986. "The Strategic Bombing of Germany in World War II: Costs and Accomplishments." *Journal of American History* 73 (3): 702–13.

Werth, Alexander. 1964. *Russia at War, 1941–1945.* London: Barrie and Rockliff.

Werth, Nicholas. 2003. "Mechanism of a Mass Crime: The Great Terror in the Soviet Union, 1937–38." In Gellately and Kiernan 2003.

———. 2012. "The Soviet Union, 1937–38." In *The Specter of Genocide: Mass Murder in Historical Perspective*, edited by Robert Gellately and Ben Kiernan, p. 232. Cambridge: Cambridge University Press.

Westerlund, Lars. 2008. "Prisoners of War in Finland in WW II: An Introduction." In *Sotoavangit ja Internoidut: Kansallisarkiston artikkelikirja (Prisoners of War and Internees: A Book of Articles by the National Archives)*, edited by Lars Westerlund, pp. 8–16. Helsinki: Oy Nord Print Ab.

Wheatcroft, S. G. 1983. "Famine and Epidemic Crises in Russia, 1918–1922: The Case of Saratov." *Annales de démographie historique*, 329–52.

———. 1993. "Famine and Food Consumption Records in Early Soviet History, 1917–25." In *Food, Diet and Economic Change Past and Present*, edited by C. Geissler and D. J. Oddy, pp. 151–74. Totnes, United Kingdom: Leicester University Press.

———. 1996. "The Scale and Nature of German and Soviet Mass Killings, 1930–45." *Europe-Asia Studies* 48 (8): 1319–53.

———. 1997. "Soviet Statistics of Nutrition and Mortality during Times of Famine, 1917–1922 and 1931–1933." *Cahiers du monde russe* 38 (4): 525–57.

————. 2012. "The Soviet Famine of 1946–1947, the Weather and Human Agency in Historical Perspective." *Europe-Asia Studies* 64 (6): 987–1005.

————. 2017. "Eastern Europe: Russia and the USSR." In Alfani and C. Ó Gráda 2017: 212–39.

————. 2024. "Hunger and Two Famines Redraw the Map of the Russian Empire Twice and Creates the Soviet State, 1914–19 and 1920–22." In *Hunger Redraws the Map: Food, State and Society in the Era of the First World War*, edited by Hew Strachan, Claire Morelon, and Mary Elizabeth Cox. Oxford: International Research Network.

Wheatcroft, S. G., and C. Ó Gráda. 2017. "The European Famines of World Wars 1 and 2." In Alfani and C. Ó Gráda 2017: 240–68.

White, Theodore H., and Annalee Jacoby. 1946. *Thunder out of China*. New York: William Sloane.

Wieck, Michael. 2003. *A Childhood under Hitler and Stalin: Memoirs of a "Certified Jew."* Madison: University of Wisconsin Press.

Wikipedia. 2020. "Civilian Casualties of Strategic Bombing." https://en.wikipedia.org/wiki/Civilian_casualties_of_strategic_bombing.

Wilcox, Vanda. 2021. *The Italian Empire and the Great War*. Oxford: Oxford University Press.

Wildt, Michael. 2002. *Generation des Unbedingten: Das Führungskorps des Reichssicherheit-shauptamtes*. Hamburg: Hamburger Edition.

Wilson, Peter H. 2017. "Was the Thirty Years War a 'Total War'?" In Charters, Rosenhaft, and Smith 2017: 21–35.

Wilson, Ward. 2007. "The Winning Weapon? Rethinking Nuclear Weapons in Light of Hiroshima." *International Security* 31 (4): 162–79.

Winick, Myron. 1979. *Hunger Disease: Studies by the Jewish Physicians in the Warsaw Ghetto*. New York: Wiley.

Winter, Jay M. 1977. "The Impact of the First World War on Civilian Health in Britain." *Economic History Review* 30 (3): 487–507.

————. 1988. "Some Paradoxes of the First World War." In *The Upheaval of War: Family, Work and Welfare in Europe, 1914–1918*, edited by Richard Wall and Jay Winter, pp. 9–42. Cambridge: Cambridge University Press.

————. 1997. "Surviving the War: Life Expectation, Illness, and Mortality Rates in Paris, London, and Berlin, 1914–1919." In *Capital Cities at War: Paris, London, Berlin, 1914–1919*, edited by Jay Winter and Jean-Louis Robert, pp. 487–524. Cambridge: Cambridge University Press.

————, ed. 2000. "Shell-Shock and the Cultural History of the Great War." *Journal of Contemporary History* 35 (1): 7–11.

————, ed. 2003a. *America and the Armenian Genocide of 1915*. Cambridge: Cambridge University Press.

————. 2003b. "Under Cover of War: The Armenian Genocide in the Context of Total War." In Winter 2003a: 37–50.

————. 2010. "Demography." In Horne 2010.

————. 2014. *The Cambridge History of the First World War*. 3 vols. Cambridge: Cambridge University Press.

————. 2022. *The Day the Great War Ended, 24 July 1923: The Civilianization of War*. Oxford: Oxford University Press.

Winter, Jay M., and Joshua Cole. 1993. "Fluctuations in Infant Mortality Rates in Berlin during and after the First World War." *European Journal of Population* 9 (3): 235–63.

Wischnitzer, Mark. 1940. "Jewish Emigration from Germany, 1933–1938." *Jewish Social Studies* 2 (1): 23–44.

Withuis, Jolande, and Annet Mooij, eds. 2010. *The Politics of War Trauma: The Aftermath of World War II in Eleven European Countries*. Amsterdam: Aksant.

Wnęk, Konrad. 2023. "Poland's Population Losses Caused by Germany during the Second World War." In *The Report on the Losses Sustained by Poland as a Result of German Aggression and*

Occupation During the Second World War, 1939–1945, edited by Konrad Wnęk and Lidia A. Zyblikiewicz, pp. 103–171. Warsaw: Jan Karski Institute of War Losses.

Wollacott, Angela. 1994. *On Her Their Lives Depend: Munitions Workers in the Great War*. Berkeley: University of California Press.

Worobey, Michael, Jim Cox, and Douglas Gill. 2019. "The Origins of the Great Pandemic." *Evolution, Medicine, and Public Health*, 18–25. https://doi.org.10.1093/emph/eoz001.

Wright, Michael. 2010. "In Search of 'Silver Rice': Starvation and Deprivation in World War II-Era Japan." *Studies on Asia*, series 4, 1 (1): 57–85.

Wyrwich, Michael. 2020. "Migration Restrictions and Long-Term Regional Development: Evidence from Large-Scale Expulsions of Germans after World War II." *Journal of Economic Geography* 20 (2): 481–507.

Xu, Ming-Qing, Wen-Sheng Sun, Ben-Xiu Liu, et al. 2009. "Prenatal Malnutrition and Adult Schizophrenia: Further Evidence from the 1959–1961 Chinese Famine." *Schizophrenia Bulletin* 35 (3): 568–76.

Yamada, Michiko, and Shizue Izumi. 2002. "Psychiatric Sequelae in Atomic Bomb Survivors in Hiroshima and Nagasaki Two Decades after the Explosions." *Social Psychiatry and Psychiatric Epidemiology* 37 (2002): 409–15.

Yarov, Sergey. 2017. *Leningrad, 1941–42: Morality in a City under Siege*. Cambridge: Polity Press.

Yehuda, Rachel, Nikolaus Daskalatis, Amy Lehrner, et al. 2014. "Influences of Maternal and Paternal PTSD on Epigenetic Regulation of the Glucocorticoid Receptor Gene in Holocaust Survivor Offspring." *American Journal of Psychiatry* 171 (8): 872–80.

Zalkin, Mordechai. 2010. "Antisemitism in Lithuania." In *Antisemitism in Eastern Europe: History and Present in Comparison*, edited by Hans-Christian Petersen and Samuel Salzborn, pp. 135–70. Frankfurt: Peter Lang.

Zavadivker, Polly. 2020. "Jewish Fever: Myths and Realities in the History of Russia's Typhus Epidemic, 1914–22." *Jewish Social Studies* 26 (1): 101–12.

Zelikow, Philip. 2021. *The Road Less Traveled: The Secret Battle to End the Great War, 1916–1917*. New York: Public Affairs.

Zeller, Joseph. 2018. "Coal: A Significant Factor in Germany's Defeat in World War I." *Canadian Military History* 27 (1): article 15. http://scholars.wlu.ca/cmh/vol27/iss1/15.

Zhou, Xun. 2012. *The Great Famine in China, 1958–1962: A Documentary History*. New Haven, CT: Yale University Press.

Zierenberg, Malte. 2015. *Berlin's Black Market: 1939–1950*. London: Palgrave Macmillan. Originally published in German as *Stadt der Schieber: Der Berliner Schwarzmarkt, 1939–1950*. Göttingen: Vandenhoeck and Ruprecht, 2008.

Zimmermann, Michael. 2007. "Jews, Gypsies and Soviet Prisoners of War: Comparing Nazi Persecutions." In Stauber and Vago 2007: 31–53.

Zimmet, P., Z. Shi, A. El Osta, and L. Ji. 2018. "Epidemic T2DM, Early Development and Epigenetics: Implications of the Chinese Famine." *Nature Reviews Endocrinology* 14: 738–46.

Zraly, Maggie, and Laetitia Nyirazinyoye. 2010. "Don't Let the Suffering Make You Fade Away: An Ethnographic Study of Resilience among Survivors of Genocide-Rape in Southern Rwanda." *Social Science and Medicine* 70:1656–64.

Zuckerman, Solly. 1978. *From Apes to Warlords, 1904–1946: The Autobiography of Solly Zuckerman (1904–1946)*. London: Hamish Hamilton.

Zuckerman, Yitzhak. 1993. *A Surplus of Meaning: Chronicle of the Warsaw Uprising*. Berkeley: University of California Press.

Zweiniger-Barbielowska, Ina. 2000. *Austerity in Britain: Rationing, Controls, and Consumption, 1939–1955*. Oxford: Oxford University Press.

Zwigenberg, Ran. 2017. "'Wounds of the Heart': Psychiatric Trauma and Denial in Hiroshima." *History Workshop Journal* 84:67–88.

INDEX

The Princeton Economic History of the Western World
Joel Mokyr, Series Editor

Recent titles